Chuck Van Eaton

W9-BZF-942

READINGS IN
THE ECONOMICS OF TAXATION

THE SERIES OF REPUBLISHED
ARTICLES ON ECONOMICS
Volume IX

Selection Committee for This Volume

RICHARD A. MUSGRAVE

CARL S. SHOUP

The participation of the American Economic Association in the presentation of this series consists in the appointment of a committee to determine the subjects of the volumes and of special committees to select the articles for each volume

READINGS IN THE
ECONOMICS
OF TAXATION

Selected by a Committee of

THE AMERICAN ECONOMIC ASSOCIATION

1959

Published for the Association by

RICHARD D. IRWIN, INC.

HOMEWOOD, ILLINOIS

© 1959 BY RICHARD D. IRWIN, INC.

ALL RIGHTS RESERVED. THIS BOOK OR ANY PART THEREOF MAY NOT BE
REPRODUCED WITHOUT THE WRITTEN PERMISSION OF THE PUBLISHER

First Printing, February, 1959

Library of Congress Catalogue Card No. 59–7389

PRINTED IN THE UNITED STATES OF AMERICA

Foreword

In preparing this selection of readings, we had to make an initial choice between a broad coverage of public finance and a more intensive treatment of a part of the field. We chose the latter alternative, on the grounds that the product would be of more lasting value to the research worker and teacher, while the area could be so delimited that editors of subsequent *Readings* in public finance would not find it difficult to avoid overlapping, or gaps.

The question then was what particular area to select. Our decision to focus on the economics of taxation was influenced by the need to avoid duplicating material covered in other readings, particularly an earlier volume in the present series, *Readings in Fiscal Policy,* and a volume published recently by the International Economic Association, *Classics in the Theory of Public Finance,* which contains readings on the theory of tax and expenditure determination. Beyond this, the economics of taxation appeared the most appropriate topic for the present series of *Readings,* since it represents the area of public finance in which the major body of economic analysis has been developed. At the same time, we do not wish to suggest that other areas, such as public expenditures, debt, and the budget, as well as the more specialized problems of tax structure, are of lesser importance. On the contrary, we hope that companion volumes in these fields will be made available before long.

We include only readings that seem useful in current research and teaching in public finance, but limitations of space forbid us to follow this principle alone; to it we add that of relative nonavailability. Articles about to be incorporated in books should give way in this volume to others (of equal merit) that are not. For the same reason, some material has been reproduced from books that are now difficult to obtain.

Then there is the Principle of Aging, or the Deterioration Principle. Anyone who reads last month's journals and then skims an issue of ten years ago, tends to be impressed with the seeming superiority of the former. Thus a temptation arises to include a large amount of recent material in a volume of *Readings,* the more so since selection among the most recent vintage is most difficult. Yet, near vision is not always to be trusted. Material that appears important now may sink rapidly in rank as the years go by, while important contributions of the past are being overlooked. Accordingly, we have made particular effort to include earlier contributions that are of continuing value, and, on the other hand, have excluded articles published during the last five years, that is, after 1952. This latter step, somewhat arbitrary, has of course led to the exclusion of some articles that will in fact pass the test of aging. However, at least for the time being, they are more readily accessible than those included in this volume.

Following the precedent of earlier volumes in this series, all selections are in English. Resources were not available for extensive translating, but we have included two brief translations and a series of bibliographies of foreign-language items, compiled at our request by distinguished scholars abroad: Erik Lindahl, Bent Hansen, Fritz Neumark, Sergio Steve, and Pierre Tabatoni. To them, our sincere thanks for their generous co-operation.

Beyond this, we are indebted to far too many of our colleagues to attempt individual recognition here; we use this occasion to express again our appreciation of the assistance we have received, although the responsibility for the final decision rests entirely with us as the editors.

RICHARD A. MUSGRAVE
CARL S. SHOUP

January, 1959

Table of Contents

I. EQUITY AND WELFARE

A. EQUITY

B. WELFARE

II. INCIDENCE AND INCENTIVE EFFECTS

A. CONCEPTS AND METHODOLOGY

BIBLIOGRAPHY

INDEX OF AUTHORS

I. EQUITY AND WELFARE

A. EQUITY

1

The Utility of Income and Progressive Taxation*

By S. J. CHAPMAN

The purpose of this paper is to bring forward certain considerations bearing upon the relation between Utility[1] and Income and the practical application of the commonly accepted doctrine, which may seem to be of a somewhat heretical bent. Its argument falls naturally into three parts: (1) a constructive treatment of the relation between Utility and Income; (2) an examination of certain fundamental grounds on which the law of diminishing utility, as commonly interpreted, has been supported; and (3) a discussion of the alleged connection between the principle of progressive taxation and the law of diminishing utility.

The best way of making clear the fundamental notion to be expounded is to approach it gradually. First, then, we may notice that, even if income is generally subject to diminishing utility, there are certainly points of discontinuity too important to be overlooked. Thus in Fig. 1, units of income being measured along OX and units of utility along OY, let the successive ordinates of lg represent the increases in the total utility of income to a given person[2] as income advances up to Ob. When his income is Ob, say, he decides to have a motor car; and, in order to have a very simple case to deal with, let us imagine that the possession of a motor car would not in the least affect the manner in which he would spend income on other things or the utility attributed to them. Suppose the cost of the car, expressed as a continuous annual charge, is ab. Then the annual value of the car to him must be af when bf is such that $cde = efg$.

* *Economic Journal,* Vol. XXIII, No. 89 (March, 1913).

[1] Utility is taken merely as a symbol representative of degrees of preference or choice, which are not to be regarded as necessarily measuring impulses or feelings. Through choices or decisions subjective human experiences are transformed into action. By "utilities" I mean the quantitative relations between these decisions or choices, which express, while leaving screened, the internal happenings which the psychologist studies. (See also page 10.)

[2] Throughout this paper, to avoid circumlocution, individuals will invariably be spoken of, though it would frequently be more appropriate to speak of families.

Now, if, after getting the car, his income still increases, the curve of the new marginal utilities will obviously start at h (when $hh = da$), and fall from that point; for the car has displaced the things which brought the marginal utility of money below da. So, when this person's income is a little less than Ob, its marginal utility approximates to bg; but, when it is a little more than Ob, its marginal utility approximates to bh, which is substantially greater than bg.

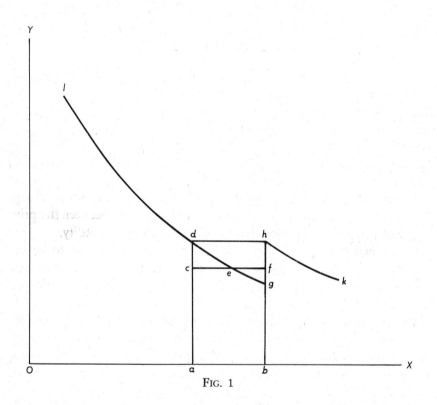

FIG. 1

This demonstration holds of all expenditure on costly things, on the assumptions stated. But we cannot stop at this recognition of discontinuity. The new expensive thing, besides displacing certain things, may alter substantially the values attributed to other things—and is, indeed, almost bound to do so in some degree—so that a thorough-going rearrangement of the scheme of consumption in question is involved. Most schemes of consumption are discovered on close inspection to be coherent systems (of an organic nature, as one might say) the parts of which fit into one another and determine one another's subjective value. Nor is this all. It will be found in addition (as the doctrine of class standards of living lays it down) that different schemes of consumption are as a rule variations of certain distinguishable types, which are kept comparatively intact over lengthy periods by habit and social assimilation, though they are never so well-defined that their existence cannot be overlooked. Objectively viewed these types may merge into one another, but subjectively —to the individual—they exist as discontinuous. People usually advance in the social scale by distinct steps.

Let us consider the effects of spending different incomes with reference to some specific standard of living the cost of barely realising which is £300 a year. When the income is just about £300 a year, and the standard is aimed at, the person in question feels pinched—that is to say, the marginal utility of money to him is high. When, on the contrary, the income is well over £300 a year, he feels himself to be in easy circumstances —that is to say, the marginal utility of money is low. The case, up to a point, is analogous to the much-quoted one of the collector who aims at a complete collection.[3] As in that case, so in this, the marginal utility gets greater as the object pursued is approached. Hence it would seem as if incomes devoted to realising a given type or standard of expenditure obeyed some such law as is exhibited by the curve of marginal utilities *gfj* in Fig. 2, where the axes stand for the same as in Fig. 1.[4]

Next let us consider what happens to the adaptable person when his income advances from about £300 a year to a considerably larger one. Let the curve *gfj* indicate the successive additions to total utility as his income varies when he spends it according to the £300 standard. Sooner or later, however, he alters his standard of living. Now the law of utility with respect to the new type will be of the same order as that with respect to the old, but the maximum of marginal utility of money will be reached, say, at £600. Let the curve *gh* in Fig. 2 represent the variations of the marginal utility of income with reference to this type. This curve must, for a time at least, rise less steeply than the curve *gf* because increments of income just in excess of *Oa* have relation to a further removed end when expended with reference to the higher type.[5] Let us suppose that

---

[3] The reader may be referred to Dr. W. R. Scott's admirable analysis of this case in his paper printed as one of the monographs published by St. Andrews University at the time of its quincentenary celebrations.

[4] The shape of the curve probably resembles that of a lop-sided cocked hat. But, despite the more gradual descent on the right, the curve must soon get close to *Ox*, so far as the individual's expenditure on himself is concerned, because many possibilities are excluded by the constraints of the type.

[5] For example, money laid out on clothes, when the lowest type was aimed at, would be spent with a view merely to comfort; but, when a higher type was aimed at, some comfort would be sacrificed to appearances, though the sacrifice would yield nothing appreciable in utility till income was large enough for the type to be substantially realised. It may be re-

the minimum income necessary for subsistence is Oa, and ignore any utility connected with this. Then the higher standard will be adopted when income is Ob, Ob being such that $gfe = cde$. So, as income advanced from a to k (on the assumptions that there is no simpler type of expenditure than the one of which the variations in utility are shown by the curve gj, and that yet a third type of expenditure is not assumed) the marginal utility of income would be traced out by the line $gfcdh$, those parts of the curves which are marked gd and cj remaining hypothetical. In Fig. 2 expenditure according to two standards only is admitted, but, of course, more than two might have to be allowed for.

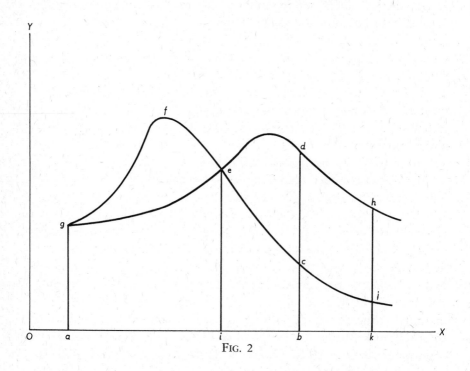

FIG. 2

A few words may be said here to prevent any misunderstanding as to the nature of the curves of marginal utilities of income in Fig. 2.[6] Neither curve must be confounded with a successive utility curve. By the latter is meant a curve whose ordinates stand for the incremental additions

---

marked that there seems to be no unanswerable reason for supposing that the peaks of successive curves like those in Fig. 2 could never, even for the shortest period, range upwards in height from left to right.

[6] The equation to each of them is $y = \dfrac{dU}{dx}$ when U stands for utility and x for income, and an assumption is made in each case as to the standard of living to which expenditure has reference.

made to utility as equal units of an income of a given amount are successively spent, on the assumption that each unit of income in turn is laid out so as to realise the greatest immediate utility, consistently, nevertheless, with the end finally desired; or, to put the same thing in another way, a curve whose ordinates mark from right to left the sacrifices of utility that would be entailed were the things purchased with the income instantly removed in the order in which the consumer would elect to relinquish them, all things being taken in units of equal cost. For every size of income a curve of successive utilities can be drawn theoretically. Now, for an income of any given size, say Oi, the sum of the successive utilities (apart from the utility of the minimum income Oa) would, of course, equal $aiefg$ if gfe is the curve of the marginal utility of income as previously explained. But, for such an income, the final one of the successive utilities would be greater than ei, and the initial one would be less than ag; and similarly for all other sizes of income. The larger the income the lower is the initial one of the successive utilities (beyond the necessity minimum), because it is spent in some degree with reference to a more distant end. The extra height of the final successive utility over the marginal utility of income is caused by the fact that *ex hypothesi* the former, regarded as a sacrifice, cannot be reduced by modifying the expenditure of the rest of the income when the sacrifice is made. Further, it may be observed that, when the curve of marginal utility of income begins by ascending, the curve of successive utilities must ascend at first. It might be thought that the latter could not because it expresses, when read from right to left, the effects of losing successively what can be dispensed with at least cost of utility. But this reasoning is unsound, as can be demonstrated formally as follows. If x and y are two things, or two groups of things, consumed, and U_{x+y} stands for the utility of x and y when taken together, U_x for the utility of x in the absence of y, and U_y similarly for the utility of y in the absence of x; then the reasoning implies that:

$$\text{(i)} \quad U_{x+y} - U_x < U_x$$

can be directly deduced from:

$$\text{(ii)} \quad U_{x+y} > U_x > U_y$$

and obviously it cannot (see also page 10). When this false inference is drawn, the erroneous assumption (implying an atomistic view of experience) is made that:

$$U_{x+y} = U_x + U_y.$$

However, it ordinarily happens that, when (ii) holds, (i) holds also.

It seems likely that the curves of Fig. 2 and the relations between them are such that the individual who is not very poor is generally, if not always, on an eastern slope, so to speak. When he steps to the higher type, he comes, as a rule, to such a position that money in his new circumstances is still subject to diminishing utility. So there are jumps; but there is seldom, if ever, any continuous increasing utility of income when people are not passing out of a state of extreme poverty. Nevertheless—and this is the important point—the view here expounded does involve the hard saying that the marginal utility of money may be greater to a man after his circumstances have improved.[7] I am sure that this is so in an appreciable number of cases; I think it is not infrequently the case; and it may be the ruling case when certain income limits (which vary with the individual) are passed by inconsiderable amounts. It is a common experience to meet with people who have obtained a slight accession of income, and whose enjoyment of life has obviously been increased quite out of proportion to the accession of income. This cannot be explained satisfactorily if additions to income can only bring diminishing additions to utility. Such people (after taking a larger house, say) are quite likely to be more careful about casual expenditure (though possibly careless with pence for reasons to be expounded), and people do not get more careful with things as the things fall in value to them. Again, the wastefulness, or open-handedness, of many unusually well-paid working men long after their old habits, formed when they were much poorer, have had time to crumble away, as contrasted with the penuriousness of many men in a somewhat better-paid economic class, at least suggests that the marginal utility of money is less for the former than the latter, if the two marginal utilities may be compared (see, below, page 10). Illustrations might be indefinitely multiplied. Of course, the ultimate test is furnished by the judgment of people who have had, in a reasonably short period, wide experiences of different incomes and who realise the points at issue; but, unfortunately, most people are not good at introspection.

II

It behoves us now to consider the chief reasons for which the view opposed to that advanced in this paper is held. Three main reasons are ordinarily given for the view that the utility of money invariably becomes

---

[7] It should be pointed out that the doctrine is involved also in such a case as is dealt with in Fig. 1, which does not incorporate the fundamental notion here advanced. Such a case might be waived aside as an exception, but I should doubt whether, in view of the many very expensive items in the budgets of the rich, the number of such exceptions is so few that they may be lightly dismissed.

less to a man when he becomes rich. Two are empirical, and the other is *a priori.*

Empirically, it is pointed out that, when well-to-do, a man is apt to be more careless about pence than when he is not so well off; which must mean, it is said, that the penny has a lower marginal utility to him in the former case. But must it? The following explanation is equally plausible for many instances, namely, that the penny ceases to figure as the unit of account in deliberations about expenditure when a man achieves wealth. The penny might have risen in utility, but, nevertheless, be neglected because of the greater aggregate utility of income. Time is too limited, in relation to the income to be spent, for the rich man to think of a penny—or, so to speak, his wealth makes his leisure too valuable for it to be worth his while to throw it away in devising plans for the saving of pennies.[8] The poor man saves pounds by looking after the pence; but the rich man, by looking after the pence, would lose pounds in value. Moreover, there is this further consideration, that the rich man is encouraged to think in large units by the high average price of the things bought by him. So, despite the rich man's carelessness about pence, his money might have been endowed with an access of utility on his becoming rich. In instituting a comparison, obviously we must not take as the standard unit a sum which is disregarded in one of the cases compared.

Again, still empirically, it is maintained that the richer a man is the higher is the pay needed to induce him to do more than a given amount of work; and that this must be because money has less utility to him when he is rich. But, assuming for the sake of argument that the first statement holds universally, the conclusion drawn does not necessarily follow. Greater wealth generally means that leisure has a higher value, so that a larger absolute sacrifice is made in undertaking extra work when a man has become wealthier. Moreover, in the case in which the greater wealth results from greater earnings, the person in question will obviously be unwilling to under-cut himself, so to speak, by accepting work at a low rate of remuneration; and, apart from this, he will naturally take into account that the time given to the low-paid work might reduce his capacity to earn at the highly-paid work. These considerations make it evident that any abbreviating effect which rising incomes may have on the

---

[8] The explanation may be put crudely in this way. A man with, say, £200 a year, has 48,000 penny units of expenditure per year to think about, and he has just time for the task. But a man with £500 a year would have 120,000 units of expenditure to think about if he made the unit of account the penny, and for so extensive a task he might not have time. He, therefore, makes his income manageable by falling back on a higher unit of account and thinking of the problem as made up of 60,000 twopenny units or 40,000 threepenny units.

time given to earning can be explained without reference to the marginal utility of income.

The *a priori* argument puts it that the most pressing wants are satisfied first, and that as we get wealthier less pressing wants are left to be satisfied, so that in satisfying them we get less utility. This argument seems so convincing because it is self-evident in one sense, which, however, does not happen to be the sense that must be read into it when a contrast is drawn between incomes of different sizes. The mere fact that, when I have £200 a year, I buy six imitation Chippendale chairs, rather than a single genuine one which costs as much as the other six put together, proves that I prefer the six imitations to the one original chair when I have an income of £200 a year. But it does not prove that, when I have the larger income and have bought the costly chair, and compare my enjoyment of it under the new income conditions with my enjoyment of the six cheap chairs under the old income conditions—that then I must judge the former enjoyment to have been greater than the latter.[9]

Some of the defences of the doctrine that the marginal utility of money must always be less for the larger than for the smaller income are, it would seem, less impregnable than they appear at first sight.

III

Another important line of defence remains. Some of my readers may be prevented from according full assent to the notions brought forward in this article by their acceptance of a principle of taxation that is steadily winning the confidence of the public, namely, the progressive principle, which recommends taxing the higher incomes at a higher rate. This principle is not uncommonly deduced from two propositions: (1) that equal proportional sacrifice should be entailed by taxation, and (2) that the marginal utility of income falls continuously in such a way, as income increases, that taxation of all incomes at the same rate would cause proportional sacrifice of utility to vary inversely as income, other things being equal.[10]

It is first necessary to bridge the gulf which has been left yawning between the experiences of different individuals (see note on page 3), since the kind of taxation referred to above aims, as it is put, at making the sacrifices in utility or satisfaction of different people equal in relation to their incomes of utility or satisfaction. There is no gulf to bridge if we

---

[9] See also pp. 7, 8.
[10] Every conceivable kind of diminishing utility of income does not, of course, necessitate progressive taxation if equal proportional sacrifice is to be secured.

can think of satisfaction as homogeneous and measurable (at least theoretically) as between different people.[11] But I am unable to think of it in this way; and, to be on the safe side, and avoid dogmatising about a psychological question, I never mean by utilities or satisfactions more than conventional symbols representative of the relations between an individual's preferences.[12] Consequently, the satisfaction of one person cannot be contrasted with that of another person, according to this view, for obviously no preferential relation can link the two experiences together. However, there is no real difficulty when we come to a political question like taxation, since the gulf is at once bridged by the doctrine, which is essential to much political doctrine, that people who in all external relations seem to be the same must be treated as if they were the same, or, in other words, that the State must not be a respecter of persons. In short, the fiction on which we proceed in taxation (which need not be defended here) is to regard different people in the same or different circumstances as the same people in the same or different circumstances.

Now, given the correctness of the theory in this paper, the second proposition referred to above does not hold with any overwhelming degree of universality at least. On the contrary, it would seem likely that, in many cases, a man's proportional sacrifice of utility would be increased when his income became greater, were his income still taxed at the same rate. Does acceptance of the ideas here expounded, then, involve discarding belief in the progressive principle, and even maintaining, for not a few circumstances, that the rate of taxation of the higher income ought to be less than that of the smaller one? If it does, we are certainly in a predicament, for most political philosophers, I imagine, have a sort of instinctive belief that the progressive principle is somehow right. But happily it does not, as I shall hope to show. With an easy mind we may deny the truth of the second premiss given above to justify progressive taxation (namely, that income must be subject to diminishing utility), because there are grounds for holding that the first premiss (that equal proportional sacrifices of utility should be aimed at) is untrue also. Indeed, the real basis of taxation may be quite other than a principle of distribution of utility-sacrifice.

Let us put the crucial question to ourselves in this way. Should we think it fair to reduce the rate of taxation of large incomes if, by a miracle, income above a certain amount became subject to immensely increasing utility? An answer in the affirmative is entailed if we believe that

---

[11] I am taking "satisfaction" to refer to a purely subjective state, and "utility" to refer to what is predicated of the thing producing it.

[12] See note on p. 3.

taxation should aim at equal proportional sacrifices of utility; but it seems absurd to suggest collecting less money for the State from the rich and more from the poor on the ground that the rich have become really richer. This crude *reductio ad absurdum* may serve to make the reader doubt whether the principle of equal proportional sacrifice of utility can be sound.

But, if this principle is not sound, what is the basis of progressive taxation? It is, in part at any rate, somewhat as follows, I should suggest: that the wants satisfied by the earlier increments to income are usually of more importance socially than the wants satisfied by later increments to income, whether the satisfaction of the former causes more utility or not. In speaking of the equity of taxation, we are obviously talking ethics, and therefore the wants primarily dealt with must be adjudged not according to the value of their satisfaction in fact (positive value), but according to the value of their satisfaction in a moral scheme of consumption (normative value). The poorer a man is, the more likely is some confiscation of income to cause him deprivation of comforts which add to efficiency (meaning the social value of his life) or even of necessities of efficiency; the richer he is, the more likely is the curtailment of his consumption to be effected at the expense of luxuries which add little or nothing to efficiency, or may even diminish it. So the right basis has a certain reference to faculty. If it is put in terms of sacrifice, it may be said that equal proportional sacrifice is the right thing to aim at, only the sacrifice meant must not be one of utility (positive value) as commonly understood. If this kind of utility comes into the reason for progressive taxation at all, it can only do so, according to the opinions expressed here, in the event of its being arguable that the man who enjoys more utility than his fellows has social obligations much greater than theirs; and, if it figures in this way, the case for progressive taxation, so far as it depends upon utility, would be strengthened rather than weakened by the contentions in this paper as regards the connection between utility and the magnitude of income. What seems to me false doctrine, as regards the basis of progressive taxation, has no doubt been occasioned, in some degree, by a confusion between the urgency and the importance of wants, and by the assumption that, when wants are satisfied according to degrees of urgency, their progressive satisfaction must result in continuously decreasing accessions of utility.[13]

---

[13] To make the argument definite, I have selected for examination the utility-sacrifice theory which seems to me most plausible. But the argument in general holds when any other utility-sacrifice theory is held, since, to deduce the necessity of progressive taxation from any of them, diminishing utility of income must be assumed. (See Edgeworth, *Economic Journal,* Vol. VII, p. 550 *et seq.*)

2

A. C. Pigou: A Study in Public Finance*

Review by ALLYN A. YOUNG

A Study in Public Finance. By A. C. PIGOU, M.A. (London: Macmillan & Co., Ltd. 1928. xvii + 323 pp.)

This is a difficult book to review. It is not, however, a difficult book to appraise. It has the qualities which have given its author the high position which he occupies among the world's economists. Because it deals always with real problems (particularly with such problems of public finance as come within the competence of the economist *qua* economist), and because it is conspicuously free from academic padding, it is a much more valuable book than the ordinary systematic treatise on public finance. But its difficulties (for the reviewer) are intimately related to these admirable qualities. Professor Pigou hews his way forward in a straight line through a succession of tangled problems. He evades no difficulties, and never pauses to give himself or his readers a rest. Nor is any time wasted in surveying familiar ground. Professor Pigou is consistently an explorer. His interest is always in the margins or frontiers where, by dint of painstaking analysis, new knowledge is to be had. Every chapter, therefore, bristles with difficulties. Almost every page, in fact, invites the reader to ponder either premises or inferences. Generally the result of such pondering will be to reassure the reader that he could have no safer guide than Professor Pigou. At a few points, however, he may be led to surmise that difficulties have been disposed of in too summary a fashion. For such reasons a really adequate review would take the form of a running commentary on the text. That being impracticable, the best that can be done is to select a few topics for comment.

One feature which sets the book apart from most of the older discussions of similar groups of problems and which helps to give it its value is the emphasis put upon the distinction between "transfer expenditures,"

* *Economic Journal,* Vol. XXXIX (March, 1929).

which merely redistribute the money incomes of the members of the community, and "exhaustive expenditures," which determine directly the uses to which part of the community's productive resources shall be put. This distinction is fundamental, not only in public finance, but also, as I believe, in the theory of money (in respect of both private and public expenditures) and even in general economic theory. Professor Pigou's analysis of the grounds upon which the distinction rests (in public finance) and his discussions, immediately following, of the sources of funds for exhaustive expenditure and of "the relation between what Government gets and what taxpayers and loan-makers surrender" are particularly good summaries, marked by clarity and penetration. Emphasis is also put upon the distinction between the "distributional" and the "announcement" aspects of taxation, and the distinction is employed in a helpful and fruitful way.

In what is said about the criteria of justice in taxation familiar matters are dealt with, but nothing is taken for granted and a satisfactory basis is sought for each conclusion. The minimum-sacrifice principle is approved, but it is suggested that the equal-sacrifice principle, properly interpreted, also points towards progressive taxation. On Bernouilli's hypothesis income receivers attach equal importance to equal percentage decrements from their incomes. (Why do writers take pains to deduce this result from the hypothesis? It *is* the hypothesis.) But Professor Pigou argues that some of the importance attached to the final increments of large incomes by their recipients is purely relative, so that the sacrifice which taxation requires of a large taxpayer is measurably reduced when others in the same income class are similarly treated. Against this finding it might be argued, I suppose, that what matters is the relative position which incomes of a given size have in the general income scale, and that progressive taxation alters that scale, while proportional taxation leaves it unchanged. These are matters of conjecture, however, and not perhaps of very profitable conjecture. Even on utilitarian principles, the taxpayer's "sacrifice" is related only loosely to the immediate pangs associated with the reduction of his income. Even if welfare be held to consist of "states of consciousness," we have no right to turn our backs upon the wisdom of the ages by assuming that a man's experienced happiness is some mathematical function of the size of his income. Progressive taxation really rests, not upon the premise that a small taxpayer attaches (at the time of "announcement") more importance to the marginal tenth of his income than a large taxpayer attaches to his marginal tenth, but upon the circumstance that the community as a whole, expressing its opinion through Government, regards the uses of the marginal tenth of the small taxpayer's income as more important than the uses of the large taxpayer's marginal tenth.

With reference to differentiation in taxation according to the way in which it affects different sorts of expenditures, Professor Pigou suggests that, neglecting effects on distribution, "the best way of raising a given revenue, when the supply of work is not rigidly fixed, is by a system of taxes under which the rates become progressively higher as we pass from uses of very elastic demand or supply to uses where demand or supply are progressively less elastic." This suggestion is joined to Mr. Ramsey's findings (in the *Economic Journal*, March 1927) that, provided such independent demand and supply curves as exist are straight lines, and again neglecting distributional effects, the optimum system of proportional taxes yielding a given revenue will cut down the production of all commodities and services in equal proportions. These are important conclusions. I propose to examine them with the aid of a simple apparatus, which is independent, so far as may be, of particular assumptions respecting the nature of demand functions. For the sake of simplicity, I shall assume that costs are constant. It will be unnecessary, therefore, to take account of elasticity of supply as something apart from elasticity of demand.

A representative consumer purchases annually x units of commodity a and y units of b. The units are the amounts which can be purchased (before a tax is imposed) for a unit of money. With an income of OC (equal to OD) the consumer is able (costs being constant) to choose any combination x,y indicated by a point on the line DC. Let the point preferred be E, indicating an even distribution of expenditure, so that BE and AE are equal. A tax of 100 per cent *ad valorem* is imposed on b. The consumer's range of choice is then restricted to points on the line BC. What point he chooses will depend upon the relative elasticities of his demands for the two commodities. I shall define the point on one side of which demand is relatively elastic and on the other side of which it is relatively inelastic as the point of equal elasticity of demand. But just where and how will equal elasticity of demand show itself?

The point F (where $AF = FE$) represents unchanged expenditure for each of the two commodities. It is also the point at which BC is tangent to an indifference curve which has the form of a rectangular hyperbola and which has another point of tangency at G. But the indifference-curve clue is worthless, for any number of points can be found between H and C at which BC is tangent to the graph of some function of x and y which has positive curvature and is symmetrical with respect to OE. The point which really corresponds best with the conception of equal elasticity of demand is H, where the ratio y/x has the same value as at E. In fact, whatever the form of their utility or demand functions, provided only that they are *alike* and are also *independent* (which does not exclude displacement disutility as a factor affecting demand), the two commodities will continue to be bought in fixed proportions, and *H* will be the preferred point. The presence of either joint demand or rival demand is not, in general, consistent with this result. At *H* two-thirds of the buyer's income will be expended for the taxed commodity, *b*, and one-third for *a*. His consumption of each will be smaller by a third than before the tax was imposed. Relatively inelastic demand for *b*, then, will show itself between *H* and *B* and relatively elastic demand between *H* and *F*. Between *F* and *C* the influence of rival demand becomes so potent a factor that the demand for both commodities might well be called elastic.

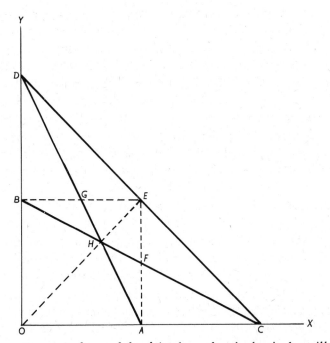

If the consumer's demand for *b* is altogether inelastic, he will station himself at *B*, doing without *a* entirely, and paying half of his income in taxes. If the tax had been imposed on *a*, the rate being the same, the range of choice would be defined by the line *DA*. In view of his inelastic demand for *b*, the consumer would station himself at *G*. He will be better off than if *b* were taxed, because he will be paying only half as much in taxes. An equal *amount* of revenue, however, could have been secured by taxing *b* at half as high a rate. In such case the point *B* would be moved upwards, and the line of choice, *BC*, would pass through *G*, which is the point which the consumer would choose. If a given amount of revenue is to be secured, which commodity is taxed is a matter of indifference to the consumer. It does not appear that the situation could be bettered by taxing both commodities.

We have not yet, however, considered the effects of returning the proceeds of taxation through transfer expenditures. The purpose will be served by supposing that our representative consumer is also a representative creditor of the Government, and that in that capacity he gets back precisely what he pays as taxes. If *b* is taxed, if the consumer's demand for *b* is inelastic, and if, as before, he is stationed at *G*, his income will be increased by an amount equal to *GE*. This will enable him to get back to *E*. If *a* is taxed, and if the consumer is again stationed at *G*, an amount equal to *GE* will again be returned to him. By expending this amount for further increments of *a*, he again increases his income and again is enabled to increase his purchases. The final outcome will be the same regardless of whether the increase of revenue (and of transfer expenditure) is not checked or whether the *rate* of taxation is reduced so as to provide no more than the amount of revenue required. In either event the consumer's total money income, in the end, must be equal both to $x(1 + r) + y$ (where r is the rate of taxation) and to $2y + rx$, whence it follows that $x = y$. Again, therefore, he returns to *E*, and his economic welfare is unaffected by the circumstance that part of his money income has passed through the Treasury and back again or by the incidental circumstance that the relative prices of the commodities which he is accustomed to buy have been altered.

The precision of this result hinges upon the presence of rigidity in the demand for one or both commodities, showing itself either in complete inelasticity of demand for one commodity or in equal elasticity of demand for the two. It is obvious, however, that if a revenue equal to *GE* is to be secured from him, the consumer must be induced to station himself somewhere on a line drawn through *G*, parallel to *DC*. Unless the consumer's demand for the taxed commodity is exceedingly elastic, there will be one rate of taxation, and generally (though not invariably) only one rate, by means of which the desired result can be secured. The same end could be achieved by taxing the other commodity at (generally) a different rate, or by taxing both commodities, in which case any one of various combinations of rates would serve the purpose. The point upon this imaginary line which the consumer would prefer, and accordingly, as we must infer, the point at which his welfare is a maximum, is the point which he would choose if he had to pay income tax in an amount equal to *GE*. Because there is no large probability that this would be the point *H*, Mr. Ramsey's theorem does not seem to have much practical significance.

To get the closest possible approximation to the preferred point, *both* commodities (or, more generally, *all* commodities) should be taxed at the same rate, so that the price of one commodity in terms of another will not be altered. If the proceeds of taxation are returned to the consumer, he would, in such case, resume his original station at *E*. A fairly good approximation to the optimum result could be secured by taxing only commodities which are known to be objects of distinctly inelastic demand. Unless the rates of taxation are excessive, the consumption of the taxed commodities will not generally be reduced much more than it would have been reduced by an equally productive income tax, and, in general, the composition of the consumer's budget will be much like what it would have been if the revenue had been secured by means of an income tax. Conceivably, however, an equally close approximation to the desired result might be secured, though more awkwardly, by *exempting* from taxation all commodities which are objects of distinctly inelastic demand, while taxing *all other* commodities at a uniform rate. If only a small number of commodities are taxed, and if the demand for some of them is distinctly elastic, there will be, of course, a considerable rearrangement of consumers' budgets. I do not think that even in such case the loss of welfare would be large, beyond what would have been occasioned by an income tax, apart from the costs entailed by the transfer of productive resources from one use to another. I am not even sure that it would necessarily be any greater than what would be inflicted by any other scheme of indirect taxation, other than the optimum scheme (uniform taxation).

It is easy to exaggerate the difference between the burden of a tax upon consumption and that of a tax of equal amount upon consumers' incomes. Neglecting distributive effects, there seems to be no reason to depart from the familiar rule (commonly held to rest upon administrative considerations) that commodities for which demand is inelastic should be selected as the objects of taxation. Nor is there any reason to diminish the weight which should be attached to the distributive considerations which indicate that luxuries, even when demand for them is elastic, may sometimes be proper objects of relatively heavy taxation.

3

Recent and Contemporary Theories of Progressive Taxation*

By ELMER D. FAGAN[1]

Since the appearance of Seligman's *Progressive Taxation* (2d ed.) in 1908 and Suret's *Théorie de l'impôt progressif* in 1909, there have been numerous restatements and refinements of certain earlier arguments for progressive taxation. In what follows an attempt will be made to evaluate those arguments which occupy an important place in recent and contemporary literature of the subject.

The persistent theories of progressive taxation may be classified as follows:

    I. The sacrifice theories
        A. The equal sacrifice theory
        B. The proportional sacrifice theory
        C. The equimarginal sacrifice theory
        D. The minimum sacrifice theory
    II. The faculty theory
   III. The surplus-income theory
   IV. The social importance theory
    V. The socio-political theory

The analysis will follow the foregoing outline, considering first the various doctrines that focus particular attention upon sacrifice.

I. THE SACRIFICE THEORIES

Students of public finance have long been familiar with the several sacrifice theories. But, despite this fact, it is desirable at the outset to define clearly the various sacrifice doctrines which are treated in this study.

According to the equal sacrifice theory, taxes should be so levied that

---

* *Journal of Political Economy,* Vol. XLVI, No. 4 (August, 1938).
[1] In the preparation of this article I have profited greatly from constructive criticism by my colleagues, Professors Bernard F. Haley and Karl F. Bode.

every taxpayer would give up the same absolute amount (equal area) of utility as every other taxpayer; according to the proportional sacrifice theory, each taxpayer would surrender the same proportion of the total utility of his income; according to the equimarginal sacrifice theory, the marginal disutility incurred by each taxpayer should be equal; and, according to the minimum sacrifice theory, the sum of the areas of utility sacrificed, both directly and indirectly, by all taxpayers "shall be as small as possible in proportion to the revenue secured."[2]

Whether or not the sacrifice theories logically demand progressive taxation is a question which cannot be answered except in the light of their underlying assumptions.[3] Nowhere in fiscal literature is there an adequately comprehensive statement of these assumptions. But in the writings of the more careful scholars who have discussed the sacrifice theories, nine postulates are either stated explicitly or implied. Seven of these assumptions are common to all the sacrifice doctrines. They are the following:

1. That the question of progressive taxation is relevant only to a rate of income which exceeds the minimum of subsistence

2. That the principle of diminishing marginal utility is valid for increasing rates of money income

3. That the sensibilities of the recipient of income remain constant for each several rate of income; in other words, there is no change in the sensibilities of the individual as the rate of his income increases

4. That the curve which shows the relationship between decreasing marginal utility of income and increasing rates of income also shows the relationship between increasing marginal utility of income and the decreasing rates of income which follow the imposition of a tax

5. That the marginal utility of income for every taxpayer is equal for each several rate of income; in other words, the curve of diminishing marginal utility of income has the same shape and position for every taxpayer

---

[2] Until Edgeworth had made clear the distinction between equal and proportional sacrifice, the former term had carried the meaning which is now generally conveyed by the latter. Seligman, in fact, in the second and latest edition of his *Progressive Taxation* still employs the earlier terminology and denies the importance of Edgeworth's distinction.

In a footnote Edgeworth states: "The honor of clearly distinguishing these principles appears to belong to Mr. Cohen Stuart (*Bijdrage tot de Theorie der Progressieve Inkomsten-belastung*, ch. i, § 4)." (See F. Y. Edgeworth, *Papers Relating to Political Economy* [London, 1925], II, 107, 234–35; and E. R. A. Seligman, *Progressive Taxation in Theory and Practice* [2d ed.; Princeton, 1908], p. 215 n.) For an excellent statement of the equimarginal and minimum sacrifice theories see T. N. Carver, "The Minimum Sacrifice Theory of Taxation," *Political Science Quarterly*, XIX (March, 1904), 72–79. Carver uses the term "minimum direct sacrifice" instead of "equimarginal sacrifice."

[3] Throughout this paper the arguments for and against progressive taxation have reference to the rate structure of the tax system as a whole. Therefore, to simplify the analysis, it is assumed that a single personal net income tax is levied on everyone.

6. That the marginal utility of income is unchanged by the public expenditure of tax revenue[4]
7. That (*a*) the real cost of a given rate of income is equal for all taxpayers and (*b*) the domestic needs of different taxpayers are identical

Readers to whom this article is addressed will understand, without demonstration, that unless these seven assumptions correspond with actual conditions none of the sacrifice theories necessarily leads logically to progressive taxation.

The practical significance of the sacrifice theories as bases for progression depends, therefore, upon the degree of reality of the assumptions which are indispensable for their theoretical validity. It is to the problem of testing the reality of these seven common assumptions that attention will next be directed.

1. When by assumption the question of progressive taxation is made relevant only to a rate of income in excess of the minimum of subsistence, there arises a question not of the reality of the assumption but of its reasonableness. And, in support of this latter quality, it is correct to argue that, for a rate of income less than a subsistence amount, the marginal utility is infinity; and, of course, it is impossible to compare areas of sacrifice when infinity is one of the dimensions of the areas to be compared. Less technically, it might be contended that the recipient of only a subsistence income has taxpaying ability equal to zero; and that any entrenchment upon his income would cost him his life—a sacrifice incommensurable both qualitatively and quantitatively with the sacrifice occasioned by tax payments from incomes above the subsistence level.[5]

2. "It was not until the marginal theory was thoroughly worked out on its psychological side," writes Sir Josiah Stamp, "that progressive taxation obtained a really secure basis in principle."[6] If Sir Josiah has reference to the hedonistic psychology of Jevons and his followers, modern psychologists easily could prove his statement false. Two courses have been followed by modern writers who have developed creditable arguments for the validity of the principle of diminishing marginal utility: first, "desiredness" has been substituted for utility; second, the hedonism of Jevons has been replaced by a psychological basis which is compatible

---

[4] All forms of nontax revenue are excluded from consideration under the sacrifice theories of taxation.

[5] For further discussion of this point see J. S. Nicholson, *Principles of Political Economy* (New York and London, 1901), III, 270–71; H. W. Peck, *Taxation and Welfare* (New York, 1925), pp. 247–48; G. P. Watkins, *Welfare as an Economic Quantity* (Boston, 1915), pp. 125–30; and U. Ricci, "Modifications of the Utility Curve for Money," *Economica*, II (new ser.), 181–85.

[6] *The Fundamental Principles of Taxation* (London, 1929), p. 40.

with modern psychology. These arguments have been treated comprehensively by others, and, therefore, suffice it for me to state my belief in the greater significance of the latter of the foregoing two approaches.[7]

But it is one thing to accept the principle of diminishing utility as a law relating to the consumption of homogeneous commodities and services and quite another to hold that it is applicable to increases in the rate of money income.[8] It is precisely in this latter capacity that the principle has been made the basis of progressive taxation.

The main arguments upon which the principle of diminishing marginal utility of income have been based have been repeated and ably criticized by Sir Sydney Chapman.[9] These arguments, three in number, are: (1) that the well-to-do man is likely to be more careless about his pence; (2) that the richer a man is, the higher is the pay needed to induce him to do more than a given amount of work and that this must be because money has less utility to him when he is rich; and (3) that the most pressing wants are satisfied first, and, as we become wealthier, less pressing wants are left to be satisfied, so that in satisfying them we get less utility.

To the first, Chapman answers that the penny ceases to figure as a unit of account in deliberations about expending by the wealthy; that their time is too valuable to be spent in devising ways of saving pennies; that the poor man saves pounds by looking after the pence, but the rich man by looking after the pence would lose pounds; and that, in instituting a comparison, we must not take as a standard unit a sum which is disregarded in one of the cases compared.

In his treatment of the second, he grants for the sake of argument the first part of the statement but contends that the conclusion drawn does not follow:

---

[7] Two of the ablest discussions of this question are by B. F. Haley, "The Psychological Basis of the Marginal Utility Theory of Value," *Proceedings of the Sixth Annual Meeting of the Pacific Collegiate Economic and Commercial Conference, Dec. 28, 29, 1927* (New York, 1928), pp. 1–10; and Jacob Viner, "The Utility Concept in Value Theory and Its Critics," *Journal of Political Economy*, XXXIII, 369–87, 638–59.

[8] Marshall makes a qualification of the principle of diminishing marginal utility even when its application is confined to homogeneous commodities. He writes: "A small quantity of a commodity may be insufficient to meet a certain special want; and then there will be a more than proportionate increase of pleasure when the consumer gets enough of it to enable him to attain the desired end" (*Principles of Economics* [7th ed.; London, 1916], p. 94 n.).

When Jevons stated his general law that "the degree of utility varies with the quantity of commodity, and ultimately decreases as that quantity increases," he used as an illustration not money income but food (*The Theory of Political Economy* [4th ed.; London, 1911], pp. 37–74).

[9] "The Utility of Income and Progressive Taxation," *Economic Journal*, XXIII, 31–32. [Article 1, pp. 3–12 of this volume. Ed.]

Greater wealth generally means that leisure has a higher value, so that a larger absolute sacrifice is made in undertaking extra work when a man has become wealthier. Moreover, in the case in which the greater wealth results from greater earnings, the person in question will obviously be unwilling to under-cut himself, so to speak, by accepting work at a low rate of remuneration; and, apart from this, he will naturally take into account that the time given to low-paid work might reduce his capacity to earn at highly paid work.

The third, he refutes by the statement of the following hypothetical case:

The mere fact that, when I have £200 a year, I buy six imitation Chippendale chairs, rather than a single genuine one which costs as much as the other six put together, proves that I prefer the six imitations to the one original chair when I have an income of £200 a year. But it does not prove that, when I have the larger income and have bought the costly chair, and compare my enjoyment of it under the new income conditions with my enjoyment of the six cheap chairs under the old conditions—that then I must judge the former enjoyment to have been greater than the latter.

There are also other arguments which cast doubt upon the reality of the diminishing marginal utility of money income. One of these is the fact that money is desired not only as a means of securing consumable commodities and services but also as an agency to economic and political power and ostentatious display. It seems unreasonable to believe that either the desire for or the satisfaction derived from additional increments of any one of these intangibles follows a curve which is negatively inclined; or, for that matter, a curve typically of any particular conformation.[10]

It is generally recognized that the principle of diminishing marginal utility is operative in the case of homogeneous goods. But it is doubtful whether money income—the means to variety and complementary utility in consumption—is subject to the principle of diminishing marginal utility.[11] The individual's desire for an additional unit of the same consum-

---

[10] In the development of this point, I make no claim to originality. Earlier arguments along the same line have been presented by the following economists: H. C. Adams, *The Science of Finance* (1898; 1924 reprint), p. 348; Frank Knight, "Value and Price," *Encyclopaedia of the Social Sciences*, XV, 219–23; Marshall, *op. cit.*, p. 87 (marginal note); F. W. Taussig, *Principles of Economics* (3d ed.; New York, 1921), I, 118; Thorstein Veblen, "The Limitations of Marginal Utility," *Journal of Political Economy*, XVII, 634–35; and Mark A. May and Leonard W. Doob, *Competition and Cooperation* (Social Science Research Council Bull. No. 25 [April, 1937]).

[11] Watkins (*op. cit.*) says that "the utility of a good is complementary in so far as the utility is due to association with other goods in consumption." An elaboration of this concept and its significance can be found in *ibid.*, chaps. ii, vii, viii, ix, and xii. This volume is an en-

able good may be zero and, at the same time, his desire for new or different things may be very great. "He wants to harmonize and round out the furnishings of his residence"—to own a country home, not as another house but as a complement to his city home.[12] It is conceivable that a tremendous income could be spent in rounding out consumption groups, without a decrease in the utility secured per dollar of expenditure.

3. If sufficient evidence has not been presented to shake one's faith in the reality of a principle of diminishing marginal utility of money income, the fact should be stressed that this alleged principle is based upon the assumption that there is no change in the sensibilities of the individual as his rate of income increases. That this static postulate is often contrary to the facts of life cannot be gainsaid by anyone with the slightest understanding of human nature. Chapman writes:

> It is a common experience to meet with people who have obtained a slight accession of income, and whose enjoyment of life has obviously been increased quite out of proportion to the accession of income. This cannot be explained satisfactorily if additions to income can only bring diminishing additions to utility.[13]

The conclusion that there is a change in the sensibilities of the individual as his rate of income increases, invalidates the alleged principle of diminishing marginal utility of money income as a description of the relationship which actually exists between the marginal utility and the rate of income. Professor J. M. Clark is correct when he states:

> The principle of diminishing utility holds true only apart from changes in the consumer himself; it is, in other words, a static principle. It does not go so far as to deny that the consumer may change, but it takes no active notice of the fact. This is always legitimate as a temporary expedient, and it may be legitimate as a permanent attitude, but only if the things ignored are things that do not concern the economist.[14]

4. Because an individual's sensibilities are continually changing, even independently of changes in the rate of his income, the assumption of the

---

lightening elaboration of the thesis that "there are different kinds of utility and the type of variation is not the same for all." Complementary utility does not, of course, lead logically to the absence of diminishing marginal utility of money income. It does, however, help us to understand why it is possible to have an increase in the rate of money income without an accompanying decrease in its marginal utility.

[12] *Ibid.*, p. 85.

[13] Chapman believes that such an increase in enjoyment is a lasting one. Unlike the proponents of any of the sacrifice theories, Chapman distinguishes carefully between the short-run utility consequences of a change in income and long-run utility consequences associated with different stable levels of income (*op. cit.*, pp. 27–31. [Article 1, pp. 3–12 of this volume. Ed.]

[14] *Preface to Social Economics* (New York, 1936), p. 108.

historical reversibility of the alleged diminishing marginal utility curve of money income is obviously unreal.[15]

Another factor which precludes the historical reversal of this curve is the alteration in relative economic and social status which takes place under either progressive or regressive taxation. For example, under progressive taxation, a taxpayer in the higher income brackets will be made to feel the effects not only of an absolute but also of a relative lowering of economic and social status.[16] The sacrifice incident to a relative reduction in economic position will not be shown, unless by accident, by an area measured beneath the original curve of diminishing marginal utility. In other words, Smith's sacrifice from a given tax payment is a function not only of the size of his own tax bill but also of that of Jones, Brown, and other of his fellow-citizens. Smith has not one sacrifice curve but many.[17]

5. A belief in the identity of diminishing marginal utility curves would be reasonable only if the nature and nurture of all men were identical. "The falsity of the assumption of identical diminishing marginal utility curves," a friend writes to the author, "is obvious empirically, since if all men were alike in this respect, it would be the one instance known of absolute identity with respect to *any* characteristic."

The fact that it is impossible to compare the satisfactions of different people appears to have been the reason why the proponents of the sacrifice theories have adopted the assumption of identical marginal utility curves as the most reasonable (or least unreasonable) assumption upon which to establish the theoretical validity of their arguments for progressive taxation.[18] A theory of progression whose logical validity and practical application depend upon so heroic an assumption as the identity of marginal utility curves will not be accepted by those who refuse to decide

---

[15] An illustration of the unreality of this assumption is the condition mentioned by Professor Taussig, and greatly emphasized by Leopold von Wiese, that while the satisfaction from many of the conventional luxuries, e.g., equipages and horses of the Continental aristocracy or the starched linen and close-fitting clothes of the well to do, is chiefly negative, "their loss would be more keenly felt than their presence is enjoyed" (Taussig, *op. cit.*, p. 128; von Wiese, "Das Prinzip der Progression in der Einkommensteuer," *Festgabe für Georg von Schanz*, II [1928], 261–72). Pantaleoni also makes and defends the statement that "the positive expansion of wants is, as a matter of fact, different from the negative expansion" (*Pure Economics* [London, 1898], p. 53).

[16] Penetrating observations concerning this point have been made by A. C. Pigou, *A Study in Public Finance* (London, 1928), pp. 111–13. [See Article 3, pp. 13–18, of this volume for a review of the book. Ed.]

[17] The marginal utility of an individual's income is a function not only of his own rate of income but also of the relative proportion of his rate of income to other persons' rates of income. Therefore, the individual has not one marginal utility curve of income but a "family" of marginal utility curves of income.

[18] See, for example, Carver, *op. cit.*, p. 74.

the case for or against progressive taxation by the bold and obvious practice of psychological legerdemain.

6. The assumption that the marginal utility of income is unchanged by the public expenditure of tax revenue must now be tested for its harmony or conflict with reality.

According to the generally accepted definition of a tax, one of its characteristics which distinguishes it from a fee, special assessment, or public price is the absence of special benefit to the taxpayer from the expenditure of tax revenue. Therefore, in the distribution of the burden of taxation it is common practice to exclude completely any consideration of the *quid pro quo* relationship. But despite the wide adoption of the assumption of "common benefit only" in taxation, general observation compels the recognition of the fact that our assumption does not square completely with actual conditions. There is a clear recognition of this fact by De Viti de Marco, who shows how "the classes which are politically inferior or weak pay for public services which they would not demand of their own accord."[19] Sir Josiah Stamp also observes that the pure-benefit principle is rarely absent altogether from most forms of taxation.[20]

The hypothesis which excludes the effect of public expenditures from the calculation of sacrifice in taxation is clearly a fiction, the adoption of which can be justified, if at all, only by political expediency.

7. It will be recalled that, according to the seventh postulate which is common to all the sacrifice theories, (*a*) the real cost of a given rate of income is equal for all taxpayers and (*b*) the domestic needs of different taxpayers are identical.

For the early steps in a purely theoretical discussion of sacrifice in taxation, this hypothesis is highly valuable if not indispensable. But, in order to estimate sacrifice in the real world, such factors as (1) differences in the real cost of a given rate of income and (2) differences in the domestic needs (number of dependents, etc.) must also receive careful consideration. For example, a schedule of graduated rates which would produce equal sacrifice under our theoretical assumption would need to be supplemented by a system of judicious discriminations and deductions in order to yield equal sacrifice under actual conditions.

The evaluation of the seven heroic assumptions which underlie all the sacrifice theories of progressive taxation has now been completed. This lengthy appraisal yields, however, a very brief conclusion. It is this: If any one of these underlying assumptions of the sacrifice theories is ex-

---

[19] Antonio de Viti de Marco, *First Principles of Public Finance*, translated from the Italian by Edith Pavlo Marget (New York, 1936), p. 117.

[20] *Op. cit.*, p. 7.

cluded, none of the sacrifice theories leads logically to progressive taxation; if all these assumptions are admitted, the sacrifice doctrines are robbed of practical significance.

8. An eighth assumption which is common to all the sacrifice theories, with the exception of the minimum sacrifice theory, is that no indirect sacrifice is incident to the imposition of the tax.[21] In other words, no significance is accorded to the indirect sacrifices which are due to the repressive effects of some forms of taxation upon "certain desirable industries and enterprises." The actual importance of these indirect effects means that any theory which precludes their consideration has little practical significance. But from the fact that the minimum sacrifice theory gives a prominent role to the indirect and long-run sacrifice as well as to direct and immediate sacrifice in taxation, it follows that the practicality of this theory is dependent, in part at least, upon the statesman's ability to make a summation of two psychic magnitudes of different time dimensions. Even if it were possible to make such a calculation, the significant limitations imposed upon the theory of minimum sacrifice by the first seven of the foregoing assumptions are sufficient to make it untenable as a basis for progressive taxation.

9. The validity of the equal sacrifice theory as a basis for progressive taxation depends not only upon the eight assumptions which have already been discussed but also upon the hypothesis that the curve of diminishing marginal utility of money income is steeper than a rectangular hyperbola.[22] The denial of the reality of the principle of diminishing marginal

---

21 For able presentations of the theory of minimum sacrifice see Carver, *op. cit.*, pp. 66–79, and Edgeworth, "The Pure Theory of Taxation" [Article 24 of this volume. Ed.] and "Minimum Sacrifice versus Equal Sacrifice," in *op. cit.*, pp. 63–125, 234–42. Carver gives more attention to indirect sacrifice than does Edgeworth; but M. E. Robinson is unfair to Edgeworth when in *Public Finance* (New York, 1922), p. 24, it is implied that Edgeworth's minimum sacrifice theory "ignored the reaction [of taxation] upon future wealth production." Edgeworth states specifically that "the principle of least sacrifice in trumpet tones proclaims that the rate of taxation ought to be progressive; *except so far as this distributional presumption is cut into by the productional and other utilitarian conditions*" (*op. cit.*, p. 240). (Italics are mine.)

22 For a mathematical demonstration of the proposition that, other things equal, equal sacrifice demands progression only on condition that the curve of diminishing marginal utility of income is steeper than a rectangular hyperbola, see Hugh Dalton, *Principles of Public Finance* (6th ed.; London, 1930), pp. 96–98; and Ragnar Frisch, *New Methods of Measuring Marginal Utility* (Tübingen, 1932), pp. 118–22.

If we grant all other assumptions necessary for the theoretical validity of the equal sacrifice theory of progressive taxation and if we assume identical marginal utility of income for all individuals for the smallest taxable income, progressive taxation would also be required under the following conditions: (1) dissimilar diminishing marginal utility curves, but varying directly in steepness with size of income, from a rectangular hyperbola in the case of the smallest taxable income to the steepest slope for the largest taxable income; (2) dissimilar diminishing marginal utility curves, with all curves steeper than a rectangular hyperbola, but with the degree of steepness varying directly with the rate of taxable income.

utility of money income carries with it, of course, a belief in the futility of any attempt to establish the characteristic slope of the diminishing marginal utility curve. The efforts of Harrod, Fisher, and Frisch toward this goal are, however, of sufficient theoretical importance to warrant careful analysis.[23]

Mr. Harrod, in four pages of purely deductive reasoning, attempts to refute Pigou's contention that "plainly it is impossible to decide whether the income-utility curve of the members of the community (all of whom are assumed to be alike) is of this character (viz., a rectangular hyperbola) or of some other defined character by any process of general reasoning."[24] Harrod, on the contrary, writes:

> I propose . . . to suggest a process of general reasoning by which we may establish a probability in favor of the steeper curve. . . . Professor Pigou confesses that the supposition of a steeper curve is "plausible." It is proposed to contend for something more than mere plausibility.

Believing it impossible to determine the slope of the income-utility curve directly, Harrod attempts to establish it inferentially from study of the nature of the effort or disutility curve. His argument is introduced by three explicit assumptions and one questionable pronouncement. The assumptions are: (1) that the taxable members of the community are alike in respect to the utility of the income to them and that the Xth unit of effort has the same disutility to them all; (2) that the whole income is derived from the reward of effort; and (3) that the recipient is at liberty to vary the amount of his effort. The questionable pronouncement is that

---

[23] It is well known, of course, that unverified hypotheses relative to the slope of the curve of diminishing marginal utility have been made by Bernoulli, Cramer, Cohen-Stuart, and Sax. These assumptions are discussed in Edgeworth, *op. cit.*, pp. 108–13; Marshall, *op. cit.*, pp. 134–35 n., 842–43; Seligman, *op. cit.*, pp. 82 n. 219–23, 279–84; and Emil Sax, "Die Progressivsteuer," *Zeitschrift für Volkswirtschaft, Socialpolitik und Verwaltung*, I (1892), 43–101. See also Daniel Bernoulli, *Die Grundlage der Modernen Wertlehre*, translated from the Latin by Dr. Alfred Pringsheim (Leipzig, 1896).

Some of these early hypotheses antedate the formulation of the Weber-Fechner Law; and later ones seem to have been made independently of it. In fact, this law affords no valid psychological basis for generalizations concerning the relationship between marginal utility and the rate of income. This is true because the Weber-Fechner Law is a statement of the relation between stimulus and sensation, a relationship which the principle of diminishing marginal utility does not attempt to express. And even in regard to the relation between stimulus and sensation, Hudson Hoagland states, "Evidence is present from the fields of vision, pressure sense, and muscular sense, to show that the logarithmic relation [between stimulus and sensation] known as the Weber-Fechner Law rarely actually exists as such" ("The Weber-Fechner Law and the All-or-None Theory," *Journal of General Psychology*, III, No. 3 [July, 1930], 370). For statements concerning the Weber-Fechner Law which are regarded as true by a leading contemporary psychologist see Edwin G. Boring, *The Physical Dimensions of Consciousness* (New York and London, 1933), p. 60.

[24] R. F. Harrod, "Progressive Taxation and Equal Sacrifice," *Economic Journal*, XL, 704–7. The quotation is from Pigou, *op. cit.*, p. 110.

"the utility of a man's last pound of income is equal to the disutility of the last unit of effort expended to earn that pound."

He next examines three possible types of relationship between effort, rate of pay per unit of effort, and income; and from each draws a logical inference concerning this relationship.

First he assumes that a man will put forth a constant amount (equal units) of effort regardless of the rate of pay per unit of effort or of the total amount of income. From this supposition it follows that the Kth unit of effort and its disutility remain constant. And, since it is given that marginal disutility of effort and marginal utility of the corresponding unit of income are equated, it follows that the marginal utility of income per unit of effort is constant. Now obviously, the total income will vary in direct proportion with the rate of pay per unit of effort because, by hypothesis, the amount (number of units) of effort is constant. This means, for example, that if the rate of pay per unit of effort is £4, the total income will be twice as great as for a rate of pay of only £2. It means also that, when the rate of pay is £4 and the total income is a, £4 measure the same magnitude of marginal disutility as do £2 when the rate of pay is £2 and the total income is $a/2$. In other words, the marginal disutility per £ of income varies in inverse proportion to its quantity. Since marginal disutility and marginal utility are always equated, it must be concluded that the marginal utility of income varies in inverse proportion to its amount. This leads finally to the conclusion that the marginal utility curve of income is a rectangular hyperbola; therefore, equal sacrifice requires proportional taxation.

Having analyzed the case of an "effort demand for income curve" of unitary elasticity, Harrod treats the two remaining effort-income relationships as follows:

If the effort demand for income curve has other than unitary elasticity, it is not identical with the income-utility curve, since the marginal unit of effort expended to obtain income is not always the Kth unit and we are deprived of our fixed rod for measuring income utility. Certain general relations may, however, be established. If the effort demand for income curve has for part of its course less than unitary elasticity, the last pound of income is, as income increases, pitted against units of effort of successively decreasing disutility. Consequently the marginal utility of a pound of income declines more rapidly than the effort demand for a pound. If the effort demand curve is steeper than a rectangular hyperbola, the income-utility curve is steeper still. If the effort demand curve is flatter than a rectangular hyperbola, the income-utility curve is by parity of reasoning flatter still. Consequently, taxation should be progressive or regressive according to whether the representative man's effort demand for income is inelastic or elastic.[25]

---

[25] Op cit., p. 705.

It remains therefore only to determine the elasticity of the representative man's effort demand for income. Harrod says:

> A man of great virtue might always work 100 per cent of capacity whatever his pay. His effort-demand curve would be the innermost of a family of rectangular hyperbolas, each showing willingness to work a given per cent of capacity whatever the remuneration. The actual effort demand of a representative man impinges on that of a man of great virtue at one point at least, namely, when he is at the subsistence level.[26]

However, the effort-demand curve of the representative man will soon drop away from that of a man of great virtue, finally falling to zero when the point of satiety has been reached. With the reservation that the income-utility curve refers to "a representative individual whose income, along with the consumable incomes of all other similar individuals is supposed to vary," Harrod maintains that

> it seems quite irrational not to suppose a limit to the quantity of means to secure which a man is prepared to undergo pain. Desire springs ever; but beyond a certain point it would be directed to new applications of existing means rather than to a further extension of them.[27]

Briefly, this is the line of reasoning from which Harrod concludes that for the representative individual the effort-demand curve has an elasticity of less than *one*. And from this, as we have seen, it follows that equal sacrifice requires progressive taxation.

Harrod admits that his argument seems to imply that "the richer a man is, the less work he will do" and also that this generalization might be regarded as too sweeping. He then immediately adds:

> The following points must, however, be *remembered*. 1. We are supposing the individuals to be similarly situated in their social environment. 2. We suppose similarity of temperament. 3. Work may be undertaken for other than income-getting motives, to obtain power, etc. 4. Some work is pleasant. Units of effort must be measured so as to show the same curve of increasing disutility of units of effort for similar individuals in different professions. Difficulties as to how to determine these units no doubt arise. But they need not be held to obstruct us from reaching our main conclusion.[28]

But, when these factors are remembered and are also conjoined with his earlier assumptions, his whole argument gives the reader the feeling

---

[26] *Ibid.*, p. 706.

[27] *Ibid.*, pp. 706–7.

[28] Points nos. 1, 3, and 4 are mentioned for the first time at this late stage of his argument. (Italics are mine.)

that he has had a delightful dialectical excursion into a world of make-believe in which a disciple of Jevons entertained him by performing miracles with hedonic units.

More specifically, Harrod's argument is unconvincing because it is based upon a felicific calculus of very doubtful psychological validity. Professor Frank Knight points out that

critical students are more and more doubtful not only as to the degree to which people really foresee the consequences of their acts, but even as to the extent to which choices are consistently made with a view to any intended result, especially any result desired for its own sake. In modern psychology there is an increasing emphasis on unconscious motivation as well as on the "prejudice" and caprice in the conscious motives of men.[29]

In Harrod's discussion no mention is made of the psychological difficulty of equating the marginal disutility of effort and the marginal utility of money income. But a psychological problem there is.

It is well known that the utility derived from the expenditure of a given sum of money may vary widely from that which was anticipated. But this familiar hiatus between desire and utility, a very important phenomenon in real life, finds no place in Harrod's purely theoretical analysis.[30]

The assumption that "the recipient [of income] is at liberty to vary the amount of his effort" is a condition far from typical in modern industry. Today the legally free laborer is not able to equate even roughly the sacrifice of his last hour of daily labor and the utility of the income therefrom. And not only does he have little or no freedom as to the length of the working day but he also has, in many lines of agricultural and industrial activity, little freedom as to the number of days and months which he may work.

Harrod's argument in support of the generalization that the effort-demand curve of income is more inelastic than *one* is too sweeping. It is reasonable, as he maintains, to expect the effort demand to stand at 100 per cent of capacity at the subsistence income level and at zero at the

---

[29] Knight, *op. cit.*, p. 219.

[30] On this point, Marshall states: "It cannot be too much insisted that to measure directly, or *per se*, either desires or the satisfaction which results from their fulfillment is impossible, if not inconceivable. If we could, we should have two accounts to make up, one of desires, and the other of realized satisfactions. And the two might differ considerably. For, to say nothing of higher aspirations, some of those desires with which economics is chiefly concerned, and especially those connected with emulation, are impulsive; many result from the force of habit; some are morbid and lead only to hurt; and many are based on expectations that are never fulfilled" (*op. cit.*, p. 92 n.; see also Viner, *op. cit.*).

point of complete satiety. But a belief in the existence of a point of satiety for money income as a means to power and prestige is open to reasonable doubt; and, furthermore, Harrod himself goes so far as to admit that the effort-demand curve may have "kinks and irregularities in various parts, but it must be predominantly inelastic."[31] The belief in the existence of these "kinks and irregularities" in the effort-demand-for-income curve between the extremes of subsistence and satiety would lead Harrod logically to hold that there are also corresponding kinks and irregularities in the curve of diminishing marginal utility of income. In other words, he must believe that this latter curve has different degrees of elasticity in its various segments. This belief would force him logically to the conclusion that no valid generalization can be made a priori as to the relationship between the rate of taxation and the area of sacrifice in the case of rates of income between subsistence and satiety.

Harrod's argument cannot be strengthened by the fact that Professor Douglas, from a statistical study, has arrived at the conclusion that the effort-demand curve for income is less elastic than *one*.[32] The curve which Professor Douglas has derived is the result of the measurement, under actual conditions, of the effort demand for income of workers in seventeen different industries in the United States from 1890 to 1926, inclusive. Under actual conditions of modern industry, the effort demand for income is influenced to a significant extent, if not determined, by such factors as technological and seasonal conditions, legislative enactment, and labor-union policies. The individual member of a labor union has very limited freedom, in the short run, in balancing the marginal disutility of his effort and the marginal utility of his income. And even in the long run it is doubtful whether labor-union members have deliberately attempted to follow a policy of choosing between shorter hours (less effort) and greater wages-income. It seems more probable that the phenomenon of historical concomitance of shorter hours and higher wage rates which Douglas has discovered is the product of the combined influence of several factors, e.g., (1) technological improvements and the consequent increase in the productivity of labor; (2) the general desire of individual laborers and of labor unions to distribute the advantages of this greater productivity between shorter hours and greater wages-income (the basic factor in Douglas' explanation of the historical concomitance of shorter hours and higher wage rates); (3) the familiar labor-union policy not

---

[31] *Op. cit.*, p. 707. For an illuminating argument against the possibility of the *a priori* determination of the elasticity of the effort demand for income, see Lionel Robbins, "On the Elasticity of Demand for Income in Terms of Effort," *Economica*, X (1930), 123–29.

[32] Paul H. Douglas, *The Theory of Wages* (New York, 1934), pp. 295–314.

of distributing the advantages of the greater productivity between shorter hours and greater wages-income but of seeking to secure an advantage in one direction only, e.g., the policy of demanding, and often receiving, shorter hours with the same wages-income, or the alternative policy of demanding greater wages-income for the same number of hours, the choice between these two policies often depending upon their strategic advantages at a given time and place; (4) the desire of labor unions to spread work among members; and (5) legislative enactment relative to wages and hours of female workers, which may or may not have represented the choice of a majority of workers in this group.

Certainly, the last three of these factors which have combined to produce the relationship between hours and wage rates which Douglas discovered are of such character and importance to make unreasonable the belief that this relationship is to any significant degree the result of the free, deliberate, and successful attempt on the part of workers to equate marginal disutility of effort and marginal utility of income.

The effort-demand curve which Harrod attempts to determine a priori is one which would exist only under conditions of freedom on the part of the individual to vary the amount of his effort. Obviously, therefore, the curve which Douglas has determined statistically affords no basis for an inference concerning the nature of the curve which Harrod has attempted to establish a priori. Furthermore, no valid inference concerning the slope of the marginal utility curve of income can be drawn from the effort-demand curve which Professor Douglas has determined statistically. Such an inference would be absurd unless based upon the assumption of freedom of the individual to vary the amount of his effort and to equate marginal disutility of effort and marginal utility of income. The conditions under which Douglas studied the effort demand for income were contrary to this assumption.

Another criticism of Harrod's general treatment relates to the significant role which he has given to the "representative man." It must be remembered that taxation has to do not with the "representative man" but with many unlike men. An evaluation of the assumption of identical diminishing marginal utility curves of income has been presented in an earlier section of this article (p. 25); therefore, no further discussion of this assumption is necessary.

Regarding the assumption that all income is derived from the reward to effort, Harrod states that

this assumption was only made in order to establish the general character of our test curve [of income utility]. The assumption is not necessary to the conclusion about income utility. If the test curve *would* be of this character in the assumed circumstances, the income-utility curve *is* of this character.[33]

These statements are acceptable, however, only on condition that the phrase "under the same assumptions" be added to Harrod's last sentence.

In the light of the foregoing critique of Harrod's thesis, it seems fair to conclude that he has failed to establish a probability in favor of an income-utility curve of an elasticity of less than *one*. Professor Pigou's contention that the character of the income-utility curve cannot be decided by any process of general reasoning stands unshaken.[34]

In radical contrast with Harrod's purely deductive analysis stands Fisher's method for measuring the "marginal utility" of money income statistically.[35] Fisher shares Jevons' skepticism as to the possibility of measuring psychic magnitudes directly. He believes with Jevons, however, that "it is from the quantitative effects of the feelings that we must estimate their comparative amounts."

For numerical data from which to measure "the feelings of the human heart," Fisher would so utilize

data of family budgets and prices as to compare the wants of two typical families of different incomes, in the same community, by using as a yardstick or criterion, a third typical family having identical tastes, but differing in the amount of income, and living under a different scale of prices for foods, rents, clothing and other items of consumption.

More specifically, he outlines his method as follows:

Let us, then, imagine three typical workingmen's families, each consisting, say, of five people, the man himself, his wife, and three typical children.

It is further assumed that, between these three families, which we may distinguish as Case 1, Case 2, and Case 3 respectively, there is no difference in the want schedules. That is, we assume that all three families' appetites and tastes are the same, so that in all three cases they will react in precisely the same way to the same opportunities to spend money. These opportunities, however, are *not* supposed to be the same, because of two variables, namely, (1) the *incomes* are supposed to be different in the three cases, and (2) the *prices* in the two countries, England and America, are supposed to be different. Because of these differences, in prices and incomes, the family budgets will necessarily differ. We shall see that

---

[33] *Op. cit.*, p. 707.

[34] *Op. cit.*, p. 110.

[35] Irving Fisher, "A Statistical Method for Measuring 'Marginal Utility' and Testing the Justice of a Progressive Income Tax," in *Economic Essays Contributed in Honor of John Bates Clark* (New York, 1927), pp. 157–93. The following statement and evaluation of Fisher's method is based entirely upon the study cited above.

the behavior of the families, in response to the changes in price and income, can be used to reveal the varying strength of their wants or desires in accordance with their want schedules. While their three want *schedules* are identical, their positions in this common schedule are not. That is, the three families *would* behave alike if their circumstances were alike, but actually *do* behave differently because their circumstances are different.

Fisher next presents an ingenious numerical illustration of his statistical method for measuring the "want-for-one-more dollar" of income. Although the reproduction of this illustration in the present article is not feasible, it should be pointed out that the equations employed are based upon the following assumptions: (1) the marginal dollar of an average or typical family is worth the same subjectively in every direction; (2) wants of different groups of individuals are assumed to be practically comparable; (3) each want is dependent exclusively on the provision for that want; (4) price indexes applicable to Cases 1 and 2 (in Fisher's numerical illustration) are equal; and (5) the ratio between the income and expenditure of any family is constant, i.e., either exact equality of income and expenditure or, more generally, a slight excess of income over expenditure, that excess being the same percentage for all cases.

Granted these assumptions, Fisher maintains that it is possible to determine the slope of the "want-for-one-more dollar" of income and, further, that such a curve is of some significance in solving the problem of the proper rate of income taxation. He writes:

According to which way this product [income multiplied by "want-for-one-more dollar"] differs from unity, we have a justification for progressive or regressive taxation, while if their product is exactly unity, taxation should be neither progressive nor regressive, but strictly proportional to income. This is all on the assumption that the tax is to be laid according to the principle of equal sacrifices to taxpayers of different incomes.[36]

Enough has been said concerning the nature of Fisher's method. It is now in order to evaluate its significance in relation to the problem of determining the proper rate structure for equal sacrifice in taxation. Because the practical significance of a method or theory, as distinct from its logical validity, depends upon the degree of realism represented in its assumptions, an appraisal of Fisher's assumptions follows logically.

The unreality of two of his assumptions—namely, that the marginal dollar of an average or typical family is worth the same subjectively in every direction and that each want is dependent exclusively on the pro-

---

[36] *Ibid.*, p. 185.

vision for that want—has been established effectively by the Italian economist F. Vinci.[37]

After stressing the difficulties which will be encountered in the selection of "typical families" answering the many conditions established by Fisher, Vinci states that

the tendency to equalize the marginal utility of money in the various classes of expenditure of a given family, even in the case of consumption that is typical and distributed over a suitable lapse of time, is a theorem which in the most favorable cases can be regarded as a broad approximation.

In support of this statement, Vinci offers a number of valid reasons. Certain of the more significant of these reasons are as follows:

1. The greater or lesser divisibility of certain commodities;
2. Some expenditures concern consumption and others use [i.e., expenditures for consumption goods versus expenditures for production goods];
3. Some expenditures are made long before the consumption or use of the goods acquired;
4. The existence of savings, which usually present widely varying proportions between one family and another, even if they have the same income, and also from time to time, with relation to the course of prices and the monetary regime;
5. Some expenditures (coal, bread, vegetables, milk, etc.) are generally made by the wife, who often saves without her husband's knowledge; others (wine or beer, tobacco, etc.) are usually made by the husband; others again (housing, clothing) perhaps by both, and sometimes not without more or less evident disagreements, which prevent either spouse or both from pushing their own consumption in the several directions to the point of equalizing the utility of the last penny spent in each of them. Actually the family expenditure—even excluding the children—is the resultant of two very different systems of utility curves and—as happens even in the most amicable transactions—does not fully satisfy either system;
6. The estimates of utility [the subjective valuations] are most variable from one instant to the next, changing with the humor of the individual and the environment in which the expenditure takes place. Here is a housewife, who is going to buy two yards of cloth with the thrifty intention of spending not more than twenty lire: the skillful salesman shows her a good-looking dress pattern and an enticing fashion-journal [fashion plate], stimulates her vanity, and upsetting all the system of subjective valuations makes her spend with joy and without regrets twice what she had intended.

---

[37] "L'Utilita della moneta e l'imposta progressiva," *Rivista italiana di statistica, economia e finanza*, V, No. 2 (1933), 209–42. All quotations from Vinci are from the article just cited. The writer wishes to acknowledge his indebtedness to Dr. Mary Wildman, of Stanford University, for her assistance in the translation of Vinci's article.

Concerning the assumption that each want is dependent exclusively on the provision for that want, Vinci correctly observes that, in reality,

> the utility of a commodity and also the utility of groups of commodities are for the most part closely dependent upon the utility of many other commodities and groups of commodities. For the working-class families considered by Fisher it cannot be seriously assumed that the utility of food is independent of that of housing. Is it perhaps not true [can it be untrue?] that an empty third of the typical lodging would be more pleasing to a workman with a wife and two children, if the family should be well nourished than if it should be undernourished? The same may be said for clothing, etc., and all the more forcibly for the individual items of expenditure, for which often the connection is very close because of the complementary or substitute relations which may exist between them.

The unreality of the two assumptions which have just been discussed is enough, in the opinion of Vinci and in that of the present writer, to destroy one's faith in the practical significance of results attainable by Fisher's method.

The assumption that wants of different individuals are practically comparable has already been discussed on pages 25 and 33; the supposition of equality of price indexes, as Fisher has stated, is not a necessary assumption; and the hypothesis of a constant ratio between the income and expenditure of any family is patently unreal.

Fisher himself questions the reality of his assumptions but answers his own questions with surprising naïveté. He asks and answers the following questions:

> But can we properly compare her [a housewife's] particular want for eggs or dollars with that of another woman by her side who is going through the same process? Can we even compare her own individual wants at two different times? Finally, are we justified in taking her market decision as representative of the wants of other members of her family?
> To all these questions I would answer "yes"—approximately at least. But the only, or only important, reason I can give for this answer is that, in actual practical human life, we do proceed on just such assumptions. Academically we may have philosophic doubts as to bridging the gulf between mind and mind, or even between one time and another time for the same mind. . . .
> Philosophic doubt is right and proper, but the problems of life cannot, and do not wait.

When this answer and the reason supporting it are added to the foregoing evaluation of Fisher's assumptions, the desirability of finding a more acceptable method than Fisher's of deciding the case for or against progressive taxation becomes obvious.

A final criticism of Fisher's study concerns the ethical aspects of his attempt to relate his statistical method of determining the curve of "marginal utility" of money income to the problem of progressive taxation.

Early in his paper, Fisher makes it plain that for him the term "utility" is devoid of psychological content.[38] The curve of diminishing "marginal utility" of income is a curve of diminishing desire-for-one-more dollar. For Fisher, the question of the hiatus between desire and satisfaction is irrelevant.

But now there arises the troublesome question: How relate this non-psychological diminishing marginal desire curve to the ethical criterion of equal sacrifice in taxation? The obvious answer is that no relationship can be established unless equal sacrifice is made to mean equal sacrifice of desire for income as distinct from the generally accepted notion of equal sacrifice of satisfaction actually derived from income by the taxpayer.

To adopt the former rather than the latter meaning of equal sacrifice is to substitute a pure desire ethics for ethical hedonism. And this substitution, it is believed, would be regarded as a poor exchange by most modern ethicists—even those who find hedonistic ethics unacceptable. The adoption of a desire ethics leaves untouched the fundamental ethical problem of distinguishing concretely between the desired and the desirable.[39]

Stimulated by Fisher, Professor Ragnar Frisch, in his *New Methods of Measuring Marginal Utility*, attempts to determine the slope of the curve of diminishing marginal utility of income by a statistical analysis of data in the *Bureau of Labor Statistics Budget Study* (1918–19), *Bulletin No. 357.* He selected thirteen of the ninety-two cities covered by the bureau's investigation. "For each of these cities the food expenditure curve was plotted using logarithmic scale along both the income axis and the food expenditure axis."[40] And for each city were plotted both the curve showing the relation between family expenditure and family income and the curve showing the relation between individual adult male expenditure for food and the individual adult male income.[41] Nine of the thirteen ex-

---

[38] Fisher writes as follows: "I hope the term 'utility' in particular may be abandoned, because it has to-day other economic connotations, such as in 'A Public Utility' referring, say, to a telephone company, and because it seems to imply a commital to the old utilitarian 'calculus of pleasure and pain' of Bentham and his school. *The true meaning needed is based primarily not on pleasure but desire*" (*op. cit.*, p. 157 n. [italics mine]; see also his *Mathematical Investigations in the Theory of Value and Prices* [New Haven, 1892; 1925 reprint], pp. 11 and 23).

[39] See A. B. Wolfe, "On the Content of Welfare," *American Economic Review*, XXI, No. 2 (June, 1931), 209.

[40] Frisch, *op. cit.*, p. 59.

[41] *Ibid.*

penditure curves were selected for detailed analysis. Then by the use of statistical techniques too involved to permit of adequate summary reproduction, Frisch establishes the curve of diminishing marginal utility of income.[42]

For the small incomes this curve is steeper, and for medium incomes flatter, than a rectangular hyperbola. Frisch concludes that, if equal area sacrifice is accepted as an objective, such a curve leads to a heavily progressive tax for small incomes and a regressive tax for medium incomes.[43] The nature of this conclusion leads him to make the surprising remark: "I feel that this implausible result is due to the fallacy of the area-difference [equal area sacrifice] principle rather than to errors in the statistical results."[44]

But more surprising still is his belief that a statistical determination of the relationship between the variable x (quantity of food consumed), the covariable r (income), and the constant a (price) in a few American cities will enable him to derive the curve of diminishing marginal utility of money income.[45] In fact, Frisch makes so many qualifications and admits so many limitations in the closing pages of his study that the final results of his analysis are entirely too meager to have significant bearing upon the questions to which he relates them, namely, "Should the income tax be made progressive? And if so, what should the exact rate of progression be?"[46]

In discussing the shortcomings of his investigation, Frisch classifies expenditures into three groups, (A), (B), and (C). Expenditure group (A) consists of current expenditures for food, clothing, shelter, etc.; in short, all those things which enter into the type of budget examined in his statistical study. Expenditure group (B) includes all the expenditures entering into (A) and, in addition, certain expenditures connected with wants that may cumulate in intensity over a long period of years and then, if the means are available, be satisfied in a relatively short period of time. "Such things as 'expenditure' for saving might also be classified under group (B)." Expenditure group (C) includes not only all expenditures in (A) and (B) but also those which have no definite relation to the actual consumption of the individual but are nevertheless of great concern to him, e.g., expenditures which will increase industrial or political power.

---

[42] *Ibid.*, pp. 60 ff.
[43] *Ibid.*, p. 122.
[44] *Ibid.*
[45] *Ibid.*, p. 33.
[46] *Ibid.*, p. 114.

Frisch sees that his statistical analysis is relevant only to the type of expenditure in class (A). He also admits that group (B) expenditures play an important role in the life of the middle class, and that they are made for "a large number of items which therefore cannot be given a significant analysis unless by considering the interrelationship between income and expenditure budgets for a long period of years."[47] Concerning class (C) expenditures, Frisch states that such outlays are the most significant items in the disbursements of nearly every great businessman or speculator and that the way such a man looks upon his income and expenditure has nothing to do with his personal consumption.

Because his statistical method can throw no light upon those expenditures which belong exclusively to either class (B) or class (C), Frisch outlines an interview method as a means of measuring the marginal utility of income for "great businessmen" and "speculators."[48] Even if it were assumed that the interviews yielded any reliable basis for prediction as to human behavior, they could serve only as a means of establishing an individual's scale of time preference for income. Frisch does not, and I am convinced that he cannot, demonstrate how information concerning an individual's scale of time preference can be made the basis for establishing the slope of his curve of diminishing marginal utility of income.

Another limitation of Frisch's analysis is the fact that the relationship which he attempts to establish between s (sum of the tax) and r (income) concerns the same individual in different situations instead of different individuals. He admits, however, that in practical application the relation between s and r would have to be applied also to cases where the different magnitudes of r stand for the incomes of different individuals.[49] Earlier in his study, Frisch states that he "doubts very much" whether interindividual or interfamily utility comparisons will ever be made.[50] He believes that such comparisons are possible but extremely difficult. Frisch dodges the difficulty, if not the impossibility, of such comparisons by adopting the fiction of the representative or average man.[51]

Frisch admits that the defects of his method which have just been pointed out constitute valid objections to his analysis even in static theory.[52] He also concedes that his theory needs "dynamification."[53] He sees that, in its present form, his method is unable to make possible the solu-

---

[47] *Ibid.*, p. 138.
[48] *Ibid.*, pp. 140–42.
[49] *Ibid.*, p. 120.
[50] *Ibid.*, pp. 20–21.
[51] *Ibid.*, p. 120.
[52] *Ibid.*, p. 138.
[53] *Ibid.*, p. 136.

tion of the problem of structural changes. Such changes he illustrates by the following example:

> Suppose we have a spiral spring. If we attach a weight to the end of the spring, we will notice a lengthening of the spring. And by experiment we may find a definite law connecting the size of the weight and the extent of the lengthening. This law would hold good for weights that are not too heavy *and not left on the spring for too long a time.* If we leave a very heavy weight on the spring for a long period of time, we would, when we got back, find that the original law connecting weight and lengthening had changed. In economics we have many phenomena of a similar sort. For instance: If a person gets more income, the representative point on his money utility curve will move along the curve downwards and to the right. But if the point is left in this position for a considerable time, this will have the effect of *shifting the whole curve upwards,* so that the money utility as represented by the ordinate of the point in question again starts increasing, even though the new income remains constant.[54]

Frisch next suggests "several ways in which we could attempt to draw this phenomenon [structural change] into the analysis." But none of the methods suggested seems capable of measuring such nebulous phenomena as structural changes in psychic magnitudes.

The candor shown by Professor Frisch in setting forth the true limitations of his method is indeed admirable. But it is difficult to understand how he could see so clearly the shortcomings of his own method and still believe that it could possibly yield results having any significant bearing upon the problem of the measurement of actual psychic sacrifice in taxation.[55]

The preceding appraisal of past attempts to determine the slope of the diminishing marginal utility curve of money income leads to the conclusion that such efforts have been futile. And, because the magnitudes involved in this problem are subjective, the probability is great that future attempts to solve it will also prove fruitless. Until there is established a reasonable basis for a belief not only in the reality of the hypothesis that the curve of diminishing marginal utility of money income is steeper than a rectangular hyperbola but also in the reality of the eight preceding assumptions, the case for progressive taxation cannot be based upon the theory of equal sacrifice.[56]

A discussion of the sacrifice theories would be incomplete without

---

[54] *Ibid.,* pp. 136–37.

[55] For further criticism of Frisch's methods and results, see Vinci, *op. cit.,* pp. 222–42.

[56] It should be pointed out, not as an argument based upon authority but purely as a matter of professional interest, that the opinion that it is impossible either to determine the rate at which the marginal utility of an individual's income diminishes or to make interindividual utility comparisons is one which is widely held.

Mr. John Pagani, a graduate student in economics at Stanford, has found that this posi-

mention of their ethical validity. But, to deal with the normative aspects of these theories, the economist must exchange his cloak for that of the ethicist. And, although the new garment may be loose-fitting, the economist will find that in its pockets the ethicist has stored the material with which the ethical limitations of the sacrifice theories can be effectively demonstrated.

All the sacrifice theories ignore completely the question of the *quality* of the satisfactions which are sacrificed in taxation. To use a classical illustration, they put the satisfaction from scratching on the same level with that which is derived from philosophical speculation. Hawtrey puts the matter as follows: "The aggregate of satisfactions is not an aggregate of welfare at all. It represents good satisfactions which are welfare and bad satisfactions which are the reverse."[57] And Professor Pigou sets forth the limitations of a naïve utilitarian ethic as follows:

It must, indeed, be admitted that no test which is centered in sacrifice, in the sense of loss of satisfaction [utility], goes quite to the root of things. For, of equal satisfactions, one may embody more *good* than another: as between a greater and a less sacrifice of satisfaction, the greater may carry the smaller amount of evil. When this happens, it is, of course, the aggregate of good and evil, not the aggregate of satisfaction and dissatisfaction, to which the wise government will look.[58]

---

tion is well established in contemporary fiscal literature in Italy. Emilio Cossa, M. Fanno, A. Graziani, and Antonio de Viti de Marco are among the Italian writers who maintain that it is impossible to establish the slope of the diminishing marginal utility curve.

Among other economists who hold this opinion are Lionel Robbins, *The Nature and Significance of Economic Science* (2d ed.; London, 1935), p. 140; Seligman, *op. cit.*, p. 246; Stamp, *op. cit.*, pp. 53–54; and Taussig, *op. cit.*, p. 129.

[57] R. G. Hawtrey, *The Economic Problem* (London, 1926), p. 215. Sir Sydney Chapman, although discussing the ethics of the theory of proportional sacrifice, shows the absurdity of attaching ethical significance to the quantity of utility sacrificed. He writes: "Should we think it fair to reduce the rate of taxation of large incomes if, by a miracle, income above a certain amount became subject to immensely increasing utility? An answer in the affirmative is entailed if we believe that taxation should aim at equal proportional sacrifices of utility; but it seems absurd to suggest collecting less money for the State from the rich and more from the poor on the ground that the rich have become richer. This crude *reductio ad absurdum* may serve to make the reader doubt whether the principle of equal proportional sacrifice of utility can be sound" (*op. cit.*, p. 34).

[58] *Op. cit.*, p. 57. In the treatment of equal sacrifice it is argued convincingly by Professor Pigou that "there is at least as good a case for taxation that makes net satisfactions equal as for taxation that makes sacrifices equal. Indeed there is a better case. For people's economic well-being depends on the whole system of law, including the laws of property, contract and bequest, and not merely upon the law about taxes. To hold that the law about taxes ought to affect different people's satisfactions equally, while allowing that the rest of the legal system may properly affect them very unequally, seems not a little arbitrary" (*ibid.*, p. 60).

John Stuart Mill could find no better ethical justification of his theory of equal sacrifice in taxation than that equality ought to be the rule in all affairs of government (*Principles of Political Economy*, Book V, chap. ii, sec. 2). It is clear that the general precept of equality in political affairs does not necessarily dictate equality of sacrifice of utility in taxation.

It should also be pointed out that the state cannot accept existing wants as data because such wants themselves are in part a reflection of political policy.

II. THE FACULTY THEORY

The nebulous nature of the magnitudes involved in the measurement of psychic sacrifice has served as a significant stimulus to the demand for an objective criterion of justice in taxation. The wide popularity of the faculty or ability-to-pay theory is to be explained in part by the belief of certain economists that it possesses a greater degree of objectivity than does any one of the sacrifice theories.[59]

But in the minds of others its superiority over the sacrifice theories which were treated in Section I lies in the fact that it is cognizant not only of the "sacrifice of disposition" but also of the "sacrifice of acquisition" of income.[60] Seligman says:

Now if by sacrifice, we mean cost involved, i.e., the costs of acquisition as well as disposition, then indeed the sacrifice theory is correct in the sense that from the point of view of economic psychology the test of ability to pay taxes is an amalgam of both of these costs or sacrifices.[61]

The proponents of both the objective and the subjective faculty theories generally regard personal net income as the most satisfactory measure of taxpaying ability. They recognize, however, that equal personal net incomes do not necessarily represent equal taxable faculties. They readily admit the necessity of such supplementary considerations as: (1) domestic circumstances, (2) earned versus unearned income, (3) surplus versus cost elements, and (4) capital gains versus regularly recurring income.

But when the proponents of the objective faculty theory recognize these factors, they are motivated by the desire to secure the best possible measure of the individual's ability to bear the sacrifice incident to taxation. In other words, they are tacitly admitting that ability to pay is an

---

59 J. S. Nicholson states: "The faculty theory does not look to the feelings of the taxpayer, but to the money value of his taxable capacity. The State takes more from the rich, not because they will feel it less in proportion, but because they have more to give" (op. cit., p. 275). Clyde L. King writes: "Possibly some of the ease with which it [ability to pay] is accepted is due to disagreement as to what ability to pay means" (Public Finance [New York, 1935], pp. 205–6; see also Sumner H. Slichter, Modern Economic Society [New York, 1931], p. 736).

60 Seligman, Studies in Public Finance (New York, 1925), p. 187.

61 Seligman seems tacitly to assume that the marginal sacrifice curve of income does not accurately reflect the real cost of acquiring the income taken by taxation. In my opinion, Seligman's tacit assumption is a reasonable one. See above, pp. 31 ff., for my argument in support of this opinion.

empty concept unless given subjective content. Thus the objective faculty theory becomes the subjective sacrifice theory with all the limitations which have been discussed in the foregoing section of this article.

The faculty theory as interpreted and defended by Seligman is highly subjective. Its successful application would involve, among other things, a summation of (1) the psychic magnitudes sacrificed in the payment of a tax and (2) the *real cost* of production of the income which is sacrificed. The difficulties of measuring these psychic magnitudes are insuperable.

In addition to this important practical limitation, Seligman's theory rests upon a fundamental assumption of questionable reality. Seligman maintains that, other things being equal, the ability to make money increases more rapidly than in direct proportion to the quantity of money income. His defense of the validity of this assumption rests entirely upon such phrases as "money makes money," and "a rich man may be said to be subject to a certain sense to the law of increasing returns"; and upon such historical support as he finds in quotations from Rousseau and Adam Smith.[62]

The validity of this hypothesis has been challenged by Sir Josiah Stamp, who argues:

> This [increasing rate of productivity] cannot, however, be said to apply to a large income made up of various mixed investments, but only to a business income in the hands of a powerful and highly intelligent direction. . . . But if the larger business is not in fact more profitable—what then? If its proceeds formed part of a large number of smaller incomes, the ability, tested on the spending side, is in direct conflict with ability on the production side.[63]

Sir Josiah's argument implies that the assumption that increases in income make possible more than proportionate increases in ability to make money might have been valid for the days of individual entrepreneurship but that it does not square with the facts in an age of the corporation in which management is divorced from investment and in which the large and the small investors have the privilege of buying the same type of securities in the open market.

In spite of the weight of the foregoing argument, there is, however, something to be said in support of Seligman's hypothesis.[64] Ignoring for the moment the question of the rate of income, everyone will admit that money has the power, under our present economic system, to earn some

---

[62] *Progressive Taxation*, pp. 290–303.

[63] *Op. cit.*, p. 42.

[64] The following argument was suggested to me by one of my former students, Mr. John P. Allen.

income for the investor. From this it follows that the man who has a surplus of money over the bare needs of subsistence can put that surplus to work and thereby receive funded income over and above his unfunded income. Compare his status with that of an individual whose income is completely absorbed in the satisfaction of the elemental needs of life. Obviously, the ability of the former to make funded income is more than proportionately greater in relation to his income than that of the latter because in this case a positive magnitude is being compared with zero.

In this illustration the reality of Seligman's assumption is obvious; but is it valid as between two men both of whom are able to save, but different amounts? According to Seligman's critics, it is not. They would argue that, because in this case both men have equal opportunities of investment, their respective investment returns should be in proportion to the amount of their respective investments.[65]

The acceptance of this argument is, however, tantamount to a denial of the economic justification for such institutions as investment trusts, investment councils, and the like.

To the man who is able to accumulate only a small surplus, few avenues of investment are open. According to the best investment practice, the first concern is the establishment of a reserve fund for contingencies, this fund to be kept where it can be obtained in emergencies. The most obvious and most popular place for such a fund is a savings bank. But the interest rate paid by savings banks is always relatively low. Therefore, it follows that the man with only a small surplus who wishes to allow for contingencies is at a relative disadvantage in increasing his earning power as contrasted with the man with a larger surplus who can actually invest his money.[66] Therefore, the ability of this latter man to make money is increased more than proportionately to his income.

Consider next the case of two men, both of whom are in a position to invest for higher returns, for example, the man with $1,000 and the man with $100,000. Will the latter's earning power increase only in proportion to his wealth? Again the answer is "No."

To obtain a high rate of return upon investment, risk must be taken. In fact, the rate of return and estimated degree of safety are inversely related. Witness the contrast between rates of return on United States Government bonds and the bonds of the Soviet Union. Investment theory

---

[65] This argument clearly ignores the fact that "inside information" concerning money-making opportunities is more likely to be enjoyed by the very large than by the very small investor. In other words, the large investor has all the investment opportunities of the small investor, and more.

[66] This reasoning is based upon the reasonable assumption that emergency funds are a smaller percentage of large than of small capitals.

permits the taking of risks where diversification of securities is obtained. This is done on the theory that, if the investment in any one security is kept small, the high rate of return on the profitable investments will more than offset any individual losses that may be sustained. Obviously, the man with the $1,000 cannot obtain wide diversification to insure the safety of his principal. Therefore, he must content himself with a comparatively low yield on his investment. The man with the $100,000 can diversify and obtain a higher yield. Again it has been demonstrated that ability to make money increases more than in direct proportion to the increase in income.

It is not clear just how far this point could be carried. Certainly the man with more money can better afford expert advice, the use of investment services, etc., which theoretically at least should increase his earning power more than proportionately. Obviously, after a certain point is reached, additional income will no longer bring additional benefit through diversification alone. The man with one million dollars can probably diversify his investments just as successfully as the man with ten million. However, the cost of investing, the cost of investment services, and to a large extent the analytical and clerical staff costs do not vary proportionately with the amount invested. Therefore, they will impose less relative financial burden upon the wealthier man and thereby enable him to secure more than a proportionate return on his investment.

It may be concluded, therefore, that even in these days of the corporation, Seligman's assumption carries more truth than his critics would have us believe.[67] Whether or not this assumption leads logically to progressive taxation is another question.

It is possible, however, to admit that the ability to make money increases at a faster rate than does the quantity of income, and still find it necessary to reject the faculty theory as a legitimate basis for progressive taxation. First, even on the production side, it is still necessary to measure and compare the *real cost* of the incomes originally invested.[68] It is necessary, for example, to know whether or not they were "windfalls," or derived from labor. Second, the application of the faculty theory requires the measurement and comparison of the psychic "sacrifices of disposition" of income in taxation. This demand carries with it, of course, the difficul-

---

[67] Seligman's argument for the validity of the assumption that "money makes money" is based upon the size of the income. The argument in the present article turns upon the absolute amount of investment funds and also upon the fact that the ratio of investment funds to the subsistence funds of an individual increases with successive increases in his income.

[68] "A man's ability to pay taxes," writes Seligman, "is to be measured not only by the relative burden imposed upon him in parting with this wealth, but also by the relative ease with which he has acquired his wealth" (*Studies in Public Finance*, p. 188).

ties and limitations of the sacrifice theories. And, third, because the faculty theory is in reality a Janus-faced sacrifice theory, it shares the ethical shortcomings of the other members of the sacrifice family.

III. THE SURPLUS-INCOME THEORY

A case for progressive taxation is constructed by J. A. Hobson upon two postulates: (1) that only the "surplus" element in income is indicative of ability to bear taxes and (2) that the greater the income, the greater the ratio of the "surplus" to the "cost" element.[69]

Briefly, Hobson defines surplus income as those "elements of income which do not 'dry up' under taxation and the taxing of which does not disturb industry."[70] The characteristics of the cost element in income are, of course, the reverse. Taxes levied upon cost elements will, in the long run, be shifted; those levied on surplus elements will not. Shifting takes place through a reduction of the supply in the schedule sense with a consequent decrease in demand in the market sense. Therefore, taxes which are shifted have repressive effects on both production and consumption. On the other hand, taxes upon surplus elements leave the supply schedules of the taxed factors unchanged and, therefore, do not alter the position of the points at which they cut the respective demand schedules.

Hobson recognizes, however, that in the taxation of either the cost or the surplus elements there is a decrease in private purchasing power which is presumably offset by an increase in public purchasing power. But, while total purchasing power may remain the same, it may undergo significant qualitative changes. For example, when the government taxes surplus income, it diminishes the funds which are the principal source of savings and investments. The government might then spend these funds in such manner as to increase the demand for consumption goods. When, however, the government levies taxes only against the cost elements, it decreases private demand for consumption goods but leaves practically undiminished the quantity of funds destined for investment channels.

In his general argument, Hobson attempts to establish the verity of the following generalizations: (1) that oversaving or underconsumption is the cause of the business cycle, (2) that savings come primarily from surplus income, and (3) that the greater the income, the greater the ratio of surplus to cost elements. He accordingly concludes that progressive taxation is one means of mitigating industrial fluctuations.

---

[69] J. A. Hobson, *Taxation in the New State* (London, 1919); *Economics and Ethics* (Boston, 1929); *Economics of Unemployment* (London, 1922).
[70] *Taxation in the New State*, pp. 24–25.

Hobson assumes the dual role of ethicist and economist. His theory of progressive taxation is at once normative and scientific. As an ethicist, he regards industrial fluctuations as undesirable economic phenomena and their mitigation as a desirable social objective. As an economist, he attempts to show that progressive taxation is a logical and effective means to this end. And whether or not Hobson's ethical or economic position is found acceptable, it must be admitted that he has stated and related the ethical question of end and the economic question of means in such fashion as to make possible their intelligent discussion.

Sir Josiah Stamp questions the reality of Hobson's assumption that the greater the income, the greater the ratio of surplus to the cost element.[71] He also points out that Hobson himself recognizes the difficulty of distinguishing, in practice, between the surplus and cost elements of income.[72]

In reply to Stamp, Hobson could argue legitimately that the soundness of his general argument for progression does not depend wholly upon the distinction between surplus and cost. He could maintain that the validity of his oversaving theory of the business cycle rests not upon the assumption that the greater the income the greater the ratio of surplus to cost elements, but upon the fact that the ratio of savings to expenditures for consumption goods is much greater in the case of the large than in that of the small incomes.[73]

It is a familiar fact that oversaving is not widely accepted by competent students of the business cycle as the one and only important antecedent condition to industrial depression. However, many would agree with Professor Hansen's statement:

> We know that one of the characteristic features of a boom period is a tendency toward an excess investment in fixed capital. Indeed, one may say that the essence of the ups and downs of business is a general rise in investment in fixed capital in a boom and a substantial cessation of investment in fixed capital in depression.[74]

It seems, therefore, that statistical data relative to the ratio of savings to size of income and modern business cycle theory establish a general presumption in favor of progressive as distinct from either proportional or regressive taxation as a means to greater industrial stability.

---

[71] *Op. cit.*, pp. 43–44.

[72] *Ibid.*, p. 43.

[73] H. G. Moulton, *The Formation of Capital* (Washington, D.C., 1935), pp. 136–54; *Income and Economic Progress* (Washington, D.C., 1935), pp. 40–46; Hobson, *Economics of Unemployment*, pp. 29–84.

[74] Alvin H. Hansen, *Hearings before the Committee on Ways and Means, House of Representatives, on H.R. 4120* (74th Cong., 1st sess.), p. 374.

To many the desirability of greater industrial stability doubtless seems obvious. Ethicists would require, however, that Hobson define "the desirable" and also that he give his reasons for believing that it would be secured in higher degree by greater industrial stability. "Nowhere," writes Wolfe, "does Hobson get down to a concrete and definite statement of the content of welfare, or give us an objective standard by which the difference between 'higher' and 'lower' values can be measured. . . . Failure to make any such attempt is a great deficiency, one feels, in Hobson's work."[75]

IV. THE SOCIAL IMPORTANCE THEORY

In an earlier section of this article it was explained why Sir Sydney Chapman refused to accept the principle of diminishing marginal utility as a basis for progressive taxation. In the development of his positive theory of progression, Sir Sydney discards the psychological preconceptions of the sacrifice theories and substitutes in their stead the ethical postulate that

the wants satisfied by the earlier increments to income are usually of more importance socially than the wants satisfied by later increments to income whether the satisfaction of the former causes more utility or not. In speaking of the equity of taxation, we are obviously talking ethics, and therefore the wants primarily dealt with must be adjudged not according to the value of their satisfaction in fact (positive value), but according to the value of their satisfaction in a moral scheme of consumption (normative value).[76]

Here is definitely a theory which represents a step, although only a short one, in the right direction. Like Hobson, Chapman recognizes that the question of the proper distribution of the burden of taxation is primarily an ethical rather than a psychological problem. He fails, however, to establish adequately specific standards by which social importance or moral worth may be measured. It is this fact which makes it impossible to determine the degree of relationship between the social importance and the rate of income. Without the knowledge of this relationship, and with no standards suggested for its determination, Chapman's theory is without practical significance.

V. THE SOCIO-POLITICAL THEORY

The merit of the socio-political theory as a basis for progression lies in the fact that it is cognizant of the necessity of "following through"

---

[75] *Op. cit.*, pp. 216–17.
[76] *Op. cit.*, p. 34.

along the path which both Hobson and Chapman abandoned after too short a distance..

Both Hobson and Chapman accept the fundamental thesis of the socio-political theorist. That is to say, they recognize that "the question of equity in taxation cannot be discussed independently of the equity of the whole existing order."[77] Like Adolph Wagner, they base their case for progression upon the belief that the existing social order is incompatible with maximum welfare.[78] They do not go so far, however, as did Wagner in setting up the objective conditions of welfare. And Wagner failed to go so far in this direction as Wesley C. Mitchell would have the economist go.

In his treatment of welfare, Professor Mitchell writes:

> In becoming consciously a science of human behavior economics will lay less stress upon wealth and more stress upon welfare. Welfare will mean not merely an abundant supply of serviceable goods, but also a satisfactory working life filled with interesting activities.
>
> At present welfare thus conceived is rather vague, but it is capable of being made objective and definite in reference to such matters as food, clothing, shelter, sanitation, education, fatigue, leisure. And this realm of the definite in welfare will be expanded steadily by quantitative methods, so that we shall develop a criterion of welfare applicable to many lines of effort.[79]

Mitchell suggests the direction which the development of the socio-political theory should take, but the implications of his suggestion remain to be worked out. The remainder of this article will be devoted to this task.

Objective criteria of welfare are not ends in themselves. They must be thought of as the basic economic, political, and social conditions under which there would be the optimum opportunity for the fullest development of the intellectual, moral, and physical capacities of every member of the state.

With objective criteria of welfare established, it would be possible to decide in favor of or against progressive taxation upon the basis of its

---

[77] Taussig, *op. cit.*, p. 509.

[78] For a concise statement of Wagner's position see the excerpts in Bullock's *Selected Readings in Public Finance* (Boston, 1924), pp. 254–58; and in Donald O. Wagner, *Social Reformers* (New York, 1935), pp. 490–506.

[79] W. C. Mitchell, "The Prospects of Economics," in *The Trend of Economics*, ed. R. G. Tugwell (New York, 1924), p. 31. Professor J. J. Spengler argues for the construction of a composite index of welfare expressed in objective terms without psychological implications ("Have Values a Place in Economics?" *International Journal of Ethics*, XLIV [1933–34], 313–31).

probable effect upon these desiderata.[80] For example, if both regularity of production and employment are adopted as objective criteria of welfare, a proposal for progressive taxation would be accepted or rejected, other things being equal, upon the evidence that progression would mitigate or accentuate industrial fluctuations.[81] It would be necessary, of

---

[80] Individuals might be agreed as to ends but in disagreement as to the best means to their attainment. For example, Lutz, Stamp, and Taussig have little or no respect for progressive taxation as a means of improving social conditions, yet they would agree that social improvement is desirable. Wagner would agree that social improvement is desirable and would argue that progressive taxation is one of the most effective means to that end. Here we have the basis for an honest difference of opinion.

The opinion of Lutz, Stamp, and Taussig rests upon the reasoning that progressive taxation must be an ineffective means of social improvement because it deals with "results" and not with "causes." In modern scientific discussion, "cause" means only "a significant antecedent condition." With this concept of "cause," it is evident that what is "cause" and what is "result" depends upon the point at which we first break the chain of circular concatenation of the phenomena under investigation.

For example, let us start with the statement that the "cause" of great inequality in the distribution of wealth is the unequal ability of individuals. Therefore, progressive taxation would deal with "results" and not with "causes." But suppose we start with unequal opportunities and see that they are a significant antecedent condition to or the "cause" of unequal abilities. What was "cause" from the old starting-point is now "result" under the new. Unequal opportunities have become the "cause." Obviously, progressive taxation by mitigating inequalities in the distribution of wealth could, if coupled with a wise program of public expenditures, decrease the inequalities of opportunity.

The penetrating discussions of causality which are to be found in Wilhelm Windelband's *Introduction to Philosophy* (New York, 1921) and in Karl Pearson's *The Grammar of Science* (3d ed.; London, 1911), cause one to doubt the validity of the position of Lutz, Stamp, and Taussig. And, even if one thinks only in terms of cause and effect in the sense in which these terms are used by Lutz, Stamp, and Taussig, he must acknowledge the wisdom of Marshall's statement that "in economics the full effects of a cause seldom come at once, but often spread themselves out after it has ceased to exist" (*op. cit.*, p. 109).

For the opinion of Lutz, see his *Public Finance* (3d ed.; New York, 1936), pp. 369–78. Stamp's position is set forth in *op. cit.*, pp. 170–77. Taussig's argument appears in *op. cit.*, pp. 513–14.

[81] To my knowledge, the closest approximation to this method of reaching a decision for or against progressive taxation has been made by Professor Henry C. Simons. On the first page of his brochure, *A Positive Program for Laissez Faire*, Professor Simons writes: "There is in America *no important disagreement* as to the proper objectives of economic policy— larger real income, greater regularity of production and employment, *reduction of inequality*, preservation of democratic institutions. The real issues have to do merely with means, not with ends (or intentions). . . ." (Italics are mine.) Later in his study (pp. 26–30), Professor Simons advocates progressive taxation as a means of reducing inequality. He makes his argument convincing without resort to any of the heroic psychological assumptions of the sacrifice theories. In chap. i of a more recent study, *Personal Income Taxation* (Chicago, 1938), a volume which did not reach me until I had completed my present manuscript, Professor Simons subjects the sacrifice theories to brief but stimulating criticism.

Mr. J. M. Keynes also approaches this method. He writes: "The outstanding faults of the economic society in which we live are its failure to provide for full employment and its arbitrary and inequitable distribution of wealth and incomes." He then argues for the income tax and surtax and death duties [progressive taxation] as means of correcting these faults (*The General Theory of Employment Interest and Money* [London, 1936], pp. 372–74). Keynes's method has, however, the identical ethical limitations of the Hobsonian method (see above, p. 49).

course, to weigh the probable effects of progression upon these two desiderata against its probable effects upon other selected desiderata, final decision being made in favor of a tax rate structure which would affect most favorably the totality of conditions embraced in the entire list of objective desiderata.

This method of reaching a decision presents grave difficulties; and it cannot give complete assurance that the best decision will always be reached. It is reasonable, however, to expect that with this method the best decision is most probable. And this is because of the fact that by the use of this method the most significant questions arise logically.

In a world in which change is inevitable the criteria of welfare themselves cannot be static. But the fact that criteria of welfare are subject to change is not a valid reason for rejecting Mitchell's proposal. In a democratic state we are repeatedly faced with the problem of making and remaking decisions as to whether more or less of this or of that will serve to maximize welfare.[82]

In these decisions conflicts between objective criteria, e.g., better housing versus less leisure, and conflicts of individual interest, e.g., more leisure for Jones versus less leisure for Smith, must be settled by intersubjective agreement reached by free citizens under political conditions most conducive to the plasticity and mutuality of individual interests.[83] It is under such conditions that a decision for or against progressive taxation is most likely to be made with maximum rationality and greatest probability of increasing welfare.

The superiority of this approach over that of the sacrifice theories as a basis upon which to decide the case for or against progressive taxation rests upon the following considerations:[84]

1. According to my version of the socio-political theory, the question of progressive versus proportional or regressive taxation is one which must be decided by ethical judgment rather than by psychological measurement.

---

[82] The difficulties in the way of the construction and use of objective criteria in economics are discussed by Viner, *op. cit.*, pp. 642–59.

[83] The prescription of such political conditions is beyond the scope of this paper. It seems obvious, however, that they could exist only in a democracy.

Students of ethics will recognize my general acceptance of Professor R. B. Perry's ethical imperative that the individual should conform himself "to those principles which harmonize life with life, and bring an abundance on the whole out of the fruitfulness of individual effort" (*The Moral Economy* [New York, 1909], p. 113).

In the development of the concluding section of this article, I have had the benefit of the suggestions and criticisms of Professor Henry Waldgrave Stuart, of the department of philosophy of Stanford University.

[84] The nature of the superiority of the socio-political theory over the surplus-income and social importance theories was pointed out on p. 50. The superiority of my adaptation of the socio-political theory over the two latter theories is greater in degree, but not different in kind, than the superiority of Wagner's socio-political theory over these theories.

2. As social beings, we do and must make ethical judgments, but we are not called upon to attempt to measure the psychic magnitudes involved in the sacrifice theories.

3. The socio-political theory, in the form proposed in this article, offers suggestions not only as to the nature of the judgments which must be made but also as to the conditions under which rational judgments are most probable.

4. Many, if not all, of the objective criteria of welfare, e.g., food, clothing, shelter, leisure, employment, etc., lend themselves to quantitive measurement. Psychic magnitudes do not.

5. The substitution of the proposed socio-political theory for the sacrifice theories replaces a naïve utilitarian ethic with an ethic more in harmony with recent and contemporary ethical theory.

The validity and significance of the considerations which have just been enumerated are, I believe, sufficient to establish my version of the socio-political theory as the most reasonable basis upon which to decide the case for or against progressive taxation. This method does not, of course, permit us to reach a decision a priori.

Progressive taxation cannot be declared to be more desirable than either regressive or proportional taxation unless it can be shown that progression will increase to a higher degree than will either regression or proportionality the objective desiderata which have been established by intersubjective agreement. In a state in which there is intersubjective agreement that the objective criteria of welfare are already at their optimum, both progressive and regressive taxation will be rejected in favor of proportionality. Proportional taxation will cause the least disturbance of the *status quo*.

In short, my conclusion is this: There is no categorical answer to the question, "Should taxation be progressive?" There is, however, one most rational method of arriving at the correct answer to this question.

4

The Concept of Income— Economic and Legal Aspects*

By ROBERT MURRAY HAIG

The Sixteenth Amendment to the Constitution gives Congress power to tax "incomes, from whatever source derived." Acting under this grant of authority, Congress has, for eight years past, collected taxes upon what it has been pleased to term income. In no one of the three statutes passed during that time has Congress attempted to formulate definitely a positive definition of income. Moreover, eight years have proved insufficient to secure from the courts a fully adjudicated definition. It is true that certain important items, notably stock dividends, which Congress has sought to include within the scope of the term, have been eliminated by court decisions. Much more important items, however, await judicial consideration. Even such questions as the taxability of gains from appreciations of property values are still unsettled. Such decisions as have been handed down appear to be leading toward a definition of income so narrow and artificial as to bring about results which from the economic point of view are certainly eccentric and in certain cases little less than absurd. The unsettled status of the definition and the wide differences of opinion which exist as to what the term *income*, as used in the Sixteenth Amendment, did, does, or ought to mean justifies an examination of its content from the point of view of the economics of the problem and from the point of view of the practice elsewhere.

In this paper no attempt is made to evaluate or criticise the interpretation of the statutes or the Sixteenth Amendment by the courts from the point of view of general legal and constitutional principles involved. This will be done in other papers to follow. The approach here taken is the broader one of fundamental economics and equity.

First of all, consider what the economist means when he speaks of

---

* R. M. Haig (ed.), *The Federal Income Tax* (New York, 1921).

income. In this case, as in so many others, the economist uses a term in approximately the same sense as it is used in ordinary intercourse. It has merely been necessary for him to be more precise as to exact limits and distinctions. There has been no revolutionary contribution to economic thought on this topic since the passage of the Sixteenth Amendment. The economist and the man in the street both use the term now as they used it in 1913.

Modern economic analysis recognizes that fundamentally income is a flow of satisfactions, of intangible psychological experiences. If one receives a dollar he receives something which he ordinarily can and does spend—perhaps for a dinner. Is his income the dollar, or is it the dinner which he buys with the dollar, or is it, at bottom, the satisfaction of his wants which he derives from eating the dinner—the comfort and the sustenance it yields to him? If one spends his dollar for something more durable than a dinner—say a book or a pipe—is his true income the book or the pipe, or the series of satisfactions or "usances" arising from reading the book or smoking the pipe? There is no doubt as to the answer to these questions. A man strives for the satisfaction of his wants and desires and not for objects for their own sake.

How universal is the acceptance of this general view may be gauged from the following pronouncements of the writers of some of the most recent and widely used texts dealing with the principles of economics. Thus Professor Taussig, of Harvard, disposes of the question:

Now just as all production in the last analysis consists in the creation of utilities, so all income consists in the utilities or satisfactions created. Economic goods are not ends in themselves but means to the end of satisfying wants. . . . Our food, clothing, furniture, may be said to yield psychic income. They shed utilities, so to speak, as long as they last.[1]

Professor Irving Fisher, of Yale, in his book asserts more categorically that "Income consists of benefits," and, again, that "A flow of benefits during a period of time is called income."[2]

Professor Ely, of Wisconsin, emphasizes the same point in these words:

Wealth refers to the stock of goods on hand at a particular time. Real income, on the other hand, has reference to the satisfaction we derive from the use of material things or personal services during a period of time.[3]

---

[1] *Principles of Economics,* Vol. X (1916), p. 134.
[2] *Elementary Principles of Economics,* 1911, p. 34.
[3] *Outlines of Economics,* 1908, p. 98.

Finally, Professor Seligman, in his *Principles of Economics*,[4] declares that "We desire things at bottom because of their utility. They can impart this utility only in the shape of a succession of pleasurable sensations. These sensations are our true income."

The testimony of our leading economists on this point is unanimous. Even in England, where the concept of taxable income is different from our own in important respects, the modern economists recognize the validity of the analysis set forth above. Thus Professor Alfred Marshall, of Cambridge, states that:

> . . . a woman who makes her own clothes, or a man who digs in his own garden or repairs his own house, is earning income just as would the dressmaker, gardener, or carpenter who might be hired to do the work. . . . For scientific purposes, it would be best if the word income when occurring alone should always mean total real income.[5]

However, the economist, while recognizing all this, realizes that before he can proceed far with his analysis of economic phenomena he must arrive at something more definite and more homogeneous—less diaphanous and elusive than these psychic satisfactions. An individual, it is true, can compare the relative worth to him of a pipe or a book or a dinner and arrange his order of consumption without the use of any formal common denominator such as money. Yet this individual would have great difficulty in telling you exactly how much satisfaction he derived from his pipe or his book. How much more difficult would it be for a second person to measure those satisfactions for him without the aid of some common unit! How impossible it is to compare one man's satisfaction with a book with another man's satisfaction with his dinner! Thus Professor Taussig is led to conclude that:

> . . . for almost all purposes of economic study, it is best to content ourselves with a statement, and an attempt at measurement, in terms not of utility but of money income. . . . The reason for this rejection of a principle which is in itself sound lies in the conclusion . . . regarding total utility and consumer's surplus: They cannot be measured.[6]

The basis of comparison, the foundation upon which economic interaction and exchange take place is, of course, that of the common, universally-acceptable unit of value—money. The usances and satisfactions and the goods and services supplying them which are of significance to

---

[4] 1914, p. 16.
[5] *Economics of Industry*, 1901, p. 51.
[6] Taussig, *loc. cit.*

the economist in his analysis are those which are susceptible of evaluation in terms of money. This, of course, involves the element of scarcity, relative to demand. When one can express his wants and satisfaction in terms of dollars and cents he can use a language which other men can understand and which means something to the economic community generally.

It should be carefully noted, however, that, first, when one abandons "usances" and satisfactions and substitutes the goods and services yielding these satisfactions, he is taking a step away from the fundamentals, for two equal sets of goods and services may yield very different satisfactions; and second, if one takes the next step, as most income tax laws do in the main, and substitutes money received during a period in place of goods and services used, as the content of the term income, he has really moved a very appreciable distance from the fundamental conception, for not only does everyone receive goods and services of greater or less amount without buying them with money, but also everyone is, in effect, considered to be in receipt of his income when he gets the money with which to buy the goods and services which will yield the usances and satisfactions which go to make up his true income. Indeed, the purchase of the goods and services may, of course, be postponed indefinitely. In the words of Professor Ely:

> Money income should, perhaps, refer to the value of the goods consumed and the services enjoyed, although in popular speech and by many economists the word is used in the literal sense of the net amount of money that comes in, whether it is spent for enjoyable things or is saved.[7]

It is apparent from what has been said that when taxable income is identified with money received in a given period two approximations have been introduced, each of which involves anomalies and inequalities as between members of the same class ostensibly on equal terms. For example, two persons who receive precisely equal amounts of goods and services may derive therefrom very unequal "usances" and satisfactions. If "usances" and satisfactions are really the proper theoretical basis for apportioning the tax burden there is here an inequality. Certainly, everyone will agree that they constitute an entirely impracticable basis. Consequently, any theoretical injustice involved must necessarily be incurred if we are to have an income tax at all. But is there, after all, any theoretical injustice? Who, for instance, would seriously defend the proposition that taxes should be apportioned according to capacity for appreciation rather than according to the capacity to command the goods and services which

---

[7] Ely, *loc. cit.*

are appreciated? The only economically significant goods are those which are susceptible of evaluation in terms of money.

In the next place, two persons who receive precisely equal amounts of money-income may receive very unequal amounts of goods and services, either because one has postponed spending a larger portion of his money than the other, or because one has received more income *in kind*. No great harm is done if the person who postpones spending his money is taxed upon it when he receives it rather than when he spends it. However, it is a different matter in the case of income *in kind*, such as the fire-wood the farmer cuts from his wood lot or the vegetables for his table which he gathers from his garden. Certainly, the fact that one man buys his fire-wood or his vegetables, rather than receives them without the formality of a money sale, should not operate so as to increase the weight of his income tax. The economics of this situation is very clear. The statement made in the preceding paragraph is that the goods and services which are of significance are those which are susceptible of evaluation in terms of money. It is not necessary that they should actually have passed through the process of a sale. From the point of view of equity it is theoretically important that all goods[8] and services received without payment should be accounted for in case it is possible to value them in terms of money.

Perhaps it is clear, then, how and why the fundamental economic conception of income as a flow of satisfactions must undergo substantial modification to classify for use in economic analysis generally and for use particularly as a basis for apportioning a tax burden. The satisfactions themselves become economically significant for the purpose only when they are susceptible of evaluation in terms of money. It is necessary as a practical proposition to disregard the intangible psychological factors and have regard either for the money-worth of the goods and services utilized during a given period or for the money itself received during the period supplemented by the money-worth of such goods and services as are received directly without a money transaction.

If the first option is taken, *viz.*, the money-worth of the goods and services utilized during a given period, we arrive at a pure consumption tax, unless indeed we attempt an evaluation of the satisfactions arising from the consciousness of a saved surplus which is obviously an impracticable procedure. It is interesting to recall that this is the result which the English economist, John Stuart Mill, sought to establish a half-century ago, although the analysis underlying his conclusions was a quite dif-

---

8 For gifts, *cf. infra.*, p. 74.

ferent one. To tax saved income and then in future years to tax the income from those savings was, he contended, double taxation.[9] The same conclusion has been reached by certain Italian writers, notably Einaudi.[10]

The second option, however, has been the one generally adopted as the definition of income in modern income tax acts. Under this conception, income becomes the increase or accretion in one's power to satisfy his wants in a given period in so far as that power consists of (a) money itself, or, (b) anything susceptible of valuation in terms of money. More simply stated, the definition of income which the economist offers is this: Income is the *money value of the net accretion to one's economic power between two points of time.*

It will be observed that this definition departs in only one important respect from the fundamental economic conception of income as a flow of satisfactions. It defines income in terms of power to satisfy economic wants rather than in terms of the satisfactions themselves. It has the effect of taxing the recipient of income when he receives the power to attain satisfactions rather than when he elects to exercise that power. This should do no violence to our sense of equity, however. The fact that a man chooses to postpone the gratification of his desires is no sufficient reason for postponing his tax.

It will be readily agreed that this definition, *viz.,* that income is the net accretion to one's economic strength in a given period, constitutes, then, the closest practicable approximation of true income. It coincides very closely indeed with the flow of economic "usances" and satisfactions expressed in terms of money, which all economists agree constitutes the thing after all we are attempting to measure. Certainly this definition is scientific in the sense that it is broad enough to include everything of like nature. Anomalies are avoided by the very simple expedient of casting the definition in broad terms. On the other hand, is the definition so broad that it includes items fundamentally dissimilar? The test of similarity applied is power in terms of money to command goods and services yielding usances and satisfactions. Is it possible to add any other test without so restricting the definition as to exclude items which should be included and thus introduce inequities and discriminations as between persons in substantially identical economic positions? Professor Seligman believes that in addition to the criteria of money-value, periodicity, and realization in-

---

[9] The source of this and several other statements made in this paper with respect to the theories of foreign economists is an unpublished monograph by Mr. Clarence Heer, a former student of Professor Seligman.

[10] Luigi Einaudi, *Corso di Scienza della Finanza,* 3rd Edition, Capitalo 4.

cluded in the definition as stated above, there should also be applied the test of separation as a necessary attribute of income.[11] Much depends upon precisely what is meant by separation. Included in the test of "susceptibility of evaluation" is certainly the condition that the valuation attached to the accretion must be sufficiently definite to form the basis for a realiza-tion. The item must be realizable and separable, certainly. That there must be an actual physical separation, however, before economic income is realized, cannot, I believe, be conceded, for, with a definition so narrowed it is not possible, in the stock-dividend case, for example, to remove the inequity as between different classes of security holders. The adoption of the definition as developed above leads to the same conclusion as that reached by Professor Seligman, *viz.*, that stock-dividends are not income, but the reason is not that the income has not yet accrued to the shareholder when the stock-dividend is declared, but rather that, economically, it has accrued to the shareholders even before the stock-dividend was declared, *viz.*, if and when the improved economic position of the corporation was reflected in the holdings of the stockholder with sufficient definiteness to be susceptible of evaluation.

What more narrow definition than the one suggested will solve the problems presented by the following three questions?

1. Are stock-dividends income?
2. Is undistributed surplus income to the shareholder?
3. Are appreciations in property values income?

1. *Are stock-dividends income?* The Supreme Court has decided that stock-dividends are not income.[12] What is the effect of this decision upon the economic position of the three following persons, *A*, *B*, and *C*, who are shareholders in similar corporations, each owning ten per cent of the stock? Assume that each company makes $1,000,000 in the given accounting period. On the day of the directors' meeting when the question of the declaration of a dividend will be considered, the economic position of all three men is the same, and no one would deny that the economic strength of each had been increased by virtue of his ten per cent interest in a corporation which has earned a million dollars net income. *A's* corporation declares a cash dividend of $1,000,000, *A's* share being $100,000 in money. *B's* corporation declares a stock-dividend of $1,000,000, *B's* share being $100,000 in stock. *C's* corporation declares no dividend, *C's*

[11] Edwin R. A. Seligman, "Are Stock Dividends Income?" *American Economic Review*, September, 1919.

[12] Towne *v*. Eisner, 245 U.S. 418; Eisner *v*. Macomber, 252 U.S. 189.

interest in the earnings of that year being reflected presumably in an increase in the market value of his stock. Before the stock dividend decision A's share and B's share were both considered taxable income. C was taxed only if and when the profits were distributed—unless in truth he were taxed indirectly in case he sold his stock at an appreciated value. A and B were together in one class. C was alone in a second class. As between the two classes there was a marked difference of treatment. The stock dividend decision disassociated B from A and placed him in the class with C. The line marking the difference of treatment is now no longer drawn between B and C. It is drawn between A and B. But the point is that the difference persists. Can justice be established in an income tax as among A, B, and C by any action short of making each of them subject to income tax upon the increase in his economic strength resulting from the earnings of the corporation in which he is interested? In this case A should account for the $100,000 cash dividend in his income tax return. B should account for the market value of his stock dividend on the last day of the year, minus any decline, if any, in the market value of his original block of stock during the year. C should be taxed on the increased market value of his block of stock. All of them, under the assumption, have received a net accretion of economic strength during the year definite enough to be susceptible of evaluation. Can a more narrow concept of income than this solve the problem here presented?

2. *Is undistributed surplus income to the shareholder?* The problem with respect to the taxation of undivided surplus may be presented best by a similar example. Assume that A owns ten per cent of the stock of a corporation and that B owns a ten per cent interest in a partnership, each of which earns $1,000,000 during a given accounting period. B must include in his individual income tax return his distributive share of the profits, $100,000, which item becomes subject to both normal and surtax rates. On the other hand, A includes in his personal income tax return his share of the profits in his corporation only if and when these profits are declared as dividends. If they are never distributed, they never become subject to the individual surtax rates. The corporation, it is true, pays the so-called normal tax at the time when the profits are earned, and A may take credit for part of this normal tax in his individual return when he receives the dividend. It is also true that the excess profits tax applies to corporate profits and not to partnership or individual profits and that for the present this has brought about a condition of poise which will be sadly disturbed if the excess profits tax should disappear. But what precise solution is there for this badly muddled situation short of the adoption of a concept of income broad enough to tax A on the in-

creased market value of his stock which presumably results from plough-
ing the earnings back into the business of the corporation? In the absence
of dependable market quotations, would not the accounts of the corporation, as to undistributed surplus, furnish light as to the increase in *A's*
economic position?

3. *Are appreciations in property values income?* At the present time
we consider appreciations of property values taxable income.[13] But we
inventory nothing except stock-in-trade. In other words, we say in effect
that nothing appreciates in value until it is sold. This, of course, is not in
accord with economic facts, however perfectly it may synchronize with
accounting practice. The truth is that certain so-called accounting principles have been evolved with other ends primarily in view than the accurate determination of relative taxpaying ability. The general result
may be illustrated as follows: *A* and *B* each buy houses in 1914 for
$10,000. Both houses appreciate in value until they are worth $20,000
each in 1916. *A* sells his house in 1916 and becomes taxable on the
$10,000 profit. The highest surtax rates in 1916 were thirteen per cent.
He holds his $10,000 uninvested. *B* retains his house, but after 1916 the
value remains stationary. He sells in 1920 and realizes $10,000 profit. In
1920 the rates range as high as seventy-three per cent. Here are two men
whose economic strength has varied in precisely the same manner. They
are called upon to pay quite different amounts in federal income taxes.
Can any proposal offer a satisfactory solution of this problem which does
not assume a concept of income similar to that outlined above? To achieve
exact justice the increased economic strength of the two men must be
measured *period for period*.

The general conclusion from the foregoing discussion is this: That
the economist when asked whether a particular item is income or is not
income, must, in the opinion of the writer, make his reply depend upon
whether the receipt of that item has increased the economic power of the
recipient to command satisfaction-yielding goods or services. If it does, it
is income; if it does not, it is not income. The answer would then be based
on practically the bed-rock of economic principle—not quite, perhaps,
because of the approximations already pointed out, but certainly on a level
as near as is practicable to that bed-rock. If courts are to base their decisions on economic principle, the answer to their queries should be in
terms of the most fundamental of principles.

---

13 In a decision published after this paper was written, Judge J. D. Thomas, of the District Court of the United States, District of Connecticut, has decided, in the case of Brewster
v. Walsh, Collector (No. 2133 at law), that the increase in the value of capital assets when
realized by sale or other disposition, by one not a trader or dealer therein, is not income, and
hence is not taxable as such. The Government has announced an appeal to the Supreme Court.

These statements present nothing which is really novel. This same doctrine has long been taught by that faithful handservant of the practical business man—the accountant. When one examines the standard books dealing with the theory of accounting he finds the definition of the net profit of a business undertaking stated in almost the precise words used in the general definition given above. Thus, A. Lowes Dickinson in his *Accounting Practice and Procedure*[14] says:

In the widest possible view, profits may be stated as the realized increment in the value of the whole amount invested in an undertaking; and, conversely, loss is the realized decrement.

Again, Robert H. Montgomery in his *Auditing* remarks:

If an absolutely accurate balance sheet could be prepared at the beginning and the end of a period, the difference would constitute the net profit or the net loss for the term.

The economist and the accountant are also, of course, in complete accord as to the theoretical distinction between income on the one hand and capital, or property, or wealth on the other. The accountant's "absolutely accurate balance sheet," to use Montgomery's phrase,[15] is synonymous with the economist's "fund relating to a given instant,"[16] to use Professor Fisher's language, or, "accumulation of . . . utilities or income at an instant of time,"[17] to use Professor Seligman's expression. The establishment of "net income," both agree, must not involve an impairment of the capital sum.

Confusion of thought is sometimes caused by the fact that the accountant usually speaks in terms of a business enterprise as a separate entity, while the economist usually speaks in terms of the individual person. The distinction between gross and net income—which occupies so large a part of the attention of the accountant—is summarily dismissed by the economist whose typical income receiver is the man whose expenditures are predominantly for purposes of personal consumption. The definitions and reasoning of the accountant, however, are very readily fitted to the case of this typical economic man if the accounting period is reduced to its true economic length, which in the case of the wage earner is a week and the salaried worker a month. In the typical business the

---

[14] p. 67.
[15] 1916, p. 206.
[16] Fisher, *op. cit.*, pp. 56–57.
[17] Seligman, *loc. cit.*

period is, of course, a year, the net income not being determined and distributed until the end of that period.

The detailed technique of determining the precise deductions which should properly be made as business expenses, as contrasted with expenditures of a capital nature, has been developed by the accountants along lines entirely acceptable to the economist. Many interesting theoretical questions are involved, such, for example, as the degree to which risk may properly be insured against by means of various reserves, but a survey of this portion of the field—while germane to the topic—cannot be developed in the time available. Ordinarily the economist contents himself with the assertion that the income must be *net*, that all expenses connected with its production must have been met.

The problem of distinguishing sharply between business expense and personal expense is one which is the occasion of much practical difficulty and upon which wide differences of opinion exist. Certain German writers, *e.g.*, Weissenborn,[18] go so far as to classify all personal and family expenditures for food, clothing, and shelter as deductible expenses, rendering the income tax substantially a tax on merely saved income. This is a result diametrically opposite to that reached by the English and Italian economists referred to above[19]—and it is a conception which does not find any considerable response except in so far as the relief of a bare minimum of subsistence, under the various personal exemptions, may be conceived to be such a response.

It is often a long step, however, between the accountant's theory and his practice; between his abstract statement as to what net profit is and the actual figure certified as such on a balance sheet. It is an equally long step for the economist between his general definition of income and the content of the category which in his opinion forms the best basis for the imposition of an income tax. This is a practical, workaday world full of imperfections. Most economists, popular superstition to the contrary, are fairly conversant with the facts of modern business life and are fairly well aware of the practical difficulties of fitting abstract conceptions to the environment of the market-place. Certainly modifications—serious modifications—must be made in the general definition of income, as formulated above, to fit it for use as the item of net income entered on Form 1040 or Form 1120, and the scientific economist in advising the legislator would be the last to suggest an attempt to follow the implications of his analysis without regard to the limitations imposed by the

---

[18] *Die Besteuerung nach Ueberfluss*, 1911.
[19] *Cf. supra*, pp. 58 and 59.

actual conditions under which the law must function. Such a course would be anything but scientific. The point to be grasped very clearly, however, is this: Those modifications to which he would consent and which, indeed, he is among the first to urge, are, after all is said and done, merely modifications—merely concessions made to the exigencies of a given situation. For example, one might urge that no tax be placed on a gain arising from the appreciation of a fixed asset until it is actually sold. But the recommendation should not be urged on the ground that the appreciation is not income until it is sold. The economic fact is that the owner of that asset comes into possession of economic income whenever the increase in the value of that asset is sufficient in amount and definite enough in character to be susceptible of precise evaluation in terms of money. Again, one might urge that no tax be placed on the services which one actually enjoys when he lives in his own home rather than a rented one. But, again, that recommendation should not be supported by the assertion that this item is not income. It is income whenever it is susceptible of evaluation in terms of money. Neither the economist nor the courts should express their opinions in the forms of an assertion that it is not income. That, it seems to the writer, is not the real question in either of the illustrations given. The real question is, rather: Is it justifiable to treat this item of income in some special way as compared with other items of income because of special circumstances surrounding its receipt? Thus, it may be futile and silly, from an administrative point of view, to attempt to include in the income tax return a money estimate of the income which the man receives when he lives in his own house. The Wisconsin authorities, after attempting to list such income for several years, have decided that the game is not worth the candle. Or, it may be impracticable as an accounting proposition, to reflect the varying worth of capital assets on the balance sheet. As the accountant, Dickinson, points out:

> Inasmuch . . . as the ultimate realization of the original investment is from the nature of things deferred for a long period of years, during which partial realizations are continually taking place, it becomes necessary to fall back on estimates of value at certain definite periods, and to consider as profit and loss the estimated increase or decrease between any two such periods.[20]

If the difficulties of complete periodical revaluations are so great as to make it impracticable to tax appreciations as they accrue, they ought not to be so taxed, and the question is transformed into these new queries: "When may these appreciations best be taxed?" and "If they are taxed

---

[20] *Loc. cit.*

sporadically is the result so unjust that no attempt should be made to tax them at all?"

To the writer it seems unfortunate that the questions as to the constitutionality of the federal income tax on specific items are turning so largely on the question as to whether the items are or are not income. The items most controverted certainly fall within the definition of income established by the analysis of business facts made by both the economist and the accountant. Moreover, the concept of income is, after all, essentially an economic concept, and if the legal concept established by court interpretation under a particular constitutional provision or amendment departs in any very fundamental fashion from the economic concept, injustices may arise of such magnitude as to necessitate either the abandonment of the income tax or the adoption of a constitutional amendment which will give a positive and comprehensive definition of income. The difficulty could be avoided if the broad economic concept of income were frankly accepted with its single test as to whether the item resulted in an improvement in economic power capable of being evaluated. The questions which the courts would then be called upon to consider would be as to whether the modifications made by Congress and by the Treasury, in attempting to construct a concept of taxable income which will be at once workable and approximately just, are modifications which are reasonable and in conformity with the various constitutional guaranties.

It goes without saying that taxable income under an income tax law should approximate as nearly as practicable the true net income as defined by the analysis of the economist and the accountant. How close an approximation is possible depends upon the perfection of the environment in which the tax must live. No unnecessary departure from the true concept should be made. The imperfections of our present economic environment which are of most significance to this problem fall into three classes:

1. The imperfections of the economic standard of value;
2. The imperfections of accounting practice; and
3. The imperfections of the administration.

A perfect income tax is unattainable so long as modifications must be made because of imperfections in our standard of value, our accounting, and our administration. These classes will be taken up in turn.

1. *Imperfections of the economic standard of value.* That variations occur from time to time in the price level and in the value of money is well known to every person whose resources during recent years have

been sufficiently limited to compel him to have any regard at all for his expenditures. If income is defined as the total accretion in one's economic strength between two points of time, as valued in terms of money, it is clear that his income will reflect every change in the value of money between those two points of time in so far as the items entered on the balance sheets at those times affect the computation. If the level of prices goes up ten per cent the money value of my assets will ordinarily follow at a like rate. That particular increase in value does not really indicate an increase in my economic strength. My power to command economic goods and services has not increased, for the money-value of these goods and services has likewise increased. So long as we have a money standard which varies, we shall find that even a perfect accounting system will show a net income which is not identical with the true accretion of economic power. Indeed, the more perfect the valuation and the accounting, the greater will this injustice be.

It must be borne in mind, however, that this is an evil which is with us under our present law. A man who sold an asset in 1920 which he had purchased in 1914, making an apparent profit of 100 per cent and receiving his pay in fifty-cent dollars is, under our statute, subject to tax on his gain, although that gain is only apparent and not real. Moreover, the situation is particularly unjust under our present system. If complete periodical revaluations were used in determining income there would still be relative equality as between different taxpayers. But as the situation now stands, the transactions are closed in a haphazard and uneven fashion. A man who happens to sell out at the peak of the price curves, is taxed very unequally as compared with the man who continues his transaction until a period of lower price levels.

It should also be borne in mind that this element is of some influence even in an income tax such as that in force in Great Britain where appreciations in property values are not taxed, for an item of inventory included in one's accounts at the beginning of the year and sold in the course of the year will reflect the change in the prices during the period held.

If it were possible to modify the concept of taxable income so as to eliminate this variation it would certainly be desirable to do so. The prospect for a complete solution of the difficulty pointed out, however, is identical with the prospect for a perfect monetary standard. But an approximate solution might be realized if we were able to evolve a satisfactory index of the level of prices. If it were accurately known what the change in price level in a given year had been, it might be possible to qualify the results shown by a comparison of the balance sheets for the beginning and the end of the period in such a way as to eliminate the influence of the changing standard. But even this refinement is not likely to be introduced soon. Indeed, the desirability and urgency of its introduction is dependent largely upon the complete solution of the accounting problem, which solution is certainly not imminent.

2. *The imperfections of accounting practice.* The wide gap which stretches between theory and practice in the field of accounting has already been remarked. Until such time as everyone keeps accounts and the accounts furnish a perfect record of everyone's economic position, the concept of taxable income must be modified in order to meet the problem presented by the shortcomings of accounting practice. Dozens of illustrations of how the concept is modified in our statute because of the necessity of allowing for the imperfections and incompleteness of accounts will occur to everyone.

While the accounting ideal as stated by the leading theorists in the accounting field is in entire harmony with the economic analysis, it should be pointed out that many so-called accounting principles which are generally accepted are little more than rules of action formulated during an obsolete period when the use of accounts for tax purposes did not exist. So long as the chief purposes of the accounts were to provide a basis for applications for credit, and for the distribution of dividends, rules which tended toward a conservative statement of profits were certainly full of virtue. The increase in the tax burden has added a new primary use for the accounts, a use which demands certain qualities which are not important in the other cases. To form an entirely satisfactory basis for the imposition of income taxes the accounts must reflect the full, true, economic position of the taxpayer; and in so far as arbitrary rules of inventory valuations operate to build up hidden reserves, or other accounting practices tend to befog the picture, they must ultimately be eliminated and they have no place in truly scientific accounting.

3. *The imperfections of the administration.* A lively regard for the limitations of the administration is essential to the successful formulation of a tax statute. This is a factor which we have failed to recognize sufficiently in this country. Many of the modifications which our statute makes in the concept of income are obviously designed to simplify the problem of administration, but in spite of the number and character of these modifications there appears to be grave question as to whether they have been sufficient to reduce the administrative task to manageable proportions. The British, with their splendid civil service, are appalled at the burden we place upon our inadequate treasury staff. Certainly such changes in

the abstract definition of income as are necessary to make the statute practical and workable must be accepted, provided the cost in terms of equity is not so great as to make some available alternative tax a more attractive method of raising the revenue.

In addition to modifications on the above grounds, modifications of two additional types are often urged. Those who are convinced that taxation should be used for the furtherance of social ends often demand special modifications. For example, those who are deeply impressed with the desirability of increasing the amount of economic capital, demand special treatment of the individual surplus of corporations, or reduced surtax rates upon that portion of individual incomes which are saved and reinvested. There are others who on social grounds believe in a differentiation between earned and unearned income.

Again, the fiscal necessities of the Government are sometimes urged as adequate ground for declining to bring the concept of taxable income into closer harmony with the concept of economic income, as in the case of the recent letter of the Secretary of the Treasury.

If time permitted it would be interesting to trace the historical evolution of the concept of economic income and of taxable income from the time these concepts became important down to the present. Only the barest summary, however, is here possible. The British income tax places very heavy stress upon the annual character of income. For an explanation of this conception, which results in the exclusion from taxable income of gains of an irregular nature, one must go back as far as the fifteenth century, when, with an agricultural society where few fortuitous gains developed, the idea of receipts as being annual in character became deeply impressed upon the minds of the people. It became the habit to think of one's regular receipts as his income, and to consider irregular receipts as additions to capital. Adam Smith spoke of income both as what remains free after maintaining the capital and as what people can consume without encroaching upon their capital. Ricardo accepted Adam Smith's conception of economic capital but protested vigorously against a concept of taxable income which would include legacies and even wages. McCulloch developed a theory of differentiated income under which income from personal services was to be fully insured in order to put it on a fair basis as compared with the income from a building from which depreciation allowances had been subtracted. Despairing of the practicability of such a proposal, he concluded that income taxation was fundamentally unfair. John Stuart Mill disapproved of McCulloch's theory of differentiation, but insisted upon exemption for savings. Because of the practical difficulties in the way of this he urged a remission of an arbitrary percentage of the income from "temporary" sources.[21] This is essentially the plan which has been incorporated into the Italian income tax of to-day. As has been noted, Marshall defines income in the broadest possible fashion.[22]

Just as the British income tax has served as the model for the various continental income taxes, so English writers have influenced the thought of the writers in other countries. Thus the German writers since Schmoller have broken away from the concept of yield and have emphasized the subjective concept. These Germans all agree that income includes all goods which are placed at the disposal of the individual for the satisfaction of his wants, but they disagree considerably as to the exact composition of that income and its relationship to the concept of capital. The idea of the durability of the source plays a considerable rôle in their discussions. Schanz calls income the net inflow of means during a given period, including all usances and services having a money value.[23]

To Roscher, income is a rather restricted category consisting of the aggregate of goods which, arising within a given period of time as the yields of durable sources of revenue, are at the disposal of the individual for the satisfaction of his personal wants and those of his family. Wagner and his associates, including Cohn, Newman, and Philippovitch, emphasize both periodicity and permanency of source. Income to them is either the sum total of goods which at regularly recurring intervals flow into the treasury of the individual, or those commodities, valuable services of third parties, and usances which, as periodic fruits of permanent productive sources, flow into the possession of the individual and over which he has absolute control.[24] It should be noted that here again appears the idea of separation emphasized by Professor Seligman.[25]

If this is what the foreign writers say about the economic concept of income, what do the foreign legislators do about establishing the limits of the concept of taxable income? Both the British and the German statutes construct a concept much more narrow than ours. Both attempt to differentiate between regular and fortuitous gains. A British salaried man who dabbles in the stock exchange is not called to account for his gains or losses. The owner of a residence in Germany is not asked to include a profit realized on its sale. Gains and losses on property are recognized

---

[21] Heer, *op. cit.*
[22] *Cf. supra*, p. 56.
[23] Heer, *op. cit.*
[24] *Ibid.*
[25] *Cf. supra*, p. 59.

only when they accrue with respect to the stock-in-trade of a dealer. In Great Britain, if one sells his mine at a profit, that profit is not subject to income tax, but neither are depletion allowances deductible in making one's annual returns. The consideration paid for a lease is not taxed, but depreciation in the lease may not be deducted. The British do not tax gains from appreciation in the value of real estate, which reduces considerably the significance of the late-lamented British Increment Value Duty. As a matter of fact, the effect of this Duty was to operate as a fairly reasonable income tax on the profits from such transactions.

Having formulated a definition of economic income, having presented the broad grounds upon which modifications may properly be made in order to fit the concept to the necessities of the business situation, and having made a very brief survey of foreign theory and practice, let us examine the meaning of the term income as used in the Revenue Act of 1918 to ascertain how closely it approaches the ideal conception of income. Such a discussion will bring clearly to the fore the implications of the proposed definition; it will test the adequacy of that definition to resolve the anomalies of our present practice; and will raise questions as to the desirability of changes in our present statutory concept.

The Revenue Act of 1918 states that "there shall be levied, collected, and paid for each taxable year upon the *net income* of every individual (and corporation) a tax."[26] Net income is defined as gross income minus certain specific deductions.[27] Gross income, in turn, is described by specifying certain items which it shall include and exclude. This establishes the outer, the inclusive limits. But it is apparent that this merely describes certain specific sources, the income arising from which is taxed. In the familiar language of the statute, gross income "includes gains, profits, and income derived from salaries, wages or compensation for personal service . . . , of whatever kind and in whatever form paid, or from professions, vocations, trades, businesses, commerce, or sales, or dealings in property, whether real or personal, growing out of the ownership or use of or interest in such property; also from interest, rents, dividends, securities, or the transaction of any business carried on for gain or profit, or gains or profits, and income derived from any source whatever."

The first point which impresses one with respect to our statutory concept is its breadth as compared with the concepts used elsewhere. It attempts to draw no line between capital gains and gains of other types. It places no emphasis at all upon the permanence of the source or the regu-

---

[26] Secs. 210 and 230.
[27] Secs. 212 and 232.

larity of the income. In its general scope it approaches almost to the point of complete identity the working concept of profit used by the accountant. It is by all odds the most theoretically perfect income tax law extant, from the point of view of its general scope. Whether it is, after all, the most scientific law is another question, for that involves the degree of skill that has been used in modifying the theoretical concept to meet our actual conditions. In that we have not been strikingly successful.

It is interesting to note the dependence which our lawmakers are beginning to place upon the accountants and their standards of practice. The 1918 law, for the first time, specifically directs that certain results be reached by methods in accordance with accepted accounting procedure. This appears to be the modern tendency and is certainly a laudable one. Thus the German Excess Profits Law passed in 1915 is an exceedingly simple document which meets the whole problem of defining profits by stating that they shall be taken to be the "balance of profit duly reckoned in accordance with the legal prescriptions and recognized principles and methods of mercantile accounting."[28]

The net income which our 1918 Act attempts to reach is in the main money income. There are these exceptions: (1) There is a specific provision to the effect that income from personal services "of whatever kind and in whatever form paid"[29] shall be accounted for. (2) Stock dividends are declared taxable but this declaration is nullified by the recent decisions of the Supreme Court.[30] (3) In the case of exchanges, the property received in exchange is "treated as the equivalent of cash to the amount of its fair market value, if any,"[31] with the qualification that in the case of reorganizations the transactions are not closed in case the par value of the securities received in exchange for the old securities is not in excess of the securities surrendered.

It will be recalled that our definition demands the taxation of the net accretion of one's power measured in money or money-worth. Should the statute go further than it does in taxing real income even when received in some form other than money? The problem is largely an administrative one. The specific case of the income one really receives when he lives in the house he himself owns has become rather acute, the favored position of such an owner being vigorously used by real-estate promoters, particularly those interested in the sale of high-class apartment buildings on the coöperative plan. Such real income should certainly be taxed if it is prac-

---

[28] *Reichs Gesetzblatt*, No. 187, Year 1915.
[29] Sec. 213.
[30] *Cf. supra*, p. 60.
[31] Sec. 202 (b).

ticable to evaluate it. The present position is anomalous, particularly when one remembers that such owners, while they may not deduct insurance and upkeep, may, nevertheless, deduct the taxes on the property and the interest on any money they may have borrowed to carry the property. The way to remove the anomaly is to approach the definition of income more closely in practice.

The statute includes as taxable income appreciations of property values, whether those appreciations are in stock-in-trade, in capital assets, or in miscellaneous bits of property owned incidentally. In this it has the sanction of our definition. A distinct departure is made from the definition, however, by the practice of taxing those appreciations only irregularly as sales are consummated, and at the rates in force in the year during which the consummation occurs. This practice lies at the root of the present widespread dissatisfaction with the taxation of appreciations. Our definition demands their taxation whenever they become susceptible of a definite evaluation. A scheme of arbitrary apportionment of the gain over the period of accrual would be infinitely superior to the present practice. With rates varying as they have during the past few years, there has been a tremendous incentive to the business man to resort to methods of postponing the closing of his transactions. The tax on appreciations has in fact operated as a substantial force restraining the alienation of property.

So long as our accounting methods are not equal to the task of furnishing a complete revaluation of assets at the beginning and the close of each accounting period there is no complete solution to this problem. However, unless the administrative burden of the plan of arbitrary apportionment of gains actually made at times of sale is too great to be borne, that plan should certainly be given a trial.

Too much importance may easily be attached to British precedents in determining whether gains from appreciations in property values should or should not be included within the definition of income. The British concept of taxable income, which excludes such gains, is a product of a practical local situation which differs in essential respects from our own. The exclusion of such gains is acknowledged to be illogical and was the cause of much evasion of the Excess Profits Duty. In fact in the administration of that Duty is was found necessary to make important modifications in the direction of the acknowledgment of capital gains and losses as factors in the determination of income.[32] Finally the *Report of the Royal Commission on the Income Tax*, recently submitted, not only rec-

---

[32] *Cf.* Haig, *The Taxation of Excess Profits in Great Britain*, 1920, pp. 69–73 *et passim*.

ommends the recognition of depletion to a limited extent but urges that, hereafter, gains from incidental business transactions, even where the property which appreciates is not worthy of the designation of "inventory," be included within the scope of taxable income.[33]

There is an interesting incidental point in connection with this problem. We have been accustomed to consider the income tax as one of our elastic taxes whose rates may be conveniently varied to meet the needs of a variable budget. Has not our recent experience with our income tax which taxes appreciation shown that with an income tax of this type variable rates must be avoided until the day of perfect accounting arrives? If the business man were certain that present rates would continue indefinitely, the present game of postponing realizations would quickly cease. On the other hand, it may be well to meet this problem by adopting the British procedure of taxing business profits on the basis of an average of previous years.

The present statute does not regard gifts received by individuals as taxable income. Ordinarily gifts may not be subtracted in arriving at the taxable income of the giver, but charitable contributions made to certain corporations may be deducted by an individual, subject to a fifteen per cent limitation. Until recently the Treasury permitted such an individual to deduct from his taxable income the value of the gift when made. This procedure, however, has been changed and he may now subtract merely the original cost or the value on March 1, 1913, if purchased before that date. Gifts to relatives of property upon which one wishes to realize are becoming a common method of evasion, for profit to the recipient is measured from the value of the gift at time of receipt.

In view of suggested legislative action with reference to gifts it is of interest to consider them in relation to the definition as developed above. Are gifts income? Under the terms of the definition, they are if they increase the economic strength of the recipient. But most gifts are either to relatives or to charitable institutions. With respect to family gifts a case may be made out for ignoring the transfer of title on the ground of the essential economic unity of the family. The family, as a matter of fact, is even now to a considerable extent the basic unit for income tax purposes. Gifts to charitable institutions are now, within the fifteen per cent limit, deductible to the giver and exempt to the recipient. On the ground of public policy much can be said for continuing this practice although it is also true that, speaking in terms of economic fundamentals, the man who makes a gift to some person or corporation outside his immediate

---

[33] Cmd. 615, p. 20 et seq., p. 41, et seq.

family deliberately chooses that way of spending his money because it yields him a greater satisfaction than some alternative use. In any case appreciations in the property given away would, under the proposed definition, become taxable gradually as they emerged in definite enough form to be susceptible of an evaluation.

In summary, then, it must be apparent that the differences among economists as to the definition of income are really more on questions of policy than on questions of principle. There is substantial agreement as to its fundamental character, but some disagreement as to how far the definition ought to be narrowed so as to make it useful for purposes of an income tax base.

The formal definition of *economic* income, which, in the opinion of the writer, provides the most acceptable concept of income, may be stated as follows: *Income is the money-value of the net accretion to economic power between two points of time.* This definition cannot be written into a statute in literal form because of the technical disadvantages in determining income as so defined, but so long as taxable income differs appreciably from this definition there will be anomalies and injustices in income taxation, and every step marking a closer approximation of this definition will result in the elimination of irregular and eccentric results.

The concept of *taxable* income is a living, mutable concept which has varied widely from time to time and from country to country with the conditions under which it has had to operate.

The concept as it stands in our own law is probably the closest approach to true economic income yet achieved by any country. The primary limiting factors are our varying level of prices, our inadequate accounting—including imperfections of valuation, and our incompetence of administration. Possibilities of further progress depend primarily upon our ability to improve our standard of value, our accounting, and our administration.

It is very undesirable from the point of view of economics and equity that the judicial definition of income should develop along narrow lines by the process of definitely eliminating from the concept certain items as not being income. The real question is not often "Is the item income?" but rather "Is the method used for reaching this class of income justified?" In other words, have Congress and the Treasury provided an equitable answer to the practical question as to how and when such income shall be taxed, taking into account the imperfections of the situation in which the tax must function? Under a given statute, is income taxed at such times and in such a manner as to bring about the necessary degree and the highest practicable degree of equity to the taxpayer and between taxpayers? The definition of income should rest on fundamental economic principles. The definition must be broad enough to iron out all the theoretical difficulties and solve all of the inequities and anomalies. The situation should be held in a mobile, flexible state which will permit the statutory definition of income to become progressively more precise and accurate with the improvement of the technique of our economic environment.

5

Averaging of Income for Income-Tax Purposes*

By WILLIAM VICKREY

It has long been considered one of the principal defects of the graduated individual income tax that fluctuating incomes are, on the whole, subjected to much heavier tax burdens than incomes of comparable average magnitude which are relatively steady from year to year. That changes in the allocation of income, which often have no relation either to physical realities or to the real financial status of the taxpayer, should substantially affect his income-tax burden is obviously not in accordance with the principle of taxation according to ability to pay.

Two notable attempts have been made to remedy this situation by the introduction of an averaging process. In the state of Wisconsin from 1928 to 1932 the state income tax was assessed on the basis of the average income for the last three years, with certain adjustments at the transition years. However, legal difficulties arose in the collection of the tax from individuals who left the jurisdiction of the state and in the case of corporations dissolving; moreover, as incomes fell drastically with the onset of the depression, there was widespread objection to paying taxes during lean years based in part on the larger incomes of the more prosperous years. This experiment had therefore to be abandoned after only five years of operation.[1]

The Commonwealth of Australia in 1921 enacted a provision that the rate of tax to be applied to the income of the current year was to be determined by reference to an average of the income for the last five years. New South Wales had had a similar provision applying only to income

---

* *Journal of Political Economy*, Vol. XLVII, No. 3 (June, 1939).

[1] For the details of the Wisconsin averaging method see Wisconsin Tax Commission, *Rules and Regulations of the Wisconsin Tax Commission under the Income Tax Act of 1931* (Madison, 1932), pp. 215–19.

from "primary production" (pastoral, agricultural, and mining) since 1912. This type of provision seems to avoid the difficulty encountered by the Wisconsin scheme of requiring heavy tax payments in years of reduced income. The application of this provision has again been restricted to income from primary production beginning with 1938 by the 1936 revision of the Commonwealth law.[2]

From 1812 to 1926 England also assessed portions of its income tax on the basis of averages. This, however, was not done for the purpose of avoiding excessive taxes on fluctuating incomes but appears, rather, to have originated as an attempt to estimate current income from the income of past years in cases where collection by withholding at the source proved impracticable. As this averaging applied directly only to the flat-rate normal tax, the effect in equalizing tax burdens was negligible.[3]

In the United States the special provisions concerning capital gains are founded in part on the theory that such gains frequently cause large fluctuations in the income of the taxpayer and so subject him to higher rates; they also, however, constitute, in part at least, a concession to those who maintain that capital gains should not be taxed as income at all. Unfortunately, the relief thus granted is capricious in its incidence, probably excessive in most cases, and opens considerable loopholes for tax avoidance.

Inequality of burden as between taxpayers of fluctuating and of steady incomes is not the only difficulty that is introduced by arbitrarily cutting up the income of the taxpayer according to time periods and assessing the tax for each period independently. In theory the determination of the accrued income between two points of time requires that valuations of all assets be made both at the beginning and at the end of the time period —an almost impossible task when the period is short, and an especially difficult one when there is no regular market for the assets in question. Supreme Court decisions and administrative exigencies have made it necessary to use so-called "realized income" as a base; one result of the use of this base has been that opportunities for manipulations designed to reduce the tax burden by shifting income from one year to another

---

[2] For the details of the Australian averaging method see Norman Bede Rydge and J. B. Collier, *Commonwealth Income Tax Acts, 1922–1929* (Sydney, 1929), pp. 82–113; also J. B. Collier and Norman Bede Rydge, *New South Wales Income Tax Acts* (Sydney, 1930), pp. 30–35.

[3] For a discussion of the British averaging provisions see H. B. Spaulding, *Income Tax in Great Britain and the United States* (London, 1927), pp. 211–28. A summary of the history of these provisions is given in: Great Britain: Royal Commission on the Income Tax (The "Colwyn Commission"), *Report* (London, 1920), Appen. 7(*m*). Testimony on the averaging provisions is indexed under "Assessment, average basis of."

have been multiplied. Such manipulations have in turn evoked a complex system of rules and penalties designed to prevent such tax avoidance, such as the undistributed-profits tax, the regulations concerning allowances for depreciation and obsolescence, the penalty taxes on personal holding companies, and the disallowance of wash sales, sales among members of one family, and the deduction of large net capital losses from other income. These provisions, on the whole, have not only failed effectively to stop the avoidance but have also in many cases dealt excessively harshly with individuals who happened to be caught by the legal provisions without having had any intention of avoiding taxes.

Now a method of taxation which considers as a whole the income of the taxpayer over a long period in assessing the tax should, if properly designed, leave the total burden of tax unaffected by such shifts of income between the various years within the period, and should also result in a much closer approach to equality in the burdens of taxpayers with steady and fluctuating incomes than is possible under the crude averaging devices cited above. It is an obvious extension of the principle of taxation according to ability to pay that no taxpayer should bear a heavier or lighter burden merely because certain items of his income happen to be earned or realized in one year or another, regardless of whether this be by chance or by design of the taxpayer and regardless of any fluctuations in the needs of the government for revenue or the rates of tax in effect at various times. If a practicable system of taxation which satisfies this criterion can be put into effect, then many of the arbitrary, unpopular, and complicated provisions designed chiefly to prevent the manipulation by the taxpayer of his income in his own favor will no longer be necessary and may be discarded.

To be practicable, a method of assessment must meet certain requirements. The most important of these, for present purposes, may be summarized as follows:

1. The discounted value of the series of tax payments made by any taxpayer should be independent of the way in which his income is allocated to the various income years.

2. The revenue for any given year should be capable of being raised or lowered by suitable modifications of the rates without too long notice.

3. If the taxpayer leaves the jurisdiction at any time, there should be no accumulations of untaxed income left behind and no tax due except possibly

the regular tax for the last year. (This was one difficulty with the Wisconsin method.)

4. Any given tax payment should not be too large in relation to the income of the period immediately preceding.

5. Transition to and from other methods of assessing income tax should be simple.

6. The method of computing the tax should not be beyond the ordinary taxpayer's capacity.

7. The administrative burden should not be excessive.

There are two steps in devising a method of assessment which will meet these criteria. The first is to determine a method of computing the final closing payment at the end of the averaging period (for example, at the death of the taxpayer) which will satisfy criterion 1; the second is to provide for the payment of suitable instalments during the averaging period which will satisfy criterions 2, 3, and 4.

Consider first two taxpayers, A and B, both of whom start with the same capital, obtain the same rate of return, and have identical earnings and expenditures during the period, the only difference being that A pays taxes on his income during the period, whereas B manages, by one method or another, to postpone the payment of the taxes until the end of the period. B's total income for the period will then exceed A's total income by the compound interest on the amounts which A paid as instalments on his income tax but which B avoided paying and so was able to invest. If, then, to A's total income is added the compound interest on the taxes which A has paid from the time they were paid to the end of the period, an amount which will be called the "adjusted total income" is obtained which is the income A would have had if he had paid no taxes during the period. It may readily be seen that this adjusted total income will remain the same for any given taxpayer, regardless of any changes that may occur in the allocation of the realization of his income to the various years within the averaging period. If the final payment is determined in such a way that the aggregate present value of the taxes paid with respect to the income period is dependent only on this adjusted total income, then criterion 1 will be satisfied. A standard for the graduation of the tax that immediately suggests itself is that the taxpayer with a steady income throughout the averaging period shall be unaffected by the change in method of assessment, so that the taxes paid by a given individual A with a fluctuating income shall have the same present value as the taxes that would have been paid on an annual basis of assessment by a taxpayer C with a steady income of such magnitude that C's adjusted total income is equal to that of A. This standard satisfies criterion 2, at least with respect to the total payments of any one taxpayer.

In providing for the payment of annual instalments previous to the end of the income period, criterion 3 suggests that each year be treated as if it were the end of an averaging period, except that, instead of requiring a final and conclusive valuation of the capital assets of the taxpayer, any reasonable valuation tendered by the taxpayer may be accepted for the purpose of computing the accrued capital gain or loss. Any errors in valuation at this point will make no difference whatever in the total burden ultimately imposed upon the taxpayer but will merely alter somewhat the time of payment. This treatment will avoid any questions of unpaid and uncollectible taxes, will keep the tax payments fairly well in step with the income of the taxpayer, and will cause revenues to respond promptly to increases or decreases in the rates.

The principles involved in the computation of the tax for each year will then be as follows: First, the adjusted total income of the taxpayer for the period from the beginning of his averaging period to the present will be calculated by adding to his total income for the period the compound interest on the taxes which he has paid with respect to this income. The size of the constant income which would have yielded the same adjusted total income over this period is then calculated. The next step is to calculate the present value of the taxes that would have been payable on such a constant income according to the present methods of assessment and the rates for the various years of the income period. The present accumulated value of the taxes already paid by the original taxpayer is then deducted from this sum, and the remainder is the tax currently due.

At first sight this method of determining the annual payments to be made by the taxpayer may seem hopelessly complex; it is possible, however, by constructing special tables and carrying figures forward from previous returns, so to arrange the computation that the actual work required of the taxpayer will be considerably less than that at present required of taxpayers having capital gains and losses. The special tables would be prepared by the Treasury, would be comparable in every respect to the surtax tables now in use, and would give the total tax payable on given amounts of adjusted total income, with marginal rates to be applied to income between the bracket limits given in the table. There would be one such table prepared for each number of years for which individual taxpayers will have been subject to this averaging method of assessment.[4] Then from a previous return or certified transcript the taxpayer would copy the total adjusted income and the total value of tax payments as of last year. The total value of taxes previously paid is then multiplied by the rate of interest fixed by the Treasury to obtain the interest accrued during the past year upon taxes previously paid. This interest is then added to the value of taxes paid as of last year to get the present value of taxes paid, and is added together with the adjusted total income from the previous return and the income reported for the past year to get the new adjusted total income. From the appropriate surtax table the taxpayer then obtains the total present value of tax corresponding to this adjusted total income by exactly the same procedure as is used at present in computing the surtax corresponding to a given surtax net income; from this total value of tax the taxpayer then deducts the total present value of past taxes paid, and the remainder is the payment due for the

---

[4] The following is a sample of such a table for taxpayers averaging over two years. The rates taken are the surtax rates of the revenue act of 1936 for both years, with interest at 5 per cent.

Adjusted Total Income (Dollars)	Total Present Value of Tax (Dollars)	Rate of Tax on Excess within Next Bracket (Per Cent)
0	0	0.0000
8,000	0	4.0959
12,004	164	5.1186
16,009	369	6.1408
20,015	615	7.1625
24,022	902	8.1836
28,030	1,230	9.2043
32,039	1,599	11.2441
36,050	2,050	13.2818
40,063	2,583	15.3176
. . . . . .	. . . . .	. . . .

This table is precisely similar to present surtax tables except for the facts that the figures are not rounded and that the amounts in the first two columns are a little over twice the corresponding amounts in present tables. These amounts would be a little more than three times as large for a table for taxpayers averaging for three years, and so on.

The figures given in the table are computed as follows: A taxpayer with a steady annual income (after exemptions) of $12,000 pays a surtax each year, under the present law, of $440. Interest on the first year's tax at 5 per cent is $22. This $22, added to the total income for the two-year period of $24,000, gives the adjusted total income of $24,022 given in the first column. The total present value of the tax is $440 + $440 + $22 = $902. The next higher level of income in the present tables is $14,000, giving similarly an adjusted total income of $28,030 and a total present value of tax of $1,230; thus, the size of the total adjusted income bracket is $4,008, and the tax on this bracket is $1,230 − $902, or $328. The rate of tax on this bracket is therefore $328 ÷ $4,008, or 8.1836 per cent.

current year.[5] These computations are fairly simple compared with many less equitable proposals for averaging and with the present computations required in the case of capital gains.

The chief drawback seems to be that a separate table is needed for each number of years for which taxpayers are permitted to average their income. Thus, after fifteen years of operation, fifteen separate tables would need to be drawn up; and while the individual taxpayer would need to consult only one, either the burden of selecting the proper table will have to be placed upon the taxpayer or the Treasury will have to undertake to mail each taxpayer the proper table on the basis of the records of previous returns. Whichever method is chosen, this should not prove an insuperable obstacle. Criterions 6 and 7 are thus fairly well satisfied.

Failure of the current tax liability to keep pace with the ability to pay of the taxpayer in accordance with criterion 4 has been a serious obstacle to the adoption of other forms of averaging, and actually was a contributing cause in the repeal of the Wisconsin averaging provision. It is possible to show, however, that under the foregoing method of computation the amounts of tax successively due will, under very general conditions, not bear too high a relation to the income of the preceding year. Under

---

[5] The required computations might be set out as follows on the income-tax return.

1. Net income this year (after exemptions) $18,500.00
2. Adjusted total income as of previous year (copied from item 5 of previous year's return) 9,200.00
3. Total value of income taxes paid as of previous year (copied from item 6 of previous year's return) 252.00
4. Interest for past year on taxes paid (5 per cent of item 3) . . 12.60
   (The rate of interest may be varied from year to year by the Treasury in accordance with current economic conditions. The rate of interest must, of course, be the same as that used in the computation of the surtax tables.)
5. Adjusted total income (sum of items 1, 2, and 4) 27,712.60
6. Present value of tax on item 5 (computed from surtax table) 1,204.02
7. Present value of past income taxes paid (sum of items 3 and 4) 264.60
8. Tax due (item 6 minus item 7) 939.42

The figures given are for the 1938 return of a taxpayer who is averaging over the two years 1937–38, having a net income, after exemptions, of $9,200 in 1937 and $18,500 in 1938. For the first year, items 2, 3, and 4 are zero, so that item 5 for the first year is simply the income of that year, and so appears unaltered in item 2 above.

Item 6 is calculated as follows: The largest amount in the first column of the surtax table not greater than item 5 is $24,022.00, the excess being $3,690.60. The tax on the first $24,022.00 is given in the second column, $902.00; the tax on the excess at the rate given in the third column, 8.1836 per cent, is $302.02, a total of $1,204.02. Except for the unrounded figures, this computation is precisely the same as that now required in computing surtax.

the Wisconsin method, a man with a sharply reduced income found that he still had to pay a tax based on the relatively high income obtained by averaging the income of the last three years. Here, on the other hand, a reduction in current income below the average of past years will cause the average, including the current year, to fall below the average on which the tax for previous years was based, and therefore will reduce the tax which should be payable with respect to those years. The excess of tax actually paid over the tax assessable in view of the reduced average is, in effect, credited to the taxpayer and applied in reducing the tax for the current year. In fact, it can be shown mathematically that, if the rate remains unchanged and the income for the current year is less than the average income, the tax payable for the current year will be less than, or at most equal to, the tax that would have been payable for that year on a straight annual basis of assessment. Actually, the only case where the payment due in any given year can bear an unreasonable relationship to the income of the year immediately preceding is the case of a drastic rise in the scale of basic surtax rates accompanied by a sharp decrease in the income of the individual taxpayer.[6] Thus, no provision for the relief of

---

[6] If for the sake of simplicity it is assumed that income accrues and tax is assessed continuously, the equivalent constant income $\bar{r}$ of taxpayer C is determined by the following relation expressing the equality between the adjusted total incomes of A and C (see pp. 79 to 81):

$$\int_0^t \{r(\tau) + s(\tau)[e^{i(t-\tau)} - 1]\}\, d\tau = \int_0^t \{\bar{r}(t) + z(\bar{r}, \tau)[e^{i(t-\tau)} - 1]\}\, d\tau,$$

where $r(\tau)$ is the income of A at time τ, $s(\tau)$ is the tax payable, i is the rate of interest, e is the base of natural logarithms, $\tau = t$ is the time at which the current computations are being made, $\tau = $ zero is the beginning of the current averaging period, and $z(r, \tau)$ is the tax payable on a nonaveraging basis on an income r according to the schedule in effect at time τ; $\bar{r}$ may be called the "average income" of A.

The total present value of the taxes on the incomes of A and C are to be equal; therefore,

$$\int_0^t s(\tau) e^{i(t-\tau)}\, d\tau = \int_0^t z(\bar{r}, \tau) e^{i(t-\tau)}\, d\tau.$$

Differentiating these two expressions with respect to t and solving for $s(t)$,

$$s(t) = z(\bar{r}, t) + [r(t) - \bar{r}(t)]\bar{m},$$

where $\bar{m}$ is the "mean effective marginal tax rate" given by the equations:

$$\frac{1}{\bar{m}} = 1 + \frac{\displaystyle\int_0^t [1 - m(\tau)]\, d\tau}{\displaystyle\int_0^t m(\tau) e^{i(t-\tau)}\, d\tau}, \qquad m(\tau) = \frac{\partial z(\bar{r}, \tau)}{\partial r}.$$

m thus corresponds to the rate of tax on the top bracket of income.

If the rates are progressive, it follows that

$$\frac{\partial^2 z}{\partial r^2} > 0.$$

hard cases need be made except in the years immediately following a sharp increase in rates. Even in the years when such relief is necessary, the form of the relief may be made fairly simple without opening any very serious loopholes, since the number of taxpayers who will be eligible for relief will be relatively small. The relief might take the form of a provision that the tax payable in any one year shall not exceed an amount determined by applying a supplementary rate schedule, somewhat higher than the regular basic one, to the income of the taxpayer for the previous year. The reduced tax payment may be carried over as a basis for calculating subsequent payments, so that in most cases the government will not, in the long run, lose any revenue through the granting of this relief except in the most extreme cases.

Unlike such moving average plans as the Wisconsin plan discussed on page 77, no particular problems arise at the time of inauguration or abandonment of an averaging plan such as that outlined in the preceding four paragraphs. At the start, the basis that is already calculated for property in the hands of the taxpayer is all that is necessary to obtain an initial value for the capital assets of the taxpayer. If at any future time it is desired to abandon this method of assessment, the basis may again be taken as that last declared by the taxpayer or as corrected by whatever restric-

---

Then, if $r < \bar{r}$ and if $m < \bar{m}$, which in particular will be the case when rate schedules are kept unchanged or lowered (and even if rates are raised slightly), then

$$s < z(\bar{r}, t) + (r - \bar{r})m + \tfrac{1}{2}(r - \bar{r})^2 \frac{\partial^2 z(\rho, t)}{\partial r^2} = z(r, t)$$

where $r \leq \rho \leq \bar{r}$. Thus, the tax is less than it would be without averaging.

If, on the other hand, $r > \bar{r}$, then, since $\bar{m} < 1$,

$$r - s = (r - \bar{r})(1 - \bar{m}) - z(\bar{r}) + \bar{r} > \bar{r} - z(\bar{r});$$

that is, the residue after the tax is greater than the residue from an income equal to the average income.

If $z(\bar{r})/\bar{r} < \bar{m}$ (which will permit the current rate to be considerably higher than past rates), then

$$s = z(\bar{r}) - \bar{m}\bar{r} + \bar{m}r < \bar{m}r,$$

that is, the overall rate of tax will be less than $\bar{m}$.

Finally, if $r > \bar{r}$ and $z(\bar{r})/\bar{r} > \bar{m}$ (which implies that current rates are considerably higher than past rates), then

$$\frac{s}{r} = \frac{1}{r}(r - \bar{r})\left(\bar{m} - \frac{z(\bar{r})}{\bar{r}}\right) + \frac{z(\bar{r})}{\bar{r}} < \frac{z(\bar{r})}{r};$$

that is, the overall rate of tax will be less than that on the average income.

The only case left out of the foregoing limitations on the tax is the case where $r < \bar{r}$ and current rates are so much higher than previous rates that $z(\bar{r})/\bar{r} > \bar{m}$. This is the only case in which there is a possibility of relief provisions being required.

The conclusions arrived at on the assumption of continuous payments are a fortiori true in the case where the payments are made annually, since similar relations can be obtained from those above by integrating the continuous payments over successive yearly intervals.

tions it is deemed necessary to reimpose. These problems of allocation of income occur in any case with even greater frequency under a straight annual basis of assessment.

It is apparent that such an averaging device can prevent the avoidance of tax by the shifting of income only with respect to shifts of income between years within the averaging period. If it is permitted to shift income between years included in an averaging period and previous or subsequent years, whether or not they are included in other averaging periods, the possibility of avoidance will re-emerge. It will therefore be necessary to reintroduce at the close and commencement of each averaging period such safeguards as may be available to prevent such shifting of income between one averaging period and another.

The simplest method of preventing such shifting of income is to require that an inventory of the assets of the taxpayer be made at the end of each averaging period and that the capital gains and accruals so revealed be included in the income of the last year of the preceding averaging period. While this procedure might involve a prohibitive amount of administrative work if valuation each year were required, as is the case when assessment on a strict accrual basis is proposed, only a small fraction of this work would be required here, since the valuations would be made only at relatively long intervals.

There are many reasons why the averaging period should be made as long as possible. Obviously, the longer the averaging period, the smaller will be the administrative task of valuation and checking valuations. If the averaging periods are arranged so that their ends are staggered, then the effect of the valuation date upon the markets may be reduced by lengthening the averaging period, since then the amount to be valued at any one time will be smaller. The incentive for the taxpayer to attempt to shift his income from one period to another will be smaller the longer the averaging period, since it will be more difficult for him to forecast for the longer period what the size of his income will be and to what rates he will be subject; moreover, the actual variations in average income and average rates as between one period and another are likely to be smaller. However, the saving in interest to the taxpayer who transfers income from the last year of one period to the first year of the next will be substantially greater, since the interval between the average date of payment of the tax will be not one year but an entire averaging period. In general, the increase in equity afforded by the averaging method of assessment will become greater as the period is made longer.

The logical limit would seem to be to extend the averaging period from the majority of the taxpayer until his death. (Although it would be possible to start the averaging period at birth, the difficulties involved seem to outweigh any possible advantages, especially as such a procedure would tend to favor those who had taxable incomes during their minority.) If this plan is adopted, then only two valuations throughout the life of each taxpayer become necessary: one at the majority of the taxpayer and one at his death. The valuation at death is in most cases already required for estate-tax purposes, while the valuation at the time of the taxpayer's attainment of majority would usually involve only a very small amount of property and would be relatively easy to enforce, since in general it would be to the taxpayer's advantage to report as completely as possible.

This plan involves the imposition of a tax upon the capital gains accrued upon the taxpayer's property at the time of his death. That such gains should be taken into account in the return for the year in which the taxpayer dies has already been proposed as an independent reform designed to plug an important loophole. Doubts have been expressed, however, as to the constitutionality of such an assessment. If the direct imposition of such a tax does prove unconstitutional, indirect methods of accomplishing the same end will probably not be difficult to find. There is the possible device of offering the averaging plan, coupled with the voluntary acceptance of such an assessment by the taxpayer, as an alternative to being taxed on an annual basis as at present; since in most cases the averaging method would, under identical rate schedules, result in a reduction of the tax burden, most taxpayers would probably elect the averaging plan. The rates applicable to those electing the annual basis of assessment might even be made somewhat higher, in order to offset any advantage that this election might have in affording loopholes for avoidance. Another method of inducing the taxpayer to accept such an assessment voluntarily might be to impose a special estate tax upon the transfer of assets containing such unrealized gains. The tax on the unrealized gains might even avoid the constitutional issue by being formulated as such an estate tax graduated according to the average income of the taxpayer.

Extending the averaging period from the majority of the taxpayer to his death automatically provides for a staggering of the ends of the averaging periods of different taxpayers so as to reduce to a minimum the influence on markets of the necessary valuations. The problem immediately arises, however, of how to treat taxpayers whose family status changes. One solution would be to cut the averaging period arbitrarily at the time of marriage, divorce, or death of spouse. Such a procedure, however, imposes a fairly heavy tax burden upon marriage, since the individual who marries will not be able to average his previous low incomes with his subsequent presumably higher incomes (or, in less frequent cases, vice versa) and will therefore have to pay heavier taxes than the man who remains single and is able to average over the longer period. This factor may altogether outweigh the concessions given the family man in increased exemptions; and if it does so, will run directly counter to most accepted notions of ability to pay. Another method of dealing with the problem would require separate returns to be filed and the tax computed and paid separately by each member of the family.

A more radical but probably more satisfactory method in the long run would be to go one step farther than the community-property states and consolidate the entire family income in one return, apportion this family income among the various members of the family according to proportions fixed by statute, and compute a tax separately for each member of the family, using for each person the appropriate previous total adjusted income. This method has the advantage that it is likely to prevent to a very large extent the avoidance of tax by various methods of redistributing income between members of the family. Moreover, it would eliminate the arbitrary and unjustified advantage now enjoyed by residents of the community-property states. On the whole, this seems a more equitable method of taxation than that at present in effect, even if not used in conjunction with any averaging basis of assessment. In order that this change should not be thought of merely as a method of increasing the relief given the wealthy on account of their families, it should be accompanied by a decrease of about 50 per cent in the income levels at which various rates of tax become effective, so that the actual change in the tax burden of the married will be relatively slight, with a substantial increase in the burdens of those individuals of large incomes who have no family with which they share this income.

Another important question is how far the averaging device should be extended to individuals with the lower incomes. A rigorously thoroughgoing application of the first criterion would result in requiring every adult to file a return no matter how small his income, and in permitting individuals to accumulate, as a deficit to be offset against any future income, any excess of exemptions and allowable deductions over gross income. This procedure is open to two very serious objections. The administrative job of auditing this vast number of returns would be staggering, especially as it would be necessary to check even those returns that were obviously not taxable, since if the taxpayer later has a large income, the amount of deficit reported in previous returns will affect his tax in such a year. The statistics might be interesting but would probably be rather expensive! The other serious drawback is that Congress might at some later time find that, having previously been somewhat more generous with exemptions and deductions than it would want to be at that time, the taxpayers would have accumulated such a backlog of deficits against which to offset any current income that no matter how far exemptions were then reduced, very little income from the lower brackets could then be made subject to tax. Thus, the result could conceivably be considerable financial embarrassment on the part of the government, or alternatively a breach of faith with the taxpayer through the abrogation of the right to set off these accumulated deficits against current income.

A simple method of getting around these difficulties is to permit personal exemptions to be deducted only to the extent of net income. This would restrict the carrying-forward of negative income to cases where business losses, capital losses, and other deductions exceed net income; in such cases a slight penalty would attach in that the benefit of the exemption for that year would be lost. Under such limitations there would be no incentive in the bulk of cases for the filing of nontaxable returns in the expectation of future increased income.

In connection with a flat-rate tax at a fairly low rate, such as the present normal tax, the application of the averaging method of assessment under the foregoing restrictions would make a slight but on the whole insignificant difference, provided only that full carry-over of losses is permitted. It may therefore be quite sufficient, at least at first, to apply the averaging method to the computation of surtax only, continuing to calculate the normal tax on an annual basis as heretofore. This plan would cut the initial administrative load down very sharply; and after experience has been gained with these returns, the plan might be extended to cover the normal tax of those paying surtax, or all taxpayers, as seems desirable on the basis of such experience.

In the case of corporations the opportunities for avoiding taxation by shifting income from year to year are more limited than in the case of individuals, since the corporation income-tax rates are but slightly graduated and since the rates themselves seem to have been, at least in the past, rather more stable from year to year than the rates of the individual income tax. Nevertheless, the application of this averaging method, or some modification of it, may be of advantage even here, since the Treasury would thereby be freed from the necessity of checking inventory, depreciation, obsolescence, and the like, except at times of reorganization and to make sure of the absence of double counting. The question is not as important as with the individual income tax, however, since the need for the undistributed-profits tax and the special capital-gains provisions would not be affected, these being largely devices to patch up the unsatisfactory operation of the individual income tax.

Any averaging device will, of course, require a certain amount of record-keeping. The current records required under the present proposal consist of only four items: the year in which the taxpayer commenced to average, the adjusted total income, the total present value of past taxes, and the total value of the capital assets of the taxpayer as declared in his latest return. Further information may be filed but is not normally necessary for the checking of future assessments. It is probable that the decrease in other administrative work which is made possible by the employment of this method of assessment, such as the checking of capital-gains computations and checking deductions for depreciation and the like, will more than make up for the keeping of more complete records.

The averaging method of assessing income tax is not without its drawbacks. The keeping of records, the slightly more complicated method of computing the tax, the required final valuation at death (and perhaps at times of change of marital status), the existence of several surtax tables among which the correct one must be selected, the occasional need for the payment of refunds (in addition to refunds of overpayments resulting from error), and the more detailed treatment of family returns are the chief points at which objections may be raised. Special groups will also require particular attention: some approximate method of dealing with part-year returns must be devised, unless the number of surtax tables to be used is to be multiplied to an extent that may be considered intolerable; aliens who draw their income from foreign sources in some years may obtain unfair advantages under the normal operation of such an averaging device and may require special provisions; changes of residence status may present difficult problems in the case of states employing such an averaging device, as may the taxation of nonresidents. These difficulties and the many possible methods of dealing with them cannot, however, be discussed at length here.

Against these minor drawbacks are to be set substantial gains in equity as between taxpayers with steady and those with fluctuating incomes, taxpayers with fixed and those with readily manipulated incomes, taxpayers with capital gains and those with other forms of income, and single and family taxpayers. The fact that similarly circumstanced taxpayers are treated similarly produces, in turn, still further desirable results, such as a substantial decrease in the worry, expense, and economic waste which now result when taxpayers seek to minimize their tax burden, a reduction in the amount of litigation, and a decrease in the influence of the income tax upon business transactions and the economic life of the community. For example, the securities market should be freer from the extraneous influence of the arbitrary rules concerning capital gains and losses, while the influence of the income tax in reducing the amount of capital for risky enterprises should be diminished, as abnormal profits in one or two years will no longer subject the taxpayer to such high rates.

The undistributed-profits tax, as well as the surtaxes on personal holding companies and corporations improperly accumulating surplus, could be repealed completely without fear of reopening loopholes for tax avoidance. The special provisions for the taxation of capital gains could also be repealed, as such gains could be included in net income without imposing any special hardships upon the recipients of such gains, while the limitations on the deduction of capital losses could be removed without thereby opening any loopholes.[7] The removal of the incentive to shift income from depression years, when rates are high, to prosperous years, when rates are low, should increase the cyclical stability of yield and in turn reduce the pressure to limit the deductibility of losses in times of depression, as was done in 1932. It is possible that this factor may also have some influence in reducing the severity of the business cycle.

The method of assessment outlined in this article has been developed on the assumption that the base to be adopted for income taxation is "accrued income" as opposed to the "paid-income" or "accrued-income-less-net-savings" base advocated by Irving Fisher.[8] It is possible to adapt this method of assessment, with a few slight changes (changes which, on the whole, make its operation even simpler), to operate on the latter

---

[7] Many of the complicated, controversial, and often arbitrary regulations for determining when gains are realized may be discarded; or, if this is not done, at least there will no longer be any incentive for contention on either side. The only necessary requirement is that any amounts received from property be either reported as income or applied to reduce the basis of the property. Indeed, separate accounting for individual assets is no longer necessary; a simple declaration by the taxpayer of the estimated total value of his capital assets as of the end of the year is all that is necessary, and accuracy need not be insisted upon. Similarly, regulations for the allowance of depreciation and obsolescence may be discarded and the allowance made as the taxpayer sees fit. The problem becomes chiefly one of avoiding double counting and seeing to it that taxpayers do not postpone realization of income to the point where there is danger of loss of tax through insolvency, or realize prematurely in the hope of being able to gain through the application of relief when in later years the taxpayers report lower incomes. This latter danger is already taken care of through the provisions in existing law for jeopardy assessments; further protection could be added by stiffening the qualifications for the application of the relief provisions. It may be desirable to provide a slight incentive to taxpayers to report income and pay taxes as early as possible by setting the interest rate used in the computation of the tax slightly above the market rate.

[8] The expenditure tax advocated by Irving Fisher is expounded in greatest detail in "Income in Theory and Income Taxation in Practice," *Econometrica*, Vol. V, No. 1 (January, 1937); also less technically in "A Practical Schedule for an Income Tax," *Tax Magazine*, July, 1937.

base; in the case of a "paid-income" tax, however, the advantages of the averaging method are much less striking than is the case with the accrued-income tax. The paid-income tax is said to be inherently less difficult of administration than the various forms of accrued-income tax; if so, there would be less room for improvement in that direction; in any case, the administrative difficulties, if they exist, are not of the variety that would be reduced to any large extent by an averaging method. On the other hand, the paid-income tax assessed on a straight annual basis may have a much more severe effect in accentuating the business cycle through encouraging spending in times of prosperity, when taxes are low, and discouraging it in times of depression and fiscal need, when taxes are high, than is the case with the accrued-income tax. Also, a rather severe transitory effect upon sales may be expected at times of sharp increase or decrease in rates. The application of an averaging device would substantially eliminate both of these untoward effects. The possibility of the simplification of administration in the one case, of the elimination of transitory and cyclical effects in the other case, and of the equalization of burden in both cases by means of such an average basis of assessment should make it easier to discuss the relative merit of these two bases for taxation on the basis of their long-run economic and social effects without having the issue confused by considerations of cyclical effects, relative ease of administration, and degree of discrimination against fluctuating incomes.

6

Federalism and Fiscal Equity*

By J. M. BUCHANAN

Fiscal relations between central and subordinate units of government have become an important problem area in the United States during the last two decades.[1] Increasing attention has been, and is being, given to the more practical policy proposals aimed at accomplishing specific short-run objectives. While this may have been necessary, perhaps too little attention has been placed upon the study and the formulation of the long-run objectives of an intergovernmental fiscal structure.[2] This paper seeks to formulate a specific long-run goal for policy and will discuss the advantages which might be expected to arise from its general acceptance.

I

A distinct group of problems immanently arise when a single political unit possessing financial authority in its own right contains within its geographical limits smaller political units also possessing financal authority.[3] These problems become especially important in a federal polity since the financial authority of the subordinate units is constitutionally independent of that of the central government. In a federalism, two constitutionally independent fiscal systems operate upon the fiscal resources of individual citizens.[4]

---

* *American Economic Review*, Vol. XL, No. 4 (September, 1950).

[1] The most general survey of the whole field published to date is: U. S. Congress, Senate, *Federal, State and Local Government Fiscal Relations*, Sen. Doc. 69, 78th Cong., 1st Sess. (Washington, Government Printing Office, 1943). Other competent works include: J. A. Maxwell, *The Fiscal Impact of Federalism in the United States* (Cambridge: Harvard University Press, 1946); Jane P. Clark, *The Rise of a New Federalism* (New York: Columbia University Press, 1938); G. C. S. Benson, *The New Centralization* (New York: Farrar and Rinehart, 1941).

[2] One important work in the field is concerned with this aspect. B. P. Adarkar, *The Principles and Problems of Federal Finance* (London: P. S. King and Sons, 1933).

[3] Financial authority may be defined as the power of a governmental unit to collect revenues from contained fiscal resources and to expend such revenues in the performance of governmental functions. *Cf.* Adarkar, *op. cit.*, p. 31.

[4] The individual must deal with three or more fiscal systems, federal, state, and one or more local units. Local financial authority is, however, derivative from that of the state, and for present purposes, the combined state-local fiscal system will be considered as one unit.

The fiscal system of each unit of government is limited in its operation by the geographical boundaries of that unit; it can withdraw resources for the financing of public services only from those available within this area. If the subordinate units are required independently to finance certain traditionally assigned functions, fiscal inequalities among these units will be present unless the fiscal capacities are equivalent. There will be differences in the number and/or the standard of the public services performed for and/or the burden of taxes levied upon the owners of economic resources within the separate units. The nature and the extent of these differences, and the difficulties involved in their elimination, constitute the elements of the over-all fiscal problem of the federal polity.

The situation has grown progressively more acute in the United States. This can be attributed largely to the three following parallel historical trends: First, the continual industrialization, specialization, and integration of the economy on a national scale has tended to concentrate high income receivers in specific geographical areas. Second, there has been an extension of the range of governmental activity at all levels in the political hierarchy. This has required the diversion of greater and greater shares of the total of economic resources through the fiscal mechanism. Third, this extension of governmental activity at the lower levels of government (and in peacetime at the top level) has taken place largely through the increase in the provision of the social services. This when coupled with the type of tax structure prevailing has increased the amount of real income redistribution accomplished by the operation of the fiscal system.

In 1789, a significant share of economic activity was limited to local markets; there was relatively little areal specialization of production. Governmental services were performed predominantly by the local units which were drawn up roughly to correspond in area to the extent of the local markets. Rapid developments in transportation and communication led to an ever-increasing specialization of resources. The economy grew more productive, but the inequalities in personal incomes and wealth increased. This emerging inequality was both inter-personal and inter-regional; expanding individual differences were accompanied by closer concentration of the higher income recipients in the more favored areas. This created disparities among the states in their capacities to support public services.

These fiscal divergences were not conspicuous, however, until the extension of governmental activity caused the traditional sources of revenue to become inadequate. As greater amounts of revenue were required at all levels, conflicts over revenue sources among state units, and between states and the central government, arose.

The form which the extension of governmental activity took was an important determining factor in making the problem more difficult. Even with the increasing costs of government, inter-regional disparities in fiscal capacity would not have been accentuated had not the extension taken place largely through the expanded provision of the social services. Had the rôle of government remained "protective," and thus the fiscal system conformed more closely to the benefit or *quid pro quo* principle, richer units would have needed greater governmental expenditures. Only when the "social" state appeared did the divergency between need and capacity become clear. As more government services were provided equally to all citizens, or upon some basis of personal need, the discrepancies between the capacities and needs of the subordinate units arose.

The emerging fiscal problem has been only one of many created by the progressive national integration of the economic system within a decentralized political structure. This development has caused many students to view the political structure as outmoded, and the federal spirit as a thing of the past.[5] The federal polity has outlived its usefulness, and the conditions which made it necessary as a stage in the process of political development no longer prevail.[6] It is true that complete political centralization would resolve the peculiar fiscal problem of federalism. If there were only one fiscal system, as there would be in a unitary form of government, regional differences in standards of public services and/or burdens of taxation would not exist.[7] But political centralization as a proposal for solution is precluded if we accept the desirability of maintaining the federal form. The approach taken in this paper accepts the federal political structure, with the existence of the states as constitutionally independent units sovereign within specified areas. Thus, the problem is reduced to that of formulating a solution within this given framework.

The same problem of fiscal inequality is, of course, present among local units of government within the same state unit. However, the scope for adjustment by non-fiscal means, through political or administrative devices (local government consolidation, state assumption of local functions, etc.), seems broader in state-local relations. The policy proposals stemming from the analysis which follows presume a fixed political struc-

---

[5] See Roy F. Nichols, "Federalism vs. Democracy," *Federalism as a Democratic Process* (New Brunswick: Rutgers University Press, 1942), p. 50.

[6] Gordon Greenwood, *The Future of Australian Federalism* (Melbourne: Melbourne University Press, 1946), p. viii.

[7] The proposal for integration and unification of the fiscal systems at different levels has been excellently presented by Professor S. E. Leland. See, for example, his "The Relations of Federal, State, and Local Finance," *Proceedings, National Tax Association*, Vol. XXIII (1930), pp. 94–106.

ture. But it should be emphasized that both the analysis and the policy implications can be extended to inter-local unit fiscal adjustment as well as to interstate fiscal adjustment. Subsequent discussion will, however, be limited to the latter.

II

The ideal type adjustment can be presented in reference to the relative fiscal systems of different state units which possess the same fiscal capacity. If all states were approximately identical in per capita incomes and wealth, the burden of taxation upon resources would not necessarily be equal in all. Neither would the general level nor the distribution of public services be equivalent. Some states might choose to tax more heavily and thus provide a higher level of public services than other units equal in fiscal potential. The criterion of comparison must be some balance between the two sides. Both the level of tax burden and the range of publicly provided services must be included. Units of equal fiscal capacity should be able to provide equivalent services at equivalent tax burdens.

An intergovernmental transfer system can be worked out which would allow state units originally unequal in fiscal capacity to provide equal services at equal rates of taxation. The explicit objective of such a system would be the placing of all state units in a position which would allow them to provide a national average level of public services at average tax rates.[8] Immediately there arises the difficult task of determining average rates of taxation and average standards of public service. A more important objection to the statement of the policy goal in this form is that it appears in terms of adjustment among organic state units. Equality in terms of states is difficult to comprehend,[9] and it carries with it little ethical force for its policy implementation. And, is there any ethical precept which implies that states should be placed in positions of equal fiscal ability through a system of intergovernmental transfers?

If the interstate differences in fiscal capacity can be traced through to their ultimate impact upon individuals, and a policy objective formulated in inter-personal terms, it would seem that greater support could be marshalled for interstate fiscal equalization. Any discussion of the operations of a fiscal system or systems upon different individuals or families must

---

[8] This is the policy objective of the National Adjustment Grants proposed by the Royal Commission on Dominion-Provincial Relations after a study of the problem in Canada. See *Report of the Royal Commission on Dominion-Provincial Relations*, Book II, *Recommendations* (1940).

[9] See R. McQueen, "Economic Aspects of Federalism: A Prairie View," *Canadian Journal of Economic and Political Science*, Vol. I (1935), p. 353.

be centered around some concept of fiscal justice. And although fiscal justice in its all-inclusive sense is illusory and almost purely relative to the particular social environment considered, there has been contained in all formulations the central tenet of equity in the sense of "equal treatment for equals" or equal treatment for persons dissimilar in no relevant respect.[10] This basic principle has been so widely recognized that it has not been expressly stated at all times, but rather implicitly assumed. Whether or not this principle is consistent with maximizing social utility,[11] it is essential as a guide to the operations of a liberal democratic state, stemming from the same base as the principle of the equality of individuals before the law.[12]

The statement of "equal treatment for equals" as a central principle immediately raises the question of defining precisely the conditions of equality which are relevant in fiscal policy, and more especially intergovernmental fiscal policy. Traditionally, rather objective measures or standards have been accepted, and the divergency between the equality represented in these and subjective or psychic quality has been neglected. Money income and estimated property values in money have therefore been used as the bases for judging individual standing for tax purposes. Some allowance has been made for family size, for income source, and for other differences generating real income effects, but differences in geographical location have not been held to warrant differences in tax treatment.[13] There seems no special reason why intergovernmental fiscal adjustment policy should be set apart in this regard from national government tax policy. Thus, "equals" in the following analysis are individuals equal in those objective economic circumstances traditionally employed in the calculation of national government tax burdens.[14] Through the use of this definition of equals and the adoption of the equity principle, a

---

[10] "Different persons should be treated similarly unless they are dissimilar in some relevant respect." (A. C. Pigou, *A Study in Public Finance* [London: Macmillan, 1929], p. 9.)

[11] If all aspects of equality, including utility or pleasure creation, are included in the definition of "equals," then the principle will be directed toward maximum social utility but will be useless due to the impossibility of application. This would be true because any application would require some inter-personal comparison of utility. Any realistic definition of "equals" must omit subjective attributes of equality; therefore, the application of the principle does not necessarily maximize social utility.

[12] *Cf.* J. S. Mill, *Principles of Political Economy* (Boston: Charles C. Little and James Brown, 1848), Vol. II, p. 352.

[13] Differences in geographical location perhaps cause significant differences in real incomes among particular individuals, but these would seem to be offsetting when large numbers of individuals are considered. If the real incomes of all, or large numbers of, individuals, were increased or decreased by location in particular geographical areas, then these differences would become relevant for fiscal policy.

[14] This analysis does not require any particular set of attributes of equality. All that is required is that geographical location not be included.

formal solution to the fiscal problem of federalism can be worked out. This allows the problem to be isolated and separated from the much more difficult one of the distribution of fiscal burdens and benefits among unequals, in which an explicit formulation of "justice" is impossible.

III

What is equal fiscal treatment for equals? The orthodox answer has been almost wholly in reference to the tax side alone, the implication being that if tax burdens of similarly situated individuals were identical, the equity criterion would be satisfied. The necessity of including the benefit side of the fiscal account has been overlooked completely in many cases, and understressed in all.[15] The object of comparison should be the aggregate fiscal pressure upon the individual or family, not tax treatment alone. The balance between the contributions made and the value of public services returned to the individual should be the relevant figure. This "fiscal residuum" can be negative or positive. The fiscal structure is equitable in this primary sense only if the fiscal residua of similarly situated individuals are equivalent.

It is next necessary to define the appropriate political structure to be considered in its relative impact on individuals. In a federal polity, the individual has a plurality of political units with which to deal fiscally. Two or more independent fiscal systems act upon his economic resources, subtract from those resources through compulsory taxation, and provide in return certain public services. In this situation, what becomes of the criterion of equity postulated? Each political unit may treat equals equally.[16] If this were done, individuals similarly situated would be subjected to equal fiscal treatment only if they were citizens of the same subordinate unit of government. There would be no guarantee that equals living in different subordinate units would be equally treated at all. Therefore, the principle of equity must be extended to something other than individual governmental units to be of use in solving the fiscal problem of federalism.

---

[15] For a further elaboration on this and related points, see the writer's, "The Pure Theory of Government Finance: A Suggested Approach," *Journal of Political Economy*, Vol. LVII (Dec., 1949), pp. 496–505.

[16] This requirement has been expressly stated by one student of the problem. "In a democratic society considerations of equity demand that governmental programs *at each level* treat all citizens in similar circumstances uniformly" (italics supplied). (Byron L. Johnson, *The Principle of Equalization Applied to the Allocation of Grants in Aid,* Bureau of Research and Statistics Memo. No. 66 [Washington: Social Security Administration, 1947], p. 88.)

The limitation of the application of the equity principle to single fiscal systems within a federal polity can be questioned. It can be plausibly established that the appropriate unit should be the combined "fisc," including all the units in the political hierarchy. The argument can take either or both of two forms.

(*a*) In the United States, the economy, for all practical purposes, is national in scope. In large part, resources are allocated in response to incentives provided in a nationwide market for both final products and for productive services. Goods are sold and equities are traded nationally. The fiscal system represents the political unit in its direct impact upon the economy. Therefore, since the economy is national, the matching political structure must be considered as one unit in its operations upon that economy.[17] If it be accepted that one of the guiding principles in the operation of a fiscal system should be that of "least price distortion,"[18] or least interference with efficient resource allocation consistent with the attainment of other specific objectives, the necessity of this approach becomes clear. The principle of equal treatment of equals is consistent with that of least price distortion only if the "treatment" refers to that imposed by a political unit coincident in area with the economic entity. This is, in the United States, the whole political structure, central and local. For, in a federal structure with economically heterogeneous subordinate units, some interference with the proper resource allocation necessarily arises, unless some interarea fiscal transfers are made.

Fiscal pressures are economic in nature, whether expressed as net burdens or net benefits. If states are not identical in fiscal capacity, the people in the low capacity (low income) states must be subjected to greater fiscal pressure (higher taxation and/or lower value of public services) than people in high capacity states. If "equals" are thus pressed more in one area than in another, there will be provided an incentive for migration of both human and non-human resources into the areas of least fiscal pressures. Resources respond to market-determined economic reward, plus fiscal balance. If the fiscal balance for equals is not made equivalent for all areas of the economy, a considerable distortion of resources from the allocation arising as a result of economic criteria alone might result. The whole fiscal structure should be as neutral as is possible in a geographic

---

[17] Accepting this does not imply that the political structure should be one unit as has been proposed. There may be, and in my opinion are, definite values to be gained in maintaining a decentralized political structure. The purpose of this paper is that of showing how this decentralization might be retained while still solving the fiscal problem.

[18] F. C. Benham, "What Is the Best Tax System?" *Economica*, Vol. IX (1942), p. 116.

sense.[19] An individual should have the assurance that wherever he should desire to reside in the nation, the over-all fiscal treatment which he receives will be approximately the same.

It seems somewhat anomalous that states are forced through constitutional provision to remain parts of a national economy in the market sense and yet are forced to act as if they were completely independent economic units in their fiscal operations. This was recognized by William H. Jones in 1887, when he proposed a system of centrally collected taxes shared equally per head among states.[20] Requiring state areas to remain integrated in the national economy is inconsistent with the forcing of the governmental units of these areas to act as if the economies were fiscally separate and independent. This inconsistency can only be removed by centralization of fiscal authority or by the provision of some intergovernmental fiscal adjustment.

(*b*) The appropriateness of using the whole political structure as the unit in fiscal equity considerations can be justified in another way. Prior to the impact of the fiscal system, the income distribution arises largely as a result of the payment for resources in accordance with productivity criteria and competitive conditions established on a national basis. The fiscal system is the major means through which this income distribution is redressed toward one which is more ethically acceptable. It follows, then, that the fiscal system, in carrying out this function, should operate in a general manner over the whole area of the economy determining the original distribution. The generality with which the "fisc" can be operated has been held to be one of its important advantages over redistribution methods which entail particularistic or discriminatory interference with the economic mechanism. But unless the fiscal system is considered that of the whole hierarchy this advantage of generality is lost, and the system necessarily operates in a geographically discriminatory fashion.

The application of the equity principle on the basis of considering the whole political hierarchy as the appropriate unit will yield substantially different results from its application on the basis of considering separate

---

[19] This should not be taken to imply that complete neutrality in this sense could ever be reached. Even with a transfer system worked out along the proposed lines, differences among states would always be present to provide some distortionary effects. In the non-geographic sense, the fiscal structure will, and should, have some distortionary effects, if the whole system is redistributive.

[20] ". . . so long as we persist in applying the principle of autonomous State taxation under Federal forms, and Federal principles of trade and intercourse for purposes of Federal autonomy, the malady will stick to the patient.

This mingling of autonomous State taxes and Federal principles of free interstate trade and citizenship for purposes of Federal autonomy, is contrary to both the letter and spirit of the Federal Constitution." (William H. Jones, *Federal Taxes and State Expenses* [New York: G. P. Putnam's Sons, 1887], pp. 86–87.)

governmental units in isolation. If there are subordinate units of varying economic characteristics within the central government area, the equity principle applied to the whole hierarchy will require that the central government take some action to transfer funds from one area to another. Thus, the central government, considered alone, must violate the orthodox equity precept since it must favor the equals residing in the low capacity units. The central financial authority must enter the process and treat equals unequally in order to offset the divergencies in the income and wealth levels of the subordinate units.[21]

The necessity of assigning this rôle to the central unit in no way implies that the over-all fiscal system be unified in the sense that all financial decisions be made by one authority. Subordinate units should be able to retain complete authority. Neither the tax burdens nor the standards of public service need be equal for "equals" in any of the states. Satisfaction of the equity criterion requires only that the residua be substantially the same.

The policy objective for intergovernmental transfers then becomes one, reduced to individual terms, of providing or ensuring "equal fiscal treatment for equals." If this objective is attained, the individual's place of residence will no longer have a significant effect upon his fiscal position. Persons earning the same income and possessing the same amount of property will no longer be subjected to a much greater fiscal pressure in Mississippi than in New York, solely because of residence in Mississippi.

That a much greater and more effective force can be mustered in support of a transfer system worked out on this basis does not seem open to question. Reduced in this way to a problem of fiscal equity among individuals, the need for inter-area transfers becomes meaningful. Although the results of the working out of such a proposed system would perhaps differ little, if at all, from those forthcoming from a system based upon equalizing the fiscal capacities of the state units, the former carries with it considerable ethical force for its implementation while the latter does not. The ideal of "equal treatment for equals" is superior to that of equalization among organic state units.

IV

The following arithmetical illustration is presented to show how the use of the equity principle can lead to a determinate system of transfers

---

[21] "The position that the federal government would occupy in the scheme is that of filling in the gaps of unevenness as between one state and another." (Adarkar, *op. cit.*, p. 195.)

in a simplified model. Assume that in a hypothetical federal government, X, there are two states, A and B. The total population of X is six citizens, with three residing in each state. Their names are A-1, A-2, A-3, B-1, B-2, B-3. The economic characteristics of X are such that in A, two skilled workers and one unskilled worker can be employed, while in B, one skilled worker and two unskilled workers can be employed. Differences in the natural abilities of the six men are such that only three are equipped to do the skilled work, A-1, A-2, and B-1. The other three must do unskilled work. There are no non-pecuniary advantages to employment in either state. The six men are substantially similar in all other respects. The relative money incomes for the two groups are $10,000 per year for the skilled workers, and $1,000 per year for the unskilled. Therefore, A has two citizens receiving $10,000 and one receiving $1,000, while B has one $10,000 man and two $1,000 men.

Let it be assumed further that the central government imposes a progressive income tax amounting to 10 per cent of the higher incomes and 5 per cent of the lower incomes. All of its revenue is derived from this source. States A and B impose proportional taxes at the rate of 10 per cent on incomes. All their revenue is derived from this source. The tax liability of each of the citizens then is as follows:

Name	Collected by X	Collected by A or B	Total
A-1.	$1,000	$1,000	$2,000
A-2.	1,000	1,000	2,000
A-3.	50	100	150
B-1.	1,000	1,000	2,000
B-2.	50	100	150
B-3.	50	100	150

It can be easily seen that if tax liability alone is considered, the overall fiscal structure is-equitable in the primary sense. Equals are treated equally. But if both sides of the fiscal account are included, glaring inequities in the treatment of equals appear.

Now, let it be assumed that both the central government, X, and states A and B, expend funds in such a manner that all citizens within their respective jurisdictions benefit equally from publicly provided services. The central government collects a total of $3,150 and when expended each citizen gets a value benefit of $525 from services provided by that unit. State A collects $2,100 from its three citizens, and each gets in return a value benefit of $700 from public services provided by A. State B collects $1,200, and each citizen thus receives only $400 in value benefit from public services provided by B. The final fiscal position of each of the citizens is represented in the following:

Name	Total Taxes	Total Benefits	Fiscal Residuum
A-1...................	$2,000	$1,225	$ 775
A-2...................	2,000	1,225	775
A-3...................	150	1,225	— 1,075
B-1...................	2,000	925	1,075
B-2...................	150	925	— 775
B-3...................	150	925	— 775

B-1 is taxed at equal rates with his equals, A-1 and A-2, by both the central government and the state, and receives the same benefits from the central unit, but he receives $300 less in benefits from his state. His fiscal residuum is $1,075 (taxes over benefits) as compared with $775 for his equals. Likewise, the fiscal residuum of B-2 and B-3 is a negative $775 (benefits over taxes) while that of their equal, A-3, is a negative $1,075.

If a transfer of $200 were made among the set of high income equals in this model, from State A to State B, thus reducing the residuum or net tax of B-1 by $200 and increasing that of A-1 and A-2 by $100 each, then each of this group would end up with a residuum of $875. A further transfer of $200 from A-3 to B-2 and B-3 would equalize the negative residua of the low income equals at $875. Thus, a total transfer of $400 from A to B would enable the equals to be placed in identical fiscal positions.

This model presents the use of the equity principle in its most favorable abstraction. Certain major qualifications must be made if the principle is to be universally applicable even in such structurally simple models. In the above model, both state units imposed taxes at the same flat proportional rate and distributed benefits equally per head, while the central government imposed progressive tax rates and distributed benefits equally among its citizens. It is necessary to examine these conditions and trace through the effects of possible changes upon the results. First of all, it can be shown that the central government acting alone can vary the progressiveness or redistributiveness of its fiscal system (either on the tax or expenditure side, or both) without in any way affecting the resulting transfer total.[22] This is, of course, due to the fact that the central gov-

---

22 This can be illustrated by changing the above model to one in which the central government collects all its tax revenues from the three high income receivers. The resulting individual fiscal positions are then as follows:

Name	Total Tax	Total Benefit	Residuum
A-1...................	$2,050	$1,225	$ 825
A-2...................	2,050	1,225	825
A-3...................	100	1,225	— 1.125
B-1...................	2,050	925	1,125
B-2...................	100	925	— 825
B-3...................	100	925	— 825

ernment system, in principle at least, treats equals equally, and thus no action carried out by this system alone would affect the existing inequalities among equals.

Second, it can be shown that the transfer total is not changed by a simple increase (decrease) in the desires of the citizens of one state for public services. The result will be changed only if, in the process of providing the increased (decreased) services, the redistributiveness of the state fiscal system is affected. For example, either of the states in the above model, desiring to provide additional services, could levy equal per head poll taxes of any amount without changing the required transfer total at all.

This is not the case, however, when the amount of redistribution carried out in the operation of either or both of the state fiscal systems is changed. Such a change can be carried out by shifts in the allocation of tax burdens or benefits among the different income classes, or through altering the total amounts of economic resources entering the fiscal systems. The limiting case is that in which neither state system is at all redistributive, both operating on purely benefit principles.[23] In this case, each individual receives in value benefits the equivalence of contributions made, *i.e.*, has a zero residuum. Thus, whatever the income differences among the units, equals are equally treated, and no required transfer is indicated. Thus, it can be stated that as the fiscal system of either of the state units is shifted more toward operation on a benefit basis, *i.e.*, is made less redistributive, the required transfer between the high income state and the low income state is reduced. Conversely, as either system is made more redistributive, a greater transfer is necessary to satisfy the equity criterion.[24] This dependence of the resulting transfer total upon

It can be seen that a transfer of $400 will again place equals in identical fiscal positions. Absolute differences among equals have not been changed by the increase in the progression of the central government tax structure. It will be noted, however, that the fiscal positions of the citizens of B have been improved relative to those of A's citizens.

[23] A special form of this limiting case is that in which neither state levies taxes or provides public services.

[24] These effects can easily be seen by imposing changed conditions in the original model. Assume now that State A, instead of levying proportional tax rates, adopts a progressive income tax which increases the tax burden on its high income citizens, A-1 and A-2, to $1,050 each, and reduces the tax burden on A-3 to zero. Assume that the distribution of benefits in both states and B's tax rates remain the same as before. The fiscal positions then are as follows:

Name	Total Taxes	Total Benefits	Fiscal Residuum
A-1	$2,050	$1,225	$ 825
A-2	2,050	1,225	825
A-3	50	1,225	— 1,175
B-1	2,000	925	1,075
B-2	150	925	— 775
B-3	150	925	— 775

the redistributiveness of the state fiscal systems creates difficult problems in the use of the principle as a direct guide for policy. Since a state unit can by its own action in shifting its internal fiscal structure affect the amount of funds transferred to or away from that state, the practical working out of the transfer system would make necessary some determination of a standard state fiscal structure as the basis for calculation.[25] It is also noted that the transfers are among equals; bloc transfers among states will satisfy the equity criterion only if made in a specific fashion. These and many other more technical problems make a precise application of the equity principle in the real world extremely difficult, but should not serve to prevent its use as a proximate standard for intergovernmental fiscal policy.

A specific type or method of intergovernmental fiscal adjustment is suggested from the above analysis. This is geographically discriminatory central government personal income taxation. Central government income tax rates could be made to vary from state to state so as to offset differences in state fiscal capacities.[26] This method of adjustment, by varying personal income tax rates among equals, could come closest to achieving the equity goal. In effect, it would limit the transfers to those among "equals." In the first model above, central government taxes on A-1 and A-2 would be increased from $1,000 to $1,100, while those on B-1 would be reduced from $1,000 to $800. Central government income taxes on A-3 would be increased from $50 to $250, while those on B-2 and B-3 would be reduced from $50 to a negative tax of $50.

Adjustment through the central governmental personal income tax system has another major advantage in that it allows the necessary inter-area transfer of funds to take place without any necessary increase in the total amount of federal revenue. This is an important feature in this era of big central government. Any other transfer method, either in the form of grants to states or geographically discriminatory central government expenditure, requires, initially at least, that a greater share of economic resources be diverted to flow through the central government fiscal mechanism. A further advantage of this adjustment system is that it does not conflict with either the revered principle of financial responsibility or that

---

In this model, a transfer of $166.67 among the three high income individuals, and $266.67 among the low income individuals is required, or a total of $433.34, as compared to the total of $400 before the change in A's tax structure was made.

[25] Applied to the existing structure in the United States this would not present serious difficulties since various state fiscal structures are substantially similar both on the tax and the expenditure side.

[26] Adarkar included both geographically discriminatory central government taxation and geographically discriminatory central government expenditure as appropriate adjusting devices. (*Op. cit.*, p. 195.)

of state fiscal independence, both of which are so often encountered in discussions of grant-in-aid policy.[27]

Geographically discriminatory personal income taxation by the central government probably would, however, have to hurdle a very significant constitutional barrier before coming into existence in the United States. The courts have held repeatedly that the constitutional uniformity of taxation required was geographical in nature.[28] Although accomplishing the same purpose as a system of positive revenue transfers, this method would appear more violative of traditional, though erroneous, equity precepts.[29] A more practical objection to this method is that individuals probably respond more quickly to tax burden differentials (especially direct taxes) than to differentials in public service standards. Therefore, if income tax rates vary from state to state in some direct correlation with per capita incomes, even though the system of rates were calculated so as to provide exact equality (to equals) in all states in over-all fiscal treatment, there might still be distortionary resource allocative effects due to this "tax illusion."

Any method of adjustment which involves the federal collection of revenue and subsequent transfer to state governmental units via specific or bloc grants is inferior to the tax adjustment method in so far as the equity criterion alone is considered. A system of grants based upon the equity principle could do little more than utilize the Canadian proposals. States could be placed in a position to treat citizens in the same manner fiscalwise as their equals in all other states. But states would not necessarily, or probably, choose to do so. Differences in the allocation of both burdens and benefits would be present. Nevertheless, the resultant inequities in the treatment of "equals" would be due to state political decisions, not to the fact that citizens were resident of the state *per se*. The differences in the treatment of equals could be reduced to insignificance in comparison to those now present.

V

The mere acceptance of the equity principle in discussions concerning the fiscal problem of federalism can yield important results. First of all,

---

[27] See the following section.

[28] See *Head Money Cases* 112 US 580; *Knowlton* v. *Moore* 178 US 41; *Flint* v. *Stone Tracy Co.* 220 US 107.

[29] The apparent anomaly here can be attributed in large part to the doctrinal errors made in economic and fiscal theory which have caused the expenditure side to be treated as a less important area of study than the tax side. Differing rates of federal taxation in different states would probably be declared unconstitutional. Arbitrarily differing amounts of federal expenditures per capita among states are not questioned.

upon its acceptance inter-area transfers do not represent outright sub-
sidization of the poorer areas, do not represent charitable contributions
from the rich to the poor, and are not analogous to the concept of ability
to pay in the inter-personal sense. The principle establishes a firm basis
for the claim that the citizens of the low income states within a national
economy possess the "right" that their states receive sums sufficient to
enable these citizens to be placed in positions of fiscal equality with their
equals in other states. A transfer viewed in this light is in no sense a gift
or subsidy from the citizens of the more favored regions. It is no more a
gift than that made from the citizens of the community property states to
those of the non-community property states when income splitting for tax
purposes was extended over the whole nation to make the federal tax
system more equitable. After the proposed inter-area transfer of funds,
relatively greater fiscal pressure would be imposed upon citizens of the
high income areas and relatively less upon those of the low income areas
in comparison to those now imposed. But tradition gives little ground for
continuing inequities, and we normally give short shrift to the individual
who has continued to escape a share of his fiscal burden.

The policy implications of adopting the equity principle as a long-run
goal for adjustment policy are far reaching. Applied to the existing structure of intergovernmental fiscal relations in the United States, several
steps are indicated. *First,* the elimination of the many matching provisions in the present grant-in-aid program is essential before progress can
be made in any equalization policy. These provisions have served to prevent the whole grant-in-aid system from accomplishing any fiscal equalization between the rich and poor areas at all.

A *second* and major implication is that the equity approach provides
a justification for inter-area transfers independent of any particular public service or group of services. In the past, the principle of fiscal need has
been combined with the principle of national interest with the result that
grants have been justified only in specific service areas (highways, vocational education, etc.). There is, of course, legitimate justification for
federal grants to states with the objective of furthering certain national
interests, for example, minimum standards in educational services. But
such grant-in-aid programs should be sharply divorced from the basic
equalization policy. It seems highly probable that, if an equalization
policy of the sort proposed here were carried out, national interests would
be adequately served without any national government direction of state
expenditure. The low income states provide deficient educational standards largely because of their fiscal plight; remove this, and it seems likely
that their service standards would approach those of other states without

any restraints upon state budgetary freedom. The acceptance of the equity objective, therefore, could lend support to a policy of broadening the functions for which grants are made, and of extending broadened conditional grants to other public service areas.

Ultimately, an essential step, if equalization is to be carried out *via* grants to states, and one which will not be easy to accomplish, is the elimination of directional conditions entirely in federal grants to states and the substitution of unconditional grants. The equity principle provides an adequate justification for grants wholly unconditional, but traditional barriers against the unconditional intergovernmental transfer of funds, especially in the United States, are likely to loom large. The principle of financial responsibility which says, in effect, that "legislatures can be trusted to spend if required to tax accordingly,"[30] and not otherwise, is strong and has certain intrinsic merit when considered in isolation. But as is the case with the traditional principle of equity, the substitution of a federal political structure for a unitary one transforms the setting within which the principle may be applied. The fact that the central government must enter the adjustment process and transfer funds to effectuate equity in the over-all fiscal system does not therefore imply that the central government should be allowed to direct the recipient states in the allocation of their expenditure. There seems no apparent reason why there should be more central interference or direction in the financial operation of the recipient states than in that of the non-recipient states. States are made claimant through no fault of their own or of their respective citizens. They are made claimant by the income distribution arising from a resource allocation and payment in a national economy. Once it is recognized that the transfers are adjustments which are necessary to coordinate the federal political structure with a national economy, and as such are ethically due the citizens of the low income state units, then the freedom of these citizens to choose the pattern of their states' expenditure follows.

This concept of financial responsibility is, however, so strong that progress will perhaps require some compromise with it. Substantial progress can be made in intergovernmental transfer policy by the gradual substitution of procedural for directional conditions. Movement in this direction can be made while observing the fiscal responsibility principle and still not greatly reducing the budgetary independence of the states.

However, as pointed out above, these problems which arise in any intergovernmental policy utilizing revenue transfers, disappear when the

---

[30] Henry C. Simons, "Hansen on Fiscal Policy," *Journal Political Economy*, Vol. L (1942), p. 178.

method of geographically discriminatory personal income taxation is adopted. No governmental unit receives revenue other than what is internally raised within its fiscal system; therefore, neither the principle of financial responsibility nor that of state fiscal independence is violated. This method of adjustment, however, can only be expected to become positive policy after there is a more widespread recognition of the basic elements of the fiscal problem of federalism, and the advantages of this method over others clearly impressed upon the public by competent authorities.

VI

The fiscal problem of federalism discussed here is not likely to become less acute. As the need for an ever-expanding scope of public services increases, with especial emphasis on the social services, the divergencies in fiscal capacities among state units will be more evidenced. The *laissez faire* result will be the ultimate centralization of a large share of effective political power, either directly through the assumption by the central government of traditional state and local functions, or indirectly through restraining financial conditions in an expanded grant-in-aid system. Therefore, those who desire to see maintained a truly decentralized political structure in the power sense, must take some action in support of proposals aimed at adjusting these interstate fiscal differences. Heretofore, little progress has been made, although increasing attention has been given to the problem. The failure to take positive steps may, in part, have been due to the lack of a specific long-run objective for policy. The equity principle presented here possibly offers an objective which, if accepted, can serve as the basis for the development of a rational intergovernmental fiscal adjustment system.

B. WELFARE

7

The Welfare Aspects of
Excise Taxes*

By EARL R. ROLPH and GEORGE F. BREAK[1]

I

The proposition has often been advanced that a commodity tax involves a burden on the taxpayer which an income tax of the same yield does not entail. The demonstration has generally been based in recent years upon the indifference map of an individual consumer.[2] This analytical device has now become thoroughly familiar, and we shall confine ourselves to a brief résumé of the usual arguments based upon its use.

In Figure 1 money income, M, is measured along the vertical axis, and quantities of a single commodity X along the horizontal axis. I_1 and I_2 are indifference curves for a single individual, being the loci of all combinations of X and M which yield him the same satisfaction. These curves, as representatives of his entire preference map between X and M, are assumed to remain fixed over the period of time under considera-

---

* Journal of Political Economy, Vol. LVII, No. 1 (February, 1949).

[1] The authors are indebted to Professors J. S. Bain, M. M. Davisson, and H. S. Ellis for criticisms of an earlier draft of this paper.

[2] See, e.g., M. F. W. Joseph, "The Excess Burden of Indirect Taxation," Review of Economic Studies, VI, No. 3 (June, 1939), 226–31; M. W. Reder, "Welfare Economics and Rationing," Quarterly Journal of Economics, LVII, No. 1 (November, 1942), 154; George J. Stigler, The Theory of Price (New York, 1946), pp. 81–82; J. R. Hicks, Value and Capital (Oxford, 1939), p. 41; H. P. Wald, "The Classical Indictment of Indirect Taxation," Quarterly Journal of Economics, LIX, No. 4 (August, 1945), 577–96. These writers have dealt with one commodity and one consumer; Harold Hotelling has generalized the argument to the case of n commodities and one consumer in the article, "The General Welfare in Relation to Problems of Taxation and of Railway and Utility Rates," Econometrica, VI, No. 3 (July, 1938), 242–69. [Article 12 in this volume. Ed.] The whole argument, of course, goes back to Dupuit's writings of the mid-nineteenth century and to Marshall's concept of consumer surplus (see Jules Dupuit, "De l'utilité et de sa mesure," écrits choisis et republiés par Mario de Bernardi, La Riforma sociale [Turin, 1933], and Alfred Marshall, Principles of Economics [8th ed.; London, 1930], p. 467). For a recent synthesis of the various refinements of the consumer surplus concept based upon indifference analysis see James N. Morgan, "The Measurement of Gains and Losses," Quarterly Journal of Economics, LXII, No. 2 (February, 1948), 287–308, and Paul A. Samuelson, Foundations of Economic Analysis (Cambridge, 1947), pp. 202–53.

tion. During this period of time the individual receives money income of an amount represented by OA and, in order to consume a unit of X, must pay the price represented by OA/OA', the slope of AA'. Given these conditions, he is assumed to adjust his money expenditures on X so as to achieve maximum satisfaction, as represented in the diagram by the point P. AA', then, represents the two constraints under which the individual is assumed to maximize the satisfaction obtained from the consumption of X and M (which may be taken to represent all other commodities in this context); namely, the price of X and the amount of money income at his disposal.

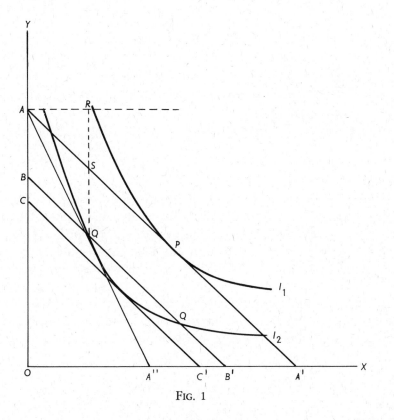

FIG. 1

A commodity tax is now assumed to be imposed upon X, thereby leading to an increase in the price of X. On the assumption that the imposition of the tax does not change the individual's money income, OA, AA'' is then the new price-income line and Q the position of maximum satisfaction. At this point the individual buys AR of X, paying RQ for it, the amount of money represented by SQ being the tax yield to the government on the amount of sales AR. If, instead of the commodity tax, an income tax yielding SQ is imposed upon the individual (regardless of the amount of X he chooses to buy), the resulting price-income situation may be represented by BB', which passes through Q and is parallel to AA' (on the argument that the price of X is unaffected by the income tax, but the individual's income is reduced by an amount $AB = SQ$).

Given that the indifference curves are convex to the origin, BB' will cut I_2 at Q and again at Q'; between these two points it will lie on higher indifference surfaces than I_2. Hence it may be argued that under the income tax the consumer will move to the point of highest satisfaction on BB', where he will be better off than under the commodity tax without reducing the yield of the tax. As a corollary, it follows that an income tax which leaves the consumer on the same indifference curve as a commodity tax will yield a greater amount of revenue to the government (AC as compared with AB).

This argument, as well as the Hotelling variation, involves two important and somewhat vulnerable assumptions. In the first place, it assumes that a person is made worse off in real terms by either an income tax or a commodity tax. For example, a person's satisfaction is supposedly decreased as a result of a tax by an amount indicated by the difference between indifference curves I_1 and I_2 (Fig. 1). This assumption can be shown to be false if generalized to an economy as a whole. In other words, income taxes or commodity taxes do not necessarily make consumers in general worse off. Second, the conventional argument implicitly or explicitly assumes that, in the absence of taxation, resource allocation is ideal. But, as will be pointed out in the following remarks, if resource allocation is not ideal, commodity taxes may improve as well as worsen it.

Both the conventional argument and the present criticism require the postulate that the concept of ideal resource allocation can be given definitive meaning. Otherwise one allocation is as good as any other, and no judgment can be made concerning the welfare consequences of the reallocation occasioned by a tax.

II

The view that taxes make people worse off is convincing at first glance. Most taxpayers undoubtedly consider it to be an obvious and sound proposition. To a particular person, an income tax appears to impoverish him when he considers the benefits he might reap by spending the money which he is required to pay to the government as taxes. The benefits which might be supposed to result from tax reduction, however, need not in fact result if taxes are generally reduced. The initial effect of a general reduction in taxes, such as provided in the Revenue Act of 1948, is to increase money incomes after taxes, which in turn leads to some increase in expenditure on output. If the economy is at or near full employment, the result is higher prices (or more rationing by nonprice methods) without any increase in output attributable to the tax reduction.

The economic arguments offered against tax reduction under conditions of full employment have been based, not upon the contention that the public should be forced to impair its real living standards (as a result of high taxes), but rather upon the view that lower taxes would lead to higher prices, impair the most efficient utilization of resources, and likely reduce rather than increase the standard of living of the low-income groups. During the war it was especially evident that higher taxes would not have impaired living standards; rather they would have reduced the need for financing governmental activities by borrowing or money creation on as large a scale as actually occurred.[3]

The costs of government arise from governmental use of resources, as Professor Pigou has pointed out.[4] To the extent that resources are directed to public ends, they are not available for private ends. Ordinarily the state acquires the use of particular resources by making money expenditures which may be financed by means of taxation, or by borrowing with or without money creation. Hence taxes need not represent the costs of government. This is not to say that it is immaterial which method of financing government expenditures is in fact chosen. Presumably that method is best which encourages, or at least interferes least with, the most efficient use of the resources left over for the private sector of the economy.[5] Thus it is seen that a reduction in taxes *may*, by leading to a system of financing which is less efficient in the above sense, actually reduce private real living standards, and an increase in taxation may do the opposite for analogous reasons. In other words, there is no a priori presumption that an increase in taxes will lower real living standards.

Applied to the issue in question, the conclusion that an income tax on an individual worsens his real position as indicated by the lower indifference curve I_2 (Fig. 1) is not generally valid. The person may even be on a higher indifference curve after the tax, provided his competitors (i.e., other consumers) are taxed more heavily. No presumption exists therefore that a person is worse off merely because of the tax.

This conclusion does not undermine the allegation that excise taxes

---

[3] Cf. William Fellner, *A Treatise on War Inflation* (Berkeley, 1942), pp. 5–6.

[4] A. C. Pigou, *A Study in Public Finance* (3d rev. ed.; London, 1947), pp. 19–23.

[5] The most efficient use may be taken to mean not only the maximum output but also the optimum system, in some ethical sense, of resource-product allocation.

involve an excess burden. Obviously, taxes may alter resource-product allocation. The essence of the excess-burden contention is that the tax-induced reallocation is always inferior from the consumer's point of view. This feature of the doctrine may now be examined.

To show the possible allocating effects of excise taxes, it is convenient to center attention at first on an economy producing only two commodities. Such a case is depicted graphically in Figure 2. Quantities of commodity X are shown along the horizontal axis and of commodity Y along the vertical axis. CP represents the combinations of X and Y which can be produced with the resources available to the economy in question. The production of any combination of X and Y which corresponds to a point on the *compound-production* curve CP[6] entails full employment of these resources. CP is drawn concave to the origin on the assumption that there is some specialization of resources to the production of each commodity and that constant physical returns to scale prevail.

Let GH be a price-expenditure line, namely,

$$M = XP_x + YP_y,$$

where M is the amount of money consumers are prepared to spend,[7] and P_x and P_y are the prices of X and Y. A position of tangency to the compound-production curve CP is arbitrarily obtained by assuming that, for any given value of M, the absolute prices of X and Y adjust to give such a position.

The indifference curves I_1, I_2, I_3, and I_4 have a special meaning. They are aggregates of the indifference curves of each consumer. This procedure is meaningful provided each consumer has the same tastes. This special assumption is made at this point to avoid interpersonal comparisons and will be dropped later in the argument.[8] Our argument also assumes that each consumer has the same amount of money to spend—an assumption which likewise will be dropped later.

---

[6] Cf. J. A. Nordin, "The Marginal Cost Controversy: A Reply," *Economica*, XIV, No. 54 (May, 1947), 134–49, which describes such a curve as a transformation curve. Transformation, however, suggests the transforming of resource-services into products (cf. Hicks, *op. cit.*, pp. 79–81). *Compound-production* curve seems a more descriptive label, since the curve shows possible combinations of products which can be produced from given resources. The point, however, is a minor one.

[7] It is customarily assumed that M is money income. This seems wrong if income means simultaneous accruals, because there must, in actual institutional settings, be some lag in time between money receipts and the expenditure of *that* money, i.e., velocity cannot be infinite. M is objectively determined by a person's cashable asset position and typically will be closely associated with that portion of a person's assets provided by the income of the preceding period.

[8] The reader may be reminded that the "excess burden" argument has generally been stated so as to avoid interpersonal comparisons.

The point of tangency, L (Fig. 2), of the highest indifference curve with CP indicates maximum consumer welfare, since I_3 is the highest indifference curve consistent with the full employment of resources. In a price system, L is also an equilibrium point, provided the prices of X and Y and the quantity of money, M, give a price-expenditure line tangent to

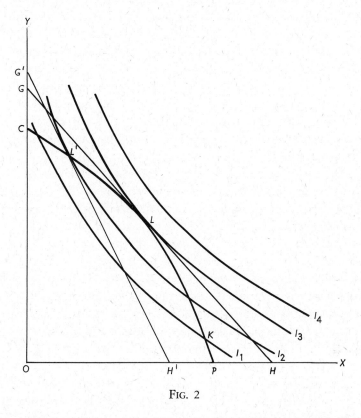

FIG. 2

both I_3 and CP. This means (1) that consumers can spend all the money they wish on X and Y (i.e., no nonprice rationing of purchases) and (2) that the quantities of X and Y produced are all taken (i.e., no nonprice rationing of sales). A further condition of equilibrium is that a unit of each kind of resource used to produce X and Y obtains the same money net income in each use, for, if this is not the case, there is an incentive to produce more of one commodity and less of the other.[9] Thus, if all these conditions are satisfied, the point L gives not only the maxi-

---

[9] For human resources differences in the attendant psychological aspects of work permit persistent differences in the money income obtained. Optimum allocation from the point of view of resource owners should, strictly speaking, be stated in terms of equating net advantages at the margin as Marshall has pointed out (*op. cit.*, pp. 73, 557).

mum welfare position for consumers but also the equilibrium conditions for a price-money system in the sense that each resource owner has reached his best income position and that prices clear all markets with full employment.

Suppose first that an income tax is levied equally against the income of all persons. The tax reduces M in subsequent periods unless offset by some compensating financial device.[10] Thus at the same prices for X and Y the price-expenditure line GH falls. Unemployment results unless P_x and P_y fall by an amount sufficient to restore GH to its original position. In a competitive environment, prices would do all the adjusting and no unemployment would emerge. It follows that consumers would be in the same real position as before, because there has been no reduction in output. Although money incomes after deducting taxes fall, prices also fall. Unless an income tax affects the compound-production curve, consumers are left at the same satisfaction levels as before the tax.

Suppose now that an excise tax is placed on commodity X accompanied by reductions in the rates of the income tax so that the two taxes together give an unchanged yield. The total income effect by assumption is zero, since the yield of the excise tax replaces the yield of the income tax. Resource owners have an incentive to produce less of commodity X and more of Y in order to equate income per unit of resources at the margin. This reallocation raises the price of X relative to the price of Y, as indicated by the new price-expenditure line $G'H'$. The point L' gives the only result consistent with the conditions that all resources are fully employed (i.e., any solution must fall on the compound-production curve) and that there is no rationing by methods other than price (i.e., L' must be at the point of tangency of the price-expenditure line $G'H'$ with the highest indifference curve touching $G'H'$). Obviously, however, L' is on a lower indifference curve than L, and there is an excess burden in this case, indicated by the difference between I_2 and I_3. This conclusion is consistent with the "excess-burden" argument.

This argument, however, is not general. It holds rigorously only if L is a point of maximum welfare. If the original position were some point K on CP, a tax on X would have put consumers on higher indifference curves as long as the production of X was reduced and Y increased thereby to the quantities indicated by L or L'. The "excess-burden" contention rests, in other words, on an empirical assumption, namely, *that the rela-*

---

[10] Government may compensate for higher taxes by (1) increased output expenditures, (2) increased transfer payments, and (3) under special conditions, sale of debt. Individuals may compensate by dishoarding or, with the connivance of the banking system, by increasing the money supply.

tive quantities of various commodities produced are ideal in the absence of excise taxes. If this is not true, there is no a priori reason for supposing that excise taxes must make consumers worse off. Furthermore, as a logical argument it does not follow that excise taxes need diminish welfare, even if allocation is already ideal. For any given tax placed on X there is a tax on Y which would leave the price-expenditure line GH in the same position. There need be no reallocation of resources if both commodities are taxed in such a way as to leave unchanged the relative net earnings of the same kind of resources in each use. In the simple case here under consideration, a uniform *ad valorem* tax would have such a result.[11]

In any actual system there is no presumption that in the absence of excise taxes resources are so allocated as to maximize living standards. Given resource mobility, if Y is sold at a monopolistic price and X at a competitive price, a tax on X would improve allocation. More generally, in an economy with many products and in which economic welfare is not maximized (i.e., any actual system), taxes upon production may move allocation toward or away from the ideal. In the absence of knowledge concerning the character of the actual allocation, no a priori judgment can be made as to whether a particular excise tax occasions an "excess burden" or an "excess gain."

III

The foregoing argument has avoided defining ideal allocation when the satisfaction of any one consumer cannot properly be taken as a perfect sample of aggregate welfare. Excise taxes are almost certain, even apart from their money income effects, to worsen standards of some consumers and to improve those of others. A tax levied on commodity X injures those who consume relatively more of X and benefits those who consume relatively more of Y.

One currently popular method for treating the problem of group welfare is to define a position of maximum welfare for society as a whole as one in which no individual can be made better off while leaving *all* other individuals at constant satisfaction levels.[12] Literally interpreted,

---

[11] A similar observation has been made by Ragnar Frisch in his criticism of Hotelling's apparently contrary view that excise taxes necessarily worsen allocation (cf. "The Dupuit Taxation Theorem," *Econometrica*, VII [April, 1939], 145–50, and "A Further Note on the Dupuit Taxation Theorem," in the same issue, pp. 156–57). [See Articles 13 and 15 in this volume. Ed.]

[12] Cf. N. Kaldor, "Welfare Propositions in Economics and Interpersonal Comparisons of Utility," *Economic Journal*, XLIX (September, 1939), 549–52; J. R. Hicks, "The Foundations of Welfare Economics," *Economic Journal*, XLIX (December, 1939), 696–712; Oscar Lange, "The Foundations of Welfare Economics," *Econometrica*, X, Nos. 3 and 4 (July–October, 1942), 215–28; and Samuelson, *op. cit.*, pp. 202–53.

this definition would rarely have any application. A tax which reallocates resources at all is almost certain to decrease the satisfaction of some persons. To avoid this limitation, the advocates of this view suggest the use of compensating devices in the form of taxes and subsidies. Those consumers injured by a reallocation are to be subsidized until they are no worse off than before. Those initially benefited are to be taxed to provide the subsidy to those injured. After those initially worsened are fully compensated, if there is something left over so that some persons remain at higher satisfaction levels whereas everyone else has been returned to a constant level, the reorganization in question has provided an increase in welfare. Maximum welfare exists only when no such reorganization is possible.

This method of handling welfare problems involving groups of individuals with different tastes and incomes does not permit any ready answer to the question of whether a particular excise tax gives rise to an excess burden or to an excess gain. If a position of maximum welfare is assumed in the sense that no reorganization of the type mentioned above is possible, any further reorganization would by definition result in a decrease in welfare. If one adopts the more likely assumption of an initial allocation of resources which is less than ideal, this approach to welfare problems does not tell us a priori in which direction the imposition of a commodity tax is likely to change the allocation. There is no presumption in favor of a movement in either (or no) direction—a conclusion which follows by analogy to the more simplified conditions considered in Section II above.

The approach under consideration does provide an experimental technique for assessing the effects of resource reallocation occasioned by a tax. The presence of an excise tax effects a transfer of money income from certain resource owners to the government[13] and a change in the composition of output so that some consumers are better off, others worse. If at the same time the resource owners who transfer money to the government under the new commodity tax are exactly compensated, say, by a reduction in their income taxes, then all money incomes, including that of the government, will be the same as before. So far no net change in money position has been brought about for any group or person. Nevertheless, three groups may be distinguished: (A) those who are better off

---

[13] The income effects of excise taxes are one of the more difficult and controversial features of tax theory. For a fuller discussion of the point see E. R. Rolph, "The Burden of Import Duties with Fixed Exchange Rates," *American Economic Review*, XXXVII (September, 1947), 604–32.

in real terms, i.e., move to higher indifference schedules; (B) those worse off; and (C) those left in the same position.

To determine whether an excise tax changes welfare, we must now effect, by positive and negative taxes, a transfer of money income from Group A to Group B until the latter have been moved into Group C. This procedure will, of course, entail a further change in relative prices and resource-product allocation because of the pressure of new demands which have now become effective, and the reduction in effectiveness of old demands. Finally, we must assess the resultant welfare position of all those initially in Group A. Presumably we have allowed none of them to be transferred to Group B, the decrease in their money incomes being stopped as soon as they move into Group C. Hence, if any individuals still remain in Group A, the commodity tax has provided an "excess-gain," i.e., an increase in welfare. On the other hand, if all those originally in Group A have been moved into Group C *before* all those in Group B have been transferred to C, the tax results in an excess burden, i.e., a decrease in welfare.

There are severe practical difficulties in the application of this concept of welfare. Compensating taxes and subsidies must be tailored to each person affected by the allocating device under consideration. Objective standards must be devised to determine when a person is restored to the same satisfaction level as before. Furthermore, the approach has little relevance when the government desires to alter its total tax yield. Other welfare approaches may therefore be sought.

One such approach commonly used in economic thinking is to let money expenditures measure welfare, i.e., the adoption of what has been called "dollar democracy."[14] Such propositions that resources are ideally allocated when the price of each product is equal to its marginal money cost, or proportional to its marginal money cost, or equal to marginal social cost illustrate the assumption that each dollar counts as one vote for welfare purposes.[15] All these propositions define maximum welfare in

---

[14] Nordin, *op. cit.*, pp. 147–48.

[15] A. P. Lerner argues in favor of the condition that price equals marginal cost on the grounds that otherwise workers are forced to take more or less leisure than they should (cf. his *Economics of Control* [New York, 1944], pp. 102–4). In this view, he is supported by R. H. Coase, "The Marginal Cost Controversy: Some Further Comments," *Economica*, XIV, No. 54 (May, 1947), 152, and by Samuelson, *op. cit.*, p. 240. Hotelling, after initially taking the same view, finally adopts the proportionality view as a result of Frisch's criticisms, stating: "It is enough that all prices be *proportional* to marginal costs" ("The Relation of Prices to Marginal Costs in an Optimum System," *Econometrica*, VII [April, 1939], 151). If leisure is thought of as a product, the proportionality theorem holds provided the "price" of leisure is proportional to its marginal cost. In fact, it is administratively difficult to im-

terms of prices alone. Hence it is assumed that products and resources are allocated only by prices and that consumer satisfaction is obtained by the expenditure of dollars. Each dollar, then, regardless of who possesses it, represents an equal claim to the output of the society, and from this fact is derived the expression "dollar democracy."

It may be noted, however, that if the "dollar-democracy" rule is accepted as a welfare guide, it does not follow that excise taxes necessarily misallocate resources. In any money-price system in which prices are neither equal nor proportional to money marginal costs, an excise tax may either worsen or improve allocation in this special sense. For the reasons set forth in the last section, an excise tax necessarily worsens allocation only when the allocation is already ideal, and only in this circumstance if the tax is neither general nor proportional to prices, as Hotelling has admitted.[16] A particular excise tax on commodities the prices of which are too low (i.e., quantities produced too large) relative to others could improve allocation. Thus a tax may give rise to an excess gain, and consumers are made better off.

But the welfare concept of dollar democracy is difficult to defend, given the wealth-ownership dispersion in actual systems. Although much of the contemporary thought on welfare problems avoids interpersonal comparisons, meaningful policy judgments concerning taxes are very difficult unless such comparisons are made. We shall postulate the ethical principle that the best system of allocation is one which treats every consumer alike. In a price-money system this is interpreted to mean that (1) each person has the same amount of money to spend, i.e., voting power is equal, and (2) resources are so allocated that quantities produced sell at prices equal to their marginal social costs. The principle that each person should, ideally, have the same vote with regard to his share of the output can be defended on the same ethical principles used to defend political democracy. Negatively, it abhors the doctrine of an élite class. Government action designed to achieve less inequality in wealth ownership involves either (1) taxing the income (or wealth) of the rich and subsidizing the poor or (2) reducing effective voting power of the

---

pose any taxes which would give this result but not much more difficult than in the case of many other implicitly priced products such as home-grown vegetables. The meaning of optimum pricing should be distinguished from the empirical methods of assuring optimum pricing. Optimum pricing refers to price relations among products only, and the prices of instrumental services are not directly relevant to the definition of the concept. Pigou, of course, holds to the condition of equality of price to marginal social cost (*Economics of Welfare* [4th ed.], pp. 151–81). This position is formally accurate, since social cost refers to the value of foregone output (including leisure) and is consistent with the proportionality theorem.

[16] See n. 15 above.

dollars of the rich as compared with the dollars of the poor. Excise taxes are particularly relevant to the accomplishment of the second objective. If items produced for the rich are taxed heavily, resources are made available to produce more output for the poor. In the absence of nonprice rationing, the effectiveness of such taxes depends upon the extent to which the rich consume things which the poor do not.[17] Although excise taxes, therefore, can directly reduce some of the inequalities in command over resources, the income effects of such taxes may work in the reverse manner. Thus a heavy tax on high-quality fur coats has some income-reducing effect on those engaging in their production, and if these groups are poor, as many in fact are,[18] they are placed at a further disadvantage as compared with other groups in the population. The cases in which excise taxes, therefore, can be justified with respect to both their allocation and income effects are not likely to be numerous.

IV

The previous comments, if correct, rob formal theory of another certainty. It is improper to suppose that excise taxes necessarily result in an excess burden. The demonstration of the excess burden argument is based on the assumption that the reduction in output of the taxed commodity is not compensated at all by an increase in the output of other commodities, and hence consumers must be worse off. Such an approach implies that the released resources disappear from the economic scene. To answer the question as to whether a particular tax changes living standards, it is at least necessary to take account of gains in the output of nontaxed items occasioned by the reorganization of resources. When the task is viewed in this manner, it is almost self-evident that excise taxes may improve as well as worsen living standards.

It does not follow that excise taxes are desirable revenue devices. Obviously, even judged on allocation grounds alone, such taxes may aggravate the problem of resource allocation and provide the public with an inferior selection of products. Conclusions concerning this point require close study of the particular commodity taxes as one aspect of a tax system, an examination of the likely character of the induced allocation, and

---

[17] Taxing "luxuries" would not satisfy this condition unless luxuries are defined to mean only those items which the rich consume and the poor do not. Commonly the notion of a luxury carries a moralistic flavor, referring to items which poor people do consume but which others think they should not (cf. Henry Simons, *Personal Income Taxation* [Chicago, 1939], p. 39).

[18] Cf. Division of Tax Research, Treasury Department, *Federal Retail Excise Taxes* (October, 1947), pp. 2, 4.

the status of those likely to be injured in real terms. A further and important consideration is the income effect of such taxes. In the preoccupation with the relation of excise taxes to resource allocation, it is easy to overlook the effects of such taxes on the pattern of money income. As compared with taxes which directly employ a means test, such as personal net income and inheritance taxes, excise taxes are not likely to be effective in reducing inequality in economic status and may in many cases lead to yet greater inequality.

Policy judgments concerning particular taxes involve, in addition to a consideration of allocation effects, investigations concerning the induced income effects and their equity, the subsequent consumption and investment expenditure effects flowing from reduced private net incomes, and, in this connection, the stabilizing or destabilizing effects of taxes ("built-in flexibility") on total expenditures over time. The allocation aspect is particularly important in the case of a commodity tax and may be the determining factor in policy judgments. Import duties illustrate such a case. As a general rule, however, all these questions must be considered in a judicious evaluation of particular taxes.

8

*Direct versus Indirect Taxes**

By I. M. D. LITTLE

The first part of this article is designed to show that the usual theoretical treatment of the problem of direct and indirect taxation is based on extraordinary assumptions, and liable to be misleading. An alternative mode of analysis is suggested. In the second part, I try to show that no case against indirect taxation can be proved from the ordinary, general, purely competitive assumptions of economic theory; and, further, that the special assumption, necessary to prove the case, involves an unplausible conclusion concerning incentives.

I

The usual analysis of direct *versus* indirect taxation (or subsidisation) runs typically as follows:[1]

A single "economic man" who spends his income on two goods (one of which may be "money") is assumed. In Fig. 1, Q_0 is the equilibrium tax-free position. When an income-tax equal to AB of X is imposed, Q_1 is reached. The same sum could be raised by an indirect tax on Y, which would result in a position such as Q_2. From the usual convexity assumption it follows that Q_2 is worse than Q_1. Q.E.D.

At first sight this result always looks like a conjuring trick. There is no overt reference to marginal costs. Yet it is well known that nothing can be proved without some such reference.[2] The covert reference is as follows: for the proof to be valid the government must be able to buy the same collection of goods whether the individual is at position Q_2 or

---

* *Economic Journal*, Vol. LXI, No. 243 (September, 1951).
[1] Cf. M. F. W. Joseph, "The Excess Burden of Indirect Taxation," *Review of Economic Studies*, June, 1939; H. P. Wald, "The Classical Indictment of Indirect Taxation," *Quarterly Journal of Economics*, August, 1945; A. M. Henderson, "The Case for Indirect Taxation," *Economic Journal*, December, 1948; A. T. Peacock and D. Berry, "A Note on the Theory of Income Redistribution," *Economica*, February, 1951.

[2] Cf. the original Frisch-Hotelling controversy—*Econometrica*, 1939, pp. 145–60; in particular Professor Hotelling's final note, pp. 158–60. [See Articles 13–16 in this volume. Ed.]

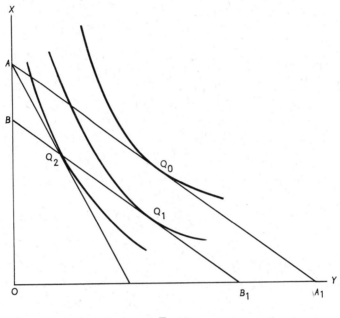

FIG. 1

at position Q_1. This it can do only if Q_2Q_1 has the same slope as the transformation curve of X and Y (the curve showing the maximum amounts of X which could be produced given varying quantities of Y, and fixed amounts of all other goods). From this it follows that the slope of BB' must equal the relative marginal costs of the two goods. Thus, in the diagram, relative marginal costs are assumed to be the same at both Q_2 and Q_1.

Although the diagram is drawn with reference to a single individual it may be presumed that it is designed to illustrate the relative effects, on each of many individuals, of two different tax systems of equal monetary incidence. Therefore, a considerable shift of production must be allowed for. This being the case, the assumption that relative marginal costs are the same at both Q_2 and Q_1 is in conflict with the normal assumption used in this connection, that of a diminishing marginal rate of transformation. The analysis is excessively and unnecessarily partial in other ways. The prices of goods, other than those represented, may change when the indirect tax is substituted for the direct. When this is allowed for, it is even conceivable that any given individual would gain as a result of the change.

But none of this invalidates the usual conclusion (that the gainers could overcompensate the losers if direct taxes were substituted for in-

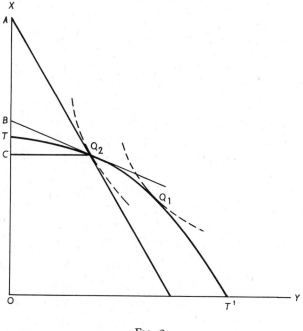

FIG. 2

direct) *given that the supply of labour is not a variable.* In Fig. 2 the curve TQ_2Q_1T' is the transformation curve of X and Y, given the quantities of all other goods, and also given the quantities of X and Y demanded by the government.[3] At Q_1 relative price is assumed equal to relative marginal cost (this is indicated by drawing in a "community indifference" curve tangential to the transformation curve at Q_1). Letting p_x, p_y, MC_x, and MC_y stand for the prices and marginal costs of X and Y, we have at Q_2,

$$\frac{p_y}{p_x} = \frac{AC}{CQ_2} \tag{1}$$

and

$$\frac{MC_y}{MC_x} = \frac{BC}{CQ_2}$$

$$= \text{Marginal rate of transformation of } Y \text{ into } X \tag{2}$$

Supposing X to be subsidised, otherwise perfect competition, and letting

---

[3] The assumption that the government's demands are absolute is made only for simplicity of exposition. We could in principle treat the government as an "economic man" with a consistent set of utility curves.

s and t stand for the rate of subsidy and tax respectively it follows from (i) and (ii) that

$$\frac{MC_y}{MC_x(1-s)} = \frac{BC}{CQ_2(1-s)} = \frac{p_y}{p_x} = \frac{AC}{CQ_2},$$

whence

$$s = \frac{AB}{AC}.$$

It is assumed above that the required revenue is raised by means of an income tax, the effects of such a tax on factor supply being ignored. Alternatively, we can suppose that Y is taxed in which case it follows that

$$\frac{MC_y(1+t)}{MC_x} = \frac{BC(1+t)}{CQ_2} = \frac{p_y}{p_x} = \frac{AC}{CQ_2},$$

whence

$$t = \frac{AB}{BC}.$$

That the position Q_2 is not "optimum" follows simply from the divergence of relative prices and relative marginal costs. No other proof is required or possible. A "community indifference" curve can, of course, be drawn tangential to AQ_2 at Q_2. This curve must pass below Q_1 on the given assumptions. This follows from the fact that Q_1 is an "optimum" position, while Q_2 is not.[4] So nothing is really added by drawing in the indifference curves. What matters is that at Q_2 the individual rates of substitution of X for Y are not equal to the transformation rate. This analysis is more general and requires fewer restrictive assumptions than those usually made. It also has the advantage that it shows quite clearly, for both subsidies and taxes, that the "case against indirect taxation" is merely a special case of conflict with one of the necessary conditions for the achievement of a Pareto "optimum," *i.e.*, that relative marginal costs be equal to relative prices. At the purely theoretical level nothing more can be said; and nothing less is valid without special "partial" assumptions.

II

In Part I it was arbitrarily assumed that the supply of labour was constant; or, to put it in another way, that the consumption of one good, leisure, was unaffected by changes in its own or other prices. This is clearly an indefensible assumption which must be removed. But, for the sake of simplicity, we will continue to ignore savings. The conclusion which we

---

[4] Cf. J. de V. Graaff, "On Optimum Tariff Structures," *Review of Economic Studies*, 1949–50, No. 42, p. 57, n. 3.

shall reach—that the case against indirect taxation is invalid—can only be reinforced if savings are considered, since an income tax is an indirect tax on savings, as well as on work.

It has been argued by Professor A. M. Henderson that the fact that all marginal taxation is a tax on work (it can also be regarded as a subsidy on leisure, as far as substitution effects are concerned) does not destroy the case against indirect taxation.[5] The argument is that both indirect and direct taxes sin against the necessary "optimum" condition that the rate of substitution of leisure for any other good must equal the rate of transformation between leisure and that good. But, it is argued, indirect taxes *also* prevent the rates of substitution between pairs of goods, excluding leisure, being equal to their respective rates of transformation. Thus Professor Henderson writes:

> If a given revenue is required then the resources available to the consumer must be limited to the same extent by either method [*i.e.*, direct or indirect taxation]. But the method of indirect taxation has the further disadvanage of reducing the efficiency with which these resources are used, and therefore imposes an added burden.[6]

I have previously accepted this argument.[7] But I now think I was wrong to do so. The argument is unsatisfactory because it assumes that the resources used are identical in both cases. In other words, it has to be assumed that the supply of labour is the same whether the taxation is direct or indirect. This amounts to saying that, for every individual, the cross-elasticity of demand for leisure with respect to all other prices is zero, *i.e.*, leisure is not substitutible for any other good. To all intents and purposes, the assumption that the amount of labour does not vary has crept into an argument designed to show that direct taxation is better than indirect taxation, even when the supply of labour is admitted as a variable. This might not matter if it were really plausible to suppose that it would, under no conditions, vary much. I shall suggest below that this is not a plausible supposition.

Consider a perfectly competitive economy with three goods, one being leisure. Designate leisure by Z and the other two goods by X and Y. Let S and T stand respectively for the marginal rate of substitution and the marginal rate of transformation. We can now distinguish three cases as follows:

---

[5] *Loc. cit.*
[6] *Loc. cit.*, p. 545.
[7] *E.g.*, in the appendix to Chapter IX of *A Critique of Welfare Economics*.

I. Direct taxation. Here we have

$$S = T \text{ for the pair } (X,Y)$$
$$S \neq T \text{ for the pair } (X,Z)$$
$$S \neq T \text{ for the pair } (Y,Z).$$

II. Indirect taxation on one good other than leisure. Letting the taxed good be X we have

$$S = T \text{ for the pair } (Y,Z)$$
$$S \neq T \text{ for the pair } (X,Y)$$
$$S \neq T \text{ for the pair } (X,Z).$$

III. Unequal indirect taxation on both goods other than leisure. Here we have

$$S \neq T \text{ for all three pairs.}$$

A comparison of Cases I and II makes it sufficiently obvious that no argument against indirect taxation can be perfectly general. The two cases are quite symmetrical. Unless special assumptions are made, whatever can be said about one can be said about the other. But even if Case III is considered to be what is normally meant by indirect taxation, nothing appears to follow.

Let us illustrate this. In Fig. 3 ABC is the production surface after subtraction of the government's fixed demands. It is assumed that the government succeeds in manipulating the budget surface so that the community's chosen point on that surface is also a point on the production surface ABC. If the chosen point were above the surface the government would not be getting the goods it required; if below it would be getting more than it required.

The points Q_0, Q_1, Q_2, Q_3 and Q_4 are points on the surface. AA', BB' and CC' are surface lines along which one of the three "optimum" conditions is satisfied. Thus at any point on the line CC', the partial rate of substitution (leisure constant) of Y for X equals the partial rate of transformation (leisure constant). These contract lines, if projected on to the planes BOC, AOC and AOB respectively, would be analogous to ordinary contract curves. The point Q_0 is the only point at which all the optimum conditions are satisfied. Case I lands us on the line CC' between C and Q_0. Case II lands us either on AA', between A' and Q_0, or on BB' between B' and Q_0. Case III brings us to some point which lies on none of the contract lines. Part of Fig. 2 is embedded in Fig. 3. The plane surface $TQ_2Q_1T'O'$ appears in both diagrams.

The advocates of direct taxation or subsidisation have to claim that every point on CC' is better than any other point on the production surface. It is intuitively obvious that there is no reason whatever for claiming that points on the line CC' are superior to those on the lines AA' and BB'.

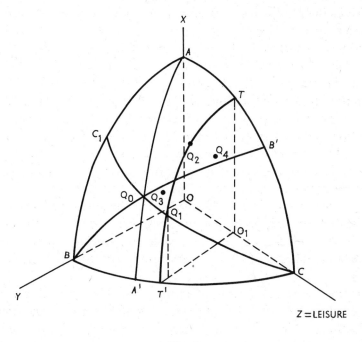

FIG. 3

The lesser claim might, however, be made that points on a contract line are superior to points not on a contract line.

What, then, can be said about the relative superiority of points such as Q_0, Q_1, Q_2, Q_3 or Q_4? First, Q_0 is "superior" to any other point because all the "optimum" conditions are satisfied. In other words, a "community indifference" surface is tangential to the production surface at Q_0, and cannot lie below the production surface at any other point. Secondly, the "community indifference" surface appropriate to Q_1 cannot lie below the production surface in the neighbourhood of the point Q_2. This is because it is tangential to the line $T'Q_1Q_2T$ at Q_1. Thirdly, it is quite consistent, both that these two conditions should be fulfilled and that the same indifference surface should or should not lie below the production surface in the neighbourhood of a point such as Q_3. There therefore appears to be no reason whatever to support any claim that Q_1 must be "superior" to Q_3.[8] A movement from Q_1 to Q_3 would reduce the amount

---

[8] By saying one point is "superior" to another we mean that its "community indifference" surface passes inside (further from the origin than) the other point in the neighbourhood of that point; which implies that the potential losers by a move from the latter to the former would be unable profitably to bribe the potential gainers to oppose the change. Therefore no point x can be "superior" to any other chosen point y if the indifference surface of x is below the production surface in the neighbourhood of y.

of leisure. But it is also conceivable, given suitable production and indifference surfaces, that the indifference surface of Q_1 should lie below the production surface in the neighbourhood of a point like Q_4, where the amount of leisure is increased. The conclusion is that nothing whatever can be said about the "superiority" of direct taxation unless it is certain that the amount of leisure will not change.

We have seen that Professor Henderson based his argument on the contention that the supply of labour would be constant. This means, in terms of Fig. 3, that it is presumed that a change from direct to indirect taxes would always cause a movement from a point like Q_1 to one like Q_2, leisure remaining constant. Taken to its logical extreme, such a contention is highly paradoxical. It implies that the amount of labour supplied is a function only of the quantities of goods consumed by the government. In the limit this implies that people would work as much even if income tax was 100% of all incomes, consumption goods being supplied free!

But, apart from subsidies, is there any reason to suppose that the supply of labour might not be greater under a suitable indirect taxation system than under direct taxation? Surely, those who have maintained that direct taxation—quite apart from any "money illusion"—is more harmful to incentives are not necessarily wrong?

Suppose that Y, in our diagram, stands for "necessities" and X for "luxuries." Let the first situation be a direct tax equilibrium. Then the equal taxation of "necessities" and "luxuries" (equivalent to direct taxation) is replaced by a relatively large tax on "necessities," and a relatively small one on "luxuries" (Case III). Is it not then plausible to suppose that the individual, while keeping his consumption of "necessities" more or less constant, might increase his consumption of "luxuries" at the expense of leisure, *i.e.*, move to a point like Q_3 which may be "superior" to Q_1? In Case II where only "necessities" are taxed the individual *must* move to a point on BB' between Q_0 and B'. Since the consumption of "necessities" is not much reduced, this may (given sets of preferences consistent with our contract lines) entail a reduction in leisure. In the extreme case, when the price-elasticity of demand for some necessity is zero, the change from an income tax, to an indirect tax on the necessity, would result in a movement from Q_1 to Q_0. The reason is as follows. Q_0 is the poll-tax position. But with no poll tax, and the price of Y raised to keep on the same production surface, Q_0 would still be the equilibrium position, since it is consistent with (a) zero price-elasticity of demand for Y, real income given, and (b) unchanged real income. It has often been held that a tax on such a good is the equivalent of an income tax.

This is wrong: it is the equivalent of a poll tax; while an income tax is itself the equivalent of a poll tax only if the supply of labour is perfectly inelastic. If, in such a case, we were interested more in incentives than "welfare," we could increase the tax on "necessities" in order to pay a subsidy on "luxuries." This would amount to a tax on leisure. Leisure would be subsidised in relation to "necessities," but this would have no substitution effect. It would also be taxed in relation to "luxuries" which would have an incentive effect.

If any general conclusion can be risked, it is simply that the best taxes are those on goods for which the demand is least elastic. The same holds true for subsidies. Income tax, which is a subsidy on leisure, is not exceptional. Only in so far as the demand for leisure is highly inelastic is it a good tax. The purely theoretical "case against indirect taxation" is an illusion.

9

The Theory of Incipient Taxes*

By C. F. BICKERDIKE

The object of this article is to call attention to some interesting generalisations which can be established when we study the tendency of very small taxes as they begin to come into operation. It is more especially in connection with international trade and the vexed question of "taxing the foreigner" that the interest of the theory lies, but the method of approaching questions of incidence by considering first the tendency of incipient taxes has some use also in connection with purely domestic taxation. In connection with international trade, the question arises whether a country, by means of taxes, can get more favourable terms of exchange with foreigners in such a way as to leave a net advantage, after allowing for the disadvantages involved in turning production from its "natural" course, as it used to be expressed.

The two propositions which I venture to put forward are:

1. That in pure theory advantage is always possible in normal circumstances from either import or export taxation when the taxes are small enough, except in one peculiar and unlikely case.[1]
2. That, in the case of incipient import taxes, the tendency to advantage is greater the more elastic the demand of the taxing country for the articles taxed.

This implies that a tax on finished articles, as a whole, would tend to give more advantage than a tax on raw materials, and that a tax on the importation of an article of which there was an untaxed home supply would give more advantage, initially, than would be the case if there were no home supply. That is to say, with taxes not exceeding some definite height, there seems to be a certain theoretical correctness in the methods followed by Protectionists. How far in any actual case such taxes could be increased to something of tangible importance and still give a balance

---

* *Economic Journal*, Vol. XVI, No. 64 (December, 1906).
[1] Below, p. 135.

of advantage, and whether this theory has anything to do with the ideas on which ordinary Protection actually rests, are questions which we defer for the present.

The propositions respecting incipient taxes can best be discussed by mathematical methods, but first of all an attempt will be made to show, by general reasoning, that they are not opposed to common sense. Consider any group of people producing a commodity, let us say milk, and selling it in competition with one another to some outside party. The competition tends to beat down the price of milk, and if the producers combine to put some check on their competition with one another, they can get better terms, provided that the buyers are not absolutely indifferent whether they buy their milk from this group of producers or not. If this group are a mere fraction of the producers, and have no advantage over others in supplying any part of the market, of course they can effect nothing by combination. If, however, those with whom they deal have some reason for dealing with them rather than elsewhere, there is room for some improvement in the terms of exchange by some degree of restriction of competition. The possibilities of improvement may be much or little, according to the degree in which the purchasers of milk are dependent on the particular group of producers, but the latter need not have a monopoly of the supply. They need only have some advantage in their particular market, so that their withdrawal would not be a matter of complete indifference to their customers.

Granting that this condition is fulfilled, an obvious method of putting a slight check on competition would be for the milksellers to agree that every time one of them sold milk, he should make a contribution to a collective fund, in token of the fact that by putting his milk on the market he is doing something to lower the price of milk to the disadvantage of his fellows. If we regard the milk-producers as receiving payment in kind, say in meat, instead of in money, how is their position likely to be affected if we suppose them to have a latent possibility of supplying themselves with meat, without recourse to strangers? Surely this fact may be expected to strengthen rather than to weaken their position as bargainers. We are presuming, of course, that they would be losers if they stopped the trade altogether; but the option of some home supply of meat to fall back upon minimises the disadvantage resulting from a diminution of the "imports," so to speak, of meat, without affecting the advantage of having to pay less, and, therefore, increases the net advantage so long as the change is within the limits within which net advantage is possible.

The fundamental resemblance between this kind of barter and international trade is commonly recognised by economists, and need not be elaborated here. The theoretical possibility of improving the terms of exchange has long been recognised by some as a debatable question, notably by Mill and Sidgwick. The only novelty in the position taken up in this article is the contention that it is all a question of degree, and that there is a general possibility of advantage not confined to exceptional circumstances.

It is very difficult to give quite a convincing proof of the propositions advanced by purely verbal reasoning. The foregoing discussion is intended rather to give an idea of the argument than to constitute by itself a satisfactory proof.

It will be evident that the kind of advantage which the writer asserts to be generally possible is simply an improvement in the terms of exchange—an increase of the excess of utility of imports over cost, or disutility, of exports. It has nothing to do with what is known as the "infant industry" argument. It is assumed all through that when an article is imported under free competition, any interference with the purchasers' freedom to buy in the cheapest market involves some disadvantage, and the advantage to be set against that has nothing to do with the possibility that in course of time home supplies may be developed in such a way that the consumer gets them cheaper than he would do if they had never been taxed. That is a kind of advantage from taxation which depends on the possibility of proving the existence of peculiar circumstances, and possesses no generality.

It will be evident also, from the discussion of the milk and meat bartering, that the most important factor in determining the extent of advantage which may accrue to the milk-producers must be the extent to which other people can compete with them in selling milk and in buying meat. At present, however, we are not concerned with the question of the extent of the advantage, but only with the fact that it is a question of degree. No great country is an absolutely insignificant quantity in the eyes of those who buy from it and of those who sell to it. There are geographical facts which give each some advantage in supplying some goods in some markets, and for this reason there is possibility in each case of securing some degree of advantage by a check on competition in foreign trade.

The existence of a general possibility of advantage is deducible from the diagrams which Professor Edgeworth contributed to *The Economic Journal* in 1894. Subjoined is his Fig. 8, p. 433. The indifference curve touches the vector OP, and a small movement of OE to the left must bring the point P into a position indicating greater advantage, provided that the foreign "supply and demand" curve *OG* is not absolutely coincident with the vector *OP*.[2]

When the home "supply and demand" curve *OE* is of the "inelastic" type (Fig. 3, *The Economic Journal*, p. 432), a different result is predicated by Professor Edgeworth of an import tax; but that is because his

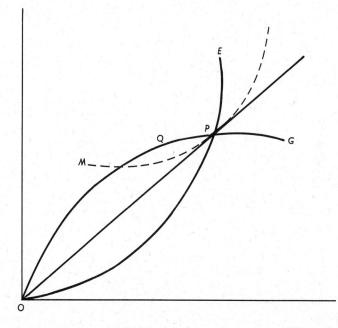

diagram represents a tax levied in kind, not in money. When the tax is in money, the change in *OE* is that represented in Fig. 3, p. 430 (*loc. cit.*), like an export tax in kind.

The only case in which there would necessarily be disadvantage in a small tax is that of inelasticity of "supply and demand" on both sides—a peculiar and unlikely case, the paradoxical result of which is explicable, but which we will not dwell on here because the case is not important.

The two propositions which have been advanced can be deduced by consideration of the diagrams which Professor Marshall has made familiar. Subjoined is a figure representing the incidence of taxation of a commodity (*vide* "Principles of Economics," p. 504).

Imagine that the tax is going to be spent for the benefit of the buyers. It is evident that they gain or lose on the whole according as *CFEK* is

---

[2] The degree of curvature of *OG* in the figure is made sufficient to show the result of a tax clearly. It is not intended to be taken as typical.

greater or less than *AKa*. If we imagine the tax to be made very small, *CFEK* becomes a line and *AKa* becomes a point, and there is, therefore, necessarily some advantage, provided that the supply curve *SS'* is not an absolutely horizontal line. In the figure the curve is made so that apparently quite a considerable advantage is possible, but that is merely for

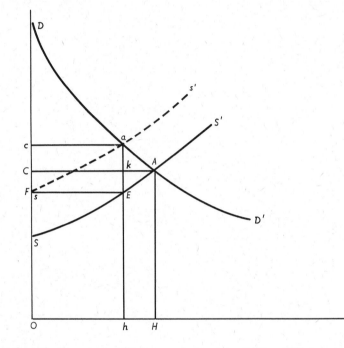

the sake of clearness. All we need suppose is that *SS'* is not perfectly horizontal.

Further, suppose the demand curve *DD'* to be made more elastic. With the small tax, *AKa* will still be a point, and *CFEK* will be a line, but, so to speak, a thicker line than before, so that the advantage will be greater.

In this diagram it is implied that money can be regarded as a constant measure, which is not a legitimate supposition when we are considering the producers and consumers to belong to different "nations." We have now to consider what difference is made when we allow for the disturbance of price-level. We shall endeavour to show that the propositions respecting advantage to the taxers hold good *a fortiori* when this correction is made. Regarding the producers as the "foreigners" and the buyers, for convenience, as ourselves, our total bill minus tax (which goes to our Government) is necessarily reduced in amount, from the rectangle *CH* to the rectangle *Fh*. In order to restore the international "equation of indebtedness," price-level here rises relatively to price-level abroad, and this is a favourable, not an unfavourable, circumstance.

In discussing the effect of taxation on international trade, people frequently argue that though there may be some tendency to gain at the expense of the foreign producer, yet there is the disturbance of price-level and the effect on exports to be considered, and they assume that this consideration is one which makes against the chance of advantage. This is not the case, however. In so far as there is a real possibility of prices in the taxing country being relatively raised, the advantage tends to be greater. (We must not say, however, that the extent of this raising of price-level is a measure of the amount of advantage. Higher money incomes are very largely discounted by higher prices of all home-made goods.)

That the reaction on price-level must be a favourable circumstance should be apparent if we consider what happens if some commodity, hitherto imported to the extent, let us say, of five million pounds, were to be superseded in the ordinary course of trade, without any taxation, by some home-made article. Our foreign indebtedness would be reduced by five millions, and there would be an effect on price-level, and, through that, on exports. Obviously, however, we should not be damaged by that kind of reaction. When the diminution of indebtedness is caused by a tax on imports, the disadvantage is not to be looked for in the effect on general prices, but in the inconvenience of those who are unable to buy the taxed article in consequence of its relatively higher price.

The more elastic the home demand for the taxed article, the stronger is the tendency to reduction of the total bill payable to the foreigner, and, therefore, the greater (but still small) the tendency to raise price-level and improve the terms of exchange.

Another point to be noticed is that we assumed that the case of what may be called a protective tax was dealt with by simply making the demand curve more elastic. It might be thought that we were ignoring the loss due to producing more of the commodity at home by presumably less efficient means. In this case, however, the demand curve DD' must be regarded as the special demand curve for the imported article. It is compounded from our total demand for the article and our supply curve (assumed to be ascending). It can be shown geometrically that the "loss" AKa comprises all the dead loss involved in the reduction of imports, including the waste of energy. It does not, however, take any account of mere transfer of wealth from the community to special interests in the taxing country, nor does the loss AEK, on the other hand, take any account of the transfer of wealth from particular interests in the export trades to the community. We simply regard the taxing country *en bloc* as one interest.

It must be admitted that to the mathematical mind there is something not quite satisfactory about this reasoning. It has not been put forward as quite sufficient. The only satisfactory procedure is to employ analytical methods, imagining each country to use a money peculiar to itself, and to levy the tax in its own money. The ratio of exchange of moneys alters, and the net result can be expressed in an algebraical formula, and we can introduce several commodities. It is on these analytical results that the propositions really rest, but it is hoped that the above reasoning may enable those who do not readily follow mathematics to see the drift of the argument.

10

*The General Welfare in Relation to Problems of Taxation and of Railway and Utility Rates**

By HAROLD HOTELLING

In this paper we shall bring down to date in revised form an argument due essentially to the engineer Jules Dupuit, to the effect that the optimum of the general welfare corresponds to the sale of everything at marginal cost. This means that toll bridges, which have recently been reintroduced around New York, are inefficient reversions; that all taxes on commodities, including sales taxes, are more objectionable than taxes on incomes, inheritances, and the site value of land; and that the latter taxes might well be applied to cover the fixed costs of electric power plants, water-works, railroads, and other industries in which the fixed costs are large, so as to reduce to the level of marginal cost the prices charged for the services and products of these industries. The common assumption, so often accepted uncritically as a basis of arguments on important public questions, that "every tub must stand on its own bottom," and that there-fore the products of every industry must be sold at prices so high as to cover not only marginal costs but also all the fixed costs, including in-terest on irrevocable and often hypothetical investments, will thus be seen to be inconsistent with the maximum of social efficiency. A method of measuring the loss of satisfactions resulting from the current scheme of pricing, a loss which appears to be extremely large, will emerge from the analysis. It will appear also that the inefficient plan of requiring that all costs, including fixed overhead, of an industry shall be paid out of the prices of its products is responsible for an important part of the instability which leads to cyclical fluctuations and unemployment of labor and other resources.

---

* *Econometrica*, Journal of the Econometric Society, Vol. VI, No. 3 (July, 1938). Pre-sented at the meeting of the Econometric Society at Atlantic City, December 28, 1937, by the retiring president.

A railway rate is of essentially the same nature as a tax. Authorized and enforced by the government, it shares with taxes a considerable degree of arbitrariness. Rate differentials have, like protective tariffs and other taxes, been used for purposes other than to raise revenue. Indeed, the difference between rail freight rates between the same points, according as the commodity is or is not moving in international transport, has been used in effect to nullify the protective tariff. While it has not generally been perceived that the problems of taxation and those of railway rate making are closely connected, so that two independent bodies of economic literature have grown up, nevertheless the underlying unity is such that the considerations applicable to taxation are very nearly identical with those involved in proper rate making. This essential unity extends itself also to other rates, such as those charged by electric, gas, and water concerns, and to the prices of the products of all industries having large fixed costs independent of the volume of output.

I. THE CLASSICAL ARGUMENT

Dupuit's work of 1844 and the following years[1] laid the foundation for the use of the diagram of Figure 1 by Marshall and other economists. A rising supply curve SB is used, and is sometimes regarded as coinciding with the marginal-cost curve. Such a coincidence would arise if there were free competition among producers, in the sense that each would regard the price as fixed beyond his control, and adjust his production so as to obtain maximum net profits. This condition is approximated, for example, in most agriculture. DB is a declining demand curve. The buyers are presumed to compete freely with each other. The actual quantity and price are the co-ordinates of the intersection B. Then it is supposed that a tax t per unit is imposed upon the sellers. Since this is a uniform increment to marginal cost, the marginal-cost curve SB is lifted bodily to the new position RL, at height $t = SR = NL$ above its former position.

Three conclusions have been derived with the help of this figure, all of which must be reviewed to take account of the interrelations of the particular commodity in question with others. One of these arguments has almost universally been accepted, but must be rejected when account is taken of related commodities. A second has been accepted, and is actually true. The third has been condemned and attacked by a long line of prominent economists, but in the light of the more thorough analysis made possible by modern mathematical methods must now in its essence

---

[1] Collected and reprinted with comments by Mario di Bernardi and Luigi Einaudi, "De l'Utilité et de sa Mesure," *La Riforma Soziale* (Turin, 1932).

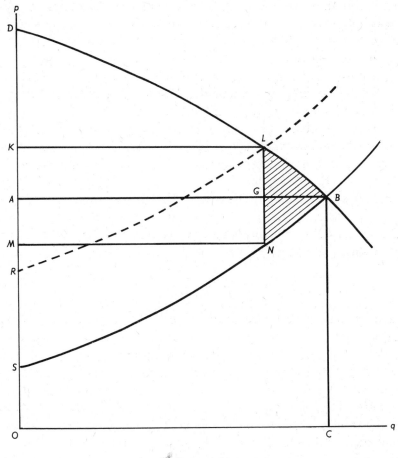

FIGURE 1

be accepted. The first is the proposition that since the point L of intersection of the demand curve with the supply curve RL is higher by GL, a
fraction of the tax rate NL, than the intersection B with the tax-free curve
SB, therefore the price is increased as a result of the tax, by an amount
less than the tax. That this conclusion is not necessarily true when account
is taken of related commodities I have shown in an earlier paper.[2] The

---

[2] "Edgeworth's Taxation Paradox and the Nature of Demand and Supply Functions,"
Journal of Political Economy, Vol. 40 (1932), pp. 577–616. Edgeworth had discovered, and
maintained against the opposition of leading economists, that a monopolist controlling two
products may after the imposition of a tax on one of them find it profitable to reduce both
prices, besides paying the tax. However he regarded this as a "mere curiosum," unlikely in
fact to occur, and peculiar to monopoly. But it is shown in the paper cited that the phenomenon is also possible with free competition, and is quite likely to occur in many cases,
either under monopoly or under competition.

second proposition—whose conclusion remains valid under certain plausible assumptions[3]—is that, since L is to the left of B, the quantity of the taxed commodity will diminish. With this diminution is associated an approximately measurable net social loss.

The third argument is based on Dupuit's, and is of primary concern here. Dupuit sought a criterion of the value to society of roads, canals, bridges, and waterworks. He pointed out the weakness of calling the value of a thing only what is paid for it, since many users would if necessary pay more than they actually do pay. The total benefit he measured by the aggregate of the maximum prices that would be paid for the individual small units of the commodity (a term used here to include services, e.g., of canals) corresponding to the costs of alternatives to the various uses. If $p = f(q)$ is the cost of the best alternative to the use of an additional small unit of the commodity when q units are already used, then, if q_0 units are used altogether,

$$\int_0^{q_0} f(q)\,dq \tag{1}$$

is the total benefit, which Dupuit called *utilité*, resulting from the existence of the canal or other such facility making possible the commodity (service) in question. Since $p = f(q)$ is the ordinate of the demand curve DB in Figure 1, this total benefit is the total area under the arc DB. To obtain what is now called the *consumers' surplus* we must subtract the amount paid by consumers, namely the product of the price by the quantity, represented by the rectangle $OCBA$. Thus the consumers' surplus is represented by the curvilinear triangle ABD. There is also a *producers' surplus* represented by the lower curvilinear triangle SBA; this is the excess of the money received by producers (the area of the rectangle $OCBA$) over the aggregate of the marginal costs, which is represented by the curvilinear figure $OCBS$. The total net benefit, representing the value to society of the commodity, and therefore the maximum worth spending from the public funds to obtain it, is the sum of consumers' and producers' surpluses, and is represented by the large curvilinear triangle SBD. It is the difference between the same limits of the marginal-cost function.

Imposition of the tax, by raising the price to the level of KL, appears to reduce the consumers' surplus to the curvilinear area KLD. The new

---

[3] On p. 600 of the paper just cited the conclusion is reached that it is reasonable to regard the matrix of the quantities h_{ij} as negative definite. From this and equation (19) of that page it follows that a positive increment in the tax t_j on the jth commodity causes a negative increment in the quantity of this commodity.

producers' surplus is the area *RLK*, which equals *SNM*. There is also a benefit on account of the government revenue, which is the product of the new quantity *MN* by the tax rate *NL*, and is therefore measured by the area of the rectangle *MNLK*. The sum of these three benefits is *SNLD*. It falls short of the original sum of producers' and consumers' surpluses by the shaded triangular area *NBL*.

This shaded area represents the net social loss due to the tax, and was discovered by Dupuit. If the tax is small enough, the arcs *BL* and *NB* may be treated as straight lines, and the area of the triangle is, to a sufficient approximation, half the product of the base *NL* by the altitude *GB*. Since *GB* is the decrement in the quantity produced and consumed because of the tax, and *NL* is the tax rate, we may say that the net loss resulting from the tax is half the product of the tax rate by the decrement in quantity. But since the decrement in quantity is, for small taxes, proportional to the tax rate, it then follows that the net loss is proportional to the *square* of the tax rate. This fact also was remarked upon by Dupuit.

This remarkable conclusion has frequently been ignored in discussions in which it should, if correct, be the controlling consideration. The open attacks upon it seem all to be based on an excessive emphasis on the shortcomings of consumers' and producers' surpluses as measures of benefits. These objections are four in number: (1) Since the demand curve for a necessity might for very small quantities rise to infinity, the integral under the curve might also be infinite. This difficulty can be avoided by measuring from some selected value of *q* greater than zero. Since in the foregoing argument it is only *differences* in the values of the surpluses that are essentially involved, it is not necessary to assign exact values. The situation is the same as in the physical theory of the potential, which involves an arbitrary additive constant and so may be measured from any convenient point, since only its differences are important. (2) Pleasure is essentially nonmeasurable and so, it is said, cannot be represented by consumers' surplus or any other numerical magnitude. We shall meet this objection by establishing a generalized form of Dupuit's conclusion on the basis of a ranking only, without measurement, of satisfactions, in the way represented graphically by indifference curves. The same analysis will dispose also of the objections (3) that the consumers' surpluses arising from different commodities are not independent and cannot be added to each other, and (4) that the surpluses of different persons cannot be added.

In connection with the last two points, it will be observed that if we have a set of *n* related commodities whose demand functions are

$$p_i = f_i(q_1, q_2, \cdots, q_n), \qquad (i = 1, 2, \cdots, n),$$

then the natural generalization of the integral representing total benefit, of which consumers' surplus is a part, is the line integral

$$\int (f_1 dq_1 + f_2 dq_2 + \cdots + f_n dq_n), \qquad (2)$$

taken from an arbitrary set of values of the q's to a set corresponding to the actual quantities consumed. The net benefit is obtained by subtracting from (2) a similar line integral in which the demand functions $f_1, f_2, \cdots, f_n$ are replaced by the marginal-cost functions

$$g_i(q_1, q_2, \cdots, q_n), \qquad (i = 1, 2, \cdots, n).$$

If we put

$$h_i = f_i - g_i,$$

the total net benefit is then measured by the line integral

$$w = \int \sum h_i dq_i. \qquad (3)$$

Such indeterminacy as exists in this measure of benefit is only that which arises with variation of the value of the integral when the path of integration between the same end points is varied. The condition that all these paths of integration shall give the same value is that the integrability conditions

$$\frac{\partial h_i}{\partial q_j} = \frac{\partial h_j}{\partial q_i}$$

be satisfied. In the paper on "Edgeworth's Taxation Paradox" already referred to, and more explicitly in a later note,[4] I have shown that there is a good reason to expect these integrability conditions to be satisfied, at least to a close approximation, in an extensive class of cases. If they are satisfied, the surpluses arising from different commodities, and also the surpluses belonging to different persons, may be added to give a meaningful measure of social value. This breaks down if the variations under consideration are too large a part of the total economy of the person or the society in question; but for moderately small variations, with a stable price level and stable conditions associated with commodities not in the group, the line integral w seems to be a very satisfactory measure of benefits. It is invariant under changes in units of measure of the various commodities, and also under a more general type of change of our way of specifying the commodities, such as replacing "bread" and "beef" by two

---

[4] "Demand Functions with Limited Budgets," *Econometrica*, Vol. 3 (1935), pp. 66–78. A different proof is given by Henry Schultz in the *Journal of Political Economy*, Vol. 41 (1933), p. 478.

different kinds of "sandwiches." For these reasons the total of all values of w seems to be the best measure of welfare that can be obtained without considering the proportions in which the total of purchasing power is subdivided among individuals, or the general level of money incomes. The change in w that will result from a proposed new public enterprise, such as building a bridge, may fairly be set against the cost of the bridge to decide whether the enterprise should be undertaken. It is certainly a better criterion of social value than the aggregate $\sum p_i q_i$ of tolls that can be collected on various classes of traffic, as Dupuit pointed out for the case of a single commodity or service. The actual calculation of w in such a case would be a matter of estimation of vehicular and pedestrian traffic originating and terminating in particular zones, with a comparison of distances by alternative routes in each case, and an evaluation of the savings in each class of movement. Determination whether to build the bridge by calculation merely of the revenue $\sum p_i q_i$ obtainable from tolls is always too conservative a criterion. Such public works will frequently be of great social value even though there is no possible system of charging for their services that will meet the cost.

II. THE FUNDAMENTAL THEOREM

But without depending in any way on consumers' or producers' surpluses, even in the form of these line integrals, we shall establish a generalization of Dupuit's result. We take our stand on the firm ground of a system of preferences expressible by a function

$$\Phi = \Phi(q_1, q_2, \cdots, q_n)$$

of the quantities $q_1, q_2, \cdots, q_n$ of goods or services consumed by an individual per unit of time. If the function Φ, Pareto's *ophélimité*, has the same value for one set of q's as for another, then the one combination of quantities is as satisfactory to the individual in question as the other. For two commodities, Φ is constant along each of a set of "indifference curves"; and likewise for n commodities, we may think of a system of hypersurfaces of which one passes through each point of a space of n dimensions, whose Cartesian co-ordinates are the quantities of the various goods. These hypersurfaces we shall refer to as *indifference loci*.

It is to be emphasized that the indifference loci, unlike measures of pleasure, are objective and capable of empirical determination. One interesting experimental attack on this problem was made by L. L. Thurstone, who by means of questionnaires succeeded in mapping out in a tentative manner the indifference loci of a group of girls for hats, shoes, and coats.[5] Quite a different method, involving the study of actual family budgets, also appears promising.[6] The function Φ, on the other hand, is not completely determinable from observations alone, unless we are prepared to make some additional postulate about independence of commodities, as was done by Irving Fisher in defining utility,[7] and by Ragnar Frisch.[8] The present argument does not depend on any such assumption, and therefore allows the replacement of Φ by an arbitrary increasing function Ψ of Φ, such as sinh Φ, or $\Phi + \Phi^3$. The statements we shall make about Φ will apply equally to every such function Ψ. Negative values of the q's are the quantities of labor, or of goods or services, produced by the individual. It is with the understanding that this kind of indeterminacy exists that we shall sometimes refer to Φ and Ψ as utility functions.

Consider now a state in which income and inheritance taxes are used to pay for the construction of bridges, roads, railroads, waterworks, electric power plants, and like facilities, together with other fixed costs of industry; and in which the facilities may be used, or the products of industry consumed, by anyone upon payment of the additional net cost occasioned by the particular use or consumption involved in each case. This additional net cost, or marginal cost, will include the cost of the additional labor and other resources required for the particular item of service or product involved, beyond what would be required without the production of that particular item. Where facilities are not adequate to meet all demands, they are made so either by enlargement, or by checking the demand through inclusion in the price of a rental charge for the facilities, adjusted so as to equate demand to supply. Such a rental cost, of which the site rental of land is an example, is an additional source of revenue to the state; it must not be confused with carrying charges on invested capital, or with overhead cost. Some such charge is necessary to discriminate economically among would-be users of the facilities. Another example is that of water in a dry country; if demand exceeds supply, and no enlargement of supply is possible, a charge must be made for the water sufficient to reduce the demand to the supply. Such a charge is an element of marginal cost as here defined.

The individual retains, after payment of taxes, a money income m. At

---

[5] "The Indifference Function," *Journal of Social Psychology*, Vol. 2 (1931), pp. 139–67, esp. pp. 151 ff.

[6] R. G. D. Allen and A. L. Bowley, *Family Expenditure* (London, 1935).

[7] *Mathematical Investigations in the Theory of Value and Prices* (New Haven, 1892).

[8] *New Methods of Measuring Marginal Utility* (Tübingen, 1932). Dr. Frisch also considered the possibility of substitute commodities in his *Confluence Analysis*, and in collaboration with Dr. F. V. Waugh made an attempt to handle this situation statistically.

prices $p_1, p_2, \cdots, p_n$ determined in the foregoing manner, he can buy or sell such quantities $q_1, q_2, \cdots, q_n$ as he pleases, subject to the condition that

$$\sum p_i q_i = m. \tag{4}$$

The combination he chooses will be such as to make his indifference function Φ a maximum, subject to the condition (4). We may put aside as infinitely improbable—having probability zero, though not impossible—the contingency that two different sets of values of the q's satisfying (4) will give the same degree of satisfaction. We therefore have that, if $q_1, \cdots, q_n$ are the quantities chosen under these conditions, and if $q_1', \cdots, q_n'$ are any other set of quantities satisfying (4), so that

$$\sum p_i q_i' = m, \tag{5}$$

then

$$\Phi = \Phi(q_1, \cdots, q_n) > \Phi(q_1', \cdots, q_n') = \Phi + \delta\Phi,$$

say. Hence, putting $q_i' = q_i + \delta q_i$ in (5) and subtracting (4), we find that any set of values of $q_1, \cdots, \delta q_n$ satisfying

$$\sum p_i \delta q_i = 0, \tag{6}$$

and not all zero, must have the property that

$$\delta\Phi = \Phi(q_1 + \delta q_1, \cdots, q_n + \delta q_n) - \Phi(q_1, \cdots, q_n) < 0. \tag{7}$$

Let us now consider an alteration of the system by the imposition of excise taxes and reduction of income taxes. Some of the taxes may be negative; that is, they may be bounties or subsidies to particular industries; or, instead of being called taxes, they may be called tolls, or charges for services or the use of facilities over and above marginal cost. There ensues a redistribution of production and consumption. Let p_i, q_i, and m be replaced respectively by

$$p_i' = p_i + \delta p_i, \quad q_i' = q_i + \delta q_i, \quad m' = m + \delta m, \tag{8}$$

where the various increments δp_i, δq_i are not constrained to be either positive or negative; some may have one sign and some the other. The yield of the new excise taxes will be the sum, over all individuals, of the quantity which for the particular individual we are considering is $\sum q_i' \delta p_i$. (We use the sign $\sum$ to denote summation over all commodities, including services.) Since this person's income tax is reduced by δm, the net increment of government revenue

$$\delta r = \sum q_i' \delta p_i - \delta m \tag{9}$$

may be imputed to him, in the sense that summation of δr over all persons gives the total increment of government revenue.[9] We neglect changes in administrative costs and the like.

The individual's budgetary limitation now takes the form $\sum p_i' q_i' = m'$, which may also be written

$$\sum (p_i + \delta p_i)(q_i + \delta q_i) = m + \delta m. \tag{10}$$

Subtracting the budget equation (4) corresponding to the former system and using (8) we find that

$$\delta m = \sum q_i' \delta p_i + \sum p_i \delta q_i. \tag{11}$$

Substituting this in (9) we find that

$$\delta r = - \sum p_i \delta q_i. \tag{12}$$

Suppose that, to avoid disturbing the existing distribution of wealth, the excise taxes paid by each individual (in the sense of incidence just defined; not in the sense of handing over the money to the government in person) are exactly offset by the decrement in his income tax. Then $\delta r = 0$. From (12) it then follows that (6) is satisfied. Except in the highly improbable case of all the δq's coming out exactly zero, it would then follow from (7) that this man's new state is worse than his old. The change from income to excise taxes has resulted in a net loss of satisfactions. Conversely, if we start from a system of excise taxes, or any system in which sales are not at marginal cost, this argument shows that there is a possible distribution of personal income taxes such that everyone will be better satisfied to change to the system of income taxes with sales at marginal cost. The problem of the distribution of wealth and income among persons or classes is not involved in this proposition.

This argument may be expressed in geometrical language as follows: Let $q_1, \cdots, q_n$ be Cartesian coordinates in a space of n dimensions. Through each point of this space passes a hypersurface whose equation may be written $\Phi(q_1, \cdots, q_n) =$ constant. The individual's satisfaction

---

[9] A friendly critic writes, "It is not clear to me why δp_i should be the exact per-unit revenue of the state from an excise tax which raises the price by δp_i from its old level. . . . I should expect (referring to Figure 1) an increase in price of GL, and a revenue to the state of NL." The answer to this is that the summation of δr over all persons includes the sellers as well as the buyers, and that the government revenue per unit of the commodity is derived in part from each—though it must be understood that the contribution of either or both may be negative. In the classical case represented by Figure 1, the buyers' δp is the height GL, while the sellers' is NG in magnitude and is negative. Since q' is positive for the buyer and negative for the seller, the product $q'\delta p$ is in each case positive. The aggregate of these positive terms is the total tax revenue from the commodity.

is enhanced by moving from one to another of these hypersurfaces if the value of the constant on the right side of the equation is thereby increased; this will usually correspond to moving in a direction along which some or all of the q's increase. The point representing the individual's combination of goods is however constrained in the first instance to lie in the hyperplane whose equation is (4). In this equation the p's and m are to be regarded as constant coefficients, while the q's vary over the hyperplane. A certain point Q on this hyperplane will be selected, corresponding to the maximum taken by the function Φ, subject to the limitation (4). If the functions involved are analytic, Q will be the point of tangency of the hyperplane with one of the "indifference loci." The change in the tax system means that the individual must find a point Q' in the new hyperplane whose equation is $\sum p_i' q_i = m'$. If we denote the coordinates of Q' by $q_1', \cdots, q_n'$, we have, upon substituting them in the equation of this new hyperplane, $\sum p_i' q_i' = m'$. If the changes in prices and m are such as to leave the government revenue unchanged, (12) must vanish; that is,

$$\sum p_i q_i' = \sum p_i q_i.$$

Since $\sum p_i q_i = m$, this shows that $\sum p_i q_i' = m$; that is, that Q' lies on the same hyperplane to which Q was confined in the first place. But since Q was chosen among all the points on this hyperplane as the one lying on the outermost possible indifference locus, for which Φ is a maximum, and since we are putting aside the infinitely improbable case of there being other points on the hyperplane having this maximizing property, it follows that Q' must lie on some other indifference locus, and that this will correspond to a lesser degree of satisfaction.

The fundamental theorem thus established is that *if a person must pay a certain sum of money in taxes, his satisfaction will be greater if the levy is made directly on him as a fixed amount than if it is made through a system of excise taxes which he can to some extent avoid by rearranging his production and consumption.* In the latter case, the excise taxes must be at rates sufficiently high to yield the required revenue *after* the person's rearrangement of his budget. The redistribution of his production and consumption then represents a loss to him without any corresponding gain to the treasury. This conclusion is not new. What we have done is to establish it in a rigorous manner free from the fallacious methods of reasoning about one commodity at a time which have led to false conclusions in other associated discussions.

The conclusion that a fixed levy such as an income or land tax is better for an individual than a system of excise taxes may be extended to the whole aggregate of individuals. In making this extension it is necessary to neglect certain interactions among the individuals that may be called "social" in character, and are separate and distinct from the interactions through the economic mechanisms of price and exchange. An example of such "social" interactions is the case of the drunkard who, after adjusting his consumption of whisky to what he considers his own maximum of satisfaction, beats his wife, and makes his automobile a public menace on the highway. The restrictive taxation and regulation of alcoholic liquors and certain other commodities do not fall under the purview of our theorems because of these social interactions which are not economic in the strict sense. With this qualification, and neglecting also certain possibilities whose total probability is zero, we have:

If government revenue is produced by any system of excise taxes, there exists a possible distribution of personal levies among the individuals of the community such that the abolition of the excise taxes and their replacement by these levies will yield the same revenue while leaving each person in a state more satisfactory to himself than before.

It is in the sense of this theorem that we shall in later sections speak of "the maximum of total satisfactions" or "the maximum of general welfare" or "the maximum national dividend" requiring as a necessary, though not sufficient, condition that the sale of goods shall be without additions to price in the nature of excise taxes. These looser expressions are in common use, and are convenient; when used in this paper, they refer to the proposition above, which depends only on rank ordering of satisfactions; there is no connotation of adding utility functions of different persons.

The inefficiency of an economic system in which there are excise taxes or bounties, or in which overhead or other charges are paid by excesses of price over marginal cost, admits of an approximate measure when the deviations from the optimum system described above are not great, if, as is customary in this and other kinds of applied mathematics, we assume continuity of the indifference function and its derivatives. Putting for brevity

$$\Phi_i = \frac{\partial \Phi}{\partial q_i}, \qquad \Phi_{ij} = \frac{\partial^2 \Phi}{\partial q_i \partial q_j},$$

we observe that the maximum of Φ, subject to the budget equation (4), requires that

$$\Phi_i = \lambda p_i, \qquad (i = 1, 2, \cdots, n), \tag{13}$$

where the Lagrange multiplier λ is the marginal utility of money. Differentiating this equation gives

$$\Phi_{ij} = \lambda \frac{\partial p_i}{\partial q_j} + p_i \frac{\partial \lambda}{\partial q_j}. \tag{14}$$

Expanding the change in the utility or indifference function we obtain, with the help of (13), (12), and (14),

$$\delta\Phi = \sum \Phi_i \delta q_i + \tfrac{1}{2} \sum\sum \Phi_{ij} \delta q_i \delta q_j + \cdots \tag{15}$$

$$= -\lambda\delta r + \tfrac{1}{2}\lambda \sum\sum \frac{\partial p_i}{\partial q_j}\delta q_i \delta q_j - \tfrac{1}{2}\delta r \sum \frac{\partial \lambda}{\partial q_j}\delta q_j + \cdots$$

where the terms omitted are of third and higher order, and are therefore on our assumptions negligible. Their omission corresponds to Dupuit's deliberate neglect of curvilinearity of the sides of the shaded triangle in Figure 1. With accuracy of this order we have further,

$$\delta p_i = \sum_j \frac{\partial p_i}{\partial q_j}\delta q_j, \qquad \delta\lambda = \sum_j \frac{\partial \lambda}{\partial q_j}\delta q_j.$$

Upon substituting for these expressions, (15) reduces to

$$\delta\Phi = -\lambda\delta r + \tfrac{1}{2}\lambda \sum \delta p_i \delta q_i - \tfrac{1}{2}\delta r \delta\lambda + \cdots \tag{16}$$

If the readjustment from the original state of selling only at marginal cost, with income taxes to pay overhead, is such as to leave $\delta r = 0$ as above, (16) reduces to

$$\delta\Phi = \tfrac{1}{2}\lambda \sum \delta p_i \delta q_i + \cdots, \tag{17}$$

where the terms omitted are of higher order.

As another possibility we may consider a substitution of excise for income tax so arranged as to leave this person's degree of satisfaction unchanged. Upon putting $\delta\Phi = 0$ in (16) and solving for δr we have, apart from terms of higher order,

$$\delta r = \tfrac{1}{2} \sum \delta p_i \delta q_i + \cdots \tag{18}$$

This is the net loss to the state in terms of money, so far as this one individual is concerned. The net loss in terms of satisfactions is merely the product of (18) by the marginal utility of money λ, that is, (17), if we neglect terms of higher order than those written. The total net loss of state revenue resulting from abandonment of the system of charging only marginal costs, and uncompensated by any gain to any individual, is the sum of (18) over all individuals. If the prices are the same for all, this sum is of exactly the same form as the right-hand member of (18), with

δq_i now denoting the increment (positive or negative) of the total quantity of the ith commodity.

The approximate net loss

$$\tfrac{1}{2}\sum \delta p_i \delta q_i \tag{19}$$

may be regarded as the sum of the areas of the shaded triangles in the older graphic demonstration. It should however be remembered that the readjustment of prices caused by excise taxes is not necessarily in the direction formerly supposed, that some of the quantities and some of the prices may increase and some decrease, and that some of the terms of the foregoing sum may be positive and some negative. But the aggregate of all these varying terms is seen by the foregoing argument to represent a dead loss, and never a gain, as a result of a change from income to excise taxes, or away from a system of sales at marginal cost. Any inaccuracy of the measure (19) is of only the same order as the error involved in replacing the short arcs LB and NB in Figure 1 by straight segments, and can never affect the sign.

It is remarkable, and may appear paradoxical, that without assuming any particular measure of utility or any means of comparison of one person's utility with another's, we have been able to arrive at (19) as a valid approximation measuring in money a total loss of satisfactions to many persons. That the result depends only on the conception of ranking, without measurement, of satisfactions by each person is readily apparent from the foregoing demonstration; or we may for any person replace Φ by another function Ψ as an index of the same system of ranks among satisfactions. If we do this in such a way that the derivatives are continuous, we shall have $\Psi = F(\Phi)$, where F is an increasing function with continuous derivatives. Upon writing the expressions for the first and second derivatives of Ψ in terms of those of F and Φ it may be seen that the foregoing formulae involving Φ are necessary and sufficient conditions for the truth of the same equations with Ψ written in place of Φ. The result (18) is independent of which system of indicating ranks is used. The fundamental fact here is that *arbitrary* analytic transformations, even of very complicated functional forms, always induce *homogeneous linear* transformations of differentials.

Not only the approximation (19) but also the whole expression indicated by (18) are absolutely invariant under all analytic transformations of the utility functions of all the persons involved. These expressions depend only on the demand and supply functions, which are capable of operational determination. They represent simply the money cost to the state of the inefficiency of the system of excise taxation, when this is arranged in such a way as to leave unchanged the satisfactions derived from his private income by each person.

The arguments based on Figure 1 have been repeated with various degrees of hesitation, or rediscovered independently, by numerous writers including Jevons, Fisher, Colson, Marshall, and Taussig. Marshall considered variations of the figure involving downward-sloping cost curves and multiple solutions, and was led to the proposal (less definite than that embodied in the criterion established by our theorem) that incomes and increasing-cost industries be taxed to subsidize decreasing-cost ones. He observed the difficulty of defining demand curves and consumers' surplus in view of the interdependence of demand for various commodities. These difficulties are indeed such that it now seems better to stop talking about demand *curves*, and to substitute demand *functions*, which will in general involve many variables, and are not susceptible of graphic representation in two or three dimensions. Marshall was one of those misled by Figure 1 into thinking that a tax of so much per unit imposed on producers of a commodity leads necessarily to an increase of price by something less than the tax.

Though the marginal-cost curve in Figure 1 slopes upward, no such assumption is involved in the present argument. It is perfectly possible that an industry may be operated by the state under conditions of diminishing marginal cost. The criterion for a small increase in production is still that its cost shall not exceed what buyers are willing to pay for it; that is, the general welfare is promoted by offering it for sale at its marginal cost. It may be that demand will grow as prices decline until marginal cost is pushed to a very low level, far below the average cost of all the units produced. In such a case the higher cost of the first units produced is of the same character as fixed costs, and is best carried by the public treasury without attempting to assess it against the users of the particular commodity as such. Our argument likewise makes no exception of cases in which more than one equilibrium is possible. Where there are multiple solutions we have that sales at marginal cost are a necessary, though not a sufficient, condition for the optimum of general welfare.

The confusion between marginal and average cost must be avoided. This confusion enters into many of the arguments for laissez-faire policies. It is frequently associated with the calm assumption, as a self-evident axiom, that the whole costs of every enterprise must be paid out of the prices of its products. This fallacious assumption appears, for example, in recent writings on government ownership of railroads. It has become so ingrained by endless repetition that it is not even stated in connection with many of the arguments it underlies.

III. TAX SYSTEMS MINIMIZING DEAD LOSS

The magnitude of the dead loss varies greatly according to the objects taxed. While graphic arguments are of suggestive value only, it may be observed from Figure 1 that the ratio of the dead loss *NBL* to the revenue *MNLK* depends greatly on the slopes of the demand and supply curves in the neighborhood of the equilibrium point *B*. It appears that if either the demand or the supply curve is very steep in this neighborhood, the dead loss will be slight. For a tax on the site rental value of land, whose supply curve is vertical, the dead loss drops to zero. A tax on site values is therefore one of the very best of all possible taxes from the standpoint of the maximum of the total national dividend. It is not difficult to substantiate this argument in dealing with related commodities; for the δq_i's corresponding to such a tax are zero. Since the incidence is on the owner of the land and cannot be shifted by any readjustment of production, it has the same advantages as an income tax from the standpoint of maximizing the national dividend. The fact that such a land tax cannot be shifted seems to account for the bitterness of the opposition to it. The proposition that there is no ethical objection to the confiscation of the site value of land by taxation, if and when the nonlandowning classes can get the power to do so, has been ably defended by H. G. Brown.[10]

Land is the most obviously important, but not by any means the only good, whose quantity is nearly or quite unresponsive to changes in price, and which is not available in such quantities as to satisfy all demands. Holiday travel sometimes leads to such a demand for the use of railroad cars as to bring about excessive and uncomfortable crowding. If the total demand the year around is not sufficiently great to lead to the construction of enough more cars to relieve the crowding, the limited space in the existing cars acquires a rental value similar to that of land. Instead of selling tickets to the first in a queue, or selling so many as to bring about an excessive crowding that would neutralize the pleasure of the holiday, the economic way to handle this situation would be to charge a sufficiently high price to limit the demand. The revenue thus obtained, like the site value of land, may properly be taken by the state. The fact that it helps to fill the treasury from which funds are drawn to pay for replacement of the cars when they wear out, and to cover interest on their cost in the meantime, does not at all mean that any attempt should be made to equate the revenue from car-space rental to the cost of having the cars in existence.

---

[10] *The Theory of Earned and Unearned Incomes* (Columbia, Missouri), 1918.

Another thing of limited quantity for which the demand exceeds the supply is the attention of people. Attention is desired for a variety of commercial, political, and other purposes, and is obtained with the help of billboards, newspaper, radio, and other advertising. Expropriation of the attention of the general public and its commercial sale and exploitation constitute a lucrative business. From some aspects this business appears to be of a similar character to that of the medieval robber barons, and therefore to be an appropriate subject for prohibition by a state democratically controlled by those from whom their attention is stolen. But attention attracting of some kinds and in some degree is bound to persist; and where it does, it may appropriately be taxed as a utilization of a limited resource. Taxation of advertising on this basis would be in addition to any taxation imposed for the purpose of diminishing its quantity with a view to restoring the property of attention to its rightful owners.

If for some reason of political expediency or civil disorders it is impossible to raise sufficient revenue by income and inheritance taxes, taxes on site values, and similar taxes which do not entail a dead loss of the kind just demonstrated, excise taxes may have to be resorted to. The problem then arises of so arranging the rates on the various commodities as to raise the required sum while making the total dead loss a minimum. A solution of this theoretical question, taking account of the interrelations among commodities, is given on p. 601 of the study of Edgeworth's taxation paradox previously referred to.

IV. EFFECT ON DISTRIBUTION OF WEALTH

We have seen that, if society should put into effect a system of sales at marginal cost, with overhead paid out of taxes on incomes, inheritances, and the site value of land, there would exist a possible system of compensations and collections such that everyone would be better off than before. As a practical matter, however, it can be argued in particular cases that such adjustments would not in fact be made; that the general well-being would be purchased at the expense of sacrifices by some; and that it is unjust that some should gain at the expense of others, even when the gain is great and the cost small. For example, it appears that the United States Government can by introducing cheap hydroelectric power into the Tennessee Valley raise the whole level of economic existence, and so of culture and intelligence, in that region, and that the benefits enjoyed by the local population will be such as to exceed greatly in money value the cost of the development, taking account of interest. But if the government demands for the electricity generated a price sufficiently high to repay the investment, or even the interest on it, the benefits will be reduced to an extent far exceeding the revenue thus obtained by the government. It is even possible that no system of rates can be found that will pay the interest on the investment; yet the benefits may at the same time greatly exceed this interest in value. It appears to be good public policy to make the investment, and to sell the electric energy at marginal cost, which is extremely small. But this will mean that the cost will have to be paid in part by residents of other parts of the country, in the form of higher income and inheritance taxes Those who are insistent on avoiding a change in the distribution of wealth at all costs will object.

One answer to this objection is that the benefits from such a development are not by any means confined to the persons and the region most immediately affected. Cheap power leads for example to production of cheap nitrates, which cut down the farmers' costs even in distant regions, and may benefit city dwellers in other distant regions. A host of other industries brought into being by cheap hydroelectric power have similar effects in diffusing general well-being. There is also the benefit to persons who on account of the new industrial development find that they can better themselves by moving into the Tennessee Valley, or by investing their funds there. Furthermore, the nation at large has a stake in eradicating poverty, with its accompaniments of contagious diseases, crime, and political corruption, wherever these may occur.

A further answer to the objection that benefits may be paid for by those who do not receive them when such a development as that of the Tennessee Valley is undertaken is that no such enterprise stands alone. A government willing to undertake such an enterprise is, for the same reasons, ready to build other dams in other and widely scattered places, and to construct a great variety of public works. Each of these entails benefits which are diffused widely among all classes. A rough randomness in distribution should be ample to ensure such a distribution of benefits that most persons in every part of the country would be better off by reason of the program as a whole.

If new electric-power, railroad, highway, bridge, and other developments are widely undertaken at public expense, always on the basis of the criterion of maximizing total benefits, the geographical distribution of the benefits, and also the distribution among different occupational, racial, age, and sex groups, would seem pretty clearly to be such that every such large group would on the whole be benefited by the program. There are, however, two groups that might with some reason expect not to benefit. One of these consists of the very wealthy. Income and inheritance taxes are likely to be graduated in such a way that increases in government spending will be paid for, both directly and ultimately, by those possessed of great wealth, more than in the proportion that the number of such persons bears to the whole population. It would not be surprising if the benefits received by such persons as a result of the program of maximum total benefit should fall short of the cost to them.

The other class that might expect not to benefit from such a program consists of land speculators. If we consider for example a bridge, it is evident that the public as a whole must pay a certain cost of construction, whether the bridge be paid for by tolls or by taxes on the site value of land in the vicinity. There will be much more use of the bridge if there are no tolls, so that the public as a whole will get more for its money if it pays in the form of land taxes. But it will not in general be possible to devise a system of land taxes that will leave everyone, without exception, in a position as good as or better than as if the bridge had not been built and the taxes had not been levied. Landowners argue that the benefits of the bridge go to others, not to them; and even in cases in which land values have been heightened materially as a result of a new bridge, the landowners have been known to be vociferous in favor of a toll system. Payment for the bridge by tolls (when this is possible) has the advantage that no one seems to be injured, since each one who pays to cross the bridge has the option of not using it, and is in that case as well off as if the bridge did not exist. This reasoning is not strictly sound, since the bridge may have put out of business a ferry which for some users was more convenient and economical. Nevertheless, it retains enough cogency to stiffen the resistance of real-estate interests to the more economical system of paying for the bridge by land taxes.

Attempts at excessive accuracy in assessing costs of public enterprises according to benefits received tend strongly to reduce the total of those benefits, as in the case of the bridge. The welfare of all is promoted rather by a generous support of projects for communal spending in ways beneficial to the public at large, without attempting to recover from each enterprise its cost by charges for services rendered by that enterprise. The notion that public projects should be "self-liquidating," on which President Hoover based his inadequate program for combating the oncoming depression, while attractive to the wealthier taxpayers, is not consistent with the nation's getting the maximum of satisfactions for its expenditure.

V. DISTINCTION OF OPTIMUM FROM COMPETITIVE CONDITIONS

The idea that all will be for the best if only competition exists is a heritage from the economic theory of Adam Smith, built up at a time when agriculture was still the dominant economic activity. The typical agricultural situation is one of rising marginal costs. Free competition, of the type that has usually existed in agriculture, leads to sales at marginal cost, if we now abstract the effects of weather and other uncertainty, which are irrelevant to our problem. Since we have seen that sales at marginal cost are a condition of maximum general welfare, this situation is a satisfactory one so far as it goes. But the free competition associated with agriculture, or with unorganized labor, is not characteristic of enterprises such as railroads, electric-power plants, bridges, and heavy industry. It is true that a toll bridge may be in competition with other bridges and ferries; but it is a very different kind of competition, more in the nature of duopoly. To rely on such competition for the efficient conduct of an economic system is to use a theorem without observing that its premises do not apply. Free competition among toll-bridge owners, of the kind necessary to make the conclusion applicable, would require that each bridge be paralleled by an infinite number of others immediately adjacent to it, all the owners being permanently engaged in cutthroat competition. If the marginal cost of letting a vehicle go over a bridge is neglected, it is clear that under such conditions the tolls would quickly drop to zero and the owners would retire in disgust to allow anyone who pleased to cross free.

The efficient way to operate a bridge—and the same applies to a railroad or a factory, if we neglect the small cost of an additional unit of product or of transportation—is to make it free to the public, so long at least as the use of it does not increase to a state of overcrowding. A free bridge costs no more to construct than a toll bridge, and costs less to operate; but society, which must pay the cost in some way or other, gets far more benefit from the bridge if it is free, since in this case it will be more used. Charging a toll, however small, causes some people to waste time and money in going around by longer but cheaper ways, and prevents others from crossing. The higher the toll, the greater is the damage done in this way; to a first approximation, for small tolls, the damage is proportional to the square of the toll rate, as Dupuit showed. There is no such damage if the bridge is paid for by income, inheritance, and land taxes, or for example by a tax on the real estate benefited, with exemption of new improvements from taxation, so as not to interfere with the use of the land. The *distribution* of wealth among members of the community is affected by the mode of payment adopted for the bridge, but not the total wealth, except that it is diminished by bridge tolls and other similar forms of excise. This is such plain common sense that toll bridges have now largely disappeared from civilized communities. But New York City's bridge and tunnels across the Hudson are

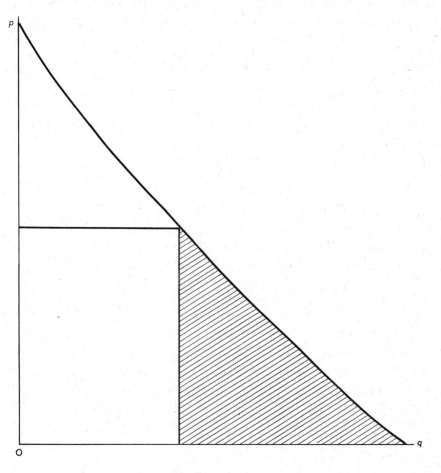

FIGURE 2

still operated on a toll basis, because of the pressure of real estate interests anxious to shift the tax burden to wayfarers, and the possibility of collecting considerable sums from persons who do not vote in the city.

If we ignore the interrelations of the services of a bridge with other goods, and also the slight wear and tear on the bridge due to its use, we may with Dupuit represent the demand for these services by a curve such as that in Figure 2. The total benefit from the bridge is then represented by the whole area enclosed between the demand curve and the axes, provided the bridge is free. All this benefit goes to users of the bridge. But if a toll is charged, of magnitude corresponding to the height of the horizontal line, the recipients of the toll are benefited to an extent represented by the area of the rectangle, whose base is the number of crossings and whose height is the charge for each crossing. But the number of crossings has diminished, the benefit to bridge users has shrunk to the small triangular area at the top, and the total benefit has decreased by the area of the shaded triangle at the right. This triangle represents the net loss to society due to the faulty method of paying for the bridge. If, for example, the demand curve is a straight line, and if the owners set the toll so as to bring them a maximum return, the net loss of benefit is 25 per cent of the total.

These are the pertinent considerations if the bridge is already in existence, or its construction definitely decided. But if we examine the general question of the circumstances in which bridges ought to be built, a further inefficiency is disclosed in the scheme of paying for bridges out of tolls. For society, it is beneficial to build the bridge if the total area in the figure exceeds the interest, amortization, and maintenance costs. But if the bridge must be paid for by tolls, it will not be built unless it is expected that these costs will be exceeded by the rectangular area alone. This area cannot, for our example of a linear demand function, be greater than half the total. We may in this case say that the toll system has 75 per cent efficiency in use, but only 50 per cent efficiency in providing new bridges. In each case the efficiency will be further diminished by reason of the cost of collecting and accounting for the tolls.

The argument about bridges applies equally to railroads, except that in the latter case there is some slight additional cost resulting from an extra passenger or an extra shipment of freight. My weight is such that when I ride on the train, more coal has to be burned in the locomotive, and I wear down the station platform by walking across it. What is more serious, I may help to overcrowd the train, diminishing the comfort of other travelers and helping to create a situation in which additional trains should be run, but often are not. The trivial nature of the extra costs of marginal use of the railroads has from the first been realized by the railroad managements themselves; indeed, it is implied in the amazingly complex rate structures they build up in the attempt to squeeze the last possible bit of revenue from freight and passenger traffic. If in a rational economic system the railroads were operated for the benefit of the people as a whole, it is plain that if people were to be induced by low rates to travel in one season rather than another, the season selected should be one in which travel would otherwise be light, leaving the cars nearly empty, and not a season in which they are normally overcrowded. Actually, our railroads run trains about the country in winter with few passengers, while crowding multitudes of travelers into their cars in summer. The rates are made high in winter, lower in summer, on the ground that the summer demand is more elastic than that of the winter travelers, who are usually on business rather than pleasure, and thus decide the question of a trip with less sensitiveness to the cost.

VI. COMPLEXITY OF ACTUAL RAILWAY RATES AND REMOTENESS FROM MARGINAL COST

The extreme and uneconomic complexity of railway freight and passenger rate structures is seldom realized by those not closely in touch with them. A few random examples will illustrate the remoteness of actual rates from what may be presumed to be marginal costs, which railway managements will find it profitable to cover even by the lowest rates. Prior to the last enforced reduction of American passenger rates the regular round-trip fare between New York City and Wilkesbarre, Pa. was $11.04. But at various times between 1932 and 1935 round-trip tickets good for limited periods were sold at $2.50, $6.00, $6.10, and $6.15. Between New York and Chicago the round-trip fare in the same period varied between $33 and $65 for identical accommodations. Between New York and Washington the ordinary round-trip fare was $18.00, but an "excursion rate" of $3.50 was applied spasmodically.

The lumber and logging activities of the country, which have been at a standstill for several years, are suffering from freight rates which in many important cases nearly equal, and even exceed, the mill price of the lumber. Thus from the large sawmills at and near Baker, Oregon, which produce lumber for the New York market, the freight amounts to $16.50 per thousand board feet. For No. 3 Common Ponderosa Pine, the grade shipped in largest quantities, the price of one-by-four inch boards ranged in the autumn of 1933 from $14.50 to $15.50 at the mill. Thus the New York wholesale buyer must pay more than double the mill price, solely on account of freight. The freight even to Chicago approximated the mill price. For No. 4 Common, also an important grade, the price was $12.50 per thousand board feet at the mill, but the New York buyer had to pay $29.00. A few months earlier, the prices were about $8 per thousand board feet less than those just given, so that the railroads received far more than the mill operators. It is hard to escape the conclusion that these high freight rates interfered seriously with the sale of lumber.

One advantage of the system of charging only marginal cost would be a great simplification of the rate structure. This is a great desideratum. It must not be assumed too readily that every purchaser distributes his budget accurately to obtain the maximum of satisfactions, or the most efficient methods of production, when the determination of the optimum requires the study of an encyclopedic railroad tariff, together with complicated trial-and-error calculations. Neither, from the standpoint of a railroad, can it be assumed that the enormously complex rate differentials have been determined at all accurately for the purposes for which they were designed. These complicated rate structures further contravene the public interest in that they enhance artificially the advantages of large over small concerns. When immense calculations are required to determine the optimum combinations of transportation with other factors of production, the large concerns are in a distinctly better position to carry out the calculations and obtain the needed information.

VII. MARGINAL COST DEPENDS ON EXTENT OF UNUSED CAPACITY

In the determination of marginal cost there are, to be sure, certain complications. When a train is completely filled, and has all the cars it can haul, the marginal cost of carrying an extra passenger is the cost of running another train. On the other hand, in the more normal situation in which the equipment does not carry more than a small part of its capacity load, the marginal cost is virtually nothing. To avoid a sharp increase in rates at the time the train is filled, an averaging process is needed in the computation of rates, based on the probability of having to run an extra train. Further, in cases in which the available equipment is actually used to capacity, and it is not feasible or is of doubtful wisdom to increase the amount of equipment, something in the nature of a rental charge for the use of the facilities should, as indicated above, be levied to discriminate among different users in such a way that those willing to pay the most, and therefore in accordance with the usual assumptions deriving the most benefit, would be the ones obtaining the limited facilities which many desire. This rental charge for equipment, which for passenger travel would largely take the place of fares, should never be so high as to limit travel to fewer persons than can comfortably be accommodated, except for unpredictable fluctuations. The proceeds from the charge could be added to the funds derived from income, inheritance, and land taxes, and used to pay a part of the overhead costs. But there should be no attempt to pay all the overhead from such rental charges alone.

Except in the most congested regions, there would, however, be no such charge for the use of track and stations until the volume of traffic comes to exceed enormously the current levels. An example is the great under-utilization of the expensive Pennsylvania Station, in New York City, whose capacity was demonstrated during the war by bringing into the city the trains of the Erie and the Baltimore and Ohio railroads. These trains are now required to stop on the New Jersey shore, constituting a wasteful nuisance which had existed before government operation, which was replaced by the more efficient procedure by the government, but which was resumed when the lines were handed back to their private owners.

VIII. THE ATTEMPT TO PAY FIXED COSTS FROM RATES AND PRICES CONTRIBUTES TO RIGIDITY AND SO TO INSTABILITY

One of the evil consequences of the attempt to pay overhead out of operating revenue is the instability which it contributes to the economic system as a whole. This is illustrated by the events leading to the depression. The immense and accelerating progress of science and technology led to the creation of new industries and the introduction of wonderfully efficient new methods. The savings from the new methods were so great that corporate profits and real incomes surged upwards. So large were the profits and so satisfactory the dividends that the operating officials of great industries did not feel under compulsion to push up the selling prices of their products to the levels corresponding to maximum monopoly profit. Because they kept their prices low, while paying relatively high wages, the physical volume of goods produced and transferred became enormous. The impulse to produce, with possibly some altruistic motives besides, tempered the desire for profits in many concerns. But under a profit system this could not last. As the prices of corporate shares rose, pressure developed to pay dividends equivalent to interest on the higher prices. This pressure would probably have led presently to gradual increases in the money prices of manufactured products, if the general level of prices had remained stationary. Such however was not the case. The general level of prices was declining.

And decline it must, according to the equation of exchange, when there was such a great new flood of goods to be sold. The vast increase in physical volume of goods, created by the new technology, called for a greater use of money, if the price level was to be maintained. This need was met for a time by increases in bank loans and deposits, and in the velocity of circulation. But neither bank loans nor velocities could continue to increase as fast as goods, and prices had to fall. The fall was not uniform. Corporations under increasing pressure to cover their overhead and pay high dividends out of earnings were strongly averse to reducing the selling prices of their products, when these selling prices were already below the points which would yield maximum profit. For several years prior to the crash, the prices of manufactured products stuck fast, while the proportion of national expenditure paid for these products continued to increase. This left a shrinking volume of money payments to be made for the remaining commodities, and these, including particularly the agricultural, had to come down in price. If, as the general price level fell, railroad, utility, and manufacturing concerns had reduced their selling prices proportionately, the prosperity of the years 1922 to 1928 might have continued. But such reductions in selling prices were not possible when an increasing volume of overhead charges had to be paid out of earnings. The intensified efforts to do this resulted in a pushing up of "real" prices of manufactured products—that is, of the ratios of their prices to the general price level—and of "real" transportation rates. Indeed, with a rapidly falling general price level, railroad freight rates, measured in money, were actually increased in 1931. This increase of 15 per cent on a large range of commodities, like the subsequent increases in suburban commuters' passenger rates, was obtained on the ground that the railroads needed the money to cover their overhead costs, though their operating costs had declined. Of course the effect was to make the depression worse, by stopping traffic which would have flowed at the lower rates. On the theory that bond interest and other such items must be paid out of operating revenues, the railroads were "entitled" to the higher rates, for their business had fallen off. But economic equilibrium calls for a rising rather than a declining supply curve; if demand falls off, the offer price must be reduced in order to have the offered services taken. This antithesis of rising railway rates, when general prices and the ability to pay are falling, well illustrates the disequilibrating consequences of the idea that overhead costs must be paid from operating revenues. There now seems to be a possibility of a repetition of the disastrous 15 per cent freight-rate increase in a time of decline.[11]

This explanation of the contrast of the prosperity of 1928 with the cessation of production in the following years rests upon the contrast of the system of prices which results from the whole-hearted devotion of different concerns to their own respective profits, with the system of prices best for the economic organism as a whole. Under free competition, with no overhead, these two systems of prices tend to become identical. Where there are overhead costs, competition of the ideally free type is not permanently possible. Monopoly prices develop; and a system of monopoly

---

[11] Since this was written the Interstate Commerce Commission has allowed a part of this proposed increase and postponed consideration of a request for a passenger fare rise.

prices is not a system which can serve human needs with maximum advantage.

IX. CRITERION AS TO WHAT INVESTMENTS ARE SOCIALLY WORTH WHILE

When a decision whether or not to construct a railway is left to the profit motive of private investors, the criterion used is that the total revenue $\sum p_i q_i$, being the sum of the products of the rates for the various services by the quantities sold, shall exceed the sum of operating costs and carrying charges on the cost of the enterprise. If no one thinks that there will be a positive excess of revenue, the construction will not be undertaken. We have seen in Section V that this rule is, from the standpoint of the general welfare, excessively conservative. What, then, should society adopt to replace it?

A less conservative criterion than that of a sufficient revenue for total costs is that *if some distribution of the burden is possible such that everyone concerned is better off than without the new investment, then there is a prima facie case for making the investment.* This leaves aside the question whether such a distribution is *practicable.* It may often be good social policy to undertake new enterprises even though some persons are put in a worse position than before, provided that the benefits to others are sufficiently great and widespread. It is on this ground that new inventions are permitted to crowd out less efficient industries. To hold otherwise would be to take the side of the hand weavers who tried to wreck the power looms that threatened their employment. But the rule must not be applied too harshly. Where losses involve serious hardship to individuals, there must be compensation, or at least relief to cover subsistence. Where there are many improvements, the law of averages may be trusted to equalize the benefits to some extent, but never completely. It will always be necessary to provide for those individuals upon whom progress inflicts special hardship; if it were not possible to do this, we should have to reconcile ourselves to greater delays in the progress of industrial efficiency.

Subject to this qualification of avoiding excessive hardship to individuals, we may adopt the criterion stated. In applying it there will be the problem of selecting a limited number of proposed investments, corresponding to the available capital, from among a larger number of possibilities. The optimum solution corresponds to application of our criterion to discriminate between each pair of combinations. The total amount of calculation and exercise of judgment required will not, however, be so great as might be suggested by the number of pairs of combinations, which is immense. Numerous means are available to shorten this labor. One of these is by the application of the line integral (3), namely

$$w = \int \sum h_i dq_i,$$

which provides a meaure of value corresponding to the sum of consumers' and producers' surpluses. The part of w constituting the generalized consumers' surplus is (2); the validity of this line integral as a measure of an individual's increment of satisfaction corresponding to sufficiently small changes in the q's may be seen merely by replacing p_i in (13) by f_i, and noticing that for small changes the marginal utility of money λ changes little, so that f_i is very nearly proportional to the derivative of the utility function Φ. Hence the increment in Φ is proportional to the sum of the integrals of the f's, apart from terms of higher order; and the factor of proportionality λ is such as to measure this increment in money so as to be comparable to an increase in income. Similar considerations apply to the part of w corresponding to producers' surplus.

Defenders of the current theory that the overhead costs of an industry must be met out of the sale of its products or services hold that this is necessary in order to find out whether the creation of the industry was a wise social policy. Nothing could be more absurd. Whether it was wise for the government to subsidize and its backers to construct the Union Pacific Railroad after the Civil War is an interesting historical question which would make a good subject for a dissertation, but it would be better, if necessary, to leave it unsolved than to ruin the country the Union Pacific was designed to serve by charging enormous freight rates and claiming that their sum constitutes a measure of the value to the country of the investment. Such an experimental solution of a historical question is too costly. In addition, it is as likely as not to give the wrong answer. The sum of the freight and passenger rates received, minus operating costs, is not the line integral $w = \int \sum h_i dq_i$, which with some accuracy measures the value to society of the investment, but is more closely related to the misleading measure of value $\sum p_i q_i$. In other words, the revenue resembles the area of the rectangle in Figure 2, while the possible benefit corresponds to the much larger triangular area. The revenue is the thing that appeals to an investor bent on his own profit, but as a criterion of whether construction ought in the public interest to be undertaken, it is biased in the direction of being too conservative.

Regardless of their own history, the fact is that we now have the railroads, and in the main are likely to have them with us for a considerable time in the future. It will be better to operate the railroads for the benefit of living human beings, while letting dead men and dead investments rest quietly in their graves, and to establish a system of rates and services calculated to assure the most efficient operation. When the question arises of building new railroads, or new major industries of any kind, or of scrapping the old, we shall face, not a historical, but a mathematical and economic problem. The question then will be whether the aggregate of the generalized surpluses of the form (3) is likely to be great enough to cover the anticipated cost of the new investment. This will call for a study of demand and cost functions by economists, statisticians, and engineers, and perhaps for a certain amount of large-scale experimentation for the sake of gaining information about these functions. The amount of such experiment and research which could easily be paid for out of the savings resulting from operation of industry in the public interest is very large indeed. Perhaps this is the way in which we shall ultimately get the materials for a scientific economics.

II. INCIDENCE AND INCENTIVE EFFECTS

11

Minutes of Royal Commission on Local Taxation, 1899

Answers by EDWIN CANNAN

QUESTIONS

These questions were sent by the Commission, in the autumn of 1897, to the financial and economic experts, whose answers will be found in the following pages. A copy of Sir Edward Hamilton's Memorandum was subsequently sent to them.

1. Is the classification of Imperial Taxation indicated in the accompanying Table a correct classification; if not, what alterations can you suggest? (*See* Table opposite.)

2. Assuming the classification, is it complete, and are the several items correctly distributed?

3. In particular should such an item as the net revenue of the Post Office, be treated as a tax, and if so, under which of the heads specified in the Table?

4. In considering the equity of any tax or system of taxation what tests should be applied?

5. Can you offer any suggestions which would assist the Commission in determining the question of the real incidence of taxation as distinguished from its primary or apparent incidence?

6. Could you, for example, state your view as to the real incidence of—
   a) The Inhabited House Duty;
   b) Rates levied on houses and trade premises;
   c) Rates levied on agricultural land;
   d) Taxes on the transfer of property;
   e) Taxes on trade profits;
   f) Death duties.

7. Is it possible to frame any criterion whereby the purposes for which taxation should be raised locally can be distinguished from those for which taxation should be raised by the central Government?

8. Should the two kinds of purposes and the expenditure on them be kept distinct or should the expenditure for local purposes be partly borne by the central Government?

9. Should local rates be divided between owners and occupiers of real property, and if so, in what proportions?

10. Should ground values be separately rated for local purposes, and if so, on what principles?

11. Under what conditions and in what manner would the rent which could be obtained by an owner of land or rateable hereditaments be affected, if at all, by—
    a) The increase of an old rate.
    b) The imposition of a new rate.
    c) The reduction or abolition of a rate.

12. Under what conditions and in what manner would the rent which could be obtained by an owner of land or rateable hereditaments be affected, if at all, if an occupier by whom a rate had hitherto been paid were empowered to deduct the whole or a portion thereof from the rent in the same manner as he is now entitled to do in the case of Income Tax (Schedule A.)?

13. What is the effect, if any, upon rent of rating property—
    a) On different scales of duty according to the value of the property.
    b) On different scales of duty according to the character of the property or the purposes for which it is used.

14. Can you make suggestions to the Commission as to any methods of raising revenue for local purposes, otherwise than by means of rates?

15. Does any point not included under any of the foregoing questions occur to you on which having regard to the terms of reference to the Commission you wish to express an opinion?

TERMS OF REFERENCE TO THE COMMISSION

To inquire into the present system under which taxation is raised for local purposes, and report whether all kinds of real and personal property contribute equitably to such taxation; and if not, what alterations in the law are desirable in order to secure that result.

ANSWERS BY MR. EDWIN CANNAN

1. It is impossible to offer useful criticism of a classification without knowing for what purpose the classification is intended. In order to discover what this is, I must have recourse to the reference to the Commission.

The reference seems to ignore the commonplace of economists which asserts that taxes cannot be defrayed by things, but must, like all other payments, be defrayed by persons. It seems to ignore this commonplace not only, as Sir Edward Hamilton observes,[1] by speaking of property "con-

---

[1] Memorandum, p. 33.

tributing" to taxation, but also by its assumption that there can be equity in taxation as between different kinds of property. Now, in spite of Blackstone's phrase, the "rights of things,"[2] things cannot be wronged or suffer inequitable treatment, whether in regard to taxation or anything else. It is necessary, therefore, to "interpret liberally" the terms of the reference, rather in the sense in which sacred writings, whether by theologians or economists, are "liberally interpreted" by modern teachers who shrink from leaving the shelter of the wings of authority. That is to say, the Commission will have to endeavour to answer not the question actually put (which is impossible), but the question which would have been put if its framers had been advised by someone familiar with the most recent scientific discussion of the subject.

The question which would have been put under those circumstances might, I think, have been divided into three branches:

1. Is the present taxation[3] of persons in respect of property equal as between the various kinds of property?
2. Is it equitable as between different persons?
3. If it is inequitable, what, if any, alterations in the law would make it more equitable?

The first two of these inquiries are perfectly distinct from one another, since a negative answer to the first does not necessarily involve a negative answer to the second, nor *vice versa*. In my opinion any confounding of the two as they are habitually confounded in the press and on the platform would render the labours of the Commission, however arduous and prolonged, wholly nugatory, if not actively pernicious.

Accordingly, it appears to me that the Commission's first object in classifying national taxes must be to discover how far the present national taxation of persons in respect of property is equal as between the various kinds of property. For the purpose of answering the second question, how far the taxation is equitable as between persons, this first classification may be, and probably will be, altogether unsuitable.

The first thing to do, in framing the classification, is to divide the various taxes into those which are equal and those which are unequal as between the various kinds of property. I take it that a tax is equal as between the various kinds of property if its abolition would neither benefit

---

[2] Quoted with the same purpose as here in Bastable, "Public Finance," 2nd Ed., p. 255, note.

[3] I omit the words of the reference "for local purposes" since it is conceivable (and is, as a matter of fact, argued) that certain inequalities and apparent inequities in the one kind of taxation are balanced by corresponding inequalities and apparent inequities in the other.

TABLE

CLASSIFYING TAXES RAISED BY PARLIAMENT IN 1895-96

NOTE: The Classification includes the Taxes assigned to the Local Taxation Accounts as well as the Taxes payable to the Exchequer. The figures represent the Net Receipts under the principal heads of Tax Revenue as given in the Finance Accounts for 1895–96, pp. 19–22.

DESCRIPTION OF TAX	TAXES INCIDENTAL TO THE OWNERSHIP, OCCUPATION, OR TRANSFER OF PROPERTY			TAXES NOT INCIDENTAL TO PROPERTY				GRAND TOTAL
	Rateable Property	Non-Rateable Property	Total	Taxes Levied in Respect of Commodities	Taxes Levied in Respect of Incomes Derived from Personal Exertion	Miscellaneous Taxes	Total	
	(1)	(2)	(3)	(1)	(2)	(3)	(4)	
	£	£	£	£	£	£	£	£
1. Customs Duties	—	—	—	20,965,000	—	—	20,965,000	20,965,000
2. Excise Duties:								
Duties on Consumable Articles (including Licenses falling on Consumable Articles)	—	—	—	29,704,000	—	—	29,704,000	29,704,000
Licenses (other than those falling on Consumable Articles)	—	—	—	—	—	1,632,000	1,632,000	1,632,000
Railway Passenger Duty	—	—	—	—	—	259,000	259,000	259,000
Total Excise Duties	—	—	—	29,704,000	—	1,891,000	31,595,000	31,595,000
3. Death Duties:								
Probate and Account Duty	48,000	133,000	181,000	—	—	—	—	181,000
Temporary Estate Duty	150,000	13,000	163,000	—	—	—	—	163,000
Estate Duty	3,540,000	6,383,000	9,923,000	—	—	—	—	9,923,000
Legacy Duty	724,000	2,007,000	2,731,000	—	—	—	—	2,731,000
Succession Duty	897,000	154,000	1,051,000	—	—	—	—	1,051,000
Corporation Duty	34,000	6,000	40,000	—	—	—	—	40,000
Total Death Duties	5,393,000	8,696,000	14,089,000	—	—	—	—	14,089,000

4. Stamp Duties:								
Deeds and other Instruments	1,946,000	2,059,000	4,005,000	—	—	—	—	4,005,000
Securities to Bearer	—	207,000	207,000	—	—	—	—	207,000
Joint Stock Companies' Capital	—	260,000	260,000	—	—	—	—	260,000
Contract Notes above 1d.	61,000	110,000	171,000	—	—	—	—	171,000
Bills of Exchange and Promissory Notes	—	673,000	673,000	—	—	—	—	673,000
Bankers' Notes and Composition for Duty on Bankers' Bills and Notes	—	124,000	124,000	—	—	—	—	124,000
Playing Cards	—	—	—	20,000	—	—	20,000	20,000
Licences and Certificates	—	—	—	—	167,000	—	167,000	167,000
Life Insurances	—	67,000	67,000	—	—	—	—	67,000
Marine Insurances	—	145,000	145,000	—	—	—	—	145,000
Patent Medicines	—	—	—	239,000	—	—	239,000	239,000
Receipts, Drafts, &c.	—	1,261,000	1,261,000	—	—	—	—	1,261,000
Total Stamp Duties	2,007,000	4,906,000	6,913,000	259,000	167,000	—	426,000	7,339,000
5. Land Tax (unredeemed)	1,021,000	—	1,021,000	—	—	—	—	1,021,000
6. Inhabited House Duty	1,487,000	—	1,487,000	—	—	—	—	1,487,000
7. Income Tax:								
Schedule A	4,766,000	28,000	4,794,000	—	—	—	—	4,794,000
Schedule B (including Farmers' profits assessed)	—	59,000	59,000	119,000	—	—	119,000	178,000
Schedule C	—	1,300,000	1,300,000	—	—	—	—	1,300,000
Schedule D:								
Fishings and Shootings	22,000	—	22,000	—	—	—	—	22,000
Railways in the United Kingdom	645,000	388,000	1,033,000	—	—	—	—	1,033,000
Quarries, Mines, &c.	447,000	404,000	851,000	—	—	—	—	851,000
Railways out of the United Kingdom	—	390,000	390,000	—	—	—	—	390,000
Foreign and Colonial Securities and Coupons	—	495,000	495,000	—	—	—	—	495,000
Municipal Interest, other Interest, and other Profits	—	239,000	239,000	—	—	—	—	239,000
Public Companies	—	1,929,000	1,929,000	—	—	—	—	1,929,000
Trades and Professions	—	726,000	726,000	2,902,000	—	—	2,902,000	3,628,000
Schedule E	—	—	—	1,124,000	—	—	1,124,000	1,124,000
Total Income Tax (at 8d. in the £)	5,880,000	5,958,000	11,838,000	4,145,000	—	—	4,145,000	15,983,000
8. Post Office (excess of Revenue over Expenditure)	—	—	—	—	—	2,994,000	2,994,000	2,994,000
Grand Total	15,788,000	19,560,000	35,348,000	50,928,000	4,145,000	5,052,000	60,125,000	95,473,000
Per-centages of Grand Total	16.5	20.5	37.0	53.4	4.3	5.3	63.0	100.0

the present owners of a particular class of property more than the present owners of another class of property, nor, by making a particular class of property a more desirable investment than another class of property, tend to increase the quantity of the first class in comparison with the quantity of the second class. In the shorter but more metaphorical and consequently dangerous language of everyday life, an equal tax in respect of property is one which "lays no peculiar burden" on any particular kind of property. The term "burden" is used because the unequal tax, so to speak, weighs or presses down either the clear value to the owner, or the quantity produced and maintained in existence.

Without going into minute details further than is done in Table D, we may say that the following taxes are obviously unequal as between different classes of property:

Customs duties	Playing cards tax
Excise duties	Marine insurance tax
Railway passenger tax	House tax
Telephone tax	Land tax
Bankers' notes tax	Patent medicine tax

The Customs and Excise duties have the effect of restricting the consumption of intoxicating beverages, tea, and tobacco. If they were abolished the capital employed in the importation and production of these commodities would increase in comparison with other forms of capital.

The abolition of the railway passenger tax would both benefit the present owners of existing railways in comparison with the present owners of other property, and, by making railways a more profitable form of investment, tend to cause an increase of railways in comparison with other forms of capital.

The telephone tax, which is none the less real because it happens to be called a "royalty" and to be hidden away in the receipts of the Post Office, is exactly like the railway passenger duty. It makes an extension of business on the part of the telephone company less profitable than it would otherwise be. Its abolition would both benefit the telephone company more than the owners of other kinds of property, and tend to increase the proportion of the capital of the country taking the form of telephone wires, instruments, and exchanges.[4]

The abolition of the tax on bankers' notes would disproportionately benefit the bankers who retain the old privilege of issuing notes.

---

[4] In short, the railway passenger duty and the telephone royalty are both vingtièmes, and liable to the objections which have always been made to tithes and other taxes on gross produce.

The abolition of the tax on playing cards would lead to an increased consumption of cards, and consequently to the investment of a larger proportion of the capital of the country in the machinery necessary for the manufacture and distribution of cards.

The abolition of the tax on marine insurance would tend to increase the proportion of the capital of the country invested in the form of shipping. The abolition of the Inhabited House Duty would disproportionately benefit the owners of the existing stock of houses of 20*l.* annual value and upwards for a time, and would eventually tend to increase the proportion of the capital of the country invested in the form of houses of 20*l.* annual value and upwards.

The abolition of the land tax would disproportionately benefit the owners of property at present subject to land tax. It would also tend to increase the proportion of the capital of the country invested in the form of rateable property on the areas which are at present subject to the tax.[5]

The abolition of the tax on patent medicines would disproportionately benefit the owners of the patents, and would tend to increase the proportion of the country's capital invested in things necessary for the manufacture and distribution of the patent medicines.

The remaining taxes are either equal, or so nearly equal, as between different kinds of property that their inequality is not worth considering. The various stamp duties, doubtless, do not, when taken together, form an absolutely equal tax, but *de minimis non curat lex*. It would be absurd to inquire whether more receipt stamps and cheques are used in connexion with houses or with ships. The income tax and the death duties are both professedly equal taxes on all kinds of property, and in spite of their necessary and unnecessary imperfections, the mere fact that Table D (taken in conjunction with the estimates of the value of property furnished to the Royal Commission on Agriculture) represents them as unequal as between rateable and unrateable property, is not nearly sufficient to destroy the presumption in favour of their equality. The great inequality indicated by the table in the case of the death duties is presumably due to the fact that the changes made in 1894 have not yet made themselves fully felt in the returns. When this has taken place we may expect to see a somewhat higher rate in the £ or percentage yielded in respect of rateable property than in respect of non-rateable property, since, as a rule, rateable property belongs to richer people, whose estates, under the progressive scale, will be chargeable at the higher rates. The inequality indicated by the table in the case of the income tax is trifling,

---

[5] I assume that reassessment within a parish does actually take place when new rateable property is created there. *See below*, Question 14, fourth paragraph.

and probably does not really exist. Here, too, we should expect to find a higher rate in respect of rateable property, since it is not much held by persons whose incomes are small enough to entitle them to exemption or abatement. But inequalities of this kind, resulting from progressive taxation, are not inequalities of taxation as between different kinds of property, but inequalities as between persons possessing different totals of all kinds of property taken together. The abolition of the progression would not make anyone more ready to buy or produce any particular kind of property.

Now in view of the classification in Table D, and the evidence given before the Royal Commission on Agriculture, it seems that the next step is to ask whether the amounts raised by the unequal taxes can be disintegrated, classified, and summed up in such a way as to show whether any inequality, and if so, how much inequality there is in taxation as between rateable property and unrateable property, each being taken as a whole. I am not prepared to deny that it is conceivable that this might be done by an omniscient statistician. He might discover and set down exactly the proportions in which the property affected by customs, excise, railway passenger duty, and the other unequal taxes, is divided between rateable and non-rateable. But no actual statistician approaches near enough omniscience to produce anything worth looking at in this direction. Moreover, even if correct figures were obtained, they would be of no use for the purposes of the Commission. The fact that one species of rateable property is more "burdened" than property in general, is not, and cannot be, counterbalanced by the fact that some species of unrateable property is more "burdened" than property in general. A special tax in respect of ships is no set-off to a special tax in respect of houses. It is not possible to set off against the land tax the fact that carriages and dogs render their owners liable to taxation. In addition to all this, we have to remember that the amount of tax collected does not measure the magnitude of the burden. The burden surely increases when the tax is made higher, whereas the amount collected does not always increase with the heightening of the tax, and seldom increases exactly in proportion to it. A tax on some non-rateable article might be made heavier and heavier till it finally prevented any new capital being invested in that form. Then, as soon as the existing stock was consumed or worn out, the article would cease to appear in Table D; but would this be any "relief" to non-rateable property? Obviously not.

2. The classification in Table D is valueless for the purposes of the Commission, because it overlooks the considerations mentioned under Question 1. But it is to be condemned for several other reasons.

In the first place, following, I admit, numerous and high authorities, it distinguishes between "taxes levied in respect of commodities" and "taxes incidental to the ownership, occupation, or transfer of property." But what commodities are not property, and what property, with the possible exception of land, is not composed of commodities? I know of no definitions of property and commodities which distinguish things into things which are property and things which are commodities. The old distinction between taxes on commodities and taxes on property is a merely temporal one, *i.e.*, a distinction based, not on the nature of the thing taxed, but on the time or times at which the taxation takes place. A barrel of beer is taxed at the time it is produced; therefore the beer tax is called a tax on a commodity. A house is taxed, not when it is built, but annually while it remains in existence; therefore it is called a tax on property. If the house duty were levied on the builder, we should call it a tax on a commodity; if the wine merchant or the private epicure were annually taxed on the stock of wine in their cellars, we should call the duties on wine taxes on property. But this distinction is of no importance to the present inquiry, and the classification, as a matter of fact, does not adopt it, since the duties exacted from public-houses annually in proportion to their annual value (on a certain arbitrary scale) do not appear under "Rateable Property" taxes, but are huddled away under "Miscellaneous Taxes," the framers of the classification having evidently thought that they were too near akin to the taxes on the gallon of beer and spirits to be classified in the other main division of the Table as a "tax incidental to the occupation of property," which they certainly are. The same confusion probably is the cause of the strange classification of the carriage tax and dog tax among "miscellaneous taxes," instead of among "non-rateable property" taxes, and to the setting down of the railway passenger duty under "Miscellaneous," instead of dividing it between "rateable" and "non-rateable" property.

If it is once recognised that the 50,928,000*l.* classified as "taxes levied in respect of commodities," and a considerable proportion of the 5,052,-000*l.* classified as miscellaneous taxes do, as indeed is obvious, affect the interests of the owners of property in diverse degrees according to the nature of their property, and also affect the distribution of the capital of the community between the various forms of property, it seems almost unnecessary to criticise the Table in further detail. I will add, however, that it seems very extraordinary to treat the 1*l.* which I pay to the income tax collector on receiving 30*l.* for a term's lectures as a "tax levied in respect of income derived from personal exertion," and then to say that the penny stamp I put on the receipt is a "tax on non-rateable property." And how is it that the receipt stamp paid for by my landlord when I pay my rent, is a tax on non-rateable property?

3. Many definitions of the word "tax" have been proposed, but I know of none which would include just so much of the Post Office revenue as happens to be in excess of the amount expended in the year and no more.

I believe that the desire to reckon this amount and no more as a tax, arises from a somewhat dim impression that it is the sum which the State exacts in excess of what a private company, without any legal or natural monopoly, would have to be satisfied with for performing the same services.[6] But it is not. In the first place, such a private company would expect and receive about 3 per cent on its capital in addition to the mere working expenses. We do not know what the capital of the Post Office is, but it must be very great, seeing that all the more important offices are owned in fee simple. Secondly, a company would raise new capital for new buildings and the purchase of more land instead of defraying the expense as if it were current working expenditure. Thirdly, a company would not "encourage thrift" by giving away upwards of 700,000*l.* a year to the depositors in the savings bank, by paying $2\frac{1}{2}$ per cent on deposits which are invested in a stock which yields less than 2 per cent.[7] Fourthly, in all sorts of ways the Post Office is not conducted as a commercial enterprise would be. For example, it spends more than a company would do in the less profitable districts.

The only argument I know of in favour of treating the so-called "net revenue" alone as a tax, thus breaks down. If any part of the gross revenue is a tax, the whole must be.

Whether the gross revenue is called a tax or not, does not strike me as being a very important question. The State revenues which are always called taxes do not appear to me to be divided by any sharp line from those which are never called taxes. If the Crown happens to have con-

---

[6] I think this is implied in Sir E. W. Hamilton's remark (*Memorandum*, p. 37) that "the amount actually expended by the State represents direct and immediate service rendered to those who write letters or send telegrams." It would be at least equally true to say that the amount received by the State represents direct service rendered. If I put a letter in the pillar box rather than walk half a mile to deliver it by hand, it is clear that I value the service rendered at one penny at least, and if its true value is to be taken as less than a penny, it must be assumed that someone would have carried the letter for less than a penny if the Post Office monopoly had been absent. But to deal thoroughly with this question it would be necessary to enter on a discussion of the Austrian theory of value and Marshall's conception of "consumer's rent."

[7] The loss does not appear in the savings bank accounts; but that is the fault of the accounts. The subsidy to depositors is paid out of the interest received by the savings bank on a fund which is the result of profitable banking in previous years, and on which present depositors have no claim.

fiscated some pretender's land in the middle ages, and still holds that land, no one calls the rent of it a tax. If the Crown by the same or similar means happens to possess some manorial right or a rent-charge on some parcel of land, no one calls that a tax. But the unredeemed portion of the charges on the parishes imposed by Parliament in the seventeenth and fixed in the eighteenth century is the "land tax." Similarly, in local finance, though receipts of all kinds are very properly included in the *Annual Local Taxation Returns,* no one calls the local authority's revenue from lands and houses or even gasworks "taxes" or "rates." About the revenue from waterworks there is occasionally a little hesitation; people are apt to say that the "water rate is not a rate," or something absurd of that kind. The revenue levied for the collection of house refuse and the disposal of sewage, on the other hand, is always called a rate and regarded as a tax. Obviously, whether a particular form of revenue is called a tax or not is only a question of degree. The water rate is more a tax than the bill for gas, partly because it is generally more difficult to dispense with the public water supply than with gas, and partly because the quantity of water taken is not measured, the payment being usually regulated by various standards in combination, such as the value of the house, number of water-closets, baths, and garden taps.

In considering the "equity of taxation" it is not desirable to adopt any narrow view of the meaning of taxation, since the action of the State must be considered as a whole. I should therefore not be inclined to exclude the whole or any part of the Post Office gross revenue from the present inquiry.

I think there is no reason for supposing that Post Office charges affect different kinds of property unequally to any extent which can be appreciated or discovered. They may, therefore, be classified along with the income tax, death duties, &c.

4. "What is equity?" is a question which has exercised the minds of philosophers for many ages, and is likely to do so for many more. It will not be finally settled, it is safe to say, by the present or any other Royal Commission. The ideas of mankind (the genus to which, after all, the species of philosophers belongs) have changed and will change, and moreover these changes do not take place at exactly the same dates in all portions of the world. But this Commission, fortunately, is not appointed to lay down rules of equity for the taxation of the inhabitants (if any) of Jupiter and Saturn, but to point out where the existing system of raising public revenues in the United Kingdom is not in accordance with the idea of equity which prevails in the United Kingdom at the end of the nineteenth century.

It will be asked at once, "Is there any 'prevailing idea of equity' as to the raising of public revenue in the United Kingdom? Are not the opinions of different classes and interests so divergent that it is hopeless to expect general agreement in any conclusions?" It is, doubtless, true that nothing can be laid down on the subject which will not be vigorously denied by some philosopher or some professor of economics. But there are, I believe, several generalisations which will be agreed to either cheerfully or with no very great reluctance by at least nine-tenths of those who are capable of understanding them.

(i) The first of these generalisations is that when a particular means of raising public revenue, *coupled with a particular way of expending that revenue*, cannot be supposed to affect the distribution of wealth between individuals in the sense of making it different from what it would be in the absence of such State action, the question of equity does not arise at all.

If, for example, it is found that of three suburban residents Smith pays a private individual 6*d.* a week to come and remove his house refuse, Jones pays him 5*d.* a week, and Robinson 3*d.*, and then the State, in the person of an extending "urban district," steps in and takes over the business of dust-collection, performing it no better and no worse than it was performed before, and charging Smith, Jones, and Robinson a penny in the £ on their houses, which are rated at 312*l.*, 260*l.*, and 156*l.*, then no question of equity can be raised as between Smith, Jones, and Robinson. The position of each compared with that of the others remains exactly as it was, and it will not occur to them as ordinary persons to allege that the fact of the State having for the general convenience taken over a particular business is a reason for altering the distribution of wealth between them. This example is typical of the whole mass of expenditure which is now usually called "beneficial," in contradistinction to "onerous" expenditure. It is true, of course, that in no one case is what may be called the "private enterprise cost" of a particular service exactly proportionate to the rateable values of all the property in the district. It is certain that with regard to dust collection, taken apart from other municipal services, rateable value does not form anything like an exact standard. But with regard to all the various municipal services of a "beneficial" character taken together, it forms as exact a standard as any which can be obtained consistently with performing the services economically. To charge accurately for dust collection, a local authority would have to send round with each cart a weighing machine to get the weight, a dry measure to get the bulk, and a smellometer to get the offensiveness. It would have to keep each person's refuse separate, so that account might be taken of the value of any special articles in it. A departmental committee of the Local Government Board would sit from time to time to determine whether pounds avoirdupois should be multiplied by cubic feet or whether the cubic root of the pounds should be multiplied by the square root of the feet. Minute account keeping of this kind prevailed in the great houses of the Middle Ages, and survives in the kitchens and butteries of some Oxford colleges, where toast and water is charged $\frac{1}{4}d.$, but is totally unsuitable to modern civilisation. Taking the various "beneficial" services together, the rateable value of the property is a sufficiently accurate standard. It was not adopted by any sudden resolution of the legislature on the recommendation of a Commission advised by experts, but has been gradually adopted all over the country by the spontaneous desire of the persons chiefly affected. In some cases other standards still survive. For example, though in many towns the local authority cleans the pavements and the cost is thus borne in proportion to rateable value, in others the occupier of each house is expected to clean the piece before his own premises, and the cost is thus borne in proportion to length of frontage multiplied by liability to splashing from the roadway. There is no probability that a change which has been accomplished so gradually and so universally as the abandonment of the old standards in favour of the standard of rateable value is regarded by any considerable proportion of the persons concerned as inequitable.

(ii) The second generalisation is that when a particular means of raising public revenue coupled with a particular way of expending that revenue, does affect the distribution of wealth between individuals, it will be inequitable if it causes the distribution to be more unequal.

The average or ordinary person holds vaguely in his mind three different and wholly inconsistent principles with regard to the distribution of wealth. He believes:

a) That incomes should be equal, with some modifications to meet differences of need.
b) That incomes should be proportionate to moral merit.
c) That incomes should be proportioned to the value of the services rendered by the receiver.

On some occasions he follows almost exclusively one or other of these three conflicting principles. Adrift in a ship's boat on the Atlantic, or in charge of the administration of a hospital, he follows the first or communist principle. In his almsgiving to individuals he follows the second, which we may call the day-nursery principle. In his ordinary business transactions he adopts the third principle. But in regard to the raising and expending of public revenue he wavers between the three.

Now it happens that a man wavering between these three principles is certain to regard any action of the State which will increase the existing inequality of wealth as inequitable. Such action will obviously be inconsistent with the first principle. It will, if general in its operation, be inconsistent with the second principle, since there is no reason at all for believing that the rich as a class are more meritorious in as great a degree as they are richer than the poor. It will also, if general in its operation, be inconsistent with the third principle, because the very rich are very rich as a class, not so much in consequence of any services performed by themselves, as in consequence of inheriting property. Any action of the State, therefore, which increases the existing inequality of wealth, except in a very partial and unusual way, will offend the ordinary person's conception of equity in distribution, no matter which of his three principles happens at the time to have most prominence in his mind.

Whether this is, so far as it goes, a correct account of the origin of the idea that it is inequitable to cause greater inequality by State action or not, there is no doubt about the fact that State action causing greater inequality is almost universally regarded as inequitable. To show that, on certain principles, it would be necessary to tax the rich at a lower percentage on income than the poor is considered a *reductio ad absurdum* of those principles.[8]

(iii) The third generalisation is that State action which reduces inequality of wealth will be inequitable unless the reduction is carried out in a fair and proportionate manner. To this generalisation universal assent will be given, except by land nationalisers. It means that no inequality of treatment shall be meted out as between individuals possessing similar amounts of wealth; to tax Sir Gorgius Midas 10,000*l.* specifically for the benefit of Mr. W. Sikes would diminish the inequality of wealth, and yet would be flagrantly unjust. This may seem an absurd example, but it is only a strong case. If a more likely one is required, take the proposal of land nationalisers for a special tax on a particular form of property, which, in this country, at any rate, is so largely held by the wealthy, that a special tax on it would probably reduce inequality. The proposal is by the ordinary person very rightly considered unjust, because it deducts unequal amounts from A, who has 10,000*l.* worth of land, and from B, who has, say, 10,000*l.* worth of ships.

---

[8] Bastable, "Public Finance," Bk. III, Ch. iii, § 2, 2nd Ed., p. 284.

(iv) The fourth generalisation is one in which all except revolutionary socialists agree. It is that it is inequitable to disappoint legitimate expectations. Of course, the difficulty here is to say what are legitimate expectations, and it is quite hopeless to expect any two persons to agree absolutely as to where legitimate expectations end and illegitimate expectations begin. It is and must remain merely a question of degree. But the generalisation is not useless. It explains to a great extent the otherwise curious phenomenon that the ordinary person is so much guided in his opinion as to the equity of new progressive taxation by the nature of the scale chosen. The establishment of a slowly rising scale, which never reaches any very large percentage on any actual income or estate, is not considered inequitable by many persons who would consider a quickly rising scale, reaching a very high percentage, grossly inequitable. The truth is that the inequity is measured by the disappointment of the persons made subject to the tax. The millionaire, most other people think, ought not to have expected to continue to be taxed only at the same percentage as the man with 10,000*l.*, but nearly everyone will admit that he might legitimately expect not to be taxed at a percentage twenty times as high. Whether it was legitimate or illegitimate for him not to expect to be taxed twice as high is a question on which opinions are divided more equally.

There are, then, four tests to be applied in the consideration of the equity of alterations in means of raising and ways of spending public revenue:

a) Will the change make any difference in the distribution of wealth? If not, whether it should be introduced or not is purely a question of production, not of equity.

b) Will the difference in distribution be in the direction of greater or less equality in distribution? If in the direction of greater inequality, it is inequitable.

c) Will the greater equality in the distribution of wealth be brought about without unfairness as between the various individuals who lose by the change and as between the various individuals who gain by it? If not, it is inequitable.

d) Will the greater equality, brought about in a fair and proportionate manner, stop short of disappointing what are regarded as the legitimate expectations of the rich?

A proposal which passes these four cumulative tests may of course be inexpedient, but it will satisfy the public conscience as an equitable measure.

5. It is usual in economic and financial treatises, as well as in parlia-

mentary and royal inquiries, to plunge into the question of the primary and ultimate incidence of taxation, without considering at all what is meant by "incidence." But this is highly dangerous.

We do not talk of the "incidence" of the cost of papering and painting houses, or of the cost of supplying a family with butcher's meat. If the price of wheat goes up owing to a bad season, we do not discuss the incidence of the addition to the price caused by the bad season. But if the cost of sewage disposal is raised (no matter whether it is by some new requirement of the Mersey and Irwell Joint Committee, or by an earthquake or some other "act of God"), or if a frontier war brings about an increase of the tax on beer, we immediately find ourselves engaged in foggy discussions about incidence. One friend has suggested that the reason why we discuss the incidence of taxes, and not the incidence of any other kind of expense, is that, as taxes can be more easily altered by public authority than any other expenses, the question of their incidence is of more practical interest than the question of the incidence of a wet August or an earthquake, and that the appropriation of a special term for use in connexion with taxes is the result of the greater practical interest. Another says that the reason is that the rain falls alike on the just and the unjust, but that legislators intend taxes to fall on certain classes of persons, and, as a matter of fact, they always fall on other classes.

However this may be, I have no doubt that it is desirable to eschew the use of the term "incidence" of taxation. It unduly restricts inquiries into the justice and expediency of taxes, since it is always held that the "real incidence" of a tax is upon the persons who ultimately pay or provide the money for the tax. But, as I have already hinted (Question 1), persons who pay a tax are often less injured by its imposition than those who pay no portion of it. The man who goes two miles out of his way daily to avoid a bridge toll would be more benefited by the freeing of the bridge than most of those who pay the toll. It is, therefore, far better to consider the *effects* of taxation. By using this more general term, we shall find it easier to avoid the usual mistake of supposing that taxes are subject to an economics of their own, instead of having effects just like any other expense. We shall also be less likely to lose our way by attempting to travel by short cuts.

The true question then, I take to be, "Can you offer any suggestions which would assist the Commission in following out the effects of taxation?"

I would suggest:

(i) That the effect of a tax can only be discovered by supposing it either (1) newly-imposed or increased, or (2) abolished or reduced. This is so obvious that I will not argue it. I only mention it because when the equity of a tax is being considered, differences of opinion constantly arise and fail to make themselves understood owing to the fact that one side is considering the tax when newly imposed, and the other is considering what would happen if it were abolished. To take an example, the present land tax would be a most inequitable tax to impose, since it would not treat holders of equal amounts of property equally, and would disappoint legitimate expectations; but after it has been imposed for one or two centuries, and both the properties subject to it and those not subject to it have been bought and sold over and over again, always on the assumption that it would continue, it would be inequitable to abolish it, since the abolition would not treat holders of equal amounts of property equally.

(ii) That "strong cases" should always be taken. It is no use to inquire what is the effect of adding a $\frac{1}{2}d.$ in the £ to the rates of Oxford. Ask rather what would be the effect of raising the rate from 3s. to 8s., or what would be the effect if a benevolent millionaire presented the city with property which would bring in enough income to pay all present expenses and return the ratepayers 1s. in the £ as well. Of course, those who have constructed theories about "economic friction" will cry out against this course, but they will do so because the shoe pinches. Nothing is more ludicrous than the argument that because a drop makes no perceptible difference in a big bucket it has produced no effect.[9] The little changes which occur in practice obviously must have just the same effect in kind, though not in degree, as the great changes which may be properly and conveniently imagined for the purpose of illustration and argument.

(iii) That as no tax is levied all over the world at the same rate, all existing taxation is local, i.e., levied in different places on different principles or at different rates. The local areas differ enormously in size, the United States being 3,500,000 square miles in area, and Furnival's Inn one acre. The larger the area and the more peculiar the language, religion, and manners which prevail in it, the more nearly is it safe to ignore the local character of its taxation, but in no case can it be altogether ignored. The areas dealt with by the Commission are small, and their populations are divided from each other in most cases by no differences of language, religion, or manners. Consequently the local character of the taxation is all-important, and any attempt to consider the effects of the taxes as if they were universal instead of local can only lead to misappre-

---

[9] The savants who disputed as to the reason why the addition of the fish to the bucket of water made no difference had a sprat rather than a whale in their minds.

hension and confusion. The pernicious practice of taking averages of local rates is to be condemned on this ground. If local rates were all at the average instead of being, as they are, very much lower in some cases, very much higher in others, and substantially different in nearly all, then almost everything with regard to the effects of the taxation would be different from what it actually is. Especially in considering the equity of taxation, is it absurd to begin by assuming that people in different places are all taxed at the same rate, when, as a matter of fact, they are not.

6. (*a* to *c*.) I do not care to accept the classification suggested in subquestions (*a*), (*b*), and (*c*). It is more convenient to deal with all these taxes together. In any case it would not be desirable to classify trade premises along with houses separately from agricultural land, which is the trade premises of the farmer.

To attempt to take short cuts in a matter of this kind only leads to waste of time, and I shall therefore approach the end in view in what will appear at first sight an unnecessarily roundabout way.

I shall ask first what is the effect of a uniform and universal *ad valorem* tax on all kinds of property levied periodically for unproductive purposes either on the true capital value or the true annual value of the property. Let us not trouble ourselves with the practical question whether such a tax has ever existed or ever can exist; it is quite conceivable that it might exist in a world where all were honest, and such a world is imaginable, though not likely to be known for some time, at any rate.

Let us suppose that this tax is now imposed for the first time, and levied directly from the owners. There appears to be no reason for supposing that they will be able *at once* to charge more for the productive contribution (as Wieser calls it) of their capital than they could before. But immediately one or both of two things must happen. The owners must curtail either their expenditure or their savings. If they curtail their expenditure only, all that happens is that the State now spends unproductively what they spent before. If, however, they curtail their savings, two results will follow, (1) the future produce will be less per head, and (2) the division of that lessened produce will be effected on terms not so advantageous to the worker. In the first case, the Government expenditure, to defray which the tax was levied, would damage nobody but the owners of property. In the second case the evil effect would be felt by the whole community. As a matter of fact, of course, the owners would curtail both their expenditure and their savings; the evil of the expenditure would consequently be felt both by them and the rest of the community, but would be felt somewhat more lightly by the rest of the community than if it had all been met by a curtailment of owners' savings. On the whole, therefore, it seems probable that the effect of a universal *ad valorem* property tax would not be very substantially different from that of a universal income-tax.

Now let us consider the effect of a universal uniform tax on some one particular class of property, the smaller the better, let us say 2*s*. in the £ on the capital value of bicycles. Now here, if we think only of the majority of cyclists who own their own machines, we will at once declare that "the incidence" of this tax is on the owners of bicycles. But when we recollect that large numbers of machines are kept for hiring out, we begin to question this conclusion. We see that though he would not be able to do so at the very first, the cycle-shop man would very soon be able to charge hirers of machines more than he could before the imposition of the tax, since the relative advantages of hiring and purchase would be altered as soon as the purchaser was made subject to a tax which the hirer is not asked to pay directly. We should then alter our previous opinion, and say that "the incidence" of the tax was on, not the owner, at any rate *quâ* owner, but upon the consumer, or more accurately, the user of bicycles, and the people who benefit (*e.g.*, by having their errands done cheaper) by the fact that other people use bicycles. Then, reflecting a little more, we should see that whatever may be the case with the "incidence" of the tax, its effect reaches not only to those who use bicycles and benefit because other people use them, but also to those who would have used bicycles or would have benefited by other people using them if the obstruction of the tax had not intervened. This last class, of course, has kept its money and been able to spend it in some other way, but not to so great advantage.

To take as another example the one mentioned in sub-question (*a*), let us suppose that there has hitherto been no house tax, and that a universal tax of 5*s*. in the £ for unproductive purposes is placed on all dwelling-houses and levied from the occupiers. Let us suppose also that the occupiers are on quarterly tenancies, all of which expire between the passing of the Act and its coming into force. The immediate effect must be a fall in house rent. All occupiers must restrict either their expenditure or their savings in some direction, and enough of them will try to reduce their expenditure in rent-plus-house-tax to make a great diminution in the demand for house room. As the number of houses has not yet been altered by the tax, the supply remains the same, and consequently the price must be reduced. But this reduction of rent, of course, reduces the capital value of houses; the capital value being reduced, some professional builders retire from the business and others become bankrupt, and the supply of houses is consequently reduced. Building stops, or proceeds at a slower rate, until building profits are restored to the ordinary level by a rise of house rent and the capital value of houses. The occupiers then have to pay more for the same accommodation, or to be content with worse accommodation for the same money.

It would appear from this that while a tax on all kinds of property is what is sometimes called "diffused" over the whole community, a tax on some one particular class of property is damaging to the consumers or enjoyers of the commodity obtained by the use of that kind of property, and not to the owners of it, except, of course, in so far as they are consumers of it. The untrained mind probably often accepts the conclusion as it stands, but the more scientific inquirer sees a contradiction. "If," he points out, "this is so, you could get a different result by taxing each class of property separately from that which you get by taxing them all together in one operation, which is absurd." To meet this perfectly sound objection, the statement with regard to the effect of a tax on a particular class of property requires amendment. Something has been omitted, which, though of trifling importance in the case of a tax on a small class of property, becomes of more and more importance as the magnitude of the class or the number of the classes taxed increases. This is the fact that a tax which checks the investment of capital in any one form of property necessarily encourages investment in other forms. If less goes into one form, there will be more to put into other forms. Now if the amount invested in bicycles is reduced, the extra amount put into other forms of property and spread over the whole field will have so trifling an effect that we treat it as inappreciable, and say nothing about it. But the more of the total property made liable to the tax, the more important will the increased flow into other forms of property become. The extra influx, whether small or great, of course tends to decrease the return to capital in the untaxed forms of property. Consequently a tax on a particular form of property does damage the owners of property in general as well as the consumers of the commodity connected with the particular class of property.

For several reasons unnecessary to mention here,[10] local taxation in this country is taxation of immovables, and it is therefore desirable to consider the particular case of the effect of a universal uniform tax on all immovable property. Such a tax must differ very little in its effect on distribution from a universal uniform tax on all kinds of property. It

---

[10] *See* my "History of Local Rates in England," pp. 132–34 and *passim*. For the same reasons State taxation in the United States is tending in the same direction; *see* the Report of the Massachusetts Commission on Taxation just published (December, 1897).

would, of course, have the effect of discouraging the investment of capital in immovable, and encouraging investment in movable property, so that if there are any consumers who consume a disproportionately large amount of products which require for their production the use of disproportionately large amounts of immovable as compared with movable property, that class of consumers would suffer more than others. But there is little evidence of the existence of such a class, so that it may be supposed a universal uniform tax on all immovables for unproductive purposes would "diffuse" the burden of the unproductive expenditure over the whole community approximately in proportion to income enjoyed.

Now let us ask what difference will be occasioned by the tax on all immovables being local, *i.e.*, levied at different rates in different places between which migration of persons and property is possible. Suppose, for example, that the tax instead of being 2*s*. in the £ everywhere, is 6*d*. in one group of districts, 1*s*. in another, 3*s*. in a third, and 3*s*. 6*d*. in a fourth group, the total raised being the same as if all were taxed at 2*s*.

The important fact here is that somehow or other in spite of the difference of rate from 3*s*. 6*d*. down to 6*d*., the return to the marginal investment of capital will be the same in all these districts. Some people, of course, are fools enough to do anything, but there are not enough fools to affect the matter. The action of the people who do affect it is guided by common sense, and common sense tells the investor not to invest in a place where the return to capital is 3 per cent less 3*s*. 6*d*. in the £, when he can invest in a place where the return is 3 per cent less 6*d*. in the £.

How, then, is the equality of return brought about? The first answer that suggests itself to the rent-paying householder or farmer is that he, the occupier, equalises the return to capital by paying more in the highly rated than in the low rated places.

But this answer is obviously absurd. The occupiers do not as a body, move from one place to another after the manner of the ancient Israelites, but enough of them do or can move to prevent any such result. That the result does not actually occur is proved by the fact that an acute business man acquainted with every material circumstance may think it just as advantageous to occupy premises in some place where the rates for unproductive purposes are 3*s*. 6*d*., as in some other place where they are 6*d*. in the £. Occupiers are clearly just as well off in places where the rates for unproductive purposes have long been high as in places where they have long been low.

The second answer which suggests itself is that the consumers equalise the return by paying more for commodities in the high rated than in the low rated places. This answer is still more obviously absurd than the last. People nowadays can get many commodities from almost anywhere, and will not, therefore, pay more for them if they come from a producer or distributor who carries on his business in a high rated district. We constantly find people living in low rated districts procuring things by parcel post from high rated districts.

The true answer is that the equalisation of the returns to investment is effected by the investment of capital in immovables being stayed a little higher up in the scale in the high rated than in the low rated districts. Everywhere the most profitable known investments are chosen first, and the more capital there is to invest the lower down in the scale of profit will investment necessarily go. Investment in immovables will stop a little sooner in the high rated than in the low rated places, so that the return to the last investment may be the same everywhere in spite of the difference in the tax. We have, let us say, 10,000 houses in Oxford, where the rates are 3s. 8d., and 20,000 of the same size in Norwich, where the rates are about 9s. Builders make equal profits in the two places simply because building is carried exactly to that pitch where the profits are equal, taking into account that the different rates will have to be paid on the houses. Similarly in two rural districts, in one of which rates are double what they are in the other, the returns to the last investment in agricultural improvement will be the same simply because investment in agricultural improvements is carried exactly to that pitch in each where the returns are the same after allowing for the difference in taxation.

Everything which tends to discourage the investment of capital in immovable property in a district tends to diminish the demand for "unimproved land" or space in that district, and this diminution in the value of space of course mitigates the effect of the discouragement to investment.

The consequence then, so far as distribution is concerned, of rates being for unproductive purposes higher in one place than another is to cause less creatable immovable property to exist in the high rated and more in the low rated, and to make the value of the land lower in the high rated and higher in the low rated places than would be the case if the rates were equal in all places.

The effect of inequality of rates for unproductive purposes, so far as production is concerned, is to diminish the productiveness of industry by causing an uneconomical distribution of capital between the various districts.

The effect of rates for productive purposes is the same as the effect of any other payment for productive purposes. It is all the same to me whether I pay a "water company" or a "local authority" for my water, and whether I pay a private individual or an inspector of nuisances to remove my house refuse, provided that I pay the same in both cases, and have the work equally well done. It is all the same to the ratepayers in general if they pay to lenders as much interest as would have been obtained by private individuals doing the work under a system of private enterprise. I have endeavoured to show, in the *Economic Journal*, Vol. V, pp. 31, 32, that any equalisation of rates for purposes productive of special benefit to the particular locality would be extremely undesirable, from the point of view of production. It would also be unjust, inasmuch as there is no reason for benefiting persons who happen to own particular localities at the expense of others. If, for example, the cost of sewering and sewage disposal were to be paid from a national fund, the creation of towns in situations difficult to drain and distant from the sea would be encouraged, and the owners of land in these situations benefited, while the creation of towns in situations easy to drain and on the sea coast would be discouraged, and the owners of land in these situations damaged.

(*d.*) "Taxes on the transfer of property," *ad valorem*, are too much like "taxes on property" to be worth separate discussion. A "tax on property" is levied at regular intervals, a "tax on the transfer of property" at irregular intervals. The regular tax is, of course, to be preferred. Taxes on the transfer of property not *ad valorem*, as, *e.g.*, receipt stamps, when the charge is the same, no matter how great the property involved (after 2*l.*), are relics of barbarism, so capricious in their effect that it would be a waste of time to consider them seriously, the amount involved being so small.

(*e.*) I doubt if I understand this question. A tax on the profits of a particular trade would have the same effects as a tax on the particular property used in that particular trade. A tax on all trade profits would be an income tax, or something very like it. What is "trade"?

(*f.*) Death duties, again, are taxes on all kinds of property, levied at irregular intervals, and their effect is substantially the same as taxes on all kinds of property levied at irregular intervals. Perhaps, on account of a certain obvious peculiarity of the time at which they occur, they discourage accumulation somewhat less than annual taxes, and, consequently, are rather more favourable to the non-propertied class. (*See above* under *a.* to *c.*) If they are graduated, they necessarily tend to cause greater equality of wealth.

7. My views on this subject will be found at length in the *Economic*

Journal, January, 1895 (pp. 22–34), and the *National Review*, November, 1896. The gist of the matter is that the *raisons d'être* of local taxation are—

a) To secure economical and efficient local administration.
b) To secure economical distribution of population and capital.

The services which should be charged on local taxation for the first only of these two reasons, vary from time to time. The central Government of the United Kingdom is far more likely now to do better than local authorities in regard to many services which in the middle ages were better performed by small local authorities.

The services which should be paid for out of local taxation for the second of the two reasons, as well as for the first, are all such as tend to increase the value of the fixed property in the particular locality where they take place. If these were paid for by general taxation, towns would grow up with a disregard of advantageousness of situation which would be extremely hampering to the productiveness of industry. (*See above* under Question 6, *a* to *c*, last paragraph.)

8. When a service is paid for out of local taxation, merely because of the first of the two reasons mentioned in the answer to Question 7, the central government should endeavour to secure that no inequalities of rating for it should be allowed to exist, except such as are necessary in order to secure good management. Grants from the central Government, if made at all, ought to be directed towards reducing the inequalities of this portion of local taxation.

No grant ought to be made for purposes which, when accomplished, and not counterbalanced by a rate, raise the value of property.

Any grants made ought to be made openly, and not by metaphorical ear-marking, which confuses the accounts both of the central and local governments. (*See below*, Question 14, last paragraph and note.)

9. Local rates ought not to be divided between owners and occupiers, but should be charged on either the owners or the occupiers. At present, in case of low-priced houses in towns, it is almost universal to charge the owner. In all other cases the occupier is charged. This is a very sensible arrangement. It is better to take the rate from the person most immediately and directly affected by its expenditure whenever you can get it from that person. This is possible whenever the occupier is a "substantial man." When he is not substantial, you must be content to take it from the owner.

So much of the rates as is raised to pay off capital expenditure ought, strictly speaking, to be paid by the owners, since it is payment for a remote benefit (that of being free from the payment of interest on the loan raised for the capital expenditure).

In the case of new occupiers, the payment will be allowed for just like any other disadvantage, but some injustice is done to old occupiers unable to revise their bargains with their landlords if new and unforeseen payments for capital expenditure are saddled upon them. The amount involved, however, is so small that it is perhaps scarcely worth while to apply the remedy, which is the creation of redeemable rent charges for the payment of interest on loans for capital expenditure.[11]

10. Ground values should not be separately rated. To rate them separately would only introduce confusion, with no counterbalancing advantage whatever.

11. (*a.*) and (*b.*) The increase of an old rate, or (which is exactly the same thing), the imposition of a new rate, in any particular locality, will diminish rent in that locality by making the competition for land and other property which is not moveable and not quickly alterable in quantity less than it otherwise would be.

(*c.*) The reduction or abolition of a rate would have the contrary effect.

12. If occupiers were allowed to deduct either rates, or the cost of getting their hair cut, or any other expense, from their rents, then their rents would be that much higher.

If they were not allowed to deduct the income tax their rents would be that much lower.

13. (*a.*) This system can obviously only be applied where the properties form distinct units. I imagine that in practice it is only applied to houses and perhaps other buildings.

Rating the more expensive houses at a higher percentage must discourage to some extent the building of such houses. Where such a system has been long in operation, the supply of houses of different values will have accommodated itself exactly to the demand.

I do not feel sure whether the difference in the number of houses in each division of the scale could be called "an effect upon rent."

(*b.*) When a certain kind of property is partially exempted from the general rate, the rent of that kind of property will be higher than it otherwise would be, provided that, and in so far as, that kind of property is

---

11 The occupier receives the benefit of the things provided by the capital expenditure till the conclusion of his term of tenancy, and should therefore pay the interest on the capital. But it is no advantage to him that the capital should be sunk or written off. Therefore, let a charge be created which he has to pay during his term and let the owner redeem the charge afterwards.

insusceptible of increase by human exertion. Obviously, if the property is susceptible of increase, as, *e.g.*, houses apart from sites of houses, the exemption from rating will encourage investment of capital in that form of property till competition reduces its value to the landlord. But if the property is not susceptible of increase, as, *e.g.*, land considered apart from buildings, fences, artificial fertility, and so on, it is equally obvious that the exemption will cause the rent to be higher than it otherwise would be.

14. It would be easy to suggest other means of raising revenue for local purposes, but it would be difficult to suggest any better means than rates on all kinds of immovable property without any exceptions or exemptions. One point which should not be overlooked is, that most feasible means of raising revenue locally have very much the same effects as rates. An octroi, for example, will reduce the desirability of a town as a place for the investment of capital and a place of residence just as a rate does.

It is probable that local authorities would often find new and harmless ways of raising revenue if it were not for a superstition which prevails in many quarters that it is wicked for an authority to make a profit, even up to such an extent as is necessary to pay ordinary interest on the capital originally expended. This superstition prevails even at the Board of Trade, which interfered a few years ago to prevent the borough of Bournemouth from making a profit out of the landing of excursionists on its pier, alleging that it was a principle with the Board that local authorities were not to make a profit out of "navigation." Thus municipal enterprise is prevented from being profitable and then denounced as a failure.[12]

If the Inhabited House Duty is to be maintained, it should be given to the local authorities in place of some of the present subsidies, but I should much prefer to see it abolished. The advantage it gives to persons who choose to live in lodgings and hotels is indefensible, and its scale of graduation makes it a progressive tax on large families in the very class from which it is most desirable the population of the country should be recruited.

It is probably unnecessary to argue against the outrageous proposal that the land tax should be given to local authorities. They might as well ask for the Crown lands which happen to be situate within their jurisdiction. In order to make it clear even to the person who has to pay it that the land tax has by prescription (the foundation of all property in land)

---

12 In "The State in relation to Trade," 1883, p. 80, Lord Farrer says that Liverpool, as owner of the Liverpool docks, "taxed the trade of the country for its own benefit." But no one says that "Bristol has for many years been unselfishly subsidising the trade of the country."

become property of the State, it would be well to put a stop to further re-assessments and make the tax a permanent fixed charge on the land. The tax ceased to be re-assessable between parishes more than a century ago, and it is time the final step was taken.

As, I presume, the Commission is considering proposals for economising expenditure as well as for raising revenue, it may be desirable here to draw attention to the enormous waste which results from the insistence of the Treasury on usurious rates of interest for loans to local authorities, and the policy of the Local Government Board, which compels, or at any rate induces, local authorities to borrow money and invest it at a lower rate of interest than that which they have to pay.

Disguise it in the form of paper "terminable annuities" payable from the waistcoat pocket to the breeches pocket as best the Treasury may, there is no denying the fact that in one way or another (by the Post Office or the Supreme Court of Judicature, or some other body), seven millions of consols are bought for the nation every year at present at a large premium, which reduces the saving of true annual charge from $2\frac{3}{4}$ to less than 2 per cent.

At the same time perfectly solvent local authorities are borrowing in the open market from the public at above 2*l.* 13*s.* per cent and paying in addition 1*s.* to a bank for management and 1*s.* for stamp duty composition. In the name of common sense then, why cannot the Treasury lend at $2\frac{1}{2}$ per cent or even $2\frac{1}{4}$ instead of buying consols, and save 14*s.* per cent to the nation and the local authorities combined? Instead of doing so, it maintains a scale of rates[13] which deter all the most solvent borrowers from applying to the Public Works Loan Board.

The policy of the Local Government Board causes local authorities to borrow when it would be more profitable for them to part with their investments, partly in consequence of insistence on the absurd ear-marking of different moneys which is required by the legislation of 1875 and 1888,[14] and more largely by a method of calculating the amounts in sink-

---

[13] The scale embodies a futile attempt to discourage borrowing for long terms. Elective local authorities care little for a remote future, and consequently regard nothing but the annual payment (*i.e.*, interest plus sinking fund), and the lower amount charged for interest on short loans does not nearly counterbalance the larger amount required for sinking fund. Consequently they invariably apply for the longest term they think the Local Government Board is the least likely to disallow.

[14] The most important instance of this system is the separation of the Exchequer contribution account, the borough fund, and the general district account. There is no reason at all why the Exchequer contribution should not be paid direct into the borough fund, and the chief result of the present arrangement is to make some people imagine that the central Government still pays half the cost of pay and clothing of the police as before 1888. The only reason for keeping the borough fund and the general district account apart is that the borough rate was before the Agricultural Rates Act leviable on the full annual value of

ing funds which discourages rate-raising bodies from purchasing their own or any stock which stands at a premium. The consequence is that local authorities all take in each others' washing—they borrow with one hand and invest sinking funds, police pension funds, and other funds in a loan to some other authority, usually overlooking the fact that the stamp duty composition, the payment for management on stock issued, and the income tax on dividends or interest received on stock bought or loans made make a difference of 4s. per cent in favour of cancelling their own stock. The city of Oxford has, or lately had, about 32,000l. of consols and about 28,000l. invested in the stock of, or in loans to, Llandudno, Peterborough, Middlesbrough, Tynemouth, Wakefield, Thornaby-on-Tees; yet in all probability the city of Oxford will shortly issue another 40,000l. of Oxford Corporation stock. Instead of encouraging this course of conduct the Local Government Board should in every case require the local authority which obtains permission to borrow to show good reasons for borrowing from the public instead of using (as any private individual in a similar position would do in the absence of special reason to the contrary) their own funds.

15. My answers to the preceding questions will have shown to anyone who has done me the honour of reading them, that I take a very conservative view of the system of local taxation which evolved itself in this country down to 1896 without much interference from Parliament. I regard the allegations of injustice made by the urban occupier on the one hand, and the landed interest on the other, as equally unfounded.

But approval of the system of raising what ought to be local expenses

---

agricultural land, and is at present leviable on 50 per cent of that value, while the general district rate is only leviable on 25 per cent. But this is in practice of little importance. In many towns no borough rate and in some no general district rate is levied. In Oxford, in order to prevent the necessity of a borough rate, we keep the waterworks and the market (which bring in a sum equal to a rate of 4d. in the £ net) upon the borough fund, and put the library and school board (which cost 2d. in the £) upon the general district account. Yet, according to the rule, the former belong to the general district account, and the latter to the borough fund; and the Local Government Board, in publishing the Annual Local Taxation Returns so arranges them, thereby making our borough fund appear to have an annual deficiency of 8,000l. To satisfy the Local Government Board we have sometimes actually to personify the borough fund and the general district fund. One of my first duties as a member of the Oxford City Council was to serve on a committee which reported that the general district fund had built a new town hall on land belonging to the borough fund, and that it was "equitable" as well as "expedient," that the general district fund "should be deemed to be the lessee" of the town hall for 50 years at a ground rent of 1,500l. per annum, while the borough fund should be the tenant of the general district fund as regards certain parts of the building and pay the general district fund 800l. a year for them. At the end of the lease the borough fund, as ground landlord, will take possession of the whole. The difficulty experienced by the ordinary mind in maintaining sound finance when the accounts are encumbered by such an accumulation of fictitious payments and repayments need not be enlarged upon.

by local rates on all kinds of immovable property (levied from the occupiers, where the occupiers are substantial, and from the owners where they are not), by no means commits anyone to approval of the whole of the "present system" of local and (for the two must be considered together) national finance.

In the first place, supposing no question to arise as to what ought to be local, and what national, expenditure, the present system is unsatisfactory in regard to the absence of any impartial authority with the will as well as the power to change the local taxation areas whenever equity and expediency require it. That the central portion of a town should be in a local taxation area all by itself is bad enough, but that the various suburbs should each be in different taxation areas is much worse. In order to secure equity and economy every town should be treated as a whole. What is a town? In the vast majority of instances no difficulty arises in deciding whether a populous district is a town or the suburb of another town. No one, except, possibly, a town councillor of West Ham, believes that West Ham is not as integral a part of the economic town of London as Fulham or Woolwich. A man might live in Manchester for a year, and yet have entirely erroneous ideas as to what exactly was included in Salford without incurring any reproach for stupidity. Salford gets just as much and perhaps more benefit from the canal than Manchester, and pays no 1*s.* 8*d.* rate for it. Nearly every large town is divided into several areas for poor law taxation. Absurdities like these ought to be put an end to, whether the local authorities and the ratepayers desire a change or not. At present the principle of the Local Government Board seems to be that no alteration of any magnitude is to be effected unless both parties concerned agree to it, and as it nearly always happens that one of the two parties will at any rate gain less than the other, the difficulty of securing a change is enormous. If it were not for the fortunate fact that one political party in a town usually desires to annex one suburb and the other party another, the *morcellement* would be more ridiculous than it is.

Secondly, supposing the question of area settled, the present system is unsatisfactory inasmuch as there is no recognition of the *raisons d'être* of local taxation in the distribution between the various localities of the vast subsidies handed over by the national Government to local authorities, among whom, for the present purpose, I include voluntary school managers.

There is no denying the fact that the subsidies have been divided between the localities at haphazard.

Local authorities perform some services, *e.g.*, refuse and sewage removal, the benefit of which is almost confined to the locality. They perform other services, *e.g.*, the provision of police, which is of primary benefit to the locality, but is also of great benefit to the rest of the country and world. They perform a third set of services, *e.g.*, the provision of a night's board and lodging for vagrants, which are of no special benefit to the locality, but are of benefit to the community at large. The *administration* of these services is allotted to them by the State, because it is supposed that local knowledge and control is necessary for efficiency. The *duty of paying for* the administration of services which are of special benefit to the locality is placed upon the locality in order to secure the most economical distribution of capital and population over the country, as well as to secure economical administration. The duty of paying for the local administration of services which are of no special benefit to the locality is placed on the locality only in order to secure economical administration, and *it ought only to be placed on the locality to such an extent as is necessary in order to secure economical administration.*

If this principle were recognised, the subsidies would be distributed so as to equalise as far as is possible without removing the local authorities' motive for economy, the burden of the expenditure which is for the national benefit and not for the special benefit of the locality. In the distribution of the old subsidies before 1888 the principle was recognised, and it was attempted to carry it out by paying from the Exchequer half the cost of various services, it being hoped that the fact that the local authority had to pay the other half would prevent undue increase of expenditure. It is said that this hope was disappointed. At any rate, in 1888, Mr. Goschen proposed a plan the popular objection to which was that it would have made the local authorities too sparing in the administration of poor relief. This plan being rejected, the present system of division between administrative counties plus the county boroughs of the ancient county on the basis of the distribution which happened to prevail in 1887–88, and of division between each administrative county and the county boroughs of the ancient county on the basis of rateable value was adopted as a temporary measure, and now threatens to become as permanent as the seventeenth century distribution of the land tax.[15] Since then the condition of things has been made still worse by the haphazard distribution of the Agricultural Rates Act subsidy (which must in many cases pay not only for the whole loco-national expenditure, but also for a portion of the exclusively local expenditure, *e.g.*, that for local highways), and the voluntary schools grant, which is paid most largely to

---

[15] It is a land tax upside down. Instead of the locality paying a fixed sum to the State, the State pays a fixed sum (or, strictly speaking, a fixed proportion of a varying sum) to the locality.

those localities where the cost of education is lightest. On the other hand, the principle has been again recognised in the elaborate scale under which the additional grant to school boards has been made.

What steps should be taken to re-establish the correct principle? This is a question for others than supposed economic experts. I will only suggest that poor relief and education are the particular expenses which it is most desirable to equalise so far as that can be done without removing the motives for reasonable economy. I cannot believe that it passes the wit of man to re-arrange the apportionment of expenses in such a way as to effect this end.[16] If the whole of the subsidies, including the agricultural rates grant and the recent education grants, could not be used in this way, the Chancellor of the Exchequer might very conveniently get rid of the resulting surplus by abolishing or reducing as far as was necessary the house tax, the railway passenger tax, and some of the numerous and pernicious taxes on the transfer of property.

---

[16] Population, it should be observed, is not a good basis for the distribution of subsidies, since it inevitably leads to the falsification of the census, as was illustrated in the first census of London taken under the Equalisation of Rates Act (see *Economic Review*, Vol. VI, pp. 409–12), and is well-known to take place in the United States.

12

Introduction to *The Shifting and Incidence of Taxation**

By E. R. A. SELIGMAN

The problem of the incidence of taxation is one of the most neglected, as it is one of the most complicated, subjects in economic science. It has indeed been treated by many writers; but its discussion in scientific literature, as well as in everyday life, has frequently been marked by what Parieu calls the "simplicity of ignorance." Yet no topic in public finance is more important; for, in every system of taxation, the cardinal point is its influence on the community. Without a correct analysis of the incidence of a tax, no proper opinion can be formed as to its actual effect or its justice. It is, therefore, time for an attempt to be made not only to pass in review the theories hitherto advanced, but to contribute to the solution of some of the theoretic problems while paying special attention to the practical aspects of the discussion.

A word first as to the terminology. In the process of taxing, we must distinguish three conceptions. First, a tax may be imposed on some person; secondly, it may be transferred by him to a second person; thirdly, it may be ultimately borne by this second person or transferred to others by whom it is finally assumed. Thus the person who originally pays the tax may not be the one who bears its burden in last instance. The process of the transfer of a tax is known as the *shifting* of the tax, while the settlement of the burden on the ultimate taxpayer is called the *incidence* of the tax. The incidence of the tax is therefore the result of the shifting, and the real economic problem lies in the nature of the shiftings.

The English fiscal language is somewhat deficient in its nomenclature. While *incidence* conveys to the mind the notion of the ultimate result of the shifting, we have no word in common use to express the immediate result of the original imposition of the tax. "Assessment" of the tax looks upon the process from above downward; but what we need is a term to

---

* E. R. A. Seligman, *The Shifting and Incidence of Taxation*, 5th ed.

characterize the process as seen from below upward. The French and the Italians have the words *percussion, percussione,* to express this idea of the primary result of the assessment. They, therefore, logically term the shifting of the tax the *repercussion*[1] of taxation, the ultimate result of which is the incidence (*incidence, incidenza*).

The English term which best expresses this idea is "impact." We occasionally speak of a tax "impinging" on somebody or something, so that the "impact" of a tax would denote the act of impinging. Moreover, we ordinarily refer to the impact of a projectile in this very sense. The impact of a tax is therefore the immediate result of the imposition of a tax on the person who pays it in first instance. It corresponds to what is often, but erroneously, called the "original incidence" or the "primary incidence" of a tax. There is but one kind of incidence, namely the ultimate incidence, which emerges only when the tax finally settles, or comes to rest, on the person who bears it. We thus have the three distinct conceptions—the impact, the shifting, and the incidence of a tax, which correspond respectively to the imposition, the transfer, and the settling, or coming to rest, of the tax. The impact is the initial phenomenon, the shifting is the intermediate process, the incidence is the result. To confuse the impact with the incidence is as reprehensible as to confound the incidence with the shifting.

Strictly speaking, the impact of a tax includes not only the immediate result of the original imposition, but also the subsequent impinging of a tax on a person who is not the tax-bearer. Thus if a tax is imposed on A, shifted to B, and then again shifted to C, who finally bears the tax, we can properly speak of the impact of the tax first on A and then on B. The impact is transferred or repeated. It is only when the taxpayer is at the same time the tax-bearer that the impact is immediately followed by, or converted into, the incidence. For a similar reason, when the initial taxpayer is also the tax-bearer, the impact of the tax is at once followed by the incidence, without any intermediate process of shifting. But in all cases incidence signifies the result, while shifting, if there is any, denotes the process.

The point to be emphasized is that through the process of shifting, the taxpayer escapes the burden of the tax. There are, however, other methods of escape, which must not be confused with shifting. It is here that both the analysis and the nomenclature of the subject have been ex-

---

[1] They also use the words *translation, traslazione,* which are the same as our "transference" or "shifting." The French also speak of taxes being *"rejetés,"* our "thrown off" or "shifted."

ceedingly defective.[2] Let us endeavor to clear up the matter and to suggest what may possibly be deemed worthy of acceptance as the definitive nomenclature.

Whenever there is a shifting of taxation, the tax may be shifted forward or backward. Thus a producer, upon whom a tax has been assessed, may shift it to the consumer, or a seller may shift it to the purchaser. The tax is shifted forward to the consumer or the purchaser respectively. On the other hand, the tax may be imposed in first instance on the consumer or the purchaser, and may be shifted by him to the producer or the vendor respectively. In this case the tax is shifted backward. Finally, when the tax is shifted from the seller to an intermediate purchaser, who then sells to another person, and so on until the tax finally settles on the ultimate purchaser or consumer, we speak of the tax being shifted onward. Taxes, therefore, may be shifted forward, backward, or onward.[3]

To be contrasted, in part at all events, with the shifting of taxation is the capitalization or the amortization of taxation. The chief feature of this phenomenon, which will be fully discussed later,[4] is the fact that under certain circumstances the purchaser of a taxable object, by cutting down the purchase price, discounts all the taxes which he may be called upon to pay in the future. If, for instance, the ordinary return on investments in securities is five per cent and a tax of one per cent is imposed on a particular kind of corporate bonds selling at par, the price of these bonds will fall from par to eighty. The tax will be amortized or discounted through a depreciation of the capital value of the bonds by a sum equal to the capitalized value of the tax. The new purchaser thus escapes the tax which he is compelled to pay to the government by giving so much less for the bonds.

The few writers who have discussed this phenomenon generally consider capitalization to be a kind of shifting. In a certain sense, indeed, there is a seeming justification for this view. For the purchaser escapes the tax by throwing it off, or shifting it backward, on the seller. In reality, however, a distinction ought to be observed between shifting and capitalization. Shifting implies a process applicable to a single tax or to a tax each time that it is imposed; capitalization implies a process applicable to

---

[2] The English and the French writers have done virtually nothing to clear up the confusion. The Germans have done a little, but only a little. More has been accomplished by the Italians, especially by Maffeo Pantaleoni, *Teoria della Traslazione dei Tributi*, 1882, and more recently by Fabrizio Natoli, *Studi su gli Effetti Economici dell' Imposta*, 1909. But their analysis also is, as we shall see, not entirely free from objection.

[3] The Germans, since the time of von Hock, in 1863, have been accustomed to these conceptions, which they designate by the terms *Fortwälzung*, *Rückwälzung*, and *Weiterwälzung*—all of them subdivisions of shifting or *Ueberwälzung*.

[4] Part II, chap. i, § 1, *Shifting and Incidence of Taxation*.

a whole series of taxes and takes place *before* any of them, with the exception of the first, is paid. In the case of a dealer who shifts a tax on a commodity back to the producer, the process takes place each time that the tax is levied, and the producer reduces the selling price each time by the amount of the tax. In the case of capitalization the purchaser indeed pays the tax, but the initial possessor or vendor reduces the price by a sum equal to all the future taxes which the purchaser expects to be called upon to pay. In the one case we have the shifting back of a single tax; in the other case we have the throwing back of a whole series of taxes at once. For capitalization implies a change in price equal to the capital value of all anticipated payments. There is, therefore, a marked distinction between shifting and capitalization. If a tax is shifted, it cannot be capitalized; if a tax is capitalized, it cannot be shifted. A tax on houses, for instance, as we shall see later, if imposed on the tenant, may possibly be shifted back to the owner, but cannot be capitalized; a tax on land, imposed on the tenant, may be capitalized without being shifted to the present owner. Shifting and capitalization are in reality opposite, not complementary, conceptions.

In the case of both shifting and capitalization, however, the taxpayer escapes the burden of the tax through the mediation of the process of exchange. Without the purchase and the sale of the commodity there can be neither shifting nor capitalization. There is, however, a third method of escape possible, which is based not upon exchange, but upon production. Let us take, for instance, the case of a tax imposed either upon a finished commodity or upon the process of producing the commodity. It is possible, under certain circumstances, that the producer, fearing the loss of his market if he should add the tax to the price, will pay the tax and endeavor to recoup himself by so improving the process of production as to succeed in turning out his units of product at a lower cost. In such a case the loss occasioned by the tax may be offset, or perhaps even more than offset, by the gains resulting from the economies of production.

What shall we call such a phenomenon? The Germans term it the "throwing-off" (*Abwälzung*), while the Italians call it the "rejection" or the "removal" of the tax.[5] All these terms, however, are ill-chosen, because there is nothing distinctive in them. If a tax is shifted, it is also thrown off or removed from the taxpayer. We venture, therefore, to sug-

---

[5] The term *Abwälzung* is found first in von Hock, *Die öffentlichen Abgaben und Schulden*, 1863, although the phenomenon itself had previously been described by Rau. Pantaleoni, *op. cit.*, p. 28, calls it *rigetto dell' imposta;* Natoli, *op. cit.*, p. 22, calls it *remozione dell' imposta;* Tenerelli, *L' Azione delle Imposte Indirette sui consumi*, 1898, p. 67, calls it *rimozione dell' imposta*.

gest for this phenomenon the term "transformation of taxation." For by virtue of its operation the loss due to the tax is, or may be, transformed into a gain: the tax is transformed into its opposite. The attribute of removal or throwing-off ("rejection") of the tax is common to all three methods of escape—shifting, capitalization, and transformation; but the attribute of the conversion of loss into gain is found only in the case of transformation.

Whether there is any such phenomenon as the transformation of taxation has sometimes been questioned. The discussion is at least as old as the time of Hume, and has usually been associated with the query as to whether taxes can act as a spur to industry. As a broad generalization, the assertion is indeed open to grave doubt, for taxes on industry must indubitably be regarded on the whole as a drag or burden on industry, rather than as a spur to industry. But while it is doubtless true that under a régime of free competition the quest for profits will impel the individual to make the best use of his opportunities, it is none the less a fact that there have frequently been cases where the attention of the producer was first directed to the possibility of improving the productive process by some new burden which started a whole branch of industry out of its comparative lethargy and caused it to forsake the old rut. Take, for instance, the familiar example of the eighteenth-century Scotch tax on the whiskey distillery which led to such improvements in the process that for a time at least the distillers succeeded in transforming the loss into a gain; or the case of the European continental tax on beet sugar in the nineteenth century, the burden of which admittedly first directed the attention of the producers to the possibility of reducing the cost of extracting the sugar from the beets. It may be true that the improvements would probably have come about of themselves after a time; but this does not invalidate the accuracy of the contention that a tax may be the occasion, even if it be not the cause, of a betterment in production. Whenever we find such a phenomenon, we are in the presence of the transformation of a tax— the transformation from loss into possible gain.

The literature of finance, however, has thus far failed to put the transformation of taxation into its proper place. Some writers confuse transformation with shifting,[6] whereas, as we are now aware, the two

---

[6] This is true especially of the Germans. Although von Hock was, as stated above, the first to speak of *Abwälzung*, subsequent writers used this as a general term, synonymous with *Ueberwälzung*. So, e.g., Rau, and Prince-Smith in his essay "Ueber die Abwälzung" in the *Vierteljahrschrift für Volkswirthschaft und Kulturgeschichte*, Vol. xiii (1866). Held, in his article "Zur Lehre von der Ueberwälzung der Steuern" in the *Zeitschrift für die gesamte Staatswissenschaft*, 1868, pp. 489 and 492, first called attention to the fact that transformation is really not shifting, but he did not designate transformation by the term *Abwälzung*, which,

conceptions are entirely distinct. In the case of shifting, the tax is thrown off the taxpayer and settles upon the final tax-bearer. The incidence is on some one else than the original taxpayer. In the case of transformation, on the contrary, the incidence is on the original taxpayer. He escapes, not by a shifting of the tax, but by a transformation of the tax. Transformation depends upon incidence and is a reaction from the incidence. If there is no incidence, there can be no transformation. But if there is a shifting, there can obviously be no incidence on the original taxpayer. Transformation and shifting are hence opposites.

Others, again, confuse transformation with evasion of taxation.[7] This phenomenon, however, as will be seen immediately below, is something entirely different. Others finally seek unduly to extend the sphere of transformation, and include under this phenomenon not only economies through improvements in production, but also savings through changes in consumption[8] which, as we shall see, properly come under a quite distinct head.

The transformation of taxation is therefore a method of escape from taxation which must be classed with shifting and capitalization. Shifting is the most common, capitalization somewhat less usual, transformation rather infrequent. While shifting and capitalization are, as we have learned, separate and even opposite phenomena, both shifting and capitalization possess two attributes which differentiate them from transformation. These are the means of escape and the result. In shifting and capitalization the escape from taxation takes place through the medium of exchange of commodities; in transformation through the medium of production. In shifting and capitalization the taxpayer may escape the burden, but can never receive a benefit; in transformation the taxpayer may not only escape, but may have his loss transformed into a gain.

While shifting, capitalization, and transformation of taxation are three forms of escape from taxation, they are not the only forms. There remains, in fact, one more method of escape from taxation which is even more common than any of those hitherto mentioned—namely, the eva-

---

on the contrary, he continually employed as synonymous with *Ueberwälzung*. See, *e.g.*, *op. cit.*, p. 481, and Part I, book ii, chap. 6, of this monograph. Wagner clearly describes the phenomenon of transformation, which he calls *Abwälzung*, but he considers it one of the two forms of *Ueberwälzung* or shifting, the other being what he terms *Weiterwälzung*. See his *Finanzwissenschaft*, II[er] Theil (1880), § 331, p. 154. The same is true of the later editions. The more recent German writers employ the terms in all degrees of confusion, none of them making the correct distinction. An improvement, however, is to be noted in the recent treatment of the subject by Dr. Mildschuh in the *Handbuch der Finanzwissenschaft*, 1926, who has profited by Pantaleoni and the present writer.

[7] This is true, *e.g.*, of Wicksell, *Finanztheoretische Untersuchungen*, 1896, p. 12.

[8] This error, *e.g.*, is committed by Pantaleoni, *op. cit.*, p. 25.

sion of taxation. In each of the three methods of escape thus far discussed the government has always received a revenue, whatever may have been the facts as to the taxpayer. Whether the tax be shifted, capitalized, or transformed, it has always been paid by some one. Even in the case of transformation the tax is paid by the producer, and it is of no fiscal concern to the government whether the loss of the producer due to the payment of the tax is transformed into a gain.

In the case of evasion, however, not only does the taxpayer escape the tax, but the government loses its revenue. Evasion of the tax takes place only when there are no proceeds. If the tax is evaded in part, there are no proceeds as to the part which is evaded. Evasion of taxation is tantamount, fiscally speaking, to the absence of taxation. So far as the revenue of the government is concerned, there might as well be no tax. In all other forms of escape from taxation the government still receives its due.

Evasion of taxation assumes several forms—the most important categories being legitimate and illegitimate evasion. The conception of illegitimate evasion is simple. It consists of failure of the legal taxpayer to conform to the provisions of the law. Illegitimate evasion is of two kinds: on the one hand, the taxpayer may fail to conform to the provisions of the law by becoming a smuggler or a "tax-dodger," or by resorting to a variety of other shifts or illegal practices. Secondly, the producer may evade the tax by reducing the quality or the size of the commodity. This involves a change in the process of production similar to that described in the so-called transformation of taxation, but with the important difference that, instead of an improvement in the process, we now have a deterioration. In both smuggling and deterioration, what the taxpayer gains, the government loses.

On the other hand, the evasion may be legitimate, that is, in accordance with law. Legitimate evasion can take place only when the individual escapes the tax by refraining from the consumption of the commodity. Without a diminution of consumption there can be no legitimate evasion. Legitimate evasion, moreover, differs according as it is intended or not intended. Intentional evasion takes place when the legislator expressly desires that the tax be not paid. The object of the tax in such a case is not fiscal, but social. Thus in the case of the American tax on opium or on state bank-notes the purpose of the law is to cause the individual to refrain from using opium or emitting bank-notes. The same would be true of a high tariff. To the extent that the tariff checks, or even prohibits, imports, the tax is not paid and the purpose of the law is thus achieved. On the other hand, the legislator may desire to have the tax paid, but the imposition or the increase of the tax may engender an unexpected and entirely unwelcome falling off of consumption, thus leading to a decrease, or even to the entire disappearance, of any revenue to the treasury. Such cases have been frequent in the excise legislation of all countries. Sometimes, however, we have a combination of legitimate and illegitimate evasion, although, of course, the legitimate evasion which is here in question must be of the unintentional type. For manifestly if the government desires that the tax be not paid, non-payment is not in conflict with the law. A good illustration of such a combination of illegitimate and legitimate unintentional evasion is afforded by the experience of the American government with the whiskey tax during the Civil War period, the sudden jump of the tax from fifty cents to two dollars a gallon causing not only a great falling off in consumption, but also a marked increase in frauds on the revenue.

If we sum up the preceding discussion, we can portray the various categories of escape from taxation in the following table:*

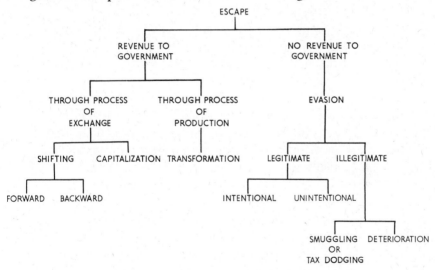

Of all these forms of escape from taxation, shifting is the really important one. Evasion of taxation is so simple that it needs little elucidation; transformation of taxation is so infrequent as to call for only slight consideration; capitalization of taxation is so closely allied to shifting that it can best be treated in connection with it. In the process that intervenes between the impact and the incidence of taxation, shifting is thus really the phenomenon that calls for an extended study.

In addition to the confusion that has been brought about by the failure to distinguish between shifting and the other forms of escape from taxation, we find another fertile source of error in the failure to distinguish between the shifting of a tax and the incidental burden which may rest on the shifter.

When we consider, for instance, the shifting of a tax as between buyer and seller, or between producer and consumer, the question that concerns us is: Will the price of the article be raised by the imposition of the tax? If the price is raised, we say that the tax is to that extent shifted. But even a complete shifting of the tax does not necessarily mean an entire absence of loss to the seller. Thus, it usually happens that an increase of the price of a commodity leads to a decrease in sales; and it may happen that these decreased sales, even at higher prices, will yield less total profits than before. In such a case, not only does the buyer pay the tax, but the seller also suffers a loss, even though the tax has been shifted completely.

These incidental burdens may be summed up under the head of pressure of taxation. We should thus have a fourth category to add to the original three mentioned above on page 203. In tracing the life history of a tax, in other words, it might seem that we should have to distinguish between (1) the impact, (2) the shifting (and other forms of escape), (3) the incidence, and (4) the pressure of taxation. In reality, however, the pressure of taxation is not simply a consequence of the incidence, but may be connected with any of the preceding stages.[9] There may be a pressure or incidental burden resulting from the impact and from the shifting or other forms of escape, as well as from the incidence. And the pressure may be felt not only by those who pay, but by those who do not pay.

That there is a distinction between the incidence of a tax and the pressure of the incidence is obvious. The incidence of a tax marks the final payment by the tax-bearer. Ordinarily, the burden upon the tax-bearer is equal to, or measured by, the amount of the tax which he is called upon to pay. But, as we shall see later, there are cases where the producer may be able, as the consequence of a tax, to raise the price of the commodity not only by the amount of the tax, but by something more than this amount. In such a case, not only is the incidence of the tax upon the consumer, but the burden resting on the consumer is greater than the amount of the tax. The loss to the tax-bearer outweighs the gain to the treasury. The pressure of incidence includes this extra loss.[10]

The pressure of the impact of a tax may be typified by the illustration mentioned in the last paragraph but two. The producer may shift the tax

---

[9] As has been pointed out by Natoli, *op. cit.*, in his criticism of Pantaleoni.

[10] Professor Adams, *Science of Finance*, p. 388, seems to overlook this when he says: "Manifestly there can be no payment by a citizen unless there is a corresponding receipt by the government." Professor Bastable, while avoiding this mistake, errs in including this extra loss under the head of incidence, rather than of pressure of incidence. *Public Finance*, 3d ed., 1903, p. 361.

entirely, and yet his restricted sales may lead to lower profits. This decrease of profit represents the pressure of the impact, which is not neutralized by the shifting of the tax. Conversely, if the tax is originally imposed upon and borne by the consumer, the loss possibly resulting to the producer through the decrease of sales represents the reaction on the producer of the pressure of the impact on the consumer. Again, if the producer who has paid the tax were able for some reason to shift to the consumer only the exact amount of the tax, not including the interest on the amount paid out, this interest lost by the producer would represent the pressure of the impact.[11]

The pressure connected with the process of escape from taxation can be well illustrated in the case of evasion. If a tax imposed on a commodity enhances its price by the amount of the tax, it is possible, and in ordinary cases even likely, that, whether the tax impinges on the consumer directly or through shifting, the consumer will restrict his consumption. He may even be led to abandon the consumption entirely. If this occurs, he, of course, pays no tax, but evades it. Yet in so far as he is compelled to resort to an inferior substitute, or to suffer the complete deprivation of the satisfaction of his want, he undoubtedly undergoes a loss. This is not a pressure of incidence, because, since he pays no tax, there is no incidence; it is a pressure of evasion. The burden of a tax may thus be felt by those who do not pay, as well as by those who do. In fact, as has been well said, "persons who pay a tax are often less injured by its imposition than those who pay no portion of it. The man who goes two miles out of his way daily to avoid a bridge toll would be more benefited by the freeing of the bridge than most of us who pay the toll."[12]

This consideration has led the writer just quoted to suggest the entire dropping of the term "incidence of taxation" and the substitution in its stead of "effects of taxation."[13] The suggestion, however, has very properly met with no favor whatsoever.[14] By effects of taxation we may mean

---

[11] Pantaleoni, *op. cit.*, p. 21, is in error in characterizing this payment of interest as a partial incidence upon the producer. As Natoli well points out, *op. cit.*, p. 37, there can be no incidence without a corresponding revenue to the treasury.

[12] Edwin Cannan in *Memoranda chiefly relating to the Classification and Incidence of Imperial and Local Taxation*, of the *Royal Commission on Taxation*, 1899, p. 166. [Article 11, p. 171 of this volume. Ed.]

[13] "I have no doubt that it is desirable to eschew the use of the term 'incidence of taxation.' It unduly restricts inquiries into the justice and expediency of taxes, since it is always held that the 'real incidence' of a tax is upon the persons who ultimately pay or provide the money for a tax. . . . It is therefore far better to consider the *effects* of taxation." Cannan, *op. cit., ibid.*

[14] The only writer who seems to lean toward the suggestion is Edgeworth, who begins his series of articles on "The Incidence of Urban Rates" in the *Economic Journal*, Vol. X (1900), p. 172 with the words: "Incidence here denotes all those effects of taxation with

two things. In the narrower sense, it denotes the immediate consequence of each of the above-mentioned steps. Thus shifting is an effect of impact, incidence is an effect of shifting, and the pressure of a tax is an effect, in turn, of the impact and of the shifting as well as of the incidence. In the wider sense, effect denotes any of the subsequent results of taxation. A tax may have a great many effects. It may diminish industry and impoverish individuals; it may stimulate production and enrich individuals; it may be an unmitigated curse to society; it may be a necessary evil; it may be an unqualified boon to the community regarded as a whole.

These problems are indeed important. They can, however, not be successfully attacked unless we previously solve the question of shifting and incidence. Scientific progress can be made only by a continually closer analysis and finer classification. To discuss nothing but the "effects" of taxation in general would be to render abortive the entire analysis which has been attempted in the preceding pages. This analysis has led us to the conclusion that the problem *par excellence* is that of shifting and incidence. With the wider questions of the general effects of taxation the student of incidence does not primarily busy himself. What he has particularly to investigate is the question: On whom does the tax ultimately fall? When we once know this, we can then proceed to the further discussion of the effects produced by the pressure of taxation on the various classes or individuals. The shifting is the process; the incidence is the result; the changes in the distribution of wealth are the effect.[15]

The discussion of incidence thus depends largely on the investigation of the shifting of taxation. The real problem before us is to ascertain the conditions according to which a tax is shifted forward, backward, or not

---

which the economist is concerned." Yet on p. 132 of the *Memoranda* mentioned in the preceding note Professor Edgeworth quotes with seeming approbation the doubt that has been raised as to whether "an effect of this sort—detrimental to a certain class, without any corresponding benefit to the exchequer—can properly be described as the *incidence* of a tax." Yet surely it is an effect "with which the economist is concerned." On the other hand Bastable thinks that "the expression is far too well established, and also far too convenient to be thus summarily abandoned." *Public Finance*, 3d ed., 1903, p. 361. Natoli says that the "remedy, as everyone can see, is worse than the evil. Once that we have reached the point of separating the phenomena into the effects of incidence and into other effects, not perhaps well designated, but clearly not the effects of incidence, it is taking a step backward to chaos to catalogue every possible effect under a rubric with no precise content whatever." *Op. cit.*, p. 311. Finally, as Row-Fogo says, "the term 'effects' is itself open to objection. Rates may have the effect of injuring the health and morals of occupiers. . . . If 'effects' is to supersede 'incidence,' the term will have to be defined more closely. . . . 'Effect' includes anything."—J. Row-Fogo, *An Essay on the Reform of Local Taxation in England*, 1902, p. 127, note and p. 131.

[15] For a discussion of some of the effects of taxation, see my article entitled "The Effects of Taxation," in the *Political Science Quarterly*, Vol. XXXVIII (1923), pp. 1–23, and my volume *Studies in Public Finance*, 1925, chapters on "Income Taxes and the Price Level," "Taxation and Prices," "The Problem of Tax-exempt Securities," and "The Reform of Municipal Taxation."

at all. Only when we understand whither, why, and how a tax is shifted, can we discover its actual incidence; and it is only when we have ascertained the incidence that we can proceed to discuss the wider effects of a tax. In the following pages an attempt will accordingly be made to attack the problem by first giving a detailed critical history of the doctrine of shifting and incidence, and then taking up the positive theory itself. In the second part, which deals with the constructive doctrine in its most recent aspects, it will be convenient to begin with a statement of some general principles, to follow this with a consideration of the chief separate taxes, one by one, and to close by drawing the general conclusions applicable to the science of finance.

13

The Terminology of Tax Analysis

By URSULA K. HICKS

The analysis of the working of taxes through the economic system is commonly built round two propositions, universally known and apparently as universally accepted. The first of these is concerned with the classification of taxes, the second with the method of analysis of their operation. These two propositions may be expressed as follows: (i) Taxes can most conveniently be divided into two categories, *direct* and *indirect*; direct being those levied immediately on the persons "who are to bear the burden" (O.E.D.); and indirect those which are not so levied. (ii) In the case of an indirect tax, the party who has to make the contribution to the revenue authorities normally proceeds to shift the "burden" somewhere else. In view of this, it follows that the analysis of the operation of taxes can most conveniently be tackled by pursuing this shifting process through the economic system to the point of "incidence," or perhaps to further points, known as "effects" or "diffusion."

Neither of these propositions is wholly satisfactory, as is evident from confusions which have arisen in classifying and analysing taxes; and it seems clear from the literature that unless they are very carefully handled they do not lead to a process of analysis which brings out clearly the factors of greatest economic importance.

In respect of the classification of taxes into direct and indirect, it is hard to disagree with the writer in the *Handwörterbuch* that "the generality of the acceptance of these terms is only equalled by the differences in their application."[1] It is natural, indeed, to expect that as the composition of tax structures changes from age to age, the usage of the terms should be modified in the course of time, and this is no doubt part of the explanation. The most famous aberration of all—the declaration by the Supreme Court of the United States that income tax is not a direct tax—

---

* *Economic Journal*, Vol. LVI, No. 221 (March, 1946).
[1] *Handwörterbuch der Staatswissenschaften*, article on direct and indirect taxes.

had an extra-economic explanation;[2] but current differences in the practice of experts are far too important to be brushed aside by explanations along these lines. To-day, for instance, we find the O.E.D. declaring that the local rate is a direct tax, while most economists, and the Central Statistical Office, would agree that it is an indirect tax. Motor-licence duties on private cars are regarded by the revenue authorities as direct taxes, most economists would probably class them as indirect, while the C.S.O. covers itself (in the notes to the Budget White Paper calculation) by stating that "they are here regarded as direct taxes." Clearly this is an unsatisfactory state of affairs, and we should be able to improve it by taking a little thought.

Parallel difficulties arise in the use of the all too familiar terms "burden" and "incidence." It is doubtful, to begin with, whether the term "burden" without qualification has any right in the discussion of a redistributive system of public finance. Apart from this consideration it is (as we shall see) used in at least two quite different connotations by different writers (by the Colwyn Committee in both, in different sections of their Report). The usage of the word "incidence" is in no better condition. The Colwyn Committee declared—on what evidence it is not clear[3] —that in popular usage the term covered "not only the intial burden of a tax, but also the whole range of consequential effects," while for economists "incidence is only concerned with where the more immediate burden of the tax, as a tax, rests."[4] Small wonder that Cannan had wanted to abandon the term altogether.[5]

I. THE CLASSIFICATION OF TAXES

It is not easy to trace the origin of the terms "direct" and "indirect" as a technical classification. In France the phrase "assise directement" was apparently in use for personal taxes at least as early as the sixteenth century.[6] Adam Smith uses the term "direct tax," but in a context which

---

[2] The decision was given in respect of the income tax of 1862, and was an effort to circumvent Article I, § 2, C3 of the U. S. Constitution, which stated that "direct taxes shall be apportioned among the several States according to their population"—an obligation which would have nullified the purpose of the income tax.

[3] This was certainly not the view of Edgeworth, see below, p. 224. Marshall, who mainly used tax analysis as a method of illustrating certain propositions of general theory, and was consequently not over-nice in his use of fiscal terms, certainly used the phrase "ultimate incidence" in a manner which is not consistent with the Colwyn Committee's dictum.

[4] *Report of the Committee on National Debt and Taxation*, Cmd. 2800 of 1927, p. 106.

[5] *Memoranda Relating to the Classification and Incidence of Imperial and Local Taxation of R.C. on Taxation*, 1899, p. 166. [Article 11, p. 171 of this volume. Ed.]

[6] Cf. Bodin, *Six Livres de la République*, 1577, quoted in the *Handwörterbuch, loc. cit.*

makes it difficult to decide whether he considered himself to be employing it in a technical sense.[7] In the United States at the time that Adam Smith was writing the term was already in very technical use, but in the highly specialised meaning of the poll tax. Prior to the introduction of the income tax, the normal English tax classification was not direct/indirect, but "assessed taxes" (on land, windows, hearths, servants and similar outward indications of wealth), on the one hand, and customs and excise, on the other. A parallel distinction in Germany was between personal taxes and excises, in France between those "assises directement" and "tarifs." In England the assessed taxes seem usually to have been regarded as direct, but on the introduction of income tax its more obvious directness, and the decline in importance of the assessed taxes, led to income tax being regarded as the direct tax *par excellence*.

The early connotation of the term "indirect" is much more shadowy, and its use much less frequent. In one sense "indirectness" apparently consisted in the tax being levied on a commodity and not on a person, but since the commodity could not pay the tax itself, this was not very satisfactory. A more sophisticated view was that the indirectness consisted in the tax being levied indirectly on one set of people by collecting it from another set of people, who would subsequently recoup themselves from the first set. It is, of course, this meaning which lies behind the analysis of shifting. It will be observed that this interpretation already implies a theory of incidence—a theory, that is, that there exists somewhere a "real" taxpayer other than the party who is in contact with the revenue authorities.

Thus a situation was reached in which, in England at least, there was general agreement that income tax (including probably death duties) was a direct tax, while customs and excise were indirect taxes. It was over the remaining (by no means unimportant) components of the tax structure that differences of opinion arose, and still arise. As so often happens, especially in this part of the economic field,[8] confusion has arisen through attempts to force distinctions proper to different types of inquiry into the procrustean bed of a single classification. In fact, there seem to be three main uses for which we need to classify taxes. For convenience we may call these the administrative, the social accounting and the analytical uses.

---

[7] *Wealth of Nations*, Vol. II, chap. 2: "There are two different circumstances which render the interest of money a much less proper subject of direct taxation than the rent of land."

[8] Cf. the controversy over the place of indirect taxes in National Income calculations, especially Bowley, *The Measurement of Real Income*, Manchester School, April, 1940; and *Studies in the National Income*, published by Cambridge University Press for N.I.E.S.R., and J. R. Hicks, "The Valuation of the Social Income," *Economica*, 1940.

A single classification has only been made to serve hitherto because over a considerable part of the territory the boundaries overlap. This does not make the strait jacket into a tailor-made.

The direct/indirect classification was clearly in origin, and is still essentially, an administrative distinction. The administrator sets out with a definite group of potential taxpayers in mind (*e.g.*, smokers, or income receivers of a certain category). He needs a distinction which makes it clear whether they are to be approached directly and personally, or through a third party. In most cases the distinction leads to an obvious classification, but there is one small difficulty.

Approach by the revenue authorities to the taxpayers may be direct, either in the sense of assessment or of collection. Thus, in the case of income-tax, assessment is direct, but collection is coming more and more to be indirect, as new methods of stoppage at source are evolved. The collection of E.P.T. is wholly indirect. On the other hand, taxpayers are in direct contact with the revenue authorities (or their deputies) when they pay their motor or wireless licences, yet these are taxes which depend not on the income of the taxpayer (from work or property), but on the fact of his desiring to enjoy the services of a particular type of capital goods. The vehicle licence duty is graded by the type of vehicle, just as the local rate is graded by the type of house; for the owner-occupier the two taxes are exactly parallel.

The British revenue authorities would appear to prefer to class as "direct" all those taxes which are *either* directly assessed or directly collected. If this is the most convenient administrative procedure, they are naturally at liberty to do so; economists cannot object if an administrative distinction does not make very good economic sense.

With the social accounting distinction we move to entirely different ground. It is now generally recognised that there are two fundamental concepts of the National Income—those which are called by the Budget White Paper the "National Income at Factor Cost," and the "National Income at Market Prices," respectively. The first of these is an objective or technical concept; the second is a subjective or welfare concept. When measuring the National Income at Factor Cost, the different commodities or services in the national output are valued according to the amounts of the factors of production which have gone to make them; the relative prices of the factors are taken to represent the rates at which the various factors are capable of being technically substituted for one another at the margin, so that the cost of a commodity is taken to represent the amount of the nation's resources which have gone into making it. The welfare concept of the National Income reduces the different commodities to a common measure, not according to their costs, but according to their marginal utilities. In most cases (though, as we shall see not in all) the relative prices of commodities represent their marginal utilities rather better than their relative money costs represent their technical rates of substitution. But this does not necessarily mean that the Welfare measure of the National Income is superior to the Factor Cost measure. The two measures are useful for different purposes; and it seems probable that the Factor Cost measure is useful for more purposes than the Welfare measure is.

In order to deduce the Welfare measure from the Factor Cost measure we have to add in the revenue from the taxes which people have to pay in order to have the right to enjoy certain commodities (and to make a similar adjustment for subsidies). Now, what precisely are the taxes which have to be added in? The White Paper says "indirect taxes"—but what are indirect taxes in this sense?

The tax distinction which is here relevant is that between the income taxes which are already included in the returns of income on which the factor cost calculation is based, and those taxes which mark a spread between the factor cost and the demand price for the article. The distinction is essentially one between taxes on income and taxes on outlay—outlay which may consist in the outright purchase of a commodity or in securing the right to its use for a prescribed period.

The taxes which have to be added in when we proceed from factor cost to *market price* are: (i) taxes which are charged to consumers as a condition of the enjoyment of particular goods or services (such as the entertainment duty or purchase tax), (ii) taxes which are paid by producers at one stage or another of the production process of such goods (such as the duty on industrial oils, or local rates on factories). These are duly added in by the White Paper; but it also adds in local rates on houses. As we shall see, it is quite proper to do this; but local rates on houses do not stand exactly on all fours with the others.

Theoretically, at least, local rates on houses are assessed on the occupier; thus it would seem more consistent to say that the *market price* for the occupation of a house is the net rent, exclusive of rates, than it is to include rates in the "market price." Nevertheless, it is right to include rates in the computation of the National Income according to the Welfare measure; for whether or not rates are part of the market price of house occupation, they are certainly part of the demand price, or marginal utility in terms of money. It is the inclusive rent (rent inclusive of rates) which the householder has to take into consideration when he is balancing his need for house-room against his need for other things.

There is therefore no doubt that domestic rates should be added in when we are calculating the National Income on the Welfare measure; what we learn from attending to this case is that "National Income at Market Prices" is a very imperfect description of the Welfare measure.

There are some other cases where the failure to attend to this distinction seems to have led the C.S.O. into actual error. Revenue from wireless licences, and that from the licence duty on privately owned motor vehicles, belong to exactly the same category as domestic rates; they do not enter into what the consumer pays "on the market," but they do enter into what he has to pay in order to acquire the right to certain satisfactions, over and above the factor cost involved. They should be reckoned as "taxes on outlay"—or indirect taxes in the social accounting sense—and added in when we proceed from factor cost to the Welfare concept of the National Income.[9]

These adjustments—particularly the transfer of the revenue from wireless licences and from vehicle duties on privately owned cars—from the direct to the indirect category—would be an improvement in the practice of National Income calculations. It is clear from the above analysis, however, that the social accounting tax distinction is at least as definite and significant in its own field as the administrative distinction is in the other. As it is unlikely that the two classifications can ever be made to coincide completely, it would seem preferable to give them separate names —for instance, retaining the terms direct/indirect for the administrative distinction, and adopting income/outlay for social accounting purposes.

In contrast to the social accounting tax distinction, which originated with, and depends on, modern methods of calculating the national income, a shadow of what we have called the "analytical" distinction has long haunted the literature,[10] in the form of a hunch that taxes which fall upon the total income or substance of the taxpayer are in a different class from other taxes, and a consequent suggestion that the term "direct" ought to be reserved for the former.

---

[9] It is probable that something of the same sort of argument should in principle be applied to the case of Stamp Duties. The C.S.O. treats Stamp Duties on the transfer of property as "direct" taxes. It could, however, be maintained that the payment of Stamp Duty on, e.g., the purchase of a house, is incurred because the purchaser seeks to acquire certain satisfactions (more accurately to exchange lesser for greater satisfaction), and that therefore it enters into the marginal utility of his expenditure as other outlay taxes do. It would even be possible to extend the same argument to the purchase of securities; but the point is a fine one, and it must be admitted that the calculation of a "price level" for deflating such refined satisfactions would probably be an impossible task. Nevertheless it is important to notice that no logical ground for the classification of Stamp Duties into those which are and which are not direct taxes appears to exist.

[10] For instance, James Mill, at least in the first ed. of his *Principles*, and in the German literature, especially J. F. Neumann and Schäffle.

To graft this point of view on to the administrative distinction is not practicable. Yet it cannot be doubted that there is an important idea behind it, which parallels closely the normal economic distinction between general and partial analysis. Just as there are some problems in economics (*e.g.* those concerned with price and output policy) which can most conveniently be tackled from the starting-point of the single firm or industry; and others which require the standpoint of the community phenomena of spending, saving and investment, so there are some taxes whose operation is best observed from the standpoint of a particular corner of the economic field, and others of which we can only make sense against the background of general phenomena.

That a distinction is required between *partial* taxes which operate (entirely at first, and always most intensively) within the framework of a limited group of industries, and *general* taxes which affect the whole level of consumption and investment, is evident from the frustrated attempts of some of the witnesses before the Colwyn Committee[11] to treat income tax by a partial analysis, and to go about looking for "mark ups" of particular selling prices as a result of a change in income tax, for all the world as if they were tracing the effects of a rise in the tea duty.

Although for the economist the analytical classification of general and partial taxes is perhaps the most important of all, it is not on a par with the other two distinctions. In the first place, it is merely a classification of convenience—partial taxes are those whose operation can most conveniently at any particular time be traced by a partial analysis, and *mutatis mutandis* for general taxes. From this it follows that the position of individual taxes may conceivably change over time. For instance, it would have been perfectly logical for a classical economist to treat a tax on bread by a general (Ricardian) analysis—emphasising its probable effect in driving the worker below the margin of subsistence; under present British conditions a tax on bread would call for just the same sort of partial analysis (effect on consumption of bread, and possible effect on production, and on the consumption and production of related commodities) as a tax on tea.

Secondly, there are some taxes (*e.g.*, the local rate) which, though partial in form, are of such widespread importance (in this case both on income and on capital account) that the analysis of their operation as partial taxes requires to be supplemented by an analysis of their general effects. The relative importance of the two lines of analysis depends to

---

[11] *Report on National Debt and Taxation, cit.*, p. 108, and more extensively in the Minutes of Evidence.

some extent on the period in which we are interested—for instance, in this case the partial analysis is sufficient so long as we are mainly interested in a period too short for a change in rates to have a noticeable effect on building; but in the longer period—in view of the importance of housebuilding as a form of investment—the effect of rates on investment may be the most important factor to consider.

I. THE METHOD OF TAX ANALYSIS

The analytical classification of taxes brings us up against the method of tax analysis. A change in a rate of tax immediately sets up economic and social reactions, and necessitates readjustments, which may conceivably be felt throughout the economic system. To describe the operation of a tax Pantaleoni used the metaphor of a stone being thrown into a pond. The economist must be prepared to trace the course of the whole circle of ripples, and should be able to say which of them does most harm to the banks of the pond.

The first step in the process is to take account of where the stone enters the water. In the case of an income tax, it is easy to see this, and consequently no "theory" of incidence is required. This is the (quite sensible) meaning behind the statement that an income tax cannot be shifted. In the case of an indirect tax the accepted procedure is to start with the party which is in contact with the revenue officials, and to find out what this party does about its financial obligation; but the ensuing search may be interpreted in either of two ways.

In the hands of some writers it is primarily a search for the party whom the Government wants to tax; in the hands of others it does include the gradual unravelling of the entire economic operation of the tax through the system. For instance, in Seligman[12] (who is mainly responsible for the shifting/incidence terminology) the emphasis is on the first of these interpretations. He speaks indeed of "effects" as well as of "incidence," but they generally appear to be no more than steps in a multiple process of shifting to the consumer.[13] In the hands of Marshall, who is using the process of tax analysis to illustrate the theory of quasirent, in following the adventures of the hard, bright stones we are taken a fairly long ride through the economic system.[14]

---

[12] E. R. A. Seligman, *The Shifting and Incidence of Taxation.*
[13] Seligman also mentions a "wider" sense of effect "which denotes any of the subsequent results of taxation," but he makes no effort to examine it. Cf. *Shifting and Incidence, cit.* definitions on p. 1. [Article 17, p. 258 of this volume. Ed.]
[14] *Principles*, 8th ed. Bk. V, ch. ix.

Now, in some circumstances the identification of the taxpayer, in the sense of the person who provides out of his income the difference between factor cost and market price, may be a matter of some little difficulty (*e.g.*, in the case of a tax on working capital, such as industrial oil, which plays a part in the production of a variety of goods). In respect of the great majority of outlay taxes, however, the taxpayer in this sense is perfectly obvious, and the answer can be found by common sense, without any elaborate mechanism of two- or three-tier shifting. Thus, when the tobacco duty is raised, there is no doubt in the minds of either the Government or the smokers that the stone is being thrown to the consumers of tobacco.

This being so, it would seem simpler and more direct to start not with the productive stage which the revenue authorities may find it most convenient to contact (which will, no doubt, differ from tax to tax), but with the consumer-taxpayer. This amounts to saying, for instance, that the lady sitting over there in a fur coat and smoking a cigarette, has paid purchase tax on her coat, and tobacco duty on her cigarette, rather than that the wholesale furrier has shifted purchase tax to the department store, who has shifted it to her, and the tobacco manufacturer has shifted the duty to the wholesaler, and so to the retailer, who has shifted it to the lady.

This direct approach is, in any case, obligatory for social accounting; it is, of course, the basis of the figures in the Budget White Paper. Estimates of the distribution of taxes on different income groups must also (although this is not always properly understood)[15] be based on the actual proportion of people's incomes during a defined period, which go not to provide the incomes of those who furnish them with goods and services, but to form the incomes of taxing authorities. The calculation is essentially one of the distribution of actual revenue collected during the period; it is not concerned with what happens as a result of consumers' incomes having been laid out in this manner.

The establishment of incidence in this sense is, of course, only the beginning of the analysis of the operation of a tax—it might even be said that it is not strictly a necessary part of that analysis. There is, however, a great convenience in starting the analysis with the consumer in this manner, especially since, unless it is very carefully handled, the shifting mechanism is apt to run on too narrow lines. The operation of a tax

---

[15] Even such a careful economist as T. Barna is hazy on this point, cf. *The Redistribution of Incomes through Public Finance in 1937*, especially the discussion of the incidence of indirect taxes on pp. 141–42. On p. 126 he excuses himself from an analysis of the distribution of the revenue collected in 1937 from Land Tax, on the ground that the incidence is on the original land owners at the time when the tax was imposed—*i.e.* in the reign of William III.

has too often been conceived in terms of the movements and counter-movements of a certain "lump" of tax, whose presence at any time can be perceived by a definite swelling in the price which is the incidence. (The lump of tax might either be transmitted whole from hand to hand, or might split up—a case of "shared" incidence—in which case the trajectories of the different fragments would have to be watched, but their behaviour would be assumed to be broadly similar to that of a complete lump.)

When the analysis is conducted along these lines it is mainly appropriate for discovering incidence in the limited Seligman sense, which is, in fact, very near the social accounting sense; as a scheme of the full operation of a tax it is obviously far too narrow. Even on its own grounds it does not allow, for instance, for the manufacturer preferring to vary quality rather than price, or the landlord increasing the repairs he is prepared to do after a rise in rates, rather than conceding a lower net rent.

Much more important, the shifting mechanism is not convenient for taking into account changes in related products or factors. Suppose, for instance, our young lady is now munching a chocolate, having given up smoking when the tax went up. The shifting mechanism can only tell us that the tobacco manufacturer cannot pass on the tax, and that the lady "evades" it—although she has no intention of defrauding the revenue, and is merely registering an adjustment of her preferences to the new price situation. We should be better employed in trying to measure the loss of (combined) surplus in the tobacco industry, and the effect of the restriction of output which it implies, and setting it against changes in surplus in the confectionery or other industries, than in sitting down under this lame result. Finally, there is the possibility that the shifting mechanism may be misapplied to the operation of income tax, with the absurd results which were produced by some of the Colwyn witnesses.

The fundamental trouble with this mechanism of analysis is that it does not go far enough or deep enough. Indeed, there has commonly been (as we have seen) some uncertainty as to how far the analysis *should* be carried; this doubt essentially arises (as has been suggested above) from different interpretations of the term "incidence," and consequently of the goal of the inquirer. Not infrequently—*e.g.*, by the Colwyn Committee—there has been an attempt to draw a line between the near and the distant ripples, designating the former "incidence" and the latter "effects" or "diffusion."

Now, as we have seen, there is a genuine difference between incidence in the social accounting sense and incidence in the sense of the economic working of the tax. In some exceptional circumstances—*e.g.*, where consumers' demand or the supply of the factors is highly inelastic—the answer to the analytical inquiry and to the statistical calculation may be practically the same, but this can only be a rare occurrence. In some other circumstances—*e.g.*, where the taxed commodity has no close relatives—there may occur a genuine discontinuity in the middle of the ripples, most of the operation being confined within narrow limits. This probably implies that for most purposes we need not bother to carry the analysis farther; but it does not alter the fact that we are concerned with an analytical, and not an accounting concept. In any case, it is never safe to assume that the discontinuity exists. In most circumstances (as the Colwyn Committee soon discovered) it is very difficult to draw a satisfactory line between the near and the further working of a tax.

It was largely the fear that the analysis would be too narrow and would stop half-way at some imaginary point called "incidence" which caused Cannan to dislike the term.[16] Edgeworth also would have no truck with any dichotomy between incidence and effects, although terminologically he was in the opposite camp from Cannan.[17] Undoubtedly they were justified in relation to what they had in mind. What neither Edgeworth nor Cannan perceived (as at the time they were writing they hardly could have done) was that there is also a distinct and important meaning in the social accounting sense of incidence, and, further, that this is a calculation which can be made with a fair degree of statistical accuracy and completeness. For the unravelling of incidence in the sense of the economic working out of a tax, on the other hand, we must largely rely—partly, but not wholly, for want of adequate data—on deduction and inference.

We arrive thus at two fundamental concepts in fiscal theory: (i) the social accounting calculation of the proportion of people's incomes paid over to taxing authorities in a defined period, and (ii) the analysis of all the economic adjustments through time and space resulting from a particular tax. These two concepts are different in kind, there is no question of one being a sort of first stage of the other. Social accounting is concerned with a *statistical* comparison at a moment of time, corresponding to the period covered by the statistics (because of the nature of the data, this will usually be a year). The analytical concept is essentially hypothetical. It is a comparison of two complete economic situations, one with

---

16 Cannan, *Memoranda before R.C. cit.*
17 Cf. especially the very interesting footnote to p. 151 in *Collected Papers*, Vol. II. Edgeworth cut the Gordian knot by blandly declaring "incidence here denotes all those effects of taxation with which the economist is concerned." His concept is entirely consistent with what is called "effective incidence" below.

a particular tax in force, the other without it. One of these set-ups will normally be imaginary, although statistical data on past changes are not entirely lacking.

The statistical calculation can, and naturally should be, extended from tax to tax, so that the income distribution of the entire tax structure can be considered at once. It can be further extended to at least parts of the expenditure structure—although this raises more difficult logical questions—to ascertain the extent of income redistribution through public finance. The analytical inquiry, on the contrary, can only be concerned with a single tax or group of taxes at a time—it makes nonsense to imagine the whole tax structure away. It follows that it is not concerned with what becomes of the revenue of the tax (which is an entirely separate analysis) except in the rare case when the two cannot be separated— *e.g.*, the sugar duty and the beet sugar subsidy. It is, of course, possible, and just as desirable, to analyse the operation of subsidies (as negative taxes) in a similar way.

If so much is accepted, it remains to determine what our two concepts are to be called. For the first the term "Burden" has already been used in a technical sense;[18] no doubt following Pigou, who declares (on what evidence is not clear) that "burden is generally conceived to be represented by the money raised in revenue."[19] It was also used in this sense by the Colwyn Committee in their extension of Sir Herbert (Lord) Samuel's calculations; but they evidently did not consider that there was anything technical about the use, since they also employed it in a much wider looser sense when discussing the effects of taxation. It is evident from this that the term "burden" will not do; apart from the fact that its implications are all wrong, it is too liable to cause confusion by being used both in a technical and in a vague non-technical sense.

It is equally apparent that the term "incidence" by itself cannot be used for either concept; yet the idea behind it, in fact, covers everything we need. In another place[20] it has been suggested that instead of the term "burden," the term "formal incidence" might be adopted for the social accounting concept; while the term "effective incidence"[21] would be appropriate for the analytical concept. It is hoped that these terms are sufficiently different from what has gone before to be confinable to tech-

---

[18] Shirras and Rostas, *The Burden of British Taxation.*

[19] *A Study in Public Finance*, p. 195.

[20] *The Incidence of Local Rates*, by J. R. and U. K. Hicks, published by Cambridge University Press, for N.I.E.S.R., 1945.

[21] These terms are derived from Goschen, *Collected Essays*, who speaks of the incidence of rates "in form and in effect."

nical usage, and at the same time sufficiently traditional to be conveniently understood.

It hardly needs emphasising that although the social accounting concept is truly formal, in the sense that in making the calculation we are not concerned with the adjustment of the lay-out of incomes as a result of public finance, it is not therefore insignificant. On the contrary, as the war-time Budget White Papers have shown, it is essential for a rational direction of policy. The term "effective incidence" seems preferable to "effects" or "diffusion" because it emphasises that we need to cast the net wider than either the primary or the secondary consequences of a tax, and acknowledges that the operational process is continuous.

B. GENERAL ANALYSIS

14

On the Principles Which Regulate the Incidence of Taxes*[1]

By FLEEMING JENKIN

It is well known that many taxes do not fall ultimately on the person from whom they are in the first instance levied. The merchant advances the duties imposed on goods, but the tax ultimately falls on the consumer. The problem of discovering the ultimate or true incidence of each tax is one of great importance, and of considerable complexity. The following paper contains an investigation of the methods by which this incidence may in some cases be experimentally determined, and of the principles regulating the incidence in all cases—these principles being stated in a mathematical form.

The author, in a paper published in *Recess Studies*, expressed the law of supply and demand by representing what may be termed the demand and supply functions as curves. The ordinates parallel to the axis OX, Fig. 1, were prices—the co-ordinates parallel to the axis OY were the supplies at each price, and the demand at each price for the respective curves—the market price is then indicated by the ordinate x of the point at which the curves intersect, this being the only price at which buyers and sellers are agreed as to the quantity to be transferred.

We might write the law algebraically as follows, calling y the quantity of goods in the market, at each price x, we have $y = \phi(x)$; and calling y_1 the quantity of goods demanded at each price, we have $y_1 = \phi_1(x)$; the market price is determined by the equation $y = y_1$. There is, however, little or no advantage in adopting this algebraic form, because we cannot suppose that in any instance $\phi(x)$ or $\phi_1(x)$ will be any tolerably simple algebraic function, whereas the curve for given goods might be determined experimentally by observing from year to year variations of quantities bought or quantities supplied at various prices.

Professor Jevons has since given a much more complex algebraic rep-

---

* Fleeming Jenkin, *Papers Literary, Scientific*, etc., Vol. II.
[1] From *Proceedings of the Royal Society of Edinburgh*, Session 1871–72.

resentation of the same law, which, however, reduces itself to the above simple form.

The graphic method may also be employed to indicate the advantage gained by each party in trade, and to show how it may be estimated in money. Let the two curves indicate the demand and supply at each price for a certain kind of goods. If all sellers were of one mind, and were willing to supply all their goods at a given price x, and were quite determined to sell no goods below that price, the supply curve would be a mere

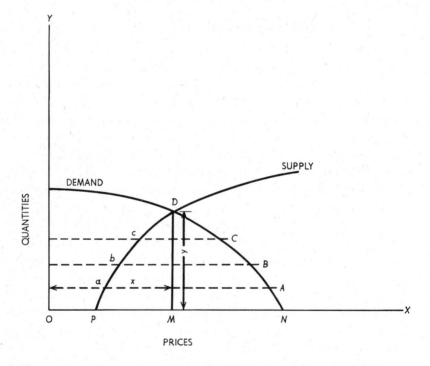

FIG. 1

straight line parallel to OX, and ending abruptly at the ordinate raised at x. Similarly, if all buyers were of one mind, and would only buy below a given price x, but were willing to buy all they want at that price, and no more at any lower price, the demand curve would be a line parallel to OX ending abruptly at the ordinate raised at x, and the price would be quite indeterminate. If the two lines overlapped, transactions might take place at any price between that at which the sellers were willing to sell and the buyers willing to buy; there would in this case be no market price. This case does not represent the true state of either buyers' or sellers' minds in any real large market. There are always a few holders who

would only sell if the price were much higher than the market price,—
these are the people who expect prices to rise; there are some who are just
willing to sell at the market price, but who will not sell a penny below;
and there are others, weak holders, who expect prices to fall, and these
would really, if pushed to extremity, sell below the market price. This
condition of things is represented by the supply curve in Fig. 1.

Similarly, there are a few buyers who, if pushed to extremity, would
buy some goods above market price; some also will just buy at market
price; some will not buy unless the price is below market price. This is
represented by the demand curve.

Now, I contend that when the market price is fixed, those traders who
are perfectly indifferent whether they buy or sell at that price reap no
benefit by the trade; but these will be few in number.

Looking at the demand curve, the ordinate x_A from the axis OY to A
represents the value set on some of the goods by some buyers, but these
buyers have got the goods for the sum represented by the ordinate $x =
OM$; the difference between these two ordinates $x_A - x$ is the difference
in price between what was given and what might have been given for a
certain small quantity Δy of goods. $\Delta y(x_A - x)$ is therefore the benefit
reaped by buyers from the purchase of the quantity Δy; and integrating
the benefits derived from the sale of each successive quantity, we find the
area $MDCBAN$ represents the whole gain to buyers by the purchase of
the quantity y of goods. Similarly, it is easy to show that the area $MDcbaP$
represents the gain to sellers by the same transaction; these areas represent the gain in money, each product $\Delta y(x_A - x)$ being the product of a
quantity by the gain in money per unit of quantity.

Thus the whole benefit to the two leading communities is represented
by the sum of the two above-named areas, and the partition of the benefit
between the two communities is perfectly definite.

Professor Jevons has used curves to integrate what he terms the utility
gained by exchange in a manner analogous to the above; but utility, as he
defines it, admits of no practical measurement, and he bases his curve, not
on the varying estimates of value set by different individuals each on
what he has or what he wants, but on the varying utility to each individual
of each increment of goods. The above estimate of the gain due to trade,
deduced from the demand and supply curves as originally drawn in my
Recess Studies article is, I believe, novel, and gives a numerical estimate
in money of the value of any given trade, which might be approximately
determined by observing the effect of a change of prices on the trade; the
curves throughout their whole lengths could certainly not, in most cases,
be determined by experiment, but statistics gathered through a few years

would show approximately the steepness of each curve near the market price, and this is the most important information.

A steep supply curve and a horizontal demand curve indicate that the buyers reap the chief benefit of the *trade*. The sellers, if producers, may, however, be making important profits as capitalists and labourers.

A steep demand curve and a level supply curve indicate that the suppliers are chiefly benefited by the trade; the community or body which is most ready to abandon the trade if the price increases a little, benefits least by the trade.

When the traders are producers and consumers, the benefits estimated in this way as due to the *trade* are not the only benefits reaped by the community from the manufacture.

In this case, what is termed the supply curve depends on the cost of production of the article, including that interest on capital and that remuneration for skilled superintendence which is necessary to induce the producer to employ his capital and skill in that way. The cost of production increases generally with the quantity of the article produced, otherwise the supply curve would be a straight vertical line; but as a matter of fact, to produce an increase of production a rise of price is necessary, indicating that only a few men with little capital are content with a small rate of interest and small remuneration for their skill, but that to induce many men with much capital to be employed in the particular manufacture, a large rate of interest and considerable remuneration are required, hence the supply curve will be such as shown in Fig. 2, where the price OP is that price or cost of production which is just sufficient to tempt a few producers to produce a little of the article.

Then if OP' is the actual cost out of pocket required to produce a small quantity of an article, and if OP is the lowest cost at which any manufacturer can afford to produce it, the area $P'D'DM$ represents the whole profit to the producing capitalist when the price is OM. The line $D'P'$ is not necessarily parallel to DP, nor vertical, the bare cost of production of the article generally increases as the quantity increases; and in that case $D'P'$ is not vertical. Again, the rate of interest required to tempt additional capital into a particular field is not constant, but increases, hence $P'D'$ is steeper than PD. I see at present no means of experimentally ascertaining the gain reaped by producers represented by the area $PDD'P'$: it can be approximately estimated by considering the prevailing rate of interest in the producing community and the amount of capital required for the production of the unit of the article.

We see that the gain of a manufacturing capitalist may be divided into two parts—the profit as a trader, and the interest as a capitalist.

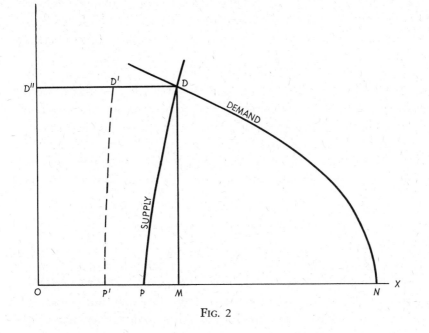

FIG. 2

In safe trades, where there are few fluctuations in price, the former gain may perhaps be the most important; in more speculative trades the latter.

There is yet a third source of gain to the manufacturing community: the labourer who produces the goods earns his wages by the manufacture, and this is an advantage to him. In the diagram, the area $OP'D'D''$ represents the wages paid for labour alone. The length of the lines between OY and $P'D'$ represents the wages of labour per unit of goods, increasing as the quantity of goods required increases. This is lost to the community if the manufacture is stopped. Thus the whole sum paid by the consumer is the area $OMDD''$; and this is made up of three parts, one of which is the profit to the trader, one the interest to the capitalist, and one the wages of the labourer; all these advantages are lost if the manufacture ceases.

The gain of the labourer does not resemble the profit of the trader, or the interest of the capitalist. The profit of the trader is the difference between his valuation of the goods and what he gets for them. If he does not sell his goods he still has his goods, he only loses the profit. Similarly, if the capitalist does not sell his capital, he still has his capital. Now, the area $P'PDD'$ represents the profit made by the capitalist on the particular employment of his capital, and this is all that he loses if unable to sell that capital; but the area $OP'D'D''$ represents the whole sum received by the labourers, not their profit. The profit of the labourer may perhaps be considered as the excess of wages which he earns in a particular trade, over that which would just tempt him to work rather than starve or go into the workhouse.

If the consumer purchases the article for simple unproductive consumption, then the loss to him is only represented by the area DMN. If, however, a community purchases goods, and consumes them productively, then, by the cessation of the trade, they in their turn lose the interest on the capital they employ, and the labourers of the community lose their wages; so that, in that case, the loss to the buyer, who cannot be classed as an immediate consumer, is made up of three parts, similar to those enumerated in the case of the seller.

TAXES ON TRADE

Having distinguished between the three distinct advantages given by trade, I will now consider the incidence of a tax on trade, levied as a fixed sum per unit of goods, as one pound per ton, or one shilling per gross.

The effect of such a tax is to produce a constant difference between the price paid by the buyer and the price received by the seller. The market prices are determined in the diagram of the supply and demand curves, by the points between which a line parallel to OX, and equal in length to the tax, can be fitted between the two curves.

Thus, if in Fig. 3, FN be the demand curve, and PE the supply curve, and if the length of the line CC' be the amount of the tax per unit of goods, then OM is the market price to the supplier, OM' the market price to the buyer, and the difference MM' is equal to the tax.

The total amount raised by the tax from the transactions represented in the diagram, is measured by the area $MCC'M'$. The portion paid by the seller is measured by the area $CC''M''M$. The portion paid by the buyer is measured by the area $C''C'M'M''$. The whole loss entailed by the tax on the two communities is measured by the area $MCDC'M'$; the loss to the sellers is measured by the area $CDM''M$; the loss to the buyers by the area $M''DC'M'$; both buyers and sellers suffer a loss beyond the tax they pay. This excess of loss is represented by the area $CC''D$ for the sellers, and $C'C''D$ for the buyers.

If the tax be large, the line CC' will approach the axis OX, the tax will be unproductive, and the area $CC'D$ representing the excess of injury to the buyers and sellers will be large, compared with the produce of the tax. This fact is one justification of free trade.

There is a certain magnitude of tax which will produce the maximum

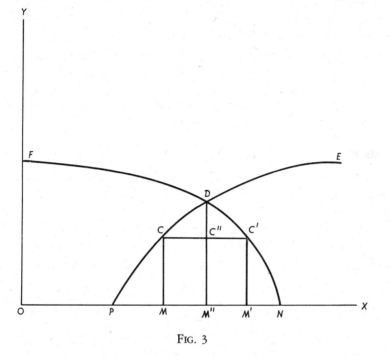

FIG. 3

revenue or value for the area $MCC'M'$. The ratio in which the tax falls, in one sense, on sellers and buyers is simply the ratio of the diminution of price obtained by the sellers to the increase of price paid by the buyers.

It is absolutely clear that this is the proportion in which the tax is actually *paid* by the two parties, although this may by no means correspond to the relative suffering inflicted on the two parties, nor is it even the proportion in which the two parties lose by the loss of trade profit. The whole loss of either party is, as the diagram shows, always greater than the tax they pay. The relative total losses of the two communities as traders, are in proportion to the areas $MCDM''$ and $M'C'DM''$; and these areas might approximately, at least, be ascertained by experiments for this purpose; treating CD and $C'D$ as straight lines, we only require to know the quantity and price of the goods before the imposition of the tax, and the quantity and price afterwards.

Thus, if a tax of $2d$. per pound were imposed on the trade in cotton between ourselves and America, if before the tax we imported 500 million lbs. at one shilling, and after the tax 300 million lbs. for which we paid $13\frac{1}{2}d$., and the Americans received $11\frac{1}{2}d$., the total loss to the two communities as traders would be $600 + 200 = 800$ million pennies, the produce of the tax 600 million pennies.

England would pay of the tax 450 million pennies. England's total loss would be 600 million pennies. America would pay of the tax 150 million pennies. America's total loss would be 200 million pennies. The incidence would be the same whichever government levied the tax.

It follows from the above principles, that if a holder sells unreservedly, trusting to the competition between the buyers to produce the market, the whole tax falls on the seller; the supply curve becomes a vertical straight line. If a buyer buys unreservedly, the whole tax falls on him; in this case the demand curve becomes a vertical straight line.

Thus, if sales by auction were subject to a tax *ad valorem* or otherwise, and if sales were quite unreserved, the number of transactions not being altered, the prices would be unaltered, but the sellers would only get the prices minus the tax.

This case does not practically arise, because, if auctions were really so taxed, although in each auction that occurred the sale might be unreserved, auctions would, as a whole, be checked; fewer people would put up their goods for sale in that way,—the prices would rise, the number of transactions would be diminished, and the tax would really be borne in part by the buyers and part by the sellers.

If the trade between two countries really consists in the exchange of goods, effected by the agency of money as a unit for expressing value, but not involving the actual transfer of coin, the above principles show the whole gain by the exchange to be the sum of two gains which each party would make by each trade if it alone existed.

If by duties one portion of the trade be extinguished or much diminished, both parties lose, but if the other portion of the trade remain uninjured, then, although there may be no exchange of commodities other than of goods for actual money, nevertheless the full gain on that which is untaxed remains intact. Thus, although the French may tax our goods, and so inflict a loss on themselves and on us, this is no reason for our inflicting an additional loss on the two communities by taxing the import of their goods.

HOUSE RENT

I will next consider the effect of a tax on house rent.

Landlords are here the sellers, and tenants the buyers of what may be termed a commodity; not the house, but the loan of a house for a term of years—the tenant buys what might be called, by the extension of a suggestion of Professor Jevons, a *house-year* from his landlord.

The difference between the house and other commodities such as food or dress is, that the house remains, whereas they are consumed. The house-year is consumed year by year, but it is reproduced year by year without material fresh expenditure on the part of the landlord. This permanency alters the incidence of taxation.

If the demand falls off the landlord cannot remove his house—he cannot cease to produce his house-year, which therefore he must dispose of. Hence, in a stationary or declining community, where no new houses are being built, but where year after year a sensible proportion remains unoccupied, the landlord must sell his house-year unreservedly, and any tax imposed on house rent would fall on him alone; that is to say, he would receive a rent diminished by the full amount of the tax, and the tenant would pay no more rent for a house of a given class than if no tax were imposed. The supply curve becomes a straight horizontal line, and is unaffected by the tax; the demand curve is equally unaffected by the tax; the number of houses let is unaltered by the tax, but the landlords lose as rent the whole amount raised by taxation.

This reasoning is based on the assumption that the supply curve has become a straight horizontal line unaffected by the tax. This condition is altered in any prosperous or growing community. There new houses must be built, and a considerable number of houses are always unlet, not because they are not required by the community, but because the speculative builders are holding out for higher terms. This produces a supply curve of the kind common to all other kinds of goods. At higher prices more goods are forthcoming. A newly-imposed tax will then be distributed between sellers and buyers, landlords and tenants in a manner depending on the form of these curves. A sensible check will be given to the letting of houses, tenants will be content with somewhat less good houses, and landlords with rather smaller rents. This is the immediate effect of the tax—the greater portion would probably fall on the landlords at first, at least in the new houses where fresh contracts are being made. But after a few years the conditions would have altered. New houses are only built because the builders obtain the usual trade profit and interest on their capital—the check to letting consequent on the imposition of the tax will therefore diminish the supply of new houses until, owing to diminution in supply, rents have risen to their old average. Then builders resume their operations. The whole tax by that time will be borne by the tenants; that is to say, if there were no tax they would get their houses cheaper by the precise amount of the tax, because rents so diminished would suffice to induce speculative builders to supply them. The rents through the whole town are ruled by those of the new districts. There is a certain relative value between every house in the town, and if the rents of new houses are dearer, the rents of the old houses are increased in due proportion. In fact, when new houses need to be supplied year by year, houses are commodities which are being produced, and the tax falls on the consumers.

The above principles determine the incidence of a tax, whether nominally levied on the landlord or tenant, but in their application account must be taken of the mental inertia of both landlords and tenants, as well as of the fact that many contracts for houses are not immediately terminable. These two conditions will for the first few years after the imposition of any new tax cause it to fall on the party from whom it is nominally levied.

Precisely as a tax on trade not only falls on the traders, but injures capitalists and labourers, a tax on house rents injures the capitalists who build houses and the labourers they employ—not that the capitalist pays the tax, but he is prevented from finding a useful investment for his money owing to the diminution in the number or quality of houses required.

TAXES ON LAND

The question of the incidence of taxes on land is peculiarly interesting. Land differs from all other commodities, inasmuch as the quantity of it does not depend on the will of any producer. The number of houses in a flourishing community does depend on the will of speculative builders; but land can only be increased in quantity by such processes as enclosing commons, or breaking up private pleasure grounds. We will neglect these small disturbing influences, and assume that all the land in a country is available for cultivation, where such cultivation is profitable; and that the absence of profit is the only reason for neglecting to cultivate any portion of it.

It is well known that the rent of each acre of [arable land is]² the excess of annual value of that acre over the annual value of the poorest land which tenants think it worth while to cultivate. We may classify all land according to the total return which it will yield per acre upon capital invested in its cultivation; and we may draw a supply curve of land such that the ordinates will be the total quantities of land which will return each successive percentage on the capital required to cultivate it. The supply diminishes as the rate of percentage increases, that is to say, there is less land which will return ten per cent on the capital than will return five per cent, and still less land which will return twenty or thirty per cent.

---

² [Editor's conjecture; type dropped in the original. Ed.]

If, therefore, tenants as a body, considered as capitalists, will not cultivate any land which does not yield twenty per cent, there will be far less land in the market than if they will be just satisfied with ten per cent.

Again, all tenants are not of one mind, and we may construct a demand curve in which the ordinates are the total quantities of land which would be let, if the land paying no rent be fixed at each successive percentage. The actual quantity of land let will be determined by the intersection of the two curves, and is represented by the height MD, Fig. 4.

If we now build a solid on the base $OD'DN$, such that its height all along each ordinate x is the number of hundreds of pounds of capital per acre required to give the percentage corresponding to the length x, then we shall have a volume standing on $OD'DN$, the contents of which will measure the total annual returns from all the land cultivated.[3] The rent is the volume standing on MDN, the profit received by the farmers is the volume standing on $OD'DM$, and this is in excess of what would have just tempted them to cultivate by the volume on MDP. We may, therefore, considering the farmer as a capitalist and a trader, call the volume on MDP his trade profit, and the volume on $OD'D$ the interest on his capital.

The effect of any tax on the land is to reduce the interest which each class of land is capable of returning on the capital employed. This it will do in very different ways according to the manner in which the tax is levied.

If the tax be an *ad valorem* duty on rent, it will modify the supply curve only between D and N. There will remain just as much land as before capable of paying rates of interest less than OM, but the quantity of land capable of paying the higher rates will be diminished; in other words, the rate of interest which the poorest land worth cultivating pays will not be affected, for this land pays no rent and remains untaxed—hence no land will be thrown out of cultivation, but the supply curve will be altered from DN to DN', diminishing the volume representing rent, but leaving the other quantities untouched; hence any tax assessed on rent is paid wholly by the landlord. The amount of the tax is the volume standing on DNN'. It is curious to remark that this tax in no way falls on the consumer. The tax on rent simply diminishes the excess of value which some land has over others; no land is thrown out of cultivation, and no less capital employed in production than before; no one suffers but the landlord. If, instead of being assessed on the rent, the tax is

---

[3] If 150*l*. per acre are required to give the percentage x of any one class of goods, the height of the ordinate perpendicular to the plane of $OD'DN$ will be 1·5.

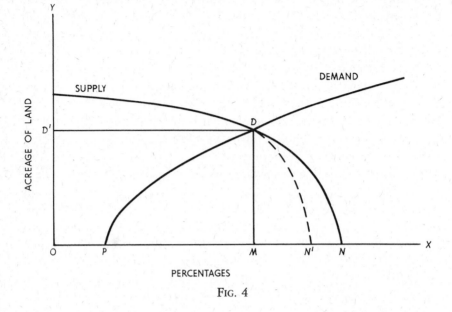

FIG. 4

assessed on the produce of the cultivation, the incidence of the tax will be greatly modified. The cultivation of land will no longer be so profitable; *i.e.* the returns from capital employed on the land will be less; in other words, the whole supply curve of the land will be modified, falling everywhere if the produce taxed be that which is produced on all qualities of land. Some land will fall out of cultivation, and only part of the tax will be borne by the landlord; part will fall in the first instance on the tenant, but he, like any other manufacturer, will recover almost the whole of his portion from the consumer. Tenants will be injured by the limitation of the number of transactions, and labourers by the diminution in the amount of work required. This is the effect of an octroi duty.

Sometimes a tax is assessed not on the rent, but on an assumed value per acre. Such a tax can never be raised on land which pays no rent, for the owner would rather abandon possession of the land than pay the tax. It might, however, lead to the abandonment of the cultivation of poorer soils; it would then injure tenants and consumers, although they would not pay one penny of the tax; for taxes cannot be paid out of lands which lie waste; assuming that the tax is always less than the rent, as it certainly always should be, it will be paid wholly by the landlords. The tax in this case does not diminish the supply of land.

A cognate question of great interest is, Who reaps the benefit of any improvements in agriculture, making land return more than it previously

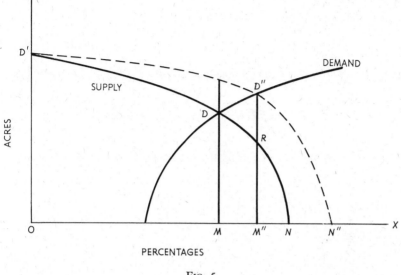

FIG. 5

did? This improvement may require, and probably will require, increased investment of capital. The whole supply curve will be raised; assuming the demand to remain the same, Fig. 5, $M''D''$ will be the new increased number of acres in cultivation, but land will be left uncultivated which would have returned the interest OM on capital. The volume standing on $D'D''N''$ will be much greater than that on $D'DN$, for the third dimension will also have increased; the average rate of interest and the trade profit of the tenant will have increased, and it is highly probable that the volume standing on $D''M''N''$ may be greater than that which stood on DNM; but this is by no means certain. It might at first be actually smaller. In all probability, however, the demand curve is very nearly vertical, a small increase of profit tempting a largely increased investment of capital in farming. If this be so, then the landlord also reaps considerable benefit from the improvement, for if the farmers were contented with nearly the same rate of interest as before, the solid standing on $DRNN''D''$ which he gains would be larger than the solid on $DRM''M$ which he loses; moreover, the volume on RNM'', which he retains, is increased. Labourers and consumers also gain.

15

*Of Monopoly and of the Influence of Taxation on Commodities Produced under a Monopoly**

By AUGUSTIN COURNOT

OF MONOPOLY[1]

26. For convenience in discussion, suppose that a man finds himself proprietor of a mineral spring which has just been found to possess salutary properties possessed by no other. He could doubtless fix the price of a *liter* of this water at 100 francs; but he would soon see by the scant demand, that this is not the way to make the most of his property. He will therefore successively reduce the price of the liter to the point which will give him the greatest possible profit; *i.e.* if $F(p)$ denotes the law of demand, he will end, after various trials, by adopting the value of p which renders the product $pF(p)$ a maximum, or which is determined by the equation

$$F(p) + pF'(p) = 0.\qquad(1)$$

The product

$$pF(p) = \frac{[F(p)]^2}{-F'(p)}$$

will be the annual revenue of the owner of the spring, and this revenue will only depend on the nature of function F.

To make equation (1) applicable, it must be supposed that for the value of p obtained from it, there will be a corresponding value of D which the owner of the spring can deliver, or which does not exceed the annual flow of this spring; otherwise the owner could not, without damage to himself, reduce the price per liter as low as would be for his

---

* Augustin Cournot, *Researches Into the Mathematical Principles of the Theory of Wealth* (1838), Chapters V and VI, translated by Nathaniel T. Bacon (New York: Macmillan Co., 1897, 1929), with "Notes on Cournot's Mathematics," by Irving Fisher, added in the 1929 edition. This volume is one of the "Economic Classics," edited by W. J. Ashley.
    [1] Chapter V.

interest were the spring more abundant. If the spring produces annually a number of liters expressed by Δ, by deducing p from the relation $F(p) = Δ$, we necessarily obtain the price per liter which must finally be fixed by the competition of customers.

27. In this simplest case, chosen for a type, the producer has no cost of production to bear, or the cost can be considered insignificant. Let us go on to that of a man who possesses the secret of a medical preparation or an artificial mineral water, for which the materials and labour must be paid for. It will no longer be the function $pF(p)$, or the annual *gross receipts*, which the producer should strive to carry to its maximum value, but the *net receipts*, or the function $pF(p) - \phi(D)$, in which $\phi(D)$ denotes the cost of making a number of liters equal to D. Since D is connected with p by the relation $D = F(p)$, the complex function $pF(p) - \phi(D)$ can be regarded as depending implicitly on the single variable p, although generally the cost of production is an explicit function, not of the price of the article produced, but of the quantity produced. Consequently the price to which the producer should bring his article will be determined by the equation

$$D + \frac{dD}{dp}\left[p - \frac{d[\phi(D)]}{dD}\right] = 0. \tag{2}$$

This price will fix in turn the annual net receipts or the revenue of the inventor, and the capital value of his secret, or his *productive property*, the ownership of which is guaranteed by law and can have commercial circulation as well as that of a piece of land or any material property. If this value is nil or insignificant, the owner of the property will obtain no pecuniary profit from it; he will abandon it gratis, or for a very small payment, to the first comer who seeks to develop it. The value of a liter will only represent the value of the raw materials, the wages or profits of the agents who coöperate in making and marketing it, and the interest on the capital necessary for development.

28. The terms of our example prevent our admitting in this case a limitation of the productive forces, which would hinder the producer from lowering the price to the rate which would give the *maximum* net receipts, according to the law of demand. But in a great many other cases there may be such a limitation, and if Δ expresses the limit which the production or the demand cannot exceed, the price will be fixed by the relation $F(p) = Δ$, as if there were no cost of production. The cost, in this case, is not borne by the consumers at all; it only diminishes the income of the producer. It falls not exactly on the proprietor (who, unless the inventor or first holder—a question of original conditions with which

theory has nothing to do—acquired the property, himself or through his agents, for a value proportioned to its revenue), but on the property itself. A decrease of this cost will only be to the advantage of the producer, so far as it does not result in the possibility of increasing his producing power.

29. Let us return to the case where this possibility exists, and where the price p is determined according to equation (2). We shall observe that the coefficient $\dfrac{d[\phi(D)]}{dD}$, though it may increase or decrease as D increases, must be supposed to be positive, for it would be absurd that the *absolute* expense of production should decrease as production increases. We shall call attention also to the fact that necessarily $p > \dfrac{d[\phi(D)]}{dD}$, for dD being the increase of production, $d[\phi(D)]$ is the increase in the cost, pdD is the increase of the gross receipts, and whatever may be the abundance of the source of production, the producer will always stop when the increase in expense exceeds the increase in receipts. This is also abundantly evident from the form of equation (2), since D is always a positive quantity, and $\dfrac{dD}{dp}$ a negative quantity.

In the course of our investigations we shall seldom have occasion to consider $\phi(D)$ directly, but only its differential coefficient $\dfrac{d[\phi(D)]}{dD}$, which we will denote by $\phi'(D)$. This differential coefficient is a new function of D, the form of which exerts very great influence on the principal problems of economic science.

The function $\phi'(D)$ is capable of increasing or decreasing as D increases, according to the nature of the producing forces and of the articles produced.

For what are properly called *manufactured articles*, it is generally the case that the cost becomes proportionally less as production increases, or, in other words, when D increases $\phi'(D)$ is a decreasing function. This comes from better organization of the work, from discounts on the price of raw materials for large purchases, and finally from the reduction of what is known to producers as *general expense*. It may happen, however, even in exploiting products of this nature, that when the exploitation is carried beyond certain limits, it induces higher prices for raw materials and labour, to the point where $\phi'(D)$ again begins to increase with D.

Whenever it is a question of working agricultural lands, of mines, or of quarries, *i.e.* of what is essentially real estate, the function $\phi'(D)$ increases with D; and, as we shall soon see, it is in consequence of this fact alone that farms, mines, and quarries yield a net revenue to their owners, long before all has been extracted from the soil which it is physically able to produce, and notwithstanding the great subdivision of these properties, which causes between producers a competition which can be considered as unlimited. On the contrary, investments made under the condition that as D increases $\phi'(D)$ decreases, can only yield a net income or a *rent* in the case of a monopoly properly so-called, or of a competition sufficiently limited to allow the effects of a monopoly collectively maintained to be still perceptible.

30. Between the two cases where the function $\phi'(D)$ is increasing and decreasing, there falls naturally the one where this function reduces to a constant, the cost being constantly proportional to the production, and where equation (2) takes the form

$$D + \frac{dD}{dp}(p - g) = 0.$$

The case must also be pointed out where $\phi(D)$ is a constant, and $\phi'(D) = 0$, so that the price is the same as if there were no cost. This case occurs more frequently than would be suspected at first glance, especially where we have to do with production under a monopoly, and where the value of the number D receives the extension of which it admits. For instance, in a theatrical enterprise D denotes the number of tickets sold, and the cost of the enterprise remains practically the same, without reference to the number of spectators. For the tolls of a bridge, which is another monopolistic investment, D denotes the number of passengers; and the costs for repairs, watching, and bookkeeping will be the same, whether the crossing is much or little used. In such cases the constant g disappears, equation (2) becomes the same as equation (1), and the price p is determined in the same manner as if there were no costs.

31. It seems a matter of course that when the cost of production increases, the price fixed by the monopolist, according to equation (2), will increase likewise; but, on consideration, it will appear that so important a proposition should be supported by a rational demonstration; and furthermore, this demonstration will lead us to an equally important observation, which only mathematics can incontestably establish.

Let p_0 be the root of equation (2) which we will put in the form

$$F(p) + F'(p)[p - \psi(p)] = 0, \tag{3}$$

as $\phi'(D) = \phi'[F(p)]$ can be more simply replaced by $\psi(p)$; and suppose that, as the function $\psi(p)$ varies by a quantity u, and becomes $\psi(p) + u$, p becomes $p_0 + \delta$. If we neglect the squares and higher powers of the increments u and δ, equation (3) will establish the following relation between these two increments:

$$\{F'(p_0)[2 - \psi'(p_0)] + F''(p_0)[p_0 - \psi(p_0)]\}\delta$$
$$- uF'(p_0) = 0;$$

(4)

the coefficient of δ in this expression being the derivative with respect to p of the first member of equation (3), in which derivative the value p_0 has been given to p.

But this coefficient of δ is necessarily negative, according to the well-known theory of maxima and minima; for if it were positive, the root p_0 of equation (3) would correspond to the minimum of the function $pF(p) - \phi(D)$, and not to the maximum of this function, as it should. Moreover $F(p)$ is by its nature a negative quantity. In general, therefore, the increment δ is of the same sign as the increment u.

32. This result has been demonstrated on the supposition that the variations u, δ are very small quantities, of which the squares and products can be neglected without sensible error, but by a very simple argument this restriction can be removed. In fact, whatever the increase of cost denoted by u, it can be supposed that the function $\psi(p)$ passes from the value $\psi(p)$ to the value $\psi(p) + u$ by a series of very small increments, u_1, u_2, u_3, etc., all of the same sign. At the same time p will pass from the value p_0 to the value $p_0 + \delta$ by a series of corresponding increments, also very small, $\delta_1, \delta_2, \delta_3$, etc.; δ_1 will be (according to the preceding paragraph) of the same sign as u_1, δ_2 as u_2, etc. Therefore,

$$\delta = \delta_1 + \delta_2 + \delta_3 + \text{etc.,}$$

will be of the same sign as

$$u = u_1 + u_2 + u_3 + \text{etc.}$$

This method of demonstration should be borne in mind, as it will be frequently recurred to.

33. From equation (4) we obtain

$$\frac{\delta}{u} = \frac{F'(p_0)}{F'(p_0)[2 - \psi'(p_0)] + F''(p_0)[p_0 - \psi(p_0)]},$$

and since both terms of the fraction in the second member are negative, we conclude that δ will be numerically greater or less than u according as we have

$$- F'(p_0) \gtrless - F'(p_0)[2 - \psi'(p_0)] - F''(p_0)[p_0 - \psi(p_0)],$$

or, in other words,

$$F'(p_0)[1 - \psi'(p_0)] + F''(p_0)[p_0 - \psi(p_0)] \gtrless 0,$$

which, by replacing $p_0 - \psi(p_0)$ by its value as deduced from equation (3), becomes

$$[F'(p_0)]^2[1 - \psi'(p_0)] - F(p_0) \times F''(p_0) \lessgtr 0.$$

34. To make this more obvious by numerical applications, let us take a fictitious case. Suppose that the function $\phi'(D)$ were at first $= 0$, and that it subsequently reduces to a constant g. The first value of p or p_0 will be given by the equation

$$F(p) + pF'(p) = 0;$$

the second value of p, which we will call p', will be given by another equation

$$F(p) + (p - g)F'(p) = 0. \tag{5}$$

Suppose, in the first place, that $F(p) = \dfrac{a}{b + p^2}$; the values of p_0 and p', according to the preceding equations, will be respectively

$$p_0 = \sqrt{b}, \text{ and } p' = g + \sqrt{b + g^2} = g + \sqrt{p_0^2 + g^2}$$

(the root of equation (5) which would give a negative value for p' must necessarily be excluded). In this case we see that p' is greater than p_0 by a quantity greater than g, i.e. greater than the amount of the new cost imposed on the production. If, for instance, the new cost is one-tenth of the original price, or if $g = \frac{1}{10}p_0$, we shall have $p' = p_0 \, 1.1488$; the increase in price will be very nearly one and one-half tenths; the old price being 20 francs and the cost 2 francs, the new price will be 23 francs, or, more exactly, 22 francs 97 centimes.[2]

Suppose, in the second place, $F(p) = \dfrac{a}{b + p^3}$, we shall have $p_0 = \sqrt[3]{\dfrac{b}{2}}$; and equation (5) will become

$$2p^3 - 3gp^2 - b = 0,$$

or

$$p^3 - \tfrac{3}{2}gp^2 - p_0^3 = 0,$$

which by the ordinary method of solution will give

$$p' = \tfrac{1}{2} \{ g + \sqrt[3]{g^3 + 4p_0^3 + 2\sqrt{2p_0^3(g^3 + 2p_0^3)}} \\ + \sqrt[3]{g^3 + 4p_0^3 - 2\sqrt{2p_0^3(g^3 + 2p_0^3)}} \} .$$

---

[2] Note by the Translator: The figures given above are as they appear in the original French, but there was evidently a mistake in arithmetic made by the author, who used under the radical $p_0^2 + g$ instead of $p_0^2 + g^2$. The figures should be $p' = p_0 \times 1.1050$, and the new price 22 francs and 10 centimes.

In this case the excess of p' over p_0 will be less than g. If $g = \frac{1}{10}p_0$, we shall have $p' = p_0 \times 1.0505$. Thus if the new cost is one-tenth of the original price, the increase in price will only be one-half of one-tenth of that price. The old price being 20 francs, and the added cost 2 francs, the new price will be only 21 francs, or, more exactly, 21 francs .01 centime.

35. The result which we have just reached is well worth attention: it shows us that, according to the form of the function $F(p)$, or according to the law of demand, an increase in the cost of production augments the price of a commodity, for which there exists a monopoly, sometimes much more and sometimes much less than the increase in cost; and that, in the same manner, there is no equality between the reduction of cost and fall in the price of the commodity.

It results from this, that if the new cost were not met by the producer himself, but by the consumer, or by an intermediate agent, who would be reimbursed by the consumer, this increase in cost, which would always make the article dearer for the consumer, and which would always diminish the net income of the producer, might, according to circumstances, produce an advance or a decline in the price paid to the producer.

Reciprocally, a fall in the cost of *transmission*, or in that of passing the commodity from the possession of the producer to that of the consumer, may have the effect at one time of increasing the price paid to the producer, and at another time of diminishing it; but in all cases it will diminish the final price paid by the consumer, and will cause an increase in the net income of the producer.

All those expenses which are incurred with a view to preparing for final consumption the crude commodity as it leaves the producers' hands, must in this respect be considered in the same light as costs of transmission.

However, this calculation is only applicable in the case where the producer can meet the demand which gives him the greatest net return, and reduce his price as much as is necessary to attain this maximum return. In other cases, he will produce all he can, before as well as after the change in the cost, whether of production or of transmission, and the cost price to the consumer will remain invariable, because in a condition of equilibrium, and on a large scale, there cannot be two different prices for the same quantity marketed. The increase of cost, therefore, from whatever source, must finally be wholly borne by the producer.

OF THE INFLUENCE OF TAXATION ON COMMODITIES
PRODUCED UNDER A MONOPOLY[3]

36. The considerations developed at the close of the preceding chapter are of course applicable to the theory of taxation. The burden of taxation makes what might be called an artificial cost, adjusted according to a more or less systematic plan, and of which at least the distribution, if not the general rate, is within the power of the legislator to determine; and consequently the theory of the incidence of taxation is one of the great objects of investigations in Political Economy.

The forms of taxation may vary widely. At the time when public affairs were conducted in secret, it was considered a great art to be able so to diversify forms as, it was thought, to increase the supplies to the treasury without making its exactions felt. Later, according to a half-understood theory, it was considered desirable to make taxation as uniform as possible; but the financial legislation which stands to-day in France is equally removed from both these extremes and recognizes forms of taxation essentially distinct, though quite limited in number, which, from practical rather than theoretical considerations, it classes in two main categories of direct and indirect taxes. The levy assessed according to the assumed net income of a landowner or of a producer is a direct tax. The excise which must be paid on an article before it reaches the consumer's hands is an indirect tax; and we intend to consider only these two kinds of taxation. It should be borne in mind, that in this chapter only those articles are considered of which the production is controlled by a monopoly.

If a tax, either fixed or proportional to his net income, is laid upon a monopolist producer, it is plain, according to explanations in the two preceding chapters, that this tax will have no direct influence on the price of the article which he produces, and consequently none on the quantity produced, and that it will not be a burden to the consumer in any way. Its only immediate result is to diminish the income and the capitalized wealth of the producer.

It can even be said that this tax only injures first holders, inventors, and, in general, those who were profiting by the property at the time when the tax was laid, and such of their successors as have obtained the property gratuitously. For successors who have to pay regulate their purchase price according to the net returns, after deduction of the tax. If the capitalized

---

[3] Chapter VI.

value is reduced while the property is in their hands, it is a real disaster for them.

Even though this tax does not affect consumers it may be nevertheless very prejudicial to public interests, not principally because, by reducing the wealth of the producer so taxed, it reduces his means as a consumer and affects the law of demand for other articles; but especially because the part withdrawn by the tax from the income of the producer is ordinarily employed in a manner less advantageous for the increase of the annual product, the national wealth, and the comfort of the people, than if it had remained at the disposal of the producer himself. We will not consider here the effects on the distribution of the products of nature and of labour of such a levy, although this is undoubtedly the final object of all problems connected with the theory of wealth.

But it is possible to say, in agreement with all authorities, that even though it does not prevent invested capital from producing as much as before its taxation, a tax on the income of the producer is an obstacle to the creation of new investments and even to the improvement of existing ones, if a proportional tax is to be considered. No one will embark his capital in new investments, nor in the improvement of existing investments, if he can no longer obtain the ordinary interest brought in by capital in enterprises of the same kind, on account of the tax imposed on the net income from his investment. It is by closing an avenue of employment for labour and industry, that such a tax, when exaggerated, has its most disastrous effect.

Bounties, an invention of modern times, are the opposite of taxes. To use an algebraic expression, they are a negative tax, so that the same analytical formulas are applicable to taxation and bounties. But bounties differ from taxes in being reckoned on the gross product; it has never been proposed to grant a bounty on the net product, so that it is only for the sake of system that we mention bounties at all here in connection with taxation on income or net product.

37. The tax may and generally does consist in a fixed charge levied on each unit of a commodity, or one of which the product is proportional to D. Its effects are the same as if the function $\phi'(D)$ were increased by a constant i. An increase in cost to the consumer must always result from it, and a decrease of consumption or production; but, according to circumstances, the increase of cost to the consumer may be greater or less than i. It makes no difference in the absolute effects of taxation to producer or consumers, from whom the tax is collected, or at what period the revenue collector reaches the commodity; only the apparent effects will vary according as the producer does or does not pay the tax in ad-

vance; *i.e.* if he advances it, the price of the commodity as it leaves his hands will always be increased by taxation; in the opposite case this price may rise in some cases and fall in others.

However, in saying that the absolute effects of taxation are the same, whether the producer does or does not pay the tax in advance, we mean to restrict this proposition to the case in which only the principal is considered, and where the additional charges arising from interest on this principal are neglected. When the commodity must pass through many hands before reaching consumers, as each intermediate agent must employ additional capital, if the article has already paid its tribute, so evidently the commodity will be sold at a higher price to consumers just in proportion as the tax is prematurely collected; and the consumption will be further reduced correspondingly. It is important, therefore, to consumers, to producers, and even to the treasury, that the tax should be paid late, and, if possible, by the consumer himself; although, on the other hand, the collection of a tax becomes more expensive by subdivisions, and tends more to excite complaints by the masses, *i.e.* the consumers, because it makes the operation of the revenue department more evident to them.

38. Let us call p_0 the price of the commodity before the tax, and p' the price which follows imposition of the tax. p_0 will be the root of the equation

$$F(p) + [p - \psi(p)]F'(p) = 0;$$

and p' that of the equation

$$F(p) + [p - \psi(p) - i]F'(p) = 0.$$

With an approximation proportionally greater as i becomes smaller relatively to p_0, we shall have

$$p' - p_0 = \frac{i[F'(p_0)]^2}{[F'(p_0)]^2[2 - \psi'(p_0)] - F(p_0)F''(p_0)}.$$

The pecuinary loss borne by consumers, who continue to buy the commodity notwithstanding the increased price, will be

$$(p' - p_0)F(p');$$

the *gross* profit of the treasury will be

$$iF(p');$$

so that the loss of consumers alone will exceed this gross profit in all cases where we have

$$p' - p_0 > i;$$

i.e. in the same cases where imposition of the tax would increase the price on leaving the producer's hands when he does not pay the tax in advance.

The loss of net income borne by the monopolist will be

$$p_0F(p_0) - \phi[F(p_0)] - \{p'F(p') - \phi[F(p')] - iF(p')\}$$
$$= p_0F(p_0) - \phi[F(p_0)] - \{p'F(p') - \phi[F(p')]\} + iF(p').$$

But, since p_0 is the value of p which renders the function

$$pF(p) - \phi[F(p)]$$

a maximum, we must necessarily have

$$p_0F(p_0) - \phi[F(p_0)] > p'F(p') - \phi[F(p')],$$

and therefore the loss to the monopolist alone will exceed the gross profit of the treasury. The loss borne by consumers will therefore remain without any compensation, and there is no doubt that the doctrine of Quesnay's school is perfectly applicable to the products of monopoly; namely, that it is better to levy a direct tax on the net income of the monopolist than to lay a specific tax on the commodity.

The amount spent in consumption of the article before the tax was $p_0F(p_0)$; after the tax it becomes $p'F(p')$ and we must necessarily have

$$p_0F(p_0) > p'F(p').$$

This results from the inequality just proved

$$p_0F(p_0) - \phi[F(p_0)] > p'F(p') - \phi[F(p')]$$

and from this other inequality

$$\phi[F(p_0)] > \phi[F(p')],$$

which is self-evident, since the absolute amount of the cost of production cannot change except by decreasing when the quantity produced decreases.

The value of i, or the rate of tax, which will make the gross profit of the treasury a maximum, can be obtained from the following equation:

$$\frac{d[iF(p')]}{di} = F(p') + iF'(p')\frac{dp'}{di} = 0,$$

and p' is furthermore a function of i which is given by the equation

$$F(p') + [p' - \psi(p') - i]F'(p') = 0.$$

39. If the law of demand and the productive property are such that the producer, whether before or after imposition of the tax, is unable to supply the demand which would produce the greatest profit, he will sell all his product, as well after as before imposition of the tax, and will sell it at the same price, because, in a stable condition of things, there can-

not be two prices corresponding to the same output. The tax will therefore fall entirely on the producer.

From this it seems as if, in fixing the amount of this tax, the treasury would only be limited by the condition of not entirely absorbing the net income of the producer. But this consequence would be inexact, and the error can be proved at least in one case; namely, that where $\phi'(D)$ increases with D, and where we have at the same time $p' - p_0 > i$, p_0 and p' being respectively the roots of the equations

$$F(p) + [p - \phi'(D)]F'(p) = 0, \tag{1}$$

and

$$F(p) + [p - \phi'(D) - i]F'(p) = 0.$$

In fact, if Δ is the necessary limit of production, and π the value of p derived from the relation $F(p) = \Delta$, it would be necessary for the hypothesis that $\pi > p'$, and *a fortiori* $\pi > p_0 + i$, i being equal to $\pi - \dfrac{\phi(\Delta)}{\Delta}$. We should therefore have

$$\pi > p_0 + \pi - \frac{\phi(\Delta)}{\Delta}, \text{ or } p_0 < \frac{\phi(\Delta)}{\Delta}.$$

But this last inequality certainly cannot hold true if $\phi'(D)$ is (according to the hypothesis) a function which increases with D; for then, p_0 being smaller than π, the demand D_0 corresponding to p_0 is greater than Δ, and $\dfrac{\phi(D_0)}{D_0}$ is greater than $\dfrac{\phi(\Delta)}{\Delta}$; p_0 would therefore be less than $\dfrac{\phi(D_0)}{D_0}$. This value of p_0 would therefore cause a loss to the producer and consequently could not be the root of equation (1).

40. If the government, instead of imposing a tax, grants a bounty i to the producer under a monopoly, the price, which was p_0 before the bounty, will fall, and will become p'. According to circumstances, we shall have $p_0 - p' \gtreqless i$. The loss to the public treasury will be $iF(p')$; the gain to such consumers as were buying before the bounty will be $(p_0 - p')F(p_0)$, and will have no necessary relation to $iF(p')$. As for the consumers who only buy after the fall in price resulting from the bounty, it is impossible to assert that the premium has benefited them pecuniarily; it has only diverted their money from one line of use to apply it to the line thus favoured.

The change in the net income of the producer which occurs as a consequence of the bounty is:

$$p'F(p') - \phi[F(p')] + iF(p') - [p_0F(p_0) - \phi[F(p_0)]]$$
$$= iF(p') - \{p_0F(p_0) - \phi[F(p_0)] - [p'F(p') - \phi[F(p')]]\}.$$

But, since p_0 is the value of p which renders a maximum the function

$$pF(p) - \phi[F(p)],$$

it always follows that

$$p_0F(p_0) - \phi[F(p_0)] > p'F(p') - \phi[F(p')],$$

so that the gain resulting from the premium to the producer (and in general it is the interest of the producer, and not that of the consumers, which is considered in establishing a bounty) is essentially less than the public sacrifice at the cost of which this gain is attained.

41. Taxation may be imposed according to a rate not specific but proportional to the selling price; in other words, the tax, instead of being expressed by the constant i, is expressed by the term np.[4] In this case, if the commodity were produced and delivered without appreciable cost between producer and consumers, the price being determined by the condition that the producer shall derive the greatest possible profit, or that $(1 - n)pF(p)$ shall be a maximum, the presence of the constant factor $(1 - n)$ will not alter the value of p in the least; the tax will fall wholly on the producer, and might go so far as to absorb all his net income.

In the opposite case, the only one which can ordinarily be realized, the condition would be that the function

$$(1 - n)pF(p) - \phi(D)$$

should attain a maximum, or that we should have

$$F(p) + \left\{ p - \frac{1}{1 - n} \phi'[F(p)] \right\} F'(p) = 0 ; \qquad (2)$$

so that imposition of the tax would have absolutely the same effects as if all the items of cost requisite for the production of the commodity and its distribution to the consumers were increased in the proportion of $1 \div \frac{1}{1 - n}$; a very simple result, and one which merits attention.[6]

Thus a tax of this nature, circumstances being otherwise unchanged, will be the heavier the higher the costs of production and distribution already are, or the smaller the proportion of the price of the commodity represented by the profit of the monopolist.

---

[4] There is a portion of the cost which may be considered to act as such a tax, *i.e.* as being proportional to the price[5] of the commodity. This is the portion which pays the interest on the capital employed in marketing the commodity.

[5] [Mistranslated "cost." Cf. Augustin Cournot, Recherches sur les principes mathématiques de la théorie des richesses, Georges Lutfalla (ed.) (Paris: Marcel Rivière & Cie, 1938), p. 83: "c'est-à-dire comme étant proportionelle au prix de la denrée." Ed.]

[6] [I.e., if the original cost is to the new, increased cost as 1 is to $\frac{1}{1 - n}$. Ed.]

The gross profit of the treasury is $np'F(p')$. The value of n which makes it a maximum is given by the equation

$$\frac{d[np'F(p')]}{dn} = 0,$$

or

$$p'F(p') + \frac{dp'}{dn}n[F(p') + p'F'(p')] = 0.$$

The loss borne by consumers who continue to buy the commodity will be $(p' - p_0)F(p')$; so that this loss will be greater or less than the gross profit to the treasury according as $p' - p_0 \gtrless np'$, or as $p'(1 - n) \gtrless p_0$.

The loss borne by the producer will be

$$p_0F(p_0) - \phi[F(p_0)] - \{(1 - n)p'F(p') - \phi[F(p')]\}$$
$$= p_0F(p_0) - \phi[F(p_0)] - \{p'F(p') - \phi[F(p')]\} + np'F(p').$$

This loss alone will therefore exceed the gross profit of the treasury, as in the other kind of taxation.

42. There remains for discussion the effect of taxation *in kind* on the price of an article under a monopoly. We will take this up only very briefly, as this form of taxation everywhere tends to disappear, owing to the industrial development of nations. We will distinguish here two different cases.

It is possible that the product of a tax in kind may be applied to a consumption which would not take place if it were not for the tax, and to one which has no influence on the demand which other consumers make on the producer. Let us first suppose the amount paid in kind equal to a constant K. The equation for the maximum, from which the value of p is to be deduced, instead of

$$F(p) + \{p - \phi'[F(p)]\}F'(p) = 0,$$

will become

$$F(p) + \{p - \phi'[F(p) + K]\}F'(p) = 0, \tag{3}$$

so that such a tax will raise or lower the price of the article, according as the function $\phi'(D)$ increases or decreases for increasing values of D.

Let us next suppose the amount paid in kind to be proportional to the gross production, and to be in the ratio of $n \div 1$ to this gross production. The function which it is the producer's interest to render a maximum will be

$$pF(p) - \phi\left[\frac{F(p)}{1 - n}\right],$$

and equation (3) will be replaced by

$$F(p) + \left\{ p - \frac{1}{(1-n)}\ \phi'\left[\frac{F(p)}{1-n}\right] \right\} F'(p) = 0.$$

If, on the other hand, the law of the consumption of the commodity is supposed to remain the same before as after the taxation in kind, we shall have for the function which must be a maximum in case of a fixed payment K,

$$p[F(p) - K] - \phi[F(p)],$$

and for its differential which determines the value of p,

$$F(p) - K + \{p - \phi'[F(p)]\}F'(p) = 0.$$

An exaction proportional to the gross product, or a *tithe*, would give for the function for the maximum

$$(1 - n)pF(p) - \phi[F(p)],$$

of which the differential would be the same as the first member of equation (2). Thus the price of the commodity, the profit to the treasury, the burden on consumers, and the loss to the producer would be absolutely the same as if the commodity had had imposed on it a tax proportional to the price in the ratio of $n \div 1$.

NOTES ON COURNOT'S MATHEMATICS[7]

1. *p.* 240. Equation (1) gives $p = \dfrac{F(p)}{-F'(p)}$, which multiplied by $F(p)$ gives

$$pF(p) = \frac{[F(p)]^2}{-F'(p)}.$$

2. *p.* 241, *equation* (2). To make the net receipts $pF(p) - \phi(D)$ a maximum, its differential coefficient must be zero; *i.e.*, $F(p) + pF'(p) - \dfrac{d\phi(D)}{dp}$ $= 0$. Cournot's result (2) is the same, D being in place of $F(p)$, $\dfrac{dD}{dp}$ in place of $F'(p)$, and $\dfrac{d\phi(D)}{dD} \times \dfrac{dD}{dp}$ in place of $\dfrac{d\phi(D)}{dp}$. The form given on p. 243 (3) is nearer to that here expressed.

3. *pp.* 243, 244. Supposing $\psi(p)$ to be replaced by $\psi(p) + u$, equation (3), namely,

$$F(p) + F'(p)[p - \psi(p)] = 0 \tag{3}$$

becomes

$$F(p) + F'(p)[p - \psi(p) - u] = 0 \tag{3'}$$

[7] By Irving Fisher; reprinted from Appendix to his article "Cournot and Mathematical Economics," *Quarterly Journal of Economics*, January, 1898, and reproduced in the 1929 edition of the English translation of Cournot's work.

If the root of (3) is p_0, the root of (3)′ is called $p_0 + \delta$. (3) may then be written,

$$F(p_0) + F'(p_0)[p_0 - \psi(p_0)] = 0$$

and (3)′, $F(p_0 + \delta) + F'(p_0 + \delta)[p_0 + \delta - \psi(p_0 + \delta) - u] = 0 \,.$

Now, by Taylor's theorem, $F(p_0 + \delta) = F(p_0) + \delta F'(p_0) +$ terms involving squares and higher powers of δ, which may all be neglected, assuming δ sufficiently small and Taylor's theorem applicable. Substituting this value for $F(p_0 + \delta)$ and, in like manner, $F'(p_0) + \delta F''(p_0)$ for $F'(p_0 + \delta)$ and $\psi(p_0) + \delta \psi'(p_0)$ for $\psi(p_0 + \delta)$, we obtain another form of (3)′. If (3) be subtracted from this, the result is (4), after neglecting any terms which may remain involving increments of the second order, such as δ^2 or δu. The process, here exemplified, of deriving the relation between a small cause such as u and its effect δ, is so repeatedly employed by Cournot that the careful student will do well to master it once for all.

4. *p.* 245. The formula immediately preceding § 34 is obtained by substituting in the formula above it the value of $p_0 - \psi(p_0)$ derived from (3), namely,

$-\dfrac{F(p_0)}{F'(p_0)}$, and then multiplying through by the *negative* quantity $F'(p_0)$, which reverses the signs of inequality.

5. *p.* 249. The value of $p' - p_0$ is derived just as was equation (4) on p. 244. In fact, (4), p. 244, and the present equation are identical except in form. The tax i here takes the place of the increase of cost, u; and $p' - p_0$, the increase of price, is the same magnitude as δ. The identity is seen by obtaining the value of δ from (4), p. 244, multiplying numerator and denominator by $F'(p_0)$, and substituting for $F'(p_0)[p_0 - \psi(p_0)]$ in the denominator its equal, $-F(p_0)$, as given by the third equation on p. 249.

6. *p.* 250, *line* 4. *I.e.*, the loss is the difference between the net income at price p_0 and the net income at price p', which latter net income involves the deduction of the tax $iF(p')$.

7. *p.* 250, *line* 9. The left member, being the *maximum* value of the function two lines above, is necessarily greater than the right member, which is *another* value of that function.

8. *p.* 250, *line* 18. This formula is obtained by adding the two inequalities which follow.

9. *p.* 250, *line* 30. See note 3. [Note 3 reads: "The value of p which will render $pF(p)$ a maximum is the root of the equation formed by putting the differential coefficient of $pF(p)$, namely, $F(p) + pF'(p)$, equal to zero." Ed.]

10. *p.* 251, *last equation.* See note 6.

11. *p.* 253, *line* 17. Of the two cases, the second begins on p. 254, line 2, *not* on p. 253, last paragraph, which relates only to a subdivision of case one.

16

*Taxation in the Monopoly Case**

By KNUT WICKSELL

Let annual demand for a monopoly good be expressed as a stable function $F(p)$ of unit price p. Gross receipts then equal $p \cdot F(p)$. Now let fixed costs of the monopolist equal K per annum and let variable unit cost equal k, so that the monopolist's net revenue equals

$$(p - k) \cdot F(p) - K$$

This expression reaches a maximum when the derivative with respect to p becomes zero, that is when

$$(p - k)F'(p) + F(p) = 0$$

or

$$-\frac{F(p)}{F'(p)} = p - k$$

This expression may be readily interpreted geometrically since the expression on the left is the subtangent of the demand curve (where p is the abcissa and $F(p)$ the ordinate) at the particular point.

As our equation shows, fixed costs have no influence on price determination; and the same holds for a lump-sum tax, independent of output. If such a tax should consume total net revenue, it would render the entire operation impossible.

The situation is just as simple for a tax which takes away a specified fraction of net revenue. Such a tax again would have no effect on price determination, as follows from our equation. It would merely reduce net revenue by the amount of tax, neither more nor less, and would have no effect on the consumer. Even a progressive tax on net revenue would have no other effects.

If, however, the tax is imposed at a fixed rate per unit of output, the effect will be such as to increase variable unit cost by the amount of tax. If the unit tax equals s, the most profitable price is now determined where

---

* This piece appears as an appendix to Chapter 2, pp. 19–21 in Knut Wicksell, *Finanztheoretische Untersuchungen, nebst Darstellung und Kritik des Steuerwesens Schwedens* (Jena: Gustav Fischer, 1896). The translation was prepared by Richard A. Musgrave.

$$-\frac{F(p)}{F'(p)} = p - k - s$$

which, as may be readily shown, always implies an increase in price.

Now suppose that the tax equals a given fraction $\frac{1}{n}$ of gross receipts or, which is the same, of price. In this case, the net revenue of the monopolist is measured by

$$\left(\frac{n-1}{n} \cdot p - k\right)F(p) - K$$

and this amount reaches a maximum where

$$-\frac{F(p)}{F'(p)} = p - \frac{n}{n-1}k$$

This price will be the same as from the earlier case of a unit tax with fixed rate, provided that the latter equals $\frac{1}{n-1}$ of variable unit cost. Thus, an ad valorem tax at a rate of $\frac{1}{10}$ would lead to the same price as a unit tax equal to $\frac{1}{9}$ of variable cost; an ad valorem tax which takes one half of gross receipts would be equal in this respect to a unit tax at a rate equal to variable unit cost and so forth. This somewhat peculiar relationship is wholly independent of the shape of the demand curve.

However, it is readily shown on the basis of the above equation, that the yield of the ad valorem tax would be greater, in this case, than that of the unit tax. Since the expression on the left is always positive, we have

$$p > \frac{n}{n-1}k, \qquad \text{hence } \frac{p}{n} > \frac{k}{n-1} \text{ etc.}$$

By the same token, the increase in price must be less if the same yield is obtained by way of an ad valorem tax than by way of a unit tax. The ad valorem tax will thus be preferable to the consumer—and it will be preferable to the monopolist as well, since he will lose the more, the higher is the price which he must set after the tax is imposed. . . . The relative gain which the monopolist may derive by increasing price will decline by the square of the tax rate, provided it is small. This may be proven readily if we replace the demand function in the neighborhood of the monopoly price by a linear function, such as $F(p) = a - m \cdot p$.

17

*The Pure Theory of Taxation**

By F. Y. EDGEWORTH

[This article, published in the *Economic Journal*, 1897, discusses the incidence of taxes, and the criterion of a good tax system, the rule according to which the burden of taxation ought to be distributed among the tax-payers. For the first purpose there is introduced a new classification formed by four dichotomic cross divisions. The leading case defined by the first, or positive, attribute of each division is, contrary to classical tradition, international trade, including dealings among non-competing groups within the same country. The incidence of taxation in this case having been already considered generally (Sect. IV.), there are here discussed only special cases. One such occurs when there is perfect inelasticity on one side of the market, or even on both. Other peculiar cases arise when commodities are *correlated* in respect of Consumption or Production. The genus correlation includes two species, "rivals" or mutual substitutes, when an increase in the possession of one renders the possession of the other less desirable, or an increase in the production of one renders the production of the other more difficult; and "complementary" articles with converse properties. It is shown that (even in a regime of competition) when demand and production are complementary, a tax on one may cause the price of *either* article to fall; with advantage to the consumers as a whole. It might have been added that if the commodities are rivals both in production and consumption, a tax on one may cause the price of *both* to fall. This *curiosum* does not depend on a change in the marginal value of money. The ordinary assumption that the total utility of consumption and cost of production is measured by money of stable value is throughout retained. Corresponding to the last-named paradox is the incident that when both supply and demand are rival, the producers may benefit by the imposition of a tax. *Both* prices may be raised; that of the taxed article to an extent in excess of the tax. A somewhat different paradox—a tax on both commodities (correlated as partial substitutes for each other) benefiting the producers of one of them—is instanced in the text. The instance is furnished by house rent; a topic which is treated at length as illustrating the effects of taxation where mobility of capital and labour acts. The effects of an impost like the Inhabited House Duty vary greatly with the length of the period under consideration.

Monopoly is treated on much the same lines as, but in less technical terms than, in the article of the same date (1897) in the *Giornale* (above, E).[1]

---

* From Vol. II of F. Y. Edgeworth, Papers Relating to Political Economy. Published on behalf of the Royal Economic Society by Macmillan and Co., Limited, London, 1925. Reproduced with permission of the Royal Economic Society. [Apparent typographical errors are corrected, with footnote reference to original, by Carl S. Shoup. Ed.]

1 [Section E is not reprinted in this volume. Ed.]

The *curiosa* of the subjects are treated more fully there and in subsequent Papers (see Index, *sub voce* "Paradox"). Attention is called to a peculiar species of semi-monopoly. As mentioned above (D),[2] it is one of the concrete cases in which differential prices may prove advantageous to both consumers and producers.

In the latter part of the article there is advocated as the criterion of good taxation, minimum aggregate sacrifice, distinguished from equal sacrifice in the obvious sense of the term, or proportional sacrifice, as the peculiar conception of Professor Seligman and Cohen-Stuart may be called.

The principle of *minimum* sacrifice is now very generally accepted, praised by Cannan, and used by Marshall (see *Economic Journal*, 1921, p. 350, and 1917, p. 407). Professor T. N. Carver, who was the first to propound this doctrine, has exhibited its application with convincing clearness in his last work, *National Economy*.]

* * * * *

The science of taxation comprises two subjects to which the character of pure theory may be ascribed: the laws of incidence, and the principle of equal sacrifice.

The first subject presents a variety of distinct cases demarcated by several cross divisions. Of these divisions the following four appear to me the most important for the purposes of theory:

Either (A) all the transactions[3] under consideration are exposed to competition; or (a) among the parties with whom we are concerned there is at least one monopolist.[4]

Either (B) all the products with which we are concerned obey the law of increasing cost; or (b) some do not.[5]

---

[2] [Section D is not reprinted in this volume. Ed.]

[3] I suppose in each case parties to an exchange, the play of demand and supply. Taxation in a regime of socialism or of slavery is not considered.

[4] I understand by a monopolist an individual, or a combination, having the sole control of an article of exchange, and dealing with it solely in the interest of the monopolist. I agree with Professor Walras in thinking that much confusion has been caused by extending the term to cases in which a commodity absolutely limited, such as land of a certain sort is in the hands of a *plurality* of uncombined possessors (*Éléments d'Économie Politique*, 2nd edition, Art. 408. Cp. *Dictionnaire d'Économie Politique*, Art. "Monopole"). As to the definition of maximum advantage in the case of a *combination*, see the present writer's article on "The Pure Theory of Monopoly" in the *Giornale degli Economisti* for 1897.

[5] I define the laws of increasing and decreasing cost thus. If $\phi(x)$ be the expense—or more generally the equivalent in money of the "real cost"—of producing the quantity x of a certain commodity, the law of increasing cost holds, when $\frac{d_2\phi}{dx^2}$ is *positive;* the law of decreasing cost, when $\frac{d_2\phi}{dx^2}$ is *negative* (*cp.* Cournot, *Principes Mathématiques*, Art. 29). [p. 242 of this volume. Ed.] Generally if $\phi(x, y, z \ldots)$ is the cost of producing the quantities $x, y, z \ldots$ of several commodities, the law of decreasing returns does or does not hold, according as the second term of variation of ϕ does or does not fulfil the conditions of a *maximum*. "Decreasing and increasing returns" will be here used as synonyms of increasing and decreasing cost. For fuller explanations and variant definitions, see C. [Section C is not reprinted in this volume. Ed.]

Either (C) the mobility of capital and labour[6] is not taken account of, or (c) exists and is taken account of.

Either (D) the taxation considered varies with the quantities of articles exchanged (including money, as in the case of a specific or an *ad valorem* tax, or one in kind), and so may be described as a tax on *margin*; or (d) it does not so vary (as in the case of a tax on profits, or a poll-tax), and so may be described as a tax on *surplus*.[7]

I proceed to consider the more important of the cases formed by the combination of these attributes, giving priority to the first member of each division, the one designated by a capital letter. According to the order adopted, the case first to be considered is that which is defined by taking the first member of each division and which may accordingly be designated as A B C D; indicating that (A) the parties considered consist of two or more groups, the members of each group supplying the same article[8] in competition with each other; (B) each additional increment of every product is obtained by a more than proportional increase of outlay; (C) the groups are "non-competing" in Cairnes' sense, "industrial competition" is not supposed to exist; (D) the tax is of the same genus as an export or import tax.

A B C D. The case thus defined is nearly coincident with the case which I have discussed in a former article; that of an export or import tax on an article of international trade; understanding international trade in the generalised sense of "exchange without mobility."[9] Following Mill, we may begin with the simplest variety where there are only two "nations." The case as conceived by us comprises not only international trade (in the proper sense), say between two islands isolated from the rest of the commercial world, but also a simple abstract market, such as the corn market, of which Professor Marshall has described the "temporary equilibrium"[10] or his ideal nut and apple-market;[11] also the dealings by which the shares of the parties in distribution are determined, the labour market, the loan

---

[6] As mobility may exist with respect to some—but not all—of the agents of production (*cp.* article on "International Values" in the *Economic Journal*, Vol. IV, p. 35), the more exact distinction might be between (C) a greater and (c) a less degree of mobility.

[7] For certain theoretic purposes it might be better to distinguish the cases in which the tax (D) strikes the variables by the variation of which the parties under consideration seek each his maximum advantage; or (d) strikes the quantity which it is sought to maximise. The distinction between *margin* and *surplus* hovers between this one and the one in the text. (See "Margin," *Palgrave's Dictionary. Cp.* below, p. 270.)

[8] Or articles in the case of joint or more generally correlated production (below, p. 266).

[9] Above, R, p. 5. [Section R is not reprinted in this volume. Ed.]

[10] *Principles*, Book V, ch. ii, § 1.

[11] *Ibid.*, § 1, *note on Barter* (latter part).

market, the land market, each considered at first abstractedly by itself, and not yet in its true interdependence with the others.[12]

A tax of the kind now under consideration, affecting such a market, will in general prejudice both parties more or less. If, in the metaphor of a distinguished economist, we represent the undisturbed relation of the parties by the equilibrium of two balls resting against each other in a bowl, it may seem, at first sight, that a wedge inserted between the two balls will raise one of them to the full extent of the thickness of the wedge. But on reflection it is evident that this only occurs in the limiting case when the mass of one ball may be neglected in comparison with that of the other. In the absence of data respecting the relative masses of the balls all we can say is that the distance between them will be equal to the thickness of the interposed lamina. Corresponding to the masses of the two balls are the elasticities of demand and supply for the two parties. The general principle is that the tax inflicts more loss on either party, the less the elasticity of that party's demand or supply; other things, including the other party's elasticity, being the same.[13]

This proposition has been demonstrated at length in former articles.[14] It must suffice here to add some remarks suggested by an examination of certain extreme cases.

An instance of infinite elasticity of supply is afforded by the labour market upon the Ricardian hypothesis that, in Mill's words, "there is everywhere a minimum rate of wages, that they can never be lower beyond the length of time required for a diminished rate of increase [of population] to make itself felt, and can never long continue higher."[15] Upon this assumption, it is "hypothetically true" that a tax on wages would not permanently rest on the working classes;[16] a conclusion which

---

[12] One of the best, and I believe the first statements of the simultaneity, in the mathematical sense, of the several equations pertaining to value and distribution is given by Professor Walras in his *Éléments d'Économie Politique Pure*.

[13] When, as in my Articles on International Value, we make abstraction of money, and consider *price* in the generalised sense of M. Walras, *i.e.* rate-of-exchange, then it is unnecessary to distinguish the elasticity of supply from that of demand. The less the extension of the demand attending a fall of price, the less is the extension of supply attending a rise of price. After the point at which demand becomes perfectly inelastic the elasticity may be said to become *negative*. This is the case alluded to in the criticism of Messrs. Auspitz and Lieben (above, R, p. 59) [Section R is not reprinted in this volume. Ed.] as not adapted to a curve which represents the variations of supply with money-price.

[14] The general principle is well stated by Professor Carver in his article on "Shifting of Taxation" in the *Yale Review* for November 1896.

[15] *Political Economy*, Bk. II, ch. xi, § 2.

[16] See Mill's application of the principle, *Political Economy*, Book V, ch. iii, § 4, par. 4.

is justly regarded as the opprobrium of pure theory, if it is applied to justify a tax on wages or on the necessities of the wage-earner. We have, however, Mill's authority for saying that "the assumption contains sufficient truth to render it admissible for the purposes of abstract science."[17]

It should be observed that this perfect elasticity of the supply of labour is predicated only of long periods; for short periods to evoke more work there would presumably be required a higher rate of wages. A similar difference in respect of elasticity between long and short periods is to be noticed in other markets. Thus, according to Professor Seligman, "an equal tax on all capital must fall on the lender, that is the capitalist. There would be no way for him to shift the burden."[18] But he admits that further accumulations might be discouraged. *Pro tanto* then the rate of interest in a long period would be increased.[19] Thus, too, we may partly account for Mill's statement respecting the "attempt to tax all purchases and sales" that "neither class [buyers or sellers] could throw the burden upon the other."[20] This is true for instantaneous periods, at least of sellers, so far as they are under the necessity of selling what they have brought to market. But can it be affirmed in general of a tax like the Spanish *alcavala*, that "if levied from the sellers" in the long run it would burden sellers more than buyers?[21]

The difference between the elasticity of supply according as short or long periods are considered is conspicuous in the case of houses.

For times so short and in places so limited that the number of houses offered may be regarded as a fixed quantity,[22] a tax on house rent, whether imposed on the occupier or owner of the house, is in general borne alto-

---

[17] *Cp.* Adam Smith on taxes upon the wages of labour and the necessaries of life (*Wealth of Nations*, Book V, ch. ii). McCulloch's remarks on these passages (McCulloch's edition of Adam Smith, Vol. IV, note xxiv) seem just; his own views (*ibid.*, p. 544) human. On this point Professor Seligman, as always where *friction* is the subject, is instructive (*Shifting and Incidence*, p. 174). Among the numbers of other writers who might be referred to, Professor Bastable may be distinguished (*Public Finance*, pp. 358–60, and 436, 2nd edition).

[18] *Shifting and Incidence*, p. 132. Cp. *Wealth of Nations*, Book V, ch. ii: "a tax upon the interest of money could not raise the rate of interest; the quantity of stock or money in the country . . . being supposed to remain the same." But it would not remain the same (*ibid. infra*).

[19] *Cp.* Bastable, *Public Finance*, Book III, ch. v, § 7.

[20] *Political Economy*, Book V, ch. v.

[21] The effect attributed to a "tax on all commodities" by Mill in an earlier passage (Book V, ch. iv, § 1, par. 2) would require a long period.

[22] The case of a commodity of which the quantity cannot be increased may be regarded as a limiting case of one which can only be increased at an increasing cost; and so belongs to our class B.

gether by the owner. This conclusion of the older economists[23] is verified by the newer methods.[24]

---

[23] Mill, *Political Economy*, Book V, ch. iii, § 6, par. 3; Ricardo, *Political Economy*, ch. xiv, first two pars.

[24] In the accompanying figure *SS'* and *DD'* are taken as, in Professor Marshall's phrase, "the typical diagram for stable equilibrium for a commodity that obeys the law of diminishing returns" (*Principles of Economics*, p. 425, ed. 3; *cp.* p. 524). A is the position of undisturbed equilibrium, *OH* is then the supply. When equilibrium is disturbed by a tax (of the kind now under consideration) on the producer, the supply is reduced to *Oh; hE* is the price received by the producer, *Ea* the tax paid per unit of commodity (Marshall, *loc. cit.*). The figure shows that, if the tax is levied from the consumer, the result is the same. For *dd'*, the demand-curve as displaced by the tax, strikes the original supply-curve in *E*. This theorem is given by Professor Carver in his article on "Shifting of Taxes" in the *Yale Review* for November, 1896 (compare Auspitz and Lieben, *Theorie der Preise*, Art. 82).

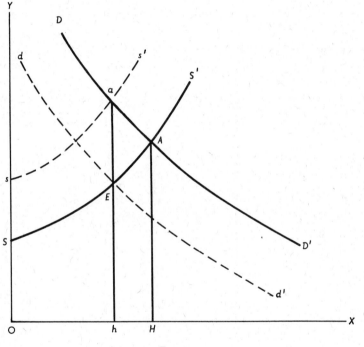

FIG. 11

Fig. 12 represents the two limiting cases of this theorem. *SS'* is the perfectly elastic curve of constant cost, *ss'* the same displaced by a tax, as in Professor Marshall's Fig. 33; *dd'* has the same import as in the last paragraph.

In the other limiting case, when the supply is perfectly inelastic, let it equal *Oκ*. Then *κα* is the supply-curve. If it is imagined as sloping a little outward, the limiting form not quite reached, the effect of a tax on supply would, as before, be represented by moving (every point of) the curve vertically upwards through a distance corresponding to the extent of the tax. The intersection of this displaced supply-curve—not shown in the figure—would cut the demand-curve in the neighbourhood of *α*, and accordingly the price paid by the consumer is nearly—in the limit quite—the same as before; the whole tax falls on the other party.

Some confusion appears to be caused by supposing the law of demand to alter concurrently with the imposition of the tax.[25] Is it not competent to the "mechanics of industry" to treat superposed disturbances independently and one at a time? If a person wears high heels, may we not estimate the elevation due to that cause without putting him on a hill? If indeed there is some connection between the artificial elongation and

---

But it is simpler to use the theorem that it comes to the same whether the tax is on supply or on consumption. In the latter case, if dd' is as before the demand-curve displaced by the tax, κa the price paid by the consumer is unaltered, the whole tax falls on the other party.

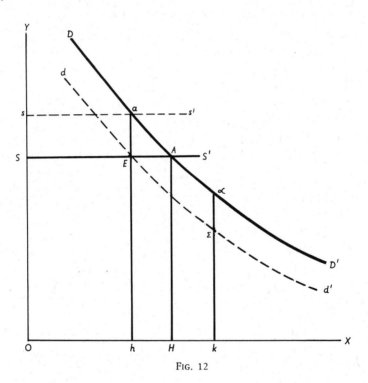

FIG. 12

Compare Fleeming Jenkin: "If a holder sells unreservedly . . . the whole tax falls on the seller; the supply curve becomes a vertical straight line" ("Incidence of Taxes," p. 114 of *Papers Literary and Scientific*). [p. 234, Article 14 of this volume. Ed.]

Or is it easier to say that, if with Cournot (*Principes Mathématiques*, Art. 51) we represent the equality of *demand* and *supply* before the tax by the equation $F(p) = \Omega(p)$ and after the tax (of u per unit imposed on the supply) by the equation $F(p') = \Omega(p' + u)$; then if Ω is degraded to a constant the equation for p' the disturbed price is the same as the equation for p the original price.

[25] Thus the Report of the London County Council Committee (Lord Farrer, chairman) concludes that in prosperous communities house-rate falls on tenants; in declining ones on landlords. Similarly the *Dictionnaire d'Écon. Pol.*, art. "Incidence de l'Impôt." So Lord Farrer in his evidence before the Town Holdings Commission (Q. 1,244): "The best authorities

the position of the wearer, it may be proper to note this. Xenophon tells us that the great king alone among the ancient Persians wore his tiara erect. If then the king—as according to Dryden, the conqueror—of the Persians sate "aloft in awful state," the apex of the royal tiara would have been elevated both in itself and on account of the wearer's position. Yet Xenophon's statement is intelligible by itself. So rates on houses when expended in improving the neighbourhood tend to increase the demand for houses.[26] Yet in measuring the burden of the tax to the owner it is allowable in pure theory to abstract its influence on demand.

Another reflex influence of a house-rate on the demand for houses already built—reflected from the quarters where new building is possible —as it presupposes the mobility of capital, must be deferred to a later section. At present we are supposing the offer of built houses to be constant—the *fourth* of the cases so lucidly distinguished and discussed by Mr. Pierson in the second edition of his *Leerboek*.[27]

When it is affirmed that under these circumstances the burden of the tax falls altogether on the owner it is understood that the demand of the occupant is of an ordinary kind—not of that extreme or limiting variety which is perfectly inelastic. The contrary assumption is made by some writers; Mr. Blunden, for instance, who puts houses in the category of those "absolute necessaries of life" of which the "prices may rise considerably without appreciably affecting the demand."[28]

---

seem to think that it depends very much on the state of the market." If it is asserted that the incidence of a tax depends on whether the demand is rising in the sense of the demand-curve being raised as a whole, I altogether dissent; if it is meant that the incidence depends on whether the demand becomes more urgent in the sense of the demand-curve becoming steeper, I give only a qualified assent (see p. 266). It is too true that the "best authorities" express themselves carelessly. Pantaleoni forms a brilliant exception when he explains that a rise of rents does not mean shifting of tax (from the owner to the occupier) if the rents would have risen independently of the tax (*Teoria della Traslazione dei Tributi*, p. 226 *et seq.*).

[26] Mr. Fletcher Moulton, in his evidence before the Town Holdings Commission, has dwelt forcibly on this incident.

[27] Noticed in the Review III, 78. [This review in Vol. III of Edgeworth *Papers* is not reprinted in this volume. Ed.]

[28] *Local Taxation and Finance*, p. 49. Compare the author's recapitulations of his views in the *Journal of the Statistical Society* for December 1896.

Similarly Professor Seligman: "The landowner is not compelled to part with his land, but the tenant is compelled to occupy some apartments" (*Shifting and Incidence*, p. 111). Elsewhere, indeed (*ibid.*, p. 120), he admits that the tax might be "so high as to cause the tenant to content himself with meaner apartments, or rooms in a less desirable locality."

I regard it as the general case, that the tax on the occupier *tends* to diminish his demand for house accommodation. Thus Mr. Bourne, steward of the London estates of the Duke of Bedford, affirmed, "with the greatest confidence," "from the knowledge that I have of everyday work for many years in London," "that the person taking the house is so free in his choice, that he can afford to throw up the houses when he takes into consideration what the rates and taxes are" (Town Holdings Committee, 1887. Q. 11,288–9).

No doubt it is so in particular instances, for instance, in the case of the dwelling-houses of the labouring classes in certain localities.[29] But can it be affirmed generally that the demand for dwelling-houses is perfectly inelastic? "If the tax, indeed, was very high," says Adam Smith, "the greater part of people would endeavour to evade it as much as they could by contenting themselves with smaller houses." And even if the tax be not high, is not a consequence similar in kind, if less in degree, to be apprehended by the owner who offers it for hire?

In fine, even granted the premiss that the demand for houses is inelastic, the conclusion that the tax falls wholly or chiefly on the occupier does not follow. The supply of houses (already built) being, as here supposed, also inelastic, the price or rent becomes *indeterminate*.[30]

The extreme cases which have been instanced form rather limits than exceptions to the rule that both sides of the market suffer by a tax. An exception is presented by a species of export-tax analysed in a preceding article;[31] the abstraction of a certain portion of the exports in kind, to be disposed of in a manner not affecting the market under consideration.[32] An instance would be the virtual export-tax which is imposed by the capture of smuggled goods; the intercepted goods being destroyed, or so disposed of as to produce the same effect on the demand and supply in the two countries as if they were destroyed. It is not contended that the exception is of any practical importance.[33]

Another class of exceptions comprises what Mill has called "peculiar" or "anomalous" cases of value.[34] Such is the case of "joint production," as defined by Mill, when "the same outlay would have to be incurred for either of the two [commodities] if the other were not wanted or used at

---

[29] *Cp.* Cliffe Leslie, *Taxation of the Working Classes.*

[30] The intersection of two coincident perpendiculars!

What the actual effect of a tax under such conditions will be would seem to depend on circumstances which from the point of view of pure theory may be called accidents; among which no doubt the circumstance whether the demand is rising or falling (above, p. 264) may in practice be important.

[31] Above, p. 38. [Page 38 of the originally published text is not reprinted in this volume. Ed.]

[32] The condition is stated with much precision by Cournot with respect to the taxation of *monopolies:* "Il peut se faire que le produit de l'impôt en nature soit appliqué à une consommation qui n'aurait pas eu lieu sans l'impôt, et qui n'influe en rien sur la demande que les autres consommateurs font au producteurs" (*Principes Mathématiqes*, Art. 42). [Article 15, p. 253 of this volume. Ed.]

[33] As this kind of tax is in practice rare, I have to acknowledge that I have, in a preceding article (*Economic Journal*, Vol. IV) exaggerated the asymmetry between export and import taxes; and to retract my criticism of Professor Bastable on that point (*ibid.*, p. 624). *Cp.* above, R, pp. 3, 12, 38. [Section R is not reprinted in this volume. Ed.]

[34] *Political Economy*, Book III, ch. xvi *passim*, and last par.

all." Akin to this case is that in which the increase of the production of either commodity, though it does not necessitate, yet facilitates, the increased production of the other.[35] I propose to call products connected by this relation, which I have elsewhere defined more precisely,[36] *complementary*.

If we suppose the degrees of complementariness to be gradually diminished, we shall pass through the zero point of absolute independence to a relation which may be distinguished as *rival* production; when the increased production of one commodity renders the increase of the other more difficult. For instance, where a limited amount of time, strength, or other resources may be spent in either of two sorts of otherwise unconnected production.

The following propositions respecting the taxation of products correlated in either of the two ways just defined may easily be proved; it being supposed that the demand for one commodity is independent of the demand for the other. A tax upon one of two rival products will raise the price of the taxed one, and lower the price of the untaxed one. A tax on one of two complementary products will raise the price of both. In the former case,[37] it is conceivable that the consumers as a whole might be advantaged by the tax, if we may set the gain of one class against the loss of another.

The gain and loss to be balanced would appertain to the same persons in the corresponding case of correlated demand. The demand for two products may be called *complementary* when a rise in the price of one is attended by a fall in the price of the other, *rival* when a rise in the price of one is attended with a rise in the price of the other.[38]

The following propositions respecting the taxation of commodities for which the demand is correlated may be proved. A tax on one of two rival commodities will raise the price of both. A tax on one of two complementary commodities will raise the price of the taxed one, and lower the price of the one which is not taxed. It is conceivable that the latter effect should so exceed the former that, on balance, a gain results to the consumers.

---

35 *Cp*. Marshall, *Principles*, Book V, ch. vi.

36 *Giornale degli Economisti*, 1897. E, Vol. I.

37 [In *Papers:* "A tax upon one of two rival products will raise the price of both. A tax on one of two complementary products will raise the price of the taxed one, and lower the price of the untaxed one. In the latter case, . . ." Ed.]

38 *Ceteris paribus*, and in particular the marginal utility of money being supposed constant. I have used a more essential attribute for the definition of *rival* and *complementary* demand in my paper on "Monopoly" already referred to.

The possibility of a positive gain resulting to one side of the market
—one of the two "nations"—from the imposition of a tax[39] is more evident in the case of commodities which are complementary, both as regards production and consumption.[40] In this compound case it may be
shown—but not, I think, very easily, perhaps not without the use of
mathematics—that a tax on one commodity may lower the price of either,
but not of both.[41]

Our estimate of the importance of these exceptions to the rule that
neither party gains by a restriction of trade depends partly on the question
whether the "peculiar cases" are frequent. According to Jevons the cases
of joint production, "far from being 'some peculiar cases,' form the general rule, to which it is difficult to point out any clear or important exceptions."[42]

---

[39] Exclusive of the gain accruing from the tax to the importing country, a gain which
must in general be included in order that an import-tax may result in a net gain to the
importing country; as maintained by Messrs. Auspitz and Lieben (*Theorie der Preise*, Art.
81), and by the present writer (*Economic Journal*, Vol. IV).

[40] For a fuller statement see the added note at the end of this Paper.

[41] x and y being the quantities purchased, consider the collective total utility (the
Gesammtnutzlichkeit of Messrs. Auspitz and Lieben), and also the collective total cost (the
Gesammtkoste of the same authors), each as a function of x and y. Before the tax, the price
of the first commodity = its marginal utility (*i.e.* the differential of the total utility with respect to x) = its marginal cost (*i.e.* the differential of the total cost with respect to x). The
price of the second quantity is similarly determined. After the tax—which may be at first
supposed small and specific, say u per unit of x, and levied from the producer—if x' and y'
be the new quantities then (1) marginal utility of x' = the marginal cost thereof + u; (2)
the marginal utility of y' = its marginal cost. Substituting $x + \Delta x, y + \Delta y$ for x' [In *Papers*:
"z'." Ed.] and y', expanding and neglecting higher powers, we obtain two simultaneous
linear equations for Δx and Δy. Solving these, we can find the increments of the prices and
the decrement of Consumers' Rent, in terms of three kinds of data: (1) the extent of the
tax, (2) the rate of decrease of utility and the rate of increase of cost, and (3) the measures
of the correlation between the two commodities in demand, and also in supply (the second
differential with regard to x and y of the utility-function, and also that of the cost function).
These magnitudes must comply with certain conditions; but those conditions are not inconsistent with the statements in the text. But, if only one of these correlations exists, though
the price of the taxed commodity cannot fall, yet the Consumers' Rent may rise.

By parity of reasoning it may be shown that though in the case of a single commodity,
"if the commodity obey the law of diminishing return . . . the result [of a tax] will be to
raise the supply price by something less than the full amount of the tax" (Marshall, *Principles*, Book V, ch. xii, § 4), yet in the case of *correlated* commodities it is possible that the
result of a tax on one may be to raise its price by more than the full amount of the tax; that
though in general, the producers' surplus is diminished by a tax, yet in the case of correlated
commodities it may be increased. The negative case of this paradox is, that a bounty may
prejudice the bountied parties (directly and apart from ulterior effects, and from the cost
to their Government).

What has been proved of a small specific tax may be extended (by neglecting higher
powers of small quantities) to *any* small marginal tax (increasing with the increase of the
commodity). What has been proved for an indefinitely small tax may be extended to a finite
tax by reasoning which Cournot has made familiar. (For further explanations see my article
on "The Pure Theory of Monopoly," in the *Giornale degli Economisti*, E, Vol. I.)

[42] *Theory*, p. 217. *Cp.* Preface, p. liii. Jevons is speaking of "joint" products in the

However that may be, the exceptions which have been adduced do not militate against the general rule considered as expressing the most frequent, the typical case. In all the varieties of correlated demand and supply it is still true that most frequently the price of the taxed commodity will be raised, while the price of the correlated commodity will as often be raised as it will be lowered in consequence of the tax. Whence it follows that the cases in which a balance of gain results to one party are a minority.

In these examples we have insensibly passed the frontier, not very important for the present purpose, which separates the case of two "non-competing groups" from that of several. We may now restore to the various markets involved in "Distribution and Exchange," the interdependence which we at first abstracted. We may now suppose a whole system of countries connected by international trade.

The reader may be referred to a former article for a discussion of this general case—the case of several balls in the bowl. It may be well to remark that when in equilibrium one ball presses against another, and that other against a third, it is not in general indifferent between which two balls a wedge shall be inserted. For example, suppose three islands, A, B, C, engaged in this sort of international trade. A imports from B goods, for the manufacture of which B has to import materials from C.[43] An import tax in A (or an export tax in B) on the goods exported from B to A will not come to the same as an import tax in B (or an export tax in C) on the materials imported by B from C. As an extreme case, suppose that the materials imported from our island C are supplied there yearly in constant quantities independently of human effort—*e.g.* seaweed deposited on the shores of C. A tax on the price charged by inhabitants of C for permission to inhabitants of B to remove this seaweed would fall altogether on the inhabitants of C; the price of the goods imported from B into A would not be affected. But a tax on these latter imports would be followed by a rise in the price of those imports, and a fall in the price of the materials imported from C; all three parties will be worse off—in general, and except in the limiting case in which the demand in A for the imports from B is perfectly inelastic; in which case the entire burden of the tax will fall on A, B and C will be unaffected.

---

narrow sense above attributed to Mill. If Jevons is right in using such strong language (which I am disposed to doubt), then *a fortiori* with reference to the wider category of goods that are *complementary* either in production or consumption.

[43] Compare Professor Carver's correct decision on the case of a tax that is placed upon an article on its way through the hands of a merchant from the producer to the consumer. (*Yale Review*, Nov., 1896.)

ABCd.[44] The possibility which has been shown in the preceding section, that a tax upon products may be in part shifted by the producer, even though he has not the power of changing his occupation, no longer exists when the tax is imposed on profits, or generally *surplus*.[45] The case is not now that of a wedge inserted between two balls in a bowl; it is rather as if the position from which one of the two balls was started to run down to equilibrium was lowered. The height at which it would finally settle would not be altered by this abbreviation of its descent to equilibrium[46] (the bowl being supposed spherical). The conditions of economic equilibrium are not affected by a tax on surplus.

This is the first approximation. But it must be remembered that in general it is not possible for the tax-collector to hit a surplus which is altogether "intramarginal." A tax on profits—such as Schedule D of our Income Tax, or such as a payment for a licence to carry on a trade—cannot be levied without some little disturbance of economic margins. This proposition might be illustrated by considering the classical theorem that the remission of rent to all farmers would not lower the price of corn. That is the first approximation. But if the farmers' "margin of saving" was displaced by their increased income, they might be willing to invest more capital in agricultural improvement, and so lower the marginal cost of produce.[47] Contrariwise there might be now required a higher rate of remuneration to evoke the same exertion from the cultivator; his new affluence having displaced the margin at which the decrements of the utility of consumption become equal to the increment of the discommodity of labour.[48] If with Jevons, or still more elegantly with Gossen,[49]

---

[44] See the explanation of these symbols above, pp. 259–60.

It would have been agreeable to classical tradition to place in this section the theorem, that a tax on rent falls entirely on the landlord. Thus James Mill: "To him [the capitalist cultivator] it is a matter of perfect indifference whether he pays the surplus in the shape of rent, to an individual proprietor, or in that of revenue, to a government collector" *Elements*, chap. iv, § v, par. 1). So Florez Estrada, Book IV, chap. v; Professor Seligman, *Shifting and Incidence*, p. 35 and p. 184, and many other authorities.

Yet in spite of the almost universal practice, I venture to think that there is some advantage in the classification here adopted. It may be observed that though under a regime of competition, a tax imposed upon the payment for an article absolutely limited in quantity, such as land, may be viewed as falling either upon margin or surplus, it is otherwise in a regime of monopoly: the tax is there certainly marginal.

[45] Compare Hadley, *Economics*, 512, 3.

[46] Energy representing total utility by a metaphor familiar to the mathematical economist. *Cp.* Irving Fisher's *Mathematical Investigations*, Part II, ch. iii (*Mechanical Analogies*).

[47] *Cp.* Ricardo, *Political Economy*, chap. viii: "There are no taxes which have not a tendency to lessen the power to accumulate."

[48] Against the probability that taxation will diminish accumulation, there is the possibility that "curtailment of profit may act as a stimulus" (Mill, Book V, chap. iii, § 3). A very bare possibility, according to Bastable (*Public Finance*, Book III, 2nd ed.). For the cognate doctrine that the impoverishment of the labourer will act as a stimulus, see the apt quotations at p. 16 of Professor Seligman's *Shifting and Incidence*.

[49] See Palgrave's *Dictionary*, Art. "Gossen," Fig. 3.

we represent that margin by the point along a line at which the ordinates to certain two curves become equal, it will be evident that neither tax on profits, nor poll tax, nor licences, nor any other form of impost under category d will be able to reduce the area representing surplus, without disturbing its boundary.

Some little disturbance of this kind is to be attributed to an income tax, in so far as it strikes the shareholders in a joint stock company. But in so far as it strikes those who are entitled to a fixed payment from the proceeds of a going concern, it affects economic margins only in so far as the reduction of income may cause an alteration in the consumers' scale of demand.[50]

To the present section belong also consumers'—as well as producers' —licences. A tax on licence to consume a thing differs in its effect from a tax upon the thing, when more than one unit of the thing are, or would be in the absence of taxation, consumed during the period within which the licence must be renewed, say a year. If no sportsman wanted more than one gun a year, the effect of a sporting licence in checking demand would be much the same as that of a specific tax on guns. But the licence to drink tea for which, as Adam Smith tells us,[51] people used to pay so much a head in Holland, would act differently from a tax of so much per pound on tea. It would be a tax on surplus. It would knock off all those consumers who do not derive from the consumption of tea a consumers' rent or surplus more than equivalent to the payment of the licence. On the remaining consumers it would act simply as a tax on their income.

A Bc.[52] Let us now remove the barriers which have so far been supposed to separate our "non-competing groups." Let us introduce that mobility of the agents of production which is the essential attribute of domestic as distinguished from international trade, which is an important property of long periods as distinguished from short ones. Admitting the classical hypothesis respecting the freedom of capital and labour, we must accept the classical theorems concerning the effects of taxation: that, in the words of Adam Smith—

A tax . . . upon the profits of stock employed in any particular branch of trade can never fall finally upon the dealers . . . but always upon the consumers, who must be obliged to pay in the price of the goods the tax which the dealer advances (*Wealth of Nations*, Book V, chap. ii, art. 2).

In the words of Ricardo—

---

50 The effect of changes in income upon prices is well analysed by Professor Irving Fisher in his *Mathematical Investigations on Prices*.

51 *Wealth of Nations*, Book V, ch. ii.

52 The category thus designated comprises both A B c D [In *Papers:* "A B c A." Ed.] and A B c d.

A tax on the profits of the farmer would raise the price of corn; a tax on the profits of the clothier, the price of cloth (*Principles*, chap. xv, par. 3).

In the words of J. S. Mill—

If a tax were laid on the profits of any one branch of productive employment, the tax would be virtually an increase of the cost of production, and the value and price of the article would rise accordingly; by which the tax would be thrown upon the consumers of the commodity, and would not affect profits (*Principles*, Book V, chap. iii, § 2, par. 1).

I do not know that these expressions can be improved upon. Yet as the attempt to paraphrase our literary classics, which is sometimes made a school exercise, however feeble in itself, brings out more fully the inimitable excellence of the originals, in the like humble spirit it may be allowable to expand the above cited authoritative dicta.

As I understand the "industrial competition" with which we are now concerned, the conditions of equilibrium are twofold—(1)[53] one common to the "commercial competition," which was supposed to exist in our first two sections, namely, that in any business the outlay in every direction should be pushed up to the "margin of profitableness,"[54] and (2) one which forms the differentia of industrial competition, namely, that the "net advantages" in all businesses between which there is mobility should be equal.[55]

Now let a tax on profits disturb the second condition. If equilibrium is restored by the consumers being "obliged to pay in the price of the goods the tax," it follows from condition (1) that the marginal costs of the business taxed must be raised.

This would, I think, be generally allowed in the most familiar case, that of the "margin of cultivation." Consider the following simplified version of an example which Mill has put among "peculiar cases of value."[56] "For simplicity we will confine our supposition to two kinds of agricultural produce; for instance, wheat and oats." There are supposed (by us, not Mill) to exist only "medium soils which, without being specifically adapted to either, are about equally suited to both" products.

---

[53] See *Address to the British Association, Sec. F*, Report for 1889. I have endeavoured to defend this view in an article in the *Revue d'Économie Politique* for January, 1891, and in a passage in the *Economic Journal* for 1896, Vol. V, p. 173.

[54] *Cp.* Marshall, *Principles of Economics*, p. 433 *et passim*.

[55] Or rather equally attractive, as explained by Professor Marshall in the *Principles of Economics*. I suppose the condition to hold not only for the typical entrepreneur, but also when enterprise delegates the task of superintendence—*e.g.* shareholders in a joint-stock undertaking. *Ceteris paribus*, the chance of profit tends to be the same in one undertaking as another.

[56] *Principles*, Book III, ch. xvi, § 2.

The relative value of the two grains will of course be determined by the productivity of the marginal dose of outlay on each species of cultivation. Now let a tax be laid on the profits of oat growers. There will be a rush from the cultivation of oats to that of wheat. There will be established a new equilibrium in which, if the demand is constant, the area of wheat-growing is widened, the marginal cost of cultivation diminished; while the converse is true of oats.[57]

I have been supposing the land to be owned by the cultivators. It comes to the same if the land is rented from competing landlords, and a tax is imposed on the rent of oats-growing land. We have then an example of Professor Marshall's theorem that *partial* rent does enter into the cost of production, taking as a test of such "entrance" the circumstance that a tax on rent will affect price.

The action of mobility is similar when the tax is not on *surplus*, as we began in this section by supposing, but on *margin*—specific, *ad valorem*, or in kind.[58]

I propose to illustrate these principles by considering a tax affecting an industry which presumably obeys the law of decreasing returns,[59] a tax on the rent of urban dwelling-houses.

Let us take as sufficiently general the case put by the Select Committee on Town Holdings in their Final Report:[60]

> The typical condition of a town holding under this system [the "leasehold system"] as regards the parties and their respective interests . . . may be described as follows:
>
> (A) The occupier of the house holding at a rack-rent, whether on a yearly tenancy or for a longer or shorter term.
>
> (B) His immediate landlord, the receiver of the rack-rent, who is ordinarily called "the owner of the house," and who holds for a term of years, paying during such term to the freeholder a fixed annual sum, generally called the "ground rent" . . .
>
> (C) The freeholder, who receives the ground rent during the term, and on its completion is entitled to the entire property absolutely.

For a first approximation, neglecting the distance in time between the different bargains, we may substitute for the three interests A, B, C, de-

---

[57] *Cp.* Marshall, *Principles of Economics*, p. 483, note; 3rd edition.

[58] Regarding the ascending curve *SS'* on Fig. 11 as an ordinary short-period supply-curve, we are to consider that it is first raised up, as explained in that context, by a marginal tax, and then further—in general and except when the demand of the consumer is perfectly inelastic—furled in by the migration of entrepreneurs from the industry. In the case of a tax on surplus the curve is not raised up; it is (theoretically) always, not merely generally, furled in.

[59] See Marshall, *Principles of Economics*, *sub voce* "Margin of building."

[60] 1892, No. 214, p. 6.

scribed in the Report the three "nations" A, B, C defined at the end of our first section;[61] A importing from B, goods for the manufacture of which B has to import materials from C, materials obtained in constant quantities independently of human effort. Only now B is no longer completely insulated, but is connected with a continent of capitalists, whereby the producers in B are kept as it were at a constant level of advantage. With allowance for this difference the solution is as before. A tax on the product houses—whether levied from the occupant or owner—will have the following effects. The occupants will suffer by having to pay a raised price, not in general raised to the full extent of the tax. The capitalist owners will not suffer though the price which they receive for their product falls;[62] the net advantage of the industry being kept constant by migration into other industries. The ground landlord will suffer by a diminution of the ground rent. A tax on ground rent, whether levied from the ground landlord or the "owner," falls entirely on the ground landlord.

This is, of course, very pure theory, making abstraction of differences in time, that great source of complications in Economics.[63]

For a second approximation let us distinguish three periods, (1) the average duration of the occupant's lease, (2) the average duration of the owner's lease, (3) longer periods.

(1) It is not questioned that a tax imposed while the occupant's lease is running rests where it strikes during that period.

(2) A first approximation has already been obtained for this case,[64] on the assumption that during this period the offer consists entirely of houses already built. On that supposition the tax falls entirely upon the owner.[65] But we have now to take into account that the offer in general consists partly of houses already built in parts of the town already occupied, say the central area, partly of new houses which may be built on land which has hitherto been agricultural, say for brevity the suburbs.[66] Now if we had an exact measure of the advantage of the central area above the suburban periphery we should have an exact measure of the

---

[61] Above, p. 269.

[62] The law of decreasing returns being supposed to act.

[63] *Cp.* Marshall, Preface to *Principles of Economics.*

[64] Above, p. 262.

[65] Mr. Cannan clenches the matter thus, "We are not really 'mostly fools.' Who will stand up and confess that he took 76 —— Street at £100 a year, and subject to £20 of rates, when an exactly similar house next door, but in another parish, was to let at £100 a year, and only £12 of rates?" (*History of Local Taxation*, p. 134.)

[66] Our problem is here the same as that which forms Mr. Pierson's *third* case (noticed in the *Economic Journal*, Vol. V, p. 436); but our solution is not quite the same as his.

effect of the tax on house-rent. Suppose, for instance, in the vein of von Thünen, that the net advantage offered by houses of equally costly structure in the respective sites differed only on account of the different fares from each site to a central point. Then since the landlord at the suburbs can only stand out for a certain minimum of rent, that which he might have obtained in the way of agriculture,[67] the occupant in the suburbs has in general to pay the entire tax, except so far as he reduces his use of house-accommodation; and since the occupants of the central area are better off only in respect of the fares they also have to pay the same price for the same accommodation. The case would be exactly parallel to the familiar case of a tax on agricultural produce. The consumer thereof pays the tax except so far as he reduces his consumption; otherwise the landlords are untouched. This would be the solution, if there were perfect rivalry between central and suburban habitations.

But of course the capacity of houses at the circumference to act as substitutes for houses in the centre is not perfect; there is only a partial rivalry.[68] Since, then, when there is no rivalry, the owners of the central area suffer to the full extent of the tax, and when there is perfect rivalry, they do not suffer at all, it might be inferred that in the intermediate case of partial rivalry the owners would suffer, but not to the full extent of the tax. The inference, however, would not be correct. It is one of the *curiosa* of the theory of *correlated* demand[69] that a tax on house rent might so disturb the balance of demand for urban and suburban accommodation respectively as to cause a positive benefit to the owners.[70] The

---

67 Professor Seligman is alone, as far as I know, in disputing this theorem (*Shifting and Incidence*, p. 106). I cannot agree with him that Mill's reasoning postulates the existence of a no-rent tract. The reasoning is akin to that on pp. 272–73 above, relating to the taxation of rent.

68 Compare Fleeming Jenkin: "The rents through the whole town are ruled by those of the new districts. There is a certain relative [In *Papers:* "selective." Ed.] value between every house in the town, and if the rents of the new houses are dearer, the rents of the old houses are increased in due proportion" ("Incidence of Taxes," p. 117 [Article 14, pp. 235–36 of this volume. Ed.], *Papers, Literary and Scientific.*)

69 *Cp.* above, p. 267.

70 Suppose, for simplicity of enunciation, that all the houses in the suburbs are of one kind; and also all the houses in the central area of another kind. Before the tax, let p_1 be the rent of a house, and x the number of houses taken, in the suburbs; and let the corresponding amounts for the central area be p_2 and y. By hypothesis, y is constant. Also, for a first approximation, we may make the classical assumption that p_1, the rent received by the capitalist-builder in the suburbs, does not vary with the tax. Under these conditions, if a tax proportional to the rent, say the ith part thereof (where i is small), is levied from the occupiers in both quarters; for the disturbed equilibrium we have the following equations:—

$$\begin{cases} (1+i)p_1 = p_1 + dx\left(\dfrac{dp_1}{dx}\right) \\ (1+i)(p_2 + dp_2) = p_2 + dx\left(\dfrac{dp_2}{dx}\right) \end{cases}$$

truth of this proposition is not impaired, because there may be in fact from other causes a centrifugal movement of residents from central quarters. *Pro tanto* the tax may have the effect of diminishing the loss which from other causes is accruing to the owners of residential houses in these quarters.[71]

(3) For long periods the solution above given[72] as a first approximation holds good. We might regard the three interests A, B, C, as three bodies held one above the other by a press or "vice," so that the sum of the depths of three bodies is constant. A wedge being driven in between A and B, the bodies—each obeying its peculiar law of compressibility and resilience—will behave as follows. At first A will be compressed to the full extent of the thickness of the wedge; B and C retaining their full dimensions. After a time A will re-expand, in part at least; B will be compressed to some extent, perhaps nearly to the whole extent of the thickness of the wedge; C will remain firm. But leave the bodies alone for a longer time and B will regain its original amplitude, and the compression due to the insertion of the wedge will be divided in uncertain proportions between A and C. It is not to be denied that during the long time required for the working out of these forces, other forces may have come into play. The bodies may have expanded from other causes, the press may have been warped so as to allow room for their expansion. But because the given forces are compounded with others known imperfectly, we are not precluded from calculating the resultant of the given ones.

Whence

$$dp_2 = ip_2\left(-1 + \frac{1}{p_2}\left(\frac{dp_2}{dx}\right) \div \frac{1}{p_1}\left(\frac{dp_1}{dx}\right)\right)$$

Whence it appears that the rent received by the urban owner falls to the full extent of the tax when the demands for residence in the respective quarters are quite independent, and does not fall at all when the two articles are perfect substitutes. In the intermediate case the owner's rent falls, or rises, according as $\frac{1}{p_1}\left(\frac{dp_1}{dx}\right) >$, or $< \frac{1}{p_2}\left(\frac{dp_3}{dx}\right)$. The former case is, I think, the more probable; but the latter is by no means impossible; for all that we know about the relative magnitude of these partial differentials is that $\left(\frac{dp_1}{dx}\right) \times \left(\frac{dp_2}{dy}\right) > \left(\frac{dp_2}{dx}\right)^2$. (*Cp.* E, p. 117.) [Section E is not reprinted in this volume. Ed.] Probably $\left(\frac{dp_2}{dx}\right)$ is less than either of the two factors of which the product is greater than its square; but not necessarily. *Ceteris paribus*, the event is more likely to occur when the demand for urban houses is very inelastic; for suburban houses very elastic. As to the conditions which the demand-functions must fulfil, see article on "Monopoly" in the *Giornale degli Economisti*, 1897, (E).

The proposition is less likely to be true when p_1 is supposed to be lowered (in virtue of the law of diminishing returns). It is strictly proved only for infinitesimal values of i, but may with probability be extended further. (See Index, s.v. *Differential*.) [The Index is not reprinted in this volume. Ed.]

[71] *Cp.* above, pp. 264–65.

[72] Above, pp. 273–74.

The proof of the general theory relating to long periods may be verified by an examination of some limiting cases in which the statement of the theory requires modification; the frequent occurrence of which cases may account for the prevalence of opposed theories.

(*a*) In the limiting case when the demand of the consumer, the occupier, is perfectly inelastic he will bear the whole tax. This assumption is more readily made, as it is usual, perhaps proper, to make it in problems about agricultural rent. The possibility of this incident has already been admitted with respect to the comparatively short period (2), and may also, though I think less easily, be admitted with regard to period (3).

(*β*) Suppose that ground-rents are in general very small in comparison with the tax, then of course, they can only bear a small part of the tax. May we not explain by this supposition Ricardo's *dictum*?

In ordinary cases it may be presumed that the whole tax would be paid both immediately and finally by the occupier.[73]

So J. S. Mill:—[74]

In the vast majority of houses, the ground rent forms but a small proportion of the annual payment of the house.[75]

This is of course true of houses in the country;[76] not so true now as fifty years ago of urban rents.[77, 78]

(*γ*) Again, suppose conditions such that only one "dose," so to speak, of building capital can be applied to one parcel of land—say in China or Peru—through the fixity of custom and the mobility of the earth, only a single-storied dwelling of uniform pattern can be placed on each unit of the area available for building. On such a supposition a tax on house-rent would fall in general entirely on ground-rent. For the accommodation of the occupants could not be reduced without some of the sites being left unoccupied. Each landlord threatened with the loss of his entire ground-rent will lower his terms until ground-rent all round has been, if it can be, reduced to the full extent of the tax.

Upon this or some adjacent less extreme hypothesis, we may account

---

[73] *Political Economy*, chap. xiv, par. 3.

[74] A different view of the Ricardian dictum appears to be taken by Esquiros de Parieu, *Traité de l'Impôt*, p. 74, and some other eminent writers.

[75] *Political Economy*, Book V, chap. iii, § 6, par. 5.

[76] Cp. *Wealth of Nations*, Book V, ch. ii.

[77] Of course supposing the tax not to exceed the rent.

[78] [In *Papers:* "rates." Ed.]

for the opinion of some distinguished writers that the tax on house rent in the long run tends to be mostly borne by the ground landlord. Thus, too, we may perhaps explain what otherwise may seem inexplicable—why the successors of Ricardo should attempt to allocate a certain portion of the house rent to the ground rent.

Thus McCulloch:—

Were the supply of houses easily diminished and increased, a tax on their rents would fall wholly on the occupiers and ground landlords, and be divided between them in the proportion which the profit of the capital required to build them bears to the rent of the ground on which they stand.[79]

So J. S. Mill:—[80]

A tax of so much per cent. on the gross rent falls on both these portions [ground rent and building rent]. . . . The incidence, however, of these two portions of the tax must be considered separately.

As much of it as is a tax on building rent must ultimately fall on the consumer, in other words the occupier.[81]

So Professor Sidgwick distinguishes "the portion of the tax which is paid for the value of the house itself" and the "portion that falls on the ground rent."[82]

Now on our present hypothesis (γ) these statements would be true in a particular case, namely, when the tax was equal to the original ground rent plus the constant building rent.[83] In that case the effects of the tax would be exactly as Mill and McCulloch lay it down. And it was, perhaps, natural to regard this case as typical; at any rate, when the consumer's demand is supposed perfectly inelastic, when our (α) as well as (γ) is present. In that sub-case the true solution, I submit, is that the division of the burden between the occupier and the ground landlord is indeterminate. But the divisions suggested by McCulloch and Mill are plausible.

The consonance of this incident (γ) with authoritative *dicta* moves me to suppose the prevalence of the incident. A house is naturally thought of by Jevons as an instance of an "indivisible" commodity which forms

---

[79] *Taxation and Funding*, Part I, chap. i, § 2.

[80] As against Mill's precise apportionment, Mr. Sidney Webb's contention that "the free-holder . . . has no fixed point of resistance" (*Town Holdings Commission*, 1890, Q. 42–44) is just. His "large jump in value" from agricultural to building land, is not necessary for this conclusion.

[81] *Political Economy*, Book V, chap. iii, § 6.

[82] *Principles of Political Economy*, Book III, chap. viii, § 8.

[83] In the spirit of the classical writers we may here suppose the cost of building constant, even though the supply of buildings should be reduced.

an exception to the general theory of value.[84] And yet, though a house is indivisible, residential accommodation is not. There may be many "mansions" not only in the archaic sense, but in that which is applicable to the modern "flats." "Increments of villa accommodation," in Professor Marshall's phrase, may be added up to the point[85] where the price just measures both the marginal cost and the marginal utility of an increment. In short, the law of value for house accommodation is (for long periods) essentially the same for house accommodation as for corn. It might be all very well for Adam Smith, who held that "in the price of corn . . . one part pays the rent of the landlord,"[86] to say that "the rent of a house may be distinguished into two parts,[87] . . . the building rent and the ground rent." But what have we to do with such apportionment of price, or tax, we who have received the doctrine of Ricardo that "rent does not and cannot enter in the least degree as a component of price"; the doctrine of Professor Marshall that "ground rent does not enter into the expenses of manufacture," on an understanding "exactly parallel to that which has to be supplied in order to make Ricardo's doctrine true, when applied to agriculture?"[88]

Dwelling-houses, then, belonging to the general category of consumable products, as the highest authorities are agreed,[89] the taxation of such houses obeys the general laws of the taxation of products which have been enunciated above as pertaining to long periods (3);[90] abstracting the peculiarities of the "leasehold system" which have been allowed for with reference to short periods (2).

A practical corollary is that a tax on ground rent hurts the ground landlord more, and the occupier less, than *ceteris paribus* a tax on the occupation rent, in the long run;[91] theoretically even, and apart from

[84] *Theory*, chap. iv.

[85] "The cases in which a man has to live in a house of a size widely different from that which he prefers, because there is none other available," are exceptional (*Principles of Economics*, Book V, p. 592, note, 3rd ed.).

[86] *Wealth of Nations*, Book I.

[87] *Ibid.*, Book V, chap. i.

[88] See the whole passage relating to the margin of building, in *Principles of Economics*, Book V.

[89] Thus Mr. Goschen in his *Draft Report on Local Taxation*: "The inhabitant of the house . . . is in reality the consumer of the commodity produced by the builder" (*Local Taxation*, p. 164). So Professor Bastable regards "houses as a particular manufactured commodity" (*Public Finance*, p. 371, 2nd ed.). Cp. Mr. Pierson, *Leerboek*, p. 146, 2nd ed.

[90] Above, p. 276. I am confirmed in this view by finding myself able to agree with all that Professor Bastable has said on this subject (*Public Finance*, Book IV, chap. ii, § 5). I concur with his criticism of Professor Seligman that "he seems to give too little weight to the forces that shift taxation on the ground owner."

[91] The reluctance on the part of common-sense and even of trained intelligence to accept the theory here maintained, that there is an essential difference between the effects of a tax on ground rent and a tax on occupation rent, may be accounted for by the tacit assumption

friction (*a fortiori*, of course, when we restore the concrete circumstance that taxes are very apt to rest where they strike).[92]

In this argument no use has been made of the circumstance that all the leases do not fall in simultaneously. But it will be found that this concrete circumstance does not invalidate the broad conclusion of pure theory, that there is an essential distinction between the effect of a tax on ground rent, and that of a tax on occupation rent. To fix the ideas, we might suppose occupation leases to be on an average for seven years, ground leases for seventy years. Thus every year on an average the leases of a seventh part of the houses in any given urban area would fall in; and in a tenth of these cases the ground leases would also fall in, and the sites would be offered to capitalist-builders; supposing as a first approximation that the duration of the ground lease coincides with the duration of the house. Upon this supposition a tax on ground rent would as before fall entirely on the landlord; a tax on occupation rent would not in general have that effect. The effect of the latter kind of tax would not indeed be exactly the same in the concrete case of rotation and the imaginary case of simultaneous bargains.

But the differences between the abstract and concrete cases will not, I think, repay examination. I am already sensible indeed that the investigation of economic forces which require some seventy years to work themselves out may seem to have been prolonged beyond the limits of applied theory. I submit, however, that the argument is not so abstract, the reasoning is not deduced through so artificial a chain of remote consequences as at least one of the classical theorems of taxation which are still accepted by economists;[93] I mean Senior's doctrine of tithes. In this argument, as interpreted by Mill, the links seem to be as follows: rise in the price of agricultural wages, check to profits, check to accumulation, check to the production of food, check to the growth of population, check to the rise of rent; comparatively to what would have occurred in the absence of the tax. But it is not my design to determine the limits of applied theory, or

---

that the amount of building is given and constant, irrespectively of the tax. Consider, for instance, the remarkably clear statements of Mr. Clements in his evidence before the Town Holdings Commission (Q. 1,969).

The argument which he illustrated by the example of a particular actual house (Q. 1,970) tacitly assumes that the amount of house accommodation demanded by the occupier is constant, whether or not the occupier pays an *ad valorem tax* (see notes).

For other direct contradictions of the theory here advanced see *Town Holdings Committee*, 1887, Q. 3,360; 1888, Q. 2,736, 2,837, 4,446, 9,357 *et passim;* or put the question to any practical man.

[92] Professor Thorold Rogers advocated this view very strongly in his evidence before the Town Holdings Commission.

[93] *E.g.* Bastable, *Public Finance*, and Seligman, *Shifting and Incidence*.

to uniformly cover with examples the field so demarcated. I aim only, at least in this first article, at a restatement, with slight modifications, of the classical laws of incidence, and a partial exemplification of the restated theory.

It will be understood that the application of the theory in this section has been adapted to the typical case propounded; modifications of statement would be required by the circumstances that there may be not only one, but several lessees between the ground landlord A, and the occupier C; that the duration of a house may exceed the period of the building lease; that the transfer of accommodation may be effected by sale or "feu," instead of lease; that houses may be used for business, as well as for habitation; that the ground landlord may act as a capitalist; that rates may differ in different parts of the same town; that house accommodation in different towns forms "rival" commodities; and many other incidents more or less important in practice.

From the point of view of pure theory the following modifications are more interesting. Perhaps the investments which are open as an alternative to an intending builder are not indefinitely extensive in comparison with the house-building industry—at any rate for periods not indefinitely long. The effect of mobility would then be to have connected our island B, not with a vast continent, but only with another island.[94] The joint island might then form a "nation" of capitalists, virtually appertaining to our first section, rather than the present one, obliged to submit in consequence of the house-tax to some permanent reduction in profits.[95]

Again, the building industry may be affected by the law of increasing returns, the operation of which we have next to consider.

A b. The old distinction between increasing and constant (or decreasing) cost presents difficulties to the newer analysis. For if any producer can continually increase his supply at a constant or diminished cost, there appears no general reason why he should not, cutting out his competitors, supply the entire market.[96] The classical conception of constant cost presupposes a limit to the production of each individual. The newer idea of expenditure pushed up to the margin of profitableness, in a regime of competition, implies the law of increased cost.[97] The law of diminishing

---

[94] Above, p. 274.

[95] This sort of intermediate case between perfect mobility and immobility is treated by Professor Pantaleoni in his highly original *Traslazione dei Tributi*.

[96] *Cp.* Marshall's *Principles of Economics*, 2nd and 3rd ed., Book V, ch. xi, *et passim*.

[97] Thus in the luminous illustration which Professor Marshall has given in note xiv of the Appendix to his *Principles*, 3rd edition, the total outlay of a master builder, considered as a function of different classes of labour x_1, x_2, and different kinds of raw materials y_1, y_2, etc., and other kinds of variables, must be such that the second term of its expansion fulfils all the

costs, as Cournot argues, is only intelligible on the supposition of monopoly.[98]

How then can the law of diminishing cost co-exist with competition? How can a larger offer go with a smaller price? How can the supply-curves of the kind which Professor Marshall has made familiar be ever conceived as *descending*?

The better opinion appears to be that such a downward trending *locus* is not to be regarded as a supply-curve in the primary[99] and obvious sense, not as representing the offer which in a given state of industry would be forthcoming at different prices; but as compounded of, or derived from, a series of such primary curves, which Mr. Cunynghame in his path-breaking essay on the subject[100] has called "successive cost curves."

It has happened to some of us to ascend a mountain slope just up to the point where the desire was just compensated by the difficulty, of further progress. Such is the position of the economic man on a primary short-period supply-curve sloping upwards.

Suppose that, as a party of mountaineers press up a steep slope, the opposing crest gives way, and they are carried down by a sort of avalanche, and landed on a new inclined plane. Again they urge their toilsome march upwards; and again, before the crest is reached, they are precipitated on to another ledge below; and so on till they are brought to a stop on some steep and comparatively firm slope. Their path in space, though in reality saw-shaped, might appear to one taking a general view to be a curve-line. Such, perhaps, is the nature of a competitive industry obeying the law of increasing returns: confined for short periods on an ascending supply-curve, extended during long periods down a descending supply-curve.[101]

Suppose that our party, after coming to a stop on a short slope, were to be incited by some fresh stimulus; they might break through another crest and descend through a distance out of all proportion to the exciting cause. Conversely, the imposition of a new burden might have prevented

conditions of a *maximum;* otherwise the statements made, *e.g. op. cit.*, p. 802, par. 2, would not hold good.

The theoretical difficulties connected with the law of increasing returns are frequently referred to by Professor Marshall in his later editions.

[98] *Principes Mathématiques*, Art. 50, p. 102.

[99] See the reference to the subject in a former article, *Economic Journal*, Vol. IV, p. 436.

[100] *Economic Journal*, Vol. II, p. 41.

[101] The idea of a curve of many branches was propounded by the present writer in his Address to Section F of the British Association (note J), 1889. The date explains one serious omission, that of "external economies," pointed out by Professor Marshall in the *Principles of Economics*. (See *d*, below, p. 305). [Not reprinted in this volume. Ed.]

such progress from occurring. It is thus that, in an industrial regime of the kind considered, a bounty is apt to lower price,[102] a tax to raise it,[103] to a disproportionate extent.[104]

But, if the law of decreasing[104a] cost is fulfilled in its natural and obvious sense, if the primary or short-period curves are descending, presumably the case belongs to *Monopoly*, the subject to which we next proceed.

Monopoly,[105] the branch of the subject we have now reached, presents a bifurcation peculiar to itself. There is an essential difference between (a₁) the cases in which we are concerned with only one monopolist, and (a₂) those in which two or more monopolists enter. The first subdivision presents ramifications parallel to those which have been traced in the case of competition. The first of these varieties is obtained by combining the just now defined attribute a₁ with the attributes which form the first members of cross divisions enunciated in the first article: namely, B prevalence of the law of decreasing returns, C immobility of capital and labour, D taxation of margin (*e.g.* specific or *ad valorem*, or in kind).

a₁ B C D. The simplest case under this head is obtained from the case which was first discussed under the heading A B C D, namely a simple market, by supposing one side of the market to be as it were solidified into a monopoly. We have thus the typical case discussed by Cournot: a single monopolist dealing with a body of customers competing with each other,

---

[102] Marshall, *Principles of Economics*, Book V, chap. xii, § 4.

[103] *Ibid. Cp.* Mill, *Political Economy*, Book V, chap. iv, § 2, end.

[104] A tax on a rival might of course act as a bounty; *e.g.* duty on foreign imports as a bounty to native producers.

Professor Carver's argument (*Yale Review*, November, 1896) that, when an import tax is levied on a commodity which is produced at home under the law of increasing returns, the consumers may possibly bear no part of the tax, is not, I think, as he seems to apprehend, "opposed to the best orthodox teaching"; unless orthodoxy be defined very straitly. The argument is used by some of the highest modern authorities, to whom I have referred in a former article [*Economic Journal*, Vol. IV, p. 48, E]. I don't know that they would accept his reply to the objection that the price—after being lowered in consequence of the tax— "might be further lowered by removing the tax." "This might be temporarily," says Professor Carver, "while it is probable that the same forces which kept the price up before the duty was first levied would ultimately bring about the same conditions after it was removed."

[104a] [In *Papers:* "increasing cost." Ed.]

[105] The taxation of monopolists and monopolised goods, which is the subject of this article, is not to be confounded with the taxation by monopoly which is practised by several modern governments. The pure theory of the latter form of taxation is simply the pure theory of monopoly in general—a subject which I have attempted to handle in the *Giornale degli Economisti* for 1897 (E). The taxation of monopoly and the taxation by monopoly are connected by a certain analogy, which, as indicated by Messrs. Auspitz and Lieben (*Theorie*, p. 427 and context), exists between monopoly and taxation in general. In ordinary taxation government alters, in taxation by monopoly it makes, prices in its own interest—or rather at its own discretion, as Government need not be perfectly self-interested (*see* Marshall on "Compromise Benefit," *Principles of Economics*, Book V, ch. xiii).

at the same price for all the customers. As demonstrated by Cournot,[106] the effect of a specific tax on the product will be to raise its price to an extent which may be either greater than, equal to, or less than the amount of the tax "selon les circonstances."[107] To which it may be added, I think, that it will probably be less, at least for the case of decreasing returns.[108] In general the addition to the price will be a substantial proportion of the tax.

What is said by many popular writers, and even by some distinguished economists, that a tax (of the kind now under consideration) will not affect the consumer, for that the monopolist has already done his worst, is true only in two special cases. (1) Where it is not in the power of the monopolist to increase or limit his output at will, he will very generally have to bear the whole tax. Cournot has noticed the case of the monopolist who is unable to increase his output.[109] The converse exception may be illustrated by an owner of urban land, if prevented by public opinion from keeping it out of the market. (2) The second exception is where the monopolist is a sole *buyer*, and the supply of the article bought is perfectly inelastic: for instance, a combination of tenants dealing with landlords

---

[106] *Principes Mathématiques*, chs. v and vi. [Article 15 of this volume. Ed.]

Professor Seligman appears to be under the impression that the only reason advanced by Cournot for the phenomenon that a tax on a monopolised article may raise the price to an extent greater than the amount of the tax was that the price paid by the consumer must include not only the tax but also interest on the sum advanced in order to pay the tax and the profits of middlemen (*Shifting and Incidence*, p. 156). "This theory," says Professor Seligman, "which Cournot invested with elaborate apparatus of mathematical diagrams, is, however, nothing but the accepted doctrine of Adam Smith, Ricardo, and Mill" (*ibid.*, p. 157; *cp.* p. 159, par. 1). But it will be evident to any one who studies Cournot's theory of monopoly (*Principes Mathématiques*, p. 78, referred to by Mr. Seligman) [p. 249 of this volume. Ed.] that Cournot rests the phenomenon in question, in the case of monopoly, upon a principle other than the accepted doctrine of Adam Smith. Cournot in the passage referred to, has "invested with mathematical apparatus" the law of taxation stated in our text; which is so far from being the accepted doctrine of Adam Smith that it has escaped even Mr. Seligman.

I do not deny that Cournot has also employed the "accepted doctrine"; whether mistakenly, as Professor Seligman holds, will depend on the validity of "the old doctrine of normal or natural profits" (Seligman, p. 158 and *cp.* p. 145), a subject on which I am not called upon in this connection to express an opinion (*cp.* ante, p. 77).

[107] *Principes Mathématiques*, p. 77 [p. 248 of this volume. Ed.]

[108] As proved by Cournot (*Principes Mathématiques*, Art. 31) the increase of price due to a small tax u per unit of commodity is of the form $u \times A \div (2A + B + C)$ where A is always negative; B is negative when the law of decreasing returns prevails (and positive in the converse case); of C nothing is known in general, either as to its sign or magnitude, except that the expression $(2A + B + C)$ must be always negative. In such a case, I submit, we are justified in regarding it as probable that A will be (in absolute quantity) less than $2A + B + C$, and therefore the addition to the price less than u—at any rate when B is of the same sign as A, as in the present section. [See pp. 243–44 of this volume. Ed.]

[109] *Principes Mathématiques*, last paragraph of ch. v; first paragraph of Art. 39 [pp. 246, 250 of this volume. Ed.]

incapable of combining. But in general the addition to the price will not be zero. I am unable to follow Professor Seligman when he asserts the contrary.

These theorems may be extended from a specific to an *ad valorem* tax. The demonstration is given by Cournot in a passage already referred to (*Principes Mathématiques*, p. 78 *et seq.*). I have endeavoured to give a simplified version of Cournot's reasoning in a note.[110]

Cournot's reasoning may be extended to any (small) marginal tax, provided that the aggregate tax increases with the amount supplied.[111]

Throughout all the cases which have so far been considered, there pre-

---

[110] Before the tax, the monopolist will have fixed the price which renders his net profits a *maximum*. He may be supposed to begin tentatively with a very low price, and to go on raising the price as long as the increment of net profit which corresponds to a rise of price continues positive. He will stop just at the point at which that increment ceases to be positive and begins to be negative. That is the required position of *maximum*. A rise of price above that point is attended with a fall in *gross* receipts. For, by hypothesis, the rise of price is [In *Papers:* "price of rise." Ed.] attended with a fall in net receipts; and net receipts equal gross receipts *minus* total cost; and total cost decreases with the rise of price, since total cost diminishes with the diminution of the quantity supplied, and that quantity diminishes with the rise of price. If, then, gross receipts minus total cost diminishes while the subtrahend total cost diminishes, much more must gross receipts diminish.

After the tax, the quantity which the monopolist seeks to maximise is the net profits in the same sense as before (that is, gross receipts minus total cost) *minus* the amount of the tax, a certain percentage of gross receipts. This quantity will not be a maximum at the point before determined. For if the price be raised above that point, the increment of the quantity to be maximised (net profits *minus* tax) will be 0 minus increment of the amount abstracted by the tax. But the increment of the amount abstracted is negative, since when the price is raised the gross receipts are diminished (as shown in the last paragraph), and therefore the tax which is a fixed percentage of the gross returns is diminished. It will be the interest then of the monopolist to raise the price beyond the old maximum point up to a new limit; at which the loss in respect of net profits (gross receipts *minus* total cost, which diminishes as the price is raised above the old maximum point) is just compensated by the gain in respect of the diminution of the tax. The new price therefore will be higher than the old.

A scruple may be felt whether, as the price is raised above the old maximum point the loss will overtake the gain, as the reasoning requires. The answer is that the loss (attending the increase of price above the old maximum point) is proportional to the *square* at the increment of the price, while the gain is simply proportional, it being supposed that the tax is small (*cp.* above, p. 268). Whence in general there is a determinate value for the increase of the new price above the old, such that the gain of the monopolist—the net receipts *minus* the tax—should be a maximum.

The mathematical reader will not expect the accuracy of a purist in this popular version; the general reader will perhaps be disappointed in his expectation of simplicity. I don't know that much has been effected by this cumbrous simplification, except to show the great superiority of the genuine mathematical method.

[111] As pointed out by Professor Marshall in the passage to which Professor Seligman refers when he says that "most writers, including Marshall (*Principles*, 460) [see p. 462, 1st ed., note, par. 1, p. 538, 3rd ed.] and Pantaleoni (*Traslazione*, 76), overlook this, and confuse a tax on gross receipts with a tax on sales or amount produced."

If the views, here stated summarily, and more explicitly in my article on "The Pure Theory of Monopoly" (*Giornale degli Economisti*, 1897), are correct, there is not the slightest confusion or mistake to be attributed to either of the authors thus disparagingly referred to by Professor Seligman. It is to be regretted that his intellectual sympathy is not always proportioned to his learning.

vails what may be called the general rule, both for competition and monopoly, that both parties suffer more or less from a tax. It remains to point out that in monopoly, as in competition, there are exceptions to this rule. The monopolist, indeed, always suffers, but his customers may be benefited in certain cases.

There is first a peculiar tax in kind noticed by Cournot with respect to monopoly, and described in our former article with respect to competition: "the abstraction of a certain portion of the exports in kind, to be disposed of in a manner not affecting the market under consideration."[112]

The case of several commodities presents a second class of exceptions, even more paradoxical in a regime of monopoly than in that of competition. If a monopolist supply two commodities for which the demand is *correlated*, that is either "rival" or "complementary," then a tax on one commodity may benefit the consumers of both.[113] To fix the ideas, let there be a railway, like our Midland, with two classes of passengers, first class and third class. Let there be imposed a small tax of say 2 or 3 per cent *ad valorem* on the gross receipts of the first class passenger traffic; or there being, as in fact, a tax already, let there be superimposed a small additional tax; I say the consequence of the new tax on first-class tickets may be to benefit passengers by lowering the fares of both kinds, both the third class and also the first class.

A mathematical demonstration of this theorem has been offered elsewhere.[114] The reader who has seen how difficult it is to state in ordinary language the proof of the simple proposition that a tax on a monopolised article tends to raise its price (above p. 285, note), will not expect here a full statement of the more complicated argument relating to two commodities. He may be put on the track of the investigation by the following hints.

---

[112] Above, p. 266. This kind of tax is presupposed in Colonel Barone's theorem respecting a contribution proportional to the quantity; forming the fourth theorem of his "Teoria Matematica dell' Imposta" (*Giornale degli Economisti*, March 1894), p. 207. [Article 27, p. 436 of this volume. Ed.]

[113] In the case of *rival* demand, the theorem makes no postulate about the cost of production. Either the law of increasing or decreasing (marginal) cost may prevail. There may even be no cost, two "mineral springs" controlled by a monopolist (*cp.* Cournot and Marshall) supplying without human effort two waters which may, to some extent, act as substitutes for each other. Or the (total) cost may be constant, not changing with that change in the amounts produced which is consequent on the tax; as it is allowable, though not necessary, to suppose in our example of first and third class accommodation. In the case of *complementary* demand, it must be postulated that production is *correlated* in a certain manner.

[114] See *Giornale degli Economisti*, 1887, Vol. I, p. 131 (E). In that article I give an explicit example of a possible curve, or rather numerical law, of demand for first and third class accommodation, such that if a tax of 2 or 3 per cent is put on first-class tickets, it will be the interest of the management to lower *both* fares.

Let x and y be respectively the first and third class fares (per mile or other unit) before the tax. After the tax let us suppose the directorate of the railway to alter the fares one at a time; and first the first-class fares.[115] By the theory above stated, the first-class fares will be raised in consequence of the tax (the third class being for the time fixed), say to x_1. There will result a diversion from first-class traffic, a rise in the demand for third-class accommodation. There might be expected then a rise of third-class fares in sympathy with the rise in the price of the rival accommodation; for when the demand for an article is raised it is probable[116] that its price will rise, *ceteris paribus*. But other things are not the same here. For, while the purchasers are now disposed to give more for third-class accommodation, the sellers are more ready to offer third-class accommodation now that it has an advantage over the first-class in not being taxed. Thus the change in the third-class fare will be the resultant of two tendencies, one making for a rise, the other for a fall. There is nothing to show that the latter tendency may not preponderate. Accordingly, the new y, say y_1, may be less than the old one. This low third-class fare will tend —by the sort of sympathy between the prices of substitutes which has just been noticed—to drag down the first-class fare, when we come to the third step, which consists in determining the first-class fare, x_2, which is most profitable to the monopolist, the third-class fare being fixed at y_1. It is probable then that x_2 will be less than x_1. And there is nothing to show that it may not possibly be less even than x. There is nothing to show that the series of subsequent steps will not converge to a system of two fares each of which is lower than the original one.[117]

---

[115] Of course I do not suppose so delicate an adjustment—such a frictionless movement towards the position of maximum profit—to be realised in the concrete management of an English railway. But I think that it may be of scientific interest to establish the theoretic possibility of the paradox enounced in the text.

[116] Though in a regime of monopoly, not necessary. See Index, s.v. *Paradox*. [The Index is not reprinted in this volume. Ed.]

[117] An acute friend has objected: If it is advantageous to the monopolist to lower prices after the imposition of the tax, why is it not before? I reply: Because the conditions of maximum profit are altered by the tax. Let x be the price of first-class accommodation, and y that of third-class accommodation, before the tax; and let the corresponding quantities demanded be D_1 and D_2. After the tax, let x' and y' be the prices, D'_1 and D'_2 the corresponding quantities. Then the profit of the monopolist is $D_1x + D_2y$ before the tax, after the tax $\frac{19}{20}D'_1x' + D'_2y'$; if, to fix the ideas, we suppose the tax to be 5 per cent *ad valorem* (on the proceeds of first-class tickets), and for simplicity we abstract expenses of production (supposed constant). There is no inconsistency in supposing that it is neither the interest of the monopolist to change the fares from x and y to x' and y' before the tax, nor from x' and y' to x and y after the tax; x being greater than x', and y than y'. It is necessary only that $D_1x + D_2y$ should be greater than $D'_1x' + D'_2y'$, and also $\frac{19}{20}D'_1x' + D'_2y'$ greater than $\frac{19}{20}D_1x + D_2y$; or that we should have at the same time $(D'_2y' - D_2y)$ less than $(D_1x - D'_1x')$, and $(D'_2y' - D_2y)$ greater than $\frac{19}{20}(D_1x - D'_1x')$. It is not surprising that of two

The preceding theorem illustrates a general characteristic of monopoly, that the laws of incidence relating to that regime resemble, but are less exact than, those relating to a regime of competition.[118] To take another example from the case of *correlation*. We have seen that when production only is correlated, "it being supposed that the demand for one commodity is independent of the demand for the other," in a regime of competition (1) a tax upon two rival products will raise the price of the taxed one, and lower the price of the untaxed one; (2) a tax on one of two complementary products will raise the price of both.[119]

Now let the correlated production be in the hands of a monopolist, the demands as before being uncorrelated. Then (1), as before, a tax upon one of two rival products will raise the price of the taxed one; but it will not, as before, necessarily—it will only probably—lower the price of the untaxed one. Also (2) as before, a tax on one of two complementary products will certainly raise the price of the taxed one, but will only probably raise the price of the untaxed one.

For example in a regime of monopoly it is probable, though not so certain as in a regime of competition, that a tax on malt would tend to lower the price of wheat in a country dependent on a limited area for its

---

quantities which are known not to be widely different (the tax being small), one should be greater than nineteen-twentieths, and less than the whole, of the other, provided that the quantities are *positive*. Now it is probable that $D_1x - D'_1x'$ is positive, if x is greater than x_1', as D_1 is probably greater than D_1' (the monopolist reducing his offer of the taxed commodity). Nor is it improbable that $D'_2y' - D_2y$ should be positive; nor inconsistent with the supposition that y' is less than y.

The objector may still insist: If D_1x [In *Papers:* "Dx." Ed.] is greater than D'_1x' [In *Papers:* "$D'x'$." Ed.], why not raise x' to x, leaving y' what it is? To which I reply that the proceeds of the first-class traffic will no longer be D_1x [In *Papers:* "Dx." Ed.] in that case, but $x \times$ first-class accommodation demanded at the prices x (first-class) and y' (third class), say $x \times \Delta$. Now Δ may fall off so rapidly, as the first-class fare is raised from x' to x, owing to the counter attractions of the third class (at the price y') that the monopolist will lose more by the decrease in the demand for first class than he gains by that increased demand for the third class which he at the same time causes.

[118] This greater latitude is explained by the circumstance that in monopoly, unlike competition, the producer [or, *mutatis mutandis*, the monopolist buyer] must take account of the change in demand price caused by variation in the amount of product which he may offer (*cp.* Marshall, *Principles of Economics*, Part II, p. 802, 3rd ed.). If β be that amount and p the price (*ibid.*), the marginal cost is equated in competition to $p\Delta\beta$, in monopoly $p\Delta\beta + \beta\Delta p$. Accordingly, in determining the variation in the position of equilibrium due to a (small) tax (*cp.* Cournot, *Principes Mathématiques*, ch. vi) [Article 15 of this volume. Ed.], whereas in competition the highest order of differential (of p with respect to β, taking β as the independent variable) which we need take account of, is of the form $\frac{dp}{d\beta}$, in monopoly we have also to take account of differentials of the form $\frac{d_2p}{d\beta^2}$. The sign of the former is given by the law of diminishing utility. But the sign of the latter is not usually a *datum*.

[119] Above, p. 267, where, by a misprint, or *lapsus plumæ*, the predicates of two propositions were transposed in the original version. [Corrected in this volume. See footnote 37. In text here, read "a tax upon one of two rival products. . . ." Ed.]

supply of both products; assuming that the production was not (other-wise) correlated. Contrariwise if the products are *complementary* in re-spect of the rotation of crops, as the Malt Tax Committee of 1862 sup-pose. "The effect of the malt tax," they say, "is to interfere with the due rotation of crops,"[120] and therefore presumably to cause wheat to be grown in more unfavourable conditions, at a higher price.

Some peculiar cases of rival production are constituted by the property that in monopoly identical objects may be sold at different prices: for in-stance seats for men or women at a theatre. If instead of the theatre tax which is now levied in Italy there were imposed a tax on men's tickets only, the ladies would be likely to gain not only in exemption from the tax, but also in having less to pay for their tickets. That is supposing the demand for one kind of ticket to be independent of the demand for the other kind. *A fortiori* if, as it is natural to suppose, the demands are *com-plementary*.[121] For it is probable in monopoly, as it is normally true in competition, that "a tax on one of two complementary commodities [*i.e.* "for which the demand is correlated"] will raise the price of the taxed one, and lower the price of the one which is not taxed."[122]

Following an order similar to that of the corresponding section on competition, we shall now leave correlation out of sight, and go on to consider the general case in which a monopolist deals with two or more competitive groups. For example, we might imagine one of our islands A, B, C,[123] to be now held by a monopolist. As before, we shall find that it is not indifferent whether a certain tax is levied on transactions between A and B, or on transactions between B and C. If, as before, we suppose the materials supplied by C to be constant in quantity and independent of human effort, we have now three cases, according as A (the consumers), B (the manufacturers), C (the landlords) form a monopoly. In the first case a tax on the product will prejudice both parties, not only in general as in competition, but always—correlation of supply or demand not being now supposed. For the circumstance which forms an exception in com-petition, the inelasticity of the consumer's[124] demand, cannot occur in monopoly.[125] In the second case a tax on the goods produced by the mo-nopolist B will not prejudice C; for the monopolist will have already done

---

[120] Parly. Papers, 1868, 420. Cp. *Evidence*, 1867: Q. 2616, 2952, 3023, 3305.

[121] The young man who treats his lady friends to tickets, and the paterfamilias who provides for mixed parties, would be disposed *ceteris paribus* to give more for men's tickets if ladies' tickets were lowered, or more for ladies' tickets if men's tickets were lowered.

[122] Above, p. 267.

[123] Above, p. 269.

[124] Above, *loc. cit.*

[125] This may be elegantly exhibited by the curves which Messrs. Auspitz and Lieben have employed to illustrate the case in which the monopolist is a sole *buyer*.

his worst.[126] In the third case a tax on the product will, on the general supposition that the demand of the consumers is not perfectly inelastic, prejudice the landlord in general in monopoly as in competition; but not in monopoly always. For, though in consequence of the tax the demand on the part of the (competitive) producers in B for the (monopolised) article supplied by C falls, yet it does not follow that the price of C will fall. For it is one of the irregularities of monopoly as compared with competition that a rise [or fall] in the demand for a monopolised article is not necessarily, but only probably, attended with a rise [or fall] in its price.[127]

This survey of marginal taxes of monopolised articles may conclude with the reflection that the consequence of such taxes appear to be in general more unpredictable in monopoly than in competition.

$a_1 B C d$. That taxation upon the profits of a monopolist cannot be shifted is universally acknowledged. It may be observed that this is true not only as stated in the books of a capitation tax consisting of a lump sum, and an *ad valorem* tax directly proportionate to profits, but also of a *progressive* tax on profits (the proportional contribution increasing with the amount).[128] Of course the alteration of the monopolist's revenue may produce, as in the case of competition,[129] an indirect result on the margins of work and saving.

$a_1 B c$. To attribute mobility to monopoly may appear a contradiction in terms. The designation may, however, be appropriate to a certain mixed case intermediate between monopoly and competition when there is pres-

---

[126] See E, Vol. I, p. 113.

[127] Suppose that the demand for the monopolised commodity increases in the sense that the average consumer "will buy more of it than he would before at the same price, and that he will buy as much of it as before at a higher price" (*Principles of Economics*, Book III, chap. iii, § 4, 3rd ed.). Then the demand-curve will be shifted outwards, as in Professor Marshall's figures 26, 27, 28. The *Monopoly revenue curve* (*ibid.*) will accordingly be modified. The new q_3 will be on a *constant revenue curve* (*ibid.*), which is further "out," or away from the axis than the corresponding old curve. But there is nothing to prove that the new Lq_1 is greater than the old one; the displacement of the demand curve may be such that—whatever the shape of the "supply-curve"—the new Lq_1 is less than the old one.

The rationale of this uncertainty, as well as others which have been noticed, is to be found in the same "dominant fact in the theory of Monopoly" (above, p. 288, note). In competition we are concerned only with the rise in the amount demanded at each price, the *variation* of Cournot's function $F(p)$, say $\delta F(p)$. If this is positive, the price must rise, the law of decreasing returns prevailing. In monopoly we have also to look to the sign of $\frac{d}{dp} \delta F(p)$, which is not usually given.

[128] See article in *Giornale degli Economisti* (E).

[129] Above, p. 270. The effect of such a tax on the margin of production is exhibited by Colonel Barone in the second theorem of "Teoria Matematica dell' Imposta" (*Giornale degli Economisti*), 1894. [See p. 438. Ed.]

ent mobility of labour and capital, but not the other characteristic of perfect competition, unique price determined by higgling of the market.

Crossing Mont Blanc from Italy into France, at a little mountain inn which is perched high above Chamonix I had some refreshment in the charge for which one item was a franc for a slice of bread. I don't suppose that this franc had any exact correspondence with the marginal efforts and sacrifices requisite to produce bread and carry it up to that height. It might have been so if several of the Chamonix bakers had erected each a shop or booth on the rock and competed with each other. Supposing this to be impracticable under the circumstances, it might still be open to any citizens of Chamonix to start a rival *auberge*, if it appeared that the proprietor of the existing one was making more than ordinary profits (account being taken of all the hardships incident to the business). In such a case we have "industrial" without "commercial" competition. The case is perhaps common where there is a large establishment and a comparatively small number of customers.

As Professor Walras has well observed, these conditions are realised much more often than is supposed—

tel fabricant de chocolat, qui vend son chocolat 3 francs la livre quand il le débite sous le nom modeste de "chocolat superfin" enveloppé simplement de papier glacé le vendra 4 francs la livre à la condition de le parfumer à la vanille et de le débiter sous le nom de "chocolat des princes," enveloppé de papier doré. Il en est de même des différentes places d'un théâtre, dont les différents prix ne sont nullement proportionels au frais de production de ces places.[130]

In such cases the incidence of taxation will partly obey the law of monopoly and partly that of competition. For marginal taxes not large enough to overcome the friction which resists mobility, it should seem that the law is rather that of monopoly than of commercial competition, our a B C D rather than our A B C D. One difference would be that, where the demand of the consumer is very urgent, the tax would fall on the producer to a greater extent than is to be expected in a regime of perfect competition.[131] In general the consequences of the tax become more un-

---

[130] *Économie Politique Pure*, p. 416; *cp.* Schönberg's *Handbuch;* article by F. Neumann, especially ii, 3; Acworth, *Railways and Traders*, ch. iv. So Hermann (*Untersuchungen*, ch. vi, p. 419, ed. 1870) of a shopkeeper who uses smuggled wares along with wares which have paid duty: "Stellen sich die preise höher als die schmuggelpreise tiefer als die preise der verzollten waare." It is not easy to see how this can be, unless the shopkeeper enjoys some of the properties of a monopolist. Professor Marshall points out that the "dominant fact in the theory of monopolies" (*cp.* above, p. 288) "is dominant also in the case of any producer who has a limited trade connection which he cannot quickly enlarge."

[131] Above, p. 284, note 108.

predictable in virtue of the property under consideration; a difference which is perhaps aggravated by the circumstance that the case is apt to be one of joint production.

a₁ b. The law of "increasing returns" does not constitute such an important subdivision of monopoly as of competition. There is no difficulty in the case of monopoly in understanding how production should stop short in the full career of the law of increasing returns, the diminution of the cost being more than counterbalanced by the falling off of demand.[132] The principal difference between the case of increasing and decreasing cost, is, I think, that the price is apt to be raised—will be raised *ceteris paribus*—to a greater extent in the case of decreasing than in that of increasing cost.[133]

a₂. The remaining branch is the shortest, yet not perhaps the least fruitful with regard to general economic theory, which rather than finance is here cultivated. Where two or more monopolists take part in a system of bargains there are no laws of incidence, for there are none of value. It has long been recognised that the bargain between two monopolists[134] is indeterminate; it is now submitted that a system of bargains in which two or more monopolists deal, not directly with each other, but with one or more competitive-groups, is also indeterminate. Suppose, for instance, a miller dealing with two monopolists, one the owner of the ground, the other of the water-power—as in an example put by Professor Marshall,[135] the only writer, so far as I know, who has given a hint of this theory. Let there be a number of such millers in competition with each other; and let the ground rent and the water rent be subject to revision from time to time, *e.g.* every year. The monopolists might go on for ever shifting the

---

[132] Regarding the action of increasing returns as essentially different in the case of monopoly and competition, I cannot quite accept Professor Seligman's statement with respect to a (specific) tax on a monopolised article. "Of course the same qualifications are to be introduced as before [in a regime of competition] according as the monopoly industry obeys the law of the constant diminishing or increasing returns" (*Shifting and Incidence*, p. 161). Not "of course," surely.

[133] I am compelled to differ from Professor Graziani (*Istituzioni delle Finanze*, p. 338) on this point. As already pointed out (above, p. 284) the imposition of a tax *u* per unit of commodity is in general of the form $u \times A \div (2A + B + C)$; where A is always negative, B is negative or positive according as the law of decreasing or increasing returns prevails; nothing is known of the sign of C—it represents the element of chance in the theory of monopoly (Index, *A priori probabilities*). Accordingly, *ceteris paribus*, A and C being constant, the increase of price is *greater* when the law of increasing returns prevails. [In second line of this note, after "the," read: "increase in price due to the." Ed.]

[134] Sidgwick, *Political Economy*, Book II, ch. x, § 3; Jevons, *State in Relation to Labour*, p. 154; Böhm-Bawerk, *Positive Theory of Capital*, Book IV, ch. ii; cp. *Mathematical Psychics*, pp. 21 *et seq.*, by the present writer.

[135] *Principles of Economics*, Book V, ch. x.

rents, making moves against each other like two chess-players when on each side there survives only the king with one or two inferior pieces.

The theorem may have some bearing on a system which is regarded by some as the ideal of the economic future, that each industry should be consolidated into a "Trust" or combination. Such a system would be characterised by instability, by fluctuations of prices such as now occur in railway wars, but more prolonged; for in so far as the combatants, like the two landlords in the example given, are not direct competitors, the combat seems less likely to be terminated by either the ruin of one party or the amalgamation of the two. That consummation may be more apt to occur when the two monopolists supply, not complementary articles, like land and water-power, but rival commodities. But even in this case the proposition that value is between certain limits—over a certain range of price—indeterminate may well be of considerable theoretical importance.[136]

For further discussion of this and other subjects touched upon here, I once more refer to the contemporary article on the Pure Theory of Monopoly in the *Giornale degli Economisti*.

[Let $F(x, y)$ be the money measure of the satisfaction attending the acquisition of the quantities of the commodity x and y. Let $f(x, y)$ be the cost of producing those quantities. What the consumers seek to maximise is then

---

[136] The case of wayleaves on mines to which Professor Marshall directs attention (*loc. cit.*) may illustrate the general principle, or rather absence of principle. It appears from evidence given before the Commission on Mining Royalties that it is not always possible to make the negotiation for royalty and wayleave concurrent (Q. 590). The lessee who, having sunk much capital on a mine, wants to take up an adjoining mine "deals with a halter round his neck" (Q. 561); he has been "got into a cleft stick" (Q. 673; *cp.*.Q. 5690). There is also much evidence that "the royalty is reduced by the rate of wayleave paid" (Q. 13,151). "A lower royalty is taken than would be if not subject to wayleave" (Q. 1933; *cp.* Q. 13,218, 11,306, 13,151, 13,749, etc.). Let us imagine these transactions to be effected successively, as thus: The first step is to take a lease of a coal-field for a certain period. The second step is to take a wayleave or some other subsidiary privilege. The terms exacted for this privilege being onerous, the third step would be on a revision of the first lease to lower the rent for the coal-field. The fourth step, it may be supposed, would be on a revision of the other lease to still further raise the wayleave. But this result is not certain, or not certain to continue as the series of steps is prolonged. It may become the interest of the owner of the subsidiary privilege to lower his terms in order to encourage the industry, wayleave being a charge of so much per ton. The principal landlord may retort by raising his terms; and the see-saw may go on *ad infinitum*. The lessee would not necessarily be worse off than if he had to deal (for both coalfield and subsidiary privileges) with a single monopolist—except so far as the instability of value is harassing to industry.

Of course I do not suppose such a prolonged series of steps as I have described to occur in the concrete. But I think it is a legitimate fiction in order to bring out the contrast that, whereas in a regime of competition a series thus continued theoretically tends to a definite position of equilibrium (as illustrated *e.g.* by Professor Walras in his *Économie Politique Pure*), in a regime of monopoly there does not exist, even theoretically, a determinate position of equilibrium.

$$(1)\ F(x, y) - p_1 x - p_2 y;$$

where p_1, p_2, are the prices of the respective commodities. What the producers seek to maximise is

$$(2)\ x p_1 + y p_2 - f(x, y).$$

Whence

$$(3)\ \left(\frac{dF}{dx}\right) = p_1 = \left(\frac{df}{dx}\right);$$

$$(4)\ \left(\frac{dF}{dy}\right) = p_2 = \left(\frac{df}{dy}\right);$$

together with certain conditions which must be fulfilled by the second differential coefficients of the functions in order that (1) and (2) may be each a maximum. We must have $\left(\frac{d^2F}{dx^2}\right)$ and $\left(\frac{d^2F}{dy^2}\right)$ each negative; say $-A$ and $-B$, where A and B are always positive. Also $\left(\frac{d^2f}{dx^2}\right)$, $\left(\frac{d^2f}{dy^2}\right)$ must each be positive, say $+a$ and $+b$, where a and b are always positive. Let $\left(\frac{d^2F}{dxdy}\right) = \mp C$, where C is always positive; the upper sign being used when the demand is rival, the lower when it is complementary. Likewise let $\left(\frac{d^2f}{dxdy}\right) = \pm c$, c always positive; the upper sign being used where the supply is rival, the lower when it is complementary. Then the two remaining conditions which must be satisfied by (1) and (2) may be written,

$$(5)\ AB > C^2; \qquad (6)\ ab > c^2.$$

Now let a tax of τ per unit be imposed on one of the commodities, say x. Thereby there is added to the cost of producing x the amount of the tax, viz., τx; and accordingly to the value of $\left(\frac{df}{dx}\right)$ for any x there is added τ. Equation (3) with this addition and equation (4) will now be true of the new values of x and y consequent on the impost, say $x' + \Delta x$, $y' + \Delta y$, where x', y' are the original quantities. Substituting these values and expanding (3) and (4) thus modified in ascending powers of Δx and Δy, recollecting that those equations are satisfied by x' and y', we obtain

$$(7)\ \Delta x \times -A + \Delta y \times \mp C = \Delta p_1 = \Delta x \times a + \Delta y \times \pm c + \tau;$$
$$(8)\ \Delta x \times \mp C + \Delta y \times -B = \Delta p_2 = \Delta x \times \pm c + \Delta y \times b;$$

whence

$$(9)\ \Delta x \times -(A + a) + \Delta y \times \mp (C + c) = \tau;$$
$$(10)\ \Delta x \times \mp (C + c) + \Delta y \times -(B + b) = 0.$$

Solving these simultaneous equations for Δx and Δy we obtain

$$\Delta x = \tau \times -(B + b)/D^2; \qquad \Delta y = \pm (C + c)\tau/D^2;$$

where D^2 is the determinant $(A + a)(B + b) - (C + c)^2$; which is known to be positive, whether a priori as the condition that the total advantage of both producers and consumers in globo should be a maximum (cp. Marshall, Principles of Economics, mathematical note xiv); or as a deduction from the aforesaid conditions of maximum pertaining to each party separately, in equations (5) and (6). Substituting these values in the expressions for Δp_1 and Δp_2 given by (7) and (8) we obtain

$$(11) \quad \frac{D^2}{\tau}\Delta p_1 = -A \times - (B+b) \mp C \times \pm (C+c);$$

$$(12) \quad \frac{D^2}{\cdot r}\Delta p_2 = \mp C \times - (B+b) - B \times \pm (C+c).$$

Let us begin with the case in which it is proper to take the upper signs before C and c; that is the case of rival demand and rival production. In this case it appears from (11) and (12) that both prices will fall if

(13) $A(B+b) < C(C+c)$;
(14) $C(B+b) < B(C+c)$; $Cb < Bc$.

These conditions are far from exacting. They are satisfied by values of the constants of which two are quite arbitrary, except for the conditions that they must be positive, and the remainder are very slightly restricted. Take *any* (positive) values of a and b and any value of $c < \sqrt{ab}$ (> 0); and *any* (positive) proper fractions r, s, t. Let $C = r\sqrt{AB}$; and for the inequations (13) and (14) write the equations

(15) $A(B+b) = sr^2AB + sr\sqrt{AB} \times c$;
(16) $r\sqrt{AB}\, b = sr^2t \times Bc$.

From (15) we have

$$AB(1 - sr^2) + Ab = src\sqrt{AB}$$
$$B(1 - sr^2) + b = src\sqrt{B/A}$$
$$(17) \quad \sqrt{B/A} = (B(1 - sr^2) + b)/src.$$

From (16) we have

$$(18) \quad rb = sr^2tc\sqrt{B/A}; \quad \sqrt{B/A} = b/srct.$$

Substituting this value of $\sqrt{B/A}$ in (17) and reducing we obtain for B $b(1/t - 1)/(1 - sr^2)$. Whence from (17) or (18) $A = \dfrac{s^2r^2c^2t^2}{b}\dfrac{(1/t - 1)}{1 - sr^2}$. $C = r\sqrt{AB} = r^2sct\left(\dfrac{1}{t} - 1\right)/(1 - sr^2)$. The reader may verify the fulfilment of inequations (13) and (14) by assigning values almost at random to the symbols in (15) and (16). Thus let $a = 1$, $b = 1$, $c(<\sqrt{ab}) = \frac{1}{2}$; $r = s = t = \frac{1}{2}$. Then $A = \frac{1}{224}$, $B = \frac{8}{7}$, $C = \frac{1}{28}$, $A(B+b) = \frac{1}{224}(\frac{15}{7}) < \frac{1}{28} \times \frac{15}{28} = C(C+c)$. $Cb = \frac{1}{28} < \frac{4}{7} = Bc$.

Whence $(D^2 = 1\cdot865$ nearly$)$ $\Delta p_1 = -\ \cdot005\tau$, $\Delta p_2 = -\ \cdot287\tau$; both prices fall in consequence of the tax.

So far of rival production and rival consumption. When both correlations belong to the other species, "complementary," the tax of one article may, as stated in the text, cause the rise of *either* of the articles but not of both. This case differs from the preceding in that the lower signs in (7) and (8) and the sequel are to be used (C and c still treated as positive). Then, if it be possible, let there coexist the inequations

$$(19) \quad -A \times - (B+b) < -C \times - (C+c),$$

i.e. $\quad A(B+b) < C(C+c);$

$$(20) \quad +C \times - (B+b) - B \times - (C+c) < O,$$

i.e. $\quad B(C+c) < C(B+b).$

$$Bc < bC; \quad c < bC/B.$$

Since $AB > C^2$ we infer from the inequation (19) $Ab < cC$. Substituting in this inequation the superior limit for c derived from the inequation (20) we obtain

$$Ab < bC^2/B; \quad AB < C^2;$$

which is absurd, being contrary to (5).

By putting now c, now $C = 0$ we may verify other statements in the text.]

C. TAXES ON INCOME AND PROFITS

18

The Colwyn Committee, the Income Tax and the Price Level*

By D. H. ROBERTSON

§ 1. The purpose of this note is to examine the validity of some of the arguments with which Sir Josiah Stamp and other members of the Colwyn Committee on National Debt and Taxation belaboured, in the name of "orthodox economic science," the unhappy business men who sought to prove before them that income tax "enters into" the price of goods. It will be suggested that some of these arguments are fallacious, and that others, whether valid or not, involve at the least a radical departure from the teaching of that authority to whom most frequent reference was made—Professor Alfred Marshall.

§ 2. The argument on which the Committee placed most reliance was thus set out by Mr. W. T. Layton in his evidence-in-chief (§ 11, M. 177).[1] "In theory the income tax should not affect the economic action of any income-tax payer. It is not directly an item in the cost of production. Whether we consider a whole industry or a particular business, production under competition continues up to that point where the last unit of output makes no contribution towards profit, and therefore nothing towards the revenue of the State. This is the unit of production which determines prices, which should therefore be unaffected by a tax on those units which yield some profit. On the same reasoning, the amount of output should remain unchanged." Mr. Layton proceeds to draw attention to certain qualifications of this theory, but explained in his cross-examination that he regarded them as being of very little importance, and "the economic theory" as expounded above as being substantially correct (Q. 2544, M. 186).

It appears, therefore, that in the view of this high authority economic theory teaches that price is determined by the marginal costs of produc-

---

* *Economic Journal*, Vol. XXXVII, No. 148, (December, 1927).

[1] The references are to the pages of the volume of Appendices (A) and Minutes of Evidence (M).

tion, those costs including no element of profit, so that profit appears as a surplus above price-determining costs, and is indistinguishable in this respect from economic rent. The same argument is developed at greater length in Professor Seligman's paper on "Income taxes and the price level," reprinted as Appendix No. XII in the volume of appendices to the Committee's report. "Inasmuch," writes Professor Seligman, "as the price is fixed at the cost of producing the most expensive portion of the supply that is actually sold, the difference between the lowest cost and the actual price—that is, the difference between the cost of producing the article and bringing it to market under the most disadvantageous circumstances and that of producing it under more favourable conditions—constitutes *the producers' surplus or profits*.[2] Profits are the result of the industrial process; they represent not cost, but surplus over costs" (A. 120).

Further study, however, reveals, in my opinion, a certain looseness in Professor Seligman's conception both of what constitutes the "costs" of the marginal producer and of the sense in which the profits of the intramarginal producer constitute a "producer's surplus." "The man at the margin who makes no profits, *or who makes only the minimum profits which correspond to wages of management or recompense for the risk*, pays no tax because he makes no profits or pays *only a negligible tax* upon these minimum profits" (A. 121). It makes surely all the difference in the world whether we are or are not to reckon among the costs of the marginal producer, which *ex hypothesi* determine price, all such profits as may properly be regarded as wages of management or remuneration for risk; yet Professor Seligman leaves us uncertain. If we *are* to include them, it can surely scarcely be argued that even in America the Golden, still less in highly-taxed Britain, the aggregate tax upon all such profits is "negligible."

But Professor Seligman does not appear to adhere firmly to his conception that only those profits (if any) which are made at the margin constitute the necessary reward of risk. For in discussing the remoter effects of taxation (A. 124) he admits that "the continual growth of a country's prosperity depends largely upon the readiness of the able and the venturesome to start new enterprises and to take the risk of the unknown. Where the hazard is great, the profits must be correspondingly great; for in the long run in new and untried fields the profits of some are likely to be counterbalanced by the losses of others. If the Government, however, demands too large a percentage of these anticipated profits, the individual may prefer not to subject himself to the risk and

---

[2] Italics, in this and all other quotations, mine.

may decide to be content with a smaller, but a surer, return." There is no indication that this argument is intended to apply only to the "minimum" profits (if any) of the marginal man; but if it is not, what exactly is meant by the doctrine that profits in general are "a surplus"?

§ 3. By far the most elaborate and ingenious analysis of the theory of value put before the Committee was that constructed by Mr. W. H. Coates as a setting for his interesting and important statistical evidence. Mr. Coates, unlike the authorities hitherto quoted, attempts to take ino account Marshall's doctrines of "normal profits" and of the "representative firm," and it will be convenient, therefore, at this point to refresh our memory of Marshall's teaching.

We are explicitly told (*Principles*, p. 343) that in constructing the normal supply schedule for any commodity we must include in the supply price for any quantity supplied "interest and insurance on all the capital" and "the gross earnings of management (including insurance against loss) by those who undertake the risks, who engineer and superintend the working." This normal supply price is to be conceived as the normal expenses of production (including gross earnings of management), not of a firm of sub-normal efficiency, but of a "representative firm." "On the one hand, we shall not want to select some new producer just struggling into business, who works under many disadvantages, and has to be content for a time with little or no profits, but who is satisfied with the fact that he is establishing a connection and taking the first steps towards building up a successful business; nor, on the other hand, shall we want to take a firm which by exceptionally long-sustained ability and good fortune has got together a vast business, and huge well-ordered workshops that give it a superiority over almost all its rivals. But our representative firm must be one which has had a fairly long life, and fair success, which is managed with normal ability, and which has normal access to the economics, external and internal, which belong to that aggregate volume of production" (*Principles*, p. 317). Again, we learn (p. 362 n.) that "the supplementary costs, which the owner of a factory expects to be able to add to the prime cost of its products, are the source of the quasi-rents which it will yield to him.[3] If they come up to his expectation, then his business so far yields good profits: if they fall much short of it, his business tends to go to the bad." I do not think any warrant can be found in Marshall's pages either for the view that the costs of production which are relevant to the determination of normal value are those of the most inefficient or

---

[3] Contrast Q. 9006 (M. 650). (Professor Hall) There are really three elements: the prime cost, the supplementary cost and the element of profit? (Mr. Coates) Yes.

unfortunate producers, or for the view that they do not comprise a substantial element of profit. I venture to suggest that Sir Josiah Stamp's attempts (Qq. 4705–19, M. 337–8) to bludgeon Mr. P. D. Leake with the authority of Marshall's name was based on a misunderstanding of the part played by "the marginal principle" in Marshall's theory of value.

§ 4. Mr. Coates, as was to be expected, shows his familiarity with the Marshallian doctrine of normal profits as a constituent element of costs (§ 7, A. 67); but it is not quite easy to determine what relation to this doctrine he conceives his own analysis to hold. There are moments when he seems to accept the validity of the Marshallian theory as an expression of long-run tendencies, and to be concerned merely to point out, like Marshall himself, that the price prevailing at any given moment is influenced by the temporary oscillations of demand and supply. Now if all Mr. Coates means is that in short periods of sub-normal demand prices will be charged which are insufficient to cover profits (or other supplementary costs), that is, of course, entirely consistent with Marshall's teaching. Where he appears to depart from that teaching is (a) in ignoring Marshall's emphasis on the strength and persistency of the forces which operate, even in times of sub-normal demand, against cutting prices so far as to "spoil the market,"[4] (b) in writing as though all short periods were short periods of sub-normal demand. "The conclusion of economic analysis," he writes (A. 68), "is thus that, while the broad trend of price is governed by the lowest or most efficient[5] cost of production, that cost including normal profit and therefore such portion of normal profit as is taken by taxation of income, this stage is rarely reached in the actual conditions of life. In these conditions, the temporary positions of demand and supply are the governing factors, and price is determined by the cost of the marginal products, the sale of which yields no profit, and may indeed yield a loss." Mr. Coates thus appears to conceive of the so-called "normal," not, like Marshall himself and Pigou,[6] as a *mean* around which actual conditions fluctuate, but as a *maximum* which they are always striving unsuccessfully to attain.

It is, indeed, hard to resist the suspicion that in question and answer both Mr. Coates himself and other witnesses and committee-men were constantly slipping into arguments relevant only to conditions of sub-

---

[4] *Principles*, p. 375. Cf. Pigou, *Industrial Fluctuations*, pp. 167–71 and 281.

[5] In this, I think, Mr. Coates flies to the opposite extreme.

[6] Cf. the diagrammatic treatment in Economics of Welfare, p. 755, where a certain area "represents normal returns to supplementary costs, and is equal to the *average* of producers' surpluses (from a short-period point of view) that result from the various positions assumed by the demand schedule *from time to time.*"

normal demand. Thus Sir Josiah Stamp inquires (Q. 5899, M. 435): "If you have a lot of ships and existing capital, would you not rather have something from them than nothing at all?" And Mr. Coates, having committed himself to the contention that even debenture interest does not "enter into" prices, is reduced to arguing (Q. 8989, M. 649): "Your debenture-holders, of course, have a right of recovery against you; but I should imagine, *in a period of very bad trade*, when debenture interest is not paid and the circumstances are explained, they are not likely to say, 'We are going to put in a Receiver at once.' " Mr. Coates is, of course, entitled to think (A. 67) that since "real life is . . . concerned, not with the long-run trend, but with the facts of the moment," "most attention . . . must be given to the short-period relation of demand price and supply price," though no one is entitled, in my view, to attempt to bluff the businessman into supposing that Marshall thought so. But since a long period is after all made up of a number of short ones, we are entitled to demand either that Mr. Coates' long-period theory and his short-period theory should be ultimately reconcilable with one another, or that one of them should be definitely repudiated as inaccurate. The long-period theory must not be left, with a perfunctory blessing hanging in the void.

§ 5. Mr. Coates, indeed, seems to be sub-consciously aware of this, for, having patted the theory of normal profits on the back as a long-run tendency, he proceeds to criticise it on grounds which, if valid, would be as fatal to it in this capacity as in any other (§§ 13–16, A. 70–71). It might, he suggests, be true if all producers were equal in ability. But in real life production is in the hands of numerous producers of very varying strength and ability, some of whom are so weak that they are making no profits or even making losses. The goods supplied by these producers form part of the total supply of goods, by the magnitude of which, taken in conjunction with the conditions of demand, price is determined. Therefore (so the argument appears to run) the magnitude of net profits is irrelevant to the determination of that price.

Now it is precisely this type of argument that Marshall's conception of the "representative firm" was designed, as it seems to me, to forestall. It becomes relevant, therefore, at this point to inquire whether the valuable statistics of the dispersion of profits furnished by Mr. Coates (A. 71–85) are such as to cast discredit on this conception. Mr. Keynes holds (*Economic Journal*, June 1927, p. 205) that the magnitude of the dispersion is so considerable as to do the conception "some damage." I venture to think that the shape of the normal curve of error disclosed by Mr. Coates for the normal year 1912–13, and even for the abnormal year 1922–23, would not greatly have surprised Marshall; but nobody can know.[7] In any case Marshall's doctrine clearly contemplates the possibility that some part of the supply is always being turned out at a loss. It is still, therefore, of at least academic interest to inquire what are the implications of the doctrine of the "representative firm" as to the effects of this part of the supply upon price, and as to the mode in which impediments to supply may be expected to affect price and output.

That, as Mr. Coates points out, the output of the least efficient producers forms part of the total output whose magnitude helps to determine price is, of course, evident; but to argue from this that there is some special relation between price and the costs of the least efficient producers is a complete *non sequitur*.[8] Indeed, as Mr. Coates himself points out, the existence of a supply from these producers, so far from raising prices above the costs (however interpreted) of stronger producers, makes it lower than it would be if, other things remaining the same, that supply were wiped out. (Of course, according to Marshall's doctrine, other things would *not* remain the same; for price having now risen above the costs of representative firms, representative firms would either expand their output or increase in number or both until price was brought down again to equal their costs.) The whole purport of Marshall's doctrine is that the least efficient producers are no more "marginal" than any other producers in the only sense of the word that is relevant to the determination of price. According to that doctrine there will always be some firms which, for what seem to them good and sufficient reasons, are ready to carry on production at a sub-normal profit or even at a loss; and the very fact that they are not covering their full costs (including profit) shows that they are *not* specially "marginal" in the only relevant sense, *i.e.* in the sense that they *must* cover their full costs if equilibrium is to be preserved.

---

[7] For convenience of reference I append the summarised statement (A. 92). Profit as per cent of turnover in seven groups of trades, taken together:—

	Median	Lower quartile	Upper quartile	Mean deviation from median
1912–13	4·61	2·53	7·67	3·59
1922–23	4·11	1·24	8·46	6·01

[8] "Concerns which are on the point of withdrawal from the market have been contributing their supplies to the total offered, and their influence on the supply side has been a factor in the determination of price, for, on the economic argument, this tends to be settled in any given unit of time by the demand which is effective in relation to the total quantity on offer. The addition to supply, which their activities have produced, will, by its enlargement of supply, have tended to depress the price to meet the effective demand. Yet the price influenced by this marginal production of the weak producers will have been insufficient to yield these producers a residuum of profit. Into that price can enter no element of any tax which is levied on profit, for, in the conditions which exist, no tax will be levied on those weak producers whose incremental supply on the market is a factor in the determination of price" (A. 71).

This would be true even if the least efficient firm at work were covering its costs, excluding profit. But the fact that some firms are working at an actual loss, while it raises no additional difficulties on the theory that there is a special relation between price and the costs (including profit) of the representative producer, makes nonsense of the theory that there is a special relation between price and the costs (excluding profit) of the "marginal" producer. For the latter doctrine loses entirely its apparent simplicity of outline when we discover that in fact the "marginal" producer is not a man who is making neither profit nor loss, but a man who is making a loss of an undefined and unpredictable amount.

§ 6. The trouble seems to arise partly from making an illegitimate analytical use of the device, appropriate enough for purposes of statistical demonstration, of ranging the various producers from left to right in ascending order of magnitude of their costs (excluding profits). If the curve so obtained is brought into connection with a demand curve, it is natural to infer that anything which raises the curve throughout its length, so that it cuts the demand curve somewhat further to the left, will leave the output of all but the weakest producers unaffected, and concentrate on the latter the whole curtailment of supply. So soon as this inference is put into words, it is seen to be fallacious. That, for instance, a uniform tax or raw materials should leave the output of the considerable majority of producers in any industry unaffected, is not to be believed.[9] The theory of price as depending on the activities of the "marginal producers" proves a good deal too much!

The fact is, of course, that we have no right thus to bring the weakest producers alone into proximity with the lowest regions of the demand curve. *Unless we are content, like Marshall, with a supply curve derived from the conditions of a representative producer*, the situation can only be treated diagrammatically by setting a partial demand curve against a partial supply curve for each separate cost-group of producers. The assumption of a single competitive price dictates that in the case of supernormal producers the two curves will not intersect, while in the case of sub-normal producers the point of equilibrium will lie to the right of their intersection. The effect of any change in the conditions of supply must be studied separately for each cost-group.

But once it is conceded that we must consider the effects of an impediment to supply on the actions of *all* producers, and not only of those "near the margin," the *a priori* distinction which it is sought to establish be-

---

[9] Though Mr. Coates, with perfect logic, was driven to adopt such a position with regard to a general increase in salaries (Q. 8887, M. 644) and even in wages (Q. 8900, M. 664).

tween the effects of a tax on raw materials and a tax on profits melts away. In either case, if it can be established statistically that the actions of the majority of producers are not affected, that will be not because of the existence of firms "at the margin," but because for the majority of producers the supply of the taxed factor is, for the period of time under consideration, inelastic. Some of the business men contended that the supply of business enterprise has a certain elasticity even over short periods,[10] and most of the economists were willing to admit that, at any rate for large changes of reward, it might have over long periods. The point at the moment is not whether or no this is true in fact, but whether or no the existence of "marginal concerns" makes it absurd to suppose it to be true. Clearly, in my opinion, it does not.[11]

§ 7. A good deal of the blame for the confusion and misunderstanding which arose must, I think, be laid on the shoulders of the Committee for the barren form in which they posited their question—whether or no income tax "enters into" prices. Several of the business men fell an easy prey, and made extravagant statements which they could not substantiate; but the more thoughtful of them showed that they conceived the rise in prices as indissolubly bound up with a contraction of supply.[12] The

---

[10] *E.g.* Q. 7306 (M. 518). "(Lord Colwyn) In making up the price, including the amount of profit, do you include income tax?—(Mr. Tredwen) It works in this way. In many cases I have declined to do business because the reward for doing it would be inadequate."

Professor Macgregor argues (Q. 5887, M. 435) that there can only be such a short-period check to enterprise in the case of producers who are individually strong enough to affect prices by checking their own supply. I see no reason to accept this limitation.

[11] In Mr. Coates' diagram 5 (A. 91) the very point which it is desired to prove, namely, the immobility of the supply-curve *SS'*, is assumed from the start. Further, this supply curve (in spite of its downward trend) is apparently supposed to represent momentary conditions, and therefore throws little light on the validity of the doctrine of "normal profits."

In diagram 4 (A. 89) Mr. Coates attempts to apply the conception of marginal production to individual firms, but as he does not appear to attach much importance to the result as compared with the conception of marginal firms (§ 35), the difficulties involved will not be further pursued here. It may be mentioned, however, that the shape of the curves of "cost as per cent of price" for individual firms—first descending owing to increasing returns and then ascending because "after [a] point, increased supplies begin to affect demand price"— appears to assume a power of charging differential prices.

The true Marshallian doctrine is admirably expounded by Henderson, *Supply and Demand*, ch. v, § 4. "The marginal concern," he writes (p. 59), "must be conceived as that working under the least advantageous conditions in respect of the assistance it derives from the strictly limited resources of nature, *but under average conditions as regards managerial capacity and human qualities in general.*"

[12] Mr. Glenday says (Q. 4867, M. 358): "I have started off with the idea that Income Tax has no direct effect on prices, but I say it has an indirect effect in this way, that it reduces the amount of goods which you sell." See also Qs. 8463–4 (M. 604): (Professor Hall) Should I be right in putting your view into these words: that it reduces your inducement to continue to extend production?—(Sir Hugh Bell) Yes, I think so. (Prof. Hall) And by curtailing production it does tend to reduce supply and to send up prices? Is that, roughly, it?—(Sir Hugh Bell) I think so.

economists, habituated to the conception of the mutual determination of economic quantities (Marshall, *Principles*, p. 818), and to the consideration of "the things which are not seen," might have been expected to give the business men a lead in this respect, and to point out that it makes no difference to the equilibrium attained whether the temporal sequence of events is (1) rise of price, (2) contraction of quantity demanded, (3) contraction of quantity supplied, or (1) contraction of quantity supplied, (2) rise of price, (3) contraction of quantity demanded. But instead the Committee preferred to harp on an unfruitful distinction between the "incidence" of a tax and its "effects." Even Professor Pigou, though quick to recognise in cross-examination that the question at issue was largely one of words, allowed himself to follow the Committee's lead in his original answer, and so to give it in a form which appears to presuppose monopoly conditions. "If," he writes (§ 30, M. 4; cf. Q. 617, M. 47), "as may be presumed, people are already charging the prices *that yield them the best profit*, the removal by the State of a proportion of the profit will not tempt them to fix prices differently." Mr. J. A. Hobson, though twitted by Sir Josiah Stamp with heresy, seems to me on this occasion to have sustained almost alone the unwonted rôle of champion of Marshallian orthodoxy.[13]

It remains to be added that once it is realised that increased prices are indissolubly bound up with contraction of supply, the suggestion of Sir Josiah Stamp (Q. 5882, M. 435), that, if prices really are raised, "the burden on the capitalist has ceased to be a burden because he has passed it on to somebody else," falls to the ground. For, as Professor Seligman admits (A. 122), "even though the producer should be able to add the income tax to the price of his goods and thus increase his profit per unit of output, he would, in all probability, sell so many less units as to diminish his total net profits. The business man, therefore, is quite justified in objecting to high taxes on business profits, even if he thinks he is able to shift them on to the consumer."

§ 8. I pass to some of the subsidiary arguments which were used to support the contention that income tax cannot "enter into" prices. The common weakness of all these arguments for the purpose in hand is that they seem to be equally applicable to local rates or to a general tax on raw

---

[13] I have sought in vain in Marshall's work for a direct expression of opinion on the effects of a general income tax. The nearest approach I can find is the following reply to the Questionnaire of the Royal Commission on Land Taxation (1897): "Generally speaking, the incidence of taxes on profits is widely and evenly diffused; they run over rapidly from one part of a trade to another and from one trade to other trades" (*Official Papers*, p. 357). I venture to think that so far as it goes this quotation supports my view of the implication of the Marshallian theory.

materials—imposts which by common consent do form part of the costs of production. The first argument is derived from the quantity theory of money, and points out that unless either the supply of money or its velocity of circulation is increased, the old total quantity of goods cannot be sold at an enhanced price-level. Mr. Hobson allowed himself to be temporarily blinded with this argument by Sir Josiah Stamp (Qq. 1626–38, M. 126–7), but after reflection gave correctly the obvious answer, that "the rise of prices would occur through a shrinkage of supply of goods" (M. 127, note). Professor Seligman, in the paper already alluded to, quotes with approval Ricardo's form of the same argument (A. 123, note). "The income tax, were it fairly imposed, would leave every member of the community in the same relative situation in which it found him. Each man's expenses must be diminished to the amount of his tax; and if the seller would wish to relieve himself from the burthen of the tax by raising the price of his commodity, the buyer for the same reason would wish to buy cheaper. These contending interests would so exactly counteract each other, that prices would undergo no alteration." In this form, the doctrine avowedly assumes that all working-class consumers are income-tax payers; and apparently also implicitly assumes that the money collected by the State is not spent but thrown into the sea. It seems to require little further comment.

The second subsidiary argument (used, *e.g.*, by Sir Josiah Stamp, Q. 621, M. 48) is that since the British income tax is progressive, and therefore falls on different producers at different rates, it cannot affect prices, because it would not know, so to speak, to what extent to affect them. Even if we disbelieve in the representative firm, the resources of algebra are equal in Professor Pigou's hands[14] (though not in mine) to analysing the effect upon price of differential taxes upon various sources of supply. One might as well argue that because foreign sugar and Empire sugar are taxed at different rates, no part of the sugar tax falls upon the consumer.

The third subsidiary argument urges that since there is a common price-level throughout the world for goods which enter into international trade, there is a theoretical absurdity about holding that the price of such goods can have been affected by the fact that the income tax is higher in Britain than in other countries. But clearly, if the British supply forms an appreciable part of the world's supply, there is not; and clearly too the argument would be equally valid as applied to local rates. In any case the substantial contention of the business men seems to have been that the

---

[14] *Economics of Welfare*, App. III, B, pp. 745–49.

high British taxation made it difficult to compete *at world prices*, and so restricted the volume of trade. In answer to this contention, Professor Hall and Mr. Coates seem to have taken up the untenable position that *no* taxation can diminish the volume of foreign trade (Q. 1378, M. 109, Q. 9080, M. 653), though Sir Josiah Stamp (Q. 1379, M. 109) and Professor Macgregor (Q. 5892, M. 435) were too wise to acquiesce.

§ 9. I pass to consider two pieces of direct statistical evidence on which Mr. Coates laid great emphasis in support of his contention that income tax does not in fact (even through the medium of restricted supply and reduced enterprise), affect prices. The first, derived from the same data as the measurement of dispersion of profits (§ 5), is the fact that, while the standard rate of income tax was 4·28 times and the average effective rate (including super-tax) 3·09 times as great in 1922–23 as in 1912–13, the median rate of profit on turnover, in the seven groups of trades considered, was only 4·11 per cent in 1922–23 as compared with 4·61 per cent in 1912–13 (A. 92–6, M. 638, § 14). I cannot help feeling, with Sir Alan Anderson, that the impressiveness of this result is very much diminished when we remember the respective positions occupied by the years concerned in the trade cycle. As Sir Alan suggests (Q. 9386, M. 677), "what you have proved is that the net return per unit with a heavy income tax in that very bad year was the same as the net return without the same income tax in a normal good year"—or rather, he might have said, the peak year of the cycle. Everyone will agree with Mr. Coates that there were plenty of other causes besides high income tax for the reduced volume of trade in 1922–23; but we are here thrown back into the region of common-sense and general reasoning. The particular statistical fact established seems to me, for the reason given, to carry little weight.

§ 10. Mr. Coates' second main statistical weapon is as follows. On the basis of figures presented by Mr. A. H. Gibson in the Financial Supplement of the *Spectator*, March 7, 1925, and extending for over 100 years, he finds a very high correlation, + 0·903, between an index-number of wholesale prices and the gross yield of Consols in the succeeding year (A. 101). For the sub-period 1908–24 he finds an equally close correlation, + 0·91, while for the same sub-period the correlation between the price-index and the *net* yield of Consols (*i.e.* after deduction of income tax) in the succeeding year is found to be only + 0·72 (A. 102–3). "The implication is that the income tax is an effective burden on the income, not thrown off through a movement in the yield." The argument, which is not, however, very clearly expressed, seems to be as follows. In fixing the gross money rate of interest which they demand, people are affected by variations in the value of money, and not by variations in the value of money *cum* variations in income tax, since if they were affected by the latter combination, it is the net rate of interest and not the gross which they would seek to keep stable in commodity value.

Now the significance of the high correlation between gross interest and the price-level is, as Mr. Coates himself admits, obscure. For year to year variations, the tendency of demanders and suppliers of capital to alter (though with a lag) the money rate of interest offered and demanded so as to compensate for the change in the real rate which an expected rise or fall in prices would otherwise produce, plays, no doubt, in accordance with the well-known theorem of Professor Irving Fisher, an important part. So probably do the variations in the intensity of the real demand for capital which occur, more or less synchronously with variations in the price-level, in the successive phases of the trade cycle. But in making a broad comparison between interest-rates in a period of high prices and in a period of low prices, neither of these explanations will serve. In particular, for the purposes of such a comparison, the whole notion of the supply price of capital as depending on the level of commodity prices is invalid. For of course interest, unlike wages, etc., is expressed as a rate per cent on capital, so that in comparing 1924, say, with 1913, both capital and interest are affected alike by the fall in the value of money. So far as the high correlation between gross interest and the price-level results from the fact that both the rate of interest and the price-level fluctuate about a higher mean level in post-war than in pre-war years, it is quite clearly not significant, since the cause of the raised mean level is unquestionably different in the two cases. The higher mean level of prices is by universal consent mainly due to the increased supplies of money (including bank-credit) in circulation; while, as argued above, the higher mean level of interest rates cannot possibly be due to this cause, either directly or through the mediation of the price-level, but must be due to a relative shortage in the supply of capital as compared with the demand. Once this is realised, the comparative lowness of the correlation between *net* interest and the price-level ceases also to be significant. It is largely a reflection of the fact that the war, which caused an inflation of prices and a shortage of capital, led also to the imposition of a high income tax.

The fact which leaps to the eye from Mr. Coates' tables is that the net rate of interest is now about the same as it was in the years immediately preceding the war, *i.e.* the gross rate has gone up by just about the amount of the increase in income tax. Sir Alan Anderson seems to have been amply justified in pointing out (Qq. 9322–39, M. 674–5) that, if we are to talk statistics at all, the prima facie suggestion of the statistical evidence is that the tax has been added to the supply price of capital. In his reply to this suggestion, Mr. Coates seems to have taken a headlong leap (which Sir Alan was not quick enough to expose) into the fallacy explained above. For he suggested in effect (Q. 9324–6) that since the net money rate of interest was unchanged, the net real rate had fallen (so that the gross real rate might therefore be substantially unchanged).[15] As already stated, since both capital and interest are expressed in depreciated pounds, this argument is fallacious. There *has* been a real rise in the gross rate of interest, and its prima facie significance is what Sir Alan stated it to be—a relative shortage in the supply of savings. How far this shortage is due to the high income tax and how far to other causes is, of course, another matter: we are here back in the realm of opinion and general reasoning.

§ 11. But Mr. Coates also uses the high correlation of prices with the gross rate of interest in another manner. In Q. 9105 (M. 655) he constructs the following syllogism:

> Prices move with gross rate of interest,
> Prices do not move with income tax,
> ∴ income tax does not move with gross rate of interest.

The minor premiss is apparently based on Mr. Coates' own previous general reasonings about the marginal firm, and not on statistics; and since it asserts the very point which it is sought to prove (namely, that income tax does not affect prices even through the medium of the rate of interest), it seems to form rather a weak logical link in the chain of argument. Statistically, it is inconsistent with the very fact on which Mr. Coates lays special stress in his argument summarised in § 10 above—the lower correlation between net interest and prices than between gross interest and prices. If it comes to correlations, it is worth noting that for the period 1908–24 the correlation between the rate of income tax and the price-level is + 0·94 and that between the rate of income tax and the gross rate of interest is + 0·93.[16]

§ 12. In conclusion, I wish to make it plain that it is to the specific arguments which impressed the Committee, and not to their general conclusions, that I demur. While there is no theoretical absurdity in suppos-

---

[15] "(Sir Alan) The net reward to the investor in gilt-edged investments has, it so happens, gone up so that he gets as much now as he would before the war.—(Mr. Coates) In terms of money?—(Sir Alan) In terms of money.—(Mr. Coates) Not in terms of commodities?—(Sir Alan) No, not in terms of commodities, but in terms of money. . . .—(Mr. Coates) I think when you turn it into terms of commodities it loses its whole point."

[16] I am indebted to Mr. D. Barber, of Trinity College, for help in seeing through this particular tangle and for working out the correlations.

ing that even over short periods the supply of existing business enterprise may be elastic, so that, in Mr. Tredwen's words, people "decline to do business because the reward for doing it would be inadequate," there are strong reasons, based on common observation, for doubting whether this is, in fact, the case to any important extent. A high income tax will only have an *important* effect in reducing output and (monetary conditions remaining unchanged) raising prices if it checks the supply of *new* capital and business ability. But here again the whole history of social legislation and Trade Union activity suggests that even in the long period the elasticity of supply of these factors is far less than used to be supposed by economists, and far less than business men as a class are naturally inclined to suppose even now. Economists are familiar with the notion that the demand and supply schedules of any commodity are not really independent of one another, so that a *permanent* alteration of the demand schedule may lead to a change in the whole schedule of supply. It is quite possible that as a result of a prolonged high level of taxation business men as a class should revise their conceptions of what constitutes a reasonable rate of reward for enterprise, and it is not impossible that, as Mr. Coates argues in an interesting passage of his evidence, something of the kind has already happened.[17] Further, the whole tendency of modern economic reasoning is to lay less stress on the effects of this or that action in stimulating or checking the *motives* for displaying this or that kind of activity, and more stress on its effects in expanding or contracting the *sources* from which that activity emanates. A high income tax, the proceeds of which are devoted partly to debt reduction and partly to measures of public health and education, may well have a beneficial effect on the sources both of savings and business enterprise far outweighing any discouraging effect it may exercise on the incentives to display those activities. Finally, it is now realised that even if it can be definitely proved that a given measure has a perceptible effect on the balance in retarding the rate of accumulation of material wealth, that measure does not necessarily stand condemned. The time has come to substitute reasoned judgments about what proportion of our national income it is proper for us to save for the blind fear of doing anything which may make that proportion less than it would otherwise have been.

For these reasons, the general attitude of the Committee and their

---

[17] Q. 9406, M. 678. "Man's comparison between disutility and utility, effort and reward, is not a constant factor; it is a moving factor, and it is conditioned by the terms and circumstances in which the man lives. . . . One judges things differently according to the circumstances that may exist, and what may be not enough to tempt a man of fifty-five, may to-day tempt a man of twenty-five strongly, and you have got every degree in between."

advisers—that if you throw enough taxation mud at the business man a good deal of it will stick—and their conclusion that the reduction of the present rate of income tax is not a matter of pressing importance, seem to me wholly sound and admirable. That the technical arguments by which they believed themselves to be moved were unsound is not a matter of great importance, except in so far as accurate thinking is a good in itself, and except for the danger that those arguments, reinforced by the authority of great and respected names, may do damage in other connections.

19

*Fiscal Control of Monopoly**

By BENJAMIN HIGGINS

With the growing recognition that size as such is not always a threat to social welfare, and the waning confidence in "trust-busting" as a device for control of monopoly, proposals for regulating monopolies through fiscal means take on new interest. This article is concerned with a variety of tax proposals, all designed to make the monopolist behave as though he were operating in a competitive market. That is, instead of penalizing bigness, these measures are aimed at making it profitable for monopolists to utilize their capacity to the full.

I

From a purely logical point of view, the best fiscal device for control of monopoly is the one suggested by Mrs. Robinson. She states that a subsidy equal to marginal cost minus marginal revenue for the purely competitive output of a firm operating under monopoly conditions will induce the entrepreneur to produce that output, and that a tax equal to the whole of supernormal profits, including the subsidy, can then be collected without altering the equilibrium position.[1] Mrs. Robinson makes no use of the

---

* This paper presents a slightly condensed version of the earlier article, "Post-War Tax Policy (Part I)," *Canadian Journal of Economics and Political Science*, Vol. IX, No. 3 (August, 1943).

[1] Joan Robinson, *Economics of Imperfect Competition* (London, 1933), pp. 164–65. Mrs. Robinson attributes the scheme to an examination paper written by her husband. Considering the general acceptance by later economists of Adam Smith's dictum that a tax on profits cannot be shifted and Cournot's clear demonstration that a subsidy on output will lead a monopolist to expand output, it is remarkable that this "tax-and-bounty" scheme should have waited so long for precise formulation.

Professor Dalton, it is true, hit upon the idea of "a tax whose total amount diminishes with output" as a device for stimulating monopolists to expand production (*Principles of Public Finance*, London, 1936, p. 60) but this tool is haphazard compared to Mrs. Robinson's. Professor Pigou proposes a system of bounties to industries operating under decreasing costs and taxes on industries operating under increasing costs, both in his *Economics of Welfare* (chap xi, London, 1932) and in his *Public Finance* (chap. viii, London, 1928). However, he considered his system applicable only under "simple competition," and rejected fiscal controls of monopoly altogether: "Where self-interest works, not through simple competition, but through monopoly, fiscal intervention evidently ceases to be effective. A bounty might,

device, feeling that the indefiniteness and instability of demand curves makes it impractical.

Actually, it can be very simply demonstrated that a subsidy per unit of output equal to marginal cost minus marginal revenue for *any* chosen output $\bar{x}$ will lead to the production of $\bar{x}$, if the entrepreneur maximizes profits and if the demand and cost curves are not altered by the subsidy. Let us denote output by x, total revenue by $R(x)$ and total cost by $C(x)$ and the subsidy per unit as S, which is not a function of x. Then in equilibrium before payment of the subsidy,

$$R'(x) = C'(x).$$

Let us now pay a subsidy $S = C'(\bar{x}) - R'(\bar{x})$. Marginal revenue with the subsidy is then simply,

$$R'(x)_s = R'(x) + C'(\bar{x}) - R'(\bar{x}).$$

Thus if $x = \bar{x}$, $R'(x)_s = C'(x)$. That is, when the subsidy is paid, equilibrium is established with output equal to $\bar{x}$. By the same reasoning, a subsidy per man-hour equal to marginal wages bill minus marginal productivity of labour for any desired level of employment $\bar{n}$ will induce a monopsonistic employer to utilize $\bar{n}$ man-hours, and so forth, and a tax on profits cannot be shifted.

A diagrammatic illustration of the device is given in Figure 1. For this purpose, demand is D_2D_2 and average cost is $(AC - R)$, marginal revenue is MR_2, and marginal cost is $(MC - R)$. If we define $\bar{x}$ as the perfectly competitive output ($\bar{x}_2$ in Figure 1) the subsidy per unit will be equal to BC_2 or S. Adding this amount to D_2 we get the curve $D_2 + S$. The curve which is marginal to this one, $MR_2 + S$, will cut $(MC - R)$ in C_2, so that equilibrium is established with an output equal to $\bar{x}_2$. The geometric proof that $MR_2 + S$ will cut $MC - R$ in C_2 is simple enough, but too cumbersome to be presented here.

An instrument for allocation so powerful on the analytical level deserves examination, despite administrative difficulties which seem more complex than is usual even in the realm of new fiscal policies. The purely statistical problem of estimating the shapes of cost and demand curves is not an insuperable one. It is a problem met implicitly by any business firm, and by any government agency concerned with allocation, no matter what technique is used. Nothing is gained by using other devices which simply

---

indeed, be so contrived as to prevent restrictions of output below what is socially desirable, but only at the cost of enabling the monopolist to add to his already excessive profits a large ransom from the State" (*Economics of Welfare*, p. 336). This dictum has been echoed by Dr. Benham in a recent article ("What Is the Best Tax System?" *Economica*, May, 1942): "Such imperfections should be removed by direct action."

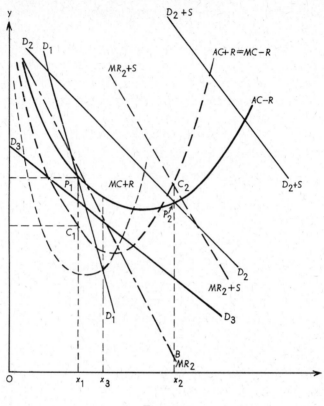

FIGURE 1

fail to make the problem explicit. Given a reasonably stable economy, the general character of the curves could eventually be determined. By a series of trial-and-error approximations, something approaching the right size of subsidy and tax could be estimated. To begin with, both tax and bounty could be set considerably lower than is estimated to be correct. Any move in the right direction would be a net gain, and it would be better to fall short of perfection than to drive a firm out of business altogether. Unless Mrs. Robinson's "indefiniteness and instability of demand and cost curves" are either more deepseated, or a product of the use of the device itself, they do not constitute sufficient reason for abandoning the plan without an analytical trial.

II

As a general rule, the fiscal authority would define $\bar{x}$ as the purely competitive output for each firm. Given pure competition in related fields, this output would be the one equating long-run average (and marginal) costs with price, since this output then equates relative marginal significances of output with relative marginal displacement costs. Unfortunately, such a definition of $\bar{x}$ would leave excess capacity in every industry where the demand curve cuts the average cost curve to the left of its minimum, which is probably the typical situation under monopolistic competition, if not in the economy as a whole.

Since we are accustomed to thinking of the "optimum" as a situation minimizing average costs as well as equating average and marginal costs with prices and eliminating monopoly gains, it may be well to state the conditions under which excess capacity is compatible with an optimum situation: (1) technical factors must make it impossible to produce the commodity with a smaller fixed plant at the same or lower average costs; (2) consumers must want a small amount of the commodity badly enough to pay a price covering costs for a small volume of output; (3) relative marginal significance (demand) of the commodity must fall more rapidly than costs, for outputs greater than the one where demand price is equal to or above costs. This constellation of conditions is perfectly possible in the real world, and there is no escape from excess capacity under such conditions except a reduction of the costs of small-scale production or a flattening of demand curves.

If the minimum average cost position were chosen, a net tax could be collected whenever the demand curve cut the cost curve to the right of its minimum point. There is no assurance that the redistribution of income involved in collection of this net tax on profits and, say, corresponding expansion of public-work expenditures or reduction of commodity taxes, would not raise the level of satisfaction more than expanding output to the level equating average cost and price. However, in reality it seems likely that more demand curves will cut to the left than to the right of the minimum cost position, and in any case the choice of this position as optimum involves interpersonal utility comparisons in a manner which is avoided by defining $\bar{x}$ as the output equating price with average cost.

Strictly speaking, the costs to which price should be equated are not average but marginal. Marginal costs are the true measure of alternative output sacrificed if there are any significant differences between production functions for commodities using the same factors—that is to say, unless costs are constant. However, if we were to define $\bar{x}$ as the output equating marginal cost and price, not only would excess capacity still exist whenever the demand curve cuts the average cost curve to the left of its minimum point, but in addition, it would be necessary to pay a net subsidy. Conversely, if demand cut to the right of minimum average costs, a net tax could be collected. In reality, it seems likely that a net subsidy would have to be paid in the economy as a whole. That being the case, the advantage of the output equating marginal cost and price is no longer clear-cut. Even admitting that part of the subsidy could be met by monetary expansion because it leads to increased output, the net change in total satisfaction in proceeding from the output where average cost equals price to the one where marginal cost equals price depends upon how the remaining subsidy is raised, upon the indifference maps of consumers, and upon the relative importance to the entrepreneurs of money income on the one hand and such things as desire for leisure and to own a big business on the other. Anyone with a strong preference for equation of price and marginal cost as a norm can easily experiment for himself with the tools presented herein, to determine their merits and demerits in terms of his own criterion.[2]

If unemployment existed among the variable factors and no more productive employment were available, their use in conjunction with the fixed plant of the monopolist would be socially costless. It would pay the society to operate the plant to capacity, even if doing so would require appropriation of the plant by the government or payment of a net subsidy to the entrepreneur. Similarly, if the plant is unnecessarily large from a technical point of view because the entrepreneur lacked foresight or is interested in maximizing returns to the fixed plant, not all rents on fixed factors constitute social costs. The optimum output would then be defined in terms of costs exclusive of these irrelevant rents.

In Figure 1, $(AC + R)$ is average costs including all rents and $(AC - R)$ is average costs exclusive of all rents. In the absence of economies of scale $(AC + R)$ is marginal to $(AC - R)$. There is always some definition of "factor of production" that will make the production function linear and homogeneous, and in this paper we shall assume that it is. Strictly speaking, the curve of "average costs minus irrelevant rents"

---

2 While his analysis is somewhat muddled for the contemporary reader by his terminology and by his concepts of "representative industry" and "equilibrium firm," Professor Pigou's definition of optimum as the point where "marginal social net product" equals "the central value of marginal social net products" no doubt means the same thing as equation of price with marginal cost. However, his discussion makes it quite clear that he thinks in terms of minimizing average cost more than in terms of equating marginal cost and price. In his "simple competition" context, there is, of course, no conflict between these two norms and the equation of price with average cost. Professor Pigou also qualifies his support for the scheme with the proviso that "the funds for the bounty can be raised by mere transfer that does not inflict any indirect injury on production" (*Economics of Welfare*, p. 224) and with the warning that administrative difficulties might outweigh the benefits of the plan (*Public Finance*, p. 119).

would not be identical with the $(AC - R)$ curve of Figure 1, since part of the rents would be social costs—the part required to replace the existing plant with one of the proper size. The true curve would lie between $(AC - R)$ and $(AC + R)$, but would still cut $(AC - R)$ at its minimum point unless diminishing returns set in at a lower level of output for part of the fixed plant than for the rest of it. Since we want $(AC - R)$ for another purpose later, we shall assume for the sake of diagrammatic economy that $(AC - R)$ is relevant for the case of oversized plant. It will be noted that definition of $\bar{x}$ in terms of this curve in cases where the monopolist has counted all rents as costs will carry production still further into the stage of diminishing returns if the demand curve cuts to the right of minimum $(AC - R)$, as in the case of D_2D_2, and will leave the firm with still more excess capacity if the demand curve cuts to the left of minimum $(AC - R)$, as in the case of D_1D_1.

Where the oversized plant is due to mistaken foresight, but the entrepreneur does not realize it because he counts all rents as costs and makes a good profit in terms of these costs, production may be carried on and plant fully replaced although the demand curve lies entirely below the relevant curve of social costs, as in the case of D_3D_3. In such cases, $\bar{x}$ should be defined so as to minimize $[(AC - R) - (\text{price})]x$: The tax-and-bounty, however, must be defined so as to leave the entrepreneur a net loss in terms of $(AC + R)$ equal to the social loss in terms of $(AC - R)$. Under these conditions, the tax-and-bounty will yield a net return to the public treasury. It will pay to abandon the plant immediately only if price does not cover prime costs; since prime costs are the same for society as for the entrepreneur, they will presumably be covered in the case under discussion. The tax-and-bounty is simply a means of compelling the entrepreneur to reduce the size of his plant by making him aware of its unprofitability on the present scale. In order to be sure of the right reaction, the tax might be stated as a tax on fixed plant instead of on profits, scaled so as to make the proper-sized plant the most profitable one when subsidy and tax are taken into account.

If, on the other hand, technical considerations prevent the use of smaller plant, but the entrepreneur fails to include rents on fixed factors as costs, there is again a discrepancy between the cost curves determining entrepreneurial behaviour and the curves which measure social costs. The curve relevant to social policy in this case includes rents, and the proper definition of $\bar{x}$ would entail a reduction in output whenever the demand curve cuts $(AC - R)$ to the right of the point where $(AC + R)$ is at its minimum.

III

While the administrative difficulties are not so insuperable as to preclude a trial-and-error approach to the tax-and-bounty scheme in industries where the degree of monopoly power is high, they are clearly serious enough to warrant consideration of alternative fiscal devices which, while logically less perfect, are easier to handle in practice. In this section, I shall discuss a few alternatives, in hopes that others may be sufficiently interested to look for better ones.

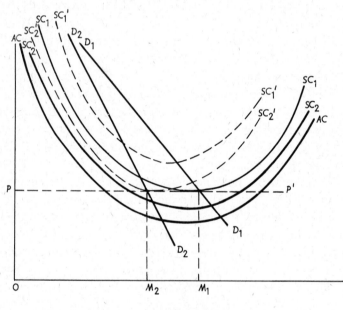

FIGURE 2

Where monopoly is based solely upon differentiation through incurrence of selling costs, one is tempted to suggest a high tax on selling costs. However, the effect of such a tax in itself is to reduce sales as well as selling costs, so that excess capacity is increased rather than diminished.[3] Only if the reduction of selling costs removes the differentiation in the

---

[3] In Figure 2, AC is average cost, SC_1 average cost plus the selling cost that produces the demand curve D_1, SC_2 average cost plus the selling cost that produces the demand curve D_2, PP' is the price. SC_1 is accordingly the equilibrium average-plus-selling cost, and output is QM_1. Now suppose a tax is imposed on selling costs, so that the curve of average costs plus selling costs plus tax which produces the demand curve D_1 becomes SC'_1, the curve which produces demand D_2 becomes SC'_2, etc. The equilibrium cost curve will now be SC'_2, which represents a lower expenditure on selling costs than SC_1, but sales will be reduced to OM_2.

minds of the consumers among rival products, and so flattens the demand curves facing each firm in the "industry," will there be any net gain. To assure this result, it might be well to use the revenues from the tax for the support of a government consumers' research organization which would distribute factual material as to the true nature of various commodities on the market.

If differentiation has a technical basis, so that complete knowledge of the nature of rival products would still leave some consumers with a preference for one product over the others, the definition of one product as "standard," and imposition of taxes on products deviating from the "standard," will not necessarily raise the level of satisfaction. If the tax is made prohibitive for the production of deviations from the "standard," the demand curves for the firms producing a given type of product (say, cigarettes) will indeed flatten and the equilibrium position will come closer to meeting the criteria of a purely competitive equilibrium. On the other hand, the loss of the "preferred" variant of the product will result in a reduction of consumer satisfaction. It is impossible to say which factor will weigh heaviest in any particular case, but the argument for such a tax policy would be strongest where the technical differentiation seems slight and the degree of excess capacity seems large.

IV

With some loss of precision, the administrative problem can be greatly reduced by a "tax on profits in excess of a fair return on utilized capacity." The application of this tax is illustrated in Figure 3. In this diagram TR_1 is total revenue, TC total costs, and TP_1 total profits. The monopoly equilibrium output is OM_1, the perfectly competitive output OC_1. Suppose profits are taxed 100 per cent in excess of, say, 5 per cent on capital value, and that 5 per cent of capital value comes to $\$OA$. The curve of total profits, or gains, will follow TP_1 to G, go along GG' to G', and then along TP_1 again. Equilibrium is indeterminate between G and G'. Suppose now that tax-free profits are calculated as 5 per cent of *utilized* capacity, with "capacity" defined in such a way as to make it vary directly with output. The curve of net gains now becomes OG'', and the equilibrium position is where this curve cuts TP_1.

In order to establish equilibrium as near to the competitive one as possible, the rate of profit, and the rate at which "utilization" increases with output, should be kept as low as they can be and still have entrepreneurs react to them. The tax must be at or near 100 per cent to guarantee an increase of output with its imposition; otherwise gross profits may fall

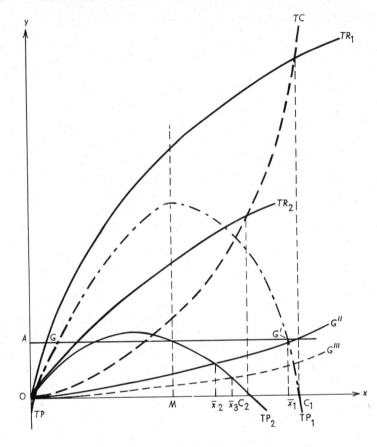

FIGURE 3

more rapidly than tax liability as output increases, and no change in output would result from the application of the device.

The attraction of this scheme is its simplicity and its virtually foolproof character. It is unnecessary to know the exact shapes and positions of the cost and revenue curves, or even to have an accurate definition of capacity. It works equally well for monopsony and for monopoly, and for mixed cases. It is only necessary that profits after payment of taxes should rise continuously with output. Provided the rate at which net profits rise with output is enough to make the entrepreneur aware of it, a movement in the right direction is inevitable. If, therefore, the tax does not result in any increase in output, it is only necessary to raise slightly the rate of profit which is made tax-free. It is unlikely that output will be contracted below the previous monopoly level, but if output does shrink it can be stopped in the same manner, by raising the profit rate. The worst that can happen is that the rate is left unnecessarily high, and output accordingly falls short of the competitive level to an unnecessary extent.

This device does not give as perfect results as would precise application of the tax-and-bounty scheme outlined in section 1 above; but it will usually result in an output very close to the competitive one, and it is no more complicated from an administrative point of view than existing excess profit taxes. An advantage of the proposed system over the usual excess profit tax is that since "utilization" is defined in terms of output, there is an incentive not only to utilize existing plant and equipment more fully but to operate the part that is utilized as efficiently as possible. To avoid discouraging new enterprise in risky fields, *bona fide* new firms might be exempt from excess profits taxes for a year or so after production starts, and some allowance for risk might be made for all firms by using a ten-year moving average of profits for tax purposes.

20

Incidence of the Corporation Income Tax: Capital Structure and Turnover Rates*

By CARL SHOUP

The proposition advanced here is that the shifting of a corporation income tax of the kind that is levied by the Federal Government depends largely upon (1) the rate of the tax, (2) the capital structure of the corporation, and (3) the nature of the industry with respect to the normal speed of turnover of assets. Depending on the answers that are given to these questions in any particular case, it seems likely that such a corporation tax will have no effect, a decided effect, or an uncertain effect on the prices charged by the corporation for its products. Reference here is to immediate effect on price policy by the conscious action of the management, induced by the tax. The discussion does not refer to a hypothetical profits tax of a type that strikes only some form of economic rent and hence does not touch real costs. Only forward shifting is covered in the present analysis; this is not intended to imply that backward shifting is not possible.

RATE OF TAX

There is substantial disagreement or doubt as to whether a change in rate of "the" corporation income tax may be expected to have an immediate effect on price policy.[1] The doubt would probably diminish, if not disappear, if the change in tax were specified to be extremely large or

* *National Tax Journal of the National Tax Association*, Vol. I, No. 1 (March, 1948).

[1] See H. R. Bowen, "Taxation of Net Income from Business," *Bulletin of the National Tax Association*, XXXI (December, 1945), 72–80, and "The Incidence of the Corporation Income Tax: A Reply [to Goode]," *American Economic Review*, XXXVI (March, 1946), 146–48; Paul W. Ellis, *The Effect of Taxes Upon Corporate Policy* (National Industrial

extremely small. Suppose that the corporation income tax were increased from the current level of 38 per cent (for corporations with net income of $50,000 or more) to, say, 88 per cent, and that practically everyone expected the new rate to remain in force indefinitely. It seems unlikely that the leading firms in most industries would keep the prices of their products unchanged, in the face of so drastic a diminution of the profits available to the owners of the concerns. The tax would provide the occasion for simultaneous, if not concerted, increases in the prices of the products of each of the leading companies, and the smaller concerns would presumably follow. This conclusion assumes that by such action the firms would be enabled to obtain larger profits before tax than they had been obtaining under their former prices, and that they had been deterred from reaching this level of profit, prior to the increase in the tax rate, by competition or fear of competition. This assumption seems to be a reasonable one, for industries where the market is shared by a number of large concerns, perhaps from three to a dozen, and by a considerable number of smaller firms.

Suppose, on the other hand, that the increase in tax rate was only from 38 per cent to 39 per cent. It seems unlikely that any of the firms would be impelled to give the change more than a passing thought, with respect to the price structure for its products.

These remarks imply that at least a part of the taxable profit, as defined in the income tax laws in the United States at the present time, is a cost that enters directly into price policy, but is only loosely linked to price policy; it may be increased or decreased by taxation slightly, perhaps even substantially, without an appreciable immediate effect on price policy, but if the change is very great, the reaction will be immediate and appreciable. The subsequent effects of the rise in prices on the volume of business are not explored here; but, in any event, such effects would not be likely to prevent the attainment of a new equilibrium in which the prices of most of the firm's products would be somewhat higher than before the tax change.

A large increase in the corporation income tax rate tends to have a

---

Conference Board, 1943); Richard Goode, "The Corporation Income Tax and the Price Level," *American Economic Review*, XXXV (March, 1945), 40–58, and "A Rejoinder [to Bowen]," *American Economic Review*, XXXVI (March, 1946), 147–48; Oscar Litterer, "Corporation Income Tax and Production," *Bulletin of the National Tax Association*, XXXII (April, 1946), 199–205; H. M. Groves, "Personal Versus Corporate Income Taxes," *American Economic Association Proceedings*, XXXVI (May, 1946), 241–49; C. Ward Macy, "The Corporation Net Income Tax and the Cost-Price Structure," *Bulletin of the National Tax Association*, XXX (May, 1944), 231–35, and "Corporation Income Tax: Incidence or Effects," *American Economic Review*, XXXVI (December, 1946), 903–6.

more pronounced effect upon price policy than does a small increase, for still another, or supplementary reason. As the firm raises its selling prices in an effort to recoup the tax, it creates a still larger taxable profit, and therefore has to pay still more tax. Suppose that a concern is earning a profit of $1,000 before tax, and the corporation tax rate is raised from 38 per cent to, say, 88 per cent; its tax payment is increased from $380 to $880, an increase of $500. The concern now considers what it must do if it is to obtain its former profit after tax (that is, $620). It finds that it must increase its profit before tax by much more than the $500 increase in tax, for some of the increase will itself be taken in tax. In this particular case, the concern's profit before tax must increase from $1,000, not to $1,500, but to $5,166.67.[2] This spiral, or cumulative, effect operates the more strongly, in terms of what has to be done to the price structure if the tax increase is to be recouped, the higher the rate of tax after the increase has been made.

If the tax change is a reduction instead of an increase, the degree of lowering of selling prices that is consistent with just retaining the former profits after tax is greater, the higher the level of the tax rate before the change. A drop of, say, 30 percentage points from 68 to 38 per cent would tend to allow a much greater decrease in selling prices than a drop of 30 percentage points from 38 to 8 per cent.

RATIO OF PREFERRED STOCK DIVIDENDS TO NET INCOME

If the relevant rate of tax to profit were never any higher than 38 per cent, the issues raised in the section above would still be of some importance; but in fact the present corporation tax imposes in many instances a rate much more than 38 per cent on the profits available for the common stockholders, which is presumably the profit that is most relevant for studying the effect of the tax on price policy. This higher rate results from the existence of preferred dividend requirements. The tax is levied as a percentage of net income available for all types of stockholders; preferred dividends paid are not deductible in computing the amount subject to tax. But it is the common stockholders, not the preferred stockholders,

---

[2] The formula for the increase in profit before tax that will maintain the old absolute amount of profit after tax may be stated as follows: p_o is the old profit before tax; p_n is the new profit before tax; t_o is the old tax rate; t_n is the new tax rate. For the profit after tax to remain unchanged, it is necessary that the profit before tax increase by the amount of the tax increase: $p_n - p_o = t_n p_n - t_o p_o$; therefore, $p_n = \dfrac{p_o(1-t_o)}{1-t_n}$; $p_n - p_o = \dfrac{p_o(t_n - t_o)}{1-t_n}$.

who bear the burden of the entire tax (if it is not shifted to others). The preferred stockholders receive their fixed rate of return, and the entire tax must be met out of the proceeds available for the common stockholders. There are some qualifications to this point, but they do not seriously affect its importance for purposes of the present analysis: holders of non-cumulative preferred stock may be directly harmed by the tax in years of low income; holders even of cumulative preferred stock may find their income impaired by the tax if the dividends fall in arrears and are finally made up only in part, in recapitalization; and public utility companies are allowed to deduct preferred dividends paid, with certain restrictions, under sections 15(a) and 26(h) of the Internal Revenue Code, with respect to that part of the corporation income tax that is designated "surtax" rather than normal tax.

The present 38 per cent corporation income tax may therefore be much more than 38 per cent of the profit available to common stockholders (hereafter referred to as "common stock profit"). For example: if a corporation has outstanding so much preferred stock, at so high a dividend rate, that the preferred dividend requirements equal 57 per cent of the corporation's taxable income, the corporation tax of 38 per cent equals 88 per cent of the common stock profit.[3] If the preferred dividend requirements equal 62 per cent of the taxable income, the rate of tax on the common stock profit is 100 per cent. In such cases the management will surely give serious consideration to changes in price policy. The company might instead call the preferred stock and borrow an equivalent amount; but this procedure is not always practicable, especially if the preferred stock outstanding, issued perhaps many years ago at a high dividend rate, is noncallable.

If the management attempts to increase profits before tax in an effort to maintain unchanged the amount of profit available, after taxes, to the common stockholder, the conclusions reached in the preceding section apply. The entry of the preferred dividends into the analysis does not change the formula derived there. For instance, if preferred dividends equal 62 per cent of the taxable income, and if a corporation tax is intro-

---

[3] If p is the profit before tax; t, the rate of tax on p; and e, the common stock profit (before tax); then tp is the absolute amount of tax; and the ratio of the absolute amount of tax to the common stock profit is $\frac{tp}{e}$. Hence, if t is 38 per cent, the tax is 88 per cent of the common stock profit. In the illustration above, $\frac{p}{e}$ is $\frac{100}{43}$, and t is $\frac{38}{100}$, so that the rate of tax on the common stock profit is: $\frac{38}{100} \times \frac{100}{43} = 88$ per cent.

duced at a rate of 38 per cent, this tax, amounting to 100 per cent on the common stock profit, can be recouped by an increase of taxable income of 61.3 per cent.

RATE OF TURNOVER OF EQUITY CAPITAL

The degree to which the corporation's selling prices must be raised, if it is to recoup the income tax from its customers, depends upon the ratio of sales to the taxable income. (To isolate the point at issue, the falling off of unit sales resulting from the rise in price is neglected.) This ratio of sales to taxable income will vary from industry to industry and from firm to firm. It will vary from industry to industry, first, because some industries habitually turn over the property that is used in the business at a faster rate than do others; the ratio of sales to such property is high in some industries, the retail grocery trade, for instance, and is low in others, as in the electric power industry. But the ratio of sales to taxable income will vary for a second reason, independent of the nature of the industry: namely, the extent to which the property used in the business is either leased by the corporation or has been purchased with borrowed money, or, on the other hand, has been purchased by money from stock issues or from retained earnings. The difference in the ratio arises from the fact that in computing taxable income the corporation can deduct rental and lease payments, and interest payments, while, as already noted, it cannot deduct dividends paid.

For purposes of the present analysis, only that part of the lease or rental payment that corresponds to an interest charge should be considered. Another part of the payment customarily goes to cover depreciation and repairs for which the owner is responsible; but these amounts would also be deductible, as such, by the corporation if it owned the property, and regardless of how the money had been obtained to purchase it. In the analysis to follow, therefore, "rental" or "lease payment" will be understood to refer only to the interest-charge element in such payment.

"Operating profit" is used here to denote the net income as ordinarily computed except that no deduction is made for either interest on debt or the interest element in the lease or rental payment. Operating profit is thus the amount that is available to compensate owners of the property that is used in the business, and to pay income tax on the corporation.

For any particular firm, the amount by which its prices will have to be raised to recoup the income tax on the corporation will be less if the corporation uses more leased or rented property, or property purchased with borrowed money.[4] For example, let the rate of turnover of the property used in the business be, in a given case, 2; that is, the property is turned over twice a year; the sales for one year equal twice the value of the property employed in the business. Suppose further that the ratio of operating profit to total property used is 5 per cent; and that, of the operating profit, one-half goes in interest or rentals (as above defined). Then, if a 38 per cent corporation income tax is imposed, sales must rise by 0.766 per cent, if the profit to the stockholders after the new tax is to be as large as it was before the tax was imposed.[5] But if two-thirds of the operating profit is used to cover interest or rentals, the required increase in sales, to recoup the corporation income tax, is only 0.511 per cent.

The turnover ratio—the number of times the property used in the business is turned over in sales during the period—becomes the more important, in determining the percentage increase in sales needed to recoup the tax, as less of the operating profit is paid out in interest or rental. In the case immediately above, where two-thirds of the operating income was paid out in interest, or rental, it was seen that sales would have to increase by 0.511 per cent to recoup a tax of 38 per cent, when the turnover ratio was 2. With a turnover ratio of only 1, sales would have to increase by 1.022 per cent to recoup the tax. Suppose instead that none of the operating income is paid out in interest or rental; it all goes to stockholders, preferred or common. Then, with a turnover ratio of 2, sales must increase by 1.53 per cent; while, if the turnover ratio is only 1, the necessary sales increase, to recoup the tax, is 3.06 per cent. In each illustration the needed percentage increase of sales doubles when the turnover

---

[4] If the analysis were broadened to include possible recoupment of the income tax that is imposed on the recipients of the interest or the rental or lease income, the relations expressed here would be replaced by more complex expressions, but the present discussion is limited to the corporation income tax and the motivation of a corporate official, in attempting to recoup the tax that is imposed directly on his corporation.

[5] If [before the tax is introduced] s is the dollar value of sales; n is the turnover ratio, that is, the ratio of sales to value of total property used in the business; v is the rate of return on property used in the business, that is, the ratio of operating profit to value of property used in the business; f is the ratio of interest and lease and rental payments (as defined above) to operating profit; and the other terms are as in footnote 2 above; [since $p_1 - p_0$ equals the increase in receipts from sales] the percentage increase in sales [the physical volume of sales remaining unchanged] necessary to cover the increase in tax is: $\dfrac{1}{s} \cdot \dfrac{p_0(t_n - t_0)}{1 - t_n}$.

If r is the profit margin on sales (ratio of operating profit to sales), $p_0 = rs - frs = rs(1 - f)$.

But $r = \dfrac{v}{n}$.

Therefore: $\dfrac{1}{s} \cdot \dfrac{p_0(t_n - t_0)}{1 - t_n} = \dfrac{v}{n}\left[\dfrac{(1 - f)(t_n - t_0)}{(1 - t_n)}\right]$. [Bracketed material in lines 1, 5–7 of note is added to original article.]

rate is halved, but in the second illustration the needed percentages are on a higher level, owing to the absence of interest and rental payments, and the doubling of the 1.53 percentage increase is of course a more serious matter than the doubling of a 0.511 percentage increase.

COMPETITIVE CONDITIONS: RESEARCH REQUIRED

The practical importance of the conclusions reached above depends in part on whether, in the real world of business, substantial differences exist between competing firms in the same industry with respect to their capital structures (including leaseholds and rental contracts) and with respect to the ratio of sales to property used in the business. If the competitors differ appreciably in that turnover rate, and with respect to the percentage of operating income that is paid out in rentals (as here defined) or interest, and if these two types of difference are not offsetting in nature, some of the corporations are likely to find it much more difficult than others to recoup the tax through a rise in prices, for some of them will have to raise their sales by a larger percentage than others, to recoup any given proportion of the tax. And if the firms differ with respect to the amount of taxable income that must be paid out in preferred dividends, they will be under unequal degrees of pressure to recoup the tax, whether or not they differ in their ability to recoup it. The most unfortunate of all, from a competitive standpoint, will be the corporation that has a large proportion of its taxable income earmarked for preferred dividends, with none of its operating profit going to interest or rentals, and with a low turnover rate. It will badly need to pass at least part of the tax on to its consumers, or to someone, if its stockholders are not to suffer a drastic decline in the rate of return on their investment (net, after tax), and it will be relatively unable to do so because of the large percentage increase in sales revenue that will be required to this end. And finally, if the given increase in tax, expressed as so many percentage points, comes on top of an already fairly high level of tax, all corporations will exhibit this condition of finding it more difficult to pass on the tax increment than if the increment had been added to a low tax rate, since the increase in profit needed to recoup is itself taxed, and, the higher the new total tax rate, the greater is this effect.

It should be possible, by some small-scale research with respect to corporate capital structures and turnover rates, to ascertain whether these considerations are likely to be of importance; some work is now being started at the School of Business at Columbia University on these points.

The assumption was made, at the beginning of the present analysis, that even in the short run it would be to the advantage of the owners of the corporation to have the selling prices of its products raised, if a large increase occurred in the rate of the corporation income tax. This is one of the issues that has been most discussed in recent articles on the incidence of the corporate income tax. The limited scope of the present article does not allow of an analysis of this point, except to say that the assumption made here is based upon two hypotheses suggested by common observation and by a somewhat intensive study of a few industries by the present writer. The first hypothesis, a double-barrelled one, is that the larger part of the corporation income tax is paid by corporations that (*a*) are engaged in monopolistic competition of the kind where most of the business in the industry is done by firms who take into account their rivals' reactions to any change in pricing policy that the firm in question may make, and (*b*) do not charge prices that are as high as they would charge if they were consolidated into one firm. The second hypothesis is that the corporation income tax strikes even some of the short-run costs, particularly the imputed interest and profit return on equity capital tied up in inventory, and that therefore in the absence of any immediate change in the operating profit, after the increase in corporation tax, it would be to the advantage of the owners to shrink production somewhat, fairly quickly, to release capital which they could invest elsewhere at a greater net return.

21

The Incidence of a General Output or a General Sales Tax*

By HARRY GUNNISON BROWN

It is generally recognized by students of taxation that a tax on the output of a particular commodity raises the price of such a commodity by decreasing its supply. But what if there is a tax on the production of all commodities and services—an equal proportionate tax on all lines of production? Will such a tax raise prices? Clearly it cannot make any particular kind of commodity, such as cigarettes, relatively scarce by driving producers of it into other lines, for other lines of production are then equally taxed, and there is no advantage in leaving one taxed line for another line which is taxed to the same extent. Where, then, does the burden of the tax rest?

A good many persons too readily conclude that such a general tax must raise all prices. But there are important considerations which such persons overlook. Such a general tax cannot reduce the output of goods unless workers are willing to remain idle—for there is no untaxed line to go into—or unless owners of capital or land are willing to let their capital or land lie idle and to receive no income at all from it. Surely, most men would, in time, accept wages very considerably lower rather than be chronically idle, and most owners of capital would rather have very greatly reduced returns on their capital rather than let their capital depreciate unused and get no returns at all. Similarly, landowners—other than vacant-land speculators (and we need hardly conclude that a general output tax, apart from any incident reduction in land-value taxes, would increase the number of these)—would presumably rather receive lower

---

* Reproduced in H. G. Brown, *Fiscal Policy, Taxation, and Free Enterprise* (Columbia, Mo.: Lucas Bros., 1946), pp. 97–106, from two articles in the *Journal of Political Economy:* "The Incidence of a General Output or a General Sales Tax," Vol. XLVII, No. 2, (April, 1939), pp. 254–62; and "A Correction," 1939, pp. 418–20. The University of Chicago Press is publisher of the *Journal;* copyright by the University of Chicago.

rent than no rent.[1] We cannot expect, therefore, that a general tax on output would cause permanent cessation of production or that it would, as a long-run phenomenon, bring any appreciable decrease. Why suppose, then, that it could, in the long run, make prices higher?

An increase in the volume of circulating medium, whether it be through the issue of additional money or an expansion of bank credit, tends definitely toward a higher range of prices. But there is certainly no obvious connection between a general tax on the output of goods and an increase of the volume of circulating medium. There is, therefore, no basis in monetary theory for supposing that a general tax on all goods will make average prices permanently higher. To raise the general level of prices there must be either a decrease of supply of goods in general or an increase of demand (as through an increased volume of money). If a tax on the output of all goods neither decreases supply nor increases demand, on what basis is it to be argued that such a tax will raise prices?

If a tax on all goods does not raise prices, it must lower the money incomes of (the number of dollars received by) workers, capitalists, and landowners. We shall begin with the workers. Here, let us say, is a coal-mine worker who is able to add to the output of a given mine one ton of coal a day. The coal is worth, at the mine mouth, $2.00 a ton. At a wage of $2.00 a day, this worker is barely worth hiring. Now, suppose there is an output tax of 10 per cent. When the coal is produced and sold, 20 cents must be paid as a tax to the government. That leaves only $1.80. The coal-mine worker whose labor adds this ton to the total output is no longer worth a maximum of $2.00 to the employing company but only a maximum of $1.80. For, if the company can sell this coal for no more than $2.00 and must pay 20 cents of this to the government, the ton of coal is worth, to the company, not over $1.80, and it cannot afford to hire the mine worker at any greater wage than $1.80. So far as the community is concerned, the worker's marginal productivity is $2.00. But, since the government takes 10 per cent of this, his marginal productivity is, to the employing company, only $1.80. If he wants to work, he cannot expect greater wages than his work is worth to the employing company. Nor, as we have seen, can the price of coal be permanently raised, for a similar tax is applied in every other industry and there is consequently no escape from the tax by changing to some other line. Thus, such a tax on the output of all commodities and services necessarily reduces wages.

---

[1] Of course vacant-land speculators, like other human beings, commonly prefer something to nothing. The circumstances which nevertheless make them hold their land unused, for a time receiving no rent, are set forth, at least partially, in my book on *The Economic Basis of Tax Reform* (Columbia, Mo.: Lucas Bros., 1932), pp. 268–74.

Let us follow out one more illustration. A farm worker adds to the output of wheat 400 bushels a year. This is a "marginal" addition, what the worker can do on no-rent land or as the "final" worker hired on a piece of high-grade land (intensive margin). At a price of $1.00 per bushel, this comes to $400. But if government, by an output tax, takes $40 of the price, the farm worker cannot possibly be worth, to an employer (or to himself, if he is self-employed), $400, but only $360. If the 10 per cent tax is levied at each stage of production and there are several stages (e.g., wheat, flour, bread, retail distribution), we must, to avoid having duplication of taxation, levy the tax at each stage only on the addition of value made to the product at that stage. Or the tax might be levied at the very last stage (retail sales), in which case it will be reflected back through the various stages to the recipients of the various kinds of income, as will be shown, with due qualification, in succeeding paragraphs.

Such a tax on all output will reduce the income of the capitalist and of the landowner in the same proportion that it reduces the income of the worker,[2] but not in any greater proportion. And since wages are a much larger part of the total product of industry than is either interest on capital or rent of land, a general output tax takes more from the wages of labor than it takes from interest or rent.

Let us now see just how a general output tax reduces the return received by owners of capital. Suppose that a farmer believes that an investment of $1,000 in fertilizing or otherwise improving his farm will add to the output which his labor can bring, every year, by some sixty bushels or $60 (in excess of an allowance for depreciation). He could then afford to pay not over $60 annual interest, or 6 per cent, for a $1,000 loan. But if a general output tax takes $6.00 of the $60, the improvement adds only $54 to that value of the output which the farmer will have after paying the tax, and he would be losing money to pay more than 5.4 per cent interest. Were the lender himself to invest his savings in production under his own direction, the tax would take an equal per cent of the output; hence, he might as well lend to someone else for a lower rate than before. And necessarily, under these conditions, the demand for loans will decline until lenders are receiving 10 per cent lower interest than previously, just as wage-earners must receive 10 per cent lower wages than before. (The part of the output required to offset capital depreciation is, of course, "imputable" to the labor and other factors used in constructing

---

[2] *Ibid.*, pp. 128–29.

the capital, and the proportionate tax on that part of the output is shifted back upon these factors.)

It is the same in regard to the rent of land. Suppose, for example, that a coal-mine operator could afford to pay $10,000 a year, as royalty, for permission to exploit a given coal mine, the coal being worth $2.00 a ton. Is it not obvious that, if the coal output is taxed 10 per cent, so that the operator receives, in effect, only $1.80 per ton, he cannot afford to pay as high a royalty? And is it not also clear that, since no other would-be operator can afford to pay as high a royalty as before, the possible competition of operators will be reduced and royalties must fall?

Or let us suppose the case of a farmer who has too little land to employ his labor most effectively. By hiring a neighboring piece of land he can, we may suppose, add fifty bushels a year to his output of wheat, without working any harder or longer than before. Obviously, he could afford to pay not over fifty bushels a year as rent for the use of this extra piece of land, or, with wheat at $1.00 a bushel, not over $50. But if an output tax takes $5.00 of the $50, he cannot afford to pay over $45. Clearly, the net rent received by the landowner must be reduced.

If, then, there is a general tax on output, the money incomes received by laborers, capitalists, and landowners must all be reduced. Since, of the prices paid for goods, a part (in our illustration 10 per cent) is taken by government, only the remainder can go as wages, interest, and rent for the factors of production. The incidence of a general output tax is, then, in practical effect, the same as if it raised all prices (as most of the public seems to suppose it does) without either decreasing or increasing money incomes. For in either case there is a subtraction, proportioned to the tax, from the real incomes of wage receivers, interest receivers, and recipients of land rent. Whether commodity prices remain the same and money incomes fall or commodity prices rise and money incomes remain unchanged, the distribution of the tax burden would appear to be identical.

A general tax on output will easily commend itself to those persons who believe that taxes should rest on everybody in about equal proportion to their respective incomes or spendings, however small these may be, and *with no distinction as to sources* of income or as to kinds of property owned.[3]

The general output tax with which a majority of us are now most

---

[3] The reasons why I cannot subscribe to any such belief but consider it essential to distinguish between sources of income and, therefore, between kinds of property, I have set forth at length in *The Economic Basis of Tax Reform* (Columbia, Mo.: Lucas Bros., 1932).

familiar is the general retail sales tax. In the American states where this tax has been adopted, it does not really apply to all retail transactions. There are various exceptions to its generality, depending on the jurisdiction, e.g., newspapers, haircuts, laundry and cleaning service, shelter, foods. But in many of the states, retail food sales are taxed the same as any other sales. In so far as the retail sales tax, as above indicated, is not all-inclusive, but bears on some lines of production and exempts others, it tends to make some prices higher than others. But since this tax, in several of the states, is so nearly a general tax, we shall, for purposes of the present analysis, assume it to apply in all lines equally.

Nevertheless, no purely retail sales tax which is not at the same time ubiquitous can apply to the entire output of goods even in a single county or state (or country), if those who live within the given territory are engaged in trade with outsiders. And, therefore, a retail sales tax, levied on all retail sales in a given state but not levied ubiquitously, will raise retail prices in that state.

Let us consider, for example, the 3 per cent general retail sales tax in Michigan, assuming, for the present, no sales taxes in surrounding states. This means that goods on which a 3 per cent retail sales tax will be levied, if they are sold to Michigan consumers, can escape the tax if they are exported to other states. If the tax applied equally on exported goods, then the factors of production, labor, capital, and land, would have to accept lower money incomes. The money returns for wages, interest, and rent would be appreciably reduced. But since exported goods escape the tax, this result does not follow. Producers of goods face no tax—even on retailers whose demand for their goods might thus be reduced—if they ship their goods outside of the state. And they will obviously accept no lower net prices from dealers inside the state than from dealers outside. Retailers in Michigan must pay approximately as high prices for Michigan produced goods which have a ready out-of-state market as if there were no Michigan retail sales tax. And since the returns to labor, capital, and land used in retailing can hardly be kept at a permanently lower level in relation to returns in wholesaling, manufacturing, etc., than before, the prices paid for goods by Michigan consumers must presumably rise.

But can we have, in Michigan, wages, interest, and rent as high as before, producers' prices as high as before, wholesale prices as high as before, retail prices actually higher than before, and a sales tax going to the state government, while the volume of circulating medium in Michigan has not increased? The answer is that the volume of circulating medium in Michigan, under the assumed conditions, will increase. For, since the tax applies on sales in Michigan and not on sales made out of state, and since, at the start, the money incomes of residents of Michigan are not greater than before, they simply cannot buy as many goods as before if retail prices are higher. Yet retail prices must be higher unless producers sell goods to Michigan retailers for less than before, since otherwise the retailers' incomes would be relatively too low. (If this is not at once obvious in the case of a 3 per cent sales tax, it certainly would be so if the tax were, say, 10 or 15 per cent.) And producers surely will not absorb the entire tax, or even any appreciable part of the tax, so long as they can avoid the tax by selling goods outside of the state. Looking at the matter, then, from any reasonable point of view, we must conclude that out-of-state sales will be relatively favored until the resulting increase of circulating medium within the state makes possible wages, interest, rents, producers' and manufacturers' prices, and wholesale prices approximately as high, in relation to the corresponding incomes and prices in surrounding states, as before, and retail prices higher by the amount of the tax. It is to be noted, of course, that the inflow of circulating medium from other states into Michigan will lower, but only to the slightest extent—since we are assuming these other states to be without general sales taxes and since only a little money would flow into Michigan from any one of them—the general price level in these states.

So far as concerns a general retail sales tax levied by a single state or by a very few states, our conclusion is that such a tax would raise retail prices in such a state or states by approximately the amount of the tax. The view of the man in the street that such a tax raises the prices of goods in general is, to this extent, confirmed.

There is another important qualification which ought to be noted here. Even if a retail sales tax is levied ubiquitously and at the same rate, there would still be some rise of retail prices. In the absence of friction (of which account is taken at a later point in this discussion), there would be an immediate adjustment of relative prices but no change in the general price level. Since the tax is levied at the point of retail sales, a wedge is driven, so to speak, between retail and wholesale prices. Wholesale prices, producers' prices, wages, interest, and rent—all these are slightly lowered. Retail prices are raised and exceed wholesale prices more than before by the amount of the tax. . . .

[At this point there is introduced material from "A Correction." Ed.]

Instead of saying "Retail prices are raised and exceed wholesale prices more than before by the amount of the tax," I should have said: "Retail prices are raised and exceed wholesale prices more than before by the amount of the tax *minus the slight reduction in the wages, interest, and rent received from retailing.*" For, since the tax lowers somewhat, in money terms, wages, interest, and rent generally, we must suppose that the wages, interest, and rent received from retail operations will go down proportionally. That is, we must suppose this *on the assumption of a relatively frictionless society in which the levy of the sales tax is followed almost at once by the re-establishment of perfect equilibrium*. To anyone who may criticize such an assumption as unrealistic, I would reply that *the existence of friction is specifically allowed for and some of its consequences pointed out* in later paragraphs of my paper.

The later sentences of the pargraph here being amended ought to be as follows:

> The decrease in the money incomes of workers, capitalists, and landowners is so balanced by the new tax receipts of the government that the total of the money incomes of individuals and government will buy as much as the incomes of individuals (and any previous government income) would formerly buy. Individually, the people have less money to spend. Collectively—through the sales-tax receipts, to be spent by the government—they have more to spend. The average of manufacturers' and other producers' prices, wholesale prices, retail prices, individual money incomes in the form of wages, interest, and rent, and government income remains unchanged, but manufacturers' and other producers' and wholesale prices are lower while retail prices are higher.

The reason for rephrasing is that the article, as first printed, gives the impression that the total of individual wages, interest, and rent, plus the new tax receipts of government, are precisely equal in money terms to the total of individual wages, interest, and rent prior to the tax; while retail prices are higher. This means that if the total of the incomes of individuals and government before the tax would just suffice to buy the annual output of goods at retail, after the tax these incomes would not suffice. Of course, a great many government purchases may be at wholesale and, therefore, at somewhat lower prices than before and, even if government purchases at retail, it may buy at a price not including the tax. Nevertheless, the statement should be so formulated as to allow for the possibility that the income of government consequent on the tax may be increased, in terms of money, more than wages, interest, and rent to individuals are decreased. This is quite consistent with an unchanged general price level, since wholesale prices, manufacturers' prices, and raw-material prices are all somewhat reduced.

In order that the long footnote on next page may be entirely consistent with the above correction, the next to the last sentence should be amended to read as follows: "But the essential point I am trying to stress now is that average prices (counting producers', wholesale, and retail prices and also individually received wages, interest, and rent and the governmentally received tax money) as actually charged and paid in the markets, are not made either higher or lower by output or sales taxes, and that the average is, therefore, the same regardless of where the 'wedge' is driven."

Some critics may still complain that the collecting of the tax is itself, in a sense, an addition to the total of transactions and that, conceivably, it may thereby slightly delay the spending of money directly for goods, thus modifying—but hardly more than infinitesimally—the conclusions. ["Correction" ends. Ed.]

If the tax were levied at some earlier stage in production, instead of on retail sales, then we could speak of the "wedge" as being driven between prices at this earlier stage, the prices preceding this stage being lowered and those succeeding it being raised. But the average of all prices would still not be affected.[4]

If a tax were levied at each stage of production, but only at a proportionate rate on the value added at that stage, then no commodity prices, whether producers' prices, wholesale dealers' prices, or retail prices, would be changed at all; but all money incomes received by individuals—wages, interest, and rent—would be lowered; and the money income received by the government for collective spending would be raised by an equivalent amount.[5] (This is on the assumption that this tax is not a substitute for

---

[4] If the tax is thus levied at an earlier stage, i.e., the "wedge" driven at an earlier stage, fewer prices are, of course, reduced by the tax and more prices are raised by it. Therefore, if the average commodity price level is to be the same, those relatively few prices which are reduced must be reduced to a greater degree, and the larger number which are raised must be only slightly raised. Perhaps one way of putting the matter—though I suspect it is a way that to most persons will be more confusing than illuminating—is to say that when the "wedge" is driven at an earlier stage, the "tax addition" (if we may so speak) to the price which the buyer at retail pays must also be paid by the retailer to the wholesaler, and so on, to the point of government collection. In a sense we may then say that the tax money paid by purchasers at retail goes through several hands on its way to government and that, therefore, this tax money is, during the period of such passing, prevented from acting on "net" prices (in the sense of prices minus tax) as quickly as if it did not pass through so many stages. Thus, "net" commodity prices (in this special sense of prices minus tax) will average lower than if the tax were collected at the point of retail sale. This was probably (or so I hope!) one of the ideas I had vaguely in mind in writing "Some Frequently Neglected Factors in the Incidence of Taxation" (*Journal of Political Economy*, Vol. XXVIII, No. 6 [June, 1920]), although enough in that article is definitely fallacious so that I am sure I could not then have really thought the problem through or fully understood it. But the essential point I am trying to stress now is that average prices (counting producers', wholesale, and retail prices) actually charged in the markets are not made either higher or lower by output or sales taxes, and that the average is, therefore, the same regardless of where the "wedge" is driven. And I want to take this opportunity to disavow anything in the earlier article here referred to which is inconsistent with the present treatment.

[5] Of course, less individual spending and more collective spending might change the relative demands for and marginal cost of various kinds of goods and so have some effect on their relative prices.

other previously levied taxes but is to provide new revenue.) Such a tax really would be a "proportional" income tax "collected at source" and having "no exemptions."

Returning, now, to the general fact that retail sales taxes levied in one state, or only a few states, make retail prices higher by the amount of the tax than in areas where such a tax is not levied, we may take note of a qualification hitherto not commented on. Persons living in a state where a retail sales tax is levied, but near the borders of a state or states where there is no such tax, may do a considerable amount of shopping in such a near-by state or states. Conceivably, some retail establishments in towns near the borders of a state levying no sales tax could keep down their prices a bit, to avoid losing trade, perhaps paying less to some employees who would nevertheless continue to clerk for them because of immobility and lack of acceptable alternatives, and less as rentals for stores and sites having no equally good alternative use. But it is doubtful if this would occur to any noticeable extent, and the probability is that only those consumers would avoid the tax in any appreciable degree who really did shop beyond the state borders.

In most of the previous discussion we have been assuming absence of friction and, therefore, immediate adjustment of relative prices (including incomes) to the tax levy. Especially has no attention been paid to the theory of "sticky" prices, e.g., "sticky" wages and rentals. But when attention is paid to this theory, it is seen that the rapid and general introduction of sales taxes, though perhaps brought about, in part, by certain consequences and ideologies resulting from depression, itself tends to produce depression.

We have seen that a general and ubiquitous sales tax cannot, as a normal, long-run proposition, increase the general level of commodity prices. But now we may note that any general attempt to increase commodity prices when there is no increase in purchasing power must tend to a decrease of sales and to dull business.

But if commodity prices are not increased, then, as we have seen, money wages, interest, and rent must fall. And if these (wages, interest, and rent) are "sticky" and so cannot be quickly adjusted, then there must obviously ensue a period of unemployment and generally dull business. The rapid introduction of sales taxes certainly tends to bring business depression and, if depression already exists, the introduction of such taxes must, it would seem, tend to retard recovery and to make the depression worse. (In a similar way, if wages are "sticky," the rapid introduction and increase of pay-roll taxes to provide for unemployment insurance and old age benefits must operate in the direction of unemployment.)[6]

So here we are apparently treated to another of the various contradictions of this remarkable New Deal era. Depression has made more vocal and persistent the demands of real estate owners for "tax relief for real estate." Depression has increased the need for funds to care for the jobless. Depression has, therefore, promoted the spread of sales taxes. Yet, if the analysis presented above is, in any essential degree, correct, the spread of such taxes has also fostered depression, has put more workers out of jobs and caused increasing pressure for more sales taxes to care for these increasing unemployed, and has, by virtue of the consequent heavier taxes on the poor, brought nearer to the level of "relievers"—perhaps not infrequently below the level—not a few of those who have continued to have comparatively steady employment. As the government, under the N.R.A., to a considerable extent offset its borrowing and spending recovery program directed to the increase of purchasing power by encouraging monopolistic price rises, and as it adopted a farm-aid program which put many tenants (especially in the South) out of employment, so it has followed a tax policy for the relief (partly) of those injured by the depression, which, itself, must have tended to cause and accentuate depression.

---

[6] While taxes on output result in reduced wages and interest and rent, the incidence of pay-roll taxes, like the incidence of compulsory insurance of workers against accident, is on wages. The subject of accident insurance I discussed in this connection in an article in the *Journal of Political Economy*, Vol. XXX, No. 1 (February, 1922), entitled "The Incidence of Compulsory Insurance of Workmen"; and this discussion was later republished as chap. vi of *The Economics of Taxation*. For a clear presentation of the theory of incidence as it relates to the new program of social security, with some reference to minor qualifying influences, see Russell S. Bauder, "Probable Incidence of Social Security Taxes," *American Economic Review*, Vol. XXVI, No. 3 (September, 1936).

22

Monopolistic Competition and the Incidence of Special Sales Taxes[*]

By JOHN F. DUE[†]

INTRODUCTION

The discussion in the previous chapter was based upon the assumption that the demand curves for the firms were not subject to modification as a result of any action taken by the latter. As pointed out in the introductory chapter, however, in practically all cases in which firms do possess some control over price, they are subject to varying degrees of competition from other firms having similar power. In these cases, changes in price and in profits earned will produce reactions on the part of these competitors in such a manner as to affect the demand curve of the first firm. It is necessary, therefore, to extend the analysis of incidence to take into consideration this intermediate sector characterized by the presence of elements of both competition and monopoly.[1]

---

[*] From *The Theory of Incidence of Sales Taxation* (New York: Kings Crown Press, 1942). Reprinted by permission. The author wishes it noted that "the term Monopolistic Competition in the title to the chapter was used with reference to the entire range of market conditions between pure competition on the one hand and complete monopoly on the other, in contrast to the more limited use of the term which has become common in recent years."

[†] University of Illinois.

[1] This problem has been almost entirely neglected up to the present time. Nothing more than a few very brief suggestions as to the effect of monopolistic competition on incidence and a few references to the need for exploring this field are to be found. R. M. Haig, in the article on taxation in the *Encyclopedia of Social Sciences* points out the need for extension of the theory of incidence: "Pure monopoly and free competition are not often encountered in modern business life. . . . The discussions of shifting and incidence in the literature of Public Finance have only slightly been affected by the recent work of economists in the field of prices. It even seems doubtful whether the implications of the writings of Alfred Marshall have been given the consideration they deserve. The studies of supply and demand curves by statisticians, such as Ezekiel and Shultz, the conception of the bulkline producer developed by Taussig and Secrist, the importance of overhead costs as a factor in price determination emphasized in the writings of J. M. Clark, and the new studies of imperfect and monopolistic competition are full of suggestions for the student of public finance." (New York, 1934, Vol. 14, p. 537.)

In the pamphlet entitled, "Sales Taxes," published by the League of Minnesota Municipalities, brief treatment of the problem, with no analysis of the means by which the conclusions are reached, is presented: "More common than either perfect competition or complete monopoly is the situation where several large producers control the market. This partial monopoly, or monopolistic competition, has only recently been the subject of extended analysis. Although there are various situations, generally the price increase will be somewhat less than under monopoly. The greater the number of producers in the market, the more will the changes approximate those which occur under competition." (*Sales Taxes, op. cit.,* p. 62.)

E. D. Fagan stresses more strongly the inadequacy of present incidence theory: "This assumption (of free competition) must be abandoned or significantly modified if our conclusions are to be of value as guides to fiscal policy. One must include both the competitive and non-competitive elements affecting the particular as well as the general supply and demand schedules. This cannot be done satisfactorily by shifting from the assumption of free competition to that of pure monopoly." ("Tax Shifting and the Laws of Cost," *Quarterly Journal of Economics*, 47:690.)

In this article, rather than attempting to develop any theoretical analysis, Fagan concludes: "Conclusions applicable to policy can be deduced only from a realistic study of the forces which determine the elasticity of demand and of supply in the actual market to which they really belong." (*Ibid.*)

In an article appearing in the August, 1939, *Quarterly Journal of Economics* ("Tax Shifting in the Short Run," *op. cit.*, 153:576–89), Fagan, in conjunction with Roy Jastram, considered the problem in some detail, but only for short run incidence.

Meyers, in *Modern Economic Problems* (*op. cit.*, pp. 44–50) treats the problem briefly; the essential part of his discussion is to be found in the following paragraph (p. 47): "A tax per unit of output on the firms operating in an industry under conditions of monopolistic competition constitutes an addition to marginal cost. Here again, however, we must consider the most likely changes in demand as well as the change in cost, so that the analysis that we made for this type of tax on perfect monopoly is no longer applicable. All we can say definitely is that because the individual firm's demand curves will be shifted somewhat (as all firms attempt to raise prices to shift the tax), the proportion of the tax shifted will tend to be somewhat greater than it would be in the case of a perfect monopoly. We cannot assume, however, that each firm's demand curve will be shifted by the amount of the tax, particularly if the competing products sold at different prices before the tax was imposed."

Likewise Dalton, Bastable, and Buehler indicate the need for modifying the theory of incidence in the light of conditions characterized by the presence of elements of both monopoly and competition. In "Public Finance," Dalton points out: "The argument of the preceding chapter regarding the incidence of taxes on a monopolist must be applied with discretion to practical problems. In reality, perfect competition is rare, and perfect monopoly is still rarer. Some element of monopoly enters into the determination of nearly all prices, and fear of competition, actual or potential, actuates nearly all apparent monopolists. Price may be influenced by the exercise of monopoly price as soon as a single seller, or group of sellers acting in combination, controls a considerable proportion of the commodity to be sold. But where monopoly power exists, though we may assume that it is seldom neglected, yet it is not always fully exercised." (*Public Finance, op. cit.*, p. 67.)

In his "Public Finance," Bastable states: "But the theoretical concept of a pure monopoly is of little direct service in dealing with the question of incidence; for in very few cases is a monopoly strictly so called to be found. There is in truth rather a number of limited or qualified monopolies, arising in part from natural, in part from legal limitations. Both monopoly and competition have to be considered, and in particular the interaction of these opposed conditions, as well as the effect of financial change, in readjusting these areas." (*Public Finance, op. cit.*, p. 375.)

Finally, Buehler, in *General Sales Taxation:* "The problem here would be greatly simplified if every case could be treated as one where free and unrestricted competition or complete monopoly prevailed, but unfortunately the conditions of conducting business are subject to varying degrees of competition and monopoly. For the sake of our theoretical discussion, it may be assumed, however, that either free competition or complete monopoly prevail." (*Op. cit.*, p. 178.)

And in his more recent *Public Finance:* "In the business world competition is seldom free and monopolies are seldom absolute, but there exists a regulated competition, which may be a mixture of competition and monopoly. Because there are all degrees of competition and monopoly, theories of tax incidence must be modified according to the conditions prevailing in each case." (*Op. cit.*, p. 236.)

The method of approach to the problem involves consideration of two general cases. The first concerns the situation in which elimination of all excess profits through perfectly free entry of firms has brought average revenue and average cost curves of all firms in the field to tangency. In the second case, limitation of entry and excess profits are assumed. In subsequent sections, the significance of selling costs, oligopoly, non-uniform demand and cost curves, multiple lines, average cost pricing, and other phenomena of monopolistic competition are introduced.

The situation characterized by tangency of the average revenue and average cost curves is commonly considered as the typical feature of the condition of monopolistic competition. Only under such circumstances are the elements usually regarded as fundamental attributes of monopolistic competition, excess capacity and improper utilization of resources, inevitable. It must be emphasized, however, that completely free entry is necessary for realization of this position; with various consumer preferences established, it will commonly be possible for firms to maintain a sheltered position, with excess profits, over a long period of time. Nevertheless, the condition provides a suitable basis for introduction of the analysis, and also is of significance in itself, as it represents the equilibrium position in cases in which preferences as between firms are relatively weak. It is assumed at first that demand and cost curves are uniform, that selling activities and oligopoly are absent, and that each firm produces only one product. Modifications of these assumptions will be introduced at later stages in the analysis.

THE PROCESS OF READJUSTMENT

When a tax per unit of output is first imposed, each firm raises its price (and thus lessens its output) to the extent that marginal revenue will equal the new and higher marginal cost. The short run marginal cost curve after the tax will be lower than the new long run marginal, and the curve is not necessarily of decreasing cost nature; thus the price rise will be less than that which would occur if adjustment were made at once on the basis of long run marginal cost. On Figure 1, short run cost curves are eliminated for purposes of simplification; it is assumed that the long and short run curves are identical. The difference is only one of degree. On this chart, each firm will raise its price to PN, the demand price of that level of output at which MR again intersects MC (MC'). However, the AR curve is drawn on the assumption that the other firms keep their prices constant. Actually, each firm finds that when it raises its price to PN it loses much less in unit sales than it would have supposed, judging from its own individual demand curve AR; this result arises from the fact that all other firms are raising their prices likewise, at the same time. The individual firm's sales drop, not to OS, but only to Oy, as shown by the slope of DD.[2] In the face of this slight decline in sales, which calls for a recomputation of AR, the individual firm is induced to put the price still higher in its striving for minimizing losses. This will continue until the point is reached where the output actually sold after the price change will be such that MC and MR are again equal.[3] Price will come to P^2, the increase being an amount approximately three-fourths as great as the tax.[4]

However, AR' remains below AC'. Seemingly, by proper output reduction, tangency of these two curves could be obtained. But, when the point is reached that MR' equals MC', no firm will reduce output so long as each acts independently of the others, since to do so would apparently involve increase in losses. Actually, all would gain if they acted in unison in making the price increase, but this will not occur in the absence of oligopoly. DD and AR' cannot intersect at the tangency of the latter with AC', so long as AR' does not change its slope as it moves; thus, when AR' is tangent to AC, the actual revenue will not be that expected; average costs will not actually be covered.[5] If each firm produced temporarily just the output which could allow all to cover average costs, it would be profitable for each to lower prices slightly, as AR' would be slightly above AC' to the right of the intersection of DD and AC'. Thus all will be pulled down into a situation of loss.

The only escape is through exodus of firms. As time passes, average variable cost of some firms will rise above the average revenue line, and the firms will cease to operate. As this process continues, the DD curve for the remaining firms will shift to the right; this must continue until the DD curve (DD') intersects the AR' curve for each firm at the point

---

[2] The DD curve indicates the amounts that can be sold at each price level, provided the prices of other firms in the industry are the same as those of the firm in question. AR indicates the amounts that can be sold at the various levels assuming that the prices charged by the other firms remain unchanged at the figure at which the curve is intersected by DD.

[3] It would seem as if the price rise resulting from the initial action of the firms would be to PX instead of P_n. This would be the case if the firms adjusted output to the level which would be the optimum, and then sold it at the price which could be obtained. Actually, however, under monopolistic competition the technique is characteristically that of setting the price and selling the amount that can be disposed of at that price; under such conditions the result will be as indicated. The final result will be the same; if price did go up to PX, it would be at once profitable for each firm to start cutting prices, as MR would greatly exceed MC; this would take place until price falls to the level indicated above.

[4] The firm's AR curve is now AR'.

[5] For detailed explanation of the relation of DD and AR, see Chamberlin, *Monopolistic Competition, op. cit.*, pp. 92–93. This is a very difficult matter to express in words.

FIGURE 1

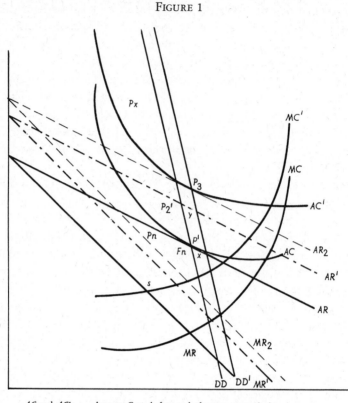

AC and *AC'*:	Average Cost, before and after tax, respectively.
MC and *MC'*:	Marginal curves of *AC* and *AC'*.
AR and *MR*:	Average Revenue and Marginal Revenue, before tax.
AR':	Temporary equilibrium Average Revenue, after tax.
AR₂:	Permanent equilibrium Average Revenue, after tax.
MR' and *MR₂*:	Marginal curves of *AR'* and *AR₂* respectively.
DD and *DD'*:	Average Revenue curves, assuming prices of other firms to be identical to prices of this firm, before and after tax respectively.

of tangency of *AR* (*AR₂*) and *AC'* (at *P₃* on Figure 1). Only when this has happened will *MR* equal *MC'* at such a point that average cost is just covered by average revenue.

THE AMOUNT OF PRICE RISE

General Statement of Incidence. If the demand curve does not change slope in the process of output reduction, the individual average revenue curve will move up by the exact amount of the increase in the average cost curve (from *P'* to *P₃* on Figure 1), as the new point of tangency is necessarily, under the conditions, directly above the old. Thus, if the cost curve of the firm does not shift as a result of the exodus of firms, the price will rise by exactly the amount of the tax; the incidence is the same as under pure competition. If the industry as a whole is one of increasing or decreasing cost, the cost curves of the firm will shift, and price will rise by less or more than the amount of the tax. There seems to be no reason why, cet. par., the existence of monopolistic competition should significantly affect the degree of decreasing or increasing cost from external economies; thus, the long run incidence is the same under monopolistic competition as under pure competition, so long as there is complete free entry and no monopoly profits in the former.

After the complete readjustment has taken place, each firm remaining will be producing the same volume as before the tax, as with the given slopes of cost and demand curves, and the assumption of tangency, only at the old output level can losses be avoided. The temporary output reductions, necessary to reduce losses so long as the number of firms in the field remains too great, are no longer profitable. If any readjustments in capacity—temporarily advantageous—were made, it will be profitable to return to the old capacity as final equilibrium is attained. Thus under the conditions assumed, the fact that the individual firms operate under decreasing cost conditions has no significance whatsoever for incidence.

When the difference between short run and long run considerations is introduced into the analysis, it must be noted that short run marginal cost is lower than that over the longer period for ranges of output below the old optimum, once the plant is constructed. Thus the price rise will not be as great in the short run; as time passes it will be profitable to make further price increases, as more elements enter into marginal cost. This process accompanies the exodus of firms; the rise in price from the increase in marginal cost over time lessens the need for exodus of firms, and brings the final equilibrium to that indicated above.

The Significance of Oligopoly Elements. Where oligopoly exists as well as differentiation, but firms are free to enter the field, average receipts and average cost will come to tangency, but at a very much higher price level than when firms ignore the reactions of their competitors to their own action. When the tax is imposed, the slope of the marginal revenue curve for each firm approaches that for the industry as a whole,[6] since it is realized that competitors will make price increases provided the firm in question does also. The curve is much steeper than in the preceding case. The initial price increase will differ according to the nature of the marginal cost curve. If the latter is increasing, there will be more price

---

[6] Thus on Figure 1, the marginal revenue curve would be the marginal curve drawn to curve *DD*.

increase than in the absence of oligopoly; the reverse is true if cost is decreasing unless the slope of the curve increases in steepness above the old price in sufficient degree.[7] However, if tangency prevailed before the tax, no firm will be able to cover average cost by any sort of price adjustment which it is profitable to make. If other firms would hold prices constant, any one firm could restore its profits by reducing price, since its average revenue curve under these conditions[8] would pass above the AC curve at greater volumes of output. But each producer realizes that others will cut prices also if he does, that his average revenue curve is not of this nature, but very much steeper (DD on Figure 1). Accordingly, action of this nature will not be taken. Exodus of firms is necessary; this must go on until the individual demand curves are again tangent to average cost. When this has occurred, the price will have risen by the amount of the tax, provided industry costs are constant. Long run incidence is thus the same as if the oligopolistic elements were not present.

Possibility of Shift in Elasticity of Demand. The assumption has been made to this point that the demand curve confronting the individual firm does not change slope as firms leave the field. There are, however, several different possibilities of change along these lines. If the customers of the firms leaving business do not become closely attached to any of the remaining firms, the elasticity of demand for the products of the latter will be increased, the slope of the curve lessened, and the price rise will be less than otherwise; AR_2 on Figure 1 will come to tangency with AC' at a lower point. It is interesting to note that the exodus of firms must be greater; DD' must shift farther to the right to intersect AR_2 at tangency. The reduced elasticity lessens the number of firms and the amount of excess capacity. This eliminates the need for as great a price increase as otherwise, as the point of equilibrium for each firm stands at a lower cost level than before.

On the other hand, the demand curve may become more steep. The number of firms may fall sufficiently that a feeling of mutual dependence will arise among the remaining firms, or an existing oligopoly situation will be strengthened. The AR curve will appear to the firm as of the slope of the DD curve (Figure 1), and a great price increase will be made. Each firm will avoid cutting prices along the new and higher revenue curve parallel to the old AR curve because it is realized that this is not the real average curve and that the competitors would cut also if any one

---

[7] This is based on the analysis of significance of different slopes of demand curves presented in Chapter III (of *The Theory of Incidence of Sales Taxation*).

[8] Comparable to *AR* on Figure 1.

takes the initiative. Under such conditions there may be an inflow of firms into the field, and a price increase very much greater than the amount of the tax.[9] Thus there is possibility of a price increase of magnitude impossible under monopoly or pure competition[10] with similar cost conditions.

No oligopoly situation is absolute; uncertainties of various types prevent the realization of positions which would be optimum from the point of view of the firms concerned. When a tax is imposed, the oligopolistic elements are likely strengthened as far as the part of cost consisting of the tax is concerned; the latter is a definite cost which each firm knows will be imposed on all others. With more or less uniform accounting methods which encourage treatment of the tax as an element by which to increase price in full amount, each firm is likely to feel that others will act in this manner and accordingly can do so itself without significant loss in volume. However, once the price has been raised so as to eliminate all tax burden, there is no assurance that some price cutting will not take place. However, if all firms are now operating at a profit, it is entirely possible that they may not cut, even though, before the imposition of the tax, they would have taken advantage of such a situation, to some degree at least, to better themselves at the expense of their competitors. If after the imposition of the tax, despite readjustment, each firm is operating at a loss, the oligopoly may be strengthened, if each firm fears to cut prices for fear of precipitating a violent price war. On the other hand, some of the firms, struggling desperately to avoid bankruptcy, may start price cutting to gain volume, and by causing general collapse of the oligopoly elements in the situation, precipitate a very severe price decline. It is conceivable that the low levels may remain over a considerable period of time. The tax can be credited with having lowered price, a phenomenon impossible under pure competition or pure monopoly. The burden of the tax in a sense rests on those entrepreneurs who have gone out of business[11] and thus have been deprived of their returns; as a result of the process, the consumer actually benefits from lowered prices. In one sense the burden still rests upon the consumer, since the revenue which goes to the government is part of that obtained from the consumer, and of which no factor now actually engaged in production is deprived. Nevertheless,

---

[9] Assuming that the inflow will not reduce too greatly the strength of the oligopoly elements.

[10] Provided that pure competition exists after the tax as well as before.

[11] Often the plants would still be operated under new owners; the loss is borne by the old owners who lose their investment. To the extent that the old plants still operate under new owners there is less chance of price increase, and delay of establishment of a new equilibrium.

since this is more than offset by the lowered production cost, the burden may be considered to rest on those groups losing their incomes as a result of the tax.

Selling Costs. It is now necessary to consider the significance of selling costs. The location of the demand curve for the product of a firm depends not only upon prices charged by the firm's competitors, but also upon the advertising activities of the firm in question and of the other firms in the field. For each price there is an optimum expenditure on selling, given the prices and selling activities of other firms; with this there is a certain possible total sales volume. The curve connecting the points designating these latter amounts for the various prices[12] is indicated by *TR* on Figure 2. For each volume of sales, the price minus the selling cost gives a certain average net revenue figure; there is an average net revenue curve (*ANR* on Figure 2) designating these amounts for the different possible prices. When equilibrium is reached, with free entry of firms, the average cost curve, exclusive of selling costs, of the firm is tangent, not to the demand curve, but rather to the average net revenue curve; the price is that indicated on the total revenue curve for the equilibrium output. Also, through this point of tangency must pass the curve of average net revenue, formally comparable to *DD* on Figure 1, which indicates the amounts that can be sold at the various prices under the assumption that other firms also make the same adjustments in price and selling activities as the firm in question. (*ND* on Figure 2.) This curve is, of course, very much steeper than the *ANR* curve.

When a tax per unit of output is levied, marginal cost will intersect marginal revenue (the marginal of the net revenue curve) at a point of lower output, and price will be raised. The output fall will be less than anticipated; further price adjustment will be made in the same manner as indicated in the previous section, until losses are minimized. There is one essential difference between the adjustment in this case and that in the preceding section; the relationship between output reduction and price rise is different, since price is determined on the basis of the total revenue curve, which is not necessarily parallel to the average net revenue curve. The output adjustment will be made on the basis of the marginal curve of the latter, but the price rise coming about from the output reduction depends on the slope of the gross revenue curve. The analysis of the relation between the slopes of the original demand curve without advertising, the net revenue curve, and the gross receipts curve has not been

---

[12] This is, of course, the demand curve for the product of the firm, with, at each price, the optimum sales expenditure for that price.

FIGURE 2

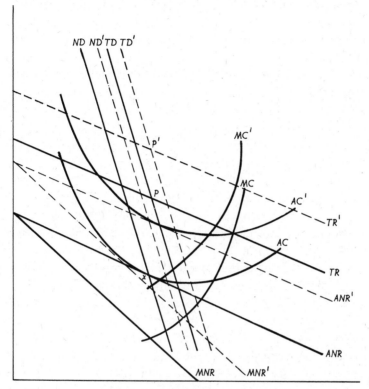

AC:	Average cost, before tax.
AC':	Average cost, after tax.
MC and MC':	Marginal curves of AC and AC' respectively.
TR:	Average gross revenue before tax.
TR':	Average gross revenue after tax.
ANR and ANR':	Average net revenue (TR minus selling cost) before and after tax.
MNR and MNR':	Marginal curves of ANR and ANR'.
TD:	Average gross revenue, assuming prices of other firms to be identical with prices of this firm, and given selling activities on part of other firms, before tax.
TD'':	TD, after tax.
ND and ND'':	Average net revenue, before and after tax, assumptions as of TD.

developed, and it is impossible to deviate in this study to consider the problem.[13] Thus nothing more can be said than to indicate the possibility that this factor may affect incidence. It is impossible to say whether there will be more or less temporary price increase, cet. par., with a situation with selling activities than in one without.

This adjustment is, however, only temporary. Each firm cannot avoid

---

[13] For brief reference, see H. Smith, "The Imputation of Advertising Costs," *Economic Journal*, 45:684, December, 1935, and A. P. Lerner, "Concept of Monopoly and the Measurement of Monopoly Power," *Review of Economic Studies*, 1:173–75 (June, 1934).

losses, as indicated in the previous section, until some of the firms leave the field, since when ANR is tangent to AC', ND will pass to the left of the point of tangency. Thus the position cannot be maintained, as with the price at the level of tangency, sales will be less than anticipated, and loss will be incurred. The exodus of firms will occur as previously indicated; the new equilibrium will be reached at the point at which ANR' is tangent to the new average cost curve (AC'), and ND (now ND') passes through the point of tangency. But price is determined on the basis of the total revenue curve rather than of the average revenue curve. So long as the ANR and TR curves remain in the same relation to each other, price will increase by the same amount as average net revenue increases, and thus by the same amount as if there were no selling cost. If one rises by a certain amount, the other must rise, at the same levels of output, by the same amount if the two curves are to remain the same distance apart. Thus, on Figure 2, the final output will be OP, being determined by the point of tangency between ANR' and AC'; ANR will have risen by the same amount as AC (assuming that the industry is one of constant cost), and price from P to P', or by the same amount.

But there is good reason to believe that the relationship between ANR and TR will shift as firms leave the field. Both the optimum amount of advertising at each price and the net return per unit of advertising expenditure are likely to shift. The reduction in the number of firms seeking the business may make it desirable to spend less to sell various volumes of output; if this is the case, the average total revenue and average net revenue curves will draw closer together, and less price increase will accompany the movement of average revenue to the new tangency with average cost. In terms of Figure 2, when ANR has reached tangency with AC', TR will not have moved up as far as ANR has moved, and the price increase will be less. This is advanced as a possibility rather than as a certain tendency; the likelihood of a shift in the TR–ANR relationship must certainly be recognized. A further potential cause of difference in incidence as compared to the condition in which there are no selling costs is the possibility of a shift in the elasticity of the average revenue curve resulting from the exodus of firms. The nature and amount of such a shift will be influenced by a number of factors, such as the buying habits of the purchasers of the firms leaving business, and cannot be analyzed in detail at this point.

As indicated in the first chapter, it is very difficult to find exactly optimum amounts of advertising expenditure. There are several practices common in determining advertising budgets which may involve probable deviation from optimum outlay for this purpose, but which make the relation between ANR and TR more definite than otherwise.[14] When selling expenditures are determined as a percentage of expected dollar sales, the selling expenditure will be greater per unit at higher price levels; thus the average net revenue curve will be less steep than the average total revenue curve, and a given output reduction will cause a greater price rise than otherwise. The same result will come about if advertising costs are determined independently of expected sales, as a fixed customary sum, etc. The divergence will be greater in the case of the latter than in the case of the former, cet. par., the steeper the demand curve.

Another factor which often influences the determination of the size of the budget is the amount of profits being made, or the amount of cash on hand. Accordingly, when taxes are imposed, and losses made, there will be a tendency to reduce advertising expenditures, a tendency which will be furthered greatly if all firms do the same thing, as the losses from failure to advertise will be less. Thus, reduction of advertising expenditure may allow each firm to return to a position of profitable operation with no exodus of firms whatsoever. If all the firms act in this manner, the total revenue curves may not fall back to any extent, yet the ANR curve, shifting to the right as selling costs are cut, may come to tangency with AC without any firms leaving. The ND curve will have shifted to the right along with the shift in ANR and thus will intersect at tangency. The position is not necessarily stable, since any one firm can gain by advertising if the others do not. Yet, if oligopoly elements are present this may not be done. Thus final equilibrium may be attained without exodus of firms even though there were no monopoly profits to start with. The entire tax will be paid by the firm, not from monopoly profits, but from that part of income formerly spent in advertising. The more that demand for the product as a whole falls as advertising is reduced, the greater is the likelihood of exodus. The burden falls in part on those formerly engaged in the production of advertising service.[15]

In summary, the existence of advertising costs allows new possibility of variations in incidence. From a short run standpoint, the reduction of output by the firm may cause a different degree of price rise than if there were no selling costs, since the average gross revenue and net average revenue curves may not be parallel. As to long run incidence there is the possibility that the gross revenue and net average revenue curves may shift in relation to each other, and that net average revenue may change

---

[14] For a discussion of means of determining the size of the advertising budget, see C. H. Sandage, *Advertising: Theory and Practice*, Chicago, 1936, pp. 555–56.

[15] There may be some burden on the consumer if the advertising has been of benefit to the latter.

slope and so affect price rise. And the existence of advertising expenditures, which are not a necessary cost of turning out the product, provides a possible outlet for absorption of the tax, under certain pricing and advertising policies. But in general selling activities apparently do not introduce significant changes in the theory of incidence. In the remaining parts of the analysis, except where otherwise indicated, it will be assumed, for simplification, that the cost curve includes optimum selling expenditure for each price, and that the demand curve indicates the demand with optimum selling expenditures at each price.

The Significance of the Existence of Monopoly Profits. When the possibility of the absence of tangency of average revenue and average cost is introduced,[16] a new problem for incidence arises. Under such circumstances there is a certain equilibrium output for each firm which allows equilibrium in the industry. This output must be such that at the level of output at which marginal revenue is equal to marginal cost, expected price is equal to realized price; in other words, DD must intersect AR directly above the MR–MC intersection.[17] Thus on Figure 3, MR intersects MC at N, directly below the intersection of AR and DD at P. Price stands at P; output is ON. Any other position will cause readjustment; unless each firm is in the situation indicated, there can be no equilibrium. For each possible higher cost curve, there is a different point of equilibrium farther to the left and higher than the previous. Thus there is a series of equilibrium volumes of output for different levels of cost, other factors, except cost, remaining the same. The curve KK, on Figure 3, indicates the location of these equilibrium points for various cost curves. For each possible cost curve, output must be less than would be the case with pure competition (curves of the industry in the latter being compared to curves of the firm in the case in question), as output in competition is determined by the intersection of average cost and average revenue (DD in this case) curves; each firm in the present case does not expand to this point, as MR would cross MC while AR is still above the latter, and thus above AC. On the other hand, output must, for each cost curve, be greater than if the case were one of pure monopoly. In the latter, output is determined by the intersection of the marginal revenue curve of the firm (MDD on Figure 3) and MC; under the case here considered, the marginal revenue curve (MR) is more elastic than in the previous case; thus the average revenue curve (AR) must also be more elastic than if the case were one of pure monopoly (DD); thus the average revenue

---

[16] This situation may be produced by legal limitation of entry, exclusive possession of raw material sources, reputation from advertising, etc.

[17] The nature of the DD curve is the same as on Figure 1.

FIGURE 3

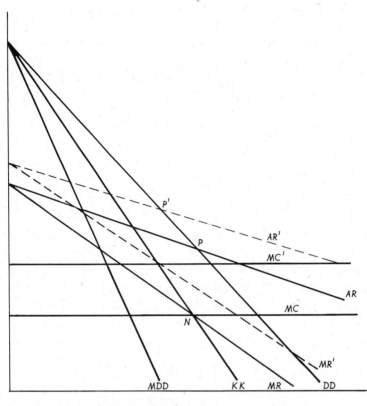

MC:	Marginal cost, before tax.
MC':	Marginal cost, after tax.
AR and AR':	Equilibrium average revenue, with cost curves MC and MC' respectively.
MR and MR':	Marginal revenue curves of AR and AR'.
DD:	Average revenue, assuming prices of other firms to be identical with prices of this firm.
MDD:	Marginal curve of DD.
KK:	Line of equilibrium levels of output, with various possible cost curves.

curve is lower than that with monopoly (DD) at the point at which the marginal curve with monopoly (MDD) intersects MC. If the firm tried to operate at this level of output, realized price would exceed expected price, and an output increase would occur until an equilibrium is reached in the manner previously discussed. This same reasoning applies for any cost curve of the same slope. Thus a line connecting these levels of equilibrium output must be of less slope than MDD, and of steeper slope than DD, and thus approach each at successively lower levels of output. (Note line KK on Figure 3.)

When a tax is imposed, the new permanent output will be determined by the intersection of the new marginal cost curve and the equilibrium line *KK*. Only at this level of output will marginal cost and marginal revenue be equal at the level of output at which actual and expected sales are the same. As this line is of less slope than the marginal revenue curve, and is steeper than the average revenue curve, the price rise resulting from the tax will be somewhat less than under pure competition and somewhat more than under monopoly.[18] In the example shown on Figure 3, the price increase is from *P* to *P'*, or 80%, almost as much as would occur under pure competition.

When the firm is one of decreasing cost, when the tax is imposed, a greater output reduction is necessary for the new optimum, regardless of the nature of competition in the industry. The line of equilibrium for different cost levels is the same, however, as under constant cost, as is indicated in Figure 4, as the same reasoning which applies to constant cost in this matter applies also under other cost conditions. When a tax is imposed, the new *AR* curve will intersect the equilibrium line farther to the left, but the change, as compared to the previous situation, is exactly the same, so long as the old and new *AR* curves are parallel, as in the case of competition or monopoly; the relative price change in the three remain the same. Exactly similar reasoning can be applied to increasing cost conditions, except that there will be less output reduction in all three cases of competition.

Where oligopoly exists with limited entry, each firm realizes that the demand curve for the product of the industry—*DD* on the charts—is its own real demand curve, and adjusts output so that the marginal of this curve is equal to its marginal cost. The price is determined in the same way as monopoly price, apart from uncertainties, differing only if the division of business among several firms instead of concentration in one affects cost at the optimum level of output. Under such conditions, a tax per unit of output will cause the same price increase as in the case of monopoly. The significance of uncertainty can be summarized briefly. To the extent that each firm is uncertain as to the policy of the others, the original price will be lower than the monopoly level. When the tax is imposed, uncertainty as to the reaction of other firms may prevent any price increase. Or, more likely, since a tax is a definitely known cost, affecting all alike, each may be certain that the others will pass on the

---

[18] The reason for the smaller price rise under conditions discussed in this section than with pure competition can be stated somewhat differently. For each equilibrium output in the former, price exceeds that of pure competition for the same cost curve by the excess of average revenue over marginal revenue. At each successively lower output this excess lessens, since marginal revenue draws nearer average revenue. Thus after the tax the price is somewhat less above the new competitive price than before.

entire tax, and thus price will rise by more than under pure monopoly, to a point nearer optimum monopoly price. It is impossible to generalize more specifically than this. Other causes of uncertainty indicated by Chamberlin[19] appear to have no particular significance for incidence theory. If the price before the tax was the optimum, it is entirely possible that the price rise from the tax will be greater than is profitable. If each

FIGURE 4

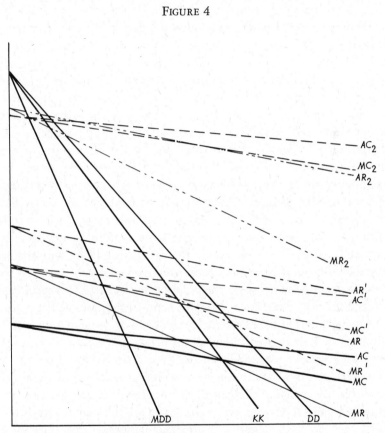

AC:	Average cost, before tax.
MC:	Marginal cost, before tax.
AC' and AC₂:	Average cost curves after relatively small and relatively large tax.
MC' and MC₂:	Marginal cost curves of AC' and AC₂.
AR and MR:	Equilibrium average and marginal revenue, before tax.
AR' and AR₂:	Equilibrium average revenue curves after imposition of the taxes of AC' and AC₂.
MR' and MR₂:	Marginal revenue curves of AR' and AR₂.
DD:	Average revenue curve, assuming prices of other firms to be identical to prices of this firm.
MDD:	Marginal curve of DD.
KK:	Line of equilibrium levels of output, with different possible cost curves.

19 *Monopolistic Competition, op. cit.,* pp. 52–53.

firm feels that the other firms will raise price by the full amount of the tax, each may raise in this manner in the fear that not to do so would precipitate a price war.[20]

Modifying Factors. Diversity of Cost Curves and Demand Curves. Several other factors must be given attention. In the first place, because of differences in cost curves and demand curves among individual firms, in most lines some firms merely cover costs, while others enjoy monopoly profits. It is difficult to generalize as to incidence under such conditions as compared to the situations previously discussed. The output reductions and price increases by the non-marginal[21] firms will increase the demand for the products of the marginal firms; this will aid them in covering cost (since all marginal firms in monopolistic competition must be in conditions of decreasing cost), and will allow more to stay in business than if all firms in the industry were marginal. Tangency between the average revenue curve and the new average cost curve can be brought about by price increases by the non-marginal firms as well as by exodus of marginal. If there is a large number of the latter compared to the non-marginal, it is unlikely that a new equilibrium can be brought about by this means, and some exodus of firms must come about. If any of the old marginal firms remain in business, the price increase in the case of the products of the marginal firms must be just the same as if there were no supra-marginal ones; the final increase in the case of the latter will ordinarily be greater than if no marginal firms were forced out of business, since they will operate farther from the point of lowest cost. There is no assurance that the final price rise will be the same in the cases of the marginal and non-marginal firms. Elasticity and location of demand curves and the nature of the cost curves differ among firms. Not only are the original prices different, but the amount of price rise from the tax is not the same in the various cases. The problem of different cost and demand curves introduces no particular difficulties for the theory of incidence, since the theoretical analysis developed by the latter applies equally well to each individual firm regardless of variations as between firms. Care must be taken, however, in applying the analysis to incidence in an actual industry. A particular tax will cause the various firms in the industry to react differently, and readjustment of relative output by the various firms will occur as a result.

---

[20] The effect of a tax under conditions of the special cases of duopoly developed by Cournot and Edgeworth could be analyzed; since these are essentially special cases, they will be ignored in this study.

[21] That is, those enjoying excess profits. The term "marginal" is used to refer to those firms having only normal profits, and thus in a somewhat different sense than in previous chapters.

Product Variation. It has been assumed thus far that the product is determined, independent of the action of the firm; actually, however, a firm may vary the quality of the product offered. At any one time each firm chooses the optimum product, the product for which net revenue, with price and advertising expenditure for that price at the most profitable levels, is the greatest. When the effect of a tax is considered, the analysis, as always when product differentiation is concerned, is difficult. Where the price for one reason or another—law, custom, etc.—cannot be changed, the increased cost may render a reduction in quality of product profitable. In fact, unless the industry is one of increasing cost, or the individual firms enjoy sufficiently great decreasing costs when no excess profits exist to start with, production must cease entirely under a fixed price condition if quality cannot be reduced. Further, even when a price rise is possible, a quality reduction may be made instead. It is very difficult for buyers to judge quality in many cases, and a poorer grade may be substituted for the better grade without realization thereof by many buyers. Of course, the tax does not render this any more profitable than before; where such is possible, the firm had not reached optimum before. But the tax may be an incentive to attempt to reach the optimum more closely. Finally, even where price adjustments are possible and are made, it may be profitable to readjust quality; this will in turn lead to further price readjustments until a final equilibrium is reached. The direction and amount of change depends on the particular circumstances, and any generalizations are impossible.[22]

When any change in quality takes place, the concept of incidence becomes less clear. If in one case price increases by a certain amount, and in another, similar in all other respects, quality changes in such degree as to allow the firms to restore similar positions of profit as in the first case, it is impossible to compare the relative burden resulting from the two changes. From the point of view of loss in satisfaction suffered by the consumer, it is impossible to compare a given price increase with a given quality reduction. Further, where the latter occurs, it is impossible to say how much of the burden is passed to consumers, as it is impossible to measure relative amounts of utility gained from two different products. However, to the extent that producers escape part of the burden by this means, it is reasonable to maintain that part of the tax is borne by the consumers, when a cheaper, poorer product is substituted for one of

---

[22] The technique developed in Chapter VIII [of *The Theory of Incidence of Sales Taxation*] is applicable to the present problem. Because of the particular significance of the technique for the subject of Chapter VIII [of *The Theory of Incidence of Sales Taxation*], the analysis is introduced in the latter.

higher cost. Yet, if the consumer never becomes aware of the difference, this is not exactly accurate. The utility of an article is determined by personal reaction to the good, and actual physical qualities are of significance only in so far as they affect this reaction.

Where products which are considered by the consumers to be of substantially different desirability are taxed at the same rate per unit of output, the tax will influence the relative desirability of the various lines. If the original prices were in proportion to the marginal utilities of the different grades to the consumer, an addition of a fixed amount to the price of each will make the cheaper grades poorer bargains, and lead to a transference of purchases as between grades, further affecting price changes according to cost conditions.[23]

Multiple Lines. Up to this point in the discussion of incidence, the possibility of the production of more than one product by a firm has been ignored. This phenomenon is, of course, possible under pure competition, but is not of particular significance under such conditions. The limit to profit making by an individual firm is the eventual increase in cost per unit when production is carried beyond a certain point, and combining of lines is profitable only if management costs per unit are thus reduced, or, in a world of uncertainty, risk is spread more widely. Under monopolistic competition, with expansion of profits checked by limited markets, and with excess capacity, which may be reduced by taking on side lines, a common phenomenon, there is a special incentive to produce more than one type of product. In some cases the establishment of an enterprise may be profitable in the first place only if several lines are carried. Such a large investment in factory, skilled personnel, distribution system, and advertising may be necessary that no one line of goods can provide sufficient excess over direct cost of production to cover the "overhead" cost, and the sum of profits in several lines is necessary to cover this overhead, which will be little greater for a series of goods than it would be for one line. Even if one line would be profitable, despite the high fixed cost per unit, the latter can be reduced and profit per unit increased by adding other lines. Further, once the enterprise is established, if part of the establishment is not fully utilized, the average cost and marginal cost of additional lines may be extremely low, as there is no overhead necessarily attributable to these lines, either in the short or long periods. If anything in excess of the special cost of producing these lines is received, it will be profitable to add them.

The total enterprise in which several lines are carried will be started

---

[23] See Silverman, *Taxation, op. cit.*, pp. 96–98.

and will remain in business over a period of time only if average total revenue from all lines covers average total cost. If completely free entry into the field exists, average revenue will equal average cost; if not, it may exceed the latter. As far as any one line is concerned, output will be expanded until marginal revenue equals marginal cost; in the short run it is profitable to keep the line if average revenue covers the average cost immediately attributable to the production of units of this good. In the long run any line will be taken on and kept only if average revenue covers direct costs attributable to this product plus the fixed costs which would not be incurred if this particular line were not produced. Even if the line contributes nothing at all to common costs,[24] there will be no reason to discontinue it so long as it pays for itself.

However, in some lines average revenue must exceed average special cost;[25] in the short run the total of such excess in the entire enterprise must be sufficiently great to equal the sum of common variable costs or operations will cease; in the long run average revenue must exceed average total special costs by the amount of common costs, fixed and variable, or the enterprise will be junked. If there is not free entry, the former may exceed the latter.

Unfortunately for purposes of analysis the situation is very unstable. There will be variations as between firms as to lines carried and profit made on various lines; one group of firms which depend upon certain lines to cover their overhead will find it profitable to extend operations to other lines which will provide some average revenue in excess of average special costs. Some of these latter will be lines which provide chief basis for support for other firms, which in turn will retaliate. The net result will be general chaos, departure of firms, and reëstablishment of some sort of a temporary equilibrium which will in turn tend to break down in the same manner. The fundamental difficulty lies in the fact that a part of the cost of any good of a group produced together is indeterminate,[26] and accordingly there is no accurate guide to the flow of capital and the determination of the direction of production. Production will be increased in certain fields, and existing firms will be forced out, by firms which are not necessarily more efficient but enjoy lower cost in this line because their common costs are borne by other goods.

The only escape from this tendency to disequilibrium is through the development of elements of oligopoly in the situation involving the fail-

---

[24] That is, those costs for which no one product is responsible.

[25] That is, those costs for which the product is directly responsible, in the sense that they would not be incurred if this product were not produced.

[26] Thus there is no true average cost for each good.

ure of firms to take advantage of immediate profit opportunities in order to avoid retaliation by the firms depending for their support on the lines in which the opportunities appear. The chief means is apparently through the use of some basis for pricing which does not necessarily lead to equating marginal revenue and marginal cost: some sort of average cost pricing which involves arbitrary allocation of a certain percentage of overhead to each line.[27] If the same basis is used by all firms in the field, the tendency to destruction will be avoided. Nevertheless, the situation is not very stable; different firms will calculate and allocate costs on different bases, and there will be constant incentive for firms to expand till marginal revenue equals marginal cost. Much trade association activity has been directed toward standardization of cost calculation and allocation to avoid "destructive" price cutting.[28]

For analysis of incidence when several lines are carried, it is necessary to assume first that an equilibrium exists at the time the tax is levied, in which certain lines yield nothing toward overhead, while other lines yield sufficient excess so that the entire enterprise covers total average cost. Complications for incidence arising out of average-cost pricing will be indicated later.

The effect of a tax per unit of output levied on a single line of such an industry will differ according to the conditions of profit on the line concerned. If the line is marginal, that is, if average special revenue just covers average direct cost, the firm will drop the line at once, if, after

---

[27] In one sense this does not necessarily involve departure from marginal pricing, if the firm takes into consideration in calculating marginal revenue the secondary reactions produced by the action of the competitors in response to the firm's own action. However, general acceptance of the average pricing method tends to divert the attention of the firms from consideration of marginal revenues and marginal cost, and leads to the establishment and maintenance of prices which would not be justifiable on the latter basis.

J. M. Clark (*Overhead Costs, op. cit.*), provides the most complete discussion of the relation of overhead and joint costs to price. He emphasizes the attention business men give to average cost as a basis for price setting, to the attempt to allocate total cost as among products in such a way as to insure that they will all be covered. He gives specific reference to the manner in which cost accounting practices serve to check destructive competition under conditions of excess capacity, indicating: "Another very important check (to price cutting), mentioned in an earlier chapter, is cost accounting. Within what Professor Taussig has called the penumbra' of supply and demand, cost accounting can and does frequently govern price policy. A 'standard burden rate,' including interest on investment, is a very powerful check on price cutting" (p. 435).

Note also pp. 64–65, 206–207, 216–57, 434–50.

The significance of average cost pricing has been emphasized by J. K. Galbraith, in "Monopoly Power and Price Rigidities," *Quarterly Journal of Economics*, 50:470–72 (May, 1936).

[28] See K. Pribram, *Cartel Problems*, Washington, 1935, pp. 31–34, 211; Burns, *Decline of Competition, op. cit.*, p. 50; Federal Trade Commission, *Open Price Trade Associations*, Washington, 1929, pp. 192–93; Bureau of Foreign and Domestic Commerce, *Trade Association Activities, Washington*, 1927, pp. 55–61.

the tax, average revenue no longer covers average direct special costs. If the latter is covered, but not average fixed special costs, the line may be dropped at once if the specialized factors can be used for some other product on which better returns can be made, or, if not, at a later period, when the specialized fixed plant wears out. The price change can come very much more quickly than if the product were turned out by a single enterprise; not only is the percentage of fixed cost attributable to the product in relation to the total cost less, but there will be less friction in departing. When entire firms must leave, the hopes of the owners, especially if they are also salaried officers, for better times, often delays exodus. When a firm is merely dropping one line, one that contributed little or nothing to net profit anyway, and one which likely can be added again with little trouble if demand increases, the action will be taken more quickly, if the firm calculates costs at all carefully.

As some of the firms drop the line, other firms will experience demand increases; a sufficient number of firms must drop the line that those remaining will again be able to cover special costs on the product. Since the average cost of the product will have risen by the amount of the tax, price must increase until average revenue also has risen by this amount. Thus, price will rise by the amount of the tax, unless the dropping of the line by some firms affects the costs of the other firms. Where the latter occurs, price increase will be modified, along lines previously indicated. In general, the price increase is the same, cet. par., as if pure competition prevailed. But the significant feature is that complete shifting of the tax occurs with no exodus of firms whatsoever.

In the case of the products for which average revenue exceeds average cost, if after the tax average revenue still covers average special cost, no firm will drop the line. But the firm, if enjoying no excess profits before, will no longer be covering total cost. However, there are several sources of relief apart from exodus of firms. As this line becomes less profitable, marginal cost for the other lines falls off (part of the non-specialized "overhead" formerly required for this product is now available for others), and total profits in the other lines may increase despite the price fall. Likewise, as marginal cost rises because of the tax in the line subject, reduction of output by other firms will allow each firm to raise its price more than otherwise. Nevertheless, these adjustments cannot allow full restoration of profits, or the firms would not have been operating at the optimum before the tax. But if the product is a relatively minor source of profits for the firms, it seems unlikely that any firms will actually be forced out of business because of the levy. It is difficult to define exactly the amount of price increase; apparently, however, the rise will be similar to that in the case in which the number of firms in a field is limited and monopoly profits exist. Marginal cost rises by the amount of the tax; the firms raise price until marginal revenue equals the new marginal cost; as they do so, the output does not fall off as much as they expect because other firms have also raised prices. A final equilibrium will be reached in which the rise will have been somewhat greater than one-half the tax and somewhat less than the tax (with constant cost conditions in the industry and straight line demand). When the firms are enjoying excess profits, or even where they are not, and the product taxed is a minor source of profits, this will be the final price rise.[29]

Where, however, a tax of considerable size is imposed on a line which supplies a large part of the support of the overhead, there can be no solution until some of the firms disappear from the field.[30] This will occur at once if total variable cost is no longer covered, or over a period of time if variable costs, but not fixed costs, are covered at first. Seemingly this process must continue until average revenue returns to its old excess over average cost, or by the amount of the tax if cost is constant. Actually, however, such will not be the case. As firms go out of business, output in the non-taxed lines falls; for the remaining firms, sales, and possibly prices, increase; profits made from these lines rise. This will lessen the need for exodus of firms, and the price rise will be less than if the good had been separately produced, simply because departure of firms from business involves reduction of output in other lines and increases profits of the firms remaining.[31] The firms which depend most heavily on the good in question will likely be the first to go out of business, but other factors, such as age of equipment, are significant also.

One further possibility must be considered. If after the tax, average direct cost of a product formerly yielding a profit is not covered, the firms will drop the line. But this will not relieve them of their difficulty, as they will be unable to meet total common cost, under the assumptions. The price rise will have come about more quickly than in the previous case; price will have risen by an amount equal to the difference between the full amount of the tax and the excess of average revenue over average special cost, except as modified by changing cost conditions as output

---

29 The part of the tax not shifted is, of course, borne by the profit receivers.

30 Unless oligopoly elements are strengthened.

31 If new firms specializing in these nontaxed lines arise to take advantage of the higher prices, or if firms in other lines add these for the same reason, the exodus of the firms in the field will be greater and the price rise greater. The less important is the product taxed in relation to the total profit of the firm, the more significant will the offsetting factor mentioned in the context be. If a large number of the nonmarginal lines are taxed, it will be of very little importance.

falls, as only then will firms again be willing to carry the line at all. But the firms are not yet covering all costs; thus exodus of firms must occur also, and the final price rise will be similar to that in the preceding case, but more of the rise will be independent of the exodus and can thus come more quickly. As this is the case, there will be less chance of check on price increase through increased output in non-taxed lines contributing more toward common cost.

One factor has been neglected as yet—namely, the significance of shifts in demand as between taxed and untaxed lines carried by the same firms. The various lines may be fairly close substitutes, and a price increase in one will lead to a shift in demand schedules in the other. This will increase profits in these other lines; the prices in the latter may fall under certain cost conditions. The increase in profits will lessen the necessity for so great an exodus of firms as would otherwise be necessary. The price increase in the taxed line may thus be less than otherwise.[32]

The significance of multiple lines for incidence can be summarized briefly. Where the products taxed are unimportant in the total profit of the firm, or yield no profit, the price adjustment will be made very much more quickly than if the product is turned out by single line firms, as firms will drop lines of unprofitable goods much faster than they will cease operation. Where no profit was earned on the line, complete shifting will occur without any exodus of firms, even though there were no excess profits in the field, an occurrence impossible under any condition previously mentioned. The amount of price increase will be the same, cet. par., as under pure competition.

Where lines are important sources of profits, the short run incidence will be similar to that of the situation in which monopolistic competition, excess profits, and limited entry exist. If excess profits exist in this case, the long run incidence will, in general, remain the same. If such is not the case, however, firms will not cover all costs after the tax; exodus will be necessary, and the final incidence will be somewhat different than in

---

[32] It is difficult to see how there could be any actual reduction in the price of the taxed article. Edgeworth maintained, in connection with a tax on railway tickets, that a tax on one class might cause the price of both to fall. ("Pure Theory," *Economic Journal, op. cit.*, 7:46; and "Mathematical Method," *Economic Journal, op. cit.*, 9:290–92.) It is clear that under decreasing cost conditions the price of the untaxed line would fall, but only with very peculiar asymmetry of cost and demand curves could the price of both possibly fall. There is no decrease in demand in the market sense comparable to the increased demand for the substitute, but merely a decrease in the sense that less will be taken at higher prices. This phenomenon seemingly would never lower prices no matter how steeply cost is of increasing nature. Rather, only a small part of the tax will be added to price. See also H. Hotelling, "Edgeworth's Taxation Paradox and The Nature of Demand and Supply Functions," *Journal of Political Economy*, 40:577–616 (October, 1932).

any of the cases previously mentioned. The amount of price increase tends to the same level as under pure competition, but the exodus of firms and price rise is prematurely checked by the increased profits on non-taxed lines as firms leave the field, and the final increase is somewhat less. Thus there is a clear case of a part of a tax being passed onto the consumers of untaxed goods. A further factor which may lead in the same direction is the tendency for demand for non-taxed lines to increase. The resulting price increases in the latter may, however, be in part offset by other forces. As output is reduced in the taxed line, marginal cost of production for the other lines falls, and output increase is encouraged. And, if decreasing marginal cost conditions prevail in the untaxed line, a price decline will result from the demand increase.

But, as previously indicated, a multiple line industry tends to instability; it is questionable whether generalizations based on the assumption of an equilibrium which is not stable, except on the basis of rather rigid assumptions that the lines carried by the different firms in the industry are substantially similar, and that no raiding of chief profit sources of other firms occurs, are very significant. As mentioned above, one of the chief means of escaping from this instability is the development of some sort of average cost pricing.

Average-Cost Pricing. As pointed out in the first chapter, price determination is often carried out on the basis of average cost of production, including "overhead," plus an additional percentage of cost depending in amount on some rate of profit which the firm feels that it can get. The implications of this for incidence must now be considered with reference first to single line and then to multiple line industries. With the former, when average revenue equals average cost before the tax, the immediate effect of average-cost pricing will be to raise price by the full amount of the tax (except as modified by a shift in average cost as output is changed), since average cost rises by the amount of the tax. This cannot, however, restore profitable operation. Exodus of firms may occur as losses are experienced; in this case the final incidence will be the same as with marginal pricing methods. The price increase in the period of readjustment, which is often quite long, will have been greater. The exodus, however, is not inevitable. The reduction in output increases average cost per unit; each firm may simply raise prices again, to such a level as to restore profitable operation.[33] If all firms act in this manner, exodus will be avoided. The consumers of the product will be burdened not only with the tax, but with an additional sum necessary to allow continued payment

---

[33] This type of reaction in itself shows the presence of oligopoly.

of returns to the owners of the original number of enterprises in the face of reduced volume of output. As indicated previously, under pure competition, with constant cost, not only does the consumer bear the entire amount of the tax, but in addition the owners of the resources forced out of the field suffer loss of incomes. In the case under consideration, the consumer is forced to carry the second burden as well as the first.

Where excess profits exist, average cost pricing will lead to a permanently greater price increase. Average cost will be raised by the amount of the tax (under constant cost), and price, being determined on the basis of this amount plus some additional percentage which the firm feels it can realize, will be increased by at least the same amount.[34] If the old price were at the optimum level, the new one will be too high for maximum profit, but so long as all the firms keep to the same basis of pricing, the high level will be maintained.[35] Actually, the old price under such pricing methods was probably not at the optimum level; the new one may be nearer than the old, and there will be even less incentive to cut the new price.

Where several lines are carried, as far as a tax on a line yielding no profit is concerned, to raise price by the amount of the tax cannot make continued carrying of the line profitable, and it will almost inevitably be dropped,[36] unless further price increases are made in the manner indicated above. Apart from the latter possibility, average-cost pricing has no particular significance for incidence in this case. Where, however, average revenue exceeds average cost in the line taxed, such a price policy will lead to a greater price increase than would a marginal policy, the incidence being the same as under pure competition. The practice is of particular significance as to the effect on prices in the untaxed lines. If the monopolist is to maximize profits, the lower marginal cost for the other lines after one is taxed dictates lower prices. But at the same time marginal cost falls, average cost rises, because a larger amount of overhead must be allocated to the non-taxed lines. So a price increase is likely in these lines, even though such is directly opposite to a policy which would maximize profits if each firm acted independently. This policy is much

---

34 Probably by more, since the percentage figure designed to supply the profit is applied to a larger base.

35 Unless, of course, the firms run at a loss because of the excessive price increase.

36 The question may well be asked, as to why it is assumed that the business man will be sufficiently rational to drop an unprofitable line, yet follow pricing practices which do not lead to maximum profits. In the first place, as previously indicated, under a multiple line situation, average cost pricing is not so irrational, from a long run view, as it might seem, and is in fact almost inevitable. Secondly, it is very much easier to find out whether a particular line is profitable or not than to determine if the price being charged is the optimum one.

more profitable, or less unprofitable, if all firms act in like manner. If one tries to raise the price of non-taxed lines while others fail to do so, his demand will be so elastic that he will be forced to reduce his price or lose a large part of his sales. If all act in the same manner, the demand is much less elastic, and the increase much more profitable. If the prices are increased by sufficiently great amounts, exodus of firms may be avoided even though there were no excess profits before the tax.

Thus, in general, average cost pricing will mean greater shifting, especially in the short run. When price is determined on the basis of average cost plus a certain desired percentage of profit, the tax will probably increase price by the amount of the levy, under constant cost, even though the optimum increase is less, since average cost is raised by this amount. Further, short run marginal cost is, for amounts below the old equilibrium, very much less likely to be of decreasing nature than average cost including overhead; this factor also involves greater price increase with average cost pricing. In the absence of excess profits, or in cases in which the firms adhere strictly to a policy of obtaining a certain rate of profit on capital, the price increase will be greater than the amount of the tax, as the overhead costs are spread over a smaller volume of output. In some cases, however, average-cost pricing will cause increases so great as actually to reduce profits to producers; not only do the latter suffer, but consumers bear a needless burden.

Variations in Constants. The same formal considerations in regard to shifts in demand, alteration of production functions, and changes in factor prices apply as in the preceding cases. The reactions of changes in these factors will, of course, be different from the previous cases; for example, the effect on price of demand increases will be different with monopolistic competition and limited entry than with pure competition. The presence of oligopoly is of particular importance in introducing differences in reaction; for example, a fall in costs may not produce a weakening of oligopoly elements comparable to the strengthening of the latter caused by the imposition of the tax; accordingly there may be no reduction of burden for consumers of the taxed article despite a general decline in factor prices. The latter is, of course, unlikely to occur on any great scale so long as the industry taxed is relatively unimportant in relation to the economy as a whole.

CONCLUSION

In concluding this chapter, it is desirable to emphasize the comparison of incidence under conditions of monopolistic competition with that under the conditions previously discussed.

There is at least one case in which incidence is similar to that under pure competition. Where monopoly elements are present, but excess profits are absent because of free entry, the price rise will be exactly the same as in the case of pure competition, apart from possible but not inevitable modifications mentioned below. With constant cost, price will rise by the entire amount of the tax in either case, since there are no other possible sources of payment; the entire direct burden of the tax rests upon the consumers, the owners of the factors forced out of use suffering additional indirect burden. In either case, complete increases come only with exodus of firms. When cost conditions for the industry are not constant, modifications will be the same with either type of competitive condition. The fact that the firm operates under conditions of decreasing cost is of no significance for incidence, as firms will operate at the same level of output after the tax as before.

However, there are numerous factors which produce differences in incidence in the two cases. In the first place, in the period prior to establishment of long-run equilibrium, the amount of price increase will be very different. In monopolistic competition, increase comes directly, from the action of the individual firms. Exodus serves primarily to allow restoration of profitable operation, though in addition it facilitates the increase. But with pure competition, no substantial increase is possible at all without exodus, since no firm can make any price change without losing all sales. It is true that, in theory, some immediate output reduction will occur with pure competition. At most, however, the rise would be slight,[37] because of the steep upward slope of the short run marginal cost curve for volumes of output within a certain range below the old equilibrium. With monopolistic competition, the marginal cost curve may be falling instead of rising in the section in which it cuts the marginal revenue curve, and a greater price increase will occur. Actually, with pure competition, no immediate output reduction at all is likely to occur in cases in which no close calculation of costs is made; price rise will come only with exodus. It is difficult to conceive of a wheat farmer cutting his output (assuming wheat to be his most profitable crop despite the tax) when the price he receives falls slightly.

Apart from theoretical considerations, there are other factors which lead to the same result. For reasons purely psychological, and inexplicable in economic terms, it seems that when in one case a certain price rise will lead to the same increase in profits as a certain output reduction would in the other case, there is more likelihood that the former would be made than that the latter would be made. Further, if comparison is made be-

---

[37] Unless, of course, the tax is relatively very high.

tween a situation in which price increases at once, output reduction coming as a result of the increase, and another, in which price increase occurs only as a result of a reduction in output, cet. par., the average price at which the goods sold in the period will have been greater in the former case. Wherever retirement from business is necessary for price increase, the process is a very slow one in many cases, especially if no actual losses (in the business world use of the term) are being made. It is difficult to transfer capital from one line to another, even over time, without serious losses. In addition, there are numerous forces, personal and otherwise, which aid in keeping firms in a particular line even if normal profit is not being earned. Thus the greater the extent to which exodus is essential to full price rise, the longer will be the period in which the consumer escapes part of the burden to which he will eventually be subject.

Furthermore, the very conditions which give rise to monopolistic competition—non-uniformity of product—is responsible in many cases for the genesis of excess profits. When consumer-preference is established and made sufficiently strong, new firms can only with great difficulty take away sufficient business to restore profits to a normal level. In addition, the large initial investment necessary in many fields serves to check the development of new enterprises. Whenever such profits exist, there is a possibility that part of the tax may be absorbed therein; with complete absence of oligopoly, this must occur. As indicated graphically above, the absorption will be less than with pure monopoly.

However, certain elements of oligopoly are likely to be present whenever monopolistic competition exists, especially because of the chain relationships in the field. The elements are commonly manifest in such practices as uniform cost accounting methods and pricing on average-cost-plus bases. With such conditions, several modifications of the analysis are necessary. In the first place, even when excess profits exist, prices are likely to be raised by the full amount of the tax, since the latter represents an addition in full to average cost; when each firm is aware that the others will treat the item as an element by which to raise prices fully, each will take similar action, and the entire tax will be passed on by means of what is essentially a strengthening of the oligopoly position. A similar increase would have yielded greater profits to all if it had been made in the absence of the tax; the degree of monopoly was not sufficiently strong to allow this until an increase in cost definite and known to all produced uniform action. Monopoly profits will, of course, fall in the process, the receivers suffering a secondary burden. The price increase is similar to that under pure competition, despite the presence of excess profits.

However, it is entirely possible that prices will be raised, with constant cost for the *industry*, by an amount greater than the tax. The reduction in output increases the cost per unit when costs for the firm are of decreasing nature, as is typically the case under the circumstances. The firms are very likely to raise prices by an additional amount to compensate for this higher cost. This is especially likely to occur where no excess profits are made; the original number of firms will be enabled to continue operation. But even with excess profits, the firms may act in similar fashion if they consider the previous rate of return as the one which they are determined to get.[38] Thus consumers will be forced to bear not only the direct burden of the tax, but that part of the secondary burden which would otherwise rest upon monopoly profits. It is not maintained that this result is inevitable with monopolistic competition; in many lines oligopoly elements are absent or are too weak to produce uniform action. But there is a definite possibility of a price rise of the nature indicated.

With strong oligopoly elements, the difference in incidence in the short run in contrast to the situation with pure competition is even more striking than in the longer period. With average cost pricing, the entire tax will be added to price at once; average cost at reduced volumes of output will almost necessarily be greater in the short run than that at the old equilibrium, provided that the capacity was properly adjusted, since the fixed cost will be spread over a reduced volume of output. Thus, the short run price increase will be greater than that in the long run if the firms follow strictly an average cost pricing basis, or will be of equal amount if merely the amount of the tax alone is added. This stands in sharp contrast to the situation with pure competition or pure monopoly. In both of the latter cases, the short run increase will be less than that which finally results when long run equilibrium is reëstablished.

There are other factors which act to produce further significant differences in incidence in the case under consideration in contrast to those previously discussed. The exact results of these factors depend upon the particular circumstances of the cases, and few generalizations can be made as to the effects beyond pointing out possible directions of modification introduced by them. In the first place, the possibility of shifts in elasticity of the demand curves of the individual firms must be mentioned. The curves may be made more elastic, for example, in the case of exodus of firms, if those formerly purchasing from the firms which cease operations have little preference as among the remaining. When any change of this type occurs, the level of output and the cost per unit for each firm

---

[38] When demand is so elastic, despite the oligopoly elements, that average revenue increases (at smaller volumes of output) less rapidly than average cost, obviously increases of this nature will not occur; there may be no price rise at all.

will be altered, and the price rise modified accordingly. With pure competition, no such change is possible since the demand curves for the products of the firms are necessarily perfectly elastic; with pure monopoly, the elasticity can be affected only through the effect of the manner in which the tax revenue is spent.

Another source of modification is introduced by the existence with monopolistic competition of expenditures on selling activities. The reduction in the number of firms and the price changes made by competitors may alter the optimum amount of selling expenditures to be made at various price levels and cause greater or less price increase. When production is carried on by the firms at different levels of output than before the tax, as when oligopoly is strengthened, the likelihood that optimum selling expenditures are different at the new volume also modifies the price change. To the extent that advertising expenditures are influenced by profits made or cash available, part of the tax will be borne out of revenue formerly paid out for this purpose.

Likewise, product variation is of particular importance with monopolistic competition; reduction in quality provides an additional means of escape from the tax burden, one especially attractive in many cases because the consumers will be less aware of the quality change than the price increase. This is not the necessary result, however; in some cases, it may be profitable to offer a more costly product as a result of the other changes. When products are varied, discussion of incidence is made difficult by the inability to measure relative utilities to the consumers of different qualities of products.

A phenomenon of particular importance with the conditions under consideration is the production of multiple lines of commodities. Not only does this factor serve to increase greatly the use of average cost pricing methods, with the results previously discussed, but it is of significance for incidence in other regards. In the case of lines which make no contribution to overhead, for example, price will increase by the full amount of the tax, without exodus of firms, even though no excess profits exist in the field. Where some contribution to overhead is made and exodus occurs, part of the burden will pass on to consumers of goods other than those of the article subject to the tax. The purchasers of the latter escape part of the burden which they would otherwise pay.

Finally, the reactions to changes in factor prices and shifts in demand schedules resulting from the manner in which the tax funds are expended will differ in this case in contrast to the other situations. The exact difference depends on the particular circumstances of the individual cases. But, in general, when only one industry is subject to the levy, changes of this nature are not likely to be of practical significance in any case.

All that has been said in this chapter applies equally well to the effects of any change in cost as well as a tax, subject to a few modifications. In regard to the latter, in the first place, the increase in cost of any other item may facilitate readjustment in relative use of different factors; an increase in wages will in many cases make profitable the use of additional capital equipment. Secondly, the expenditures on other items—for example, labor—do not vary directly with total volume produced, as does the type of tax under consideration; the cost curves will be altered in a different manner than in the latter case, and the price increase will be affected accordingly. Finally, the reaction of oligopoly elements will not necessarily be the same as in the case of a tax. This is, of course, especially true when firms do not use the same amounts (relative to output) of the commodity the cost of which has increased; there will be less certainty that the competitors will act in uniform fashion, and accordingly common action resulting in full price increase is much less likely. Very few types of increase in cost are as definite and uniform for all firms as a tax per unit of output; the less definite the cost increase, the less likelihood is there of full price increase.

Thus, in summary:

1. With monopolistic competition, in the special case of absence of excess profits, incidence will be the same as with pure competition apart from the possible operation of certain modifying factors indicated in the analysis above.

2. The importance of monopoly profits provides possibility of absorption of greater amounts of the tax. Even without any feeling of mutual interest, however, price increase will be greater, cet. par., than with pure monopoly.

3. Despite excess profits, price increase will normally approach that of pure competition. The importance of oligopoly elements, with common cost accounting and average-pricing methods, allows the tax, which appears as a common and uniform increase in cost, to facilitate a price increase by the full amount of the levy. The increase is thus greater than with pure monopoly, the price level being adjusted nearer to the full monopoly level. This is, of course, not the necessary result; few fields are entirely free of price cutters, the activities of which interfere with the price increases. The increase will be checked also in the fields in which demand for the products of the firms is very elastic for price levels higher than the old for reasons other than the presence of price cutters.

4. In many cases, not only will price be raised by the full tax, but by an additional amount to compensate the firms for reduced volumes of output. Strong oligopoly and strict average cost pricing will bring this result, and allow retention of the original number of firms even when no excess profits existed. Not only is the consumer forced to bear the entire tax, but likewise the secondary burden normally resting upon owners of the factors forced to leave the field or suffer reduced returns.

5. In the short run period, the difference is particularly striking in contrast to incidence under pure competition. The price increase, in full or in part, comes at once without exodus of firms; the latter, when it occurs, serves for the most part simply to restore profitable operation. With strict average cost pricing, the immediate price increase will be greater than that after readjustment of capacity has taken place.

APPENDIX: THE PROCESSING TAXES OF THE AGRICULTURAL ADJUSTMENT ACT

Throughout this analysis, reference to actual taxes on particular commodities has been avoided. Determination of conditions of cost and competition in any line requires extensive investigation beyond the scope of this report, and generalizations as to incidence based on external indices of these conditions are likely to lead to serious errors. One group of taxes, however, has recently received extensive empirical treatment by the Bureau of Agricultural Economics, and a summary of their findings in relation to the conclusions reached in this study are of interest. The levies in question are the processing taxes imposed under the Agricultural Adjustment Act during 1933, 1934, and 1935.[39] Before presenting the summary, it is necessary to orient these levies in terms of the analysis of the preceding chapters. The taxes, levied upon the first processing of the commodities, were of specific nature, and represented fairly high percentages of the sale prices of the articles. The tax upon hogs ranged (at different times) from $.50 to $2.25 per 100 pounds,[40] which sold for from $4.00 to $11.00 in the period.[41] The wheat tax was $.30 a bushel, the latter selling from $.50 to $1.30 during the period.[42] The tax on rye was $.30 per

---

[39] The conclusions, accompanied by statistical evidence, were published by the U.S. Treasury Department, Bureau of Internal Revenue, for the U.S. Department of Agriculture, Bureau of Agricultural Economics, entitled, *An Analysis of the Effects of the Processing Taxes Levied Under the Agricultural Adjustment Act*, Washington, 1937.

[40] *Ibid.*, p. 12.

[41] *Ibid.*, p. 75.

[42] *Ibid.*, pp. 21–22.

bushel,[43] selling from $.50 to $.85.[44] Cotton was taxed 4 cents a pound, selling from 6 to 14 cents.[45] Tobacco was taxed on an average of 3.9 cents,[46] the price ranging from 7 to 23 cents.[47] The corn tax was 5 cents,[48] the price $.39 to $1.07 a bushel.[49] The rice tax was $1.62 per barrel[50] selling from $1.51 to $3.24 per barrel.[51] Peanuts were taxed 1 cent per pound,[52] selling from 1 to 4 cents.[53] Sugar will be omitted from this summary because of the complexity of the situation and the resulting obscurity of the results. The taxes are accordingly specific taxes levied upon manufacturers, in fields characterized by the existence of monopolistic competition. Accordingly, the expected result would be immediate price increases, by fully the amount of the tax, or, more likely, more than the tax. Where, however, the industry uses the entire supply of the basic product, the supply is likely to be extremely inelastic, if not entirely so in the short run. Accordingly, it is possible that this initial price rise would be followed by a fall in price of the basic product; this would not, however, be permanent, in the absence of excess profits in agriculture, but would remain over a long period of time because of the importance of irrational elements in the determination of the volume of investment in this field.[54] No exodus of firms in processing is likely unless the demand for the product is quite elastic and raw material prices do not fall; the processors can be expected to bear little of the burden except temporarily prior to exodus when the latter is required. The burden in the short run will fall upon consumers where demand is not too elastic and other uses exist for the product, upon producers where no alternative uses exist, and upon distributors, in part at least, where other outlets are available and demand is elastic.

The method used by the Bureau can be summarized briefly. The margins of the processors were determined, before, during, and after the tax,

---

43 *Ibid.*, p. 27.
44 *Ibid.*, p. 28.
45 *Ibid.*, p. 30.
46 *Ibid.*, p. 39.
47 *Ibid.*, p. 94.
48 *Ibid.*, p. 48.
49 *Ibid.*, p. 101.
50 *Ibid.*, p. 56.
51 *Ibid.*, p. 103.
52 *Ibid.*, p. 60.
53 *Ibid.*, p. 61.
54 The period of readjustment would be lengthened, if not made indefinite, by the payment of the benefits provided under the act. Where no reduction in price to basic producers occurs, the payment of the benefits could not act to increase supply and lower price, since they are paid only for acreage reduction, on the basis of quotas depending primarily on past output. See Nourse, E. G. Davis, J. S. and J. D. Black, *Three Years of the Agricultural Adjustment Act*, Washington, 1937, pp. 90–91.

to ascertain whether or not this group had borne any of the burden; the margins of the wholesalers and retailers were similarly analyzed. The burden on the consumer was determined by an anlysis of the elasticity of demand, to see whether producers could profitably raise prices, and by study of actual retail price variations. Changes in basic price levels were considered to discover if any of the tax passed back onto producers. This type of analysis is subject to the usual difficulties of empirical technique in economics, particularly the inability to exclude the effects on the prices and margins in question of factors other than those under consideration. Likewise the analysis is essentially of short run reaction. Nevertheless, the conclusions are of interest, and because of their clear-cut nature, in several cases at least, of significance.

The studies show that in only two cases, corn and tobacco, did the processors bear any burden at all, except perhaps incidentally through reduced volume.[55] The margin of hog-processors increased by almost exactly the amount of the tax, despite the fact that the latter amounted to four times the original margin.[56] After the tax was removed, the margin fell quickly to the old level.[57] In the case of wheat and rye flour millers, the margin between wheat and flour rose by approximately the amount of the tax, falling back when the tax ended.[58] With cotton, the margin rose more than the amount of the tax, although other costs were also increasing during the period of the tax.[59] With tobacco, because of the complexity of grades, uses, and time lag between purchase and sale, the conclusions are not clear. Cigarette margins increased by three times the tax; other products experienced much smaller increases, often by amounts less than the tax. Apparently most of the tax was passed off onto cigarette buyers alone.[60] In the case of corn for human consumption, the margins rose more than the tax, but because of changes in cost and competitive conditions, it is not clear that processors escaped all burden.[61] Peanut processors apparently escaped burden.[62]

As far as wholesalers and retailers were concerned, studies of margins indicate that there was no absorption of the tax by these agencies.[63] In the

---

[55] Bureau of Agricultural Economics, *Processing Taxes, op. cit.*, p. 5.
[56] *Ibid.*, p. 10.
[57] *Ibid.*, p. 12.
[58] *Ibid.*, p. 21; pp. 27–28.
[59] *Ibid.*, p. 29.
[60] *Ibid.*, pp. 37–43.
[61] *Ibid.*, p. 54.
[62] *Ibid.*, p. 65.
[63] *Ibid.*, p. 5.

case of hog products,[64] cigars and cigarettes,[65] and peanuts,[66] the margins actually increased during the period, as would be expected in the light of markup practices to be discussed in Chapter VII. In the other lines, the margins remained virtually unchanged.[67]

In the case of wheat, rye, and cotton, study of the demand situations, of the impossibility of a substantial fall in raw material prices because of the world market, and of actual retail price changes shows that the tax was passed forward to the consumer. Inelastic demand conditions, especially with the first two products, coupled with a world demand of such nature that the decreased home consumption could be absorbed without price decline (except in cotton, in which apparently a slight decline resulted), allowed processors to increase prices without serious demand loss or fall in raw material prices.[68] With tobacco, the evidence indicates that, so far as cigarettes are concerned, price increased by an amount greater than the tax, this being made possible by the very inelastic demand for this product.[69] For other tobacco products, apparently the entire tax was not shifted, the remainder of the burden being borne by cigarette consumers.[70] In the case of peanuts, the conclusion is reached that the consumer likewise was burdened with the levy.[71]

Analysis of conditions in the producer markets indicate that in the cases just mentioned, no significant price decline to agricultural producers occurred. This situation is possible because only one use of the products was taxed; the relatively inelastic demand in the taxed line, coupled with the ability of the other markets to absorb the additional supply without serious price decline, prevented any secondary price decrease of the finished product arising from a fall in purchase price of raw materials to the processor.[72] Only in the case of cotton did the decreased consumption lower world prices sufficiently to allow a small portion of the tax to pass back onto the producer.[73]

In one case, however, namely,that of hogs, the processors were unable profitably to raise prices because of the recognized high elasticity of demand. If this commodity had been one with a world market, processors

64 *Ibid.*, p. 18.
65 *Ibid.*, p. 32.
66 *Ibid.*, p. 64.
67 *Ibid.*, p. 5.
68 *Ibid.*, p. 5.
69 *Ibid.*, p. 5.
70 *Ibid.*, pp. 44–47.
71 *Ibid.*, p. 6.
72 *Ibid.*, pp. 6–7.
73 *Ibid.*, p. 35.

would have had to absorb the tax, or, in time, except with excess profits, quit business in sufficient numbers that hog product prices would have risen to cover the tax, regardless of demand elasticity. However, the market for this product is not world wide, and few alternate uses exist. Accordingly, the price of the raw material fell. Rather than increase prices initially, which they would have done with a more inelastic demand, the meat packers were enabled by their monopolistic position to force down hog prices directly. This would have been only a short run phenomenon, however, in the absence of excess profits in hog production, were it not for the benefit payments being made. Studies of the retail prices of hog products showed that apparently no change in these prices occurred as a result of the tax or its removal;[74] studies of income received by hog producers indicated a decline in prices as a result of the tax.[75]

Thus, in general, the relevant conclusions of the preceding chapters are borne out in the main by the statistical analysis of the processing taxes. Since the processors operate under conditions of monopolistic competition, with considerable degree of oligopoly, immediate increase in prices by the full amount of the tax, which was to be expected except with very elastic demand, was found in all cases except hog products, for which demand was shown to be elastic. The tax, a definite known cost to which all were subject, produced essentially a strengthening of oligopoly, and an increase in price by the full tax, apparently without the exodus of firms necessary in the absence of oligopoly. There was no definite evidence of an increase above the tax necessary to maintain the old number of firms or the old level of excess profits. This amount may have been of such little significance with the inelastic demands as to be unnoticeable in the statistical work, or may have simply not occurred. No evidence is presented as to excess profits or exodus of firms; because of other dynamic factors involved, it is extremely difficult to measure the effect of a tax on the latter.

---

[74] *Ibid.*, p. 9.
[75] *Ibid.*, pp. 18–19.

E. TAXES ON LAND AND PROPERTY

23

Taxation of Site Values[*][1]

By C. F. BICKERDIKE

The modern demand for taxation of ground values is based on alleged injustices of the rating system. Landlords benefit from municipal improvements, and therefore ought to contribute specially towards the expenses of them; or "tenants have to pay twice over for their improvements." These are the popular arguments.

What exactly is meant by "benefit" when appeal is made to the "benefit principle"? If payment for municipal services is to be like payment for all other things, the only sort of benefit to be considered is direct use. Those pay for domestic gas who enjoy the light derived from it, and are responsible for its consumption. One does not trouble about indirect effects, though they are just as complicated as the indirect effects of a rate levied to pay for the lighting of streets. In either case, the comparative dearness of gas in one place may be prejudicial to rents, and we may if we like try to estimate what portion of the gas bill, as of the rates, falls upon landlords or leaseholders. Or the supply of gas may prove such a boon that it attracts people to the neighbourhood, and landowners may benefit. All the same, using words in their ordinary sense, we are justified in saying that a man pays his own gas bill, and few doubt that he ought to pay it. On ordinary commercial principles, those who get the direct use of a thing make the direct payment. Municipal services then should, on ordinary principles be paid for by those for whose first-hand benefit, or on whose responsibility, they are provided, *i.e.*, the whole body of inhabitants. There may be difficulty in apportioning the payment amongst those inhabitants, but that does not affect the question at issue. There is no question of apportionment between the body of inhabitants, and the body of leaseholders and of landowners.

* *Economic Journal*, Vol. XII, No. 48 (1902).
[1] The greater part of this paper is taken from the essay which won the Cobden Prize at Oxford this year. Owing to want of space, the latter portion dealing with the practical proposals of Mr. Moulton, the London County Council, and the Royal Commission Minority, has been omitted, and a summary only of the earlier part of the essay is given.

Misconception has arisen from failure to recognise that the benefit, if any, derived by landowners, is indirect, and does not exist at all unless the money value of improvements is in excess of the cost; it is simply the producer's surplus, like the rest of their rent.

Is it possible or desirable to appropriate any part of this surplus? Here we come to the well-known "unearned increment" argument. Properly speaking it has nothing to do with the incidence of rates, and the discussion of it on its own merits is reserved to another place. Many people, however, think that the surplus due to municipal enterprises is very considerable, and is chiefly responsible for the growth of land values, and justifies an attempt to improve upon ordinary commercial principles. The importance of this factor in the growth of land values is, however, usually much exaggerated through a hazy idea that the value of an improvement has a direct connection with its intrinsic utility. Really, utility enters into the value only in the same kind of way as into the value of wheat. Most of the surplus of intrinsic value, so to speak, above cost is consumer's surplus. The mistake arises from forgetting that most improvements are not peculiar to any one place, and only those places which have some natural advantage above the average yield a surplus. Apart from the growth of population and industry it is doubtful whether aggregate economic rents would be increased at all by improvements which make towns healthier and pleasanter. Professor Marshall and Ricardo have discussed the effect upon agricultural rents of improved processes, and the conclusion of the former is, that though Ricardo is wrong in arguing that such improvements must necessarily lower rents, that result is quite probable. Similar reasoning may be applied to urban rents. (For a discussion of the validity of applying to urban rents conclusions based on arguments from agricultural rents, see further on.)

The conclusion is that increments of rent due to the actions of public bodies cannot possibly be dissociated from that due to the general growth of population and business. The "unearned increment" argument must therefore be separated from the question of the justice of ordinary rates.

It is quite evident, however, that the advocates, and even the opponents of the rating of ground values do not usually recognise the fact that the one solid foundation for the proposal is this argument from the "unearned increment." It is necessary to examine, therefore, the less vulgar sources of misconception. Even amongst economists the general principle that as regards occupiers in toto the payment of rates is like other payments, is often much obscured owing to the way in which the subject is approached. First, we have the principles of benefit and ability mentioned without any discrimination between direct use and indirect advantage; then follows an intricate discussion of the incidence of a rate assumed to be purely onerous, and the verdict as to the right and wrong of rates is made to turn on the answer to the question whether an occupier shifts any definite part of the burden on to his superiors. The benefit is hazily spoken of by both parties as something shared between occupier and owner, and controversy turns on the distribution of the burden of payment. We lose sight of the fact that there is no benefit to the owner until the occupier has been at least compensated for his payment. This way of treating the question introduces many pitfalls, the detection of which is the theme of that part of the essay which now follows.

It is unfortunate that, amongst the questions put to the experts by the Royal Commission on Local Taxation, there is none which asks directly about the incidence of benefits. Consequently the question is treated much more vaguely than that of onerous rates. Professor Marshall says, "The ultimate effects of such rates (*i.e.* beneficial rates) may be discovered fairly well by discovering the effects of onerous rates and reversing those." But he leaves the reader to do the reversing. One result is that an erroneous one-sided view is frequently taken of the effects of "friction." In discussions of the incidence of onerous rates much stress is sometimes laid upon the difficulty which occupiers experience in shifting any part of the burden upon owners. Ignorance, unwillingness to move, and length of leases are made much of. Hence friction is regarded as a force which acts against the interests of the occupier. Even in regard to onerous rates it might be pointed out that friction acts both ways. If occupiers in highly-rated places are unwilling or unable to move to the more low-rated places, it is to the disadvantage of landlords in the latter. But it is more important to remember that in so far as friction is effective, it also tends to prevent landlords in places which have been improved from reaping the advantage. If people are unwilling to go to the expense of moving where onerous rates are high, they will probably be equally unwilling to move in order to go to a neighbourhood where the results of beneficial rates more than make up for their amount. If leases in the latter place are long, the owner cannot raise his rent easily. It is a favourite device of the partisan to fix attention upon the onerous rates when the occupier is talked about, but when the owner is brought in, rates are thought of as producing great conveniences. If it be a fact, as Mr. Costelloe says, that ratepayers fail to appreciate the value of the services rendered to them by municipal expenditure, whilst they fully appreciate the burden of payment, this makes it the more difficult for landlords to get any indirect benefit.

Another circumstance which is made the basis of a complaint that landowners derive undue benefit, is the system of paying sinking funds for the extinction of debt.

Let us disregard at first the complications of intermediate leaseholders, and suppose landowners to build houses and let them directly to tenants on short leases. If now an improvement is made with borrowed capital and a sinking fund established, it does not matter whether the owner or the occupier pays it. It is an element in the supply curve anyhow. On whom the incidence of the sinking fund rests depends upon whether it is a peculiarity of one place or a universal system. In the former case, the owner bears the burden, for this improvement would be charged for at a higher rate than elsewhere. If the system is universal, the occupier substantially bears it. It means that these conveniences have a higher price than would be the case if no sinking fund were judged necessary, and the only effect upon owners would be the result of a possible diminution of demand for building accommodation. Similarly, it must be remembered when the capital has all been paid off, the same considerations have to be taken into account in deciding who has the benefit of the improvement unaccompanied by a rate. If the whole thing is confined to one neighbourhood, the owner gets the advantage, which is just, since he or his predecessor bore the burden. If the system is general, the occupiers stand to get much of the benefit of cheaper accommodation in precisely the same way as their predecessors stood to bear the burden.

If sinking funds really are too large, the issue is between the present and succeeding generations. Whatever part the occupiers bear is for the benefit of future occupiers, and, whatever part the owners bear is for the benefit of future owners. People are very apt to assume tacitly that the burden is borne like a universal onerous rate, but when the advantage of having no rate to pay is thought of it is treated as a peculiarity of one locality.

When length of leases is taken into consideration, the matter is not quite so simple, for the length of the lease in this case acts only one way. If the burden is imposed after the leaseholder has made his contracts, of course he cannot shift it backwards, but when the time of freedom from rate comes, it is not an unexpected event. If the lease has been taken after the imposition of the burden, the fact that the burden would cease entirely in course of time would presumably have been allowed for. Thus the long leaseholder may have a small grievance. The ordinary occupier is not affected. These long leaseholders, however, are not usually supposed to deserve much pity, since the progress of towns has usually been quite as much an unexpected event as the imposition of sinking funds.

Apart from the more obvious popular fallacies already mentioned, there is confusion on the subject of benefit, owing to the fact that payment for municipal services cannot be made to correspond to payment for ordinary services in all particulars, for two reasons. Firstly, the majority of such services, though partially beneficial, are not so entirely. Secondly, even if they were purely beneficial, the benefit is too generally diffused to allow of the apportionment of payment on ordinary principles amongst those who directly enjoy it. It is only when regarded *in toto* that one can say that ratepayers pay for what they directly use. In the case of houses, each individual can feel that he has paid in proportion to what he has got. It is the same with gas and tramways. But in the case of street-lighting, though the majority of ratepayers presumably admit that taken altogether they have their money's worth, there is nothing to prove directly to each individual that he in particular gets his money's worth; so each one thinks that the advantage accrues to every one else. The difference between beneficial and onerous rates is largely a matter of degree. Some things, such as lighting and cleaning of streets, are advantages visible to the eye; they may be taken into account when a man is choosing a house, though they are apt to be forgotten when the rate-collector calls. Other things, such as police, schools, town halls, are also supposed to be worth the money to the community as a whole, but are not likely to be thought of very seriously by house-hunters; they are mainly then onerous. Finally, there is the poor-rate, which the majority of people approve of for unselfish reasons only. It is clear that the more the object for which the rate is levied approximates to an ordinary commodity desired by individuals for selfish enjoyment, the more possibility is there of indirect benefit to landowners. Hence, the maximum possible benefit will be found by assuming that each individual fully appreciates the money value of an improvement. If in this case the landlord's benefit is merely indirect and vague, *a fortiori* it will be the case with the majority of rates, and in many of them the net result is burdensome, at least so far as landowners are concerned. It has already been argued that a rate assumed to be purely beneficial is neither more nor less just to occupiers as a body than any other payment for commodities and services. The only effect, so far as the question of landowners is concerned, of introducing the burdensomeness into the discussion, is to minimise still further the benefit argument for taxing land values. It is useful to remember that if an improvement is really sufficiently beneficial to benefit landlords, it would be worth their while, if they could agree amongst themselves, to execute the improvement at their own expense. This test will frequently make it evident that the supposed benefits to owners are much more doubtful than people often imagine. Very few rates are really payments for commodities like ordinary commodities for which people pay a money value equal to marginal cost of production.

But there are some who maintain that apart from the benefit question, purely onerous rates should come partly from ground landowners. This idea is undoubtedly due to the popular habit of regarding a rate as a tax on property, intended to fall upon owners of property. Hence the discussion about the shares of taxation which falls upon real and personal property, or movables and immovables, the futility of which is recognised by the Royal Commission. After all, when one asks why owners of property should be taxed, the answer must be because they benefit, so that the argument about "all classes of property contributing equally" is really, so far as it means anything, the benefit discussion over again.

The intricacies of the question of incidence have had something to do with the prevailing confusion about rates. There has been much controversy over the question whether the occupier shifts any appreciable portion of the rates to the owner, and the most hotly argued question frequently comes to be regarded as the most important. It may fairly be asked why the question should be considered important. If the occupier is intended to pay, the only people who might feel interested in the question of incidence are the owners, who might urge a grievance if the tax is shifted on to them. There is some plausibility in the argument that the share of onerous rates borne by leaseholders and ground landlords is a compensation for the benefits derived from other sources, a sort of indirect taxation of unearned increment. On this question, as on the benefit question, popular opinion has been full of fallacies. Estate agents declare in one breath that onerous taxation falls practically on owners, and in the next they say that to divide rates between owner and occupier would be useless. "We should merely put up our rents by that amount."

Hopeless inconsistencies and disagreements make it impossible to attach much weight to the opinions of the "practical men." It is no use trying to find out by observation whether the addition of a few drops of water makes any difference to the height of water in an agitated bucket.

Unfortunately the highest economic authorities are not quite agreed. Professor Marshall, in reply to the Royal Commission (*Memoranda*, p. 117), says, "If a uniform imperial tax be levied on the annual value of all land and buildings, the building part of it tends to settle on the occupier, or on his customers if he uses the building for trade purposes; but the site part of it tends to settle on the owner for the time being; that is, on the interim owner in so far as it is imposed during his lease; and on the ultimate owner when he comes into possession. If, however, agricultural land is exempt from the tax, then the tenant escapes only that part of the site tax which is assessed on the excess of the value of the land for building uses over its value for agriculture."

This has all the appearance of being a careful statement, and it is difficult to avoid the conclusion that Professor Marshall really gives his support to Mill's division of a tax on rent into two parts, the incidence of each of which may be traced separately, so that any such tax is definitely, apart from friction, a tax on economic rent which the owner cannot shift. According to this view, if the tax is uniform and leases very short, the owner pays at least a fraction of the tax, the fraction being the ratio of economic rent to the whole rent, quite independently of any additional loss due to diminution of demands for buildings resulting from the other part of the tax.

Professor Edgeworth, in the *Economic Journal* (Vol. X), controverts this view, and although he refers to the language of his fellow experts as merely "infelicitous," and liable to deceive the "vulgar, who take words literally," it is impossible to avoid the conclusion that there is a real difference of opinion. "There is no objection," he says (p. 192), "to speaking of 'the portion which is a tax on ground rent', if we are careful to remember that this portion, and its proportion to gross rent has no relation whatever to the amount by which the ground rent tends to be reduced in consequence of the impost." And (p. 191) he says, substitute barley for house accommodation . . . "who ever heard, outside the pages of Adam Smith, of that part of a tax on barley which falls on rent?"

It looks an obvious criticism of this to reply, that, whereas rent does not enter into the price of barley, that price being the marginal cost of production, the rent of a building is the cost of production plus the ground rent. There is an apparent difference between the natures of urban ground rent and agricultural rent. Economists generally explain the latter as arising from the fact that fields differ in fertility, so that some doses of capital yield greater quantities of corn in one than in another.

There is also to some extent, difference of convenience in situation, but this can be taken into account by including cost of carriage amongst the expenses of production. In the case of urban rent, however, convenience of situation cannot be thus put into cost of production, and it is differences of convenience which are the chief cause of urban rent. There is not much difference between the cost of construction in different places in England. A city building could probably be duplicated in Brixton at about the same cost, or even less.

To explain urban ground rent as producers' surplus and to show the identity of the nature of rent in the two cases, it must be remembered that what is really "produced" is a power to satisfy wants, a group of conveniences. In the case of buildings, mere size is only one consideration: vertical and horizontal position are as much attributes of the building which the purchaser considers as is cubical capacity. The builder in the city can produce greater "accommodation" in the wide sense, and he applies his capital until the marginal dose produces just enough net convenience to cover the cost. The total rent is the value of the net convenience produced, the price per unit of which is the marginal cost of production, and the rent is the value of the surplus quantity. The imagination cannot well picture a "unit of building convenience," other than as a certain cubical space, but this difficulty is not confined to urban land produce. The difference between two fields of wheat might be merely a difference in quality, not quantity, of corn, but to aid the imagination one takes quantity as constituting the difference, and corn or barley is taken as short for agricultural produce generally. For it is almost as difficult to think of a unit of agricultural produce as to think of a unit of urban produce in the wide sense; each is a certain quantum of utilities measurable in money value. The theory of rent is just the same in the two cases, and Professor Edgeworth is perfectly justified in appealing to the received theories of taxes on agricultural produce.

Very likely the dynamical analogy of the effect of the resultant of two forces or velocities, which can be found by treating each force or velocity independently and combining the result, may have suggested the division of the tax on rent into two independent portions. The method, however is quite fallacious. The existence of the tax on the building part of rent entirely destroys the peculiarity of the ground rent part, and the arguments by which a tax on ground rent is proved to fall entirely on the owner completely break down. Consider agriculture first. If a tax is levied only on economic rent the price of corn (meaning agricultural produce generally) cannot be raised, for the rise of price would bring into profitable cultivation a new grade of land, or cause a further dose of capital to be applied to land. This would mean an increase of supply, whilst with the higher price, the demand at best could not be greater than before. But if the produce of the new marginal dose were taxed equally with surplus produce, the price paid by consumers could rise to the extent of the tax before new doses of capital could be profitably applied. The tax is treated as levied from producers; if levied from consumers, we should say the price could remain as before without bringing fresh land into cultivation, so that in either case the consumer would have to pay the whole tax unless he reduced his demand—hardly a genuine shifting of the burden.

It is the same with urban rates. A rate on ground rent alone could not be shifted on to consumers, because such shifting would mean an increase in the price of accommodation. A better money's worth could be got by building on land just outside the margin, or by pushing the margin of building higher (*i.e.* on the assumption that the different kinds of building convenience really do compete, and no doubt a number of people would prefer a larger house in a less convenient situation, or taller, rather than pay more for their existing accommodation). This could not last, for supply would be increased when demand could not possibly be greater. Owners would have to reduce rent. But if the new buildings on the margin had also to pay the rate, there would be no advantage in them. Apart from elasticity of demand, the price of accommodation could rise to the extent of the rate before the margin of building could be pushed higher or wider.

A tax on total building rent is like all other taxes on commodities, falling substantially on the consumer. He may reduce his consumption, and in that way indirect loss will be caused to producers for a time, and more permanently to owners of land required for the production of the commodity. But it is quite impossible to take such losses into consideration in practical politics, just as it is impracticable to take account of indirect gains. If the community, or a great part of them, alter their tastes, and spend more of their incomes, say on education, and have less to spare for house rent, those interested in real property must put up with it. If the unwilling are also compelled by law to make similar redistribution of their expenditure, the indirect effects are to some extent greater, but they are just as complicated and incalculable as if the change had been entirely voluntary. It is not meant that all discussion of incidence is futile; only that for practical purposes a tax levied in respect of any commodity must be regarded as falling upon consumers. If they shift any part by reducing their consumption they do not really escape the burden to the extent of their saving; they suffer loss of convenience. Every extra payment which does not work round so as to cause an increase of income has to be saved somehow out of saving and expenditure with indirect losses to the people concerned in the production of those commodities for which the demand is lowered. Income tax is all saved somehow, and the only difference between it and a tax levied on house rent is that in the latter case there is rather more inducement to effect the saving at the expense of house accommodation, since a reduction of house-rent means automatically a reduction of tax. But as house-rent and general expenditure are so closely connected, a house-rent tax is a much nearer approximation to an income tax than any other tax levied in respect of a particular commodity.

The more completely the question of incidence is examined, the more clearly is it seen how hopeless is the attempt to take account of anything but the loss to consumers. Professor Sidgwick points out that the beer tax is to some extent a tax on barley, and says that this should be taken into account in considering the burdens on agricultural land. Why should not the effects of government expenditure of the money also be considered? If the money goes to paying soldiers and sailors, very likely they spend as much on beer or other things that agriculturists help to produce as would have been spent on them if the money had remained at the disposal of individuals. It is still more difficult to say precisely what is the effect upon landowners generally of local rates for poor relief and education. A considerable part of the expenditure is expenditure on buildings. It may be conjectured that, even taking this into account, landowners tend to suffer rather more than they would if the tax had not been levied proportionately to house-rent. Nevertheless, it is quite useless for the practical politician to attempt to take notice of such loss; in the main it is merely the loss due to change in people's manner of spending their money, which must be borne by landowners as part of the ups and downs of fortune; the circumstance that rent is taken to measure people's ability to pay makes too little difference to be seriously considered. The question of appropriating for the state part of the increment of rent, on the ground that it is "unearned," must be considered quite apart from either incidental gains or incidental losses due to rates.

Further, it is rather an encouragement to erroneous ideas to suggest that part of rates should be directly levied from owners "for the sake of sentiment," or "to make the real and apparent incidences correspond." People grumble at rates for the same reason as they grumble at income tax, they are payments of substantial sums not immediately accompanied by a visible return. As a concession to the weakness of human nature it might be allowable to practise a little sleight of hand, as is done in imperial taxation by means of customs and excise: only if this is to be done it should not be pretended that any definite part of an onerous rate is *intended* to fall upon the landowner and leaseholder. Much less should rates be levied more highly on ground rent than on other rent for this reason. The fact that at present rates tend probably to the detriment of rent must not be allowed as a proof that they ought so to do. Specifically heavy onerous rates in any one district, if due to necessity, of course do naturally fall upon owners to something near the extent of the difference between the rate in the district considered and the average of onerous rates. This is right, since the landowner's rent is caused by special advantages of one district over another, and, if a district is badly situated for drainage or anything of that kind, of course it is not to be expected that such good rents could be had there as elsewhere. To some extent also exceptionally heavy poor-rate should fall, as it does, on owners, because it is a sign that the economic conditions are abnormal. The landowner should normally get only surplus wealth, after the producers have been remunerated. An abnormal number of paupers, as in agricultural districts, may indicate that past history has led to a distribution of wealth not in accordance with that which would have prevailed if labourers had all along been really able to look after their own interests. Landowners may have succeeded in appropriating more than the true economic rent, and in that case they should in justice bear the burden of excessive poor-rate. In so far as the inequality of onerous taxation is not due to these causes, it is mischievous. No doubt readjustments of rent should in course of time equalise the burdens so far as general inhabitants are concerned, but this is done only by causing population to be distributed and capital applied in a way which is not the most advantageous for production. Such inequalities ought therefore to be abolished. Only those inequalities which are due to natural causes should be allowed to remain. It is only, then, in these cases that one can say that any definite part of an onerous rate ought to fall upon the landowner, and it is just in these cases that it does so fall. It is impossible to agree with the Royal Commission Minority that "it is also eminently desirable that the charge which now falls indirectly and irregularly on site value, should, if possible, be made more direct and visible, as well as more accurately and evenly proportioned." As to the advisability of making it more "direct and visible" that is primarily, as Professor Edgeworth says, a question in the art of politics, not a question of economic science. But the idea of making it "more accurately and evenly proportioned" implies wrong views. Any effect there may be, due to diminution of demand, is quite outside the business of government. Why should they not try to make the effect of the beer duty on landowners more accurately and evenly proportioned? And should not the effect upon owners of brickfields and stone quarries be included? Then there are effects on quasi-rents, less durable, perhaps, but often sharper while they do last, losses to bricklayers and builders, house decorators and furniture makers, domestic servants, etc. It is rather a curious argument to say that because rates have a tendency to cause indirect losses to all these people, they are therefore intended to bear part of the burden, and further, that that part should be made more visible and its existence more certain.

Neither should this indirect effect upon rents be regarded as a set-off to indirect gains in other ways. If there were no such thing as an onerous rate the question of "unearned increment" would not be affected. Neither would it be affected if all rates were purely onerous, and every improvement which added cash value to property were undertaken by private enterprise.

24

*Capitalization and Amortization of Taxes**

By LUIGI EINAUDI

The term capitalization of taxes is properly applied to the case of an object which, being totally or partially exempted from a given general tax, rises in value by a sum equivalent to a capitalization at the current rate of interest of the amount of tax saved. The inverse case, that of an object hit by a special tax and as a result reduced in value by the capital value of the tax, may best be described as one of tax amortization. In the first case a buyer would pay for the object its original value plus the capitalized tax saving; in the second case he would pay the original value less the capital value of the tax. Thus if a special land tax reduces the net yield of a farm from $5000 to $4500, the capital value shrinks from $100,000 to $90,000. One who purchases at the latter figure continues to pay over to the state $500, but this is in effect merely interest on the $10,000 saved on the purchase price. The abolition by the state of the $500 annual charge would be equivalent to the free gift of an annuity of this amount or of its capital value, since the farm's value would again rise to $100,000.

The first conscious experiment in tax capitalization was made in 1788 by the Grand Duke Pietro Leopoldo of Tuscany. Landowners were required to pay into the treasury a sum equivalent to the capital value of the tax based on an interest rate of 3.5 per cent. The amount of tax thus redeemed, in terms of capital value, was 8,250,000 scudi out of a possible total of 12,500,000. In 1790, however, the new grand duke, Ferdinand II, yielding to the clamor of the interested parties, canceled the edicts of his predecessor and ordered that the sums paid be refunded and the land tax restored. More successful and better known is Pitt's Redemption Act of 1798 in England, which provided that the land tax, already fixed in 1775 at four shillings per pound, be made perpetual at that rate and that

* Encyclopaedia of the Social Sciences, Vol. III.

taxpayers be permitted to redeem it at the rate of twenty times the amount of the annual charge.

Amortization theory, as applied to the land tax, plays an essential part in the single tax doctrine of Henry George. Once the whole net income from land had been absorbed by taxation the capital value would have disappeared, and any purchaser would have paid only for improvements. Although the purchaser continued to pay the net rental value as a tax the burden would in effect have been thrown back on the one who owned the land when the tax was first imposed.

In 1814 it was pointed out by Craig that the amortization process was not peculiar to the land tax but extended to all "exclusive" taxes; Rau observed that sometimes the fall in capital value consequent on special taxation was obscured by a change in the rate of interest or other factors; and Schäffle stressed the general character of the theory. The classic theory received its most definite formulation at the hands of Seligman, who summarizes as follows the conditions under which amortization may take place: taxation must be unequal, since if there is no excess of a given tax over the general taxation level there is nothing to be capitalized; the object taxed must have a capital value which is susceptible of diminution; the object taxed must be relatively durable in character; the tax must not be capable of being shifted.

Of all these conditions the one which demands the most careful analysis is the first. To be amortized a tax must rest on the taxpayers with unequal weight; but this raises the question, what is equality in taxation? Clearly a flate rate general tax on all income from capital alone is not an equal tax, because it exempts labor incomes. It might lead to the investment of new savings in education, etc., and subtract them from ordinary investments. Thus it might raise the rate of interest and to this extent might reduce capital values. This would mean that such a tax is in some measure amortizable. Are we to regard as equal a general tax on all incomes (capital as well as labor), which in almost all countries is progressive, with exemptions at the bottom, and which frequently differentiates against property incomes? It is obvious that equality of taxation is a very refined and complex idea, which allows for apparent inequalities, intended to equalize the psychological burden of taxation for different taxpayers. An equal tax may be a compound of very unequal separate taxes whose total impact on the several taxpayers is evenly distributed. As this ideal of equal taxation is very difficult of attainment there will always be a residuum of inequality to which the amortization process can be applied.

In the classic theory amortization depends on the circumstance that a special or differential tax does not reduce the general rate of interest in proportion to the rate of taxation. If the rate of interest is 5 per cent a 10 per cent tax on a particular form of income does not change the rate of interest, because new savings can be invested in non-taxed fields. If the tax is general and all fields are equally hit, taxpayers can nowhere find investments free of the tax. All investments will yield a lower net return on account of the tax, but since they all suffer alike the rate of interest will be uniformly reduced from 5 to $4\frac{1}{2}$ per cent, capital values remaining therefore unchanged. In other words no amortization can take place.

It is tacitly assumed, in the classic theory of amortization, that whatever is taken from the taxpayer by either special or general taxation is lost to him completely. If $500 is taken from a $5000 income by a tax it is assumed that the situation of the taxpayer is the same as it would be if his income were diminished an equal amount by natural causes. This assumption has been challenged by Einaudi in a paper published in 1912 and republished in enlarged form in 1919. Einaudi points out that we cannot appraise the effects of an equal tax apart from the effects of the use of the proceeds of the tax. A 10 per cent general tax, as such, reduces all incomes; but without the tax and its use to the furtherance of the state ends economic society could not exist and private incomes would not be forthcoming. An equal tax is not to be regarded merely as a subtraction from private income, but as the portion of the total social income which ought to go to the state if that total income is to reach a maximum. Optimum taxation may be a composite of equal or general taxes, with special or differential taxes on windfall incomes and others which may be deemed worthy of a special burden. The ultimate effect of the introduction of an optimum tax system would in theory be an increase in the total social income and in the flow of new savings, a fall in the rate of interest and a rise in most individual incomes and their capital values. In cases of differential taxation there would be a decrease in the relative amount of the incomes affected. If the effect of this decrease were not counterbalanced by the fall in the rate of interest and the general increase in total social income, the capital value of such specially affected incomes would decline, or in other words the principle of amortization would become operative.

Actual tax systems are far from optimum either as to their structure or as to the use of their yield. Assuming small additions to the existing tax structure, to the extent that such new taxes depart from the optimum they do not increase and may even reduce total social income. The effect on the rate of interest will probably be to raise it above the level which would have obtained without the additional increment of taxation. Most individual incomes would decrease and their capital values would fall. The fall would be particularly marked in the case of incomes subject to special taxation or disproportionately burdened by the general system. Incomes less than proportionately burdened might rise and their capital value increase.

In the actual world the phenomena of capitalization and amortization of taxes rarely, if ever, present themselves in clear outline. Any extensive fiscal change, whether involving mere quantitative increase or a shift in the objects of taxation, is likely to involve both types of phenomena in more or less disguised form.[1]

---

[1] *See:* Taxation; Land Taxation; Single Tax; Property Tax; Income Tax; Capitalization; Interest (Encyclopaedia of the Social Sciences).

Consult: For literature and discussion of tax amortization and capitalization theories: Seligman, E. R. A., *The Shifting and Incidence of Taxation* (5th ed. New York, 1927) p. 174–83, 221–26.

For Tuscan experiment of land tax redemption: Gianni, F. M., "Memoria istorica dello scioglimento del debito pubblico della Toscana" in *Scritti di pubblica economia* (Florence, 1848) p. 145–58.

For variation of capital values theory: Einaudi, L., "Intorno al concetto di reddito imponibile" in R. Accademia della Scienze di Torino, *Memorie*, 2nd ser., Vol. LXIII, pt. ii (1913) 209–318, and "Osservazioni critiche intorno alla teoria dell' ammortamento dell' imposta e teoria delle variazioni neí redditi e nei valori capitali susseguenti all' imposta" in R. Accademia delle Scienze di Torino, *Atti*, Vol. LIV (1919) 1051–1131; Griziotti, B., "Teoria dell' ammortamento delle imposte e sue applicazioni" in *Giornale degli economisti*, 3rd ser., Vol. LVI (1918) 1–37, 57–87, 181–207; Einaudi, L., "Intorno alla metodologia della teoria della capitalizzazione dell' imposta" in *Beiträge zur Finanzwissenschaft; Festgabe für Georg von Schanz*, 2 vols. (Tübingen 1928) Vol. II, p. 69–86, and "Contributo alla ricerca dell' 'ottima imposta' " in *Annali di economia*, Vol. V (1929) 7–244.

All the papers by Einaudi quoted above are now collected in *Saggi sul risparmio e l'imposta* (Turin, 1958).

25

*The Income Burden of Capital Taxes**

By *NICHOLAS KALDOR*

The fundamental criterion for determining whether a particular tax falls on *capital* or on *income*, is not whether it is levied on the one or the other, but whether it is singular (a once-and-for-all-payment) or recurrent. Thus an annual tax on capital is merely a particular species of income-tax; even though it is expressed as a percentage of capital value, and not as a percentage of income; while an income tax which is only expected to remain in operation for a short period (such as the additional income-taxes levied in war-time, in so far as they are expected to be removed once the war is over) is really a levy on capital and not on income.[1] On this criterion, death duties represent a tax on capital; for though they are recurrent (in the sense that they have to be paid each time an estate passes by inheritance) the period of this recurrence is very long; the equivalent annual payment is only a small fraction of the amount payable on a single occasion. They differ moreover from other conceivable taxes on capital—such as a capital levy—in that they are not payable immediately, but at uncertain future periods, when the estate

* *Review of Economic Studies*, Vol. IX, No. 2, (Summer, 1942). Section III of this paper was prepared at the request of the National Institute of Economic and Social Research, and will appear in *The Burden of Taxation*, by F. Shirras and L. Rostas, to be published by the Institute. It is reprinted here by kind permission of the National Institute.

[1] If individuals behaved with the degree of rationality assumed in economic theory, they would charge some proportion of the income tax payable at the present time to capital account, and not to income account. From the point of view of the efficacy of war finance, this practice would no doubt be deplorable. The fact that it is not done (or at any rate not on a scale which purely rational considerations would warrant) can partly be explained by uncertainty as to the duration of the war and the levels of post-war taxation—an uncertainty which, enters, in a sense, disproportionately, into consciousness. But it is also, and perhaps mostly, due to sheer inertia: to the fact that once individuals grow accustomed to charge income taxes to income, and to treat as "net income" what the income-tax authorities regard as their net income, it takes a long time to make them depart from established practice, especially when every such departure necessitates the conscious weighing of future chances and probabilities which most people prefer to avoid. Thus there can be little doubt that if additional taxes of an equivalent yield had been imposed in the form of a special war-time levy on capital, instead of a rise of the income-tax schedules on investment incomes, the effects on consumption would have been very different; though assuming rational behaviour, they should have been the same.

passes by inheritance. The estimate of the burden of these taxes as a percentage of income involves analogous problems to those arising in connection with an immediately payable capital tax—a capital levy—but it is more complicated. It may be helpful, therefore, to consider first what is the burden on income of a capital levy, and then proceed to examine the problem in the case of death duties.

I. THE INCOME BURDEN OF A CAPITAL LEVY

1. It can be assumed that the annual burden of a capital levy from the point of view of the individual whose estate is subjected to it, cannot be less than the reduction of the annual net income of the estate occasioned by the levy. Thus if an individual owns assets whose market value is K and whose annual net income is x, and if the proportion l of the estate is taken away by a levy, we may assume, in the first approximation, that the consequent reduction in annual income is lx^2. It does not follow, however, that the burden of the capital levy lK will be *equal* to that of a permanent annual tax of the amount lx. For, if instead of the levy, the individual were subjected to an income tax of the amount lx which he expected to pay permanently, he would be better off than if he were subjected to the levy; for his annual net income would suffer an equivalent reduction in the two cases, but in the latter case he would also retain command over assets to the value of lK^3. This command over assets, since it confers power on its owner to make use of unforeseen opportunities, and also a certain social distinction, is certainly worth something, quite apart from the income it yields; the owner, therefore, if confronted with the choice of paying a levy, or paying an annual tax, will prefer the latter unless the tax exceeds by some definite amount the income-reduction due to the levy. Thus, if we write $i = \dfrac{x}{K}$ for the average yield of capital, lK the amount of capital reduction due to the levy, lKi will be the annual income reduction due to the levy, while lKr will be the annual-income-tax equivalent of the levy (i.e. the income-tax which will make the owner

---

2 We ignore here the possibility that as a result of a redistribution of assets of different kinds which comprise the estate, annual income may be reduced more or less than in proportion to the reduction of the value of the estate; and we also ignore at this stage that owing to the progression of income taxation, the reduction in *net income* (after payment of income taxes) may be less than in proportion to the reduction in *gross income*.

3 This is because it is here assumed that the imposition of income tax leaves the market value of assets unchanged—i.e., that it reduces the *net percentage yield* of assets, rather than increases their *gross percentage yield*. If it were assumed that the income tax leaves the net percentage yield unchanged, there would be no difference in the two cases. But the latter assumption is not realistic.

indifferent as between paying the tax and paying the levy) where $r > i$. In other words, to obtain the annual burden of the capital levy, we must multiply the capital sum collected with a rate of interest that is higher than the average yield of capital.

2. It can be shown, on the other hand, that the income-tax-equivalent of a capital levy, *from the point of view of the State*—assuming that the State is free to vary the size of its indebtedness—is equal to lKz, where z is the rate of interest at which the Government can borrow, on long term. For by imposing a capital levy—whether its proceeds are used to repay existing indebtedness or as a substitute for current borrowing—the State, by imposing the levy, frees itself from an annual financial obligation equal to that amount.

If we assume that $z = i$, in other words, the rate at which the Government can borrow on long term is equal to the average yield of capital of estates subjected to the levy, the loss to taxpayers will be greater than the gain to the State (both expressed in terms of annual money-value) by the proportion by which r exceeds i. If the imposition of the levy was prompted therefore by purely budgetary considerations—as a means of reducing annual taxation in the future, or of preventing an increase in future annual taxation, due to the larger volume of debt outstanding—it would be preferable to borrow (or keep the volume of debt outstanding constant) and keep annual taxation correspondingly larger, than to impose a levy. Thus a capital levy, as a form of taxation, is in a similar category to indirect taxes (as compared to an income tax), in that it causes a loss of satisfaction to tax-payers which is not compensated by the gain of the State, and which could be avoided if alternative forms of taxation were imposed.[4]

3. There are two other considerations which are sometimes raised in connection with discussions on a capital levy, both intending to show that the net gain to the State will be less than the loss of taxpayers, or even that the net gain to the State can be negative. One is based on the assumption that the average yield of capital to those subjected to the levy is higher than the yield of long-term Government obligations, $(i > z)$ so that by depriving the owner of part of his capital, and using the proceeds to repay the debt, the annual amount which the State saves (given the *rates* of income taxation) through the reduction in the Debt, will be less

---

[4] This is not intended as an exhaustive discussion of the merits of a capital levy, which should take into account other considerations as well. The main argument in favour of a post-war capital levy for repaying the National Debt is distributional: it makes it possible to fix the burden of the Debt on a particular group of taxpayers, the capitalists, rather than diffuse the burden among income-tax payers in general. (In theory, at any rate, the same result could be secured by a differential income-tax on investment incomes).

than the loss of money income to the owner of the capital. If A is obliged to sell assets which yielded him 5 per cent per annum, in order to pay capital levy, and the State uses the proceeds to repay debt which carried interest of 3 per cent, A's loss of money income will clearly exceed the gain of the State by 2 per cent per annum of the amount collected in the levy. If now the existence of income-tax and surtax is taken into account, there is a further loss of tax revenue to the State, which must be deducted in calculating the net gain to the State. This loss of tax revenue, in combination with the discrepancy between i and z, may even cause the *net gain* to the State to be negative, in the sense that the saving in interest payments resulting from the debt-repayment might prove to be less than the loss of tax revenue (at the existing *rates* of taxation) consequent upon the levy. Thus, in terms of our previous example, if A pays over 60 per cent of his marginal income in taxation, the annual loss of tax revenue will be over 3 per cent of the amount collected, as against the 3 per cent which is saved through debt repayment.[5]

These last two considerations are not, however, on the same footing as the argument mentioned earlier, in that they do not set up a discrepancy between the net gain of the State and the net loss of the *body of taxpayers* as a whole. The loss of income tax revenue, consequent upon the levy, will make the net gain of the State less than the apparent gain; but it will also make the net loss of the levy-payer less than the apparent loss. If there is a discrepancy between i and z, (the yield of the assets surrendered through the levy, and the yield of Government loans) there will be a difference between the loss of income of levy-payers and the gain of income to the State; but this difference will be precisely offset by the gain of a third group: of those who held the bonds which were repaid. For the assets which were taken over by the State in connection with the levy, or which were sold by their owners for the purpose of paying the levy, are not physically destroyed: they will, in fact, be taken over by those who were put in possession of investible funds through debt-repayment. If the percentage yield of these assets is higher than the percentage yield of Government bonds, the latter group will now receive a higher money income.[6] (In other words, the cancellation of public debt through repay-

---

[5] This assumes also that the effective rates of income taxation of those paying the capital levy are higher than those who owned the National Debt which was cancelled—otherwise, as will be shown below, there would be an offsetting increase in tax revenue from the latter group.

[6] If the income of this third group of people were taxed at the same rate as that of the capital levy-payers, the net yield of the capital levy to the State could never be negative. The latter view assumes, therefore, not only that the average yield of capital to those subjected to the levy is higher than the yield on Government loans, but also that the levy is so graded, and the ownership of the National Debt is so distributed, as to lead to a net transference of income from heavily-taxed to lightly-taxed groups.

ment will cause an increase in the average percentage yield of all capital assets.) Unless the real return of the assets is less in the hands of the new owners than in the hands of the old owners (which might be the case if the levy forces the surrender of assets for the management of which the old owners were specially qualified), the net loss of money income following upon the levy, for *capitalists as a whole* must be precisely equal to the net gain of the State—though the levy might bring about incidental redistributions of money income between different groups of capitalists. These last two considerations therefore (i.e. differences between i and z, and the subsequent loss of Government revenue from other taxation), unlike the factor mentioned earlier (the difference between r and i) do not constitute an argument against a capital levy as an inferior form of taxation as compared with income tax; though they point to the possibility of certain incidental redistributional effects of the levy, between different groups of capitalists, which however—if they are regarded as undesirable—could be taken account of, in a rough way, when the nature and scale of levy payments are determined.

II. THE INCOME BURDEN OF DEATH DUTIES

1. Death duties are also a charge on capital, and to estimate their income-burden involves the same problems of capitalisation (or rather its opposite) as is the case with the capital levy. They differ from the latter, however, in that they are definitely anticipated a long time before the payments are due, and because of this anticipation, affect the estate-owner's income a long time in advance—strictly from the moment when the estate comes into his possession. The case is similar to that of the business man who in calculating his current profit, must take into account that there are charges on his capital—such as a loan—which at some future date (it may be in the distant future) must be met. This analogy is not complete, however, for while the business man (presumably) pays interest on that part of the capital at his command which was lent to him, there is nothing similar to this in the case of death duties; the sum to be paid in death duties is like an interest-free loan for life—a "life-interest," with the difference, that the beneficiary has command, during his lifetime, over the capital assets themselves as well as over the income from them. Perhaps the best way of approaching the problem is to say that if an individual owns assets whose value is K, and whose average yield is i, so that his current income is Ki, and if the proportion d of his capital is payable in death duties,[7] that part of his current income represented by Kdi

---

[7] For simplicity, we assume at this stage that the death duties payable are a uniform proportion of capital.

is in the nature of a life interest only;[8] a further part, $(K - Kd)$ *di*, is in the nature of a life interest for the present owner *and* his immediate successor, and so on.[9]

The problem of finding the present income-burden of future death duties payable then presents itself as one of translating these series of "life annuities" into their permanent income equivalent. The difference between the width of the annuity-stream, and the width of a permanent income-stream which has the same value to the owner (i.e. which makes him indifferent as between one or the other) is the income-burden of the anticipated death duty payments.

2. That there is such a difference is best shown by applying to this problem the same kind of test which we applied for determining the income-burden of a capital levy. Supposing that the owners of estates were confronted with the choice of compounding all future death duty liabilities by paying a permanent annual tax (additional to other annual taxes to which they are liable), it is clear that there is *some* positive reduction of income which they would prefer to accept rather than leave their estates liable to inheritances taxes. The amount of this reduction may vary greatly between individuals (with estates of the same size); but as against the equivalent annual tax in the case of a capital levy, it is likely to be small. For unlike the capital levy, death duties do not imply any surrender of capital, or of income, in the life time of the individual; events occurring after death (and even more, those occurring after two or three generations), are likely to be heavily discounted (more heavily perhaps, than discounting at ordinary interest rates would warrant) in the estimation of the typical human being. Thus it is quite possible that the sum of these equivalent annual taxes, of all individuals owning estates subject to death duties, would be less than the average receipts from death duties of the State over long periods (or more precisely: that the present discounted value of these equivalent annual taxes should be less than the present discounted value of future revenue from death duties), in which case death duties represent a form of collecting revenue that is superior to income tax—by much the same test by which a capital levy, or taxes on particular commodities, were found inferior to it.

3. We have found that the concept of the "income-burden" of in-

---

[8] Remembering, of course, that it is a specially favourable sort of life interest—where the principal, as well as the interest, is at the disposal of the beneficiary.

[9] These formulae assume, of course, that the present owner (and also his successors) maintains capital constant over lifetime. If he increases it by saving out of income, or reduces it by dissaving, the amount payable in death duties will be greater or less than Kd, (and *mutatis mutandis* for the successors). But provided he has a definite life expectation, and expects to save, or dissave, at a certain rate, similar formulae can be worked out for other, more complicated, cases.

heritance taxes can be given a clear and definite meaning; it is that annual tax on income which gives the owners of the estates the same loss of satisfaction as the future liability for death duties. This can also be expressed by saying, that there is *some* rate of interest by means of which the anticipated death duty payments can be converted into a perpetual annual payment of equal significance to the owner—by discounting the future payments down to the present, and multiplying this discounted value by that rate of interest. What this rate of interest is, cannot, however, be directly inferred from statistically observable data—any more than is the case with the income-tax-equivalent of a capital levy, or with the equivalent income tax corresponding to any given sum raised by commodity taxation. It is one of those things which can only be discovered by knowing the individual's "indifference curves." It might indeed be argued that since an individual is supposed to distribute his consumption over time in such a way as to equate the marginal rate of time preference to the market rate of interest, it is this "market rate" which should be used in discounting future payments into their equivalent in terms of present capital value, and in converting present capital value into an annual flow. But there is really no necessity why the results reached in this way should be identical with that obtained (theoretically) by our first test. For one thing, recent work in the theory of saving has cast doubt on the proposition that the individual's marginal rate of time preference, and the market rate, are equal;[10] but even if the proposition were true (and the "market rate" were something entirely unambiguous and tangible, which it is not) it is only when discounting payments (or receipts) anticipated in the *near future*, that we could rely on it. There is no necessity why the psychological rate of discount applicable for long periods should be identical with that applying to short periods; and it is with the problem of discounting over relatively long periods that we are concerned here.

Unless one gives up the attempt of forming some quantitative estimate of the actual burden of death duties as a proportion of income altogether, it is imperative, however, that *some* rate of interest should be chosen, for converting the future loss of income consequent upon death duties, or the future death duty payments, into the equivalent in terms of an annual tax on present income, and for the purposes of the estimate which is given below, it was decided to employ the "average yield of capital"—i.e. the rate of interest which emerges by dividing the estate owner's "statutory income," with the market value of his assets (as assessed for death duty purposes).[11] In the light of the considerations above, this must be con-

---

[10] Cf. Pigou, *Employment and Equilibrium*, p. 126.
[11] In 1937–38 this rate was around 4 per cent on the average.

sidered arbitrary; but the choice of any other rate would have been even more arbitrary; this element of arbitrariness is in the nature of the problem, and cannot be eliminated, whatever method of calculation is chosen.[12]

III. A QUANTITATIVE ESTIMATE OF THE ANNUAL BURDEN OF DEATH DUTIES IN GREAT BRITAIN

1. It follows from the argument of the previous section that the annual burden of death duties is a sum standing in the same proportion to the present annual net income as the present discounted value of all future death duties payable bears to the present value of the total estate. This formula, however, requires some modification when account is taken of the existence of income tax and surtax. In so far as the payment of death duties reduces the size of the estate, it also relieves the estate from some of the taxes which would otherwise be payable in the form of income tax and surtax. The present discounted value which is relevant for calculating the net burden of death duties is not, therefore, the discounted value of the future death duties as such, but the *difference caused by death duties in the discounted value of all future tax payments;* in other words, the difference between (*a*) the discounted value of all future payments on account of income tax, surtax, and the death duties; and (*b*) the discounted value of the income tax and surtax that would have to be paid in the future if there were no death duties to be paid. It is the ratio which this difference bears to the total value of the estate which determines the proportion of net income which should be allocated to death duties.

Looked at in another way, the burden of death duties is the net reduction of the income-stream of an estate occasioned by it. This is shown, as a proportion of current net income, by comparing the discounted value of the expected net income-stream of an estate when there are no death duties, with the discounted value of the net income-stream, when future net income is reduced by successive death-duty payments. The proportion by which the second of these discounted values falls short of the first is the proportion of current net income which should be allocated to death duties. These two ways of approach must yield identical results if the rate

---

[12] If a higher rate of interest had been chosen, this would have made the amount of the annual burden, in any given case, less, for the reduction in terms of present discounted value, due to discounting future payments at a higher rate, would have more than compensated for the higher income-loss corresponding to any given magnitude of this discounted value. Some indication of the sensitivity of these estimates to changes in the interest rate is given in note 24, page 408 below.

of interest employed in discounting is the same as that which relates the income of the estate to the capital.

2. It follows from these considerations that the annual burden of death duties on present income can only be determined if definite assumptions are made not only as to the future rates of taxation (the future rates of income tax and surtax, as well as the future rate of death duties payable), and the future rates of interest; but also as regards the changes in the *size* of the estate in the lifetime of each generation, i.e. the rate of saving or dis-saving, both present and future. The burden of death duties as a proportion of income will be all the greater, the greater the proportion of the income devoted to saving. Thus, if an estate owner consumes the whole of his capital in his lifetime—by exchanging his capital for a life annuity, for instance—the estate escapes the payment of death duties altogether; while if the estate-owner in each generation "saves up" for death duties—so that the estate is passed on intact despite the payment of death duties—the actual amount of death duties to be paid, and thus the annual burden as a proportion of income, will be greater, and in some categories of estates much greater, than if the size of the estate is allowed to be depleted by the payment of death duties in each successive generation.

3. The "insurance method," which was adopted by the Colwyn Committee,[13] really amounts to a special case of our general formula, given above. If it is assumed that the owner in each generation saves an annual sum, the accumulated value of which is just sufficient to allow the estate to pass intact to his successor—or, what (subject to a qualification made in paragraph 7 below) amounts to the same thing, if he takes out a life-insurance policy which is sufficient to cover the total amount of death duties payable, including the increase in the duty due to the policy, and if he does not save otherwise—the net addition to the discounted value of all taxes payable caused by death duties is just equal to the discounted value of the death duties paid (since, in this case, there is no reduction in capital in successive generations, hence no reduction, consequent upon death duties, in the payments of income tax and surtax); and the annual burden of death duties (if the rate of interest used in discounting is the same as the one at which the savings are accumulated) is just equal to the annual savings. In this case, therefore, but only in this case, the annual burden of death duties can alternatively be looked upon either as the interest on the discounted value of *net* death-duty payments, or the annual

---

[13] Cf. Barna, "Death Duties in Terms of an Annual Tax," *Review of Economic Studies*, November, 1941, pp. 28 et. seq., for an account of the methods adopted in previous enquiries.

savings, made out of income, which provide a "special fund" out of which death duties are paid.

It will be readily seen, however, that by "saving up" for death duties estate-owners make the estate liable to much heavier payments of death duties than would be the case if they did not save up for it. This is partly because the size of the estate is increased by the accumulated savings; partly also because the more distant death-duty payments, made by successive heirs to the estate, will be on a *constant amount of capital*, instead of on a diminishing amount. The annual burden of death duties, as calculated by the "insurance method," cannot therefore be regarded as *the* burden of death duties, applicable in all cases; or, rather, it is only applicable in those cases where estate-owners do, in fact, save up a sufficient amount to leave their property intact to their successors. It is unlikely that this is the usual practice, especially for the larger estates.

4. For certain categories of property-owners it may well be the case that savings made during lifetime are sufficient, or more than sufficient, to cover the payment of death duties on inheritance.[14] In those cases, the insurance method, if properly calculated,[15] gives the correct approximation of the true burden. But in the case of estates beyond a certain critical size—this critical size was the estate of £331,000 with the tax system of 1937–38, and of £86,000 with the tax system of 1941–42—it would be futile for estate-owners to save up for the *full* amount of the death duties, for this policy would leave the estate with a smaller *permanent* net income (after paying income tax and surtax) than would be obtained if estate-owners saved less.[16] For still larger estates, it would be impossible to save up for the full amount; and here the assumptions of the insurance method yield nonsensical results. For these estates—which were estates of more than £1,073,000 in 1937–38 and of more than £190,000 in 1941–42—the necessary annual insurance premium, together with income tax and surtax, would amount to more than the total income of the estate, so that the insurance premia could only be paid out of capital (with the result that at death the size of the estate, and hence the death duties to be paid, would be smaller than the amount on the basis of which the insurance premia were calculated).[17] Thus the insurance method is a *sensible* method of calculating the burden only for estates *below a certain size*;

---

[14] The size of the estate might also increase through "capital gains"—unexpected capital appreciation, occurring in the future—but this factor must, of course, be ignored in calculating the burden on *current* income.

[15] Cf. paragraph 6, p. 404 below.

[16] Cf. also p. 406 below.

[17] But quite apart from this, any method of calculation which suggests that the total burden of direct taxation—income tax, surtax and death duties—amounts to more than 100 per cent of income is clearly misleading, for so long as the sum of income tax and surtax amounts to less than 100 per cent, the existence of death duties cannot make the burden *more*

and it is the *correct* method only if the typical estate-owners in those categories do, in fact, behave in the manner assumed, and save up during lifetime, either by insurance, or in some other way, an amount sufficient to cover death duties.

5. In the November, 1941, issue of the *Review of Economic Studies* Mr. T. Barna has put forward a method for measuring the annual burden of death duties which is different both from the insurance method adopted by the Colwyn Committee and the one adopted in the present inquiry. His method consists of converting death duties into an equivalent annual tax by multiplying an estate-owner's *potential death duties* (i.e. the death duties for which his estate would be liable if he died now), with the probability of death within the current year—his "rate of risk." This probability, and hence the annual burden of death duties on this method, varies of course with the age of the estate owner; but since it is possible to calculate the typical age of estate owners in any particular capital-group, we can derive the relevant annual tax, for each income-and-capital-category, by multiplying potential death duties with the mortality rates typical for the group.

An alternative way of describing Mr. Barna's method is to say that the annual burden of death duties on his definition, is equal to the insurance premium an estate owner would have to pay in order to insure against the risk of dying, and the consequent death duty liabilities, *in the current year*. His method, therefore, amounts to assuming an alternative form of insurance against death duties—an annual, instead of a whole life insurance—and if the rate of interest at which the insurance company accumulates life insurance premiums is the same as the one that is relevant to the estate-owner's own savings, the discounted value of the series of insurance premiums which the estate owner can expect to pay during his lifetime under Mr. Barna's method (by paying out an annual insurance, year by year, until his death) should be the same as the discounted value of the sum of the life-insurance premiums, for a policy of equal value. (The amount payable *annually* will not be the same, of course, with the two methods; with the whole life method, it will be a constant annual amount;

---

than 100 per cent of income as long as the rate of death duties is less than 100 per cent of capital. This becomes obvious when it is remembered that however many times an estate is subjected to death duties, the remaining part of the estate must still have some positive value. Thus, if the estate passed by inheritance n times, the $(n + 1)th$ heir would still derive some positive income from it, however large is n. The *present* net income from the estate, after allowing for taxation, must be greater than the net income of the $(n + 1)$th heir. Another demonstration of the absurdity of the insurance method when applied to very large incomes can be derived from the reflection that it asks us to believe that the higher is gross income the lower is net income (net after income tax, surtax and death duties). If it were really true that beyond a certain point, net income decreases with the size of the estate, estate owners would enrich themselves by abandoning their superfluous capital.

with Mr. Barna's method, it will be lower than the former in the early years, and higher in late years of life). Mr. Barna's method is subject, therefore, to the same kind of objection as the insurance method of the Colywn Committee: it is not applicable to *all* estate-owners, but only to those who save up a sufficient amount over their lifetime to pass their estates (*net* of death duties) intact to their successors. For the higher categories of estates this is not only an unlikely, but an impossible assumption.

6. The particular form of the insurance method adopted by the Colwyn Committee, suffers, moreover, from another defect: it was there assumed that estate-owners take out an insurance policy at the age of 45. The age at which the policy is taken out cannot, however, be arbitrarily chosen; since the purpose of the calculation is to provide the equivalent of a constant annual burden, the age assumed for taking out the life-insurance policy must be such as to provide an expectation of life which corresponds to the average length of a generation, i.e. the average interval of time during which the estate remains in the possession of a single owner. With the present life expectation, the Colwyn Committee's assumption of the age of 45 for taking out a policy implies an average length of generation of 25.5 years. The average length of a generation is, however, about 31 years.[18] Hence the right assumption is, for this method that the policy is taken out at the age of 38, since this gives an expectation of life of 31 years.

Calculations prior to the Colwyn Committee's—such as one given by the Chancellor of the Exchequer in answer to a Parliamentary question in 1918[19] and Sir Herbert Samuel's in 1919[20]—assumed the age of 40, which might well have been the right figure for that period, since it is

---

[18] Mr. Barna has calculated this figure by the following method. Assuming that the line of succession is from father to son and that the son is expected to die at the same age as the father, the length of a generation, i.e. the period which elapses from the time the son inherits his father's estate until his death, equals the age of the father when his son was born.

From preliminary data of the Bristol survey the following can be extracted (E. Grebenik; *Journal of the Royal Statistical Society*, 1940, p. 306):

In the highest occupational group the average age of mothers at the birth of their first child was 27.95, second child 30.50, third child 31.91; on the average 29.64 years.

Usually the first son inherits. The age of mother when the first son is born is the average between the age when the first child and when the second child is born, which in Bristol was 29.23 years. But as not all first sons live long enough to inherit we ought to take a figure somewhere between the age when the first son is born and the age when the average child is born.

In 1910–15, which can be considered as the relevant period for our purpose, the difference between the mean ages of bachelors and spinsters who were married was 1 9 years, the men being older (*Registrar General's Statistical Review of England and Wales*, 1937, Part II, p. 65. Mean age of bachelors marrying spinsters 27.2, of spinsters marrying bachelors 25.3 years). Hence the average age of fathers when their son who inherits is born was between 31.1 and 31.5 years. Therefore the length of generation is estimated to be 31 years.

[19] Cf. *H.C. Debates*, 11 July, 1918, 108, 53, p. 511.

[20] Cf. "The taxation of the various classes of the people," *J.R.S.S.*, 1919.

likely that the age at which parents beget children has risen somewhat in the meantime.

7. It follows from what has been said above, that the correct approximation for assessing the annual burden of death duties can only be obtained by taking into account the *expected* increment in the size of the estates between inheritance and death, as inferred from the actual rate of savings in the various income groups.[21] Unfortunately, however, there are no data available for the distribution of personal savings in various income categories. The only possible way of proceeding therefore appeared to be to work out the burden of death duties for *two special cases*, which may be looked upon as the limits within which the actual burden, in the great majority of cases, is likely to fall.[22] The estimates of burden thus derived can, with some looseness of language, be called the Minimum Burden and the Maximum Burden.

The first assumption, that of the Minimum Burden, the results of which are given in Table 1 below, is that the estate-owners of the present, and every successive generation, maintain their capital constant during lifetime (i.e. that there is *zero net saving* during the lifetime of each generation), so that the value of the estate inherited by the nth heir[23] is equal to the estate inherited by the $(n-1)$th heir minus the death duties paid on his death. Here the amount of death duties to be paid by successive generations will be a diminishing series, since the estate will be smaller on every successive inheritance. The figures in Table 1 were so arranged as to show the calculation of the burden by *both* methods mentioned in paragraph 2 above—as the difference caused by death duties in the discounted value of future net income. Thus, column (3) shows the discounted value of tax payments, on the assumption that the estate yields

---

[21] Just as in the case of indirect taxes, the actual burden is calculated on the basis of the *actual consumption* of the taxed articles (without taking into account how much this consumption is itself altered by the existence of the tax), in the case of death duties, the calculation of the burden must be based on the actual distribution of income between consumption and saving—i.e. by taking into account just that increment in the size of the estate which results from this rate of saving—since it can be presumed that, in deciding how much to save, estate-owners take the existence of death duties into account along with all the other factors (such as the rate of interest) which are relevant to their decisions.

[22] These two special cases are not true "limiting cases" in the sense that the burden cannot lie outside them *under any circumstances*. The *true minimum burden* of death duties would be reached under the assumption that the estate-owner consumes all his capital in his lifetime; in this case the burden of death duties is nil. The *true maximum burden* would be obtained if we assume that the owner of the estate, in each generation, saves up the whole of his "free income," i.e. the whole of his income after income tax and surtax have been paid. This gives the maximum possible increment in the size of the estate in the lifetime of each generation. But neither of these cases appeared to us sufficiently typical of real life to warrant its consideration.

[23] It is assumed throughout these estimates that estates pass on to a *single heir*. If they pass on to several heirs, the successive death duties paid will be smaller. On the significance of this assumption, cf. p. 411 below.

the present income permanently and no death duties are paid. Column (6) shows the present discounted value of all future death duties payable, and column (7) the present discounted value of income tax and surtax payments, when the size of the estate is reduced in successive generations by the death-duty payments. Thus the difference in the corresponding figures between column (3) and column (7) shows the reduction in the payment of other direct taxation resulting from death duties. Alternatively, column (4) and column (8) show, respectively, the discounted value of net income in the absence of death duties, and allowing for death duties. Column (9) brings the two methods together. It shows the discounted value of the net burden of death duties, and it equals *either* column (6) minus the difference between columns (3) and (7) *or* the difference between columns (4) and (8). Finally, this discounted value is converted into a net annual burden in column (10).

The second assumption, that of the Maximum Burden, the results of which are given in Table 2, is that estate-owners in each generation save out of income an amount sufficient to *maintain the net income of the estate constant over successive generations*, in spite of the payment of death duties, so far as that objective is attainable. Up to a certain capital level—the "critical level"—which, as mentioned earlier, was an estate of £331,000 in 1937–38 and of £86,000 in 1941–42, this assumption implies an annual rate of savings the accumulated value of which is just sufficient to pay the death duties (including the increase in death duties due to the accumulation) and leave the estate intact to the successor; it is identical, therefore, with the assumptions made by the Colwyn Committee. Beyond that critical level, however (i.e. for larger estates) the assumption of maintaining the capital intact would have produced a *smaller* net income than could be obtained on the critical level estate. For the owners of the larger estates it would therefore be pointless, if not impossible, to maintain the capital intâct. In fact, for the owners of thèse estates it would be pointless to save up anything at all for death duties, since by doing so, they cannot prevent the reduction in the size of the estate to the critical level; by saving they merely postpone the time at which the estate is so reduced, at the cost of sacrificing the income from the estate in the intervening period. Saving only becomes worth while after the estate has fallen to this level.

For these estates (which are those calculated by Method (*c*) in Table 2) it was assumed that annual savings out of income are equal to the savings on estates of the critical level. This, of course, is purely arbitrary; to assume that the owners in these categories saved nothing at all would have given results identical with Table 1, whereas the whole purpose of Table 2 is to show the added burden of death duties due to savings; moreover, it is justifiable to assume that owners of large estates do, in fact, save something out of their income and, to that extent, make themselves liable to larger payments of death duties.

It will be noted that these assumptions make the annual burden of death duties (the Maximum Burden) identical with annual savings for estates which are less than the critical size and more than the annual savings for estates which are greater.

For the smaller estates it was assumed that savings take either the form of direct accumulation (at the same gross rate of interest which relates the income to the capital of the estate) or else the form of life-insurance premiums, whichever secures the higher net income. For the lower categories of income (those calculated by Method (*a*) in Table 2), which are not subject to income tax, or else pay income tax at a reduced rate, direct accumulation yields the lower burden, for the reason that the income from investments of insurance companies is subject to income tax, and insurance premiums carry therefore a lower rate of interest. For higher categories of incomes (those calculated by Method (*b*) in Table 2) savings in the form of life insurance yield a higher net income, largely owing to the income tax rebates which are allowable on insurance premiums but not on other forms of saving.

Table 3 shows the total burden of direct taxation (income tax, surtax and death duties) under both assumptions. Since the net burden of death duties, especially in the higher categories of income, is greatly influenced by the payment of income tax and surtax, for purposes of comparison between different years Table 3 is the really instructive one, and not Tables 1 and 2. In particular the reduction of the net burden of death duties between 1937–38 and 1941–42 shown in Table 1, and also to some extent in Table 2, might be misleading if considered in isolation, since it was not due to any reduction in the rates of death duties payable (which were, in fact, increased between these two financial years), but is exclusively due to the compensating effect of increases in the other forms of direct taxation.

Table 4 shows the annual burden of death duties with the insurance method, assuming the policy is taken out at the age of 38 (instead of the age of 45, assumed by the Colwyn Committee). This was included in order to enable a comparison to be made with earlier calculations.

8. Throughout these calculations, which were prepared by Mr. T. Barna, the following assumptions were made:

(i) The average yield of capital was assumed to be 4 per cent both for 1937–38 and 1941–42. The Colwyn Committee assumed an average yield of 5 per cent, but this was considered too high for recent years.

(ii) The length of a generation was assumed to be 31 years, and the death duties payable in the first instance were discounted 31 years, those in the second instance 62 years, and so on. It might be objected that since all the estates in existence at a particular moment will become liable for death duties over a period which, on the average, is only 15.5 years (since, on the average, present estate-owners must already have been in possession of their estates for a period equal to half the length of a generation), the death duties payable *in the first instance* should only be discounted for 15.5 years, and not 31 years. It must be remembered, however, that the purpose of the calculation is to provide the equivalent of a constant annual burden of death duties; if the death duties payable in the first instance had been discounted only for 15.5 years, this would have implied the assumption that there had been no burden on account of death duties, on the income from the estates during the first half of the generation.

(iii) The average yield of capital, the rates of income tax, surtax and death duties were assumed to be the same for all future years as they actually were in the particular years for which the calculations were made. This, of course, is a much more realistic assumption for 1937–38 than for 1941–42 (since income tax and surtax can hardly be expected to remain permanently at their war-time level), with the result that the figures for 1937–38 have more claim to be regarded as a true representation of the burden than those for 1941–42.

(iv) Future tax payments and future net income were discounted at the same rate of interest as that assumed for the average yield of capital, i.e. at 4 per cent. This assumption of a single rate of interest, applicable to all income and capital groups, is, of course, arbitrary. It should be borne in mind, however, that the rate of discount only enters into the determination of the annual burden in so far as it affects the *relation* between two capital values (i.e. the relation between the discounted value of net income with or without death duties); and changes in the rate of discount will only affect the figures for the annual burden to a significant extent if they are considerable.[24]

---

[24] If the rate of interest employed is not the same as that assumed for the average yield of capital (the ratio between income and estate) the annual burden as calculated by discounting net incomes (column 4, *minus* column 8 in Table 1) is no longer the same as that obtained by discounting tax payments (column 6, *minus* [column 3—column 7] in Table 1); the latter method giving *lower* figures for the annual burden than the former method, if the rate of interest chosen is *lower* than the average yield of capital, and *higher* figures, if it is *higher*. But with both of these methods, the figures obtained would have been *smaller* than those actually shown, if a *higher* rate of interest had been employed, and *vice-versa*. Thus, if a 2 per cent rate had been employed, instead of the 4 per cent rate, the figures for 1937–38 in column 11 of Table 1, obtained by discounting net incomes (column 4, *minus* column 8) would have been changed from 2 to 5.4 per cent for the annual income of £100, from 4.67 to 11.65 per cent for the income of £2,000, and from 5.43 to 12.09 per cent for the income of £50,000. If instead the figures had been computed by the alternative method of discounting tax payments, the differences caused by changing the rate of interest from 4 per cent to 2 per cent would have been much smaller.

TABLE 1

Net Annual Burden of Death Duties, Assuming Zero Net Saving During Each Generation Husband, Wife and Two Dependent Children

(1) Investment Income £	(2) Equivalent Estate £	(3) Discounted Value of Income Tax and Surtax in the Absence of Death Duties £	(4) Discounted Value of Net Income in the Absence of Death Duties [(2)−(3)] £	(5) Rate of Death Duties Payable in the First Instance (See Table 5) %	(6) Discounted Value of Death Duties Payable £	(7) Discounted Value of Income Tax and Surtax Allowing for Death Duties £	(8) Discounted Value of Net Income Allowing for Death Duties [(2)−(6)−(7)] £	(9) Net Discounted Value of Burden of Death Duties [(4)−(8)] = (6)+(7)−(3) £	(10) Annual Net Burden [4 % of (9)] £ s.	(11) Annual Net Burden as Percentage of Income
						1937–38				
100	2,500	—	2,500	4.84	50	—	2,450	50	2 0	2.00
150	3,750	—	3,750	4.84	75	—	3,675	75	3 0	2.00
200	5,000	—	5,000	4.84	100	—	4,900	100	4 0	2.00
250	6,250	—	6,250	5.82	150	—	6,100	150	6 0	2.39
300	7,500	—	7,500	5.82	180	—	7,320	180	7 4	2.39
350	8,750	104	8,646	5.82	209	88	8,453	193	7 14	2.20
500	12,500	688	11,812	6.80	332	605	11,503	249	9 19	2.00
1,000	25,000	3,813	21,187	11.25	1,089	3,533	20,378	809	32 7	3.24
2,000	50,000	10,063	39,937	16.13	3,122	9,280	37,598	2,339	93 11	4.67
2,500	62,500	13,875	48,625	18.08	4,339	12,625	45,536	3,089	123 11	4.94
5,000	125,000	37,234	87,766	23.93	11,108	32,850	81,042	6,724	268 19	5.39
10,000	250,000	98,047	151,953	27.83	25,786	85,225	138,989	12,964	518 11	5.18
20,000	500,000	239,609	260,391	33.68	61,229	205,000	233,771	26,620	1,064 16	5.33
50,000	1,250,000	708,984	541,016	41.48	182,793	594,125	473,082	67,934	2,717 7	5.43
						1941–42				
100	2,500	—	2,500	4.84	50	—	2,450	50	2 0	2.00
150	3,750	—	3,750	4.84	75	—	3,675	75	3 0	2.00
200	5,000	—	5,000	4.84	100	—	4,900	100	4 0	2.00
250	6,250	81	6,169	5.82	150	58	6,042	127	5 2	2.01
300	7,500	488	7,012	5.82	180	430	6,810	122	4 18	1.62
350	8,750	894	7,856	5.82	209	826	7,715	141	5 13	1.62
500	12,500	2,528	9,972	7.78	383	2,345	9,772	200	8 0	1.60
1,000	25,000	8,778	16,222	13.01	1,290	8,138	15,572	650	26 0	2.60
2,000	50,000	21,278	28,722	18.86	3,601	19,480	26,919	1,803	72 2	3.60
2,500	62,500	28,778	33,722	22.76	5,238	25,788	31,474	2,248	89 18	3.59
5,000	125,000	70,809	54,191	30.37	13,758	60,963	50,279	3,912	156 10	3.14
10,000	250,000	171,434	78,566	35.44	31,915	146,025	72,060	6,506	260 5	2.61
20,000	500,000	404,247	95,753	43.05	74,901	335,100	90,000	5,754	230 3	1.15
50,000	1,250,000	1,135,497	114,503	53.19	224,283	917,625	108,090	6,411	256 9	0.51

TABLE 2

Net Annual Burden of Death Duties, Assuming Maintenance of Maximum Net Income
Husband, Wife and Two Dependent Children
(For an explanation of Methods (a)—(c) see note below.)

Method	(1) Investment Income £	(2) Equivalent Estate £	(3) Estate Plus Value of Accumulated Savings £	(4) Rate of Death Duties (See Table 5) %	(5) Death Duties Payable £	(6) Annual Savings £ s.	(7) Income Tax and Surtax £ s.	(8) Net Income [(1)—(6)—(7)] £	(9) Interest on Discounted Future Net Incomes £	(10) Net Burden [(6) or (1)—(7)—(9)] £ s.	(11) Annual Net Burden as % of Income
						1937–38					
(a)	100	2,500	2,627	4.84	127	2 1	—	98	—	2 1	2.06
(a)	150	3,750	3,941	4.84	191	3 2	—	147	—	3 2	2.06
(a)	200	5,000	5,309	5.82	309	5 0	—	195	—	5 0	2.50
(a)	250	6,250	6,636	5.82	386	6 5	—	244	—	6 5	2.50
(a)	300	7,500	7,963	5.82	463	8 0	—	292	—	8 0	2.66
(a)	350	8,750	9,291	5.82	541	9 6	—	337	—	9 6	2.66
(a)	500	12,500	13,555	7.78	1,055	20 9	4 3	452	—	20 9	4.09
(a)	1,000	25,000	28,484	12.23	3,484	67 12	27 10	780	—	67 12	6.76
(b)	2,000	50,000	61,035	18.08	11,035	220 0	152 10	1,377	—	220 0	11.00
(b)	2,500	62,500	78,154	20.03	15,654	315 1	402 10	1,630	—	315 1	12.60
(b)	5,000	125,000	168,645	25.88	43,645	899 14	555 0	6,211	—	899 14	24.64
(c)	10,000	250,000	366,193	31.73	116,193	2,464 5	1,489 8	3,614	6,320	2,464 5	24.64
(c)	20,000	500,000	668,390	37.58	251,181	3,597 0	3,921 18	—	15,754	4,096 0	20.48
(c)	50,000	1,250,000	1,418,390	43.44	616,149	3,597 0	9,584 8	—	—	5,887 0	11.77
						1941–42					
(a)	100	2,500	2,627	4.84	127	2 1	—	98	—	2 1	2.06
(a)	150	3,750	3,941	4.84	191	3 2	—	147	—	3 2	2.06
(a)	200	5,000	5,309	5.82	309	5 0	—	195	—	5 0	2.50
(a)	250	6,250	6,636	5.82	386	7 7	3 5	239	—	7 7	2.93
(a)	300	7,500	7,963	5.82	463	8 16	19 10	272	—	8 16	2.93
(a)	350	8,750	9,291	5.82	541	10 5	35 15	304	—	10 5	2.93
(a)	500	12,500	13,730	8.96	1,230	23 7	101 3	375	—	23 7	4.67
(a)	1,000	25,000	29,131	14.18	4,131	78 8	351 3	570	—	78 8	7.84
(b)	2,000	50,000	64,733	22.76	14,733	280 10	851 3	868	—	280 10	14.03
(b)	2,500	62,500	83,668	25.30	21,168	413 19	1,151 3	935	—	413 19	16.56
(c)	5,000	125,000	158,391	32.90	52,111	667 0	2,832 8	—	1,425	743 0	14.86
(c)	10,000	250,000	283,391	37.97	107,604	667 0	6,857 8	—	2,286	857 0	8.57
(c)	20,000	500,000	533,391	45.58	243,120	667 0	16,169 18	—	2,955	875 0	4.37
(c)	50,000	1,250,000	1,283,391	55.72	698,266	667 0	45,419 18	—	3,502	1,078 0	2.16

(v) It was assumed that the estate, on each successive occasion, is inherited by a *single heir*. The extent of the error introduced by this assumption is less than might at first be supposed. It can only affect the burden of death duties in terms of present discounted value, and thus on current income, in so far as the death duties paid on the second instance and subsequently are payable at a lower rate. But since the death duties payable in the second instance are discounted for 62 years (and those paid subsequently for 93 years or more) this factor is unlikely to cause a considerable difference to the present discounted value. The discounted value of *all* future tax payments can, of course, be considerably altered, if the estate is broken up after the death of the present owner, since the estate might then become liable to much lower income tax and surtax payments. But this latter factor is irrelevant for the purposes of our calculation, since we are not interested in the discounted value of tax payments as such, but only in the difference caused by the payments of death duties to this discounted value.

(vi) It was assumed that the whole estate is subject to death duties. Actually, some proportion of estates escape the payment of death duties altogether, since they are passed on, from one generation to the next, by settlements during lifetime. It is impossible to discover statistically what

---

NOTE TO TABLE 2

(*a*) Annual savings are accumulated in order that at death they should cover death duties payable. With the 4 per cent rate of interest used a saving of 1.62 per cent is necessary to obtain £100 31 years hence. If income tax is payable accumulation takes place at a rate of interest of $4(1 - t)$ per cent only where t is the marginal rate of income and surtax above the given income. The rates of saving for different marginal rates of income and surtax are as follows:

Marginal Rate of Income and Surtax in the £	Annual Saving to Obtain £100 at Death %
1s. 8d.	1.72
5s. 0d.	1.94
6s. 1½d.	1.99
6s. 6d.	2.05

Column (6) is Column (5) multiplied by the rate of saving, otherwise the table is similar to Table 4.

(*b*) It has been found that for incomes of £2,500 and over in 1937–38 and for all incomes liable to income tax in 1941–42, the modified insurance method as set out in detail in Table 4 yields a lower burden than the method of accumulation, therefore it was assumed that the individual insures instead of accumulating his own savings.

(*c*) For incomes which, with the insurance method, would yield less than the critical net income it was assumed that the amount of saving is just as much as was the amount of premiums paid to cover death duties on the critical estate, which amounted to £3,597 in 1937–38 and £667 in 1941–42. Estate is allowed to fall after death in successive generations until it reaches the critical level where it is maintained. Column (2)—(4) refer to the estate in the first instance.

the proportion of settled estates is in the total, and even if data were obtainable, it is questionable whether allowance should be made for them. For the proportion of estates which thus escapes the payment of death duties varies very widely from case to case; the *average* proportion therefore gives very little information of the proportion which is *typical* in the various income groups.

It should be borne in mind, however, that the omission of this factor makes the burden of death duties, in both of the assumed cases, appear *larger* than it is in reality.

TABLE 3

THE TOTAL BURDEN OF DIRECT TAXES ON INVESTMENT INCOMES

Husband, Wife and Two Dependent Children

INVESTMENT INCOME £	INCOME AND SURTAX %	ANNUAL NET BURDEN OF DEATH DUTIES		TOTAL BURDEN	
		Assumption I %	Assumption II %	Assumption I %	Assumption II %
1937-38					
100	—	2.00	2.06	2.00	2.06
150	—	2.00	2.06	2.00	2.06
200	—	2.00	2.50	2.00	2.50
250	—	2.39	2.50	2.39	2.50
300	—	2.39	2.66	2.39	2.66
350	1.19	2.20	2.66	3.39	3.85
500	5.50	2.00	4.09	7.50	9.59
1,000	15.25	3.24	6.76	18.49	22.01
2,000	20.13	4.67	11.00	24.80	31.13
2,500	22.20	4.94	12.60	27.14	34.80
5,000	29.78	5.39	17.90	35.17	47.77
10,000	39.22	5.18	24.64	44.40	63.86
20,000	47.92	5.33	20.48	53.25	68.40
50,000	56.72	5.43	11.77	62.15	68.49
1941–42					
100	—	2.00	2.06	2.00	2.06
150	—	2.00	2.06	2.00	2.06
200	—	2.00	2.50	2.00	2.50
250	1.30	2.01	2.93	3.31	4.23
300	6.50	1.62	2.93	8.12	9.43
350	10.21	1.62	2.93	11.83	13.14
500	20.23	1.60	4.67	21.83	24.90
1,000	35.11	2.60	7.84	37.71	42.95
2,000	42.56	3.60	14.03	46.16	56.59
2,500	46.05	3.59	16.56	49.64	62.61
5,000	56.64	3.14	14.86	59.78	71.50
10,000	68.57	2.61	8.57	71.18	77.14
20,000	80.85	1.15	4.37	82.00	85.22
50,000	90.84	0.51	2.16	91.35	93.00

TABLE 4

THE BURDEN OF DEATH DUTIES CALCULATED WITH THE INSURANCE METHOD
Value of Policy Included in Estate;* Policy Taken Out at Age of 38; Husband, Wife and Two Dependent Children

(1) Investment Income £	(2) Equivalent Estate £	(3) Estate Plus Value of Policy £	(4) Rate of Death Duties (See Table) %	(5) Death Duties Payable £	(6) Gross Insurance Premium £ s.	(7) Income Tax Rebate £ s.	(8) Net Insurance Premium £ s.	(9) Net Insurance Premiums as Percentage of Income
				1937–38				
100	2,500	2,627	4.84	127	2 18	—	2 18	2.92
150	3,750	3,941	4.84	191	4 8	—	4 8	2.92
200	5,000	5,309	5.82	309	7 2	—	7 2	3.56
250	6,250	6,636	5.82	386	8 18	—	8 18	3.56
300	7,500	7,963	5.82	463	10 14	—	10 14	3.56
350	8,750	9,291	5.82	541	12 9	1 1	11 8	3.26
500	12,500	13,555	7.78	1,055	24 5	3 1	21 5	4.25
1,000	25,000	28,484	12.23	3,484	80 3	10 0	70 5	7.01
2,000	50,000	61,035	18.08	11,035	253 16	31 16	222 0	11.10
2,500	62,500	78,154	20.03	15,654	360 1	45 0	315 1	12.60
5,000	125,000	168,645	25.88	43,645	1,003 17	104 3	899 14	17.99
10,000	250,000	366,193	31.73	116,193	2,672 9	208 7	2,464 5	24.64
20,000	500,000	826,856	*39.53*	*326 856*	*7,517 14*	*416 13*	*7,101 1*	*35.51*
50,000	1,250,000	2,563,576	*51.24*	*1,313,576*	*30,212 5*	*1,041 13*	*29,170 12*	*58.34*
				1941–42				
100	2,500	2,627	4.84	127	2 18	—	2 18	2.92
150	3,750	3,941	4.84	191	4 8	—	4 8	2.92
200	5,000	5,309	5.82	309	7 2	—	7 2	3.56
250	6,250	6,636	5.82	386	8 18	1 11	7 7	2.93
300	7,500	7,963	5.82	463	10 14	1 17	8 16	2.93
350	8,750	9,291	5.82	541	12 9	2 4	10 5	2.93
500	12,500	13,730	8.96	1,230	28 6	4 19	23 7	4.67
1,000	25,000	29,131	14.18	4,131	95 0	16 13	78 8	7.84
2,000	50,000	64,733	22.76	14,733	338 17	58 7	280 10	14.03
2,500	62,500	83,668	25.30	21,168	486 17	72 18	413 19	16.56
5,000	125,000	186,289	32.90	61,289	1,409 13	145 17	1,263 16	25.28
10,000	250,000	438,982	43.05	188,982	4,346 12	291 13	4,054 19	40.55
20,000	500,000	1,068,148	*53.19*	*568 148*	*13,067 8*	*583 7*	*12,484 1*	*60.24*
50,000	1,250,000	3,662,468	*65.87*	*2,412,467*	*55,486 15*	*1,458 7*	*54,028 8*	*108.06*

* For the incomes where the figures are shown in italics a smaller net income corresponds to a greater gross income, so that the assumptions yield nonsensical results.

Note on Minor Duties (Legacy and Succession Duties)
By T. Barna

Minor duties are, in practice, very much in the nature of an addition to the estate duty, and were treated as such for purposes of the present calculation. It is therefore necessary to express them in the same way as estate duties, i.e. as a rate on the capital value of the estate on which estate duties are payable.

The minor duties at present still in force (the legacy duty on personal property and the succession duty on real property) are levied in connection with the acquisition of the property by the beneficiaries.

The method adopted in previous calculations, including the Colwyn Report, was to allocate the burden of minor duties in proportion to the burden of estate duty, the proportion being the same as Exchequer receipts of minor duties to receipts of estate duty in the relevant financial year.

In fact minor duties are not paid in proportion to estate duty. Minor duties are paid by the beneficiary, whereas estate duty is payable by the estate, i.e. the legator by legal fiction. For purpose of valuation and of minor duties certain incumbrances are allowed. The main deduction is estate duty paid, and there are minor deductions also, e.g. Probate Court fees, fees of executor, etc. Minor deductions are not likely to form a significant proportion of the estate.

On the remaining part of the estate minor duties are payable at different rates. If the relationship of beneficiary to legator is close (wife or husband, linear descendant or linear ancestor) the rate is 1 per cent. For other persons higher rates (5 to 10 per cent) are payable. However, there are certain exemptions:

(i) Estates not exceeding or slightly exceeding £1,000 are exempt from minor duties.
(ii) If relationship between beneficiary and legator is close.
    (a) estates under £15,000 are exempt.
    (b) legacies under £1,000 or £2,000 are exempt.
(iii) If higher rates were payable certain small legacies (under £100) are exempt.

As can be seen there is no burden of minor duties on estates under £1,000. For estates over £1,000 we calculated two average rates, one rate for estates (after deduction of estate duties) from £1,000 to £15,000, and another average rate for estates over £15,000.

The average rate of minor duties on estates less estate duty payable was found to be:

(i) For estates £1,000 to £15,000, 1.9 per cent.
(ii) For estates of £15,000 and over, 2.5 per cent.

This calculation was based on data given in Tables 16, 21 and 22 of the Report of the Board of Inland Revenue for 1937–38, and on certain assumptions as to the proportion of administrative expenses and small legacies in the two groups.

It has been assumed that the average rates 1.9 and 2.5 per cent were the same in 1941–42, which implies that rates of minor duties on the value of estate were lower because of higher rates of estate duty.

In the following table rates of estate duty and of minor duties as percentage of estate duty capital are shown. (In Tables 1 to 4 only rates of death duties, i.e. estate duty plus minor duties, occur).

TABLE 5

THE RATE OF DEATH DUTIES

Range of Estate £	1937–38			1941–42		
	Estate Duty %	Minor Duties %	Total Death Duties %	Estate Duty %	Minor Duties %	Total Death Duties %
100– 500	0.7	—	0.7	0.7	—	0.7
500– 1,000	2	—	2	2	—	2
1,000– 5,000	3	1.84	4.84	3	1.84	4.84
5,000– 10,000	4	1.82	5.82	4	1.82	5.82
10,000– 12,500	5	1.80	6.80	6	1.78	7.78
12,500– 15,000	6	1.78	7.78	7.2	1.76	8.96
15,000– 18,000	7	2.30	9.30	8.4	2.27	10.67
18,000– 21,000	8	2.28	10.28	9.6	2.24	11.84
21,000– 25,000	9	2.25	11.25	10.8	2.21	13.01
25,000– 30,000	10	2.23	12.23	15	2.18	14.18
30,000– 35,000	11	2.21	13.21	13.2	2.15	15.35
35,000– 40,000	12	2.18	14.18	14.4	2.12	16.52
40,000– 45,000	13	2.15	15.15	15.6	2.09	17.69
45,000– 50,000	14	2.13	16.13	16.8	2.06	18.86
50,000– 55,000	15	2.10	17.10	19.5	1.99	21.49
55,000– 65,000	16	2.08	18.08	20.8	1.96	22.76
65,000– 75,000	17	2.05	19.05	22.1	1.93	24.03
75,000– 85,000	18	2.03	20.03	23.4	1.90	25.30
85,000– 100,000	19	2.01	21.01	24.7	1.86	26.56
100,000– 120,000	20	1.98	21.98	26	1.83	27.83
120,000– 150,000	22	1.93	23.93	28.6	1.77	30.37
150,000– 200,000	24	1.88	25.88	31.2	1.70	32.90
200,000– 250,000	26	1.83	27.83	33.8	1.64	35.44
250,000– 300,000	28	1.78	29.78	36.4	1.57	37.97
300,000– 400,000	30	1.73	31.73	39	1.51	40.51
400,000– 500,000	32	1.68	33.68	41.6	1.45	43.05
500,000– 600,000	34	1.63	35.63	44.2	1.38	45.58
600,000– 800,000	36	1.58	37.58	46.8	1.32	48.12
800,000–1,000,000	38	1.53	39.53	49.4	1.25	50.65
1,000,000–1,250,000	40	1.48	41.48	52	1.19	53.19
1,250,000–1,500,000	42	1.44	43.44	54.6	1.12	55.72
1,500,000–2,000,000	45	1.36	46.36	58.5	1.03	59.53
2,000,000 and over	50	1.24	51.24	65	0.87	65.8

26

The Incidence of a Tax on Urban Real Property*

By HERBERT A. SIMON

I

It is a curious fact that, although there has been common agreement among two generations of economists as to the fundamentals of tax incidence theory, no consensus has been reached with respect to the incidence of a tax on urban real property. Four principal schools of thought may be distinguished. The classical economists (including Marshall in this case) divided the tax into two portions—a tax upon site rent, and one upon improvements—considered the incidence of each, and combined the two effects.[1] Edgeworth, and some English writers who have followed him, denied the validity of this division, and concluded that, under conditions of inelastic demand, the tax would be borne entirely by the occupier.[2] Seligman distinguishes a tax upon selling value from a tax upon house rent. He follows the classical economists with respect to the incidence of the second.[3] Finally, Professor H. G. Brown, taking issue with all of these, divides the tax but concludes that a major share of the tax upon improvements will be borne by owners of capital in general.[4]

In part, these differences of opinion may be traced to explicit differences in the assumptions which are made with respect to the elasticities of

---

* Quarterly Journal of Economics, Vol. LVII, No. 3, (May, 1943).

[1] In this paper, we shall cite N. G. Pierson, *Principles of Economics* (London, 1902) as the proponent of the "classical" doctrine. Pierson develops the classical position in some detail (pp. 146–56), and is extensively cited by Edgeworth and Seligman in contrasting their own views with his.

[2] F. Y. Edgeworth, *Papers Relating to Political Economy* (London, 1925), Volume II, "The Pure Theory of Taxation," pp. 63–125 [Article 17, pp. 258–96 of this volume. Ed.], "Answers to Questions Put by the Local Taxation Commission," pp. 126–49, "Urban Rates," pp. 150–214.

[3] Edwin R. A. Seligman, *The Shifting and Incidence of Taxation*, 3d ed. (New York, 1910), pp. 277–325.

[4] Harry Gunnison Brown, *The Economics of Taxation* (New York, 1924), pp. 178–212, 213–62.

supply and demand for land and structures. In part, they may be traced to the fact that some writers give greater emphasis to frictional forces than do others. The fact remains, however, that even when these writers make the *same* explicit assumptions regarding elasticities, and even when they agree in ignoring, or abstracting from, frictional forces, they still reach different conclusions as to incidence. These disagreements can only lie in differences in unacknowledged assumptions which are implicit in the various analyses, or in faulty logic used in carrying out the deductions. It is the purpose of this paper to reconcile and amend, if possible, the doctrines to be found in published writings on the subject by discovering where the disagreements have their origin.[5] Since the four writers cited supply most of the dicta on incidence theory set forth in American and English textbooks, the inquiry is perhaps not without practical utility.

For purposes of our analysis, we shall make the following assumptions:

1. We shall consider only dwelling houses, and shall ignore the possibility of transferring land from one urban use to another (but not the possibility of taking it out of urban use altogether).

2. We shall assume that within our range of interest the house-building industry is an industry of constant costs, carried out under competitive conditions.

3. We shall assume that only a small proportion of all capital is in the house-building industry; and that there is complete elasticity of flow of capital from house-building to other uses.[6]

4. We shall assume that the demand for capital, other than in house-building, is moderately elastic.[7]

5. We shall examine both the case (*A*) where the total supply of capital is moderately elastic, and the case (*a*) where the total supply of capital is inelastic.

6. We shall assume that there is no supply of existing houses.[8]

7. We shall examine both the case (*B*) where the total demand for houses is

---

[5] I am indebted to Professor Earl R. Rolph for criticism of an earlier draft of this paper.

[6] This is, of course, the classical assumption in the "long run." Conclusions respecting incidence drawn from this assumption hold equally well in the "moderately short run," provided only that *some* new capital is required for house-building, and that there is perfect competition between old and new houses. Cf. assumption 6 below.

[7] When we speak of "high elasticity" we shall, in our deductions, assume that the elasticity is infinite. When we speak of "low elasticity" we shall assume the elasticity to be zero. When we speak of "moderate elasticity," we shall assume the elasticity to be finite.

[8] Our conclusions would not be modified in the "moderately short run" if we were to assume only that a certain proportion of existing houses wear out each year, that the demand schedule for housing is not shifting downward more rapidly than houses become obsolescent, and that there is perfect competition between old and new houses. Cf. assumption 3 above.

moderately elastic, and the case (*b*) where the total demand for houses is inelastic.

8. We shall ignore frictional forces, and restrict our analysis to a static equilibrium and the "long run."

If we can reach some measure of agreement with respect to the incidence of urban real property taxes under this particular set of assumptions, the extension of the analysis to other cases (the relaxation, for example, of assumptions 3, 6, and 8) should not be difficult.

Where the total demand for houses is inelastic (assumption 7*b* above), Pierson concludes that a tax on house rent is divided between landowner and occupier in the ratio of the site value to the improvement value. The further assumption is made (assumption 3 above) that the elasticity of supply of capital for house construction is infinite, but no explicit assumption is made with respect to the elasticity of supply of all capital.

Under these same assumptions[9] Edgeworth concludes that the entire burden of the tax is upon the occupier.

Under identical assumptions Seligman concludes that a tax on house rental is borne by the occupier, but that a tax on the value of land and house is shared by the landowner and the occupier in the ratio of site value to improvement value. Seligman rests this remarkable conclusion on the contention that the tax on value is "separable" into its components, while the tax on gross rental is not.[10]

Without explicit assumption as to the elasticity of demand for houses, Brown concludes that the tax on site value is borne by the landowner, while the tax on improvement value is shared by owners of capital in general, occupiers, and (possibly) landowners. Under the further assumption 5*a* that the total supply of capital is inelastic, he concludes that the tax on improvement value is borne almost entirely by owners of capital in general.

There are thus revealed among these economists two principal areas of contention. The first three do not trace the incidence of any part of the tax to owners of capital, while Brown asserts that a part or all of the tax upon improvement values will rest upon owners of capital. Pierson and Brown hold that an urban real property tax is separable into a tax on site values and a tax upon improvements; Edgeworth denies the validity of the separation; Seligman straddles the fence.

---

[9] The authors cited examined, of course, a large number of other alternatives as well, but we are particularly interested in discovering why they reached different conclusions even in those cases where they started from the same assumptions.

[10] *Op. cit.*, pp. 300–301.

II

Let us consider Brown's position first, and let us assume a tax on improvement values only[11]—granting for the moment the contention that the total tax is separable. Brown's theory diverges most widely from the usual one when (a) the total supply of capital is inelastic. Since, from assumption 3, house-building absorbs only a relatively small proportion of all available capital, a diversion of capital from this use (necessary in order to shift the tax to the occupier) cannot increase by more than a very small percentage the amount of capital available for other uses. Hence the diversion cannot, even if demand for capital is moderately elastic, cause a significant reduction in the price received for capital.[12] We may conclude that the net price received for capital will be only slightly reduced by the tax, and hence that occupiers will be forced to add the tax to their net rent, even though they may reduce the amount of capital demanded.[13]

Here the classical analysis ends—with the demonstration that the price paid for house-building capital (including the tax) will be increased by the full amount of the tax. The very small change in the net price received for capital is ignored. It is Brown's contribution to have shown that this change, though small, when multiplied by the total amount of capital supplied may significantly affect the total amount of interest paid.[14] The point is a subtle one, but one not at all uncommon in the realm of mathematics. It frequently happens in taking limits that the limit of the product of a very small number by a very large one is finite. So we find in the present case that the very small reduction in the price received for capital, when multiplied by the very large total amount of capital, is a quantity of the same order of magnitude as the total tax collection. More

---

[11] Seligman points out that gross house rental is a composite price "from which there must be deducted expenses of maintenance, repairs, insurance and the like, in order to ascertain the net rent." Op. cit., p. 298. In order to simplify our initial analysis, however, we shall assume that the difference between net rent and gross rental is negligible, and that a tax upon gross house rental is exactly equivalent to a tax upon income from house-building capital, or upon the capital value itself. Later we shall introduce as an additional complication the difference between gross rental and net rent.

[12] It will prove convenient in this paper to speak of interest as the "price received for capital."

[13] Brown seems to imply that this result depends on an assumption of diminishing returns for capital. Op. cit., p. 180. This, however, is not the case, as our reasoning shows.

[14] Brown attributes the origin of this doctrine to H. J. Davenport and T. S. Adams. See Adams, "Tax Exemption Through Tax Capitalization: a Fiscal Fallacy," American Economic Review 6:271–87 (June, 1916), esp. pp. 273, 278; E. R. A. Seligman, "Tax Exemption Through Tax Capitalization: A Reply," Ibid., 6:790–807 (December, 1916), esp. pp. 798–800; Davenport, "Theoretical Issues in the Single Tax," Ibid., 7:1–30 (March, 1917), esp. footnote, pp. 26–28.

precisely, the amount lost in interest to owners of capital is to the amount yielded by the tax in the same ratio as the elasticity of demand for house-building capital is to the elasticity of demand for other capital. We shall attempt in the next paragraphs a verbal demonstration of this proposition, and append a mathematical demonstration at the end of this paper.

In order for price received to increase by the full amount of the tax when (B) demand is not inelastic, and when (a) the total supply of capital is inelastic, it is necessary that some capital be transferred from the house-building field to other uses. If A is the elasticity of demand—which in this case we shall define as the percentage that demand for house-building capital will be decreased by a $1 increase in rent[15]—then the amount of capital transferred will be Axt, where x is the amount of capital previously devoted to house-building, and t is the amount of the tax.

An increase, by Axt, in the supply of capital for other purposes will decrease by Axt/By the price paid for capital—where B is the elasticity of demand for other capital, defined as above—and y is the total amount of capital for other than house-building purposes. Multiplying this price change by y, the amount of capital to which it applies, we have a total loss in interest of $A(xt)/B$. But xt is the total yield of the tax. Thus we have proved our proposition.[16]

Suppose now that (b) the demand for houses is inelastic. In this case, as before, the net price received for capital will be unchanged. But there will be no need to transfer capital from the house-building field to prevent a reduction in interest. Hence there will be no decrease in total interest received by owners of capital, nor will there be a windfall to users of capital other than building capital. This same conclusion flows from our previous line of reasoning if we set A equal to zero.[17]

Consider now the case (A) that the total supply of capital is elastic. The results are the same as for (a), except that now under assumption (B) a somewhat smaller amount of interest will be lost to owners of capital than was lost in case (a), and a somewhat smaller gain will be realized by other users of capital. This becomes plausible when it is remembered that the loss in interest results from a transfer of capital to other uses. When the supply of capital is elastic, the amount offered will

---

[15] We adopt this definition of elasticity in preference to the usual one—the percentage change in demand divided by the *percentage* change in price. Since, prior to the application of the tax, the demand prices for house-building capital and other capital are equal, the ratio of elasticities as we have defined them (A/B) is exactly equal to the ratio of elasticities (a/β) defined in the usual way.

[16] Mathematical Appendix, Note 1, p. 429.

[17] Mathematical Appendix, Note 2, p. 430.

be decreased to avoid transferring it to another use at a lower rate of interest.[18] In this case, the amount lost to owners of capital will be in the same ratio to the total tax collected as the elasticity of demand for house-building capital is to the *numerical* (not algebraic) sum of the elasticities of supply of capital and of demand for other capital.

We must now, as promised earlier, allow for the difference between gross rental and net rent. If k per cent of the gross rental represents interest on house-building capital, then a tax of t per cent on net rent will be for the occupier a tax of only kt per cent on gross rental. Hence the elasticities of demand, A and B, must be interpreted as elasticities of demand for *capital* with changes in the price of *capital*. It follows that the magnitude of these elasticities will depend upon the product of two factors: (1) the elasticities of demand for the products in which the capital is invested, and (2) the percentage which net rent, that is, interest on capital, is of gross rental for these products. If the elasticities are so interpreted, then the validity of the analysis set forth above is not affected by the difference between gross rental and net rent.

Professor Brown's position would appear, then, to be substantially correct, provided that the demand for housing is not much less elastic than the demand for other goods.[19] At this point, however, we must raise a very serious objection of method which, for that matter, Brown himself anticipates.[20] Our approach has been one of "partial equilibrium." We have disturbed certain price relationships in an equilibrium situation, and attempted to trace the consequences of the disturbance. To do so we have had to make a number of *ceteris paribus* assumptions about other prices and quantities in the economic situation which were not within our immediate purview. An analysis which makes use of partial equilibrium assumptions may be perfectly valid when it concerns only a narrow segment of a large economic area. Under such circumstances, *ceteris paribus* assumptions are a fair approximation to reality. We must view our conclusions with less confidence, however, when they extend to a large part of the economic system—when they attempt to predict changes in the rate of interest for the system as a whole. This is especially true when, as in the present case, we take very small effects and multiply them over a very wide area to arrive at a finite result.

---

[18] Mathematical Appendix, Note 3, p. 430.

[19] It should be noted, however, that Seligman's entire treatment of this incidence problem is based upon an insistence that, *in fact*, the demand for housing is very inelastic. (*Op. cit.*, pp. 310–15.) He would, therefore, undoubtedly criticize Brown, as he criticizes Edgeworth (fn., p. 314), for drawing logically correct conclusions from empirically invalid assumptions.

[20] *Op. cit.*, pp. 182–98.

For example, underlying our entire analysis are the assumptions that the demand schedule for house-building capital is independent of the price of other capital; that the demand schedule for other capital is independent of the price of house-building capital; that the two demand schedules are independent of the total amount of taxes collected; and that production costs, cost of labor, equipment and materials, in both house-building industries and other industries, remain constant even when the equilibrium is disturbed and the quantities employed are altered. To trace the consequences which follow when these assumptions are relaxed is not easy. We have made a few attempts in this direction in a note.[21] Few positive conclusions flow from the analysis, but we reach this negative result: a partial equilibrium analysis is insufficient to show the incidence and effects of a tax upon a particular use of capital. The analysis shows only that, under almost any assumptions, the price of housing is increased by the approximate amount of the tax. The further effects of the tax and its final incidence depend upon very small price changes in other parts of the economy.

Professor Brown has performed a very valuable service, however, in pointing out that a tax upon a particular use of capital has repercussions upon income from capital in general. He has supplied an important corrective to the classical analysis which ignored these repercussions, and has shown that the earlier theory is valid only if the demand for houses is entirely inelastic and independent of the demand for other commodities.

III

Let us now see what conclusions we can reach with respect to the second point at issue. Is a tax on house rental separable into a tax on site value and a tax on building value? To avoid the verbal entanglements which characterize the discussion of this issue,[22] we shall understand the word "separable" in a very precise sense. A tax on house rental, or upon selling value, is separable if its effect upon the prices and quantities ex-

---

[21] Mathematical Appendix, Note 4, p. 431. This note should be interpreted as only suggestive of the various possibilities to be anticipated. A really satisfactory analysis involves the construction of a model of the entire economic system and a determination of the effects of disturbing its equilibrium by the imposition of a tax. This has been done for a simple system by my colleague, Dr. Ronald W. Shephard, in an unpublished thesis entitled "A Mathematical Theory of the Incidence of Taxation." He finds that the incidence is a function of certain elasticities in the system.

[22] Evidence Seligman, *op. cit.*, p. 300: "To attempt to separate the entire rental paid for a house into the net rent of the land and the gross rent of the building is therefore as ill-advised as it would be, in discussing a tax on pianos, to divide it into two parts, one of which corresponds to the rent of the land which produced the raw material."

changed is exactly equal to the combined effects of an equivalent tax upon site values, followed by a subsequent tax, at the appropriate rate, upon improvement values.

Let us consider first a tax upon the value of site and building. Seligman considers this tax to be separable,[23] apparently concluding that Edgeworth's arguments, which he quotes with respect to a tax on house rental,[24] are not equally cogent when applied to a tax on values. We shall show, on the contrary, that if Edgeworth's analysis is correct for a tax on house rental, it is equally applicable to a tax on value. In the initial analysis, however, we shall ignore the difference between net rent and gross rental.

In the case where (*b*) the total demand for houses is inelastic, Edgeworth concludes that the entire tax falls upon the occupier. In criticizing the classical position as stated by Pierson, he makes very clear the assumptions from which his own conclusion flows:

The eminent Mr. N. G. Pierson, of Holland . . . has come to a different conclusion, namely, that the occupier of a house with a high ground rent, as in a central region, will, at most, pay only as much tax as what is paid by the occupier of an exactly similar house with (little or) no ground rent, as in a suburban periphery. Mr. Pierson deduces this conclusion from the assumption that the difference between the rents of the two houses may be expected to be the same after and before the imposition of the tax (or, at least, not greater after than before). This assumption would be appropriate if two similar houses dissimilarly situated . . . could be regarded as two units of the same commodity, analogous to two quarters of barley grown on a highly rented site and at the margin of cultivation respectively. But I submit that the two houses ought rather to be regarded as *different quantities of commodity*, analogous to the quantities of barley produced by the outlay of the same capital at the margin and on a highly rented site. There is no "anomaly" . . . in the supposition that the difference between the prices paid for those two quantities of produce should be increased by a tax. It is the received theory, as stated, e.g., by Mill (Book V, ch. iv, sec. 3, pars. 2, 3, 4).[25]

The dispute, then, lies in differing theories as to the nature of urban ground rent. Is urban rent analogous to that rent which a piece of agricultural land pays when the cost of transporting its product to market is less than the cost from marginal land? This is the analogy upon which Pierson's contention rests. Or is urban rent analogous to that rent which a piece of agricultural land pays when the product obtained from a given investment is greater there than on marginal land? This is the analogy which Edgeworth holds to be the correct one. Let us examine in somewhat

---

23 *Ibid.*, p. 294.
24 *Ibid.*, pp. 309–10.
25 Edgeworth, *op. cit.*, p. 136 fn.

more detail the consequences which flow from these rival concepts, retaining our assumption that the total demand for houses is inelastic.

If we accept Pierson's assumption, then the difference in the respective prices paid for housing on two different sites cannot be affected by a tax. This difference is the rent paid for site. Hence, to determine the incidence of a tax we have only to calculate the total tax on a marginal house and on a super-marginal house. Each occupier will bear a tax equal to that on the marginal site, while any excess in tax paid on a super-marginal house will be borne by the site owner. We conclude that:

1. A tax on total value or gross rental will be shared by landowner and occupier,[26] in the ratio of site rent to building rent.[27]
2. A tax on improvement value or building rental only, being equal for houses on all sites,[28] will rest entirely on the occupier. A tax on site rent only, not resting on marginal sites, will remain entirely on the landowner. Hence the combined effect of the two taxes is equal to the effect of a combined tax.[29]

If we accept Edgeworth's assumption, then the ratio between the respective prices paid for housing on two different sites cannot be affected by a tax. Hence, to determine the incidence of a tax upon a house commanding a times the rent of a marginal house, we have only to calculate the tax assessed on the super-marginal house, and determine whether this is greater or less than a times the tax assessed on a marginal house. If it is greater, the excess will be paid by the site owner; if it is less, the site owner will not only shift the entire tax on to the occupier, but he will be able to secure from the occupier an increase in rent (after payment of the tax) equal in amount to the deficiency. We conclude:

1. A tax on the total value or gross rental of a super-marginal site will be exactly a times the tax on a marginal site. Hence the entire tax will be borne by the occupier.[30]
2. A tax on the value of the building alone will be no larger on a super-marginal than upon a marginal site. Hence the occupier will pay the entire tax, and will pay to the landlord, in addition, a rent increase of a times the tax, less the tax—that is, $(a - 1)$ times the tax. A tax on site values alone will be proportional to the site rent—that is, gross rental less building rental, or $(a - 1)$ times the rent of a marginal house. Since a tax on site rent does not touch the margin, it is paid entirely by the landowner. Hence it will take

---

[26] As shown in Section II, the occupier's portion of the tax may subsequently be shifted back to owners of capital.

[27] Mathematical Appendix, Note 5, p. 432.

[28] We are assuming, as is assumed throughout the literature, that the intensive margin of house-building is the same for all pieces of land, and is not altered by the tax.

[29] Mathematical Appendix, Note 6, p. 433.

[30] Mathematical Appendix, Note 7, p. 433.

from him exactly the amount of the windfall he received from the occupier, and we conclude that the combined effects of the two taxes is exactly equal to the effect of the combined tax.[31]

Up to this point we have been assuming net rent to be equal to gross rental. We shall now consider that gross rental is made up of three parts: site rent, rent on the building investment, and operating costs. The first two of these three components we shall continue to call net rent.

The results which flow from Pierson's assumption are not materially altered:

3. With a tax on gross rental, the ratio of occupier's to landowner's contributions will be equal to the ratio between interest plus operating costs on the one hand, and site rent on the other.[32]

4. With a tax on net rent, the ratio of occupier's to landowner's contributions will be equal to the ratio of interest to site rent.[33]

The conclusions from Edgeworth's assumption undergo a somewhat more important change:

3. With a tax on gross rental, the amount assessed on a super-marginal house will be just a times the amount assessed on a marginal house. Hence the entire tax will be borne by the occupier.[34]

4. Suppose, however, the tax were levied upon net rent. We may consider the gross rental of the super-marginal house as a times the interest on a marginal house plus a times the operating cost of a marginal house. The net rent tax would increase only the first of these two elements for a marginal house. But the tax on the super-marginal house would be assessed on a times both elements, reduced only by the operating cost of the super-marginal house. Hence, for sites where a is large, the landowner and the occupier would share the tax in the ratio that operating costs bear to interest on building investment. Strictly speaking, the occupier's share would be proportional to a times the interest on building investment, while the landowner's share would be proportional to $(a - 1)$ times the operating cost.[35]

This division is very different from that under the classical assumption. In the present case, the ratio of landowner's to occupier's share is approximately the same no matter how high the site rent. In the classical case, the landowner's share increases with the site rent.

We have now examined the incidence of a number of different taxes:

---

[31] Mathematical Appendix, Note 8, p. 433.
[32] Mathematical Appendix, Note 9, p. 434.
[33] Mathematical Appendix, Note 10, p. 434.
[34] Mathematical Appendix, Note 11, p. 434.
[35] Mathematical Appendix, Note 12, p. 434.

on site rent, on gross rental, on gross rental less site rent, on net rent, and on rent for house-building capital. For each of these, we have traced the consequences of Pierson's and of Edgeworth's theories of urban rent. It is clear, first of all, that Seligman's treatment of the incidence of urban real property taxes suffers from serious inconsistencies. He treats the taxes upon site value, upon improvement value, and upon sales value on the basis of the "classical" assumptions, while he follows Edgeworth in his treatment of a tax upon gross rental. He errs, consequently, in insisting that taxes on net rents are "separable," while taxes on gross rentals are not "separable." We have seen, on the contrary, that taxes of both kinds are separable, so far as their incidence and effects are concerned, but that the incidence is divided into two parts only under Pierson's assumptions, and not under Edgeworth's.[36]

IV

Which set of assumptions concerning rent is correct—Pierson's or Edgeworth's? This is clearly an empirical question, and not one that can be decided from *a priori* considerations. As a matter of fact, both assumptions involve a gross simplification of the true situation, for they both treat houses in different locations as quantities (whether the same or different quantities) of a single mythical commodity—"housing." Thus, Pierson's position results from considering site rent as a differential price for a single commodity, when the cost of transporting it to market varies. Edgeworth assumes expressly that site rent results when more of a single commodity can be produced for a given investment on one piece of land than on another. In truth, however, two dwelling places in different locations are not quantities of a single commodity, but *different* competing commodities. The problem of incidence involves a consideration of the effect of price changes upon the related demands for these two commodities. The simple formulae of Pierson and Edgeworth are merely special cases of a much more general problem of related demand.

Peculiarly enough, Edgeworth recognizes this fact when he treats of the related demands for "suburban" and "central" housing,[37] and when he discusses the incidence of local taxes which vary in adjoining localities.[38] Why he does not extend this concept to his consideration of general real property taxes is not entirely clear. Perhaps the deficiency has a purely

---

[36] Except, of course, for the portion of the tax on net rent which the landowner pays, even under Edgeworth's assumptions.

[37] *Op. cit.*, p. 81 [p. 275 of this volume. Ed.]

[38] *Ibid.*, pp. 175–76.

verbal origin—arising from the definition of "perfect substitution" which he uses. Apparently he considers commodities as perfect substitutes only if they can be substituted for one another in a fixed proportion.[39] So defined, the prices of two perfect substitutes would necessarily maintain the same ratio under all circumstances.

A more general treatment of related demands would consider two commodities to be perfect substitutes if the price of the one commodity were a single-valued function of the price of the other. The more restricted definition would require, in addition, that this function be a simple proportion. For example, if the general rent level were low, houses in desirable sites might command a greater differential rent than if the general rent level were high, for occupiers might feel financially able to spend more on "amenities." *At a given rent level*, there would be a definite fixed price ratio at which almost all occupiers would be indifferent as to the choice of a more desirable or a less desirable site. This ratio might decrease, however, with an increase in the price level.

Edgeworth accepts the more restricted definition of perfect substitution which requires the same price ratio to be maintained between the two commodities, whatever the price level. Pierson accepts a different, but equally restricted, definition of perfect substitution which requires the same absolute difference to be maintained between the prices of the two commodities, whatever the price level. A more general treatment would require that the price ratio, or price difference between the two commodities, be a function of the price level.[40]

We may indicate briefly how incidence varies when we consider the more general relationship of substitution. The following cases may be distinguished:

1. When the price of marginal houses increases, the price of super-marginal houses may actually decrease.

2. When the price of marginal houses increases, the price of super-marginal houses may remain the same.

3. When the price of marginal houses increases, the price of super-marginal houses may increase by a lesser amount.

4. The price of super-marginal houses may increase by exactly the same amount as the price of marginal houses.

5. The price of super-marginal houses may increase by a greater amount than the price of marginal houses, but not by a proportionately greater amount.

---

[39] See his footnote 3, *op. cit.*, p. 81.

[40] It should be pointed out that Pierson is clearly aware of this more general possibility. *Op. cit.*, pp. 148–50.

6. The price of super-marginal houses may increase proportionately to the increase in price of marginal houses.

7. The increase in price of super-marginal houses may be more than proportionate to the increase in price of marginal houses.

The incidence of a gross rental tax will be different in each of these seven cases. In case 1 the landowner not only pays the entire tax on the super-marginal house, but he pays a windfall to the occupier. In case 2 the landowner pays the entire tax on the super-marginal house. In case 3 the landowner pays more than the tax assessed on the site value, but less than the whole tax. In case 4—Pierson's—the tax is shared between landowner and occupier in the ratio of site value to building value. In case 5, the landowner bears some of the tax, but less than in 4. In case 6—Edgeworth's—the occupier pays the entire tax. In case 7 the occupier pays the tax and pays a windfall to the landowner in addition. From the standpoint of related demands, this is all that needs to be said about an urban real property tax.[41]

V

We may conclude our inquiry by summarizing the results of our discussion. First, except for Brown's work, analyses of the incidence of urban property taxes are faulty in assuming that a tax on a special kind of capital can under no circumstances be shifted back to capital in general. However, substantiation of Brown's contention that such shifting *will* take place must await a thorough analysis of the problem from the standpoint of general equilibrium.

Second, Seligman is entirely incorrect in attributing the difference of viewpoint between Pierson and Edgeworth to a difference between a tax upon net rent and gross rentals respectively. Pierson's and Edgeworth's conclusions flow logically from their respective assumptions, and do not indicate a substantial difference, given the same assumptions, between a tax upon net rent and one upon gross rentals.[42]

Finally, Pierson's and Edgeworth's conclusions are seen to follow from the particular assumptions they made regarding the related demand for marginal and super-marginal houses. Generalizing their results, seven cases can be distinguished which give different results for the incidence of the tax.

---

[41] All these results of Section IV are demonstrated in Note 13 of the Mathematical Appendix, p. 343.

[42] Except, under Edgeworth's assumptions, when operating costs are of a magnitude comparable with interest on house-building capital.

It goes without saying that practical application of the theory of incidence requires investigation of the validity of some of the empirical assumptions which are crucial to it—notably the elasticity of demand for housing, and the nature of the competitive demand functions for housing on different sites.

MATHEMATICAL APPENDIX

Note 1. The verbal demonstration of the proposition is far from satisfactory. It can be made clearer by mathematical reasoning.

A. Let the following conditions hold before imposition of the tax:

x = amount of capital devoted to house-building.

y = amount of capital devoted to other uses.

p = price received for capital, which is equal to price paid for capital.

r = price paid for house-building capital (equal to p before imposition of the tax).

B. Let the supply and demand schedules satisfy the following conditions:

$-\dfrac{1}{x}\dfrac{dx}{dr} = a$ is the elasticity of demand for house-building capital.

$-\dfrac{1}{y}\dfrac{dy}{dp} = b$ is the elasticity of demand for other capital.

$\left(\text{Note that, since } p \doteq r, \dfrac{a}{b} \doteq \dfrac{\alpha}{\beta} \text{ where } \alpha \text{ and } \beta \text{ are the elasticities } \dfrac{r\,dx}{x\,dr} \text{ and } \dfrac{p\,dy}{y\,dp}.\right)$

$z = x + y$ is the constant amount of capital supplied at all prices.

C. Let dt be a small tax on house-building capital, levied on the occupier (it will be clear later that it is immaterial whether levied on occupier or on the owner of the capital).

Let dp be the resulting change in price *received* for house-building capital. Then $dr = (dt + dp)$ will be the resulting net change in price *paid* for house-building capital.

From Assumption 3 in the text, x is very small in comparison with y, hence we may take $\dfrac{x}{y} \doteq 0, \dfrac{z}{y} \doteq 1.$

D. We now have three conditions to be fulfilled:

$$\frac{1}{x}dx = -a(dt + dp)$$

$$\frac{1}{y}dy = -b\,dp$$

$$dx = -dy$$

E. Whence we derive:

$$dp = -\frac{ax}{ax + by}dt$$

(change in price received for capital)

$$dr = dt + dp = \frac{b}{a\dfrac{x}{y} + b}\, dt$$

(change in price paid for building capital)

$$-dx = dy = \frac{abx}{a\dfrac{x}{y} + b}\, dt$$

F. Using the relation $\dfrac{x}{y} \doteq 0$, we have the following approximate relations:

$$dp \doteq 0$$
$$dr \doteq dt$$
$$dy \doteq axdt$$

$$z\, dp \doteq -\frac{a}{b}xdt$$

(total loss in interest to owners of capital)

$$(x + dx)(dt + dp) \doteq (x + dx)dt \qquad \text{(total amount of tax)}$$

These conclusions involve the assumption that $\dfrac{\partial x}{\partial p} = 0$ and $\dfrac{\partial y}{\partial r} = 0$; i.e., that the demand for house-building capital is not affected by the net price of other capital, and the demand for other capital is not affected by the net price of building capital.

Note 2. In Note 1E, set $a \doteq 0$. We obtain:

$$dp \doteq 0$$
$$dr \doteq dt$$
$$dy \doteq 0$$
$$z\, dp \doteq 0$$
$$(x + dx)(dt + dp) \doteq (x + dx)dt$$

Note 3. Following the same general procedure as in Note 1, we may deduce the consequences of this tax when the elasticity of supply of capital is not zero.

$z = x + y$ is no longer a constant, and we have for our third equation of equilibrium (in place of $dx = -dy$): $\dfrac{1}{z}\dfrac{dz}{dp} = c$ for the elasticity of supply of capital. Solving, we find:

$$dp = \frac{-ax}{ax + by + cz}\, dt$$

(change in price received for capital)

$$dr = dt + dp = \frac{by + cz}{ax + by + cz}\, dt$$

(change in price paid for building capital)

$$dx = -ax\frac{(by + cz)}{ax + by + cz}\, dt$$

$$dy = \frac{abxy}{ax + by + cz}\, dt$$

$$dz = \frac{-acxz}{ax + by + cz}\, dt$$

and we obtain the following approximations:

$$dp \doteq 0$$

$$dr \doteq dt$$

$$dx \doteq -\,axdt$$

$$dy \doteq \frac{abx}{(b+c)}\,dt$$

$$dz \doteq \frac{-\,acx}{(b+c)}\,dt$$

$$z\,dp \doteq \frac{-\,ax}{(b+c)}\,dt$$

(total loss in interest to owners of capital)

$$(x+dx)dr \doteq (x+dx)dt \qquad \text{(total amount of tax)}$$

Note 4. We may show, for example, how our conclusions are altered when, instead of an inelastic supply of capital, we posit a fixed total outlay for goods of all kinds plus taxes. In this case, the three conditions for equilibrium are:

$$-\frac{1}{x}\frac{dx}{dr} = a$$

$$-\frac{1}{y}\frac{dy}{dp} = b$$

$$x(dt+dp) + pdx + pdy + ydp = 0$$

(ignoring 2d order differentials).

We find:

$$dp = \frac{-\,(1-ap)xdt}{x(1-ap) + y(1-bp)} \doteq 0$$

$$ydp = \frac{-\,(1-ap)xydt}{x(1-ap) + y(1-bp)} \doteq \frac{(1-ap)}{(1-bp)}\,xdt \doteq \frac{(1-a)}{(1-\beta)}\,xdt$$

$$dp + dt = \frac{y(1-bp)dt}{x(1-ap) + y(1-bp)} \doteq dt$$

$$dx = \frac{-\,axy(1-bp)dt}{x(1-ap) + y(1-bp)} \doteq -\,axdt \doteq -\frac{a}{p}\,xdt$$

$$dy = \frac{(1-ap)byxdt}{x(1-ap) + y(1-bp)} \doteq \frac{(1-ap)}{(1-bp)}\,bxdt \doteq \frac{(1-a)\,\beta}{(1-\beta)\,p}\,xdt$$

$$dx + dy = \frac{(b-a)xydt}{x(1-ap) + y(1-bp)} \doteq \frac{(b-a)}{(1-bp)}\,xdt \doteq \frac{(\beta-a)}{p(1-\beta)}\,xdt$$

Hence, the effects of the tax depend on whether

$$a \gtrless \beta; \quad \beta \gtrless 1; \quad \text{and } a \gtrless 1.$$

An even more general development is obtained by considering the demands for house-building capital and for other capital as related, and by considering the supply of capital to be elastic. Then we have for equilibrium

$$dx = \frac{\partial x}{\partial p} dp + \frac{\partial x}{\partial r}(dt + dp)$$

$$dy = \frac{\partial y}{\partial p} dp + \frac{\partial y}{\partial r}(dt + dp)$$

$dx + dy = \frac{\partial z}{\partial p} dp$, where $\frac{\partial x}{\partial p}, \frac{\partial x}{\partial r}, \frac{\partial y}{\partial p}$, and $\frac{\partial y}{\partial r}$ are the coefficients of demand elas-

ticity, while $\frac{\partial z}{\partial p}$ is the coefficient of supply elasticity which gives:

$$dp = \frac{-\left(\frac{\partial x}{\partial r} + \frac{\partial y}{\partial r}\right) dt}{\left(\frac{\partial x}{\partial p} + \frac{\partial y}{\partial p} + \frac{\partial x}{\partial r} + \frac{\partial y}{\partial r} - \frac{\partial z}{\partial p}\right)} \quad \text{for the price change;}$$

xdt for the yield of the tax; and

$$(x + y)dp = \frac{-\left(\frac{\partial x}{\partial r} + \frac{\partial y}{\partial r}\right)(x + y) dt}{\left(\frac{\partial x}{\partial p} + \frac{\partial y}{\partial p} + \frac{\partial x}{\partial r} + \frac{\partial y}{\partial r} - \frac{\partial z}{\partial p}\right)} \quad \text{for the loss or gain to owners of capital.}$$

Even if $\frac{\partial z}{\partial p} = 0$, owners of capital may possibly gain by the tax, i.e., it may be

that $dp > 0$. General conclusions regarding the incidence of the tax can hardly be made unless the signs and magnitudes of the partial derivatives are known.

Further complications would arise if the supply and demand functions for factors other than capital were introduced into the situation. However, we have already proceeded far enough to show that a partial equilibrium analysis does not suffice to determine the incidence of a tax upon a particular use of capital.

Note 5. Let p_a be the rent paid for a marginal house before the tax was imposed (equal to improvement rent)

p_b be the rent paid for a supermarginal house before the tax was imposed (improvement rent plus site rent).

Since the cost of building a house on both plots is the same $p_b - p_a = d$ is the site rent.

Let a tax at the rate of t be imposed on rents.

Let p'_a and p'_b be the new rents *paid*.

Then, by Pierson's assumption:

$$p'_b = p'_a + d$$

The rent *received* for the marginal house must, of course, be increased by the full amount of the tax. Hence:

$$p'_a = (1 + t)p_a$$

and

$$p'_b = (1 + t)p_a + d,$$

while the amount of the tax on the super-marginal land is:

$$tp_b = tp_a + td$$

Hence, the new rent received, rent paid less tax, is:

$$p'_b - tp_b = p_a + (1 - t)d$$

The site rent has been decreased by td, which is equal to a tax on site rent at the rate t.

Note 6. Using the symbols of Note 5, but with the tax imposed on improvements only, we have:

$$p'_a = (1 + t)p_a \qquad \text{(tax on marginal house)}$$
$$p'_b = p'_a + d = (1 + t)p_a + d \qquad \text{(Pierson's condition)}$$

But the tax on super-marginal land is only:

$$tp_a$$

Hence, the new rent received, rent paid less tax, is:

$$p'_b - tp_a = p_a + d$$

Thus, rent received is unaffected by the tax.

Now, impose a tax on site rent. This does not increase the price of the marginal house, hence does not increase the price paid for the super-marginal site. However, it decreases rent received on the latter by td, the amount of the tax. Compare this result with Note 5.

Note 7. Under Edgeworth's assumptions, in place of Pierson's equation, we have:

$$p_a = ap_a(a > 1)$$

The site rent is

$$p_b - p_a = (a - 1)p_a$$

After imposition of a gross rental tax, we have:

$$p'_b = ap'_a$$

and

$$p'_a = (1 + t)p_a$$

hence

$$p'_b = a(1 + t)p_a$$

The tax is

$$tp_b = atp_a$$

Hence, the new rent received is: $p'_b - tp_b = ap_a$, which is exactly the same as before imposition of the tax.

Note 8. If the tax is placed on improvement values alone, the new prices are the same as in Note 7, but the tax on the super-marginal land is only:

$$tp_a$$

Hence, the rent now received is:

$$p'_b - tp_a = ap_a + atp_a - tp_a = ap_a + (a - 1)tp_a$$

The rent received is actually increased by the amount of $(a - 1)tp_a$, which is equivalent to a tax at the rate of t on the site value, $(a - 1)p_a$. This "tax" is paid by the occupier to the landowner, in addition to the tax on improvements the occupier pays to the government.

A tax at the rate of t on site value will, therefore, wipe out this gain, but will not impose any tax on landowners.

Note 9. Let q be the operating cost of a house. Then, the rents paid are: $p_a + q$; $p_b + q$; $p'_a + q$; and $p'_b + q$.

$$(p_b + q) = (p_a + q) + d \qquad \text{(Pierson's condition)}$$
$$(p'_a + q) = (1 + t)(p_a + q)$$
$$\text{(after tax on marginal house)}$$
$$(p'_b + q) = (1 + t)(p_a + q) + d$$
$$\text{(Pierson's condition after tax)}$$

Hence, the rent received (rent paid, less tax) is:

$$(p'_b + q) - t(p_a + q) - td = (p_a + q) + (1 - t)d$$

Note 10.
$$(p_b + q) = (p_a + q) + d \qquad \text{(Pierson's condition)}$$
$$(p'_a + q) = (1 + t)p_a + q$$
$$\text{(after net rent tax on marginal house)}$$
$$(p'_b + q) = (1 + t)p_a + q + d$$
$$\text{(Pierson's condition after tax)}$$

Hence, the rent received (rent paid, less tax) is:

$$(p'_b + q) - tp_b = p_a(1 + t) + q + d - tp_a - td$$
$$= (p_a + q) + d - td$$

Note 11.
$$(p_b + q) = a(p_a + q) \qquad \text{(Edgeworth's condition)}$$
$$(p'_a + q) = (1 + t)(p_a + q)$$
$$\text{(tax imposed on marginal house)}$$
$$(p'_b + q) = a(1 + t)(p_a + q)$$
$$\text{(Edgeworth's condition)}$$

Hence, the new rent received is:

$$(p'_b + q) - at(p_a + q) = a(p_a + q)$$

Note 12.
$$(p_b + q) = a(p_a + q) \qquad \text{(Edgeworth's condition)}$$
$$(p'_a + q) = (1 + t)p_a + q$$
$$\text{(after net rent tax on marginal house)}$$
$$(p'_b + q) = a(1 + t)p_a + aq$$
$$\text{(Edgeworth's condition after tax)}$$

Hence, the rent received (rent paid, less tax) is:

$$(p'_b + q) - tp_b = a(1 + t)p_a + aq - at(p_a + q) + tq$$
$$= a(p_a + q) - t(a - 1)q$$

Note 13. Instead of the special relations

$$p_b = p_a + d \qquad \text{(Pierson's assumption)}$$

or

$$p_b = ap_a \qquad \text{(Edgeworth's assumption)}$$

consider the more general relation $p_b = ap_a + d$. Then, assuming that $p_b > p_a$, site rent is $p_b - p_a = (a - 1)p_a + d$.

A gross rental tax will result in a new price for a marginal site of:

$p'_a = (1 + t)p_a$, and consequently a new price for a super-marginal site of:

$$p'_b = ap'_a + d$$
$$= a(1 + t)p_a + d$$

Hence, the new rent received for the super-marginal site—gross rental less tax—is:

$$p'_b - tp_b = a(1 + t)p_a + d - atp_a - td$$
$$= ap_a + d - td$$

The tax causes a net change in site rent of $- td$.

A. Assume $a < 0$. In this case, in order to satisfy $p_a > 0$; $p_b > 0$, we must have $d > 0$; hence $td > 0$. Consequently, the landlord suffers a loss in site rent of $|td|$. The total tax assessed on his house is:

$$|atp_a + td| < |td|$$

Hence, the occupier receives a windfall of $|atp_a|$.

B. Assume $a = 0$. Again, we must have $d > 0$. Comparing the total tax assessed with the loss in site rent, we have:

$$|atp_a + td| = |td|$$

Hence the landlord pays the tax, but there is no windfall.

C. Assume $a > 0$, $a < 1$. Again, if $p_b > p_a$, $d > 0$

$$|atp_a + td| > |td|$$

Hence, the tax is shared by landowner and occupier. But:

$$|td| > |t(a - 1)p_a + td|$$

Hence, the landowner pays more than that share of the tax which is assessed on site rent.

D. Assume $a = 1$. Again, $d > 0$. Then:

$$|atp_a + td| > |td|$$

but

$$|td| = |t(a - 1)p_a + td|$$

The landowner pays the tax on site rent, the occupier the tax on building rent.

E. Assume $a > 1$. First, suppose $d > 0$. Then:

$$|atp_a + td| > |td|$$

and

$$|td| < |t(a - 1)p_a + td|$$

The landowner pays less than the tax assessed on site rent.

F. Assume $a > 1$; $d = 0$. Then $|td| = 0$. The landowner pays no part of the tax.

G. Finally, assume $a > 1$; $d < 0$. Then $td < 0$. The landowner receives a windwall of $|td|$ from the occupier. The latter pays, in addition, the entire tax.

F. INCENTIVE EFFECTS

27

About Some Fundamental Theorems on the Mathematical Theory of Taxation

By ENRICO BARONE*

1. Economists who have conducted a quantitative analysis of taxation, based on marginal utility theory, have concerned themselves from the beginning with the problem which we are going to analyze. We will try to reduce this problem to its simplest terms, and to solve it with the help of mathematics; the solution moreover will be presented in the easiest possible form.

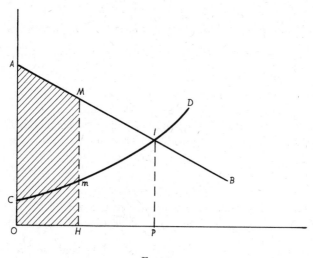

FIG. 1

Primus—whom the theory supposes to be a perfect hedonist—produces a certain good. The utility which he derives from this good is shown

---

* Enrico Barone, "Di Alcuni Teoremi Fondamentali per la Teoria Matematica dall' Imposta," *Giornale degli Economisti*, Second Series, Vol. IV, 1899, pp. 201–10. The translation was prepared by Gian Carlo Carlucci.

by curve AB (Fig. 1) and the cost of pain of producing it is shown by CD.[1] If Primus is free to enjoy the total quantity which he produces, his production—which is determined by the condition of maximum difference between the utility of the quantity produced and its cost—is given by the value which maximizes $U(x) - C(x)$; i.e., the value of x for which $u(x) = c(x)$; putting it differently, production is given by the point of intersection I. This means that Primus produces up to the point at which the marginal utility of the good equals its marginal cost.

But suppose now that an authority intervenes and compels Primus to surrender a part of his product in tax; and suppose first that this part (a for example) does not depend on the quantity produced x, and secondly that a equals a given fraction of x (for example tx, where $t < 1$).[2] Suppose moreover that Primus finds himself in a position in which he is unable to shift his obligation on to someone else; this amounts to assuming that the shifting of the tax has already occurred. The problem which we have to solve here is this: in view of such contribution, will Primus produce the same quantity as before, or more or less?

The answer is given by the following theorems; they appear to me to be productive ones, considering the further developments which can be derived from them.

2. Let us assume first that the contribution a is independent of the quantity produced, i.e., is a lump-sum tax.

The production of Primus will now no longer be determined by the

---

[1] Some explantion is perhaps useful here for those who are not familiar with the mathematical application of the theory of the marginal utility. The utility curve AB is defined in this way: every ordinate represents the marginal utility of the dose of the good equal to the corresponding abscissa; the area included between the two axes, the ordinate and the curve, is the total utility of the dose of the good. For example, MH is the final degree of utility of the quantity OH, while the total utility of the same dose of the good is the shaded area $AMHO$.

The cost or pain curve is correspondingly defined in this way: every ordinate represents the marginal cost of a dose of the good which is equal to the corresponding abscissa; the area included between the two axes, the ordinate and the curve is the total cost of this dose. For example, mH is the marginal cost of the quantity OH of the good, while the total cost of the same quantity is the shaded area $CmHO$.

If the ordinates of the curves AB and CD are represented respectively by the functions $U(x)$ and $C(x)$, $u(x)$ and $c(x)$ will be the derivatives of these functions; this is so because they represent the limit towards which tends the ratio between the increase of the utility (or of the cost) and the increase of the quantity consumed (or produced) when this increase tends to zero.

Of this one can easily convince oneself if one considers that when the increase in the quantity consumed (or produced) is very small, the area which represents the corresponding increase of the utility (or of the cost) may be thought of as a small rectangle, in which the height (ordinate) is just the ratio between the area and the base.

[2] Other and more complex cases of taxes deserve analysis, too: the method for dealing with the problem, however, would always be the one here outlined. We will speak of this in a later article.

condition of the maximum difference $U(x) - C(x)$, but by a maximum for the difference $U(x - a) - C(x)$: the value of x which satisfies this condition is the one for which $u(x - a) = c(x)$.

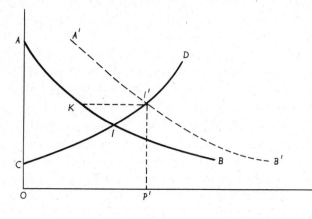

FIG. 2

Therefore:

Theorem I. In the case of a contribution independent of the quantity produced, Primus will regulate his production in such a way that the marginal cost of output equals the marginal utility of consumption. Obviously, the new point at which production will stop is the intersection I' (Fig. 2) of the cost curve with $A'B'$. This point lies on a curve defined by the equation $u = u(x - a)$, which lies to the right of curve AB, at a distance a.[3] It follows:

Theorem II. When the tax is independent of the quantity produced, Primus will increase his production and cut his consumption; this effect will be stronger, the higher is the tax.

We can give a geometric verification of these two theorems. It is indeed easy to observe:

That it does not pay Primus to produce more than OP'. If he did so, he would have to support an increase in cost in excess of the increase in utility derived from the additional consumption;

That it does not pay Primus to produce less than OP'. If he did so the loss of utility due to the decrease of the quantity available would be larger than the saving in cost from the decreased production;

That the larger is a, i.e., $I'K$, the higher is the point I'.

---

[3] [Barone wrote the utility function as $x = u(x - a)$ but evidently meant to say $u = u(x - a)$. Also, he refers to "a distance y," but evidently means "a distance a." Ed.]

3. Let us now consider the more complex case in which the tax equals tx, i.e., a fraction t of the output x, where $t < 1$. In this case Primus will determine the output of x by maximizing the difference $U(x - tx) - C(x)$; the value of x which satisfies this condition is given by the equation

$$(1-t)u(x - tx) = c(x).$$

Therefore:

Theorem III. If the contribution is proportional to output, Primus will produce to the point where marginal cost equals marginal utility, *reduced to a net value.*

4. A direct geometric illustration of theorem III is as follows:

Let OP in Figure 3 be the quantity produced and OQ the quantity available for consumption, so that the marginal cost PM of the former is equal to the marginal utility, reduced to a net value, RQ of the latter. We have $PQ = t \cdot OP$, and $NR = t \cdot NQ$.

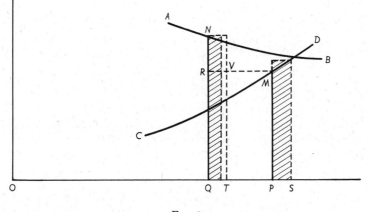

FIG. 3

It is easy to see that it does not pay for Primus to produce either more or less than OP. Indeed, if Primus produces a small additional quantity PS, with an increase of cost represented by the shaded area, the increase in the quantity available for consumption will not be $QT = PS$, but $QT(1 - t)$, since the new quantity produced will be subject to the same contribution per unit t. Now the small rectangle in the shaded area which represents the increase in utility derived from the increase in the quantity available for consumption is equivalent to the small rectangle $RVTQ$. But this is less than the increase in cost; therefore it does not pay Primus to produce beyond OP. In the same way it can be shown that it does not pay Primus to produce less than OP.

5. In this case, the quantity produced is determined no longer by the intersection of the cost curve with the utility curve $y = u(x)$, but with the net curve $y = (1 - t)u(x - tx)$. The net curve may be derived readily from the utility curve, and like it decreases with increasing quantity.[4] In order to answer the question whether Primus will increase or decrease production as a result of the tax, it is not necessary to construct the entire net curve which has the ordinates $(1 - t)u(x - tx)$; it is enough to inquire whether the point of the net curve corresponding to intersection I (Fig. 4) of the utility curve with the cost curve is higher or lower than the point I; if it is higher, Primus will increase his production, and if it is lower, Primus will decrease it.

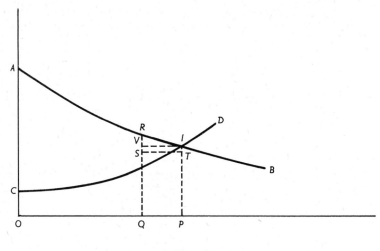

FIG. 4

The point T on the net utility curve which corresponds to point I can be determined as follows. Take $PQ = t \cdot OP$ and determine R and measure $RS = t \cdot RQ$. Then draw the parallel ST.

The ratio $\dfrac{PQ}{OP} : \dfrac{RV}{IP}$ can be designated with the letter e. It is the quantity which we will call the elasticity of the utility curve at point I, applying a term already used by Marshall in his analysis of the demand curve. The quantity so defined is clearly the one by which the percentage in-

---

[4] It can be shown in a simple way, without making use of differentiation, that with an increase in x, given $u(x)$ decreasing, the quantity $(1 - t)u(x - tx)$ must be decreasing.

Suppose we have first derived $Y = u(x - tx)$ from the curve $y = u(x)$. These two curves will be such that with the same ordinate the abscissa of the second will always be higher than the abscissa of the first; and the difference between the two abscissas corresponding to the same ordinate will be larger the higher is the ordinate. Therefore $u(x - tx)$ is decreasing with the increase of x; and, consequently, the same holds for $(1 - t)u(x - tx)$.

crease of the final degree of utility has to be multiplied in order to obtain the percentage increase in the quantity of the good.[5]

We thus have

$$TP = (1 - t)RQ = (1 - t)(RV + IP);$$

but given

$$e = \frac{PQ}{OP} : \frac{RV}{IP} = t : \frac{RV}{IP}$$

we get

$$RV = \frac{t}{e} IP$$

and hence

$$TP = \frac{(1 - t)(e + t)}{e} IP$$

Now it is easy to see that in this formula the coefficient $\dfrac{(1 - t)(e + t)}{e}$ is more or less than 1 depending on whether $1 - t$ is more or less than e, the elasticity of the utility curve at point I.[6]

Therefore:

Theorem IV. If the tax is proportional to the quantity produced, Primus will increase or decrease production depending on whether $(1 - t)$, the fraction of output per unit which is retained, will be more or less than the elasticity of the utility curve at its point of intersection with the cost curve.

6. From this theorem many others can be derived according to the various possible combinations of hypotheses about the shape of the utility and cost curves.

I will present here only one illustration, based on the hypothesis that the utility curve is concave toward the x axis. Corresponding theorems can be derived for the hypothesis that our curve is convex toward the x axis, or is in part concave, in part convex, showing points of inflexion.

Note first of all that independently of whether the curve is convex, concave or has inflexion points, the elasticity at any point is always equal to the ratio between the cotangent and the abscissa. Indeed if M and N

---

[5] It is known that in Marshall's analysis of the demand curve, elasticity represents the quantity by which the percentage change in price has to be multiplied in order to get the corresponding percentage change in consumption.

[6] In order to pass from $1 - t > e$ to $(1 - t)(e + t) > e$, we have to multiply both members of the inequality by t, add e to both members, shift all the terms of the second member, with the exception of e, to the first member and factor out for $1 - t$ in the first member.

(Fig. 5) are close enough so that we can consider MN as the tangent at M, we have

$$\frac{NR}{RM} = \frac{MP}{PT},$$

therefore

$$PT = \frac{RM \cdot MP}{NR},$$

and so

$$\frac{PT}{OP} = \frac{RM \cdot MP}{OP \cdot NR} = \frac{RM}{OP} : \frac{NR}{MP}.$$

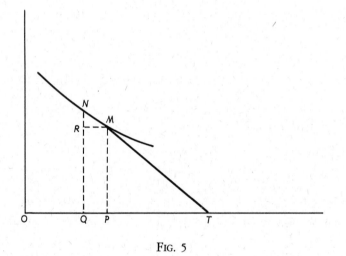

FIG. 5

7. Suppose now AB is a curve which is concave toward the x axis (Fig. 6). It can easily be shown that the elasticity is infinitely large at A, is zero at B, and between A and B is continuously decreasing. Indeed, the farther away is the point M from A, and smaller is the cotangent PT (because the leg MP and the angle in M of the triangle MPT decrease) and the larger is the abscissa OP: therefore a fortiori the smaller is the elasticity.

There is a point C at which the cotangent is equal to the abscissa and at which, consequently, the elasticity of the curve is 1. This point C I will call the *Cournot point*, for brevity's sake, and to honor one of the greatest names in our science.[7]

---

[7] At the point C of elasticity 1, the product $xu(x)$ of the abscissa times the ordinate is a maximum, because at this point we have $u(x) + xu'(x) = 0$. If AB is a demand curve, the point C is just the one that we frequently encounter in the mathematical theory of monopoly, which is dealt with in a splendid way by Cournot. The studies by this author, in-

8. If the cost curve intersects the utility curve to the *left* of the Cournot point, as at *I* in Fig. 6, the elasticity at *I* will always be more than 1; therefore the quota available for consumption per unit, $1 - t$, will be less than the elasticity of the curve at *I*. Consequently, by Theorem IV, the production of Primus will be reduced when the tax is proportional to the quantity produced; and the decrease in production will be larger the higher is the tax.

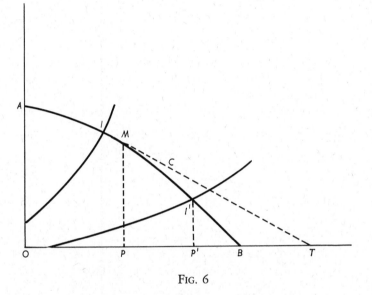

FIG. 6

Suppose instead that the cost curve intersects the utility curve to the *right* of the Cournot point, as at point *I'* of Fig. 6. The conclusion will be different. At point *I'* the elasticity is less than 1. Suppose it is $1 - h$. If the tax per unit is zero, i.e., if $t = 0$, the production of Primus is *OP'*; if the contribution is very small, so that the quantity available for consumption per unit exceeds the elasticity of the curve at *I'*, the tax will increase production. But if the contribution per unit exceeds h, the quota available for consumption becomes less than the elasticity of the curve at *I'* and production is therefore reduced. Thence the following:

Theorem V. When the tax is proportional to the quantity produced, and the cost curve intersects the utility curve to the *left* of the Cournot point, the tax causes a decrease in the production of Primus; and the de-

---

cidentally, together with those by Gossen, Jevons, Walras, Edgeworth, Launhardt, Auspitz, Marshall, Fisher and Pareto have made for progress in economic science more than all the many writings which pretend to deal "ad orecchio" with problems which are essentially quantitative.

crease in production will be larger the higher is the tax. If the intersection is to the *right* of the Cournot point, the tax will raise production as long as the amount available for consumption per unit of output remains above the elasticity of the utility curve at its point of intersection with the cost curve. Production will decrease when the amount available for consumption per unit falls below this elasticity.

28

The Transformation of Taxes[*][1]

By OTTO VON MERING

A. PRELIMINARY REMARKS

By "transformation" of a tax is understood an increase in productivity resulting from taxation. Strictly speaking, and according to our own definitions, this process is not part of the shifting of taxes. It will be discussed here because it constitutes one of those effects of a tax which, like shifting processes, is capable of exact analysis. Moreover, the significance of transformation is undoubtedly greater than is generally supposed.

We may distinguish two kinds of transformation:[2]

1. Increased productivity brought about by taxation in general,
2. Improvements of productive technique induced by particular methods of assessment.

McCulloch[3] thought he had proved a general tendency towards transformation by the following reasoning:

Man is not influenced solely by hope, he is also powerfully operated on by fear. Taxation brings the latter principle into the field. To the desire of rising in the world, implanted in the breast of every individual, an increase of taxation superadds the fear of being cast down to a lower station, of being deprived of conveniences and gratifications which habit has rendered all but indispensable; and the combined influence of the principles produces results that could not be produced by the unassisted agency of either.

McCulloch's commonsense, however, led him to admit the existence of certain limits to the tendency towards transformation of a tax. And, in a general way, he draws attention to the probability that an increase

---

* From *The Shifting and Incidence of Taxation*.

1 This term was introduced by Seligman.

2 Cf. Adolf Wagner, *Finanzwissenschaft*, part 2; *Theorie der Besteuerung, Gebührenlehre und allgemeine Steuerlehre;* 2nd ed. (Leipzig, 1890), pp. 349 ff.

3 John R. McCulloch, *A Treatise on the Principles and Practical Influence of Taxation and the Funding System* (London, 1845), p. 10.

in taxation which draws in its wake insuperable difficulties would strangle people's efforts rather than encourage them.[4]

Doubtless, McCulloch's thoughts on the matter are not without practical significance, even though his alluring analogies can hardly be said to make up for the lack of exactness. The principle of utility comes to our rescue by providing a more exact solution of the problem of transformation.[5]

B. DISCUSSION BASED ON THE CONCEPT OF MARGINAL UTILITY AND DISUTILITY

For all those whose total income is earned, not only the utility of their income but also the disutility of their labor may be considered as a function of their income. Surely, for the lawyer, physician, or other professional man, this holds true, and there is little doubt that an entrepreneur can change his income as he changes his efforts, but it might be objected that most employees, clerks, and ordinary workers who are paid on a time basis do not profit by increasing their efforts.[6] Although the relation between the quality and quantity of work on the one hand and the earned income on the other hand is not very close in the case of fixed salaries or time wages, the worker's chances of being employed continually and of getting a better position and higher salary or wages in the future depend on the quality and quantity of his work. Thus, on the whole, we may safely use the utility and disutility concept for the purpose of finding out the effects of taxation on different classes of people.

Let us consider, first, a tax of a fixed amount. What will be the effect of such a tax upon the efforts of an individual who has to bear the tax, no matter whether he must pay it or whether it is shifted upon him?

Let OU (see Fig. 1) be the total utility and OD the total disutility curve[7] of our individual's income before the imposition of the tax.[8] Then

---

[4] McCulloch, *op. cit.*, p. 11.

[5] Part of the conclusions drawn in the text were expounded long ago by Enrico Barone, ("Di alcuni teoremi fondamentali per la teoria matematica dell' imposta," *Giornale degli Economisti*, 2nd series, Vol. VIII, 1894, pp. 201–210 [Article 27 of this volume. Ed.], and "Studi di economia finanziaria," *Giornale degli Economisti Rivista di Statistica*, 1912, II, p. 72) who, to my knowledge, was the first author to use the principle of utility successfully for the solution of the problem of tax transformation. Although his method of expounding the principle differs considerably from the explanation given in this book and although his conclusions are quite incomplete, he undoubtedly is to be considered the originator of an exact theory of tax transformation.

[6] Cf. A. C. Pigou, *A Study in Public Finance* (London, 1929), p. 91. [See a review of this book in Article 2, p. 13 of this volume. Ed.]

[7] For the sake of simplicity it is assumed that the disutility of labor is always positive.

[8] The reader can easily translate the curves of total utility and disutility into curves of

he will earn an income of OX_0, since at this point the slope of his utility curve equals the slope of his disutility curve. In other words, he will stop his efforts when the marginal utility of his income equals the marginal disutility of his labor. Suppose now that a fixed tax of $OT = t$ is imposed and must be borne by our individual. In this case his total utility curve would be shifted to the right by the amount of t. Not before his income has reached point T will he enjoy his income; only at point T will his utility curve begin. Evidently the slope of the new utility curve TT' at point X_0 is now greater than the slope of OU at the same point and therefore also greater than the slope of OD. The taxed person will therefore increase his efforts until his income reaches the point X_1, at which point the slope of TT' equals the slope of OD.

The question arises whether the income which is left to our individual *after deduction of the tax* will be greater or smaller than before. It can be proved as follows that it is necessarily smaller: In order to have the same or a greater net income (i.e. income after deduction of the tax) the taxed person would have to increase his gross income (i.e. income before deduction of the tax) at least by the amount of t to OX_2 (see Fig. 1). At this point the slope of TT' equals the slope of OU at point X_0, which in turn equals the slope of OD at point X_0. But at point X_2 the slope of OD is greater than at point X_0 and therefore greater than the slope of TT' at X_2. In other words, if our individual were to increase his efforts until his net income was as great as before the tax, the marginal utility of his income would be smaller than the marginal disutility of his labor. Hence, he will not increase his efforts to that extent.

The above reasoning applies to all taxes which do not vary with income. Examples of such taxes are poll taxes, taxes on real estate which are imposed a considerable time before payment is due (as was the custom in earlier systems of taxation), certain taxes on buildings or on business and all taxes on indispensable consumption goods to the extent that they fall on the consumer. Other taxes which do not vary with earned income are taxes on wealth, insofar as they are levied on capital assets which yield an unearned return, as well as taxes on capital returns and even on income to the extent that the taxes affect only returns on capital. All these cases are characterized by the fact that the marginal utility of the *earned* returns is raised by the tax which, by assumption, does not vary with the earned returns.

A tax which varies with income has different effects. Let us assume, as

---

marginal utility and disutility. The point of maximum spread between the total curves or, that is, the point of equal slopes of these curves, corresponds to the intersection of the marginal curves.

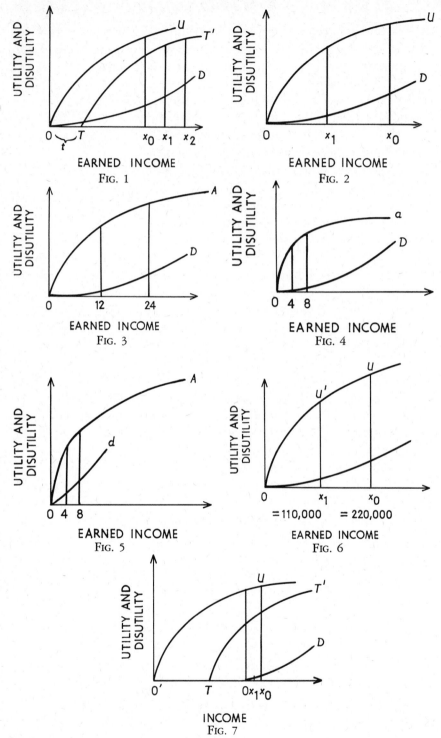

FIG. 1

FIG. 2

FIG. 3

FIG. 4

FIG. 5

FIG. 6

FIG. 7

before, that without taxation the slope of the utility function OU and the disutility function OD (see Fig. 2) are equal at point X_0, so the income is OX_0. Now, if an income tax of 50% is imposed, how will equilibrium be determined? Evidently the taxed person's net income (income after deduction of the tax) will be reduced to $\frac{1}{2}OX_0 = OX_1$. On the other hand, the 50% income tax takes away half of every increase in income and hence (roughly) half of every increase in utility. This means that marginal utility of the *taxed* income may be represented by *half* the slope of the utility curve; and our individual will increase, leave unchanged, or decrease, his income after tax according as *half* the slope of the utility curve at point X_1 is greater than, as great as, or smaller than the slope of the disutility curve at X_0.[9]

Naturally the same reasoning applies to every percentage of income tax, the net income as well as the slope of the utility curve being always reduced by the percentage taken away as tax.

Generally speaking, income taxes are less likely to be "transformed" than taxes which do not vary with income. This may be seen as follows: If a fixed tax is imposed on an income of a certain amount, the full value of the slope of the utility curve of the remaining net income has to be taken into consideration. Whereas, if an income tax is imposed, which happens to tax the same income by the same amount as the fixed tax, only a fraction of the slope of the utility curve must be taken into account.

The opinion, therefore, that income taxes will discourage effort,—an argument frequently advanced against them whenever such taxes are introduced or extended,—in a sense turns out to be valid. The suggestion that an unrepeated capital levy would be more inclined to encourage the effort of producers than a permanently high income tax, a view expressed in Germany during discussions as to how the costs of the war of 1914–18 were to be met, also appears to be valid. However, on other grounds, a permanently high income tax may be preferable to a high capital tax levied only once.

Let us turn now to the problem of how the shapes of the utility and disutility curves affect the change in effort and hence in income as a result of an income tax.

---

[9] Let $f(x)$ and $\varphi(x)$ be the utility and disutility function respectively. Let x_0 be the value of x for which $f'(x) = \varphi'(x)$ and let $q \cdot x$, $(q < 1)$ be the income tax. The taxpayer will increase, leave unchanged, or decrease his application of labor according as

$$(1 - q)f'(x_0 - qx_0) \gtreqless \varphi'(x_0).$$

The general statement of Frank H. Knight, *Risk, Uncertainty, and Profit* (London, 1933), p. 117, that an increase in earnings causes the worker to work less is not correct. This may be seen easily by application of the reasoning in the text to Mr. Knight's problem.

We shall consider, first, two different utility curves, with the corresponding disutility curve remaining the same in each case. The difference between the two utility curves is caused by the difference in the extent of the wants of the two individuals. Furthermore, let us assume that the requirement for indispensable commodities (nourishment, clothing, shelter) is equally as intensive for the individual with few as for the individual with many wants, and that therefore the utility of these commodities is the same for both. The individual with few wants is almost completely satisfied once these requirements are met, and we may, therefore, assume that he will stop working at an early stage; while the individual with more complex tastes may be supposed to continue working harder for a longer time. Under these assumptions, a high income tax will endanger the satisfaction of the indispensable wants only for the individual whose wants in general are limited. The individual with limited wants will be induced to increase his efforts despite the fact that the fruit of his efforts will only in part accrue to him. The individual with a wider range of desires, however, will apply himself less fervently, since the addition in utility resulting from the marginal units of labor applied is relatively small and is reduced by the tax to such an extent that he will not find it worthwhile to work as long as before.

This train of thought may be illustrated as follows: The curves OA and Oa in Figures 3 and 4, respectively, show the utility as a function of income of an individual with a wide range of desires (OA) and of one with limited wants (Oa). Before the tax, the income of the first individual will be 24,000; the income of the second, 8,000 units, since the slopes of OA and OD (disutility curve) and Oa and OD are the same at point 24 and point 8, respectively.

After the imposition of an income tax of 50%, the individual with the greater wants will reduce his efforts and hence his income,—half the slope of OA at point 12 being smaller than the slope of OD at point 24. But the individual with few wants will increase his efforts and hence his income,—half the slope of Oa at point 4 being greater than the slope of OD at point 8.

Let us consider, secondly, two different disutility curves,—the utility curve remaining the same and having the shape as illustrated in Figure 3. If the disutility of labor, as a function of income, rises slowly, an income tax will reduce efforts; whereas with a rapid increase in the disutility of labor, efforts will be encouraged. In the first case, the taxed person will work less hard. In view of the slow increase of the disutility of labor, he will, even after payment of the tax, still be able to satisfy his less intensive wants, and the utility of the increase in his net income will now be less than the increase in the disutility of labor. In the second case, the taxed person will work harder. As a result of the rapid increase in the disutility of labor and the low level of his income after payment of the tax implied therein, he will no longer be able to satisfy even the most intensive wants without an increase in his efforts. The marginal utility of his net income will be greater than the marginal disutility of labor.

This may be illustrated diagrammatically as follows: The utility curve *OA* in Figure 5 has the same shape as the curve *OA* in Figure 3. The curve *Od* (disutility) in Figure 5 rises at a more rapid rate than the curve *OD* in Figure 3. Before the tax, in the case of rapidly increasing disutility of labor, income will be 8,000. If a tax of 50% is imposed, it will be to the advantage of the taxed person to increase his gross income, since half the slope of the utility curve at point 4 is greater than the slope of the disutility curve at point 8.[10]

Our conclusions as to the effects of different utility and disutility curves, both lead to the result that an income tax is likely to endanger economic productivity more in that it falls on those with higher (earned) incomes than that it falls on those with lower (earned) incomes. Not only do the former generally have a wider range of desires, but also the disutility of labor usually increases more slowly for them than for those with less income.[11] There remains, however, the tax limit to be taken into consideration as pointed out by McCulloch: Too heavy taxation on those with a smaller income might result in loss of hope, and hence inefficiency.

Furthermore, we may conclude that the industrious individual, whose disutility curve rises slowly, is more likely to decrease his efforts as a result of high income taxation than the indolent individual whose disutility curve rises rapidly.

We pass to consideration of a progressive income tax. Progressive taxation is usually imposed by means of the so-called bracket system, i.e. the system by which different tax rates are applied to the different parts

---

10 It may be pointed out, however, that the above result was obtained by the assumption that the value of the second derivative of the utility function is sufficiently greater for higher values than for lower values of x. If it should be assumed—probably as a rule not in conformity with actual life—that the value of the second derivative of the utility curve is the same for every value of x, the conclusion drawn before would not hold. On the contrary, as may be seen without difficulty, the individual with a higher income would be more likely to increase his efforts than the individual with a smaller income.

11 Lionello Rossi in his analysis, "Di un caso particolare di Abwälzung," *Giornale degli Economisti*, vol. 69, October 1929, pp. 766–78, has—apparently independently—expressed the same opinion.

H. A. Silverman, *Taxation, its Incidence and Effects*, London, 1931, p. 123, rightly points out that a professional or business man who is making a large income may be persuaded to retire from economic activity sooner than he would do if the rates of taxation were lighter.

of the income. Thus, the first \$1,000 of one's income may be exempt, the second \$1,000 may be taxed at 1%, the third \$1,000 may be taxed at 2%, and so forth. The federal income tax, by means of this bracket system, reaches a ratio of 50% at an income of about \$220,000, but the last \$20,000 of this income is taxed at a rate of about $66\frac{2}{3}$%.[12] What does this mean from the viewpoint of transformation of taxes?

It means (see Figure 6) that the utility of income is reduced from $X_0 U$ to $X_1 U'$ in accordance with reduction of income by 50%, but the slope of the utility curve at point X_1, in order to be comparable with the slope of the disutility curve at point X_0, has to be reduced—not as was true in the case of a proportionate tax by 50% but—by $66\frac{2}{3}$%. Therefore, the tendency towards decreasing efforts will be still stronger in the case of a progressive income tax than in the case of a proportionate income tax. Needless to say, the above reasoning applies to every rate of progressive taxation.

There remains the problem of income taxation in the case of an income which is partly earned and partly unearned. Generally speaking, the taxation of unearned income in connection with the taxation of earned income, counteracts the possible tendency toward decreasing efforts as a result of a taxation on earned income. This is all the more true if the tax rate is higher for the unearned income than for the earned income. Diagrammatically this may be illustrated as follows. Before the tax (see Figure 7) unearned income equals $O'O$, earned income OX_0, the slope of the utility curve $O'U$ at point X_0 being the same as the slope of the disutility curve OD at the same point. Now let an income tax be imposed, the rate of which is $66\frac{2}{3}$% for the unearned and 50% for the earned income. This is to say: unearned income will be reduced to TO, TO being $\frac{1}{3}$ of $O'O$, and the utility curve will be moved from $O'U$ to TT'. Earned income, however, assuming the efforts of the taxed person being unchanged, would be reduced to OX_1, OX_1 being equal to half OX_0. Consequently, the question is now whether half the slope of TT' at point X_1 is greater, as great, or smaller than the slope of OD at X_0. Since the slope of TT' at point X_1 is necessarily much greater than the slope of $O'U$ at point X_0, the first alternative is most likely.

But is it justified to consider every taxation on income from invested capital as taxation on unearned income from the view point of transformation of taxes? In other words, may we conclude that however high a tax on income from invested capital may be, the taxation will not result in decreasing efforts of the taxed person? Surely, once capital is invested,

---

[12] Based on the law in force during the early part of 1941.

taxation will not affect the efforts of the taxed person, but the question is whether, and to what extent, the later taxation of invested capital restrains the entrepreneur and the would-be investor from applying his ability and capital. From this angle, there does not seem to be a clear borderline between earned and unearned income, and thus it may well be that too high taxation on seemingly unearned income does lead to declining productiveness.

Since the concept of utility and disutility curves has been questioned, it may seem worthwhile to show that the above propositions may also be proved by the method of indifference curves.

C. DISCUSSION BASED ON INDIFFERENCE CURVES

1. *Fixed Tax.* Let OX be the earned income, OY the hours of leisure of a given individual. Then the indifference curves plotted in Figure 8

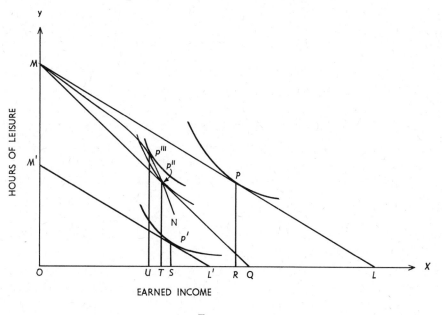

Fig. 8

show the combinations of leisure and earnings which yield the same satisfaction to the individual. The line ML indicates the market price at which the exchange of leisure for earnings may take place before the imposition of a tax. P is the point of tangency of ML to one of the indifference curves.

Now, a fixed tax of the amount $L'L$ shifts the price line ML to the left, the new price line $M'L'$ being parallel to ML.[13] P' is the point of tangency of $M'L'$ to an indifference curve.

In order to find out where this point is situated we must realise that a tax of a fixed amount may be considered as a negative gift. It is safe to say that a positive gift will tend to decrease the efforts of the individual in such a way that although his earned income will be smaller than before, his earned income plus the gift will be greater than his earnings before the gift. In other words he will increase his leisure, but at the same time he will have more money to spend. Therefore the curve which connects the point of tangency of the price lines to the indifference curves will slope upward to the right similar to the usual "expenditure curve."[14] Consequently, the ordinate of P' is smaller than the ordinate of P. The fixed tax increases the efforts. Furthermore, since $P'P$ slopes upward to the right, the difference between the abscissas of P' and P (i.e. RS) is smaller than $L'L$. That is to say, net earnings after deduction of the tax, though smaller than before imposition of the tax, are decreased by less than the amount of the tax.

2. *Proportional Income Tax.* If, on the other hand, a proportional income tax is imposed, the new price line is drawn from M to a point Q on the x-axis to the left of L. At any point of equilibrium on the line MQ, the horizontal distance between MQ and ML represents the amount of the tax imposed. In this case, it depends on the shape of the indifference curves, and it is, generally speaking, not certain, whether the point of tangency (P'') of the price line MQ to one of the indifference curves is more distant, equally distant, or less distant from the x-axis than P; $P''T \gtreqless PR$. In other words, the individual may increase, leave unchanged or decrease his efforts.[15]

3. *Progressive Income Tax.* In this case the price line is no longer a straight line but concave down, for example MN. Let us assume the rate of the progressive tax to be such that the amount of the progressive tax at the former equilibrium point P'' is the same as the amount of the proportional tax. In other words, let us assume that the price line after imposition of a progressive income tax goes through P''. It may be easily

---

[13] The reader must bear in mind that the fixed tax reduces not only the maximum income the individual can earn but also the maximum time of leisure, since part of the total available time must be devoted, after imposition of the tax, to earning the amount of the tax.

[14] In regard to the concept "expenditure curve" see J. R. Hicks and R. G. D. Allen, "A Reconsideration of the Theory of Value," *Economica*, 1934, pp. 52–76. See also J. R. Hicks, *Value and Capital*, 1939, p. 27 ff., where the curve is called "income-consumption curve." Naturally, both expressions are not quite adequate in our particular case.

[15] The same result is reached by D. Black, *The Incidence of Income Taxes*, 1939, pp. 158 ff.

seen that the price line in the case of the progressive income tax touches some indifference curve at the point P''' upward and to the left of P''; $P'''U > P''T$ and $OU < OT$. Our statement that a progressive income tax tends to decrease efforts more than a proportionate income tax is thus confirmed.

4. *Regressive Income Tax.* Regressive income taxes as such are not in use. However, taxes on necessities of life where we assume a certain amount of the tax being shifted onto the consumer, may have the same effect on productivity as a regressive income tax.

The price line in the case of a regressive income tax is obviously convex down. Again it is not certain where the point of tangency of the price line is situated; it may be upward to the left, or be downward to the right of P. The price line may even partly coincide with an indifference curve, which would mean that the equilibrium after imposition of a regressive income tax is not uniquely determined.[16]

Needless to say, the principles of transformation cannot be allowed to have too much influence on fiscal policy, since other viewpoints have to be taken into consideration. The general objection to income taxes and even progressive income taxes on the ground of unfavorable transformation effects would therefore by no means be justified.

---

[16] This result may seem peculiar at first sight. Actually it can also be shown by means of utility and disutility curves that after imposition of a regressive income tax a unique point of equilibrium may not be obtained. For marginal utility after taxation may now at several points be equal to marginal disutility for suitable choices of the tax rate structure.

29

The Income Tax and the Supply of Labor[*][1]

By RICHARD GOODE

One foundation of the case for the progressive income tax is the belief that it offers a means of reducing economic inequality with minimum sacrifice of the advantages of the price system as a guide for economic activity. Progressive taxation meets strong opposition when a defense of economic inequality on ethical or political grounds commands popular respect.[2] It becomes unnecessary when the price system is abandoned for comprehensive state control. Then any desired distribution of income can be attained by government manipulation of prices, wages, and rations.[3]

This case depends to an important degree upon the effects of the income tax on total production and on relative outputs and prices. If the tax reduces production, this loss must be charged against the benefits of the government expenditures it finances and the advantages of greater equality. If it significantly changes relative outputs and prices, some of the potential advantages of the price system are lost; and the incidence of the tax and its effect on income distribution become uncertain. The shifts in the use of economic resources that are at issue are the incidental or unintended additions to the deliberate changes in resource allocation that are always the purpose of taxation and government expenditures.

The income tax may affect production through its influence on the amount and kind of work done and on the amount and kind of investment. This paper will examine some effects of the tax on the supply of labor as a whole and in particular employments. The investment or capi-

---

[*] *Journal of Political Economy*, Vol. LVII, No. 5 (October, 1949).

[1] Adapted from a paper presented at the annual meeting of the Midwest Economic Association, St. Louis, April 22, 1949. I am indebted to Milton Friedman and O. H. Brownlee for many helpful suggestions and criticisms.

[2] This is illustrated by the opposition to progression in nineteenth-century Britain and by the debates in the United States over the income tax of 1894.

[3] The U.S.S.R., for example, makes little use of the progressive income tax; the principal source of revenue is a turnover tax.

tal-supply aspect of the problem, which has received more attention, will be considered only in connection with investment in training and preparation for work. The discussion relates to an income tax that is general in the sense that the same schedule of rates applies to all taxable income, after allowance for personal exemptions, deductions, and exclusions. This does not mean, however, that the tax is general or uniform in the economic sense. There may be differences between the economic and statutory definitions of net income and in the effectiveness of tax enforcement, which affect the taxation of economic income from various sources. For present purposes the total amount and composition of government expenditures are assumed to be given, and no account is taken of the impact of taxation and government expenditures on aggregate demand.

EFFECT ON TOTAL LABOR SUPPLY

Most formal treatments of the effect of the income tax on the total labor supply run in terms of its influence on the choice between leisure and income.[4] Clearly, the tax is not neutral between leisure and work. It reduces the money return from labor, but it diminishes the satisfaction from leisure only in so far as money income permits the enjoyment of leisure. It is not clear, however, that the imposition of an income tax will always cause a net reduction in the amount of work done. Impressed by the fact that the tax decreases the obtainable rewards, some individuals may work less. Others may work more in an effort to raise their incomes before taxes in order to maintain an accustomed or attain a desired standard of living.

In more formal terms, we may say that imposition of an income tax is equivalent to a reduction in the price of leisure and that, like other price reductions, it has a substitution effect and an income effect.[5] The substitution effect suggests that more leisure will be bought at the lower price. The income effect, however, is less clear. If government expenditures yielded no satisfactions to taxpayers, their real incomes would be reduced; and the income effect would be the opposite of that usually associated with a price decrease. On this assumption, the income effect would

---

[4] See, e.g., Duncan Black, *The Incidence of Income Taxes* (London, 1939), pp. 157–67; Haskell P. Wald, "The Classical Indictment of Indirect Taxation," *Quarterly Journal of Economics*, LIX (August, 1945), 577–96; A. Henderson, "The Case for Indirect Taxation," *Economic Journal*, LVIII (December, 1948), 538–53.

[5] Another approach is to consider an income tax as an increase in the effort price of income. See Lionel Robbins, "On the Elasticity of Demand for Income in Terms of Effort," *Economica*, X (June, 1930), 123–29, reprinted in *Readings in the Theory of Income Distribution* (Philadelphia, 1946), pp. 237–44.

suggest that less leisure would be taken unless it were an "inferior good."[6] To the extent, however, that taxpayers feel that government expenditures produce a form of income for them, the income effect of the tax is reduced; and the substitution effect becomes relatively more important. For some taxpayers the income effect may be completely eliminated. The individual taxpayer usually does not look upon the payment of taxes as an exchange transaction in which he buys government services. Nevertheless, government services may satisfy wants that the individual would try to satisfy himself if his disposable income were larger and government expenditures smaller. In the present context the income effect is only one aspect of the proposition that people may work less if conventional necessities are available without cost than if they must be bought by exchanging labor for them. Government services cost the community as a whole something, but they may be free to an individual in the sense that the amount of services received bears no relation to the amount of taxes paid by him.

The interrelation between the substitution effect and the income effect may be illustrated by supposing that the government imposes a tax on a mixed group of confirmed vegetarians and meat-eaters and uses the revenue to provide free meat for consumers. Everyone will find that an hour of leisure costs him less than formerly, but the meat-eaters will probably be more inclined to take advantage of the new price and increase their leisure. This is because the real income of the meat-eaters will be as great or greater than before, while the vegetarians will have suffered a loss of real income.

The foregoing type of analysis may help indicate the nature of the problem, but it does not tell us the net effect of the income tax on the total labor supply. Individual attitudes toward work, leisure, and the usefulness of government services are different and unpredictable. It is uncertain whether the community as a whole will do more, less, or the same amount of work after an income tax is imposed.

The considerations outlined are not peculiar to income taxes. Excises or sales taxes will also reduce the real return from labor. The most significant difference is not between income taxes and consumption taxes as such but between different rate structures.[7] An individual is more likely to be deterred from additional work if the return is subject to a progressive tax rate than if it is subject to a proportional or regressive rate. In practice, consumption taxes are seldom progressive with income over a wide range. A further possibility is that high- and low-income groups may

---

6 Cf. Wald, *op. cit.*, p. 583.

7 This important point has often been neglected, but it has been stressed by Henderson (*op. cit.*, pp. 545–46).

differ in the extent to which they try to work harder to prevent taxation from encroaching on their standard of living. If this reaction is more characteristic of low-income groups, it will be an additional reason for expecting a proportional or regressive tax to reduce the supply of labor less than a progressive tax. If, however, the reaction is more characteristic of high-income groups, it will partly offset the fact that each individual member of the community is more likely to be discouraged from additional effort by a progressive rate of tax.

Other differences in public reaction to income taxes and excise taxes are possible. If individuals have a "money illusion," they may be more conscious of income taxes than of excise taxes that reduce their real incomes by an equivalent amount. This attitude, however, seems unlikely to persist for a long period of time. When a tax increase is expected to be temporary, excise taxes differ from income taxes in that the former do not reduce the value of income currently saved and intended for use at a time when tax rates are expected to be lower.

The concept of motivation implicit in the formal analysis of the effects of taxation is subject to challenge. The tacit assumption that work in itself is always distasteful does not seem warranted. It is more plausible to suppose that most people find some amount of work satisfying for its own sake. This is especially true in the professions, managerial positions, and skilled occupations, which are ordinarily the most highly rewarded and therefore the most heavily taxed under progressive rate schedules. Moreover, customs and moral attitudes exert pressure toward work and against idleness. In Veblenian terms, we may say that social credit attaches to "leisure" only when it is taken as evidence of extraordinary pecuniary standing.[8] If the pecuniary ability is not present, "leisure" becomes "idleness."

People seem to work not only for consumption goods and for the satisfaction inherent in the activity itself. Once a low minimum has been passed, income is desired also as an indication of status or as conventional evidence of success.[9] These objectives are largely relative and are not appreciably affected by a proportional tax. A progressive tax will reduce differences in amounts of disposable income and wealth but will not change the rank order of individuals. Income before taxes may continue to be the primary measure of success.[10]

---

[8] Thorstein Veblen, *The Theory of the Leisure Class* (Modern Library ed. [New York, 1934]), pp. 35–67.

[9] Frank H. Knight, *Risk, Uncertainty and Profit* (London, 1939), pp. 52–54, 331–33.

[10] The income figures that receive publicity are nearly always for income before taxes. The newspaper stories prompted by the Treasury Department's annual lists of names of

Another objection that may be raised is that individual employees are not free to express their preferences between work and leisure because they have little control over their hours of work. There is an element of truth in this, but some flexibility can nearly always be obtained by absenteeism. Employers will be influenced by the preferences of individual workers as to hours when these preferences are reflected in the wages and other concessions that must be offered to secure labor. Organized workers as a group bargain about hours as well as wages and other working conditions. However, union demands for shorter hours and for vacations do not necessarily represent a strong preference for free time as compared with additional income. In part, such demands may indicate a drive for social status and an attempt to win prerogatives traditionally reserved for higher-income groups and white-collar workers. Shorter hours may also be a means of sharing work in slack periods.

These qualifications and objections suggest that the effect of taxation on the total labor supply may be less than has sometimes been supposed, but they do not permit a definite answer even to the simple question whether the labor supply will increase or decrease. Nor does the available inductive evidence dispel the uncertainties. The problem is analogous to that of the impact of changes in wage rates on the supply of labor. A few inductive studies have suggested that the short-run supply curve for labor of some types is negatively inclined over a significant range and that a decrease in wage rates increases the amount of labor offered.[11] This is perhaps the prevailing view. But the facts are meager and subject to different interpretations.[12]

How much of the historical reduction in working hours can be attributed to rising real wages is not clear. The decrease in hours was part of a broad social movement that included the growth of democracy, the extension of education, the rise of trade-unions, and the acceptance of new ideas about the efficiency of long and short hours of work.[13] These social developments may derive partly—but certainly not exclusively—

persons with large incomes have seldom pointed out that (before passsage of the Revenue Act of 1948) a married person living in a community-property state—California, for example—paid much less taxes on a large income than a person living in a common-law state— New York, for example.

[11] Paul H. Douglas, *The Theory of Wages* (New York, 1934), chaps. xi–xii; Erika H. Schoenberg and Paul H. Douglas, "Studies in the Supply Curve of Labor: The Relation in 1929 between Average Earnings in American Cities and the Proportions Seeking Employment," *Journal of Political Economy*, XLV (February, 1937), 45–79.

[12] John D. Durand finds both the a priori arguments and the available data "inconclusive and contradictory" (*The Labor Force in the United States, 1890–1960* [New York, 1948], pp. 84–104).

[13] Wladimir Woytinsky, "Hours of Labor," *Encyclopaedia of the Social Sciences* (New York, 1937), VII, 478–93.

from increasing real wages. Moreover, any historical relation between real wages and working hours is not necessarily reversible, especially if the reduction in wages received by individuals reflects a diversion of income to public consumption and investment rather than a decline in productivity. As government activities expand, workers receive an increasing amount of real income in the form of public services. Taxes levied to support these services reduce real wages but do not reduce the real income of workers by an equivalent amount. Workers cannot be expected to behave in the same way as at some time in the past when their real wages were the same but their total real income lower.[14]

EFFECTS ON LABOR SUPPLY IN PARTICULAR EMPLOYMENTS

The effects of the income tax on the labor supply in particular employments have received less attention than its effect on the total amount of work done. Yet taxation may influence occupational choice and also the division of time between a regular job and casual work for one's self. Such changes in the allocation of labor have a bearing on the efficiency of the market mechanism and possibly also on the incidence of taxation.

The basis for the usual neglect of the effect of a general income tax on the choice among types of work is the assumption that the impact of the tax is substantially the same on returns from all types of employment. But an income tax is never perfectly general and uniform. The income tax may affect the relative attractiveness of different types of work because of differences in (1) the adequacy of deductions allowed for necessary costs of earning income, (2) the extent to which returns from various types of work enter into the tax base, (3) the tax rates applicable to money incomes expected to be equivalent over time, and (4) the effectiveness of tax enforcement. All except the third of these four differences in the impact of the income tax might exist even with a proportional rate; under a progressive scale of rates, they are accentuated for those subject to the higher brackets but are of no consequence for the lowest income groups, who are exempt from the tax. The following discussion is focused on the present federal income tax, but a few comments are made on the feasibility of modifying the tax to eliminate its differential repercussions.

Differences in Allowable Cost Deductions. The income tax does not

---

[14] Taxation may also affect the labor supply by influencing the size of population, although this possibility seems relatively unimportant today, except in the poorest countries. For a discussion stressing the possible influence of taxation on population see Black, *op. cit.*, pp. 168–79.

allow deductions for all costs associated with entering or pursuing certain occupations. Hence the tax is not confined to pure net income. At high rates it may be expected to discourage the kinds of work that entail the largest amounts of nondeductible costs.

One type of nondeductible cost is investment in training and preparation for a particular kind of work. For example, a physician finds that an income tax delays and reduces the opportunity for amortizing the costs of his long and expensive education. The significance of this depends partly on the cause of the high rates of return on investment in certain kinds of professional training.[15] To the extent that the large returns are necessary to overcome a high rate of time preference or to compensate for risk, the delay in amortization will be especially important in curtailing entrance into the profession. But, if large earnings reflect scarcity of necessary abilities and restrictions on entry, they include elements of surplus. For professions in which large surplus earnings are possible, the lack of amortization of costs under the income tax may not greatly limit the desire to enter the field. The tax may nevertheless restrict investment in professional training because it reduces the ability of parents to pay for education for their children.[16]

Failure to allow amortization of training costs may be regarded as merely a technical defect of the income tax, which could be remedied by granting such an allowance over the expected earning period of the individual. But in practice it would be extremely hard to determine what costs should be amortized. Allowance for lack of earnings during the training period and for low earnings during the early years in an occupation would present an especially difficult problem. In an extreme case, several years of apparent idleness may be devoted to the development of an idea that will yield large future returns.

There is also a difference in the extent to which the income tax allows deductions for current expenses in excess of normal living costs associated with certain occupations. Expensive standards of respectability or perhaps of conspicuous display in dress, residence, entertaining, and the like are commonly regarded as necessary to success in many occupations. Usually, however, these outlays are not allowable as cost deductions. On the other hand, persons such as traveling salesmen and business executives may find it possible to obtain deductions for some items that would ordinarily be considered personal consumption rather than business expenses. A

---

[15] Milton Friedman and Simon Kuznets, *Income from Independent Professional Practice* (New York, 1945), pp. 83–94, 118–73.

[16] These effects will be partly offset if some of the private resources diverted from investment in vocational training are replaced by additional public funds.

high income tax may be an influence favoring choice of occupations and working arrangements in which deductions are relatively liberal. Because the line between consumption and business expenses is extremely vague, it does not seem possible to modify the income tax to eliminate completely this influence on occupational choice.

Differences in the Extent to Which Returns Are Taxed. A second type of effect of the income tax on choice of work arises out of differences in the extent to which returns from different kinds of work result in taxable income. It is not usual to impute taxable income to persons who consume their own products.[17] The most important instance is probably the services of housewives. Another clear example is farmers' consumption of home-produced food. But there are many other examples. For instance, anyone who chooses to spend a few days painting his house instead of working for someone else is earning an income that does not enter the tax base.

Any income tax, but especially a high and progressive one, will be a factor influencing choice in the direction of work resulting in nontaxed income as compared with work producing taxable income. The income tax may be especially significant for married women choosing between work in the home and work outside.[18]

This influence of the income tax is an interference with the price mechanism for the allocation of labor. Individuals who are led by the tax to alter their choice of work presumably lose some potential satisfaction. To the extent that the tax stimulates self-sufficiency it breaks down the specialization of labor. Amateur house painters, for example, are less efficient on the average than professionals; and the amateurs are doubtless less productive in painting than in their regular occupations.

The importance of the point should not be exaggerated. Much casual work is a substitute for leisure and is therefore not subject to a tax influence. Work for one's self is stimulated, on the one hand, by its quasi-recreational character and limited, on the other hand, by hesitancy to do menial jobs because of possible loss of status.

The influence of the income tax on choice between work that results in imputed income and work for money income could not be eliminated

---

[17] For a brief discussion of this problem see William Vickrey, *Agenda for Progressive Taxation* (New York, 1947), pp. 44–50.

[18] When a married woman takes a job outside the home, the family often incurs additional expenses for household maintenance and food. One expedient for reducing the tax discrimination against outside work would be to allow a special deduction for working wives on the grounds that the additional expenses are a necessary cost of earning the outside income. In strict theory, however, the additional outlays should be regarded only as evidence of the imputed value of the services formerly rendered by the housewife. Loss of the value of the housewife's services is merely an opportunity cost of her accepting outside employment.

by any feasible modification of the tax law. Valuation of services performed for one's self would involve an impossible administrative problem. Even on the conceptual level, it is usually impossible for the taxpayer, much less the tax collector, to separate the economic and recreational elements in tasks such as mowing one's lawn or growing a vegetable garden.

The income tax may affect the net advantages of different available employments because these advantages are composed of different combinations of pecuniary and nonpecuniary features. In principle, we may distinguish between jobs that are attractive mainly because of their earning opportunities and other jobs that offer smaller money earnings but larger amounts of prestige, more pleasant surroundings, greater independence, and the like. The income tax reduces the money earnings but does not directly affect the nonpecuniary advantages. To oversimplify, we may illustrate the problem by considering two jobs that would be equally attractive to an individual in the absence of an income tax. In the one case, the money earnings are $10,000 and the nonpecuniary advantages are negligible; in the second case, the money earnings are $6,000, but, for the individual, the nonpecuniary advantages are equivalent to $4,000 in money income. A proportional income tax of, say, 20 per cent will reduce the net advantages of the first job to $8,000 and of the second to $8,800. A progressive tax will change the relative advantages of the two types of jobs even more.

The income tax reduces the opportunity cost of taking a low-earning job that is attractive in itself. Of course, a choice between pecuniary and nonpecuniary advantages is not always necessary. The jobs with the greatest money income are sometimes the most pleasant and carry the greatest prestige. Prestige may be in part a reflection of high pay, but it is also possible that prestige sometimes calls forth high pay. Nevertheless, the differential impact of the income tax may be decisive in some close decisions.

Difference in Tax Rates Applicable to Equivalent Money Incomes. The third group of problems arises out of differences in the tax rates applicable to money incomes that are equivalent but differently distributed over time or subject to different ranges of probability. These problems, unlike those already discussed, are peculiar to progressive income taxation and would not exist with a proportional tax.[19]

If taxable income is not averaged over the earner's whole lifetime, an income tax at graduated rates will be heavier on an income that fluctuates

---

[19] This is true only if proportionality is defined to include negative taxation on negative incomes, as it must be in strict usage.

from year to year or that is concentrated in a few years than on an equal aggregate amount of income that is evenly distributed over time. In the United States income tax, averaging is allowed mainly for losses and not for fluctuations in income above the zero level.[20] The averaging problem has been rather fully discussed,[21] and need not be considered in detail here. It should be noted, however, that under existing rates large fluctuations in income are required at most levels to produce important differences in effective tax rates. The rate brackets are rather wide, and the changes in rates between successive brackets are small. The sharpest progression occurs where taxpayers move into the taxable area, and for earned incomes the most important part of the problem might be solved by a carry-over of unused personal exemptions.

Lack of averaging can be expected to cause a progressive income tax to influence some people to choose jobs that promise stable earnings in preference to those with equal or greater but fluctuating earnings. Furthermore, the income tax may greatly affect the attractiveness of careers such as those of the professional athlete, in which lifetime earnings may be concentrated in a few years. Other things equal, most people doubtless prefer stable earnings; therefore, the tax accentuates a tendency to choose jobs offering stable remuneration.

A progressive income tax will reduce the expected net return from a risky occupation more than from a less venturesome job. This is because the anticipated return from the more risky occupation depends to a greater extent on the chance of large earnings (before taxes). The progressive tax will reduce the net value of a chance of large earnings before taxes by a greater percentage than the net value of a chance for small earnings. This proposition may be simply illustrated by considering two occupations with expected incomes of equal value before taxes, let us say, $12,500. In the first case, the expected value is the result of equal chances that the actual income will be $10,000 or $15,000. In the second case, the chances are equal that the income before taxes will be $25,000 or zero. At the rates provided by the Revenue Act of 1948, the federal income tax on a married person with two dependents will reduce the net expected

---

[20] A net operating loss sustained in one year may be carried back against the income of the two preceding years, and any unabsorbed balance may be carried forward against the income of the following years (Internal Revenue Code, sec. 122). A limited amount of averaging is allowed for compensation for personal services extending over a period of thirty-six calendar months or more when at least 80 per cent of the total compensation is received in one taxable year. In such cases, the tax is computed after averaging the compensation over the period of performance of the services (Internal Revenue Code, sec. 107).

[21] See, e.g., Henry C. Simons, *Personal Income Taxation* (Chicago, 1938), pp .153–55 *and passim;* Harold M. Groves, *Postwar Taxation and Economic Progress* (New York, 1946), pp. 223–36; Vickrey, *op. cit.,* pp. 164–97.

value of the income from the first job to approximately $10,560 and of the second to approximately $9,760.

It is not entirely clear, however, that the progressive income tax will cause a net shift to secure as compared with venturesome jobs. If people were indifferent with respect to risk and made their decisions entirely on the basis of other advantages and disadvantages, clearly the tax would cause such a shift. But personalities differ. It seems likely that most people are attracted by security but that some place great stress on even a remote chance of large earnings.[22] For those with a preference for security, the problem is similar to that of the effect of the tax on the choice between work and leisure. They will find that the tax reduces the cost of security, but it may also reduce their real incomes. Whether they will choose more or less security depends on the balance between the substitution effect and the income effect or on whether they try to make up a loss of income by becoming more venturesome. On the other hand, those who like venturesomeness for its own sake will find its price raised, and the substitution effect and the income effect will reinforce each other.

Differences in Effectiveness of Tax Enforcement. In practice, differences in the effectiveness of tax enforcement may be more significant than the more subtle differences in the impact of the income tax. Taxation of the self-employed depends largely on voluntary compliance. In contrast, most wages and salaries are subject to withholding; and information returns are required on payments of rent, dividends, interest, and certain other items. It is commonly believed that farmers, independent professional practitioners, small businessmen, and domestic and agricultural workers (whose wages are not subject to withholding) have been less fully taxed than others.[23] With high tax rates, the opportunity for evasion may become a factor in occupational choice.

Effects of Tax Differentials. It is difficult to strike a balance among the various differential effects of the income tax. The discrimination against fluctuating incomes and against risky jobs is an influence in the direction of salaried employment as opposed to entrepreneurial activity or independent professional practice. On the other hand, opportunities for tax evasion and probably also the failure to include nonpecuniary returns in the tax base favor self-employment. The lack of amortization of investment in vocational training discriminates against professional work,

---

[22] A recent survey found that college graduates of the class of 1949 place great emphasis on security in seeking employment (*Fortune*, XXXIX [June, 1949], 84–87, 163–70).

[23] The Bureau of Internal Revenue is now engaged in a sample audit program that may reveal whether this is true. See Marius Farioletti, "The 1948 Audit Control Program for Federal Individual Income Tax Returns," *National Tax Journal*, II (June, 1949), 142–50.

whether salaried or independent; but the omission of nonpecuniary returns is a partly offsetting factor, if we may assume that they are more important in the professions than in other occupations.

It would be hard to support the hypothesis that the income tax exercises a strong influence on broad occupational choice, for little is known about the process of occupational choice. Most individuals find the range of their opportunities severely limited. Among available opportunities, choice often seems to be non-rational and, to the extent that it is rational, to be heavily influenced by non-economic considerations. Many early decisions are virtually irreversible, and most involve some commitment.[24] It seems possible, however, that the income tax may have considerable influence on choice of jobs and working arrangements within broad occupational groupings, especially on the part of members of higher-income groups.

The income tax is likely to have its chief immediate influence on people who would be making new occupational or job choices even if the tax were not in effect. Much inertia must be overcome to induce those already settled to seek a change. And, even for the long run, it would be unrealistic to put great stress on the influence of the tax. Most men seem neither willing nor able to make the exact calculations of economic advantages and disadvantages that such a view would have to assume. But it cannot be denied that the continuous pressure of the tax has some influence.

CONCLUSIONS

If the income tax changes the supply of labor in different employments, it affects relative money wages (before taxes) and consequently the pattern of production and prices. Relative money wages (before taxes) tend to rise in employments that the tax discriminates against and to fall in employments favored by the tax. Outputs tend to be lower and relative prices higher for goods produced in employments discriminated against than for other goods. Thus the tax forces consumers of some goods to pay higher prices and enables consumers of other goods

---

24 Eli Ginzberg, Sol W. Ginsburg, Sidney Axelrad, and John L. Herma, "The Problem of Occupational Choice," a research report presented at the annual meeting of the American Orthopsychiatric Association, Chicago, April, 1949, to be published in the *American Journal of Orthopsychiatry*. The authors stress the complexity of the problem and the lack of a satisfactory theory of occupational choice. For present purposes, it is interesting to note that, in a study of boys and youths aged eleven to twenty-three, the authors found among the upper age groups an increasingly "instrumental" attitude toward occupational choice with stress on returns in the form of income, pleasant working conditions, and prestige.

to pay lower prices. We do not know how much of the tax is shifted in this way; but, unless the gains and losses of consumers and workers cancel out in each income size class, the shifting that does occur modifies the redistributive effect of the progressive income tax. There is perhaps a presumption that the actual equalizing effect is less than if the tax did not change relative prices and wages,[25] but this cannot be confidently asserted.

The effects of the income tax on the labor supply and consequent changes in wages and prices are unintended additions to the deliberate shift of economic resources that accompanies diversion of private income to public uses and the redistribution of income among individuals. It could be positively asserted that these unintended changes are bad only if it were clear that the market allocation that would exist in the absence of the tax would be ideal. This cannot be taken for granted. But, simply because they are unintended, the changes in resource allocation cannot be defended as a deliberate use of the regulatory power. The presumption must be that the unintended changes represent a loss in the potential advantages of the market system.

In so far as the income tax strikes returns from some kinds of work more heavily than those from other employments, it is similar to a series of excise taxes. Unless the supply of the factors affected is completely inelastic over the relevant range, either a differentially heavy income tax or an excise tax will reduce output and raise the relative price of the commodity produced.

Despite the differential effects of the income tax discussed in this paper, it applies to a wider range of opportunities than other available taxes. This is an important advantage, since the wider the application of a tax the more likely is it to be confined to surplus and the less will it change relative outputs and prices.[26] A nominally general income tax will not fall exclusively on surplus, but it is a relatively good way of reaching it. There may be other taxes that would be confined entirely to surplus, but they are hard to find and harder yet to apply. In this important respect, the usual belief that the unintended effects on resource allocation are smaller for an income tax than for other taxes seems justifiable. It must be admitted, however, that the steeper the graduation of rates and the

---

[25] The equalizing effect of the tax will be reduced (1) if those whose gross money incomes are raised as a result of the tax have higher than average incomes—as seems likely, since highly paid occupations will be most affected by a progressive tax and those remaining in the occupations will ordinarily be better established than those shifted to other occupations—and (2) if the changes in prices affect consumers in all brackets in proportion to their total consumption outlays or total incomes.

[26] Cf. Abba P. Lerner, *The Economics of Control* (New York, 1947), pp. 228–40.

larger the number of exemptions and exclusions, the less general and uniform does the income tax become and hence the less powerful is this argument in its favor.

Our knowledge of the incidence of the income tax is less definite than has usually been assumed. Its ultimate effectiveness in reducing economic inequality is therefore somewhat uncertain and perhaps less than its apparent effectiveness. Nevertheless, the evidence here considered is not enough to discredit the income tax as a means of securing greater equality while retaining in large measure the advantages of the price system. These purposes can be furthered by any practicable refinements of the base of the income tax and by supplementing it with other appropriate taxes. Slower but also effective is an attack on the roots of inequality by programs such as those to broaden educational opportunities, to improve nutrition and public health, and to eliminate racial and religious discrimination.

30

*Taxation and Incentive in Mobilization**

By GERSHON COOPER[†]

I. INTRODUCTION

The current discussion of the relative merits of alternative fiscal policies, and the possibility that we shall have a high level of defense expenditures for many years even if we do not become involved in a major
war, raise once more the question of the effect of taxation on incentive.
It has frequently been assumed that the effect of taxation is necessarily
to reduce incentive, and though we may find it expedient or desirable to
tax rather than (say) to borrow, we do so in spite of the effect of taxation
on incentive. Thus, from the assumption that an increase in taxes will
reduce incentive it follows that the policy known (inaccurately) as "pay
as you go" necessarily has very limited applicability. In mobilization, for
example, when the magnitude of the social product is of crucial importance, it is clear that a policy which will significantly reduce the social
product (as compared with alternative policies) will have little claim
to serious consideration.

This is not to suggest that effect on incentive or output is the sole
criterion by which fiscal policies ought to be evaluated. There are clearly
a great many factors which must be taken into account—factors which
possess no common yardstick. How, for example, shall we evaluate the
relative importance of equity considerations on the one hand and incentive considerations on the other? Only if it should happen to be true that

* *Quarterly Journal of Economics*, Vol. LXVI, No. 1, (February, 1952). Reprinted by
courtesy of the Harvard University Press as publisher, and the author.

† The author wishes to acknowledge his indebtedness to a great many of his colleagues at
The Rand Corporation. Joseph Kershaw made the initial suggestion for this paper, and gave
advice and encouragement at many points. Irving Glicksburg was unbelievably patient in
remedying my mathematical misconceptions. In addition, Armen Alchian, Lawrence An-
tonellis, Charles Hitch, Norman Kaplan and Ronald Shephard all read an earlier draft of
this paper and contributed valuable criticism. The errors are mine.

a given policy is deemed superior in every relevant respect can the economist, in his professional capacity, choose between policies. It is not claimed, therefore, that the conclusions reached in this paper ought to be decisive in choosing between policies. Much has already been written on the relative merits of alternative fiscal policies, and it is not proposed to add to the *rudis indigestaque moles*. It may not be amiss to point out, however, that there are probably many economists for whom the major, if not the sole, argument against a "pay as you go" policy is the alleged harmful effect of taxation on incentive.

What, then, is meant by "incentive" in this context? "Incentive" clearly refers to that which motivates behavior or action, so that if, in the customary fashion of economists, we assume that individuals are motivated by a desire for "utility" or satisfaction, we can equate "incentive" and "desire for satisfaction." It would be patently ridiculous, however, to suggest that taxation influences the individual's "desire for satisfaction." When we speak of the influence of taxation on incentive we must mean the influence of taxation on *the actions* which a person takes as a result of his incentive, i.e., desire for satisfaction. Put otherwise, we might say that economists ordinarily assume the nature of the individual's incentive or motivation, so that what is in question is the effect of taxation on the individual's actions.

What actions of the individual are relevant to the choice between fiscal policies? There are two major effects of taxation in which the economist might be interested: that on investment activity, and that on labor services. While the former is undeniably important, it is hard to believe that it could have anything but a very minor significance during a mobilization period, when the major risks are to be borne by the government, when private investment is to be restricted, and when the pattern of future economic events is perhaps clearer than in a "normal" period. Be that as it may, we shall be concerned in this paper only with the influence of taxation on the supply of labor services.

There are, however, several aspects of the "supply of labor services" which may conceivably be important in mobilization. In the first place, we may wish to increase the total number of persons who will offer their services for sale. Secondly, we may wish to cause people to "work harder" —that is to say, to increase their output per unit of time. Thirdly, we may desire to alter the kinds of labor services which are supplied, e.g., we may wish to reallocate labor from the production of civilian goods to the production of munitions. Finally, we may wish to increase the supply of labor by increasing the number of hours which each individual works. In what follows we shall be concerned, strictly speaking, only with the last of these, although the analysis may shed some light on the factors which are relevant for other aspects of the supply of labor.

Furthermore, there are a very large number of possible changes in the tax structure which might be relevant to the general question of the influence of taxation on incentive. In this paper, however, we have confined ourselves to the analysis of the influence of income taxation. Thus the paper deals with the influence of income taxation on the number of hours which the individual will be willing to work, given freedom of choice. It may be objected, of course, that the individual's freedom of choice with respect to the number of hours which he will work is very limited, that is, he does not really have freedom of choice. If this objection be valid, perhaps the whole issue is unimportant and the influence of taxation on "incentive" to work should be ignored in determining the optimum fiscal policy.

Three further qualifications should be stated at the outset. First, the analysis proceeds by the method of comparative statics, and is rigorous only for small changes in the tax structure.[1] Secondly, we assume that individuals are rational, in the sense that they will maximize their utility, and that utility or satisfaction depends (in most of the cases dealt with) only on the income which an individual receives and upon the leisure which he enjoys. The individuals of our analysis are thus unmotivated by ideas about what constitutes an equitable tax system, by patriotic feelings, or by a "money illusion." Finally, we shall abstract from the possible influence of the *method* of tax collection, and assume simply that the individual is completely aware of the consequences for him of a given tax structure.

II. THE INFLUENCE OF INCOME TAXATION UPON HOURS OF WORK

The cases which are analyzed below may be distinguished from one another in terms of the assumptions which are made about (*a*) the tax structure, (*b*) the individual's utility function, and (*c*) inflation. Cases *A* through *H* assume the same utility function, but different kinds of tax structure. Case *I* carries through the analysis with a modified utility function. Case *J* discusses the case of inflation, as an alternative to taxation. Case *K* determines the "optimum" individual tax rate.

Case A. The utility or satisfaction which an individual enjoys is assumed to depend only upon the real income which he receives and upon

---

[1] It is hoped to remedy this in a later paper.

the number of hours of leisure which he enjoys; all three magnitudes being interpreted as quantities per unit of time. We may then write the utility function[2]

$$u = \phi(l, y) \tag{1}$$

where

    u = utility
    l = number of hours of leisure
    y = real disposable income

Further, we assume that there exists a governmentally determined tax schedule or function such that the individual pays a fixed proportion of his gross real income in taxes. We abstract from the fact that, in the real world, taxes are levied on money income.[3] If we write the tax schedule as

$$T = ag \tag{2}$$

where

    T = total tax (per unit of time)
    g = gross income per unit of time
    a = a governmentally determined parameter,

it follows that disposable income is given by

$$y = (1 - a)g \tag{3}$$

Hence we may write

$$y = (1 - a)[w(k - l)] \tag{4}$$

where

    w = the wage rate (a constant)
    k = the number of hours in the basic time unit (say, a week)
    $(k - l)$ = number of hours of work (per week)

If now we assume that the individual maximizes his utility, and takes account of the relation (4) between disposable income and hours of work (or leisure) we may easily show that, in equilibrium,

$$\frac{\phi_l(l, y)}{\phi_y(l, y)} = (1 - a)w \tag{5}$$

so that equations (4) and (5) together determine the equilibrium income and hours of work. In words, the individual will work up to the point where the ratio of the marginal utility of leisure to the marginal utility of income is equal to the wage rate after tax.

---

[2] We assume here that utility is cardinal, but merely for simplicity of exposition. The assumption of ordinal utility gives the same results, as is demonstrated in the Appendix to this article.

[3] The result is, once more, to simplify the exposition, without changing the results.

It is apparent from equation (5) that, if the tax rate a is increased, the ratio of the marginal utilities must fall, but this tells us nothing whatever about whether hours of work (or income) will increase or diminish as a result of the increase in the tax. Suppose, for example, that the individual should decide to reduce his hours of work. The marginal utility of income would (presumably) rise, the marginal utility of leisure would (presumably) fall, and the ratio would therefore fall. But this adjustment *need not* happen, for even if the individual works the same number of hours as before, the marginal utility of income will rise, the marginal utility of leisure will fall (under the same assumptions as before) and the ratio will fall. Thus, so far as we can tell by examination of (5), it is perfectly possible for the required adjustment of the ratio to take place without a reduction of hours of work.

There is, however, an additional condition which is sufficient to guarantee a maximum,[4] namely

$$\left[\phi_y + y\phi_{yy} - (k - l)\phi_{ly} \right] \frac{dl}{da} > 0 . \tag{6}$$

Here the first term, ϕ_y, is the marginal utility of income. The second term, $y\phi_{yy}$, is disposable income times the rate at which the marginal utility of income changes as income increases. The third term, $(k - l)\phi_{ly}$, is number of hours of work times the rate at which the marginal utility of leisure changes as income increases. Finally $\frac{dl}{da}$ is the change in hours of leisure due to a small increase in the tax rate a.

Now it is precisely the sign and magnitude of $\frac{dl}{da}$ in which we are interested. But the inequality (6) makes it apparent that the sign of $\frac{dl}{da}$ must be the same as the sign of the expression in parentheses. ϕ_y may be assumed positive. $y\phi_{yy}$ will be negative if we make the usual assumption of diminishing marginal utility. And the expression $- (k - l)\phi_{ly}$ will be negative if the marginal utility of leisure increases with income. Thus the sign of the expression in parentheses depends on the magnitudes of ϕ_y, $y\phi_{yy}$, etc., and cannot be determined from *a priori* considerations alone, if our assumptions be upheld. Hence $\frac{dl}{da}$ may be positive or negative. Hence it is impossible to say whether hours of work will increase or diminish as a result of the increase in the tax.[5]

---

[4] See Appendix to this article for a generalized proof of the condition displayed in (6), and other, similar, conditions employed below.

[5] Except in certain cases which are trivial. For example, if the marginal utility of leisure is independent of income and the marginal utility of income is constant, the inequality (6) demonstrates that hours of work will diminish if the tax rate increases.

The dilemma may be illustrated by a series of diagrams. Figure 1 shows the relation between taxes and gross income, before and after the tax change. Figure 2 shows the indifference map of the individual, to-

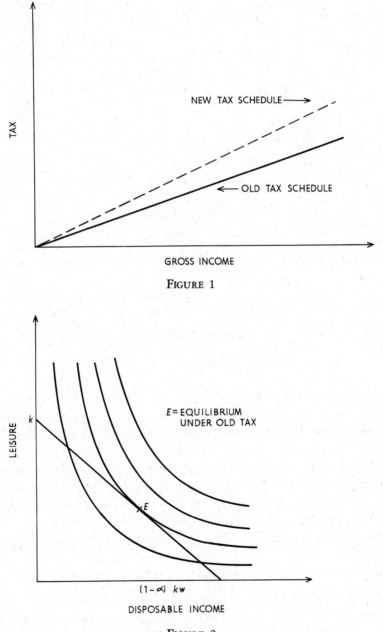

FIGURE 1

FIGURE 2

gether with the line which shows the various combinations of disposable income and leisure achievable by the individual. The point of tangency of this line with the curve of highest utility represents the equilibrium

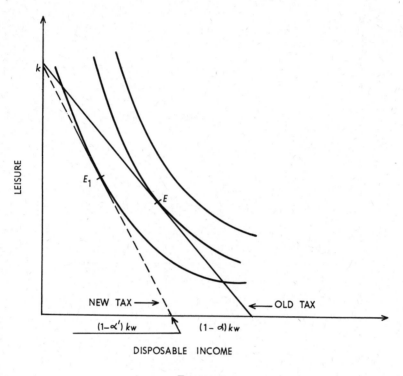

FIGURE 3

solution. Figures 3 and 4 present the effect of a change in the tax schedule, as shown in Figure 1, upon the equilibrium solution; with alternative indifference maps. In Figure 3 it is seen that hours of work will diminish; in Figure 4, increase.

The problem just dealt with is, of course, identical with the ancient question: What is the shape of the supply curve of labor? This follows from the fact that a change in the rate of a proportional tax is equivalent to a change in the wage rate. It is impossible, therefore, to determine the shape of the supply curve of labor from the usual *a priori* considerations alone.

The results of Case *A* may be summed up as follows:

Proposition A. If utility depends only on real income and leisure, and the rate of a proportional tax is increased, incentive to work (as measured by hours) may increase or diminish. Whether hours of work will increase or diminish depends on the initial values of the variables and upon properties of the utility function which cannot be adduced *a priori*.

Corollary: If the marginal utility of leisure is independent of income, hours of work will increase or diminish according to whether the elasticity of the marginal utility of income curve is greater or less than unity.[6]

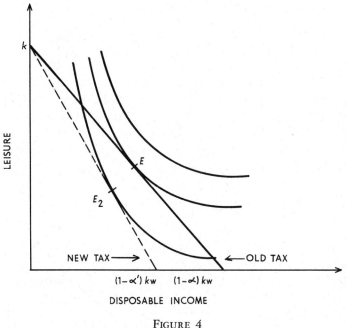

FIGURE 4

It will already have occurred to the reader that while we may not be able to say very much about the effect of an increase in a proportional tax, we may be able to give a definite answer in the case of an increase in a progressive tax. This is the subject matter of Case B.

Case B. The utility function is assumed to be the same as in Case A, but the tax function is now given by[7]

$$T = g - g^{\frac{1}{a}} \tag{7}$$

---

[6] Since marginal utility is assumed to diminish the elasticity of this curve is, of course, negative. The condition as stated refers to the absolute value of the elasticity.

[7] Progressiveness is here taken to mean that $\dfrac{d(T/g)}{dg} > 0$. The tax function [equation (7)] satisfies this requirement if $a > 1$. It should be noted, also, that the tax increases as a increases.

so that disposable income may be written as

$$y = [w(k-l)]^{\frac{1}{a}} \tag{8}$$

If we proceed exactly as before (Case *A*) we can write two conditions which must be met, namely

$$\frac{\phi_l(y,l)}{\phi_y(y,l)} = \frac{y}{a(k-l)} \tag{9}$$

and,

$$\left[\left(1 + \frac{1}{a}\log g\right)\phi_y + \frac{y}{a}(\log g)\phi_{yy} - (k-l)(\log g)\phi_{ly}\right]\frac{dl}{da} > 0. \tag{10}$$

As before, the parentheses contain one positive, one negative and one doubtful term. Therefore, as before, it is impossible to say whether hours of work will increase or decrease as a result of the increase in the tax.

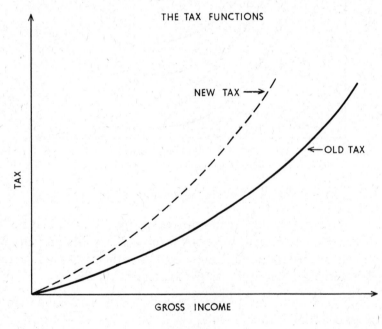

THE TAX FUNCTIONS

NEW TAX →

←OLD TAX

TAX

GROSS INCOME

FIGURE 5

The diagrammatic representation of this case follows exactly the lines of the earlier case.

The results of Case *B* may be stated as follows:

Proposition B. If utility depends only on real income and leisure, and the rate of a progressive tax is increased, incentive to work (as measured by hours) may increase or diminish. Whether hours of work will increase or diminish depends on the initial values of the variables and upon properties of the utility function which cannot be adduced *a priori*.

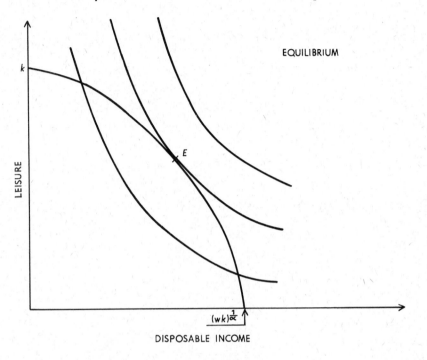

FIGURE 6

The two cases dealt with so far by no means exhaust the possibilities. For example, neither of these cases allowed for the exemption of part of gross income from taxation. Cases C and D will remedy this omission.

Case C. This case is similar to Case A, except that the tax function, while still a straight line, does not go through the origin. The point at which the tax function meets the income axis represents the exemption level. For this case theh tax function is given by

$$T = \alpha g + \beta \qquad (11)$$

where β is negative. As β increases (algebraically) the tax increases because the exemption level diminishes. Equation (10) leads to the disposable income function

$$y = (1 - \alpha)[w(k - l)] - \beta \text{ where } g > -\frac{\beta}{\alpha} \qquad (12)$$

If utility be maximized it is necessary that

$$\frac{\phi_l(y,l)}{\phi_y(y,l)} = (1-a)w \tag{13}$$

and

$$\left[w(1-a)\phi_{yy} - \phi_{ly} \right]\frac{dl}{d\beta} > 0. \tag{14}$$

If the expression in parentheses is positive (negative) hours of work will diminish (increase) as a result of the increase in the tax via a reduced exemption level. We may perhaps reasonably assume that the marginal

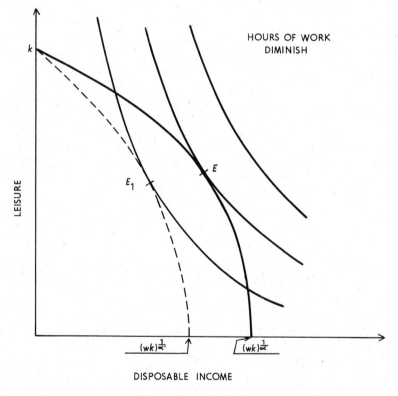

DISPOSABLE INCOME

FIGURE 7

utility of income diminishes, so that the first term is negative. Similarly, if we may assume that the marginal utility of leisure does not diminish as income increases, the second term $(-\phi_{ly})$ will be negative or zero. Hence we may state Proposition C, as follows:

Proposition C. The effect of lowering the exemption level (and thus raising the tax) is to increase incentive (hours of work), provided that *a*) utility depends only on real income and leisure,

b) the marginal utility of income diminishes,

c) the marginal utility of leisure does not diminish, as income increases,

d) the initial equilibrium is such that the individual's gross income is above the exemption level.[8]

Corollary: If the individual's initial (equilibrium) income is tax exempt, but this income would be taxable at the new level of taxation, it is easy to show that hours of work will increase or diminish under the same conditions as in Case *A*.

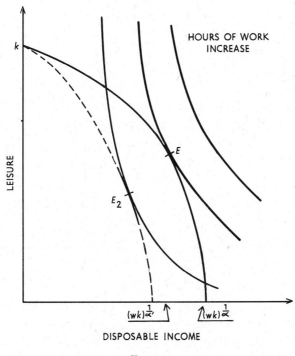

FIGURE 8

The results of Case *C* should be noted, inasmuch as they are referred to in Part III.

Case D. What happens to incentive if, assuming the same functions as in Case *C*, we change the tax rate without changing the exemption level?

---

[8] This requirement arises from the fact that the tax function (11), as written, applies only to the range of gross income above the exemption level. For the range of income up to (and including) the exemption level the tax function is, of course, $T = 0$.

Constancy of the exemption level means simply that the ratio of the parameters is constant. [This is obtained by setting $T = 0$ in the tax function.] Let us call this exemption level e. Then we may rewrite the tax function (11) in an equivalent fashion as

$$T = a(g - e) \text{ where } g > e. \tag{15}$$

The disposable income function then may be written as

$$y = (1 - a)[w(k - l)] + ae \tag{16}$$

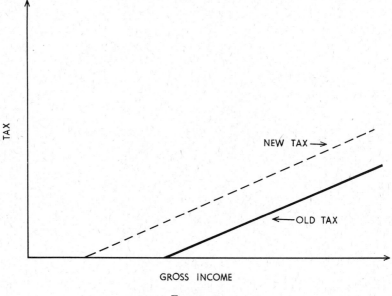

FIGURE 9

and we need only discuss the effect of increasing the single parameter a in order to determine the effect of increasing the tax rate above the exemption level. In this case the maximum conditions become

$$\frac{\phi_l(y,l)}{\phi_y(y,l)} = (1 - a)w \tag{17}$$

and

$$\left[w\phi_y + w(1 - a)(g - e)\phi_{yy} - (g - e)\phi_{ly} \right] \frac{dl}{da} > 0. \tag{18}$$

Examination of the expression in parentheses reveals the by now familiar result: it is not possible to say *a priori* what the effect of such a change in the tax will be. Proposition A, as stated, includes this result.

Case E. Just as Cases *C* and *D* extended the results of Case *A* to take account of an exemption level, so we must now extend the case of pure progression in the same way. The tax function of Case *B* may be modified so that

$$T - r = g - g^{\frac{1}{a}} \text{ where } r > 0, \tag{19}$$

r being the distance from the point where the tax function intersects the vertical axis to the origin. The kind of change in the tax function which is envisaged is displayed in Figure 10. As *r* increases (algebraically) the

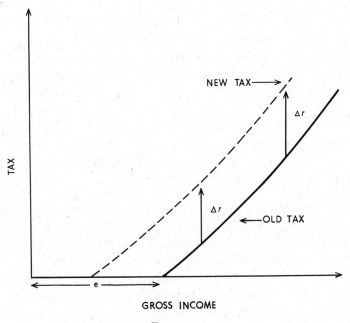

GROSS INCOME

FIGURE 10

exemption level *e* must diminish. Hence we may discuss the effect of increasing *r*, in order to determine the influence of increasing a progressive tax by lowering the exemption level. The exemption level itself is given by the solution of

$$g - g^{\frac{1}{a}} + r = 0. \tag{20}$$

It should perhaps be pointed out that the tax function has been shifted in such a way that the marginal rate of tax (at any income above the initial exemption level) is left unchanged by the change in the exemption level.

The necessary conditions for a maximum become

$$\frac{\phi_l(l,y)}{\phi_y(l,y)} = \frac{y+r}{a(k-l)} \tag{21}$$

[which is, of course, identical with equation (9) if $r = 0$] and

$$\left[\frac{y+r}{a(k-l)}\,\phi_{yy} - \phi_{ly}\right]\frac{dl}{dr} > 0. \tag{22}$$

Thus we have, in this case also, that the effect of lowering the exemption level is to increase hours of work. This conclusion is already contained in Proposition C, as stated, and should be similarly noted.

Case F. What happens if we increase the rate of a progressive tax without changing the exemption level? In other words what happens if we increase a; utilizing the tax function of Case E? Clearly the first equilibrium condition will be identical with (21). The second equilibrium condition becomes

$$\left[\left(1 + \frac{1}{a}\log g\right)\phi_y + \frac{y+r}{a}(\log g)\phi_{yy} - (k-l)(\log g)\phi_{ly}\right]\frac{dl}{da} > 0 \tag{23}$$

and, as in Case B, it is quite impossible to determine *a priori* what the influence of a change in the tax rate will be.

Case G. There remains one general kind of possible change in the tax structure which has not been discussed (except in a special case).[9] This possibility is displayed in Figure 11. Essentially, this consists in a simultaneous raising of the exemption level and of the marginal rate of tax so that the new tax schedule intersects the old at some predetermined point P. Whether this change in the structure would increase or decrease one's *total* tax liability (if no adjustment were made) of course depends on whether one's gross income were greater or less than g_o, as indicated in Figure 11, where g_o is the gross income at which the schedules intersect.

This case may be analyzed in the following way. Let the initial tax function be

$$T = ag + \beta \tag{24}$$

The assumptions of the problem require that g_o satisfy the equation

$$y = (1-a)g - \beta \tag{25}$$

and hence,

$$y = (1-a)(g-g_o) + y_o \tag{26}$$

---

[9] Given by Case A, where the tax functions intersect at the origin.

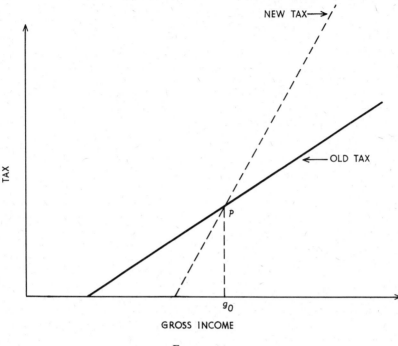

FIGURE 11

We may now proceed to discuss this case in terms of changes in the para-meter a alone.

When the marginal tax rate is increased and the exemption level *simultaneously* raised we obtain the following equilibrium conditions:

$$\frac{\phi_l(l,y)}{\phi_y(l,y)} = (1 - a)w \tag{27}$$

and,

$$\left[w\phi_y + w(1 - a)(g - g_0)\phi_{yy} - (g - g_0)\phi_{ly} \right]\frac{dl}{da} > 0. \tag{28}$$

Let us recall that g_0 is the gross income at which the old and new tax schedules coincide. Then we may regard the following proposition as having been established:

Proposition G. If utility depends only on real income and leisure; and if the tax schedule is altered in such fashion that the new and old schedules intersect at some level of gross income g_0; and the change is in the direction of raising both the exemption level and the marginal tax rate; then,

(i) For an individual whose equilibrium income before the tax change is g_o, the effect of the change will be to decrease hours of work, provided only that the marginal utility of income be positive.

(ii) For an individual whose equilibrium income before the tax change is less than g_o the effect of the change will be to reduce hours of work provided that the marginal utility of income be positive and diminishing, and that the marginal utility of leisure does not diminish as income increases.

(iii) For an individual whose equilibrium income before the tax change is greater than g_o, and whose utility function has the same properties as in (ii), the effect of the change cannot be determined *a priori*.

This result should also be noted.

Case H. The case just dealt with concerned the intersection of two straight line tax functions. Does the same result hold if the tax functions are progressive above the exemption level?

Let the initial tax function be

$$T = g - g^{\frac{1}{a}} + \beta \tag{29}$$

Then g_o, the intersection point, must satisfy

$$y = g^{\frac{1}{a}} - \beta \tag{30}$$

and hence,

$$y = g^{\frac{1}{a}} - g_o^{\frac{1}{a}} + y_o \tag{31}$$

The equilibrium conditions are

$$\frac{\phi_l(y,l)}{\phi_y(y,l)} = \frac{y + g_o^{\frac{1}{a}} - y_o}{a(k-l)} \tag{32}$$

and,

$$\left[\left(1 + \frac{\log g}{a} \right) \phi_y + \frac{1}{a} \left(g^a \log g - g_o^{\frac{1}{a}} \log g_o \right) \phi_{yy} \right.$$
$$\left. - \frac{k-l}{g^{\frac{1}{a}}} \left(g^{\frac{1}{a}} \log g - g_o^{\frac{1}{a}} \log g_o \right) \phi_{ly} \right] \frac{dl}{da} > 0.$$

Examination of (33) reveals that our result holds even where the tax functions are progressive above the exemption level. The result is contained in Proposition *G*, as stated.

The cases which have so far been discussed may be regarded as having exhausted the real alternatives with respect to income taxation, as well as the patience of the reader. Those who have persevered thus far may, nevertheless, find it useful to consider [10] three additional cases of a somewhat different variety.

The first of these takes one hesitant step in the direction of making the assumed utility function more "realistic." One may suppose that utility or satisfaction depends not only on real income and leisure, but also upon the individual's past income; and that, if he has grown accustomed to a certain standard of living, he will go to greater lengths (will work longer hours) to maintain that standard than he will to achieve a standard of living which he has not previously enjoyed. One simple way of studying the possible influence of this factor is to introduce the individual's highest past income into the utility function.[11]

Case I. Let the peak disposable income of the past be denoted by y^*. Then our hypothesis might be that utility depends upon the ratio of this peak income to current income, as well as leisure and current income. If so, we may write

$$u = \phi(y, l, z) \tag{34}$$

where z is the ratio of past peak income to current income. Let us assume the simple tax function of Case A (a proportional tax). We then have

$$z = \frac{y^*}{y} = \frac{y^*}{(1-a)[w(k-l)]} \tag{35}$$

If we now proceed as before we find that

$$\frac{\phi_l(y, l, z)}{\phi_y(y, l, z)} = (1-a)w + \frac{z}{k-l} \frac{\phi_z(y, l, z)}{\phi_y(y, l, z)} \tag{36}$$

and

$$\left[\phi_y + y\phi_{yy} - (k-l)\phi_{ly} + \frac{z}{y}\phi_z + z\phi_{zz} \right] \frac{dl}{da} > 0. \tag{37}$$

Just as it was impossible in Case A to determine the influence of the increase in taxation so it is impossible here, on an *a priori* basis. If our hypothesis be upheld, however, it is clear that ϕ_z and ϕ_{zz} are both negative—that is to say, we have two terms, not present in Case A, which will tend to increase hours of work.

The introduction of past income into the utility function for other indeterminate cases has similar results, and need not be displayed here.

---

[10] It was my inclination to write ". . . find some marginal reward in considering . . . ," until I recalled the stricture of a mathematician friend that one needs only to intersperse the text with the word "marginal" with sufficient frequency to sound like an economist.

[11] The same kind of idea, in a different connection, has been admirably set forth in Duesenberry, *Income, Saving and the Theory of Consumer Behavior* (Harvard University Press, 1949).

Case J. It will be useful for the discussion which follows if we consider one case of a different nature. We wish to answer the question: What will be the influence of inflation upon incentive, as measured by hours of work?

Let us denote the utility function by

$$u = \phi(Y/P, l) \tag{38}$$

where

$Y =$ disposable money income
$P =$ the general price level, not including wage rates.

This is the same utility function as before.

The tax function we shall write as

$$T = aG + \beta \tag{39}$$

where

$G =$ gross money income
$T =$ total tax in money

We have, therefore,

$$Y = (1 - a)[W(k - l)] + \beta \tag{40}$$

where

$W =$ the money wage rate

The first necessary condition for maximizing utility becomes

$$\frac{\phi_l}{\phi_y} = (1 - a)\frac{W}{P} . \tag{41}$$

What happens if we increase P but leave W unchanged? It is easy to show that

$$\left[\phi_y + y\phi_{yy} - \frac{y}{w(1 - a)} \phi_{ly}\right]\frac{dl}{dP} > 0 \tag{42}$$

and hence that no *a priori* determination of the consequence of "inflation" is possible; though the similarity to the inequality (6) is striking.

Case K. Finally, we may find it useful to attempt to answer the question: Given the kind of income tax (i.e., proportional, progressive, etc.) to be imposed, what should the tax schedule be in order to make the amount of work done as great as possible? Let us assume that the tax is to be proportional. If we assume that utility depends on real income and leisure, as before, the individual will work up to the point where

$$\frac{\phi_l(l, y)}{\phi_y(l, y)} = (1 - a)w \tag{43}$$

where a is the proportion of gross income which is paid in tax.

The government now desires to choose a so as to minimize l. This requirement leads to the following necessary condition:

$$w\phi_y + (1 - a)wg\phi_{yy} - g\phi_{ly} = 0 \qquad (44)$$

so that

$$a = 1 - \frac{(k - l)\phi_{ly} - \phi_y}{g\phi_{yy}} \qquad (45)$$

Hence, under the usual assumptions about marginal utility and its rates of change, the tax rate a which maximizes the amount of work done will not in general be zero. In fact, of course, this tax rate a will be different for each individual, so that the government might choose to impose a tax rate which would be a weighted sum of the tax rates given by the N equations like (45), where N is the number of workers. In particular, they might choose to weight according to gross income, so that

$$\bar{a} = \frac{\Sigma a_i g_i}{\Sigma g_i} \quad i = 1, 2, \cdots, N \qquad (46)$$

where $\bar{a}$ is the overall tax rate which is to be imposed and where a is the tax which will maximize individual i's hours of work.

III. SUMMARY AND CONCLUSION

What, then, has been accomplished by the collection of symbols in Part II? The general nature of our results may be summed up quite briefly:

(i) The tax function which will maximize the number of hours which an individual will work is not, in general, $T = 0$. Hence the assumption that "incentive" will diminish as a result of an increase in tax rates possesses no justification.

(ii) Where the change in the tax structure is such that both the average and the marginal rates of tax are increased or diminished, it is impossible to determine the effect of the tax on the basis of the assumptions usually made about the utility function.

(iii) Where the change in the tax structure is such that the average rate of tax is increased and the marginal rate diminished the effect of the change is to increase hours of work. If the average rate is reduced and the marginal rate increased hours of work will diminish.

(iv) An increase (decrease) in the average rate of tax, leaving the marginal rate unchanged, will increase (diminish) hours of work.

(v) The effect of inflation on hours of work cannot be determined on the basis of the usual assumptions about the utility function.

At first glance these conclusions may be hard to swallow, so frequently has the myth been repeated that taxation reduces incentive. Let the reader ponder on his own reactions, however, if, say, his disposable income were cut in half! Consider, too, the historical fact that leisure has increased rather than diminished as income rose. Furthermore, we may think of leisure as being a commodity which the individual purchases with his income; so that if we change the tax schedule in such a way that both the individual's income and the effective price of leisure are altered, his "purchase" of leisure will change because *both* income and the price of leisure change. If there is an increase in taxes the individual will, in general, tend to buy less leisure because his disposable income has been reduced, but he will tend to buy more leisure because the price of leisure has been reduced; and the question becomes: Which influence is dominant?

The qualifications which are relevant to these conclusions should not, of course, be forgotten. We have assumed an extremely simple utility function. We have dealt only with certain limited aspects of labor services; though we might, however, regard the earlier development (Part II) as having reference to some sort of utility function for the household, so that an increase or diminution of hours of work may be taken to refer to the hours of the household, rather than the individual. If this approach be permissible then Part II also covers the case of drawing additional persons into the labor force, in large part.[12]

Obviously, too, the analysis is inapplicable to those employed on a piece-work basis. I know of no way to handle this problem, since it would involve introducing a factor which measures "how hard a person works when he works," rather than simply "number of hours." Nor have we investigated the possible allocational influence of income taxation, though the claim sometimes made, that the reallocation of labor which is desired during mobilization is rendered more difficult by an increase in income taxes, is simply not demonstrable.[13]

Notwithstanding all of these, and perhaps other, qualifications, it seems to this writer that there is a core of solid truth in what has been demonstrated, a core of reality which is applicable to the world in which we live. If our results had been completely indeterminate, if we had found it impossible to say, in any case whatever, what the influence of a change in the tax structure would be, this fact alone would have considerable significance. For it would then be reasonable to suppose that there are

---

12 It would still exclude persons who, before mobilization, were members of households of which no individual was in the labor force.

13 For example, if two occupations pay $2.00 and $1.50 per hour, respectively, it is not true, *in general*, that the imposition of a tax which would reduce these to, say, $1.80 and $1.40 would make reallocation more difficult. It may very well make it easier.

some individuals whose hours of work would be diminished, others whose hours would be increased. The wisdom of increasing tax rates would then depend, in part, upon the relative numbers of individuals in each class, and upon the strength of their reactions to the tax change.

In fact, however, we have demonstrated that there *are* ways of increasing total tax receipts which, if our rather modest assumptions be accepted, will actually increase incentive, as measured by hours of work. Moreover, there may exist devices which will enable us to increase taxes without reducing incentive, even if the properties of the individual's utility function are such as to make this the expected result. For example, we might impose a tax on the income which the individual *would have earned* if he had worked some predetermined number of hours,[14] thus effectively making the marginal tax rate zero. Or we might simply exempt from taxation the income derived from work beyond, say, forty hours. We might have special tax provisions for *increases* in labor income. These and other devices might be used in cases where there is real ground for believing that an increase in income tax rates will have undesirable incentive effects.

In addition, it should be pointed out that, even at the price of some reduction in output, we might prefer high income taxes to alternative fiscal policies, inasmuch as these latter will inevitably have costs of their own associated with them.

There may, in the current and contemplated mobilization, be good reason for not relying on "pay as you go," but the case against it cannot rest on an *a priori* incentive argument.

APPENDIX

Given the utility function

$$U = F[\phi(l,y)] \quad F'(\phi) > 0 \tag{1}$$

and the disposable income function

$$y = f(l,a) \tag{2}$$

where a is the tax parameter.

If we maximize U with respect to l we obtain

$$\frac{\partial U}{\partial l} = F'(\phi)[\phi_l + \phi_y f_l] = 0 \tag{3}$$

so that the equilibrium (l_o, y_o) is seen to be independent of F.

It is sufficient to guarantee a maximum U if, at equilibrium,

$$\left[\frac{\partial^2 U}{\partial l^2}\right]_o < 0 \tag{4}$$

---

[14] I have been unable to trace the source of this idea, though I feel sure that it is not my own.

and the functions F, ϕ, f are taken as continuous in the neighborhood of equilibrium. From (3) we obtain

$$\left[\frac{\partial^2 U}{\partial l^2}\right]_0 = F'(\phi)\left[\phi_{ll} + 2f_l\phi_{ly} + f_l^2\phi_{yy} + f_{ll}\phi_y\right].$$ (5)

If now we treat (3) as an identity in a, and differentiate with respect to a, it may be shown that

$$\frac{dl}{da} = \frac{-\left[f_a\phi_{ly} + f_lf_a\phi_{yy} + f_{la}\phi_y\right]}{\left[\phi_{ll} + 2f_l\phi_{ly} + f_l^2\phi_{yy} + f_{ll}\phi_y\right]}$$ (6)

and, using (4) and (5)

$$\frac{dl}{da} = \frac{F'(\phi)\left[f_a\phi_{ly} + f_lf_a\phi_{yy} + f_{la}\phi_y\right]}{\left|\left(\frac{\partial^2 U}{\partial l^2}\right)_0\right|}.$$ (7)

Hence $\dfrac{dl}{da}$ has the algebraic sign of the expression

$$\left[f_a\phi_{ly} + f_lf_a\phi_{yy} + f_{la}\phi_y\right]$$ (8)

which is equivalent to the expressions displayed in the text.

The exact form of the expression displayed in the text is derived as follows. Differentiate (3), regarded as a function of l and a, with respect to a, to obtain

$$\frac{\partial^2 u}{\partial l^2}\frac{dl}{da} + \frac{\partial^2 u}{\partial l\,\partial a} = 0.$$ (9)

If $\dfrac{dl}{da} \neq 0$, then

$$\frac{\partial^2 u}{\partial l^2}\left(\frac{dl}{da}\right)^2 = -\frac{\partial^2 u}{\partial l\,\partial a}\frac{dl}{da}$$ (10)

and, using (4)

$$\left[\frac{\partial^2 u}{\partial l\,\partial a}\right]\frac{dl}{da} > 0.$$ (11)

31

*Proportional Income Taxation and Risk-Taking**

By EVSEY D. DOMAR and RICHARD A. MUSGRAVE

The effects of income taxation on investment have been discussed in economic literature with varying emphasis. Prior to the debacle of the late 'twenties the detrimental effects of taxation upon the volume of savings were stressed. During the 'thirties economic thinking and experience indicated that the decision to invest constitutes a crucial link between the setting aside of savings and the flow of funds into actual investment. Accordingly, the emphasis of the discussion was shifted to the effects of taxation on the investment of available funds, particularly on investment in risky ventures. In this paper we examine the basic aspects of this problem, which will be of vital importance after the war.

I. SUMMARY AND CONCLUSIONS

An investment involves the possibility of a loss. It will not be undertaken unless the expected return appears sufficiently promising. In every investment decision the investor must weigh the advantage of a greater return, or *yield*, against the disadvantage of a possible loss, or *risk*. These two variables serve as tools for the analysis of the problem.

The effects of taxation upon risk-taking are analyzed in two steps: first, we consider how the imposition of a tax, under varying conditions, affects the yield and the risk of an investment (or more correctly, of a whole combination of various assets); second, we inquire how the investor will react to these changes. That the tax reduces the yield, is entirely evident and has been much emphasized; but the equally important fact that the tax may also reduce the degree of risk has received little attention. Its significance has recently been pointed out by A. P. Lerner, to whom this paper owes a considerable debt.[1]

---

* *Quarterly Journal of Economics*, Vol. LVIII (May, 1944).
[1] A. P. Lerner "Functional Finance and the Federal Debt," Social Research, February,

By imposing an income tax on the investor, the Treasury appoints itself as his partner, who will always share in his gains, but whose share in his losses will depend upon the investor's ability to offset losses against other income. Three cases may be distinguished:

1. If losses cannot be offset, the investor carries the entire burden of the loss. The tax reduces the yield (and even by a higher percentage than the tax rate), but leaves the degree of risk unchanged, so that the compensation per unit of risk-taking is reduced. This is the case most frequently discussed in the literature.

2. If a complete offset of losses is possible, the result is very different. Suppose the investor receives an income of $1,000, which is independent of the investment in question, so that after a 25 per cent tax he retains $750. If he now makes an investment and suffers a loss of $200, this loss can be fully deducted from his other income, so that only $800 remains subject to tax. Accordingly, the tax is reduced to $200 and his total income remaining after the loss, net of the tax, is now $600, as compared with $750 before the investment was made and the loss suffered. The net loss is thus only $150, the remaining $50, or 25 per cent, having been absorbed by the Treasury in the form of a reduced tax bill on the investor's other income. The yield *and* the risk of the investment have been reduced by the rate of the tax, so that the return per unit of risk-taking remains unchanged.

3. If only a partial offset of losses is possible, the yield is reduced by a greater percentage than the degree of risk, and the results fall between those of cases (1) and (2).

How will the investor react to these changes in yield and risk, which the tax has produced? Prior to the tax, he was in an equilibrium position, which gave him the most advantageous combination of yield and risk available. After one or both of these variables are changed, he may wish to change his position, that is, take more or less risk. We again consider the same three cases:

1. Since, without loss offset, the yield is cut, while risk is unchanged, the compensation for risk-taking is reduced. Risk-taking has become less attractive, so that the investor will want to take less risk. But the reduc-

---

1943, pp. 45–46. A similar point was also made by Henry C. Simons in his *Personal Income Taxation* (Chicago, 1938), p. 21. Also see Twentieth Century Fund, *Facing the Tax Problem* (New York, 1937), p. 292, and M. J. Bowman and G. L. Bach, *Economic Analysis and Public Policy* (New York, 1943), p. 768. As far as we are aware, the argument is neglected in the standard texts on Public Finance.

An empirical study of some phases of our problem has appeared since this paper went to print. See J. Keith Butters and John Lintner, *Effect of Federal Taxes on Growing Enterprises*, Study No. 1, Lockheed Aircraft Corporation (Harvard Business School, Division of Research, 1944).

tion in yield also means a lower income from his investments. To restore his income, the investor will try to take more risk, since risky investments can be expected to have a higher yield. These two forces are operating in opposite directions. Theoretically the result is uncertain; practical evidence would indicate that the investor is likely to shift in the direction of less risk.

2. If losses can be offset, and the Treasury assumes part of the risk, as well as of the yield, a distinction must be drawn between *private* risk (and yield), which is carried by the investor, and the *total* risk (and yield), which includes also the share borne by the Treasury. It is the private risk (and yield) of an investment that is reduced by the tax; the total risk (and yield) remains, of course, unchanged. Since the private risk and yield are reduced by the same percentage, risk-taking has not become less attractive. The inducement to take less risk, which was present in the first case, has disappeared. The investor's income, however, has been reduced, and to restore it, he will take more risk, although the private risk taken after adjustment to the tax need not equal the pre-tax level. If the investor had retained the original asset combination, its total risk would have remained the same. But since the investor was shown to adjust his asset combination so as to increase his private risk above the unadjusted level to which it was lowered by the tax, total risk must have increased above the pre-tax level.

3. Under conditions of partial loss deduction, the yield is reduced by a greater percentage than risk. Both forces will be operating as in case (1), and the outcome will be uncertain. But there appears little doubt that the higher is the rate of loss offset, the higher will be the degree of risk taken after the tax.

The assumptions under which these conclusions have been reached are developed later on and are summarized in the final section.

A shift towards a more risky investment (or rather asset combination) may be accomplished by reducing the proportion of the investor's total assets held in cash, that is, by larger total investment, or through a change from less to more risky investments. There is no question that increased risk-taking in either or both forms is highly desirable (except during acute boom conditions) and that therefore a higher degree of loss deduction is of vital importance. The extent to which loss offset is possible in actual practice depends on the offset provisions in the tax law and upon the availability of other income in each instance.

There are limited provisions for loss offset in the tax law. Since a tax is imposed on net income, the law necessarily permits the offset of investment losses realized in a given period against income received in that period, subject, however, to the important limitation that, with minor exceptions, capital losses can be offset against capital gains only. The likelihood that sufficient other income will be available to the taxpayer is increased greatly if losses made in one period can be carried forward or backward against income made in other periods. The personal and corporation income tax law now provides for a limited carry-back and carryforward (two years each) of business net operating losses and for a fiveyear carry-forward of long-term capital losses. Possible changes in the rate schedule introduce additional uncertainties into the investor's calculations.

The extent to which investors may utilize these provisions depends upon the availability of other income. Here the position of various taxpayers differs greatly. A large corporation or a large-scale financial investor may undertake a risky investment as a side line, and know that possible losses are covered by other income which is reasonably certain to be derived from the main line of business. It is not necessary, of course, that the losses should be realized in the form of capital losses; they may also take the form of a lower taxable income resulting from depreciation costs being charged against other income. Further, a large corporation is assured of the possibility of loss offset as long as the investment in question does not exceed the minimum net income (low as it may be relative to total invested capital) which the management is reasonably certain to derive during the period of carry-over. Thus, if a public utility or a life insurance company were to make a small investment (small relative to other income from operations or interest on gilt-edged bonds) in a very risky venture, it could be quite certain of a loss offset, and would thus have a great advantage over a small competitor who might consider the same venture. The discrimination is even more flagrant in the case of loss carry-back, which gives an "old" corporation (that is, a corporation with past net income) the certainty of possible loss offset, thus placing it in a very advantageous position as compared with a new company. Inequities of this type will tend to increase economic concentration, and may lower the volume of new investment.

It is evident that the tax law should be adjusted to create the most favorable possible condition for loss offset for all types of investors. This raises numerous technical problems which are not considered in this paper. A careful analysis should be made of the length of the carry-over period required for this purpose, and, if necessary and feasible, unlimited carry-forward of losses should be permitted, supplemented by a limited carry-back. The possibilities of averaging income over a period of years should also be explored, and the present differential treatment of capital gains and losses, as well as the possibility of providing more flexible depreciation schedules, should be examined. These considerations by no means apply to the corporation tax only, but are equally if not more important with respect to the personal income tax.

A less orthodox alternative to an extended carry-over of losses might be considered, under which the Treasury would reimburse the taxpayer during the very period in which the net loss was made. Besides encouraging risk-taking, an arrangement of this kind might also contribute to cyclical stability by raising effective tax rates during prosperity and lowering them during depression. Even if some loss in revenue results, the condition for investment will be more favorable under a somewhat higher tax rate, together with more complete loss offset than under a lower tax rate accompanied by more imperfect offset conditions.

In the following five sections, the analysis is carried out in greater detail. In Section II the general rationale of investment behavior is described. In Sections III, IV and V the effects of taxation on risk-taking are examined under the assumptions of no loss offset, full loss offset, and partial loss offset, respectively. Some limitations of the analysis are reviewed in Section VI.

II. THE RATIONALE OF INVESTMENT BEHAVIOR

The essence of our problem is the change in the investor's behavior under the impact of the tax. Just as the usual theory of tax shifting is but an application of the principles of price theory to a particular change in data caused by the imposition of a tax, so the solution of the present problem consists in applying a theory of investment behavior to a similar change. Although the discussion of various investment problems is common in economic literature, no integrated theory of investment behavior applicable to the analysis of effects of taxation has come to our attention. While this is not the place to develop such a theory, it will be necessary to agree at the outset on those aspects of investment behavior which are directly related to our problem. For purposes of simplicity, our analysis is mainly concerned with the case of financial investment, some special characteristics of real investment being mentioned in the closing section. In addition, the following assumptions are made: (*a*) a *given* amount of investment funds is available to the investor; (*b*) investments are divisible into small units, that is, "lumpiness" is excluded; (*c*) the investment market is perfectly atomistic, so that the investor can neglect the effect of his decisions on yields; (*d*) the investor's expectations, gross of the tax, are unaffected by the imposition of the tax and by resulting government expenditures.

To handle our problem, quantitative values for the yield and the degree of risk of an investment are needed; and in the absence of a better approach, they are obtained by means of a probability distribution which the investor will construct for each available investment opportunity.[2] Each possible yield, positive or negative, will include the recurrent income from the investment (such as interest or dividends), as well as the change in capital value which the investor expects to realize. Thus, no distinction is made here between capital gains and other income or capital losses and other losses. Each expected yield will be net of all monetary costs of investment. The dollar amounts are transformed into percentage yields on the amount invested by a process similar to that used by Keynes in defining the marginal efficiency of capital.[3] In constructing the probability distribution, the investor will consider all those circumstances which appear significant to him, such as the period of holding, possible developments during this period, and the conditions accompanying the sale. Thus, not only expectations regarding the specific investment and general market developments will be included, but also personal circumstances, such as a sudden need of cash because of a broken arm. Since income for tax purposes is always expressed in dollar amounts, our analysis is carried out in cash terms, cash being used as the numéraire.

From the probability distribution thus constructed, the investor will

---

[2] For examples of the traditional probability approach, see Irving Fisher, *The Nature of Capital and Income* (New York, 1906), Ch. 16, and A. C. Pigou, *The Economics of Welfare* (London, 1932), Appendix I. For a bibliography of more recent writings on risk theory, see W. Fellner, "Monetary Policies and Hoarding in Periods of Stagnation," *Journal of Political Economy*, June, 1943, p. 196.

The probability approach to risk theory implies that it is "reasonable to set up the assumption of quantified probability estimates as an idealization of actual business practice." A. G. Hart, "Uncertainty and Inducements to Invest," *Review of Economic Studies*, October, 1940, p. 52. Objections may be raised to this assumption, as in fact they may be raised against most any feature of the "homo economicus." For purposes of this paper, which does not discuss risk theory as such, the probability method is adopted, because no satisfactory alternative approach to the subject of risk theory has been developed. The theory of investment behavior, as developed by G. L. S. Shakle, divides expectations into those which would and would not cause "surprise," and thus avoids having to attach numerical probabilities to all expected yields. It appears to us that the resulting indeterminacy makes it impossible to derive satisfactory tools for the comparison of relative advantages of different investments and therefore for the analysis of taxation effects. *Cf.* G. L. S. Shackle, "The Nature of the Inducement to Invest," *Review of Economic Studies*, October, 1940, pp. 44–48, and "A Theory of Investment-Decisions," *Oxford Economic Papers*, April, 1942, pp. 77–94.

[3] That is, the investor will compute the rate of discount which equates the present value of the prospective returns with the amount invested. *Cf.* J. M. Keynes, *The General Theory of Employment Interest and Money* (New York, 1936), p. 135, and Irving Fisher, *op. cit.*, Ch. 13 and 14.

compute the mathematical expectation of the percentage yields, to be indicated by y.[4] It will prove helpful in the following discussion to separate y into its negative component r and its positive component g. Thus, if $q_1, q_2 \cdots q_{k+1} \cdots q_n$ are the expected rates of return, such that $q_i < q_{i+1}$ and $q_k = 0$, and if the probability of the occurrence of q_i is p_i, so that

$$\sum_{i=1}^{n} p_i = 1,$$

we arrive at the following definitions:

$$r = -\sum_{i=1}^{k} q_i p_i \qquad (1)$$

$$g = \sum_{i=k+1}^{n} q_i p_i \qquad (2)$$

$$y = \sum_{i=1}^{n} q_i p_i = g - r \qquad (3)$$

The magnitude of the actuarial value is not the only factor determining the investor's choice. Other characteristics must also be considered, though for purposes of this analysis their number must be limited.

Investment decisions are made in spite of uncertainty with respect to the relevant data and their implications. No investor is sure that his estimated probability distribution is entirely correct, but the degree of uncertainty will vary with different investors and different investments. It will be a factor in the investment decision. Yet it is extremely difficult to express the degree of uncertainty involved in workable terms.[6] For our pur-

---

[4] The use of the mathematical expectation appears to us to be superior to that of the most probable value, employed by some other authors in similar problems. See, for instance, W. Fellner, *op. cit.*, p. 198. If, for reasons of simplicity, the probability distribution is to be represented by one variable, the latter should reflect as much as possible the changes in any part of the probability distribution. The significance of this condition for an analysis of taxation effects will be seen presently.

[5] Since the values of all q's from the beginning to q_k are negative, r is positive.

[6] The uncertainty factor has been emphasized in recent discussions of investment behavior, according to which the investor is, in fact, confronted not with a single probability distribution, but with a probability distribution of probability distributions. A. G. Hart has pointed out that the problem of uncertainty cannot be solved by boiling down the set of probability distributions into a single "super" distribution, since the latter would conceal certain characteristics of the component distributions which are relevant for economic planning. This paper being a first step in the analysis of our subject, these complications, which will hardly affect the major results, are avoided here. *Cf.* A. G. Hart in *Studies in Mathematical Economics and Econometrics* (Chicago, 1942), pp. 110–18, and *Anticipation, Uncertainty, and Dynamic Planning*, Studies in Business Administration, Vol. XI, No. 1 (University of Chicago, 1940). See also H. Makower and J. Marschak, "Assets, Prices and Monetary Theory," *Economica*, August, 1938, pp. 271 ff., and J. R. Hicks, "A Suggestion for Simplifying the Theory of Money" *Economica*, February, 1935, pp. 1–19.

pose it is sufficient to say that the prevalence of uncertainty may induce the investor to require a somewhat higher return than would be required otherwise.

The very fact that the actuarial value is based on a probability distribution indicates that the investment involves some degree of doubt as to whether or not the actual return will fall within specified limits. The investor will undoubtedly be interested in a number of limits, and in comparing two investments with different actuarial values may or may not wish to apply the same limits to each. Of all possible questions which the investor may ask, the most important one, it appears to us, is concerned with the probability of the actual yield being less than zero, that is, with the probability of a loss. This is the essence of *risk*.[7] Since the investor is not only interested in the probability of a negative return, but also in the chances of suffering losses of various magnitudes, the coefficient of risk should be defined more precisely as a function of losses and their probabilities. This can be done most simply by defining risk as the already familiar expression *r*, i.e. the summation of all possible losses multiplied by their respective probabilities as defined in (1).[8]

By considering *r*, the most relevant aspect of the dispersion of the prob-

---

[7] The terminology employed here broadly agrees with that used in recent literature; *cf.*, for instance, H. Makower and J. Marschak, *op. cit.*, p. 271, and G. Tintner and A. G. Hart in *Studies in Mathematical Economics and Econometrics* (Chicago, 1942), pp. 92 and 110.

The term "risk" has been given different connotations by various authors, but it has been generally described as a property of a known probability distribution. It has been expressed, for instance, as the probability of obtaining a smaller return than *y* (A. C. Pigou, *op. cit.*, p. 776), or as the coefficient of variation. The expression in the text appears to be most useful for our purposes, because among the factors underlying investment behavior and affected by a proportional tax we regard risk as defined in the text as by far the most important.

The term "uncertainty" usually applies to anticipations where the probability distribution itself is not exactly known. This is in general agreement with Professor Knight's use of the term, although "uncertainty" in his sense would appear to apply only where probability estimates are assumed not to be cardinal. See H. Makower and J. Marschak, *op. cit.*, p. 271, and A. G. Hart, *op. cit.*, p. 111.

[8] A further refinement of our definition of risk may be made. If the market pays a return on an entirely riskless investment, the investor when purchasing a given investment incurs not only the risk of losing a part of his present wealth, but also of losing the opportunity of obtaining a certain return from a riskless investment. If, therefore, the return on an entirely riskless investment is equal to *l*, expected losses should be measured, not from the zero point of the probability distribution, but from *l*. Thus, if in our original probability distribution of $q_1, q_2 \cdots q^k \cdots q_m \cdots q_n$ there is a $q_m = l$, the adjusted degree of risk may be redefined as

$$r' = -\sum_{i=1}^{m} (q_i - l) \, p_i = -\sum_{i=1}^{k} q_i p_i + \left(-\sum_{i=k+1}^{m} q_i p_i + l \sum_{i=1}^{m} p_i \right) = r + \lambda.$$

In an economy like that of the United States, the difference between *r* and *r'* is likely to be of minor importance, since *l* may be expected to be quite small or zero. Therefore, this correction may be omitted for most of the argument and will be mentioned only where it may be particularly significant.

ability distribution is accounted for in our analysis. If an investor is to undertake an investment involving a possible loss of his wealth, a compensation will definitely be demanded. The case is less clear in regard to other aspects of the dispersion. If a choice is to be made between investments with different probability distributions, but which have the same yield and risk, it may well be that one investor would prefer the possibility of a large gain, although the probability of obtaining an even moderate return may be low, while another investor would prefer a greater probability of obtaining a moderate return, even though the possibility of substantial gain may be small. It is thus not clear that a greater dispersion, other things being equal, represents a disutility and commands a market return. This is not to say that the dispersion of the distribution will not be a factor in investment decisions. A more elaborate analysis would allow for additional variables defining the shape of the probability distribution, for example, in terms of the standard deviation, the probability of obtaining less or more than a given "minimum yield," or the probability of suffering more or less than a given "maximum loss." For purposes of this analysis, however, it is assumed that the investor will consider changes in y and r only.[9]

From the preceding discussion we thus emerge with two tools of analysis: r — the degree of risk, and y — the yield of the investment, which is regarded as a compensation for risk-taking. Aside from the already considered question whether a compensation is needed for the uncertainty and dispersion of the probability distribution, the definition of y as the compensation for risk-taking may meet with two objections. First, it may be argued that y should also contain a compensation for the necessary "effort" of making an investment. Second, the reader will wonder what has happened to the compensation for parting with liquidity.

As stated previously, y is defined as net of all monetary costs of investment, so that the only element that is disregarded is the personal "effort" of making the investment. But this effort is subject to enormous economies of large scale, which are also available to smaller investors through the services of investment trusts. It appears to be of no great importance. In those few cases, however, where the element of personal effort may affect the results, it will be taken into consideration.[10]

The problem of liquidity remains to be considered. As expounded by

---

[9] This limitation would probably not be acceptable for the analysis of a progressive tax, for which the entire shape of the probability distribution would be important.

[10] Thus, if it can be assumed that the net investment effort requires a minimum compensation, to be indicated by e, which is a constant percentage rate on the amount invested, then the adjusted compensation for risk-taking may be redefined as $y' = y - e$.

Keynes, cash is held because of the speculative, precautionary and income (and business) motives.[11] The speculative motive refers to possible losses due to changes in interest rate, and thus represents a component of our concept of risk. The same holds true for the precautionary motive, which is concerned with the possibility of a loss due to the unavailability of cash at some future date. The analysis of the income motive results in a similar conclusion: the reason why an investor does not invest all his funds up to his last dollar is the knowledge that he will need some cash for current expenditures at an early date, so that the investment of the last portion of his funds would almost certainly result in a net loss, since investment expenses would be large relative to gross yield and a rush sale would probably be necessary. Thus, the three elements of the liquidity preference represent nothing but the fear of loss, and are therefore accounted for in our probability distribution and in the values of y and r.[12]

So far, the discussion has referred to single investments. Actually the investor is concerned with obtaining the most desirable use of all his assets, consisting of various investments and cash. It should be noted that a distinction is made here between an *investment combination*, which refers to that part of the investor's wealth which is not held in cash form, and an *asset combination*, which includes both investments and cash. It will be convenient to assume, at first, that the investor intends to invest all his funds, and then to introduce varying holdings of cash. To the extent that the probability distributions of various possible investments are independent of one another, their combination will reduce the degree of risk in accordance with the usual probability theory. But actually the probability distributions of most investments are somewhat interdependent, primarily due to their common dependence on general business conditions. A careful selection of investments may thus be more important than the choice of a large number of different investments.

Let the ordinate and abscissa of the points A and B in Figure 1 indicate the degree of risk and the yield of two different asset combinations

[11] J. M. Keynes, *op. cit.*, ch. 13 and 15.

[12] This view of the supply price for investment funds has certain implications for the theory of interest. If the return for waiting is zero (which, of course, depends upon institutional and other factors) and if Keynes' liquidity preference represents merely special types of risk, the question must be asked why the return for these elements of risk (namely, marketability and changes in the interest rate) should be separated from other risk factors and identified as *the* rate of interest. This does not mean that for certain purposes a distinction between various types of risk might not be useful, but the more inclusive is the definition of interest—that is, the more complete the different types of risk the return for which is included—the clearer becomes the need for discarding the idea of *the* rate of interest and for talking about the returns available on different investments. We hope to develop this idea at a future date.

consisting *entirely* of the investments A and B respectively. Thus no cash is held at all. If the two investments are combined, the magnitudes of the r and y of each combination will depend upon the r and y of the components, the ratio at which they are combined, and their degree of independence. If they are completely interdependent, the magnitudes of y and r of the combinations will equal the weighted averages of the components and will hence be located on a straight line AB. If, as is more likely to be the case, they are more or less independent, the r of each combination will be more or less below the weighted average of the r of the components. This reflects the principle that diversification reduces the dispersion of a probability distribution. Therefore the r's and y's will fall on a curve such as ACB.

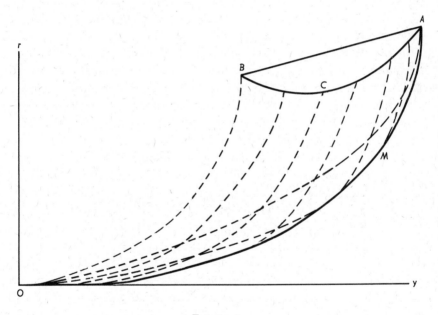

FIGURE 1
THE OPTIMUM ASSET CURVE

Besides investments, the investor's asset combination will also include a proportion of cash. Cash differs from investments by having a zero risk and zero yield. Cash holdings are riskless, since they can not give rise to losses. This is the case because opportunity costs, that is, income not received because investment opportunities were missed, do not enter our analysis. Losses or gains in the real value of cash, due to price changes, are excluded likewise, because the entire anaylsis is in terms of cash. An expected appreciation or depreciation of investments due to general price changes is already accounted for in the estimating of probable gains and losses. Therefore in Figure 1 an asset combination consisting of cash only is located at the origin.

Beginning with an asset combination consisting of investments only, such as represented by a point C, the investor can move his combination towards the origin by increasing the proportion of his assets held in cash. The dotted curve CO described by this movement will be called the *cash-investment curve*. As the proportion of cash increases, the risk and the yield of the whole asset combination decline, since cash has zero risk and yield. The point C will move towards O, not along a straight line, but rather along a curve of the type CO, since r falls faster than y. The reason is that as the proportion of cash in the asset combination increases, it becomes less likely that a forced sale under unfavorable conditions will be necessary. Therefore the risk of the *investment* combination will decline, while its yield may even rise.[13]

The cash-investment curve, as drawn in Figure 1, does not indicate the proportion of cash in the asset combination corresponding to any given point on the curve. To measure the cash ratio, a third dimension would be needed. This is an important limitation of our analysis, since it makes it impossible to allocate changes in risk to changes in cash holdings and changes in the riskiness of investments held.

In order to find the best available asset combination, the investor will draw all possible cash-investment curves between each point indicating an investment combination and the origin, as shown by the dotted curves in Figure 1. It is evident that for each level of risk there will be a large (infinite) number of asset combinations with varying proportions of the investments A, B and cash. Of these, however, only the one with the highest yield is relevant.[14] The locus of these points of maximum yield, AMO, is *the* curve which describes the investor's evaluation of the market situation and which is the principal tool for our analysis. We shall call it the *optimum-asset curve*.[15]

---

[13] It is quite possible that, as the investor moves down along the cash-investment curve, the yield of the whole asset combination may increase at first, since he will escape the probable loss that would result from the investment of the last portion of his funds. In order to analyze what happens on the upper part of the curve, it would be necessary to allow for the possibility of borrowing, which may become profitable as the investor moves up along the curve. We prefer to disregard borrowing, so as not to complicate the general discussion.

[14] It follows from subsequent analysis that the imposition of a tax will not change the yield rating of various asset combinations with the same degree of risk.

[15] The optimum-asset curve can be expected to be smooth and continuous, because we have assumed an infinite divisibility of all assets. The investor can, therefore, combine the three assets, namely, the investment A, B and cash, in an infinite number of proportions which, most likely, will eliminate kinks. The case will be even stronger if more than two investments are considered.

In order to determine the investor's choice of the best position on the optimum-asset curve, a preference map between y and r can be constructed. Again y is measured along the abscissa and r along the ordinate. The essence of the map is a comparison between the investor's advantage of obtaining income and the disadvantage of jeopardizing his wealth. In our analysis both income and losses, measured in terms of y and r, are expressed as percentage rates on a given dollar amount of wealth. Therefore, any changes in wealth will result in a change in the indifference map.[16] But since the amount of wealth is assumed to be constant, changes in percentage returns are equivalent to corresponding changes in income.

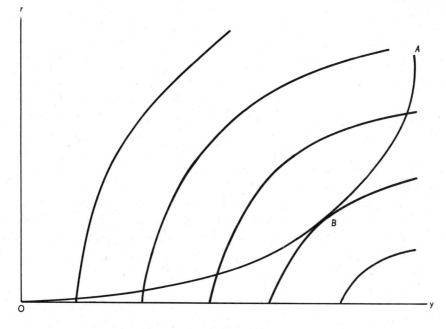

FIGURE 2
THE EQUILIBRIUM POSITION

The indifference map presented in Figure 2 and in the other figures is constructed on the basis of the following conditions: it is assumed, first, that for any individual the marginal utility of income declines with increasing income, and second, that the marginal disutility of risk-taking rises with increasing risk. We also assume the marginal utility of income

---

[16] The indifference map could also have been expressed in dollar amounts. Then the pattern would have been independent of changes in wealth, which would have been reflected in a shift of the optimum-asset curve. For the purposes of the present analysis, the approach chosen seemed more convenient.

to be independent of risk and vice versa. Our analysis being limited to the immediate effects of a tax on investment, without regard for secondary effects such as changes in wealth, this assumption appears reasonable.

Since the slope of each indifference curve, or *the marginal rate of risk-taking*, equals the ratio of the marginal utility of income to the marginal disutility of risk, the slopes of the indifference curves must be positive: an increase in y along any indifference curve must be accompanied by an increase in r and vice versa. The application of the two assumptions, stated above, to the preference map gives the indifference curves the following three properties:

1. The slope of any one indifference curve must be decreasing upward and to the right. This is the result of *either* one or both assumptions.

2. The slopes of the indifference curves must decline with increasing values of y for any given value of r — the result of the first assumption.

3. The slopes of the indifference curves must decline with increasing values of r for any given value of y — the result of the second assumption.

Property (1), used throughout our argument, is more certain than properties (2) and (3), since it holds true even if either one of the assumptions is omitted. Property (3) is not needed for our purposes.[17] Finally, property (2), which rests on the first assumption only, is used throughout our discussion, but sceptics who do not believe in it will find comfort in the footnotes below.[18]

The equilibrium position of the investor can now be easily found by establishing the point of tangency of the optimum-asset curve, ABO, with one of the indifference curves, as shown by point B on Figure 2.

III. TAXATION WITHOUT LOSS OFFSET

We turn now to the effects of a tax on investment. By imposing a tax without loss offset, the Treasury shares in the investor's gains, while leaving his losses unchanged. We consider first the effects of the tax on the magnitudes of y and r, and then the investor's reaction to this change.

---

[17] The second assumption and property (3) are included here for the sake of completeness only. They would enter into the analysis of related problems, such as the effects of insurance against loss on risk-taking.

[18] If the marginal utility of income is assumed to be constant, the slopes of the indifference curves will be constant with increasing values of y for any given value of r. In other words, the curves will be horizontally parallel. If income utility is thus assumed constant, the second assumption (increasing disutility of risk-taking) must be applied, since the tax will produce no effects on risk-taking whatsoever, if both income utility and risk disutility are held constant. See also notes 23 (p. 511), 28 (p. 515) and 35 (p. 522).

For a more thorough discussion of the properties of indifference curves, see Henry Schultz, *The Theory and Measurement of Demand* (Chicago, 1938), pp. 18–22, and J. R. Hicks, *Value and Capital* (Oxford, 1939), ch. 1.

Let the rate of the tax be indicated by t, $(0 < t < 1)$, and let y_t, r_t, and g_t indicate the magnitudes of these variables after the tax. From (1) and (2) it is evident that

$$g_t = g(1 - t) \tag{4}$$

and

$$r_t = r, \tag{5}$$

since by assumption, no losses can be deducted.[19]

Therefore,

$$y_t = g(1 - t) - r = y(1 - t) - rt \tag{6}$$

From (6) we find that

$$y_t < y(1 - t). \tag{7}$$

Thus the rate of yield is reduced by a greater percentage than the rate of the tax. This, of course, should be expected, because all gains are reduced by the rate of the tax, while all losses are left unchanged. When $t \geq \dfrac{y}{g}$ we obtain $y_t \leq 0$. In other words, if the tax is sufficiently high, the rate of yield becomes zero or negative.

It is often stated that the yield of more risky investments is hit particularly hard by a tax. It is not clear whether this statement should be interpreted in the absolute or relative sense. To the extent that more risky investments have a higher yield, they will obviously suffer a greater absolute reduction. Similarly, out of any two investments with the same degree of risk, the one with a higher yield—that is, the more attractive one—will be hit harder in the absolute sense. It appears to us, however, that the relative reduction is the more significant of the two, and there the argument is far from evident.

Let α indicate the fraction by which y is reduced by the tax so that

$$\alpha = \frac{y - y_t}{y} \tag{8}$$

Substituting the values of y and y_t from (3) and (6), we obtain[20]

$$\alpha = \left(1 + \frac{r}{y}\right) t. \tag{9}$$

---

[19] If instead of r we use r', as defined in footnote 8 (p. 500), the tax will reduce the adjusted degree of risk somewhat. Since the tax reduced the yield of a perfectly safe investment as of all other investments, λ becomes $\lambda(1 - t)$ and $r'_t = r + \lambda(1 - t)$, which is smaller than $r' = r + \lambda$. But since λ is likely to be small, the reduction in risk will not be substantial.

[20] $\alpha = \dfrac{y - y^t}{y} = \dfrac{y - y(1 - t) + r^t}{y} = \left(1 + \dfrac{r}{y}\right) t.$

Thus, a is not a function of risk, but of $\frac{r}{y}$. This expression may be called the degree of tax sensitiveness, and will be indicated by s.

Figure 3 shows that s can be interpreted geometrically as being the slope of the line connecting any point representing a given asset combination with the origin. It also demonstrates that the degree of risk and the degree of tax sensitiveness are different concepts, and that there is no apparent reason in general why a higher degree of risk should be accompanied by a higher degree of tax sensitiveness. Thus, while the degrees of risk of the points p_1, p_2 and p_3 are $r_1 > r_2 > r_3$, their degrees of tax sensitiveness are $s_3 > s_1 > s_2$. It must be noted, however, that if a com-

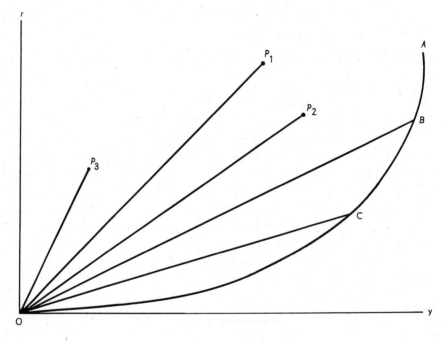

FIGURE 3

TAX SENSITIVENESS

parison is made among points located on the same optimum-asset curve, $ABCO$, a point with a higher degree of risk (B) will also be more tax sensitive than a point with a lower degree of risk (C).[21]

As the yield is cut by the tax, the investor may wish to change the

---

[21] The problem becomes more complex in the case of progressive taxation. To the extent that probability distributions with a higher degree of risk are also characterized by a longer right tail, they will probably be more tax sensitive than less risky distributions.

asset combination chosen by him prior to the imposition of the tax. The adjustment will depend upon both the reduction in yields and the investor's preferences. It will be the result of the income and substitution effects. On the one hand, the tax will reduce the compensation per unit of risk $\frac{y}{r}$ because y is reduced while r is left unchanged. The investor will therefore tend to take less risk. On the other hand, a reduction in y means that his total income is reduced, which will induce him to take more risk. The substitution and income effects will thus work in opposite directions, and the outcome will depend upon the circumstances of each case. The situation is somewhat similar to that in the labor market, where a fall in wage rates may or may not result in a decreased supply of labor. General opinion and empirical evidence would indicate, however, that a shift towards less risk appears more likely.

A geometrical analysis of the problem may permit some more definite conclusions. Let *ABO* (Figure 4) indicate the position of the optimum asset curve prior to the imposition of the tax, and let *B* be the equilibrium point. When a tax is imposed, each point of the asset curve suffers a re-

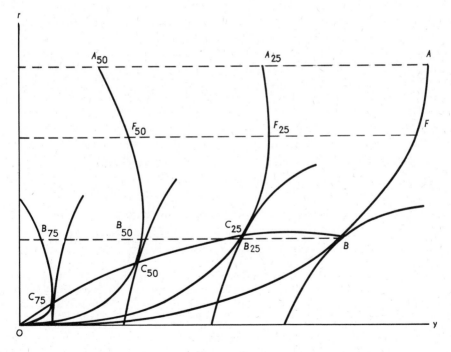

FIGURE 4
NO LOSS OFFSET

duction in y, in accordance with its degree of tax sensitiveness. It will move to the left along a horizontal line, since the degree of risk remains unchanged by the tax. Thus, any point F moves to F_{25}, F_{50}, etc., and so does the whole asset curve, ABO, which now becomes $A_{25}B_{25}O$, $A_{50}B_{50}O$, and so on, the subscripts indicating the rate of the tax. Because the tax sensitiveness of any point on the asset curve rises with risk, the upper part of the curve bends leftward as the tax rate increases, so that, as shown in Figure 4, its upper part becomes negative, if the tax is sufficiently heavy.

The investor who before the tax was located at the equilibrium point B, will, after a 25 per cent tax, find himself at B_{25}. This point is not an equilibrium position. He will therefore move up along the asset curve $A_{25}B_{25}O$ to the new equilibrium position C_{25}, located at the point of tangency of $A_{25}B_{25}O$ with an indifference curve, where his risk will exceed that taken before the tax. In the case of a 50 per cent tax, the corresponding adjustment would have been a downward move from B_{50} to C_{50}. It should be noted that the price of risk-taking $\frac{y}{r}$ falls (increases) as the investor moves up (down) the optimum asset curve, which produces a secondary substitution effect and acts as a check to his movement.

Whenever an investor shifts to a more risky asset combination, he may do so by taking more risky investments or holding less cash or, most likely, by applying both methods at the same time.

As the optimum asset curve moves to the left, the new equilibrium positions describe the curve $BC_{25}C_{50}C_{75}O$, which will be called the *tax-asset curve* (Figure 4). It first rises and then gradually falls towards the origin. Its shape, proceeding this time from left to right, can be explained in the following manner. If the return on risk-taking is close to zero—that is, if market prospects are extremely poor—the investor will take little risk, if any. As the market improves, he will take more risk. Finally, as his income increases, due to improved market conditions, he may once more become less willing to take risk. The result is determined by the interaction between the substitution and income effects.[22]

It follows that if an investor (with a given amount of wealth) is optimistic about the market outlook, so that the optimum asset curve is

---

[22] The faster the slopes of the indifference curves fall as the rate of yield increases along any given horizontal line, that is, the more the investor's marginal rate of risk-taking is (inversely) affected by the size of his income, the sooner will the tax-asset curve begin to fall. Since an increasing tax rate makes the investor move from right to left, an investor who "tires" quickly of taking risk as his income increases, is more apt to shift to more risky investments as a result of the tax than is another investor whose willingness to take risk is less affected by the size of his income. In the extreme case, the investor who insists on a given income, irrespective of the risk involved, will be taking higher and higher risk as the rate of the tax increases.

further down and to the right, the effect of a tax on risk-taking is more favorable or less detrimental than in the case of a darker market outlook. If the tax is very heavy, the investor may prefer to hold his entire assets in cash.

The subjective nature of the problem should be emphasized. The indifference curves, by their very definition, are only expressions of the investor's preferences, and the optimum asset curve represents his personal evaluation of the market situation. Since the same market situation may appear more favorable to one investor than to another, it is quite possible that a given tax may induce the more optimistic investor to take more risk, while driving his more pessimistic colleague out of the market. But the general conclusion is likely to hold that a relatively low tax imposed under depressed economic conditions, when expectations are bad, may have more harmful effects on investments than a much higher tax imposed under more favorable conditions.[23]

The argument is frequently presented that income taxes discourage risk-taking, because (1) the yield for risky investments is particularly sensitive to taxation, and (2) because more tax sensitive investments are avoided by the investor.[24] The first part of the argument has already been dealt with above (p. 507). In regard to the second part, it must be emphasized that tax sensitiveness is by no means the only factor which determines the investor's reaction to the tax. As has been shown, his choice depends both on the original position of the optimum asset curve, and on its movement, as well as on the slopes of the indifference curves. Unless special assumptions are made in respect to these factors, the choice need not be in favor of the less tax sensitive investment. As a matter of fact, the concept of tax sensitiveness is not a very essential part of the argument, and the whole problem could well be analyzed without it.

Another version of the argument runs as follows. Prior to imposition of a tax, the investor is indifferent between a more risky investment, bearing, say, ten per cent, and a less risky investment, bearing, say, three per cent, the difference of seven per cent being just sufficient to compensate the investor for the additional risk of the second investment. If now a 50 per cent tax is imposed and both yields are cut by one-half (in fact,

---

[23] As promised above, the argument is reconsidered on the assumption that the marginal utility of income remains constant with an increasing y, so that the indifference curves are horizontally parallel. In that case, there is no income effect. The tax asset curve moves downward throughout, and the investor takes less risk.

[24] See, for instance, H. G. Moulton, et. al., Capital Expansion, Employment and Economic Stability (Washington, 1940), p. 296, and for the version of the argument presented in the following paragraph, D. Black, The Incidence of Income Taxes (London, 1939), p. 222.

they are likely to be reduced by different percentages), the difference is reduced to 3.5 per cent, which is not sufficient to compensate for the difference in risk. Hence the conclusion that the investor will take the less risky investment. Evidently the argument implies that the investor will be indifferent between any two investments (or asset combinations) as long as the difference between their rates of yield remains constant, irrespective of the level of the yields themselves. This means that the indifference curves are assumed to be horizontally parallel, or in other words that the marginal utility of income is constant. For a discussion of this special case, the reader is referred to notes 18 (p. 506) and 23 (p. 511) above.

IV. TAXATION WITH FULL LOSS OFFSET

We shall now assume a complete offset of losses. This implies that the investor is assured of a sufficient amount of income derived from other sources (than the asset combination), and that adequate provisions for loss offset are made in the law. If he suffers a loss from his asset combination, he can then reduce his other taxable income by the magnitude of the loss. Thus, his total tax liability is decreased by an amount equal to the loss multiplied by the tax rate, so that this part of the loss is recovered. In other words, full loss offset means that whenever the investor suffers a loss, the Treasury reimburses him for a fraction of the loss equal to the tax rate. The Treasury thus becomes a partner who shares equally in both losses and gains.

Under these conditions, not only are the expected gains in the probability distribution cut by a percentage equal to the tax rate, but all losses are reduced likewise. We therefore have from (1), (2) and (3)

$$r_t = r(1-t) \tag{10}$$

$$g_t = g(1-t) \tag{11}$$

$$y_t = g_t - r_t = y(1-t) \tag{12}$$

Thus, both the degree of risk and the yield are reduced by a percentage exactly equal to the rate of the tax. The question of tax sensitiveness does not arise here at all, because all asset combinations (or investments) suffer the same percentage reduction.[25] These results are in sharp contrast

---

[25] This statement must be modified, if the minimum compensation for effort defined in footnote 10, p. 501, is taken into consideration. Then we have $y'_t = y_t - e$ and the percentage reduction of the adjusted yield is ·

$$a' = \frac{y' - y'_t}{y'} = \frac{y - e - y(1-t) + e}{y'} = t\left(1 + \frac{e}{y'}\right).$$

It follows, therefore, that the yield is reduced by a greater percentage than the rate of the

with those of the preceding case, where no loss offset was possible, so that we may expect the investor's reaction to be markedly different.

Before proceeding further, we must make a distinction between *total yield* and *private yield* and between *total risk* and *private risk*. The imposition of the tax reduces the yield and the degree of risk which are left to the investor, or his *private* yield and *private* risk, in the manner already described; but the *total* yield and the *total* risk of the given asset combination are entirely unaffected by the tax. The fractions of yield and risk which the tax takes away from the investor are simply transferred to the Treasury.[26] The symbols y_t and r_t refer to private yield and degree of risk, respectively. Total yield and degree of risk, being unchanged by the tax, are still denoted by y and r. Since our main problem is the effect of the tax on total *risk*-taking, not much use will be made of the difference between y and y_t; but the distinction between r and r_t will be extremely important. This distinction was not needed in the preceding case, where it was assumed that no loss offset was possible. Since in that case the Treasury did not share in risk, private risk and total risk were necessarily equal. From the point of view of the economy as a whole, it is, of course, total risk that is important, not private risk.

Faced with a reduction in private yield and private risk, the investor will try to readjust his asset combination. His reaction can again be studied in terms of the income and substitution effect. This time, however, the tax produces no initial substitution effect, because the price of risk-taking $\left(\dfrac{y}{r}\right)$ is unchanged, the yield and the degree of risk being reduced in the same proportion. The income effect will make the investor shift to an asset combination with higher risk. This increase in private risk taken (though not necessarily to or above the private risk taken before

---

tax. If $t \geqq \dfrac{y'}{y}$, we get $y'_t \leqq 0$, so that the adjusted yield can become zero or negative, if the tax is sufficiently high. But since e is small, $\dfrac{y'}{y}$ is very close to 1, and therefore, to achieve this result, the tax rate must be very high.

The adjusted degree of tax sensitiveness now becomes $s' = \dfrac{e}{y'}$. Since e is a constant, s' depends on y' only and varies inversely with it. To the extent that a higher y' is accompanied by a higher r (or r'), more risky asset combinations are less tax sensitive. Again, since e is small, this difference in tax sensitiveness is hardly important.

[26] The statement that the total degree of risk is unaffected by the tax is perhaps misleading, because it implies that public and private risk are interchangeable. Quite possibly the concept of total risk is illegitimate, because it represents a combination of heterogeneous items. *Public* risk-taking presents a most interesting problem, which certainly deserves further investigation. It remains true, however, that changes in "total risk"—which for any given investment equals private risk before the tax—reflect the changes in the magnitude and direction of capital flows.

the tax) also implies an increase in total risk, since from (10)

$$r = r_t \cdot \frac{1}{(1-t)}.$$

Thus we reach the important and somewhat unexpected conclusion that the imposition of the tax will increase the total risk taken.

A geometric demonstration will help to clarify this result. Let ABO in Figure 5 be the position of the optimum asset curve before the tax, and

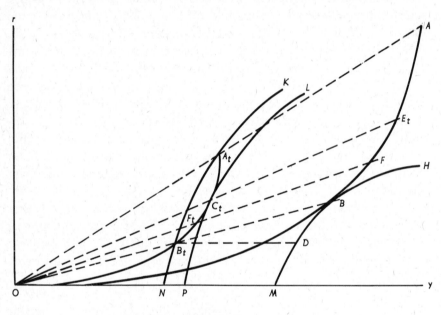

FIGURE 5

FULL LOSS OFFSET AND CONSTANT TAX

let B be the optimum point. Since the imposition of the tax reduces y and r equally by the percentage of the tax rate, any point F on ABO moves towards the origin along a straight line FO, covering a fraction of the distance from F to O equal to the tax rate, so that if the new position of F is F_t we have $\frac{FF_t}{FO} = t$. Similarly, the entire curve ABO moves to a new position, A_tB_tO, and the investor, who prior to the tax was at the equilibrium point B, now finds himself at B_t.

Finding himself at B_t, the investor discovers that, while holding the identical asset combination, his net return (after tax) has fallen by a fraction equal to the rate of the tax, and so has his private risk. He will then find that he can improve his position by moving from B_t to C_t, the point of tangency of the optimum asset curve, in its new position, with an indifference curve. Since, as shown before, the imposition of the tax will produce an income effect only, the point C_t must be above B_t. This statement can be readily proven geometrically.[27]

From the fact that private risk taken after adjustment to the tax exceeds private risk taken prior to this adjustment (although not necessarily private risk taken prior to the tax), it follows *that total risk taken after the tax will exceed total risk taken before the tax.* To find the total risk point, E_t, corresponding to the private risk point C_t, we can either apply the formulae $r = r_t \dfrac{1}{1-t} \left(\text{and } y = y_t \dfrac{1}{1-t} \right)$, or draw the line C_tO and extend it to its intersection with ABO, which gives the position of E_t. The total risk (and yield) of any optimum asset combination being unaffected by the tax, it is still represented by its original position on the optimum asset curve. Since C_t is above B_t, E_t must be above B.[28]

The relationship between the level of total risk and the rate of tax remains to be considered. As the tax rate increases, the optimum asset curve ABO moves towards the origin, taking the positions $A_{25}B_{25}O$, $A_{50}B_{50}O$, etc., as shown on Figure 6, the subscripts indicating the corresponding tax rates. The new equilibrium positions located at its tangency points with the indifference curves describe the already familiar tax asset curve, $BC_{25}C_{50}C_{75}D$. This time, however, this curve indicates only the private degree of risk (and yield) taken by the investor under given tax rates, and will be referred to as the private tax-asset curve.

---

[27] The *first* proposition is that the slope of KB_tN at B_t must be greater than the slope of HBM at B. This follows from the fact that (a) at the point B the slopes of ABO and HBM are equal and therefore are both smaller than the slope of HBM at D, since, by assumption, the slope along any given indifference curve falls with increasing y and r, and that (b) the slope of KB_tN at B_t must be equal or greater than the slope of HBM at D. A *second* proposition is that the slope of A_tB_tO at B_t will be equal to the slope of ABO at B: the slope of ABO at any point (y, r) is $\dfrac{dr}{dy}$. Similarly, the slope of A_tB_tO at a corresponding point (y_t, r_t) is $\dfrac{dr}{dy_t}$. But since $y_t = y(1-t)$ and $r_t = r(1-t)$, we have $dy_t = dy(1-t)$, $dr_t = dr(1-t)$ and hence $\dfrac{dr_t}{dy_t} = \dfrac{dr}{dy}$.

From these two propositions it follows that at B_t the slope of A_tB_tO must be smaller than the slope of KB_tN. Therefore, B_t cannot be the new point of equilibrium, at which the slopes of A_tB_tO and the indifference curve must be equal. Since the slope of A_tB_tO increases while moving upward and to the right, while that of any indifference curves decreases, the new equilibrium point C must be to the right and above B_t.

[28] Continuing the story of footnote 23, p. 511, we must review the argument on the assumption of a constant marginal utility of income. As explained in note 18, p. 506, an increasing marginal disutility of risk-taking must then be assumed. The conclusion reached in the text that the imposition of the tax will increase the level of total risk taken still holds, because the price of risk-taking is unchanged, while the marginal disutility of risk is reduced by the reduction in private risk. It should be noted that the geometric proof given in the preceding note does not depend on the assumption that the slopes of the indifference curves fall along a given horizontal line.

In Figure 6 the private tax-asset curve first rises with an increasing tax rate from B to somewhat beyond C_{25}, and then falls towards the origin, this movement again depending upon the investor's evaluation of market conditions prior to the tax, and the shapes of the indifference curves.[29] Since the equal percentage reduction of y and r leaves the ratio $\frac{y}{r}$ unchanged, it may appear surprising that the private tax-asset curve should fall at all; that is, that under certain conditions the investor should fail to recover the degree of private risk taken before the tax. When a given, say 50 per cent, tax is imposed, the investor will find his original

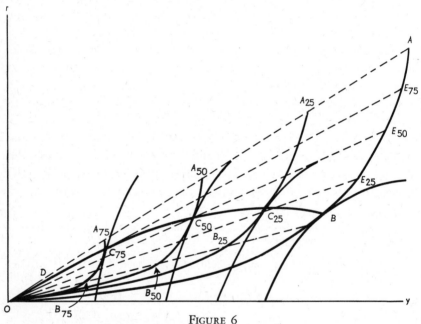

FIGURE 6

FULL LOSS OFFSET AND VARIABLE TAX

equilibrium point B moved to B_{50}, and again readjust his position in the direction of increased private risk by moving up along the new optimum asset curve $A_{50}B_{50}O$. If the latter were a straight line passing through the origin, he would be able to return to the original point B, thus taking

---

29 In Figure 6 the tax-asset curve is not continued beyond D, because as the tax continues to increase, there are no points of tangency between the subsequent positions of the optimum asset curve and the indifference curves below the line ADO. In order to make use of the tangency points above ADO, borrowing must be introduced, which is excluded in this paper. In the absence of borrowing, the tax-asset curve will proceed along the straight line DO.

just as much risk as he did prior to the tax; but as the slope of $A_{50}B_{50}O$ increases with increasing risk, the investor finds that the ratio $\frac{y}{r}$ diminishes as he goes up along $A_{50}B_{50}O$; this secondary substitution effect will finally stop his upward movement. In the general case, it cannot be said whether any given tax will cause the investor to stop short of or exceed the *private* risk taken prior to the imposition of the tax. But as in the preceding case, a comparatively favorable market and lower tax rate will be conducive to a higher level of private risk.

From the point of view of the economy, the question whether the pre-tax level of private risk is recovered is relatively unimportant. What matters is the degree of total risk taken jointly by the investor and the Government. By extending the lines $OC_{25}, OC_{50}, OC_{75}$, etc. to their intersection with ABO, we find the corresponding points E_{25}, E_{50}, E_{75}, etc., indicating the degrees of total risk which will correspond to the investor's adjustment to various tax rates. We have already proved that all these points must fall above the pre-tax equilibrium B; it can be shown by a similar proof that the degree of *total* risk taken will be the higher the higher the tax rate. This, of course, is not an argument for a tax rate approaching 100 per cent. The simplifying assumptions upon which the conclusion rests must be kept in mind. In addition, the results for the economy would obviously be chaotic, if the Government were to invite everybody to invest his funds in whatever project he chooses with a "no loss" (and "no gain") guarantee.[30]

V. THE GENERAL CASE: TAXATION WITH VARIABLE LOSS OFFSET

The discussion presented in Sections III and IV will be recognized as the two extreme cases of the same problem. This can now be treated in its more general form by assuming a variable tax rate and variable degrees of loss offset.[31] Since the two extreme cases have been developed in detail, only the more important aspects of the general case are considered here.

Let the fraction of the loss that can be offset be indicated by $z (0 \leqq z$

---

[30] If e, defined in note 10, p. 501, which will become more important at very high levels of taxation, is taken into consideration, the conclusions reached in this section will have to be somewhat modified. The case becomes more like that of partial loss deduction, discussed in Section V.

[31] A more detailed analysis of partial loss offset would include these considerations: (1) since the immediate offset of losses may not be possible, a loss of interest may result; (2) the extent to which loss offset will be possible may be uncertain, and thus in turn raise probability problems.

$\leqq 1$). Then all expected gains are reduced by a percentage equal to t, while the losses are reduced by tz only. From (1), (2), and (3) we have

$$r_t = r(1 - tz) \tag{13}$$

$$g_t = g(1 - t) \tag{14}$$

$$y_t = g(1 - t) - r(1 - tz) = y(1 - t) - rt(1 - z). \tag{15}$$

The changes in the r and y of any given asset combination, under the impact of various rates of tax with varying degrees of loss offset, may again be determined algebraically from (13) and (15) or geometrically in the following manner:

Let M in Figure 7 represent the position of an asset combination prior to the imposition of the tax. If no loss offset is possible, the imposition of the tax will move the point along the horizontal line ME_{100}, and if full

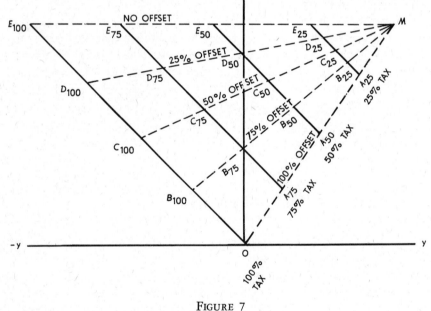

FIGURE 7

VARIABLE OFFSET AND TAX

loss offset is provided, the point will move towards the origin along the line MO. Its new position A_{50} after, say, a 50 per cent tax and full loss offset, will be such that $\dfrac{MA_{50}}{MO} = .50$. If the tax rate is kept constant at 50 per cent, but the percentage of loss offset is allowed to vary, y_t and r_t will move along the line $A_{50}E_{50}$ which is given by the expression $r_t + y_t =$

g_t, where g_t, being independent of z, is a constant. If the loss offset is, say, 75 per cent, the corresponding point on $A_{50}E_{50}$ is B_{50}, such that

$$\frac{B_{50}E_{50}}{A_{50}E_{50}} = .75 \,.[32]$$

Turning to the case of a *varying tax rate* with a constant loss offset of, say, 50 per cent, the locus of M is indicated by the straight line MC_{100} or—for varying rates of loss offset—by the family of lines MB_{100}, MC_{100}, and so forth, the slope in each case depending upon the degree of loss offset and the original position of M. Algebraically these lines[33] may be expressed as

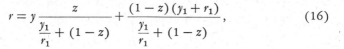

$$r = y \frac{z}{\dfrac{y_1}{r_1} + (1 - z)} + \frac{(1 - z)(y_1 + r_1)}{\dfrac{y_1}{r_1} + (1 - z)}, \tag{16}$$

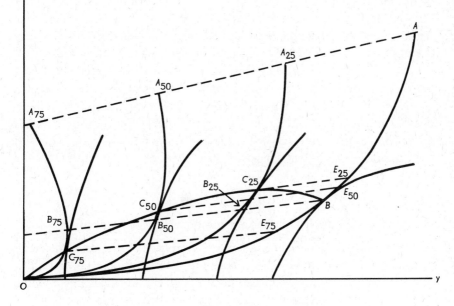

FIGURE 8

FIFTY PER CENT OFFSET AND VARIABLE TAX

---

[32] If r is the ordinate of the point M, it follows, by applying a standard procedure from analytic geometry, that the length of the line $A_{50}E_{50}$ is $rt\sqrt{2}$ and that of $B_{50}E_{50}$ is $rtz\sqrt{2}$. Their ratio is therefore z, as stated in the text.

[33] We have here the standard problem of finding an equation of a line passing through two given points, the coördinates of which are (y_1, r_1) and (y_t, r_t) respectively. It should be noted that the expression (16) is independent of t, so that all points obtained from M by applying a constant loss offset and a varying tax will be on the same straight line.

where y_1 and r_1 indicate the coördinates of the point M prior to the tax.

The movement of M in Figure 7 is restricted to the area falling between ME_{100}, MO and OE_{100}, because it relates only to tax rates and loss offsets varying from 0 to 100. By assuming the Treasury to share in losses by over 100 per cent (that is, to guarantee a minimum positive return) or to impose negative taxes (that is, to grant subsidies)—and by allowing for even odder possibilities of negative loss deductions and more than 100 per cent tax rates—the point M may reach any point on the chart.

Using the described algebraic or geometric procedure, we can now turn to the movements of the optimum asset curve and the effects of the tax upon risk-taking. In order to avoid the construction of three dimensional diagrams, it will be necessary to treat separately the case of a variable tax rate with a given loss offset and that of a variable loss offset with a given tax rate.

(*a*) *Variable tax rate with a given loss offset.* Let ABO in Figure 8 be the optimum asset curve, and let B be the equilibrium point prior to the tax. Under the assumption of a constant, say 50 per cent, loss offset and a variable tax rate, ABO moves to the left and towards the origin, taking the positions $A_{25}B_{25}O$, $A_{50}B_{50}O$, etc., the subscripts indicating the rate of the tax. The points of tangency of those curves with the indifference curves at C_{25}, C_{50}, etc. describe the familiar private tax-asset curve $BC_{25}C_{50}C_{75}O$.

In order to find the degrees of total risk corresponding to the new equilibrium points C_{25}, C_{50}, etc., we can either draw the lines $C_{25}E_{25}$, $C_{50}E_{50}$, etc. as given in (16), where y_1 and r_1 are now the coördinates of the C points, or simply make use of the expression

$$r = r_t \frac{1}{(1 - tz)} \tag{17}$$

derived from (13). It is important to note that the "multiplier" $\frac{1}{1 - tz}$ increases with an increasing tax rate. Therefore, if the same level of private risk is produced by the imposition of two different tax rates, the point corresponding to the higher rate will give a higher degree of total risk.[34] As the tax increases, the total risk rises, because the multiplier increases, and at the beginning also because the multiplicand (private risk) increases. After private risk begins to fall, total risk will continue to rise for a while, but eventually the diminution of private risk will overcome the increase in the multiplier, and therefore total risk will fall. With a given indifference map, market picture (i.e. position of the optimum asset

---

[34] The same conclusion can be reached by observing from (16) that the lines $C_t E_t$ are positively inclined, and that their slopes are the greater the smaller is the ratio $\frac{y_1}{r_1}$.

line prior to the tax), and any positive degree of loss offset, there will thus be an *optimum tax rate* which produces the highest total risk. It also holds that this optimum tax rate will be higher than the rate which produces the highest private risk. In Figure 8 a tax of about 20 per cent will cause the investor to take the highest private risk, but the maximum total risk is not reached until the tax rate becomes about 25 per cent.

(*b*) *Variable loss offset with a given tax rate.* Let ABO (Figure 9) be the optimum asset curve and B the equilibrium point before the tax.

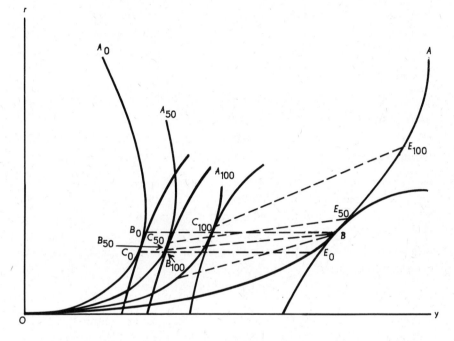

FIGURE 9
VARIABLE OFFSET AND FIFTY PER CENT TAX

Three rates of loss offset will be considered: 100 per cent, 50 per cent and zero. As a result of a given, say 50 per cent, tax, ABO will move to new positions $A_{100}B_{100}O$, $A_{50}B_{50}O$, and A_0B_0O, the subscripts indicating the percentage of loss offset. Again, these positions can be determined either algebraically or geometrically by the methods already described.

The investor will find that his original equilibrium point, B, has moved to new locations, B_{100}, B_{50} or B_0, and will try to readjust his asset combination by moving along the new optimum asset curves to C_{100}, C_{50} or C_0, determined by their tangency with the indifference curves. From Section IV we know that in the case of full loss offset the movement from B_{100} to

C_{100} must be upwards; but in the other two cases the movement may be in either direction.

In general, no definite statement can be made as to whether the level of *private* risk taken by the investor goes up or down with decreasing percentage of loss offset. A lower rate of loss offset, very similar to an increased rate of tax, reduces the ratio $\frac{y}{r}$, and thus sets into motion the income and substitution effects already discussed in Section III. Again they work in opposite directions and the outcome is uncertain.

As before, the effect on *total* risk is most important. The relative positions of the points E_{100}, E_{50} and E_0, indicating the total risk of the asset combinations chosen by the investor, may again be determined according to (16) or by the expression (17), $r = r_t \dfrac{1}{(1 - tz)}$. It was proved in Section IV that E_{100} must be above B, since, on the assumption of full loss offset, total risk taken is increased. While E_{50} and E_0 may fall either above or below B, there are strong reasons for believing that E_0 will be below E_{50}, and that E_{50} will be below E_{100}, because the multiplier $\dfrac{1}{1 - tz}$ increases with an increasing rate of loss offset. In Figure 9, where $t = 50$ per cent, this multiplier rises from 1, with no loss offset, to 4/3, with a 50 per cent offset, and to 2, when full offset is assumed. If E_0 is to fall above E_{100}, the ordinate of private risk of C_0 must be more than twice as large as that of C_{100}. An investor for whom this was true would be characterized by an unusually strong income effect, forcing him to increase his risk-taking sharply, notwithstanding a declining $\frac{y}{r}$. In general, it can be safely said that for any given tax rate the total risk of the investor's asset combination will be the greater, the higher the rate of loss offset.[35]

From the arguments presented above the following conclusions can be drawn: (1) with a given rate of loss offset, there will be an optimum tax rate at which total risk will be at its maximum; (2) with a given tax rate, total risk will, with minor exceptions, be the greater, the higher the rate of loss offset. From these two statements it also follows (3) that the optimum tax rate will be the higher, the higher is the rate of offset.

---

[35] As a final chapter of the story begun in note 23, p. 511, it is again assumed that the marginal utility of income is constant while the marginal disutility of risk is rising. In this case, since a higher percentage of loss offset (with a given tax) produces a greater reduction in r and a smaller cut in $\frac{y}{r}$, it clearly follows that the degree of total risk taken will be the higher, the greater is the percentage of loss offset. This is the same conclusion as that reached in the text, except that it can now be stated without exceptions.

VI. QUALIFICATIONS

In the preceding analysis the problem has been considered in a simplified form. A review of the major limitations is now in order.

(1) Our analysis has been based upon the probability approach to risk theory. Lacking better alternatives, this approach was introduced in order to obtain numerical values for y and r. It appears that, under the impact of a tax, these values behave in a manner quite compatible with common-sense considerations. If definitions of risk and yield were obtained on the basis of some different approach, their behavior under the impact of a tax would probably be very similar. If it is denied that numerical values *can* be obtained, no method for a precise analysis of the problem appears to be available.

(2) We have assumed that the investor's behavior is concerned with changes in y and r, only because these variables appear to us the most important. Undoubtedly there are other characteristics of the probability distribution in which the investor may be interested, such as the probability of obtaining less than a given minimum rate of return, the probability of suffering more than a given loss, the probability of obtaining very large gains, and so forth. Like r and y, each of these variables will also change as the result of a tax, but not necessarily in the same way. If the investor includes these additional variables, the outcome may in some cases differ from that described in the text.

(3) Throughout our discussion the investor's wealth was assumed to be constant. Now, it is likely that as the result of the tax the investor's wealth will change, which in turn may change his indifference pattern. That is, his general attitude towards risk-taking may become more or less favorable. This secondary adjustment has not been taken into account, since the analysis is limited to the immediate effects of the tax on the investor's decisions. The effect of taxation on wealth is in itself a complex problem, particularly because the effects of alternative taxes and/or expenditures must be taken into consideration.

(4) Our analysis omits a consideration of the "investment market." It examines the intended reactions of any one investor to the imposition of a tax, and disregards the fact that all investors may want to shift towards more or less risk, thereby lowering or raising the price of risk-taking. Moreover, the analysis assumes that the individual investor disregards the effects of his moves upon the investment market, an assumption which is clearly unrealistic with respect to important groups of investment decisions, and which we hope to reconsider at a later date.

(5) The probability approach as used here is more nearly applicable to the case of the financial investor than to "real" investment decisions. The manager of a corporation about to decide which of his plants he should expand, and what equipment he should purchase, is confronted with fewer and more unique investment alternatives than is the financial investor, and is thus unable to achieve an equal degree of diversification. Certain considerations which might be of little importance for the financial investor, such as those related to maintaining competitive advantages, might be very significant for him. On the whole, however, it is likely that the rationale of real investment decisions would move along similar lines, and that the general conclusions here arrived at would also apply to the case of real investment.

(6) The effects of a proportional tax only have been considered. If the case of a progressive tax is examined, additional complications arise. The entire shape of the probability distribution, and its right tail in particular, become of great importance, so that it is very doubtful whether it remains sufficient to describe the distribution in terms of y and r. Given a progressive rate schedule, tax savings due to loss offset are likely to be made at different (mostly lower, but possibly higher) rates than those which would have been imposed on the gains. These considerations would modify some of the conclusions reached here, but the case for loss deduction would become even stronger. In an analysis of progressive rates, the related problem of discrimination against fluctuating incomes, and its elimination through averaging, becomes of particular importance.

32

*Business-Income Taxation and Investment Incentives**

By E. CARY BROWN

Taxes can affect investment expenditures in a number of ways. They reduce the disposable income of some income recipients, decrease their consumption expenditures, and, indirectly, may reduce the level of investment. Also, they may directly reduce investment expenditures through their effect on the profitability of investment or on the funds available for investment. The reactions set up finally may affect the rate of interest, which in turn will have an impact on the level of investment expenditures.

In this paper, only one phase of these broad problems will be considered, namely, the direct effect of a business-income tax on incentives to invest in durable producers' goods. Major emphasis is placed on the definition of the tax base—the question of depreciation policy receiving most attention with incidental attention given to the treatment of losses for tax purposes.[1]

As will be shown, modifications in the timing of depreciation can affect both the *amount* of taxes expected to be paid on income arising from an investment, and the *timing* of their payment. Both effects can alter the profitability of the investment. More liberal treatment of losses can affect the amount of taxes expected to be paid, but it has a relatively insignificant effect on the timing of these payments over the life of the asset.

---

* Chapter IV in Part III in *Income, Employment and Public Policy, Essays in Honor of Alvin H. Hansen* (New York: W. W. Norton & Co., Inc., 1948).

[1] Other treatments of the question of loss offsets have been made by E. D. Domar and R. A. Musgrave, "Proportional Income Taxation and Risk-Taking," *Quarterly Journal of Economics*, May, 1944 [Article 31 of this volume. Ed.], to which this paper owes a large debt: J. K. Butters and J. Lintner, *Effect of Federal Taxes on Growing Enterprises* (Boston, 1945), especially chap. iii; H. R. Bowen, "Taxation of Net Income from Businesses," *Bulletin of the National Tax Association*, December, 1945; and A. P. Lerner, "An Integrated Full Employment Policy," *International Postwar Problems*, January, 1946. For a discussion of depreciation, see Bowen, *op. cit.;* M. Kalecki, "Three Ways to Full Employment," and E. F. Schumacher, "Public Finance—Its Relation to Full Employment," in *The Economics of Full Employment*, Oxford University Institute of Statistics (Oxford, 1944).

To summarize the conclusions reached:

1. The effect on investment incentives of a proportional tax levied only on business income can be neutralized (*a*) if the amount expended on durable producers' goods can be deducted from taxable income in the year when made, and (*b*) if the Government will pay for any "losses" of the firm at the same rate as it taxes the firm's income. Neither adjustment taken alone is sufficient for this purpose.

2. Depreciation of assets over a short period, say, three to five years, would come reasonably close to neutralizing the adverse effect of the tax, provided the excess of depreciation over income in any year can be carried forward as an offset against future taxable income.

3. If depreciation for tax purposes is spread over the economic life of an asset, the tax will adversely affect investment incentives, even though the Government reimburses business losses at the rate of tax.

4. Under such a system of economic-life depreciation, incentives to invest are more adversely affected (*a*) the longer-lived the asset in which the investment is contemplated, (*b*) the higher the cost of investment funds to the individual firm, and (*c*) the greater the uncertainty of future income. These latter two effects are particularly severe on the new or small firm.

5. Incentives to replace assets are less affected than incentives to make new investment. The existing firm would have its advantages furthered as against the new firm, replacement representing a larger proportion of investment outlays for the former than for the latter. For similar reasons the static firm is favored over the growing one.

6. The effects as indicated in points (3) to (5) are greater, the higher the rate of tax.

I. BUSINESS-INCOME TAXATION UNDER CONDITIONS OF CERTAINTY

Taxation with Full Loss Offsets and Economic-Life Depreciation. First, let us consider the effect of the business-income tax on incentives to make new investment under conditions of certainty. For our purposes, new investment is distinguished from replacement only because the latter involves the discarding of an existing asset at the time the investment is made, whereas the former does not. Nothing is implied regarding the capacity or efficiency of the replacement.

1. *New Investment.* If an entrepreneur is maximizing total profits, he invests up to the point at which the cost of funds for investment equals the investment's yield (marginal efficiency of capital). To state this condition in another way, he is willing to make any investment outlays which are expected to bring in a greater amount of net receipts in present-worth

terms.[2] By discounting to the present the algebraic sum of these changes in net receipts in each period, the present worth of the investment is determined. For a rate of discount, the entrepreneur uses the rate of interest he must pay on funds made available to him for the investment. We can think of him as ranking the various possible outlays on durable goods on the basis of the excess of the present worth of their future net receipts over their cost. He schedules all outlays for which this difference is positive, that is, in which the investment yield equals or exceeds the rate of interest.[3]

Assume now that a proportional tax is imposed on the excess of business revenues over expenses, interest expenses and dividend payments not being treated as deductions. Depreciation expense is determined by spreading the cost of durable goods over their economic life. If expenses exceed revenues in any year, the Government reimburses the entrepreneur for the loss at the rate of tax. That is to say, a $100 profit will require the payment of $50 tax, if the tax rate is 50 per cent; a $100 loss will result in a $50 refund from the Government. Thus, we have a truly proportional tax on income: each dollar of additional income will be taxed at the given rate; each dollar of additional expense will be reimbursed at the same rate. This type of system can be termed one of full loss offset, since losses will result in negative taxes whether or not past, present, or future taxable income is earned.

Under our assumptions the tax does not reduce the rate of interest at which the entrepreneur can secure funds.[4] Because the tax will reduce the prospective net receipts from investment, and because the discount factor applied to these net receipts remains unchanged, the present worth of some investment outlays will fall below their cost and they will become unprofitable.

In order to look more closely at these effects, the tax base will be separated into two parts: first, the net receipts expected from the investment before deducting depreciation; second, the deductions in the form of depreciation charges. The tax liability (or refund) for any given year is, of

---

[2] Scrap value at the end of the asset's life should be included as a receipt. Increased salaries should be included as additional payments if the investment requires additional managerial effort.

[3] However, if the entrepreneur's funds are limited, he would make only the most profitable investment which his limited resources permitted.

[4] Interest and dividend payments are not deductible in determining taxable income under our hypothetical tax. Thus the interest costs of the entrepreneur are not partially reimbursed by the Government through reduction in taxable income. Moreover, the rate of interest at which money is offered to the firm does not decrease, inasmuch as the investor can put his funds out in other ways, e.g., in Government bonds, free of the tax on business income. In the long run, of course, the interest rate may be affected.

course, determined by applying the rate of tax to the algebraic sum of these two amounts.

The next step, after separating tax liabilities into these two components, is to treat the present worth of the tax rebates (negative taxes) resulting from the depreciation deduction as an offset to the cost of the asset in which the investment is contemplated.[5] Thus we compare the cost of the asset minus the present worth of the tax reduction from depreciation with the present worth of expected net receipts minus tax (the tax applied directly to net receipts before deducting depreciation). This method permits us to concentrate on the present worth of the tax rebates from depreciation. Since the present worth of prospective net receipts (before depreciation) will be proportionately reduced by the tax, some investments will become unprofitable unless the present worth of the tax rebates from depreciation reduces the cost of the asset proportionately to the rate of tax. This statement is equivalent to saying that the cost of the asset would otherwise exceed the present worth of the net receipts after taxes.[6]

To illustrate this point, assume that net receipts of $100 per year for 5 years are anticipated through acquisition of an asset costing $400. At a rate of interest of 8 per cent, the present worth of $100 per year for 5 years would be $400. The investment would be marginal, since its cost would just equal the present worth of the anticipated net receipts from its operation. Assume now the imposition of a 50 per cent tax on business income. With a depreciation rate of 20 per cent per year, taxable income would amount to $20, and taxes to $10. The present worth of the net receipts after taxes now becomes $360. The asset's cost of $400 would

---

[5] Even casual students of business reactions to the wartime excess-profits tax will recognize that this is not an artificial construction. With an 85 per cent tax rate there was much talk of fifteen-cent dollars.

[6] Before the tax $C = RA$ for the marginal investment, where C represents the cost of the asset, R the prospective annual net receipts per year for n years, and A the present worth of a dollar a year for n years discounted at i.

After the tax is imposed, this expression becomes $C = RA - t(R - \frac{C}{d})A$, where t is the rate of tax and d the number of years over which the asset can be depreciated for tax purposes. This expression can also be transformed to $C(1 - \frac{At}{d}) = RA(1 - t)$. If $\frac{At}{d} = t$, that is, if the tax reduces net receipts and the asset's cost proportionately, the pretax equality between C and RA will be re-established.

[The following paragraph has been added by the author to the original note. Ed.] In this note it was assumed that $n = d$. More generally, the last expression would become $C = (1 - \frac{Bt}{d}) = RA(1 - t)$, where B is the present worth of $1 per year for d years discounted at i. The reestablishment of pretax equality would require $\frac{Bt}{d} = t$, and this would come about only under the condition mentioned at the end of the preceding paragraph.

now exceed the present worth of the net receipts after tax by $40 (the present worth of the tax liabilities of $10 per year). On the other hand, we can consider the present worth of the net receipts as being reduced proportionately by the tax—from $400 to $200—and the cost of the asset as being reduced by the present worth ($160) of the tax rebates (of $40 per year) from depreciation. The cost of the asset is thus reduced from $400 to $240, and the discrepancy of $40 between cost and present worth of net receipts shows up again.

It becomes clear why the tax reduces investment incentives. *It stems from the failure of the present worth of the tax rebates from depreciation to reduce the cost of the asset by an amount proportionate to the rate of tax.* The aggregate amount of depreciation deductible over an asset's life is, by definition, equal to the cost of the asset. The aggregate tax reduction resulting from the deduction will thus be proportionate to the rate of tax. But because depreciation is spread out over the life of the asset, the resulting tax reduction is similarly spread out into the future. Upon discounting to the present these future tax rebates, their present worth falls below the sum of their annual amounts. Therefore, because the tax proportionately reduces the net receipts (before depreciation), but does not proportionately reduce an asset's cost, the tax makes some of the outlays unprofitable which were previously profitable. The level of investment under any given conditions of demand is reduced.

The smaller the present worth of the tax rebates resulting from depreciation, the greater is the harmful effect of the tax on investment incentives. Their present worth is smaller, the higher the rate of discount applicable. Thus, small or new firms with very limited access to cheap capital would find a future tax rebate of less worth to them than would a large firm with abundant cheap capital. The former's investment incentives would be reduced more than would the latter's.

Similarly, the longer the tax rebate is postponed on the average, the smaller is its present worth. Since depreciation is spread over a relatively long period for long-lived assets, tax rebates are subject to a larger discount, relative to the asset's cost, than are the rebates resulting from short-lived assets. This effect may change the ranking as to their profitability of various outlays on durable goods. Shorter-lived assets would move up the scale relative to the longer-lived.[7] All outlays would, however, become absolutely less profitable.

---

[7] In a letter to the *Economist*, May 27, 1944, p. 719, a writer, obviously in business, points out that repairing an old machine may be favored under the income tax over acquiring a new asset. Repairs are deductible from taxable income in the year when made, but a new asset must be depreciated over its useful life.

The strength of these factors is indicated in Table 1 which shows the present value of depreciation deductions as a per cent of the cost of an asset under different interest rates and different lengths of asset life. Reading from left to right indicates the decrease in the present worth of the depreciation deductions as the cost of borrowing increases; reading down indicates the decrease in present worth as the life of the asset lengthens. One can notice the marked reduction in present worth of depreciation deductions as longer-lived assets and higher interest rates are considered.

TABLE 1

PRESENT WORTH OF STRAIGHT-LINE DEPRECIATION DEDUCTIONS*
AS A PER CENT OF COST OF ASSET

Economic Life	Annual De-duction	Present Worth of Depreciation Discounted at Rate of Interest (Annually Compounded) of			
		2 %	4 %	6 %	8 %
(1)	(2)	(3)	(4)	(5)	(6)
5	20 %	94.3 %	89.0 %	84.2 %	79.9 %
10	10	89.8	81.1	73.6	67.1
20	5	81.8	68.0	57.3	49.1
50	2	62.8	43.0	31.5	24.5

* Cost divided by length of life, assuming no scrap value.

The present worth of the depreciation deductions is not, of course, the factor which reduces the asset's cost in the preceding analysis, but the tax on this amount. For example, the table indicates that for a twenty-year asset and interest costs of 4 per cent (third line, Column 4) the present worth of straight-line depreciation would be 68 per cent of the asset's cost. If a 50 per cent tax were imposed, the net receipts from the asset would be cut in half, but the cost of the asset would be reduced only by 34 per cent (half of 68 per cent). Whereas before the tax, the cost was equal to the present worth of net receipts for the marginal investment, after the tax, the cost would exceed the present worth of net receipts by 16 per cent of the asset's cost: it would only have fallen to 66 per cent of its original cost after tax, whereas the net receipts after tax would have fallen to 50 per cent. With higher tax rates, these disproportions increase.

2. *Replacement.* When no tax is in effect, the decision to replace an asset is similar to that when added investment is contemplated. A comparison is made between the cost of acquiring an asset with the present worth of the net receipts it is expected to bring in.[8] The remaining undepreciated cost of the asset to be discarded should not affect this com-

---

[8] If it or the asset replaced has any scrap value, this would enter into net receipts.

parison because the cost is sunk.[9] However, when the tax is imposed, the undepreciated cost of the old asset will affect the investment decision because it will affect tax liabilities. On the new asset, the entrepreneur may take a series of depreciation deductions. On the asset discarded, the undepreciated cost may be deducted in the year of replacement rather than depreciated over its remaining useful life. If the cost of the discarded asset has not been fully depreciated, a gain results from trading a series of future tax rebates for a present tax rebate of equal aggregate amount.

The larger the remaining undepreciated cost of the asset to be discarded (the newer it is or the higher its original cost), the greater is the present worth of the tax rebate associated with it. If the remaining undepreciated cost is sufficiently high, the inducement to make a replacement can be as high or higher than it was before the tax was imposed. The present worth of the tax rebate from discarding the old asset plus the present worth of the tax rebates on the new asset can reduce the cost of this replacement in proportion to the tax. Such a favorable result cannot take place, however, if the asset to be replaced costs the same amount as the replacement, and depreciation rates are the same on both assets.

In Table 2 are indicated the magnitudes involved in telescoping depreciation on the old asset into the year of replacement, assuming an interest rate of 4 per cent, identity between the cost of the old asset and its replacement, and the same depreciation rates for both assets. Column 2 indicates the present worth of the depreciation deductions on the new asset and is taken from Column 4 of Table 1. Columns 3 to 6 show the additions to that amount which result from discarding the old asset, assuming that varying percentages of its original cost remain undepreciated. These columns are computed as the difference in present worth of deducting (e.g.) 40 per cent of the cost of the asset in the year of replacement, or depreciating it normally (e.g.) at 5 per cent a year for eight years if the asset had an original depreciable life of twenty years.

As will be noted from the table, the present worth of the additional tax rebate increases more than proportionately with increases in the undepreciated cost and length of life of the asset discarded. The effect of changes in the rate of interest is not indicated in the table, but it is clear that higher interest rates will increase this factor as they make present deductions more valuable than future deductions. For example, Column 5, line 3, of Table 2 indicates that the present worth of the deduction from discarding a twenty-year asset, 40 per cent depreciated, is 11 per

---

[9] This cost apparently is not disregarded, however, in many investment decisions. Discussions of replacement policies indicate the presence of some irrationality here.

cent of the cost of the asset at a 4 per cent rate of interest. At an 8 per cent rate, the percentage would increase to 18 per cent.

Thus another element of scrambling is introduced in the pretax ranking of investments as to their profitability. Outlays for the replacement of assets with undepreciated costs move up the scale relative to expansion of depreciable assets (investment without replacement) and to outlays for replacement when the cost of the discarded asset has been fully depreciated. It is important to notice that a large part of the asset expenditures of existing concerns represents replacement of one kind or another. They would thus hold an advantage over the new or rapidly expanding firm, because the profitability of a large part of their investment expenditure would be less affected by the tax.

TABLE 2

PRESENT WORTH OF TAX DEDUCTIONS FROM REPLACEMENT AS A
PER CENT OF COST OF NEW ASSET AT 4 PER CENT INTEREST

Economic Life of Old and New Asset	Present Worth of Depreciation on New Asset	Present Worth of Tax Deduction on Old Asset Whose Remaining Undepreciated Cost as a Per Cent of Cost of New Asset Is			
		20 %	40 %	60 %	80 %
(1)	(2)	(3)	(4)	(5)	(6)
5	89.0 %	0.0 %	0.7 %	2.2 %	4.3 %
10	81.1	0.4	2.2	5.3	9.6
20	68.0	1.1	4.8	10.8	18.7
50	43.0	3.0	11.3	23.1	37.3

Taxation with Full Loss Offsets and One-Year Depreciation. We now drop the requirement that the cost of the asset must be spread over its economic life in computing taxable income, and permit taxpayers to shorten the life use for tax purposes. As they telescope the depreciation deduction, the present worth of the tax rebates from the depreciation increases as the rebates are shifted closer to the present. In the limiting case, the asset could be written off in one year. In such an event, the tax rebate from depreciation would be proportional to the tax. Investment incentives would be restored to their pretax level, since the tax would proportionately reduce both the prospective net receipts from investment and its cost. By paying the entrepreneur the tax on the asset's cost, the Government would literally be a partner in the firm. It would make a capital contribution on new investment at the same rate at which it shared in the future net receipts of the enterprise. The contribution would be made at the same time the investment was undertaken. In contrast, the full-loss-offset system with economic-life depreciation would spread the Government's contribution out over the life of the investment, and would require the firm to carry a larger debt and interest cost until this contribution was finally received.

From the point of view of the entrepreneur such a tax would imply a substitution of Government funds for private funds in proportion to the tax, with a corresponding shift in interest payments from private lenders to the Government in the form of taxes. The tax would not increase investment incentives over what they would be if no tax were imposed. Any investment in excess of the amount that would be made if no tax were in effect would also prove to be unprofitable after these adjustments in the tax. It would still fail to earn an amount sufficient to pay for the cost of funds used to make the investment. The reduction in the relative amount the entrepreneur would have have to invest would not change the investment's relative profitability.

The type of tax necessary to neutralize the effect of the tax on investment incentives is a graft of the Kalecki system of a credit for investment onto the Domar-Musgrave system of tax refunds whenever losses arise. Both types of adjustment are theoretically necessary, and they cannot be viewed as alternatives.[10] As we have seen, a system of full loss offsets will not restore investment incentives to their pretax level when a tax on business income alone is considered, because it will not change the timing of the tax payments. A credit for investment will also fail if there is insufficient taxable income in the current year to absorb the full amount of investment undertaken.

II. BUSINESS TAXATION UNDER CONDITIONS OF UNCERTAINTY

Let us change the assumptions so that the entrepreneur is no longer sure what actual series of net receipts will be forthcoming from the asset. Future changes in prices and costs, the level of output, technologic changes, and the like, can, in various combinations, result in a wide variety of possible series of net receipts from the use of an asset. Some of the series of net receipts will have a present worth less than the cost of the asset. If one of these series turns out to be the one realized, the entrepreneur would make a loss on the outlay.[11]

---

[10] Lerner tends to look on one-year depreciation as an alternative method of offsetting losses. He rightly points out its deficiencies in this respect, but fails to appreciate the fundamental difference in the effect of the two adjustments. *Op. cit.*, pp. 98, 105.

[11] The maximum loss would equal the cost of the asset. A greater loss would imply a negative amount of future net receipts (operating costs exceeding operating revenues). Since the original investment would not commit the entrepreneur to future outlays which

The entrepreneur must somehow convert this variety of series into a present worth in order to know whether or not the asset is worth buying. The method he uses has been treated in a number of ways by different writers, some of which lead to different conclusions regarding the effect of a tax on investment incentives. Without in any way attempting a catalogue, the different implications of some of the alternative interpretations are indicated.[12]

Assume first that the business tax allows no loss offsets, and requires economic-life depreciation. The present worth of the net receipts, however it is determined, will be reduced proportionately by the tax, before taking account of depreciation, as under conditions of certainty. The issues focus on the determination of the present worth of the tax rebates from depreciation. The question is whether or not their present worth falls below the tax times the cost of the asset because of the interest discount alone, as under conditions of certainty, or is further reduced because of uncertainty.

1. The results would be the same as under conditions of certainty, if the entrepreneur adjusts the various series of net receipts *before* taxes to a representative series expected with certainty over the same time period as the unadjusted series. This representative series of net receipts would be able to absorb each year's depreciation charge. Because this deduction could be expected with certainty, the tax rebates from depreciation would be discounted only by interest.

2. If, however, the entrepreneur separately appraises the probability of a full absorption of the depreciation against a wide diversity of net receipts from the asset itself, as well as income from other assets of the firm, the depreciation deduction may be reduced by a discount for uncertainty and for interest. If some of the possible series of net receipts fall short of the cost of the asset, and if sufficient future taxable income from all sources is not certain to be large enough to absorb the depreciation deduction, the entrepreneur would determine the chances of an effective depreciation deduction in each year and then discount the resulting adjusted tax rebate to the present. The further in the future the depreciation deduction, the less sure would he be of a tax rebate. The adjustment for uncertainty would be larger.

---

failed to return their cost, he could abandon the asset when this contingency arose and avoid it.

[12] Recent articles of interest, most of which also contain useful references, are the Domar-Musgrave article; G. L. S. Shackle, "Interest Rates and the Pace of Investment," *Economic Journal*, March, 1946; M. Moonitz, "The Risk of Obsolescence and the Importance of the Rate of Interest," *Journal of Political Economy*, August, 1943; and F. A. Lutz, "The Interest Rate and Investment in a Dynamic Economy," *American Economic Review*, December, 1945.

3. An adjustment for uncertainty of an effective future depreciation deduction would also be present if the conversion of the various series of net receipts into a representative series expected with certainty were made by drastically shortening their expected duration. The entrepreneur may be quite certain that a given amount of net receipts will continue for a given period, but after that he may not be sure. The depreciation deduction would fall against this very brief period of net receipts from the asset in question, and then have to be absorbed by future taxable income from all other assets. Although the tax rebates from depreciation may be certain during the arbitrary period, after that time they depend on future income which may be uncertain. A discount for uncertainty would be applied to them.

Thus, the tendencies found under conditions of certainty would be magnified under the latter two adjustments for uncertainty. The difference between the worth of present and future deductions would increase. Lengthening of depreciation periods, or choosing longer-lived assets, would decrease the proportion of the asset likely to be effective in reducing taxes as well as increase interest costs. The tax would thus create a wider gap between long-lived and short-lived assets, between incentives to expand assets as against replacing them, and would fall most heavily on firms with uncertain prospects of future income.

Full loss offsets and one-year depreciation would cope with any of these effects. Full loss offsets would make sure that depreciation would result in a tax rebate, regardless of whether or not future income was present; it would eliminate any uncertainty regarding the tax rebate from depreciation.[13] One-year depreciation would then have the same effect as it has under conditions of certainty; it would eliminate the interest discount applicable to the tax rebates from depreciation and return investment incentives to their pretax level.

It is not believed, however, that one needs to go as far as this to eliminate most of the effect of the tax. One-year depreciation and a reasonably long carry-forward of losses would probably come very close to achieving neutrality. Studies made of investment decisions indicate the prevalence of adjusting for uncertainty by sharp reductions in the duration of the net receipts expected from the asset. The period is so short that entrepreneurs can be fairly certain of their guesses. If this is so, the total cost of the asset can be absorbed by prospective net receipts within this period. If the cost exceeded taxable income in the year of investment, some postponement

---

[13] H. W. Singer, in a letter to the *Economist*, May 13, 1944, p. 648, suggested removal of this uncertainty by reimbursing the taxpayer for depreciation in years of loss at the rate of tax.

of the Government's contribution would result. But the discount applied to the postponed tax reduction would be relatively unimportant over the very short periods within which entrepreneurs expect net receipts to continue.

III. CONCLUDING REMARKS

This analysis does not imply that one should necessarily advocate full loss offsets and a one-year write-off of outlays on depreciable assets as desirable modifications in the corporation-income tax—the present system of *ad rem* business taxation in the United States—without a consideration of other factors. Some of the more important can be indicated briefly below.

1. The business-income tax we have discussed did not permit the deduction of interest payments; the present corporation income tax does. If interest is deductible, it would not be legitimate to assume that the rate of discount used by the entrepreneur is unaffected by the tax, as we have done in our analysis. If interest payments are permitted to reduce taxable income, the net interest costs of the entrepreneur are proportionately reduced. The Government shares in these costs by foregoing taxes. Thus, while yields would be reduced by the tax, interest costs would be equivalently reduced. Investment incentives would remain unaffected. One-year depreciation for debt-financed investment would not be necessary for incentive reasons. If applied to debt-financed assets, it would raise investment incentives above their pretax level.

2. Full loss offsets carry with them substantial costs, both revenue and economic. They may place more resources at the disposal of inefficient firms than if no tax were imposed. The existing definition of taxable income is not sufficiently precise to weed out losses sustained by those attempting to maximize profits from losses sustained by those in "business" as a hobby or those who charge consumption expenses to the firm's account. Salary payments to business owners would offer a convenient way of drawing funds from the Government.

3. Shifting from the present method of computing depreciation to a system permitting a one-year write-off would result in no revenue loss, if expenditures on depreciable assets were equal to what is now termed normal depreciation, and if the cost of existing assets remaining to be depreciated could be eliminated as a tax deduction. Even in this latter event, revenue losses would arise if more were spent on depreciable assets than normal depreciation. Normal depreciation is a moving average of

capital outlays for a long period of time, moving more slowly, both up and down, than the annual outlays themselves.

However, it seems idle to discuss a depreciation policy which implies the elimination of the cost of existing assets remaining to be depreciated. If these assets are depreciated normally and future outlays written off in one year, the loss in the corporate tax base is huge. Contrary to popular belief, this substantial loss in tax base would never be recaptured so long as outlays on depreciable assets average no less than normal depreciation. Writing off the additions to depreciable assets would keep the depreciation deduction up to what it would have been if normal depreciation were taken on total assets. On top of this is added the write-off of existing facilities at a normal rate. In the first year this amount might be as great as asset expenditures; gradually it would diminish to zero when all existing assets had been discarded. At this point total depreciation would have returned approximately to what it would have been under normal depreciation because outlays on new assets, equal to normal depreciation, would continue to be written off. A permanent bulge in total depreciation charges thus arises.

Revenue losses are unimportant in themselves, but they do indicate the price tag connected with returning investment incentives to their pre-tax level. This form of revenue cut must be weighed, in its stimulus of private expenditures, against other varieties of tax reduction. In magnitude it is by no means inconsiderable.

This drawback can be substantially eliminated by a system which permits the firm to deduct either (1) current outlays (or an average of outlays for a short period) on depreciable assets or (2) normal depreciation on total assets. The additional depreciation deduction is then limited to firms which are spending more than normal depreciation on their fixed assets—new and growing firms. Under such a system the tax burden can be shifted from the dynamic to the static elements in the business community.

BIBLIOGRAPHY

Classified Bibliography of Articles on the Economics of Taxation

The items listed in the following bibliography have been arranged to correspond generally with the topical outline of the text, allowing in some cases for further subclasses. The grouping follows the conventional distinction between the analysis of incidence and incentive effects. Since this distinction is a vague one, the classification of certain items is more or less arbitrary, so that the reader who uses this bibliography may wish to search for his titles in more than one place. The topical arrangement is as follows:

A. *Equity and Welfare Economics*
  1. General Principles of Taxation
  2. Ability to Pay and Equal Sacrifice
  3. The Concept of Taxable Income and the Taxation of Saving
  4. Excess Burden of Taxation
  5. Public Pricing and Other Aspects

B. *Incidence*
  6. General Discussions
  7. Taxes on Income and Profits
  8. Estate and Inheritance Taxes
  9. Capital Levy
  10. Sales Taxes
  11. Payroll Taxes
  12. Taxes on Land and Property

C. *Incentive Effects and Tax Burden*
  13. Effects on Work Effort
  14. Effects on Investment and Business Organization
  15. Taxable Capacity
  16. Estimates of Distribution of Tax Burdens

D. *Tax Structure*
  17. Over-all Aspects
  18. Income and Profits Taxes
  19. Income Concept
  20. Other Taxes

Items 1 to 16 cover the range of problems included in the text material, while those listed under 17 to 21 extend beyond this range. Limitation of space required a selective approach to the listings for items 17 to 21, the principle being to choose those items which are of greatest interest in connection with the general economics of taxation. In connection with item 21 the reader is referred to the extensive bibliography in *Readings in Fiscal Policy*, published earlier in this series.

The bibliography for topics 1 to 21 is drawn from English speaking journals, up to and including 1956. The listings under topics 22 to 25 provide a small selection of foreign language articles in the economics of taxation. The distinguished colleagues who contributed these selections are Professor Pierre Tabatoni for the French selection, Professor Fritz Neumark for the German selection, Professor Servio Steve for the Italian selection, and Professors Eric Lindahl and Bent Hansen for the Scandinavian selection. We are greatly indebted to them and hope that their contributions will induce the reader to transcend the insularity of a volume otherwise limited to the English language.

A. EQUITY AND WELFARE ECONOMICS

1. GENERAL PRINCIPLES OF TAXATION

ADAMS, T. S., Ideals and idealism in taxation, *American Economic Review*, XVIII (1928), 1–9.

BASTABLE, C. F., The rule of taxation for revenue as a canon of public finance, *Economic Journal*, XIII (1903), 505–10.

BENHAM, F. C., Notes on the pure theory of public finance, *Economica*, N.S. I (1934), 436–58.

———, What is the best tax-system?, *Economica*, N.S. IX (1942), 115–27.

BUCHANAN, J. M., Federalism and fiscal equity, *American Economic Review*, XL (1950), 583–600.

———, Wicksell on fiscal reform: comment, *American Economic Review*, XLII (1952), 599–602.

———, The pure theory of government finance: a suggested approach, *Journal of Political Economy*, LVII (1949), 496–506.

———, Social choice, democracy, and free markets, *Journal of Political Economy*, LXII (1954), 114–23.

———, Individual choice in voting and the market, *Journal of Political Economy*, LXII (1954), 334–43.

CANNAN, EDWIN, Equity and economy in taxation, *Economic Journal*, XI (1901), 469–80.

COLM, GERHARD, Why public finance?, *National Tax Journal*, I (1948), 193–207.

———, Comments on Samuelson's theory of public finance, *Review of Economics and Statistics*, XXXVIII (1956), 408–12.

DALTON, HUGH, Some recent contributions to the study of public finance, *Economica*, I (1921), 199–206.

JENKINS, H. P., Fiscal equity in the unequal treatment of unequals: a suggested test, *Journal of Political Economy*, LIX (1951), 353–58.

JOSHI, T. M., The concept of the "optimum" of public finance, *Indian Journal of Economics*, XX (1939–40), 83–91.

MANN, FRITZ KARL, The threefold economic function of taxation, *Openbare Financiën*, 2nd year, Nos. 1 and 2 (1947), 5–16.

MARGOLIS, JULIUS, A comment on the pure theory of public expenditures, *Review of Economics and Statistics*, XXXVII (1955), 347–50.

MUSGRAVE, RICHARD ABEL, The voluntary exchange theory of public economy, *Quarterly Journal of Economics*, LIII (1938–39), 213–38.

———, The planning approach in public economy: a reply, *Quarterly Journal of Economics*, LV (1940–41), 319–25.

NEAL, ALFRED C., The "planning approach" in public economy, *Quarterly Journal of Economics*, LIV (1939–40), 246–54.

PLUMLEY, C. A., Equality in taxation, *Bulletin of the National Tax Association*, X (1924–25), 271–75.

ROLPH, EARL R., Equity versus efficiency in federal tax policy, *American Economic Review*, XL (1950), Papers and Proceedings, 391–405.

SAMUELSON, PAUL A., The pure theory of public expenditure, *Review of Economics and Statistics*, XXXVI (1954), 387–90.

———, Diagrammatic exposition of a theory of public expenditure, *Review of Economics and Statistics*, XXXVII (1955), 350–57.

SIMON, HERBERT A., The planning approach in public economy: further comment, *Quarterly Journal of Economics*, LV (1940–41), 325–31.

SULTAN, HERBERT, Public finance and national economy sociologically considered, *Bulletin of the National Tax Association*, XXI (1935–36), 40–45.

TIEBOUT, CHARLES M., A pure theory of local expenditures, *Journal of Political Economy*, LXIV (1956), 416–25.

UHR, C. G., Wicksell on fiscal reform: further comment, *American Economic Review*, XLIII (1953), 366–68.

2. ABILITY TO PAY AND EQUAL SACRIFICE

BLOUGH, ROY, Ability to pay re-examined, *Proceedings of the Thirty-Third Annual Conference (1940) of the National Tax Association*, 1941, 368–76; discussion, 376–89.

BUEHLER, ALFRED G., Taxation and minimum of subsistence, *American Economic Review*, XXIII (1933), 234–45.

CASSEL, G., The theory of progressive taxation, *Economic Journal*, XI (1901), 481–91.

CHAPMAN, S. J., The utility of income and progressive taxation, *Economic Journal*, XXIII (1913), 25–35.

DEMPSEY, BERNARD W., S. J., "Ability to pay," *Quarterly Journal of Economics*, LX (1945–46), 351–65.

DORESAMIENGAR, M. R., Some recent developments in the mathematical theory of taxation due to Edgeworth, *Indian Journal of Economics*, X (1929–30), 317–31.

EDGEWORTH, F. Y., The subjective element in the first principles of taxation, *Quarterly Journal of Economics*, XXIV (1909–10), 459–70.

———, Methods of graduating taxes on income and capital, *Economic Journal*, XXIX (1919), 138–53.

FAGAN, ELMER D., Recent and contemporary theories of progressive taxation, *Journal of Political Economy*, XLVI (1938), 457–98.

GROVES, HAROLD M., Neutrality in taxation, *National Tax Journal*, I (1948), 18–25.

————, Toward a social theory of progressive taxation, *National Tax Journal*, IX (1956), 27–35.

HARROD, R. F., Progressive taxation and equal sacrifice, *Economic Journal*, XL (1930), 704–8.

KENDRICK, M. SLADE, Ability-to-pay theory of taxation, *American Economic Review*, XXIX (1939), 92–102.

LINDHOLM, R. W., Degree of progression: the income tax, *American Economic Review*, XLIV (1954), 617–27.

MUSGRAVE, R. A. and TUN THIN, Income tax progression, 1929–48, *Journal of Political Economy*, LVI (1948), 498–515.

PREINREICH, G. A. D., Progressive taxation and sacrifice, *American Economic Review*, XXXVIII (1948), 103–18.

RAMSEY, F. P., A contribution to the theory of taxation, *Economic Journal*, XXXVII (1927), 47–62.

YOUNG, ALLYN A., Review of A. C. Pigou, A Study in Public Finance, *Economic Journal*, XXXIX (1929), 78–83.

3. THE CONCEPT OF TAXABLE INCOME AND THE TAXATION OF SAVING

CRUM, W. L., Alleged double taxation of savings, *American Economic Review*, XXIX (1939), 538–49.

FISHER, IRVING, Income theory and income taxation in practice, *Econometrica*, V (1937), 1–56.

————, Double taxation of savings, *American Economic Review*, XXIX (1939), 16–34.

————, Paradoxes in taxing savings, *Econometrica*, X (1942), 147–59.

————, Rebuttal to Professor Crum and Mr. Musgrave, *American Economic Review*, XXXII (1942), 111–17 (on double taxation of savings).

————, Income-tax revision: reply, *Econometrica*, XI (1943), 88–94.

GREEN, A. ROMNEY, The tax curve, *Economic Journal*, L (1940), 469–75.

GUILLEBAUD, C. W., Income tax and "double taxation," *Economic Journal*, XLV (1935), 484–93.

HAIG, R. M., The concept of income, *Federal Income Tax* (ed. R. M. HAIG), pp. 1–28.

HOTELLING, HAROLD, Income-tax revision as proposed by Irving Fisher, *Econometrica*, XI (1943), 83–88.

MACGREGOR, D. H., Taxation of savings, *Economica*, N.S. III (1936), 387–404.

————, Taxation of savings: a rejoinder, *Economica*, N.S. IV (1937), 206–8.

MUSGRAVE, RICHARD ABEL, Further note on double taxation of savings, *American Economic Review*, XXIX (1939), 549–50.

PIGOU, A. C., Taxation of savings: a reply, *Economica*, N.S. IV (1937), 204–6.

WEAVER, D., The double taxation of savings: a fallacy, *Economic Journal*, XLII (1932), 495–98.

4. EXCESS BURDEN OF TAXATION

ABBOTT, LAWRENCE, A theory of excise subsidies: comment, *American Economic Review*, XLIII (1953), 890–95.

ALLEN, CLARK LEE, Modern welfare economics and public policy, *Southern Economic Journal*, XIX (1952–53), 28–37 (indirect vs. direct taxes, pp. 31–32).

ARCHIBALD, G. C., Saving and the welfare theory of taxation, *Economic Record*, XXXI (1955), 90–95.

BAILEY, MARTIN J., The welfare cost of inflationary finance, *Journal of Political Economy*, LXIV (1956), 93–111.

BREAK, G. F., Excise tax burdens and benefits, *American Economic Review*, XLIV (1954), 577–95.

CORLETT, W. J. and HAGUE, D. C., Complementarity and the excess burden of taxation, *Review of Economic Studies*, XXI (1953–54), 21–31.

DAVIDSON, R. K., The alleged excess burden of an excise tax in the case of an individual consumer, *Review of Economic Studies*, XX (1952–53), 209–16.

FRASER, L. M., Taxation and returns, *Review of Economic Studies*, I (1933–34), 45–59.

——, Rejoinder to Mrs. Robinson, *Review of Economic Studies*, I (1933–34), 141–43 (on taxation and returns).

FRIEDMAN, MILTON, The "welfare" effects of an income tax and an excise tax, *Journal of Political Economy*, LX (1952), 25–34.

GOODE, RICHARD, Direct versus indirect taxes: welfare implications, *Public Finance*, XI (1956), 95–97.

HENDERSON, A., The case for indirect taxation, *Economic Journal*, LVIII (1948), 538–54.

JOSEPH, M. F. W., The excess burden of indirect taxation, *Review of Economic Studies*, VI (1938–39), 226–31.

KOO, ANTHONY Y. C., Welfare and direct taxation, *Canadian Journal of Economics and Political Science*, XXI (1955), 43–52.

LITTLE, I. M. D., Direct versus indirect taxes, *Economic Journal*, LXI (1951), 577–85.

PHIPPS, CECIL G., Friedman's "welfare" effects, *Journal of Political Economy*, LX (1952), 332–34 (answer to Friedman's article on income tax and excise tax, 1952).

RAO, K. BALAKRISHNA, The excess burden of indirect taxation, *Indian Journal of Economics*, XXXIV (1953–54), 115–23.

ROBINSON, HERBERT W., Consumer's surplus and taxation: ex ante or ex post? *South African Journal of Economics*, VII (1939), 270–80.

ROBINSON, JOAN, Mr. Fraser on taxation and returns, *Review of Economic Studies*, I (1933–34), 137–40.

ROLPH, E. R., A theory of excise subsidies, *American Economic Review*, XLII (1952), 515–28.

——, A theory of excise subsidies: a reply, *American Economic Review*, XLIII (1953), 895–98.

ROLPH, EARL R. and BREAK, GEORGE F., The welfare aspects of excise taxes, *Journal of Political Economy*, LVII (1949), 46–55.

SCHWARTZ, ELI and MOORE, D. A., The distorting effects of direct taxation: a re-evaluation, *American Economic Review*, XLI (1951), 139–49.

WALD, HASKELL P., The classical indictment of indirect taxation, *Quarterly Journal of Economics*, LIX (1944–45), 577–96.

WALKER, DAVID, The direct-indirect tax problem: fifteen years of controversy, *Public Finance*, X (1955), 153–76.

5. PUBLIC PRICING AND OTHER ASPECTS

BACKMAN, JULES and KURNOW, ERNEST, Pricing of government services, *National Tax Journal*, VII (1954), 121–41.

BICKERDIKE, C. F., The theory of incipient taxes, *Economic Journal*, XVI (1906), 529–35.

COASE, R. H., The marginal cost controversy, *Economica*, XIII (1946), 169–82.

DEBREU, GERARD, A classical tax-subsidy problem, *Econometrica*, XXII (1954), 14–23.

FORTE, FRANCISCO, Motor vehicle taxation as pricing for highway services: some theoretical notes, *Banca Nazionale del Lavoro Quarterly Review*, XXXIV (1955), 134–42.

FRISCH, RAGNAR, The Dupuit taxation theorem, *Econometrica*, VII (1939), 145–51.

——, A further note on the Dupuit taxation theorem, *Econometrica*, VII (1939), 156–57.

HENDERSON, A. M., The pricing of public utility undertakings, *Manchester School of Economics and Social Studies*, LXVI (1947), 223–50.

HOTELLING, HAROLD, The general welfare in relation to problems of taxation and of railway and utility rates, *Econometrica*, VI (1938), 242–70.

——, The relation of prices to marginal costs in an optimum system, *Econometrica*, VII (1939), 151–55.

——, A final note, *Econometrica*, VI (1939), 158–61 (on theorem stated in 1938 article).

MEADE, J. E., Price and output policy of state enterprise, *Economic Journal*, LIV (1944), 337–39.

PIGOU, A. C., Problems of compensation, *Economic Journal*, XXXV (1925), 568–83.

SHOVE, G. F., Varying costs and marginal net products, *Economic Journal*, XXXVIII (1928), 258–67.

THOMSON, PROCTER; HARBESON, ROBERT W.; FITCH, LYLE C.; MUSGRAVE, RICHARD A.; and LANDERS, FRANK M., Taxes and user charges in government finance, *Proceedings of the Forty-Eighth Annual Conference (1955) of the National Tax Association*, 1956, 140–95.

WILSON, T., Price and outlay policy of state enterprise, *Economic Journal*, LV (1945), 454–60.

B. INCIDENCE

6. GENERAL DISCUSSIONS

BATES, STEWART, Classificatory note on the theory of public finance, *Canadian Journal of Economics and Political Science*, III (1937), 163–80.

BENHAM, F. C., Taxation and the relative prices of factors of production, *Economica*, N.S. II (1935), 198–204.

BHARGAVA, R. N., Incidence of taxation, *Indian Economic Journal*, II (1954–55), 37–45.

BLOUGH, ROY, Economic research and tax policy, *American Economic Review*, XXXIV (1944), Supplement: the implemental aspects of public finance, 1–22.

BROWN, HARRY GUNNISON, Some frequently neglected factors in the incidence of taxation, *Journal of Political Economy*, XXVIII (1920), 499–504.

BROWNLEE, O. H., Taxation and the price level in the short-run, *Journal of Political Economy*, LXII (1954), 26.

BUTLIN, S. J., Incidence of taxation, *Economic Record*, XIII (1937), 189–200.

EDGEWORTH, F. Y., The pure theory of taxation, *Economic Journal*, VII (1897), 46–70, 226–38, 550–71.

FASIANI, M., Materials for a theory of the duration of the process of tax shifting—part I, *Review of Economic Studies*, I (1933–34), 81–101.

———, Materials for a theory of the duration of the process of tax shifting—part II, *Review of Economic Studies*, II (1934–35), 122–36.

FERGER, W. F., The measurement of tax shifting: economics and law, *Quarterly Journal of Economics*, LIV (1939–40), 429–54.

FISHER, IRVING, Edgeworth's papers relating to political economy, *Quarterly Journal of Economics*, XL (1925–26), 167–71.

HICKS, URSULA K., The terminology of tax analysis, *Economic Journal*, LVI (1946), 38–51.

HOLDEN, GRENVILLE, Incidence of taxation, *American Economic Review*, XXX (1940), 774–87.

HUNTER, M. H , Problem of classification: public expenditures and revenues, *American Economic Review*, XX (1930), 46–54.

JENKIN, FLEEMING, On the principles which regulate the incidence of taxes, *Papers Literary, Scientific*, etc., II (1887), 107–21.

KALECKI, M., A theory of commodity, income and capital taxation, *Economic Journal*, XLVII (1937), 444–51.

KENDRICK, M. SLADE, Public expenditure in tax incidence theory, *American Economic Review*, XX (1930), 226–31.

———, Incidence and effects of taxation, *American Economic Review*, XXVII (1937), 725–35.

KEYNES, J. M., The Colwyn report on national debt and taxation, *Economic Journal*, XXXVII (1927), 198–213.

LEAVITT, J. A., Note on "taxes and the consumer," *American Economic Review*, XXVIII (1938), 319–20.

METZLER, LLOYD A., Taxes and subsidies in Leontief's input-output model, *Quarterly Journal of Economics*, LXV (1951), 433–39.

MILLER, ADOLPH C., On incidence of taxation, *Journal of Political Economy*, I (1892–93), 450–68.

MUSGRAVE, R. A., General equilibrium aspects of incidence theory, *American Economic Review*, XLIII (1953), Papers and Proceedings, 504–18.

————, On incidence, *Journal of Political Economy*, LXI (1953), 306–24.

PODUVAL, R. N., The economic effects of taxes, *Indian Journal of Economics*, XXIV (1943-44), 117–26.

SCHUMPETER, ELIZABETH BOODY, English prices and public finance, 1660–1822, *Review of Economic Statistics*, XX (1938), 21–37.

SELIGMAN, E. R. A., On incidence of taxation, *Journal of Political Economy*, I (1892–93), 444–50.

————, The classification of public revenue, *Quarterly Journal of Economics*, IX (1894–95), 279–90.

————, The effects of taxation, *Political Science Quarterly*, XXXVIII (1923), 1–23.

————, Income taxes and the price level, *Academy of Political Science, Proceedings*, 1924 ("Wealth and Taxation"), 3–23.

SHEPHARD, RONALD W., A mathematical theory of the incidence of taxation, *Econometrica*, XII (1944), 1–19.

SOMERS, H. M., Note on "taxes and the consumer," *American Economic Review*, XXVIII (1938), 736–37.

————, Taxes as a share in distribution, *American Economic Review*, XXIX (1939), 349–50.

VINER, JACOB, Taxation and changes in price levels, *Journal of Political Economy*, XXXI (1923), 494–520.

WALKER, DAVID, Taxation and economics, *Public Finance*, XI (1956), 98–100.

WASSERMAN, MAX J., Taxes as a share in distribution, *American Economic Review*, XXVIII (1938), 103–5.

WEBB, URSULA K., Taxation and production, *Review of Economic Studies*, II (1934–35), 18–30.

WEHRWEIN, CARL F., Taxes and the consumer, *American Economic Review*, XXVIII (1938), 92–100.

WYCOFF, V. J., Tax classification and public finance, *Bulletin of the National Tax Association*, XXXI (1945–46), 110–14.

7. TAXES ON INCOME AND PROFITS

ADAMS, T. S., Tax exemption through tax capitalization: a fiscal fallacy, *American Economic Review*, VI (1916), 271–88.

BASTABLE, C. F., Taxation through monopoly, *Economic Journal*, I (1891), 307–25.

BECK, MORRIS, Ability to shift the corporate income tax, *National Tax Journal*, III (1950), 248–57.

————, Ability to shift the corporate income tax: correction, *National Tax Journal*, III (1950), 353–54.

BENEKE, RAYMOND, Some effects of income tax regulations on farming efficiency, *Journal of Farm Economics*, XXXIV (1952), 520–35.

BERNSTEIN, E. M., Public utilities and the income tax, *Quarterly Journal of Economics*, XLV (1930–31), 529–35.

BLACK, DUNCAN, The incidence of the tax on gold mining in South Africa, *South African Journal of Economics*, V (1937), 121–31.

————, The subsidy to British farming in respect of income tax, *Economica*, N.S. V (1938), 33–45.

BODENHORN, DIRAN, The shifting of the corporation income tax in a growing economy, *Quarterly Journal of Economics*, LXX (1956), 563–81.

BOULDING, K. E., The incidence of a profits tax, *American Economic Review*, XXXIV (1944), 567–72.

BOWEN, H. R., Incidence of the corporate income tax, *American Economic Review*, XXXVI (1946), 146–47.

————, Taxation of net income from business, *Bulletin of the National Tax Association*, XXXI (1945–46), 72–81.

BRADLEY, PHILIP D., Some effects of the personal income tax, *Quarterly Journal of Economics*, LVIII (1943–44), 134–41.

BROWN, E. CARY, The corporate income tax in the short-run, *National Tax Journal*, VII (1954), 240–42.

BUEHLER, ALFRED G., The capitalization of taxes, *National Tax Journal*, III (1950), 283–98.

BURKHEAD, JESSE V., The changing incidence of public utility taxation, *Journal of Land and Public Utility Economics*, XV (1939), 383–90.

BUSSCHAU, W. J., Gold mining taxation: a method of analysis, *South African Journal of Economics*, III (1935), 322–44.

BUTTERS, KEITH, Discriminatory effects of the annual computation of the corporation income tax, *Quarterly Journal of Economics*, LIV (1939–40), 51–72.

CRUM, W. L., Large-scale enterprise in the light of income tax returns, *Quarterly Journal of Economics*, XLVII (1932–33), 414–49.

DALTON, J. P., On taxation and grade in gold-mining: a study in inequalities, *South African Journal of Economics*, V (1937), 306–14.

DUE, JOHN F., The economic effects of local non-property taxes, *Public Finance*, VIII (1953), 388–96.

FAGAN, ELMER D., The economics of capital gains taxation, *Proceedings of the Thirty-Second Annual Conference (1939) of the National Tax Association*, 1940, 113–26.

FISHER, IRVING, The use of income tax statistics, *Bulletin of the National Tax Association*, II (1916–17), 245–47.

FRIDAY, DAVID, Shifting of income and profits taxes, *Proceedings of the Seventeenth Annual Conference (1924) of the National Tax Association*, 1925, 306–15.

GARVER, RAYMOND, The effect of taxation on a monopolist, *American Economic Review*, XXII (1932), 463–65.

GEMMILL, ROBERT F., The effect of the capital gains tax on asset prices, *National Tax Journal*, IX (1956), 289–302.

GITLOW, A. L., Wages and the excess profits tax, *Southern Economic Journal*, XIX (1952–53), 95–97.

GOODE, RICHARD, The corporate income tax and the price level, *American Economic Review*, XXXV (1945), 40–59.

———, Incidence of the corporate income tax: rejoinder, *American Economic Review*, XXXVI (1946), 147–48.

GOPAL, M. H., The role of the excess profits tax in modifying capitalism, *Indian Journal of Economics*, XXIV (1943–44), 387–95.

HAYES, HARRY GORDON, Tax exemption through tax capitalization, *Bulletin of the National Tax Association*, II (1916–17), 69–73.

HICKS, URSULA K., Direct taxation and economic growth, *Oxford Economic Papers*, N.S. VIII (1956), 302–17.

HIGGINS, BENJAMIN, Post-war tax policy—part I, *Canadian Journal of Economics and Political Science*, IX (1943), 408–28 (entirely theoretical).

HOLLANDER, JACOB H., An economist's examination of the theory of tax shifting as exemplified by the windfall tax, *Proceedings of the Thirtieth Annual Conference (1937) of the National Tax Association*, 1938, 135–37.

JENSEN, J. P., Tax capitalization, *Bulletin of the National Tax Association*, XXIII (1937–38), 45–57.

KHUSRO, A. M., The incidence of taxation in India: The marginal rate of tax, *Indian Journal of Economics*, XXXIII (1952–53), 449–61.

LENT, GEORGE E., Excess profits taxation in the United States, *Journal of Political Economy*, LIX (1951), 481–98.

LERNER, EUGENE M., Federal taxes on corporate income and the rate of return on investment in manufacturing, 1927 to 1952, *National Tax Journal*, IX (1956), 193–203.

LITTERER, OSCAR F., Corporation income tax and production, *Bulletin of the National Tax Association*, XXXI (1945–46), 199–206.

MACY, C. WARD, The corporation net income tax and the cost-price structure, *Bulletin of the National Tax Association*, XXIX (1943–44), 231–35.

———, Corporation income tax: incidence or effects; *American Economic Review*, XXXVI (1946), 903–6.

MEHTA, J. K., Taxation of monopoly, *Indian Journal of Economics*, XXV (1944–45), 124–30.

MILLER, MERTON H. and SHELTON, JOHN P., Effects of a shifted corporate income tax on capital structure, *National Tax Journal*, VIII (1955), 252–60.

MORGAN, LUCY, The impact of war taxation on eighty Canadian corporations, *Canadian Journal of Economics and Political Science*, VIII (1942), 566–84 (entirely descriptive and statistical).

MUNSHI, M. C., Incidence and effects of corporation taxes, *Indian Journal of Economics*, XXVII (1946–47), 503–13.

OAKES, EUGENE E., The incidence of the general income tax, *American Economic Review*, XXXII (1942), Papers and Proceedings, 76–83.

PLEHN, CARL C., Can a public utility shift its taxes to its patrons? *Bulletin of the National Tax Association*, V (1919–20), 164–67.

PREST, A. R., The royal commission on the taxation of profits and income, *Economica*, N.S. XXIII (1956), 366–75.

ROBERTSON, D. H., The Colwyn Committee, the income tax, and the price level, *Economic Journal*, XXXVII (1927), 566–82.

ROSENBERG, W., A note on the incidence of company tax under the regime of price control in New Zealand, *Economic Record*, XXVII (1951), 207–12.

SELIGMAN, EDWIN R. A., Tax exemption through tax capitalization: a reply, *American Economic Review*, VI (1916), 790–808.

SHOUP, CARL S., Incidence of the corporation income tax: capital structure and turnover rates, *National Tax Journal*, I (1948), 12–18.

——, Ricardo on the taxation of profits, *Public Finance*, V (1950), 101–18.

SMITH, JAMES G., Undistributed profits tax: reply, *American Economic Review*, XXVIII (1938), 740–42.

SMITH, R. H., Distribution of income in Great Britain and incidence of income tax, *Quarterly Journal of Economics*, XXV (1910–11), 216–38.

SNAVELY, TIPTON R., The Colwyn Committee and the incidence of income tax, *Quarterly Journal of Economics*, XLII (1927–28), 641–68.

SOLO, ROBERT, The incidence of corporate income taxation on public utilities, *National Tax Journal*, VI (1953), 298–300.

SOMERS, HAROLD M., An economic analysis of the capital gains tax, *National Tax Journal*, I (1948), 226–33.

STOCKFISCH, J. A., The capitalization, allocation, and investment effects of asset taxation, *Southern Economic Journal*, XXII (1956), 317–30.

——, Common stock financing and tax capitalization, *National Tax Journal*, VII (1954), 182–86.

STRAYER, PAUL J., The effect of a rise in prices upon the income tax, *Bulletin of the National Tax Association*, XXIV (1938–39), 165–76.

STREETEN, P. P., Some problems raised by the report of the Royal Commission on the taxation of profits and income, *Oxford Institute of Statistics Bulletin*, XVII (1955), 321–63.

STUART, A. J., Progressive taxation in Holland, *Economic Journal*, VII (1898), 325–32.

TROXEL, C. EMERY, Shifting of public utility taxes, *Bulletin of the National Tax Association*, XXV (1939–40), 104–10.

VAN ARSDELL, P. M., Economic significance of undistributed profits tax, *American Economic Review*, XXVIII (1938), 737–40.

VILJOEN, STEPHAN, Are the gold mines overtaxed? *South African Journal of Economics*, III (1935), 548–58.

WALKER, DAVID, Some economic aspects of the taxation of companies, *Manchester School*, XXII (1954), 1–37.

WARD, R. L., Are the gold mines overtaxed? A commentary, *South African Journal of Economics*, IV (1936), 75–86.

WELCH, RONALD B., Comparative tax burdens of carriers, *Proceedings of the Thirty-Sixth Annual Conference (1943) of the National Tax Association*, 1944, 125–42.

WESTON, J. FRED, Incidence and effects of the corporate income tax, *National Tax Journal*, II (1949), 300–316.

WORSWICK, G. D. N., Official papers: the Royal Commission on the taxation of profits and income, *Economic Journal*, LXVI (1956), 370–78.

ZOLLER, J. F., The incidence of business taxes, *Proceedings of the Seventeenth Annual Conference (1924) of the National Tax Association*, 1925, 315–45.

8. Estate and Inheritance Taxes

BARNA, T., The burden of death duties in terms of an annual tax, *Review of Economic Studies*, IX (1941–42), 28–39.

CARTTER, A. M., A new method of relating British capital ownership and estate duty liability to income groups, *Economica*, XX (1953), 247–59.

FIJALKOWSKI-BEREDAY, G. Z., The equalizing effects of the death duties, *Oxford Economic Papers*, N.S. II (1950), 176–97.

HALL, JAMES K., Incidence of death duties, *American Economic Review*, XXX (1940), 46–60.

HARRISS, C. LOWELL, Stock prices, death tax revenues, and tax equity, *Journal of Finance*, V (1950), 257–70.

HOOVER, GLENN E., Economic effects of inheritance taxes, *American Economic Review*, XVII (1927), 38–50.

JOHNSON, ALVIN H., Public capitalization of the inheritance tax, *Journal of Political Economy*, XXII (1914), 160–80.

RHODES, E. C., The distribution of incomes and the burden of estate duties in the United Kingdom, *Economica*, XVIII (1951), 270–78.

9. Capital Levy

BALOGH, T., The unimportance of a capital levy, *Oxford Institute of Statistics Bulletin*, VI (1944), 44–48.

BENHAM, F. C., The taxation of war wealth, *Economica*, N.S. VIII (1941), 321–25.

COMSTOCK, ALZADA, Proposals for the taxation of wealth in Great Britain, *Journal of Political Economy*, XXVIII (1920), 399–406.

FAGAN, ELMER D., Tax shifting in the market period, *American Economic Review*, XXXII (1942), 72–87.

GOTTLIEB, M., The capital levy after World War I, *Public Finance*, VII (1952), 356–84.

KALDOR, N., The income burden of capital taxes, *Review of Economic Studies*, IX (1941–42), 138–57.

VAN SICKLE, JOHN, The fallacy of a capital levy, *Journal of Political Economy*, XXXIV (1926), 181–96.

10. Sales Taxes

BAILEY, MARTIN J., Edgeworth's taxation paradox, and the nature of demand functions, *Econometrica*, XXII (1954), 72–77.

BARKAR, V. V., The role of indirect taxes in development planning, *Indian Journal of Economics*, XXXII (1951–52), 279–85.

BARNA, T., Indirect taxes, subsidies and the cost-of-living index, *Review of Economic Studies*, X (1942–43), 53–61.

BEHRMAN, J. N., Distributive effects of an excise tax on a monopolist, *Journal of Political Economy*, LVIII (1950), 546–49.

BOULDING, K. E., Sales and output taxes: comment, *American Economic Review*, XLIV (1954), 129.

BRABSON, GEORGE D., Economic aspects of state sales and use taxes, *Bulletin of the National Tax Association*, XXXII (1946–47), 148–60.

BRONFENBRENNER, M., Sales taxation and the Mints plan, *Review of Economic Statistics*, XXIX (1947), 39–43.

BROWN, HARRY GUNNISON, The shifting of taxes on sales of land and capital goods and on loans, *Journal of Political Economy*, XXIX (1921), 643–53.

———, The incidence of a general output or a general sales tax, and "A correction," *Journal of Political Economy*, XLVII (1939), 254–62 and 418–20.

BUCHANAN, J. M., The capitalization and investment aspects of excise taxes under competition: comment, *American Economic Review*, XLVI (1956), 974–77.

COLBERG, MARSHALL R., Shifting of a specific excise tax, *Public Finance*, IX (1954), 168–73.

COPELAND, JOHN, Some effects of the changes in the federal cabaret tax in 1944, *Proceedings of the Thirty-Eighth Annual Conference (1945) of the National Tax Association*, 1946, 321–41.

DUE, JOHN F., Ad valorem and specific taxes, *Quarterly Journal of Economics*, LIV (1939–40), 679–85.

———, The incidence of retail sales taxes, *Bulletin of the National Tax Association*, XXV (1939–40), 226–31.

———, A general sales tax and the level of employment: a reconsideration, *National Tax Journal*, II (1949), 122–31.

———, The incidence of a general sales tax, *Public Finance*, V (1950), 222–38.

———, Toward a general theory of sales tax incidence, *Quarterly Journal of Economics*, LXVII (1953), 253–67.

———, The effect of the 1954 reduction in federal excise taxes upon the list prices of electrical appliances—a case study, *National Tax Journal*, VII (1954), 222–27.

ELLIS, PAUL W., Taxes and the consumer—a Gestalt analysis, *American Economic Review*, XXIX (1939), 800–801.

FAGAN, ELMER D., Tax shifting and the laws of cost, *Quarterly Journal of Economics*, XLVII (1932–33), 608–711.

———, The shifting of sales taxes under joint costs, *Public Finance*, VIII (1953), 338–54.

FAGAN, E. D. and JASTRAM, R. W., Tax shifting in the short-run, *Quarterly Journal of Economics*, LIII (1938–39), 562–90.

FAWZY, ABDEL MONEM and MARTIN, JAMES W., Effect of changes in state motor fuel tax rates on prices and consumption of gasoline, *National Tax Journal*, VI (1953), 143–57.

FERBER, ROBERT, How aware are consumers of excise changes? *National Tax Journal*, VII (1954), 355–59.

FERGER, WIRTH F., Who paid the processing taxes—the first time? *Southern Economic Journal*, III (1936–37), 255–70.

———, Windfall tax and processing tax refund, *American Economic Review*, XXVII (1937), 45–61.

GARVER, RAYMOND, The Edgeworth taxation phenomenon, *Econometrica*, I (1933), 402–8.

GILBERT, DONALD W., The shifting of sales taxes, *Quarterly Journal of Economics*, LIII (1938–39), 275–86.

———, The incidence of sales taxes: rejoinder, *Quarterly Journal of Economics*, LIV (1939–40), 686–93.

GREENHUT, MELVIN L., Effects of excise tax and freight cost: a geometrical classification, *Southern Economic Journal*, XXI (1954–55), 330–36.

HALL, JAMES K., Excise tax incidence and the postwar economy, *American Economic Review*, XXXII (1942), Papers and Proceedings, 83–102.

HAYGOOD, TYLER F., How would a federal sales tax affect farmers? *Journal of Farm Economics*, XXVII (1945), 649–64.

HENDRICKS, H. G., Incidence of the gasoline tax, *American Economic Review*, XXI (1931), 88–89.

HIGGINS, B. H., The incidence of sales taxes: a note on methodology, *Quarterly Journal of Economics*, LIV (1939–40), 665–72.

HOLZMAN, FRANKLYN D., Commodity and income taxation in the Soviet Union, *Journal of Political Economy*, LVIII (1950), 425–34.

HOTELLING, HAROLD, Edgeworth's taxation paradox and the nature of demand and supply functions, *Journal of Political Economy*, XL (1932), 577–616.

———, Note on Edgeworth's taxation phenomenon and Professor Garver's additional condition on demand functions, *Econometrica*, I (1933), 408–10.

JASTRAM, R. W., The shifting of sales taxes, *Quarterly Journal of Economics*, LIV (1939–40), 673–78.

JENKINS, H. P. B., Excise-tax shifting and incidence: a money-flows approach, *Journal of Political Economy*, LXIII (1955), 125–50.

JOHNSON, H. G., General equilibrium analysis of excise taxes: comment, *American Economic Review*, XLVI (1956), 151–57.

KENDRICK, M. SLADE, Gasoline tax: a reply, *American Economic Review*, XXI (1931), 89–90.

——, The processing taxes and some problems raised by them, *Journal of Farm Economics*, XVII (1935), 307–17; discussion, 317–21.

——, Processing tax on wheat, *American Economic Review*, XVII (1936), 621–37.

LERNER, A. P., The symmetry between import and export taxes, *Economica*, N.S. III (1936), 306–14.

McGOUN, A. F., The taxation of luxuries and the rate of interest, *Quarterly Journal of Economics*, XXXIII (1918–19), 298–320.

McGREW, JAMES W., Effect of a food exemption on the incidence of a retail sales tax, *National Tax Journal*, II (1949), 362–68.

MALACH, V. W., Sales and output taxes, *American Economic Review*, XLIV (1954), 123–29.

MILLER, DONALD C., Sales-tax progressivity attributable to a food exemption, *National Tax Journal*, IV (1951), 148–60.

PRITCHARD, L. J., The effects of specific and ad valorem taxes, *Quarterly Journal of Economics*, LVIII (1943–44), 149–53.

RITTER, L. S., Consumption taxes and income: comment, *American Economic Review*, XLI (1951), 191–94.

ROLPH, EARL R., A proposed revision of excise tax theory, *Journal of Political Economy*, LX (1952), 102–18.

——, Interregional trade and state excise taxes, *National Tax Journal*, VIII (1955), 388–93.

SHEPHERD, GEOFFREY, The incidence of the AAA processing tax on hogs, *Journal of Farm Economics*, XVII (1935), 321–34; discussion, 334–40.

SHOUP, CARL, The experience of 2,000 retailers under New York City's sales tax, *Bulletin of the National Tax Association*, XXI (1935–36), 98–114.

SOLOWAY, ARNOLD M., Economic aspects of the British purchase tax, *Journal of Finance*, IX (1954), 188–209.

STOCKFISCH, J. A., The capitalization and investment aspects of excise taxes under competition, *American Economic Review*, XLIV (1954), 287–301.

——, The capitalization and investment aspects of excise taxes under competition: reply, *American Economic Review*, XLVI (1956), 977–80.

SUITS, D. B. and MUSGRAVE, R. A., Ad valorem and unit taxes compared, *Quarterly Journal of Economics*, LXVII (1953), 598–605.

WELLS, PAUL, A general equilibrium analysis of excise taxes, *American Economic Review*, XLV (1955), 345–60.

WHITTLESEY, C. R., Excise taxes as a substitute for tariffs, *American Economic Review*, XXVII (1937), 667–80.

11. PAYROLL TAXES

ARNOLD, SAM, Forward shifting of a payroll tax under monopolistic competition, *Quarterly Journal of Economics*, LXI (1945), 267–85.

BAUDER, RUSSELL, Probable incidence of social security taxes, *American Economic Review*, XXVI (1936), 463–66.

BROWN, HARRY GUNNISON, The incidence of compulsory insurance of workmen, *Journal of Political Economy*, XXX (1922), 67–77.

HALL, JAMES K., Incidence of federal social security pay roll taxes, *Quarterly Journal of Economics*, LIII (1938–39), 38–64.

ROSENSON, ALEX. MOSES, Monetary effects of wartime social security taxes, *Journal of Political Economy*, L (1942), 881–901.

UNDERHILL, H. FABIAN, The incidence of pay roll taxes, *Quarterly Journal of Economics*, LVII (1942–43), 160–63.

WINTERS, R. A. and CLARK, HARRISON, The incidence of pay roll taxes: comment, *Quarterly Journal of Economics*, LIV (1939–40), 161–64.

12. TAXES ON LAND AND PROPERTY

ADAMS, T. S., Valuation of railway property for purposes of taxation, *Journal of Political Economy*, XXIII (1915), 1–16.

ANDERSON, B. M., JR., "Unearned increments," land taxes and the building trade, *Quarterly Journal of Economics*, XXVIII (1913–14), 811–14.

BASTABLE, C. F., The taxation of ground rents, *Economic Journal*, III (1893), 255–63.

BICKERDIKE, C. F., Taxation of site values, *Economic Journal*, XII (1902), 472–84.

———, The principle of land value taxation, *Economic Journal*, XXII (1912), 1–15.

BROWN, HARRY GUNNISON, Ethics of land-value taxation, *Journal of Political Economy*, XXV (1917), 464–92.

———, An oversight in the theory of incidence, *Quarterly Journal of Economics*, XXXIII (1918–19), 734–36.

———, The single-tax complex of some contemporary economists, *Journal of Political Economy*, XXXII (1924), 164–90.

———, Is a tax on site value never shifted? *Journal of Political Economy*, XXXII (1924), 375–82.

———, Land speculation and land-value taxation, *Journal of Political Economy*, XXXV (1927), 390–402.

———, Taxing rental versus taxing salable value of land, *Journal of Political Economy*, XXXVI (1928), 164–68.

———, Should bareland values be taxed more heavily? *Journal of Land and Public Utility Economics*, IV (1928), 375–92.

CHAPMAN, HERMAN H., The taxation of forest property, *Proceedings of the Fourteenth Annual Conference (1921) of the National Tax Association*, 1922, 36–47.

CIRIACY-WANTRUP, S. V., Taxation and the conservation of resources, *Quarterly Journal of Economics*, LVIII (1943–44), 157–96.

CLARKE, SAMUEL B., The single tax and the Impôt Unique, *Quarterly Journal of Economics*, V (1890–91), 357–60.

CONNOLLY, JOHN L., The effects of personal property taxes, *Proceedings of the Forty-Second Annual Conference (1949) of the National Tax Association*, 1950, 205–12.

DARWIN, LEONARD, The taxation of site values with reference to the distribution of population, *Economic Journal*, XVII (1907), 330–44.

DAVENPORT, H. J., Exhausted farms and exhausting taxation, *Journal of Political Economy*, XVII (1909), 354–62.

———, The single tax in the English budget, *Quarterly Journal of Economics*, XXIV (1909–10), 279–92.

———, Theoretical issues in the single tax, *American Economic Review*, VII (1917), 1–30.

DODD, A. F., Taxation of land values in Australasia, *Economic Journal*, XIV (1904), 401–12.

EINAUDI, LUIGI, Taxes on property and property investments in Italy, *Quarterly Journal of Economics*, XXXV (1920–21), 108–38.

ELY, RICHARD T., The taxation of land, *Proceedings of the Fourteenth Annual Conference (1921) of the National Tax Association*, 1922, 228–301.

ENGLUND, ERIC, The place of taxation in a constructive agricultural policy, *Journal of Farm Economics*, VII (1925), 305–24.

EVANS, M. G., Burden of property taxation, *American Economic Review*, XX (1930), 685–87.

FERNS, J. HAMILTON, Single-tax in theory and in practice, *Bulletin of the National Tax Association*, V (1919–20), 75–80.

GALLETTI, R., Taxation and agricultural policy, *Indian Journal of Economics*, XXII (1941–42), 68–87.

GARLAND, J. M., The incidence of a progressive land tax, *Economic Record*, XI (1935), 145–56.

GIDE, CHARLES, The single tax and the Impôt Unique, *Quarterly Journal of Economics*, V (1890–91), 494–95.

GOODFELLOW, K. F., The effects of the new rating valuation lists, *British Tax Review*, I (1956), 52–58.

HAIG, R. M., The effects of increment taxes upon building operations, *Quarterly Journal of Economics*, XXIX (1914–15), 829–40.

HALL, BOLTON, "Land" and taxes on monopolists, *American Economic Review*, XXII (1932), 693–95.

HARRISS, C. LOWELL, The British revaluation of real estate for local taxation, *National Tax Journal*, V (1952), 239–45.

HAYES, H. G., The capitalization of the land tax, *Quarterly Journal of Economics*, XXXIV (1919–20), 373–80.

HAYGOOD, TYLER F., Analyzing the tax load of agriculture, *Journal of Farm Economics*, XXXI (1949), 668–78; discussion, 678–82.

HEATON, H., The taxation of unimproved land in Australia, *Quarterly Journal of Economics*, XXXIX (1924–25), 410–49.

HIBBARD, B. H., Taxes, a cause of agricultural distress, *Journal of Farm Economics*, XV (1933), 1–10; discussion, 10–14.

HOOK, A., The present position of the land tax, *Economic Journal*, XV (1905), 374–80.

HOXIE, GEORGE L., City taxation and skyscraper control, *Journal of Political Economy*, XXIII (1915), 166–76.

HUNTER, M. H., Shifting of taxes as applied to land, *Proceedings of the Seventeenth Annual Conference (1924) of the National Tax Association*, 1925, 298–306.

KING, WILLFORD I., The single-tax complex analyzed, *Journal of Political Economy*, XXXII (1924), 604–12.

KRISHNAN, K. C. RAM, Taxation of agricultural income, *Indian Journal of Economics*, XVII (1936–37), 461–73.

LAMKE, EDWIN ASHLEY, Comment on "incidence of real estate taxes," *American Economic Review*, XXII (1932), 462–63.

LEE, JOSEPH, Ethics of the single tax, *Quarterly Journal of Economics*, VII (1892–93), 433–58.

LELAND, SIMEON E., The real estate tax: capitalization and benefit, *Bulletin of the National Tax Association*, XVIII (1932–33), 227–32.

MARTIN, JAMES W., Relationship between the property taxes and the economy, *Proceedings of the Forty-Fifth Annual Conference (1952) of the National Tax Association*, 1953, 47–56.

MATTHEWS, NATHAN, JR., Double taxation of mortgaged real estate, *Quarterly Journal of Economics*, IV (1889–90), 339–45.

MEADE, J. E., Elasticity of substitution and the incidence of an imperial inhabited house duty, *Review of Economic Studies*, I (1933–34), 149–52.

MEHROTRA, JAYANTI SWARUP, Problem of income tax on agricultural income, *Indian Journal of Economics*, XVII (1936–37), 473–79.

NEWCOMER, MABEL, The general property tax and the farmers, *Journal of Political Economy*, XXXVIII (1930), 62–72.

PLEHN, C. C., A study of the incidence of an increment value land tax, *Quarterly Journal of Economics*, XXXII (1917–18), 487–506.

POLLOCK, WALTER W., "Normal value" versus "price" as the basis of land appraisal, *Bulletin of the National Tax Association*, I (1916), 100–103.

RANGNEKAR, S. B., The burden of land taxation in the Punjab (India) 1927–28 to 1949–50, *Indian Economic Journal*, I (1953–54), 166–84.

REYNOLDS, THOMAS J., The present status of the single-tax controversy in the United States, *Bulletin of the National Tax Association*, XXII (1936–37), 203–8.

SANGER, C. P., The report of the local taxation commission, *Economic Journal*, XI (1901), 321–33.

SELIGMAN, EDWIN R. A., A mediaeval tax problem, *American Economic Review*, XXI (1931), 672–82.

SIMON, HERBERT A., The incidence of a tax on urban real property, *Quarterly Journal of Economics*, LVII (1942–43), 398–421.

SIMPSON, HERBERT D., The incidence of real estate taxes, *American Economic Review*, XXII (1932), 219–30.

————, Changing theory of property taxation, *American Economic Review*, XXIX (1939), 453–68.

SINHA, BIMAL CHANDRA, The basis of land tax: a problem in applied economics, *Indian Journal of Economics*, XXI (1940–41), 158–67.

SPENGLER, EDWIN H., The real estate tax: capitalization and benefit: a reply, *Bulletin of the National Tax Association*, XVIII (1932–33), 232–36.

————, The taxation of urban land-value increments, *Journal of Land and Public Utility Economics*, XVII (1941), 54–58.

THOMAS, CHARLES S., Taxes and the farmer, *Bulletin of the National Tax Association*, XII (1926–27), 70–78.

TREVELYAN, CHARLES, Land value taxation and the use of land, *Economic Journal*, XVII (1907), 30–35.

TURNER, J. R., Some considerations on land taxation, *Quarterly Journal of Economics*, XXXI (1916–17), 348–54.

VAN SICKLE, J. V., Classification of land for taxation, *Quarterly Journal of Economics*, XLII (1927–28), 94–116.

VENN, J. A., The incidence of taxation in agriculture, *Economic Journal*, XXXVIII (1928), 560–73.

WEDGWOOD, J. C., The principle of land value taxation, *Economic Journal*, XXII (1912), 388–97.

WILLIAMS, ALAN, The abolition of derating: an exercise in differential incidence, *Economica*, N.S. XXIII (1956), 150–58 (local taxation in England).

WILLIAMSON, K. M., The taxation of real estate: a survey of recent discussion, *Quarterly Journal of Economics*, XLVIII (1933–34), 96–124.

WOLFBEIN, SEYMOUR L., The burden of property taxation, 1926–1936, *Bulletin of the National Tax Association*, XXIV (1938–39), 194–211.

C. INCENTIVE EFFECTS AND TAX BURDEN

13. EFFECTS ON WORK EFFORT

BOOKER, H. S., Income tax and incentive to effort, *Economica*, N.S. XII (1945), 243–48.

BREAK, GEORGE F., Income taxes, wage rates, and incentive to supply labor services, *National Tax Journal*, VI (1953), 333–53.

COOPER, GERSCHON, Taxation and incentive in mobilization, *Quarterly Journal of Economics*, LXVI (1952), 43–67.

————, Taxation and incentive in mobilization: reply, *Quarterly Journal of Economics*, LXVI (1952), 609–14.

DAVIDSON, ROBERT, Income taxes and incentive: the doctor's viewpoint, *National Tax Journal*, VI (1953), 293–98.

GIBSON, R. S., The incentive to work, as affected by unemployment insurance and the poor law respectively, *Manchester School*, I (1930), 21–28.

GOODE, RICHARD, The income tax and the supply of labor, *Journal of Political Economy*, LVII (1949), 428–38.

VON MERING, OTTO, Taxation and incentive in mobilization: further comment, *Quarterly Journal of Economics*, LXVI (1952), 605–9.

————, A note on planning and inducement to work, *National Tax Journal*, IX (1956), 69–75.

MUSGRAVE, RICHARD A., Taxation and incentives, *Preceedings of the Thirty-Ninth Annual Conference (1946) of the National Tax Association*, 1946, 400–411.

OAKES, EUGENE E., Comments on incentives and taxation, *Proceedings of the Thirty-Ninth Annual Conference (1946) of the National Tax Association*, 1946, 419–22.

PAISH, F. W., Economic incentive in wartime, *Economica*, N.S. VIII (1941), 239–49 (entirely concerned with taxation).

SCHWARTZ, HARRY S., Taxation and incentive in mobilization: comment, *Quarterly Journal of Economics*, LXVI (1952), 600–605.

SMITH, DAN THROOP, Taxation and executives, *Proceedings of the Forty-Fourth Annual Conference (1951) of the National Tax Association*, 1952, 234–51; discussion, 264–74.

SOLO, ROBERT, Accumulation, work incentive, and the expenditure tax, *National Tax Journal*, IX (1956), 283–88 (comment on Kaldor's expenditure tax).

14. EFFECTS ON INVESTMENT AND BUSINESS ORGANIZATION

ABBOTT, CHARLES C. and ZUCKERT, EUGENE M., Venture capital and taxation, *Quarterly Journal of Economics*, LV (1940–41), 667–83.

AHMAN, SVEN, Uncertainty-bearing and the income tax, *Economic Journal*, XXXIX (1929), 288–91.

BALAKRISHNA, R., Tax incentives in India, *Indian Journal of Economics*, XXXI (1950–51), 45–123.

BALOGH, T., Taxation, risk-bearing and investment, *Oxford Institute of Statistics Bulletin*, VII (1945), 181–93.

BECK, MORRIS, Carryover of business losses, *National Tax Journal*, VI (1953), 69–86.

BENEWITZ, MAURICE C., Theoretical effect of income averaging for tax purposes on investment incentives, *National Tax Journal*, VI (1953), 194–97.

BLOUGH, ROY, United States taxation and foreign investment, *Journal of Finance*, XI (1956), 180–95.

BRADLEY, PHILIP D., The direct effects of a corporate income tax, *Quarterly Journal of Economics*, LVI (1941–42), 638–55.

BREAK, GEORGE F., Capital maintenance and the concept of income, *Journal of Political Economy*, LXII (1954), 48–63.

———, The effects in capital expenditures of a shift from money to real income for tax purposes, *National Tax Journal*, IX (1956), 14–27.

BROWN, E. CARY, Tax allowances for depreciation based on changes in the price level, *National Tax Journal*, I (1948), 311–22.

———, Capital maintenance and the concept of income: a correction, *Journal of Political Economy*, LXIII (1955), 74–75 (comment on 1954 article by BREAK, G. F.).

BROWN, E. CARY and ECKAUS, RICHARD, Operation of the carry backs of World War II during the reconversion period, *National Tax Journal*, V (1952), 193–207.

BROWN, E. CARY and EDMONDS, WILLIAM J., Symposium on two years of Republican tax policy and the Internal Revenue Code of 1954: depreciation policy, *National Tax Journal*, VIII (1955), 81–114.

BROWN, E. CARY and PATTERSON, GARDNER, Accelerated depreciation: a neglected chapter in war taxation, *Quarterly Journal of Economics*, LVII (1942–43), 630–46.

BUTTERS, J. KEITH, Would the complete integration of the corporate and personal income taxes injure small business? *Proceedings of the Fortieth Annual Conference (1947) of the National Tax Association*, 1947, 189–93; discussion, 193–206.

———, Effect of federal taxes on inventory valuation procedures, *Proceedings of the Forty-Second Annual Conference (1949) of the National Tax Association*, 1950, 64–69; discussion, 75–80.

———, Tax influences on investment choices, *Proceedings of the Forty-Fourth Annual Conference (1951) of the National Tax Association*, 1952, 260–64; discussion, 264–74.

———, Taxation, incentives, and financial capacity, *American Economic Review*, XLIV (1954), Papers and Proceedings, 504–20.

BUTTERS, J. KEITH and LINTNER, JOHN, Tax and non-tax motivations for mergers, *Journal of Finance*, VI (1951), 361–83.

DOBROVOLSKY, S. P., Depreciation policies and investment decisions, *American Economic Review*, XLI (1951), 906–15.

DOBROVOLSKY, S. P.; MUSGRAVE, R. A.; BUTTERS, J. KEITH; CALKINS, F. J.; HOWELL, PAUL L.; and KETCHUM, M. D., Effects of federal personal and corporate income taxation on American business finance, *Journal of Finance*, IV (1949), 183–243.

DOMAR, EVSEY D., The case for accelerated depreciation, *Quarterly Journal of Economics*, LXVII (1953), 493–519.

———, Accelerated depreciation: a rejoinder, *Quarterly Journal of Economics*, LXIX (1955), 299–305.

DOMAR, EVSEY D. and MUSGRAVE, RICHARD A., Proportional income taxation and risk-taking, *Quarterly Journal of Economics*, LVIII (1943–44), 388–423.

DOWELL, A. A., and TOBEN, G. E., Some economic effects of graduated income tax rates on investors in farm capital, *Journal of Farm Economics*, XXVI (1944), 348–59.

DUGAN, JAMES E. and ZUBROW, REUBEN A., The influence of the excess profits tax on business decisions to invest, *National Tax Journal*, VII (1954), 242–52.

EISNER, ROBERT, Accelerated amortization, growth, and net profits, *Quarterly Journal of Economics*, LXVI (1952), 533.

———, Depreciation allowances, replacement requirements and growth, *American Economic Review*, XLII (1952), 820–32.

———, Accelerated depreciation: some further thoughts, *Quarterly Journal of Economics*, LXIX (1955), 285–96.

EITEMAN, WILFORD J., Effect of franchise taxes upon corporate location, *Southern Economic Journal*, IX (1942–43), 234–40.

ELDRIDGE, DOUGLAS H., Tax incentives for universal enterprise, *Journal of Political Economy*, LVIII (1950), 222–41.

ELLSWORTH, C. A., Would integration of corporate and individual taxes injure business? *Proceedings of the Fortieth Annual Conference (1947) of the National Tax Association*, 1947, 175–79; discussion, 193–206.

FROEHLICH, WALTER, Income determination and investment, *American Economic Review*, XXXVIII (1948), 78–92 (income determination for the purpose of taxing business incomes).

GARWOOD, JOHN D., Taxes and industrial location, *National Tax Journal*, V (1952), 365–70.

GOODE, RICHARD, Accelerated depreciation allowances as a stimulus to investment, *Quarterly Journal of Economics*, LXIX (1955), 191–221.

GOPAL, M. H., Planning of production through tax adjustments, *Indian Journal of Economics*, XXIX (1948–49), 155–65.

GOWDA, K. VENKARA GIRI, Incentive taxation and uncertainty bearing, *Indian Journal of Economics*, XXXI (1950–51), 175–89.

GUTHMANN, HARRY G., The effect of the undistributed profits tax upon the distribution of corporate earnings: a note, *Econometrica*, VIII (1940), 354–57.

GUTHMANN, HARRY G.; SOMERS, HAROLD M.; SHOUP, CARL S.; GOODE, RICHARD; MITCHELL, GEORGE W.; and FORD, ROBERT S., Taxation and business incentive, *Journal of Finance*, VI (1951), 161–211.

HALL, CHALLIS A., JR., Effects of federal taxation on deferred compensation plans, *Proceedings of the Forty-Second Annual Conference (1949) of the National Tax Association*, 1950, 48–64; discussion, 75–80.

HOOD, CLIFFORD F., Impact of taxation on production and jobs, *Proceedings of the Forty-Third Annual Conference (1950) of the National Tax Association*, 1951, 39–45.

HOUSTON, G. SIDNEY, Taxation and the investor, *Proceedings of the Forty-Fourth Annual Conference (1951) of the National Tax Association*, 1952, 254–60; discussion, 264–74.

HULCY, DECHARD A., The effect of present taxes on risk-taking in business, *Proceedings of the Forty-Fourth Annual Conference (1951) of the National Tax Association*, 1952, 274–83.

HUNTER, M. H., Effects of taxation on the localization of industry, *Proceedings of the Thirtieth Annual Conference (1937) of the National Tax Association*, 1938, 179–87; discussion, 187–91.

JENSEN, J. P., Economic aspects of bank taxation, *Proceedings of the Twenty-Third Annual Conference (1930) of the National Tax Association*, 1931, 297–305.

KAISER, ARTHUR R., The impact of state and local taxes on a merchandising business with special reference to mail-order business, *Proceedings of the Fortieth Annual Conference (1947) of the National Tax Association*, 1947, 220–33.

KEITH, E. GORDON, Some effects of current federal tax policies on business, *Proceedings of the Forty-Fifth Annual Conference (1952) of the National Tax Association*, 1953, 256–67.

KNOOP, DOUGLAS, The burden of heavy taxation on industry and trade, *Manchester School*, I (1930), 17–21.

LAYLIN, CLARENCE D., The business view of the effect of federal taxation, *Proceedings of the Forty-Second Annual Conference (1949) of the National Tax Association*, 1950, 18–28.

LENT, GEORGE E., Bond interest deduction and the federal corporation income tax, *National Tax Journal*, II (1949), 131–42.

LINDHOLM, RICHARD W., The impact of accelerated depreciation, *National Tax Journal*, IV (1951), 180–86.

LINTNER, JOHN, Effect of corporate taxation on real investment, *American Economic Review*, XLIV (1954), Papers and Proceedings, 520–35.

———, Effects of a shifted corporate income tax on real investment, *National Tax Journal*, VIII (1955), 229–52.

LISMAN, F. J., Confiscating capital and incentive by taxation, *Bulletin of the National Tax Association*, V (1919–20), 177–79.

LITTLEFIELD, R. J., The effect of state and local taxation on railroads, *Proceedings of the Forty-Seventh Annual Conference (1954) of the National Tax Association*, 1955, 101–7.

MAY, GEORGE O., Accelerated depreciation: a comment, *Quarterly Journal of Economics*, LXIX (1955), 296–99.

McINTYRE, FRANCIS, The effect of the undistributed profits tax upon the distribution of corporate earnings—a statistical appraisal, *Econometrica*, VI (1939), 336–49.

———, The effect of the undistributed profits tax: a reply, *Econometrica*, VIII (1940), 357–60.

McKEON, CHARLES P., The effects of state income taxes on business, *Proceedings of the Forty-Second Annual Conference (1949) of the National Tax Association*, 1950, 181–85.

MILLER, D. C., Corporate taxation and methods of corporate financing, *American Economic Review*, XLII (1952), 839–55.

MORAG, AMOTZ, Income tax exemptions and accelerated depreciation, *Public Finance*, XI (1956), 357–65.

NARASIMHAM, N. V. A., Price-wage-tax subsidy: policies as instruments in increasing output, *Indian Journal of Economics*, XXXIII (1952–53), 143–55.

NORTON, PAUL T., Present federal income tax practice penalizes new and small business, *Proceedings of the Forty-Second Annual Conference (1949) of the National Tax Association*, 1950, 9–18.

OHL, JOHN P.; GOODE, RICHARD; JAMES, G. F.; and LACHMANN, KARL E., Taxation and foreign investments, *Proceedings of the Forty-Sixth Annual Conference (1953) of the National Tax Association*, 1954, 208–56.

POULOPOULOS, STYLIANOS, Fiscal legislation and promotion of private investments in Greece, *Public Finance*, XI (1956), 74–93.

PRICE, L. L., Economic theory and fiscal policy, *Economic Journal*, XIV (1904), 372–87.

ROBERTSON, THOMAS, The British income tax as it affects the businessman, *Bulletin of the National Tax Association*, II (1916–17), 7–11.

RUDICK, HARRY J., The effect of the excess-profits tax on business, *Proceedings of the Forty-Fourth Annual Conference (1951) of the National Tax Association*, 1952, 404–15.

SCHUMACHER, E. F., Tax incentives for export, *Oxford Institute of Statistics Bulletin*, VII (1945), 124–28.

SEDER, A. R., The effect of federal taxation on railroads, *Proceedings of the Forty-Seventh Annual Conference (1954) of the National Tax Association*, 1955, 92–101.

SELDEN, RICHARD T., Accelerated amortization and industrial concentration, *Review of Economics and Statistics*, XXXVII (1955), 282–92.

SHELTON, J. P. and OHLIN, GORAN, A Swedish tax provision for stabilizing business investment, *American Economic Review*, XLII (1952), 375–80.

SHELTON, JOHN P., A tax incentive for stabilizing business investment, *National Tax Journal*, IX (1956), 232–47.

SHOUP, CARL, Progressive taxation to restrict production, *Bulletin of the National Tax Association*, XVII (1931–32), 257–63.

SMITH, DAN THROOP, Effects of taxation on corporate financial policy: a progress report, *Proceedings of the Forty-Second Annual Conference (1949) of the National Tax Association*, 1950, 69–75; discussion, 75–80.

———, Corporate taxation and common stock financing, *National Tax Journal*, VI (1953), 209–26.

SMITH, DAN THROOP; HELLER, WALTER W.; and SMITHIES, ARTHUR W.; Symposium on two years of Republican tax policy and the Internal Revenue Code of 1954: economic appraisal, *National Tax Journal*, VIII (1955), 2–36.

SOMERS, H. M., An economic analysis of the capital gains tax, *National Tax Journal*, I (1948), 220–26.

SPORRER, M. J., Some effects of federal income and excess profits taxes on corporate organization, *Proceedings of the Thirty-Seventh Annual Conference (1944) of the National Tax Association*, 1945, 292–99.

STAMP, JOSIAH (Sir), Taxation, risk-taking and the price level, *Economic Journal*, XXXVIII (1928), 204–16.

STREETEN, PAUL, The effect of taxation on risk-taking, *Oxford Economic Papers*, N.S. V (1953), 271–88.

THOMPSON, L. E., The effects of personal federal taxes on individuals' savings and investment policies, *Proceedings of the Forty-Second Annual Conference (1949) of the National Tax Association*, 1950, 42–48; discussion, 75–80.

THOMPSON, LAWRENCE E. and BUTTERS, J. KEITH, Needed research in finance: effects of taxation on the investment policy and capacities of individuals, *Journal of Finance*, VIII (1953), 137–52.

TILLMAN, E. K., The tax law and depreciation, *Bulletin of the National Tax Association*, XXVI (1940–41), 66–80.

TURNER, CLARENCE L.; MARTIN, C. W.; and WARNER, T. K., Depreciation, *Proceedings of the Forty-Sixth Annual Conference (1953) of the National Tax Association*, 1954, 450–87.

VAN SICKLE, J. V., Reform of federal taxes on personal and corporate income, *American Economic Review*, XXXIV (1944), 847–49.

VICKREY, WILLIAM, The effects of integration of corporate and individual income taxes on business, *Proceedings of the Fortieth Annual Conference (1947) of the National Tax Association*, 1947, 179–89; discussion, 193–206.

WEBB, URSULA K., Taxation and production, *Review of Economic Studies*, II (1934–35), 18–30.

WILES, P., Corporate taxation and depreciation, *Oxford Institute of Statistics Bulletin*, XII (1952), 115–24.

15. TAXABLE CAPACITY

BHARGAVA, R. N., The concept of taxable capacity, *Indian Economic Review*, Feb., 1954, 115–22.

BRONFENBRENNER, M., Diminishing returns in federal taxation? *Journal of Political Economy*, L (1942), 699–719.

CLARK, C., Public finances and changes in the value of money, *Economic Journal*, LV (1945), 371–89.

DOUGALL, HERBERT E., Taxation of railways in Canada: analysis of the burden, *Journal of Land and Public Utility Economics*, V (1929), 398–411.

GATES, R. C., The weight of taxation in five countries, 1938–50, *Economic Record*, XXVIII (1952), 222–36.

GHOSH, D., Optimum taxability, *Indian Journal of Economics*, XII (1931–32), 152–59.

GIBLIN, L. F., Taxable capacity, *Economic Record*, IX (1933), 235–41 (taxable capacity of different Australian states).

GOODE, RICHARD, An economic limit on taxes: some recent discussions, *National Tax Journal*, V (1952), 227–34.

HANDY, ALBERT, Some notes on taxable capacity, *Bulletin of the National Tax Association*, XXVI (1940–41), 99–105.

HELLER, WALTER W., How high can taxes go? *Proceedings of the Forty-Fifth Annual Conference (1952) of the National Tax Association*, 1953, 243–56.

KAPUR, G. P., and VENU, S., The concept of taxable capacity—a comment, *Indian Economic Review*, Aug., 1954, 104–5.

KIMMEL, LEWIS H., The effects of war-time control on taxable capacity, *Proceedings of the Thirty-Third Annual Conference (1940) of the National Tax Association*, 1941, 406–13; discussion, 413–19.

KUZNETS, SIMON, National income and taxable capacity, *American Economic Review*, XXXII (1942), Papers and Proceedings, 37–76.

OJHA, P. D., Taxable capacity in a developing economy, *Indian Economic Journal*, II (1954–55), 263–74.

PECHMAN, J. A. and MAYER, T., Colin Clark on the limits of taxation, *Review of Economics and Statistics*, XXXIV (1952), 232–42.

SCHMIDT, EMERSON, P. and HOFFMAN, CHARLES L., Incentive taxation with special reference to unemployment—discussion, *Proceedings of the Thirty-Fourth Annual Conference (1941) of the National Tax Association*, 1942, 464–79.

STAMP, JOSIAH (Sir), The taxable capacity of Ireland, *Economic Journal*, XXXI (1921), 335–49.

TRESCOTT, PAUL, The burdens of government finance, *Public Finance*, XI (1956), 164–76.

WITTE, EDWIN E., Incentive taxation with special reference to unemployment: experience rating anad other forms of incentive taxation to promote employment, *Proceedings of the Thirty-Fourth Annual Conference (1941) of the National Tax Association*, 1942, 479–84.

ZANGERLE, JOHN A., What is an excessive tax burden? *Bulletin of the National Tax Association*, XIV (1928–29), 262–66.

16. ESTIMATES OF DISTRIBUTION OF TAX BURDENS

ADAMS, T. S., The effect of income and inheritance taxes on the distribution of wealth, *American Economic Review*, V (1915), Papers and Proceedings, 234–45.

ALEXANDER-KATZ, C., On national tax realities and international tax comparisons, *Public Finance*, XI (1956), 287–345.

BAJPAI, R. G., Incidence of taxation in India, *Indian Journal of Economics*, XXXIII (1952–53), 315–25.

BOWLEY, A. L., The British super-tax and the distribution of income, *Quarterly Journal of Economics*, XXVIII (1913–14), 255–68.

COLM, GERHARD, Some international comparisons of taxation, *Social Research*, I (1934), 244–48.

COLM, GERHARD and WALD, HASKELL P.; MUSGRAVE, R. A. and FRANE, L.; TUCKER, RUFUS S., Further consideration of the distribution of the tax burden, *National Tax Journal*, V (1952), 1–39.

CONRAD, ALFRED H., On the calculation of tax burdens, *Economica*, XXII (1955), 342–49.

DONNAHOE, ALAN S., Measuring state tax burden, *Journal of Political Economy*, LV (1947), 234–45.

GUPTA, SADHANA, Incidence of taxation in India, *Indian Journal of Economics*, XXXIII (1952–53), 289–99.

HOLLAND, BERNARD, The incidence of taxation upon Ireland, *Economic Journal*, VII (1897), 214–25.

HOLZMAN, F. D., The burden of Soviet taxation, *American Economic Review*, XLIII (1953), 548–72.

KULKARNI, N. K., Incidence of taxation in India, *Indian Journal of Economics*, XXXIII (1952–53), 325–33.

LAKDAWALA, D. T., Incidence of taxation in India, *Indian Journal of Economics*, XXXIII (1952–53), 461–71.

MANNING, RAYMOND E., Techniques in computing the geographical incidence of federal, state and local taxes, *Proceedings of the Forty-Second Annual Conference (1949) of the National Tax Association*, 1950, 106–10; discussion, 110–15.

METZLER, LLOYD A., Effects of income redistribution, *Review of Economic Statistics*, XXV (1943), 49–58 (income redistribution through taxes and subsidies).

MUSGRAVE, R. A., Distribution of tax burden under sales and income taxes, *Bulletin of the National Tax Association*, XXXII (1946–47), 16–18.

——, Distribution of tax payments by income groups: a review, *Proceedings of the Forty-Fifth Annual Conference (1952) of the National Tax Association*, 1953, 179–95; discussion, 215–22.

MUSGRAVE, R. A.; CARROLL, J. J.; COOK, L. D.; and FRANE, L., Distribution of tax payments by income groups: a case study for 1948, *National Tax Journal*, IV (1951), 1–54.

MUSGRAVE, R. A. and FRANE, L., Rejoinder to Dr. Tucker, *National Tax Journal*, V (1952), 1–53.

NEISSER, ALBERT C., The dynamics of tax burden comparisons, *National Tax Journal*, V (1952), 351–65.

PEACOCK, ALAN T. and BERRY, D., A note on the theory of income redistribution, *Economica*, XVIII (1951), 83–91.

PECHMAN, JOSEPH A., Some technical problems in the measurement of tax burdens, *Proceedings of the Forty-Fifth Annual Conference (1952) of the National Tax Association*, 1953, 204–15; discussion, 215–22.

PETTENGILL, ROBERT B., Tax burden among income groups, *American Economic Review*, XXX (1940), 60–72.

PREST, A. R., Government revenue and the national income, *Public Finance*, VI (1951), 238–52.

——, Statistical calculations of tax burdens, *Economica*, XXII (1955), 234–46.

——, On the calculation of tax burdens—a rejoinder, *Economica*, N.S. XXIII (1956), 270–73.

SHIRRAS, G. F., The Pareto Law and the distribution of income, *Economic Journal*, XLV (1935), 663–82 (study of income-tax statistics of British India and implications of the Pareto Law concerning possible evasions and overtaxation).

STRAYER, PAUL J., The individual income tax and income distribution, *American Economic Review*, XLV (1955), Papers and Proceedings, 430–41.

TARASOV, HELEN, Who does pay the taxes? *Social Research*, Supplement IV (1942), 48 pp.

TODD, EDWIN S., Taxation and the redistribution of wealth, *Bulletin of the National Tax Association*, XXII (1936–37), 269–76.

TUCKER, RUFUS S., The distribution of income among income tax payers in the United States, 1863–1935, *Quarterly Journal of Economics*, LII (1937–38), 547–87.

——, Distribution of tax burdens in 1948, *National Tax Journal*, IV (1951), 269–86.

——, Dstribution of tax burdens in 1948, *Proceedings of the Forty-Fifth Annual Conference (1952) of the National Tax Association*, 1953, 195–204; discussion, 215–22.

——, The distribution of government burdens and benefits, *American Economic Review*, XLIII (1953), 518–35.

VASWANI, M. H., Incidence of taxation in India, *Indian Journal of Economics*, XXXIII (1952–53), 345–53.

WEAVER, FINDLEY, Taxation and redistribution in the United Kingdom, *Review of Economics and Statistics*, XXXII (1950), 201–14.

YAPLE, MAXINE, Direct taxes by income classes, *American Economic Review*, XXVI (1936), 691–711.

D. TAX STRUCTURE

17. OVER-ALL ASPECTS

BLOUGH, ROY, Problems of postwar federal tax policy, *Proceedings of the Thirty-Seventh Annual Conference (1944) of the National Tax Association*, 1945, 150–59; discussion, 181–93.

BROWNLEE, O. H., The C.E.D. on federal tax reform, *Journal of Political Economy*, LVI (1948), 166–73.

COLM, GERHARD, The ideal tax system, *Social Research*, I (1934), 319–43.

GRAVES, MARK, An ideal tax system, *Bulletin of the National Tax Association*, XII (1926–27), 168–74.

GROVES, HAROLD M., Revising the postwar federal tax system, *American Economic Review*, XXXIV (1944), Supplement: the implemental aspects of public finance, 27–39.

——, Postwar federal taxation, *Proceedings of the Thirty-Seventh Annual Conference (1944) of the National Tax Association*, 1945, 199–207; discussion, 207–13.

HOLZMAN, F. D., Commodity and income taxation in the Soviet Union, *Journal of Political Economy*, LVIII (1950), 425–34.

HOUSTON, G. SIDNEY, Twin Cities program for postwar taxation, *Proceedings of the Thirty-Seventh Annual Conference (1944) of the National Tax Association*, 1945, 159–67; discussion, 181–93.

SHOUP, CARL, Three plans for post-war taxation, *American Economic Review*, XXXIV (1944), 757–71.

SIMONS, HENRY, Postwar federal tax reform, *Proceedings of the Thirty-Sixth Annual Conference (1943) of the National Tax Association*, 1944, 434–43.

WALSH, J. RAYMOND, Taxation and fiscal policy in the postwar, *Proceedings of the Thirty-Seventh Annual Conference (1944) of the National Tax Association*, 1945, 174–81; discussion, 181–93.

18. INCOME AND PROFITS TAXES

ADAMS, T. S., Federal taxes upon income and excess profits, *American Economic Review*, VIII (1918), Papers and Proceedings, 18–36; discussion, 36–55.

———, Fundamental problems of federal income taxation, *Quarterly Journal of Economics*, XXXV (1920–21), 527–56.

———, Should the excess profits tax be repealed? *Quarterly Journal of Economics*, XXXV (1920–21), 363–93.

BLUNDEN, G. H., The position and function of the income tax in the British fiscal system, *Economic Journal*, II (1892), 637–52.

BOWEN, HOWARD R., The taxation of small business, *Proceedings of the Thirty-Ninth Annual Conference (1946) of the National Tax Association*, 1946, 394–400.

BUEHLER, ALFRED G., Some comments on the taxation of small business, *Proceedings of the Thirty-Ninth Annual Conference (1946) of the National Tax Association*, 1946, 415–19.

———, The taxation of small business, *American Economic Review*, XXXVI (1946), Papers and Proceedings, 250–65.

COLM, GERHARD, Don't throw the baby out with the bath, *Finanzarchiv*, N.F., Bd. 14, Heft. 3 (1953), 525–30.

———, The corporation and the corporate income tax in the American economy, *American Economic Review*, XLIV (1954), Papers and Proceedings, 486–504.

ELDRIDGE, DOUGLAS H., Extractive industries and the excess profits tax, *National Tax Journal*, IV (1951), 315–32.

FORD, ROBERT S., Some economic aspects of the present corporate income tax system, *Proceedings of the Fortieth Annual Conference (1947) of the National Tax Association*, 1947, 55–62; discussion, 80–91.

GOODE, RICHARD, Alternative approaches to the integration of corporate and individual income taxes, *Proceedings of the Fortieth Annual Conference (1947) of the National Tax Association*, 1947, 134–46; discussion, 160–75.

GROVES, HAROLD M., Personal versus corporate income taxes, *American Economic Review*, XXXVI (1946), Papers and Proceedings, 241–50.

———, Personal versus corporate income taxes, *Journal of Finance*, I (1946), 52–61.

———, Revision of the corporation income tax, *Proceedings of the Fortieth Annual Conference (1947) of the National Tax Association*, 1947, 97–105; discussion, 120–34.

———, Preliminary report of the Committee on the Federal Corporate Net Income Tax, *Proceedings of the Forty-Second Annual Conference (1949) of the National Tax Association*, 1950, 437–71.

———, Final report of the Committee on the Federal Corporate Net Income Tax, *Proceedings of the Forty-Third Annual Conference (1950) of the National Tax Association*, 1951, 54–74; discussion, 74–77.

GROVES, HAROLD M. and SOULE, DON M., A new proposal for emergency taxation of corporate profits, *National Tax Journal*, V (1952), 325–35.

HAIG, R. M., Report of the Committee of the National Tax Association on Federal Taxation of Corporations, *Proceedings of the Thirty-First Annual Conference (1938) of the National Tax Association*, 1939, 574–673.

———, Report of the Committee of the National Tax Association on Federal Taxation of Corporations, *Proceedings of the Thirty-Second Annual Conference (1939) of the National Tax Association*, 1940, 534–97; discussion, 597–638.

HALL, FRANKLIN P., Should business pay any taxes? *Bulletin of the National Tax Association*, XXVIII (1942–43), 276–78.

HEWETT, WILLIAM W., The taxation of increases in personal income, *Bulletin of the National Tax Association*, XXXIII (1947), 11–17.

HUNTER, MERLIN H., Shall we tax corporations or business? *American Economic Review*, XXVI (1936), 84–90.

KEITH, E. GORDON, The corporation in the tax system, *Proceedings of the Thirty-Ninth Annual Conference (1946) of the National Tax Association*, 1946, 384–94.

———, The future of the corporation income tax, *Journal of Finance*, XI (1956), 195–205.

KOHLER, E. L., Report of the Committee of the National Tax Association on Capital Gains, *Proceedings of the Thirty-First Annual Conference (1938) of the National Tax Association*, 1939, 806–17.

MORTON, WALTER A., Excess profits taxes versus higher regular corporate tax rates, *National Tax Journal*, III (1950), 348–53.

MUSGRAVE, RICHARD A., Should an absolute corporation tax be retained? *Proceedings of the Fortieth Annual Conference (1947) of the National Tax Association*, 1947, 111–20; discussion, 120–34.

SCHREIBER, LOUIS, The place of the corporate income tax in the tax system, *Proceedings of the Fortieth Annual Conference (1947) of the National Tax Association*, 1947, 105–11; discussion, 120–34.

SHERE, LOUIS, The fiscal significance of the corporation income tax, *Proceedings of the Fortieth Annual Conference (1947) of the National Tax Association*, 1947, 4–55; discussion, 86–91.

SHOUP, CARL S., The taxation of excess profits, *Political Science Quarterly*, LV, LVI (1940, 1941), 535–55, 84–106, 226–49.

SIMPSON, HERBERT D., Regulation vs. undistributed profits tax: a dilemma, *Journal of Land and Public Utility Economics*, XIII (1937), 228–31.

SLITOR, RICHARD E., The corporate income tax: a re-evaluation, *National Tax Journal*, V (1952), 289–310.

———, The role of corporate income taxation, *National Tax Journal*, VII (1954), 227–40.

SOMERS, HAROLD M., The place of the corporation income tax in the tax structure, *National Tax Journal*, V (1952), 279–85.

STAMP, J. C., The special taxation of business profits, *Economic Journal*, XXIX (1919), 407–27.

STUDENSKI, PAUL, Toward a theory of business taxation, *Journal of Political Economy*, XLVIII (1940), 621–55.

19. INCOME CONCEPT

BEALE, TRUXTUN, The measure of income for taxation, *Journal of Political Economy*, XIX (1911), 655–75.

BLACK, D. G. and EDWARDS, R. S., British income tax and company reserves, *Review of Economic Studies*, V (1937–38), 114–22.

BLOUGH, ROY, Measurement problems of the excess profits tax, *National Tax Journal*, I (1948), 353–66.

BOND, HENRY H., A practical aspect of the stock dividend question, *Bulletin of the National Tax Association*, III (1917–18), 237–40.

CLOE, CARL W., Capital gains and the changing price level, *National Tax Journal*, V (1952), 207–18.

CRUM, W. L., The taxation of stockholders, *Quarterly Journal of Economics*, LXIV (1950), 15–56.

DAVENPORT, H. J., The taxation of dividends, *Journal of Political Economy*, XV (1907), 552–54.

ELDRIDGE, DOUGLAS H., Issues raised by proposal to grant cost or market option with lifo, *National Tax Journal*, VI (1953), 52–69.

FAIRCHILD, FRED ROGERS, Economic nature of the stock dividend, *Bulletin of the National Tax Association*, III (1917–18), 161–64.

——, The stock dividend—a rejoinder, *Bulletin of the National Tax Association*, III (1917–18), 240–43.

FRIDAY, DAVID, The taxable income of the United States, *Journal of Political Economy*, XXVI (1918), 952–69.

HAIG, R. M., The concept of income, *Federal Income Tax* (ed. R. M. HAIG), pp. 1–28. New York: Columbia University Press, 1921.

HELLMUTH, WILLIAM F., JR., Erosion of the federal corporation income tax base, *Proceedings of the Forty-Eighth Annual Conference (1955) of the National Tax Association*, 1956, 315–50.

HEWETT, WILLIAM W., The concept of income in federal taxation, *Journal of Political Economy*, XXXIII (1925), 155–78.

HOLLAND, DANIEL M., The differential tax burden on stockholders, *American Economic Review*, XLV (1955), Papers and Proceedings, 415–30.

KENDRICK, M. SLADE, Tax on capital net gains, *American Economic Review*, XIX (1929), 648–52.

KLEM, CHARLES; DIRECTOR, AARON; and PERRY, HARVEY, Capital gain taxation, *Proceedings of the Forty-Sixth Annual Conference (1953) of the National Tax Association*, 1954, 138–64.

LACEY, K., The Tucker Report and the technique of adjusting taxable profits for price changes, *Economic Journal*, LXI (1951), 756–77.

LUTZ, H. L., The treatment of dividends in income taxation, *Journal of Political Economy*, XXXIII (1925), 129–54.

——, Should capital gains be taxed as income? *Bulletin of the National Tax Association*, XXII (1936–37), 130–36.

MANNING, RAYMOND E., Depreciation in the tax laws and practice of the United States, Australia, Canada, Great Britain, New Zealand, and South Africa, *National Tax Journal*, I (1948), 154–75.

MAY, GEORGE O., The taxation of capital gains, *Bulletin of the National Tax Association*, VIII (1922–23), 71–78.

MORGAN, JAMES N., The measurement of gains and losses, *Quarterly Journal of Economics*, LXII (1947–48), 287–309.

PECHMAN, JOSEPH A., A practical averaging proposal, *National Tax Journal*, VII (1954), 261–64.

PECHMAN, JOSEPH A. and SHOUP, CARL S., Symposium on two years of Republican tax policy and the Internal Revenue Code of 1954: dividends and other individual income tax provisions, *National Tax Journal*, VIII (1955), 114–48.

SELTZER, LAWRENCE H., Capital gains and the income tax, *American Economic Review*, XL (1950), Papers and Proceedings, 371–79.

——, Evolution of the special legal status of capital gains under the income tax, *National Tax Journal*, III (1950), 18–36.

SHERE, LOUIS, Federal corporate income tax—revenue and reform, *National Tax Journal*, II (1949), 110–22.

STEGER, WILBUR A., Averaging income for tax purposes: a statistical study, *National Tax Journal*, IX (1956), 97–115.

TIBBETTS, FRANK C., The accounting period in federal income taxation, *Southern Economic Journal*, VII (1940–41), 362–79.

VICKREY, WILLIAM, Averaging of income for income tax purposes, *Journal of Political Economy*, XLVII (1939), 379–97.

——, Rate reduction or increased exemptions: the economics of the question, *Proceedings of the Forty-Seventh Annual Conference (1954) of the National Tax Association*, 1955, 288–95.

WHITAKER, A. C., Stock dividend question, *American Economic Review*, XIX (1929), 20–43 (stock dividend as a means of income tax evasion).

20. OTHER TAXES

BLOCH, HENRY S., Economic objectives of gratuitous transfer taxation, *National Tax Journal*, IV (1951), 139–48.

BUEHLER, ALFRED G., The spendings tax, *Public Finance*, V (1950), 8–22.

DUE, JOHN F., Federal excise taxation, *Bulletin of the National Tax Association*, XXXIII (1947), 66–79.
———, The role of sales and excise taxation in the overall tax structure, *Journal of Finance*, IX (1956), 205–21.
FRIEDMAN, MILTON, The spendings tax: the tax as a wartime measure, *American Economic Review*, XXXIII (1943), 50–63.
GROVES, HAROLD M. and EDWARDS, WALLACE I., A new model for an integrated transfer tax, *National Tax Journal*, VI (1953), 353–61.
HARRISS, C. LOWELL, Revenue implications of a progressive-rate tax on expenditures, *Review of Economic Statistics*, XXV (1943), 175–92.
———, Erosion of the federal estate and gift tax bases, *Proceedings of the Forty-Eighth Annual Conference (1955) of the National Tax Association*, 1956, 350–58.
MILLS, OGDEN L., The spendings tax, *Proceedings of the Fourteenth Annual Conference (1921) of the National Tax Association*, 1922, 327–38.
MORTON, WALTER A., A progressive consumption tax, *National Tax Journal*, IV (1951), 160–67.
POOLE, K. E., The spendings tax: problems of administration and equity, *American Economic Review*, XXXIII (1943), 63–74.
SHOUP, CARL S., Theory and background of the value-added tax, *Proceedings of the Forty-Eighth Annual Conference (1955) of the National Tax Association*, 1956, 6–20.
VICKREY, WILLIAM, The rationalization of succession taxation, *Econometrica*, XII (1944), 215–37.

E. TAX POLICY FOR STABILIZATION

21. GENERAL

BECK, MORRIS, British anti-inflationary tax on distributed corporate profits, *National Tax Journal*, I (1948), 275–78.
BERGSON, ABRAM, The incidence of an income tax on saving, *Quarterly Journal of Economics*, LVI (1941–42), 337–41.
BIGHAM, TRUMAN C., Economic effects of the New Deal tax policy, *Southern Economic Journal*, III (1936–37), 270–81.
BRETHERTON, R. F., The sensitivity of taxes to fluctuations of trade, *Econometrica*, V (1937), 171–84.
BROWN, E. CARY, The static theory of automatic fiscal stabilization, *Journal of Political Economy*, LXIII (1955), 427–41.
———, Fiscal policy in the thirties: a reappraisal, *American Economic Review*, XLVI (1956), 857–80.
———, Analysis consumption taxes in terms of the theory of income determination, *American Economic Review*, XL (1950), 74–90.
CARTER, C. F., Personal saving and public finance, *Public Finance*, X (1955), 105–19.
CHENG, PAO LUN, A note on the progressive consumption tax, *Journal of Finance*, VIII (1953), 333–43.
CLARK, J. M., Effects of income redistribution on consumers' expenditures: note, *American Economic Review*, XXVII (1947), 931.
COLM, GERHARD and LEHMANN, FRITZ, Economic consequences of recent American tax policy, *Social Research*, Supplement I (1938), 108 pp.
DUE, JOHN F., The sales tax as an anti-inflationary measure, *Public Finance*, VI (1951), 385–94.
EDELBERG, V., Flexibility of the yield of taxation—some econometric investigations, *Journal of Royal Statistical Society*, III (1940), 153–79.
GILBERT, DONALD W., Cycles in municipal finance, *Review of Economic Statistics*, XXII (1940), 190–202.
———, Taxation and economic stability, *Quarterly Journal of Economics*, LVI (1942), 406–29.
GROVES, H. M. and KAHN, C. H., The stability of state and local tax yields, *American Economic Review*, XLII (1952), 87–103.

HAMILTON, C. J., The growth of taxation in relation to population and price, *Indian Journal of Economics*, V (1924–25), 370–84; discussion, 384–89.

HICKS, URSULA K., Lags in tax collection: a neglected problem of war finance, *Review of Economic Studies*, VIII (1940–41), 89–99.

HIGGINS, BENJAMIN, Post-war tax policy—part II, *Canadian Journal of Economics and Political Science*, IX (1943), 532–56.

——, A note on taxation and inflation, *Canadian Journal of Economics and Political Science*, XIX (1953), 392–402.

HOLT, CHARLES C., Averaging of income for tax purposes: equity and fiscal-policy consideration, *National Tax Journal*, II (1949), 349–62.

HUBBARD, J. C., The proportional personal income tax as an instrument of income creation, *Economic Journal*, LIX (1949), 56–68.

JHA, DIVAKAR, The theory of taxation and saving, *Indian Economic Journal*, IV (1956–57), 22–33.

JOHNSON, HARRY G., A note on the effect of income redistribution on aggregate consumption with interdependent consumer preferences, *Economica*, XVIII (1951), 295–98.

——, The effects of income-redistribution on aggregate consumption with interdependence of consumers' preferences, *Economica*, XIX (1952), 131–48.

LINDHOLM, R. W., Note on the effect of tax reduction, *American Economic Review*, XXXVI (1946), 910–11.

LUBELL, HAROLD, Effects of income redistribution on consumers' expenditures, *American Economic Review*, XXXVII (1947), 157–70.

——, Effects of income redistribution on consumers' expenditures: a correction, *American Economic Review*, XXXVII (1947), 930–31.

MISRA, J. K., Role of taxation in economic planning, *Indian Journal of Economics*, XXXII (1951–52), 237–49.

MORAG, AMOTZ, Escalator clauses and indirect taxation, *Indian Economic Journal*, III (1955–56), 154–68.

MUSGRAVE, R. A., and MILLER, M. H., Built-in flexibility, *American Economic Review*, XXXVIII (1948), 122–28.

MUSGRAVE, RICHARD A., and PAINTER, MARY S., The impact of alternative tax structures on personal consumption and saving, *Quarterly Journal of Economics*, LXII (1947–48), 475–500.

PEACOCK, ALAN T., Social security and inflation: a study of the economic effects of an adjustable pensions scheme, *Review of Economic Studies*, XX (1952–53), 169–74.

PECHMAN, JOSEPH A., Yield of the individual income tax during a recession, *National Tax Journal*, VII (1954), 1–17.

PEN, J., The theory of public finance and the theory of saving, *Public Finance*, V (1950), 38–44.

PRUEFER, CLIFFORD H., The excess profits tax and defense financing, *Southern Economic Journal*, VIII (1941–42), 40–53.

RUML, BEARDSLEY, Fiscal policy and taxation, *Proceedings of the Thirty-Seventh Annual Conference (1944) of the National Tax Association*, 1945, 167–74; discussion, 181–93.

——, Tax policies for prosperity, *American Economic Review*, XXXVI (1946), Papers and Proceedings, 265–75.

——, Tax policies for prosperity, *Journal of Finance*, I (1946), 81–91.

SALERA, VIRGIL, Taxation and economic stability, *Quarterly Journal of Economics*, LVII (1942–43), 323–26.

SHACKLE, G. L. S., The deflative or inflative tendency of government receipts and disbursements, *Oxford Economic Papers*, VIII (1947), 46–65.

SHULTZ, WILLIAM J., The proposed currency-and-deposits tax, *Bulletin of the National Tax Association*, XXIV (1938–39), 182–84.

SLITOR, RICHARD E., The flexibility of income-tax yield under averaging, *Journal of Political Economy*, LIV (1946), 266–69.

——, The measurement of progressivity and built-in flexibility, *Quarterly Journal of Economics*, LXII (1947–48), 309–14.

SOLOWAY, A., Purchase tax and fiscal policy, *National Tax Journal*, IV (1951), 304–14.

STEIN, HERBERT, Stability and flexibility in federal tax policy, *Proceedings of the Thirty-Ninth Annual Conference (1946) of the National Tax Association*, 1946, 260–66; discussion, 269–77.

STEINER, GEORGE A., The tax system and industrial development, *Bulletin of the National Tax Association*, XXIII (1937–38), 98–111.

SUMBERG, THEODORE A., Leakage problems in flexible taxation, *Journal of Political Economy*, LV (1947), 572–76.

TRESCOTT, PAUL B., The idea of "built-in flexibility" 1837–1860, *Public Finance*, XI (1956), 366–70.

TURVEY, RALPH, Dr. Pen on the theory of public finance: a criticism and reply by Pen, *Public Finance*, V (1950), 250–52.

VICKREY, WILLIAM, The effect of averaging on the cyclical sensitivity of the yield of the income tax, *Journal of Political Economy*, LIII (1945), 275–78.

————, Some limits to the income elasticity of income tax yields, *Review of Economics and Statistics*, XXXI (1949), 140–45.

WALKER, DAVID, Some comments on the taxation of personal income and expenditure in the United Kingdom, 1945–53, *Public Finance*, IX (1954), 190–211.

WALTER, JAMES E., Tax sensitivity, *Southern Economic Journal*, XVII (1950–51), 422–37.

WAUGH, FREDERICK V., Excise taxes and economic stability, *Journal of Farm Economics*, XXX (1948), 399–411.

WHITE, M. I., Personal income tax reduction in a hypothetical contraction, *Review of Economics and Statistics*, XXXI (1949), 63–69.

F. SELECTIONS FROM FOREIGN-LANGUAGE BOOKS AND JOURNALS

22. FRENCH SELECTION (PROFESSOR PIERRE TABATONI)

a) *Impôt et Théories du bien-être*

WALRAS, L., Eléments d'économie pure (Ed. déf., Paris, 1938, 42ème leçon "des Impôts"), p. 448–65.

PERROUX, F., Les choix de l'Etat producteur et la théorie des surplus du producteur et du consommateur (Proceedings of the International Statistical Conferences, 1947), Vol. V.

KRIER, H., La charge des impôts sur l'économie (Librairie Générale de Droit et de Jurisprudence) Paris, 1944.

DUPUIT, J., "De l'Utilité et de sa mesure"—"De l'utilité publique" (Journal des economistes, S.I., Tome XXXVI, 1853) p. 1–27. Différents articles de J. DUPUIT ont été publiés par M. DE BERNARDI, "La réforme sociale," (Turin, 1933).

b) *Incidence des Impôts*

MARCHAL, J., L'incidence des impôts cédulaires sur le revenu ("Finances Publiques," 1949), p. 323–40).

LA GARRIGUE, V. ROUQUET, Les éléments d'une Théorie de la repercussion fiscale (Actualités Economiques (Canada), 1952, Octobre-Decembre, p. 489 et 1953, Janvier-Mars).

TABATONI, P., Concepts et méthode dans la théorie de l'incidence des impôts (Revue de Sciences et Législation Financières, 1952), p. 707–30.

DEHOVE, G., Pression fiscale et équilibre économique (Presses Universitaires de France, 1947), p. 218–80.

c) *Tarification*

COLSON, CL., La tarification des chemins de fer (Annales des Ponts et Chaussées, 1892—2—p. 44; et 1894—2—p. 152).

LEROY, TH., Détermination des prix de revient et tarification des transports par chemin de fer (Annales des Mines, 1939, S. XII–IX) p . 79.

DUPUIT, J., De l'influence des péages sur l'utilité des voies de communciation (Annales des Ponts et Chaussées, 1849, SII, T. XVII) p. 170–248.

d) *Mesure de la pression fiscale—Progressivité—Justice fiscale*

NEUMARK, F., Problème de la progressivité dans une fiscalité rationnelle, (Rev. de Sciences et de Législation Financières, 1950), p. 390–413.

REYNAUD, P. L., La psychologie du Contribuable devant l'impôt (Revue de Sciences et de Législation Financières, 1947, p. 394–411; et 1948, p. 276–90).

MERIGOT, J. C., La justice fiscale: Variations sur un thème connu (Revue de Sciences et de Législation Financières, Janv.–Mars, 1955).

D'ALBERGO, E., Sur la double taxation de l'épargne (Rev. de Sciences et de Legislation Financières, 1953, p. 239–58; et 1954, p. 126–38).

LAURÉ, M., Influence de la fiscalité sur la formation de l'épargne, (Rev. de Sciences et de Législation Financières, 1954), p. 290–309.

VISINE, F., La signification des statistiques fiscales et leur utilisation (Finances Publiques, 1955) p. 8–82.

e) *Théories générales de l'impôt dans les manuels*

LEROY-BEAULIEU, P., Traité de la Science des Finances (Paris, 1877, Guillaumin & Cº, Tome I, chap. II) "L'Impôt proportionnel et l'impôt progressif," p. 126–63.

JEZE, G., Cours de Finances publiques (Paris, M. Giard, 1931, Livre III, chap. III) "Théorie générale de l'impôt," p. 445–84.

LAUFENBURGER, H., Précis d'Economie et de Législation Financières (Sirey, 1943, Tome I) "Revenu et impôt," IIe partie, chap. I et II, p. 96–147.

23. GERMAN SELECTION (PROFESSOR FRITZ NEUMARK)

A. Equity

NEUMANN, FR. J., Die Steuer nach der Steuerfähigkeit, Jahrbücher f. Nat. u. Stat. N.F. Bd. 2, 1881.

ALTMANN, S. D., Das Problem der Gerechtigkeit in der Besteuerung, Archiv für Sozialwissenschaft und Sozialpolitik, Bd. 33/1911, S. 77 ff.

SAX, E., Die Wertungstheorie der Steuer, Zeitschr. f. Volkswirtsch. u. Sozialpol. N.F. Bd. 4, 1924, S. 91 ff.

PETER, HANS, Das Problem der Gerechtigkeit und die Theorie der Steuerverteilung, Finanzarchiv, N.F., Bd., 1933.

GERLOFF, W., Steuerwirtschaftslehre, HBdFinwiss., 2. Aufl. 2. Bd. Tübingen, 1956.

HAYEK, F. A., Ungerechtigkeit der Steuerprogression, Schweizer Monatshefte, 1952.

B. Excess Burdens

Zum Teil unter I A, zum Teil unter II B (insbes. Föhl).

C. Public Pricing

KELLER, THEO, Die Eigenwirtschaft öffentlicher Gemeinwesen, HBdFinwiss, 2. Aufl. 2. Bd., Tübingen, 1956.

D. Incidence and Incentive Effects, General

MANN, F. K., Überwälzung der Steuer, HwbdStw., 4. Aufl., Bd. 8, Jena, 1928.

NEUMARK, F., Zum Problem der Klassifikation der Steuerformen, Beiträge zur Geld-und Finanztheorie, Festschr. f. Wilhelm Gerloff, Tübingen, 1951.

E. Incidence of Taxes on Income and Profits

FÖHL, CARL, Kritik der progressiven Einkommensbesteurerung, Fin. Arch. N.F. Bd. 14, 1953.

DERS., Das Steuerparadoxon, Fin. Arch. N.F. Bd. 17, 1956/57.

ALBERS, WILLI, Preisliche Wirkungen der Besteuerung, Fin. Arch. N.F. Bd. 16, 1956.
KRELLE, WILHELM, Zur Wirkung der progressiven Einkommensbesteuerung, Fin. Arch. N.F., Bd. 16, 1956.
MANN, F. K., Die Überwälzbarkeit der Einkommen-, Vermögen-, Vermögenszuwachs- und Erbschaftsteuern, Veröffentlichungen der Friedrich List-Gesellschaft, 3. Bd. "Kapitalbildung und Steuersystem," Verhandlungen und Gutachten der Konferenz von Eilsen, hrsg. v. G. Colm und H. Neisser.
HELANDER, SVEN, Überwälzbarkeit der spezifischen Unternehmungssteuern, *ibid.*

noch Einkommensteuer—generell:

LAMPE, A., Reine Theorie der Finanzreform, Fin. Arch. N.F., Bd. 2, 1934.
DERS., Neue Verteidigung der Einkommensteuer, *ibid.*, Bd. 3, 1935.
WILKEN, FOLKERT, Organische Finanzreform, *ibid.*
NEUMARK, F., Internationale Entwicklungstendenzen auf dem Gebiete der Einkommensbesteuerung, Weltw. Arch., 63, 1949.
V. WIESE, L., Das Prinzip der Progression in der Einkommensteuer, Beiträge zur Finanzwiss., Festgabe für G. v. Schanz, Bd. II, hrsg. v. H. Teschemacher, Tübingen, 1928.

F. Taxes on Products and Sales

SCHMÖLDERS, G., Die Umsatzsteuern, HBdFinw. 2. Aufl., 2. Bd., Tübingen, 1956.

G. Taxes on Land and Property

s. Mann unter D
DIEHL, KARL, Die einmalige Vermögensabgabe, Schriften des Vereins für Sozialpolitik, 156. Bd., München und Leipzig, 1918.
STUCKEN, R., Die grosse Vermögensabgabe und das heutige Finanzproblem, Fin. Arch. N.F. Bd. 11, 1949.

H. Incentive Effects

GERLOFF, W., Die Problematik hoher Steuerbelastung in der Marktwirtschaft, Beiträge zur Finanzwissenschaft und zur Geldtheorie, Festschr. f. Rudolf Stucken, hrsg. Fritz Voigt, Göttingen, 1953.
LANDMANN, J., Die Grenzen der Besteuerung—Produktionspolitische Gesichtspunkte der Besteuerung, Kapitalbildung und Steuersystem, Bd. I, 1930.

24. ITALIAN SELECTION (PROFESSOR SERVIO STEVE)*

BARONE, E., Studi di economia finanziaria, *Giornale degli economisti*, XLIV (1912), 309–53, 469–505; XLV (1912), 1–75.
BORGATTA, G., Contributi critici alla finanza teoretica (A proposito di una memoria di Luigi Einaudi), *Giornale degli economisti*, LX (1920), 321–40.
———, La rendita del consumatore e le sue applicazioni finanziarie, *Giornale degli economisti*, LXI (1921), 157–74, 248–71.

———

* This list does not include articles which were collected in book form, or were extensively used in books by their authors. Mention is to be made specially of the following: E. BARONE, Le opere economiche, Vol. I: Scritti vari, Bologna, 1936; C. COSCIANI, Principii di scienza delle finanze, Torino, 1953; E. D'ALBERGO, Economia della finanza pubblica, Bologna, 1952; A. DE VITI DE MARCO, Principii di economia finanziaria, Torino, 1934; L. EINAUDI, Saggi sul risparmio e l'imposta, Torino, 1941; U. GOBBI, Scritti vari di economia, Milano, 1934; B. GRIZIOTTI, Studi di scienza delle finanze e diritto finanziario, Milano, 1956; P. JANNACCONE, Discussioni e indagini economiche e finanziarie, Torino, 1954; M. PANTALEONI, Scritti di finanza e statistica, Bologna, 1938; G. U. PAPI, Teoria della condotta economica dello Stato, Milano, 1956.

———, Intorno alla pressione di qualunque imposta a parità di prelievo, *Giornale degli economisti*, LXI (1921), 290–97.

CABIATI, A., Per riempire alcune "empty boxes" finanziarie, *Giornale degli economisti*, LXVIII (1928), 81–98.

———, La "Finanza" di Antonio De Viti De Marco, *Giornale degli economisti*, LXVIII (1928), 881–98.

EINAUDI, L., Contributo alla ricerca dell' "ottima imposta," *Annali di Economia*, V (1929).

FASIANI, M., Sulla doppia tassazione del risparmio, *La Riforma sociale*, XXXIX (1928), 123–40.

———, Elementi per una teoria della durata del processo traslativo dell' imposta in una società statica, *Giornale degli economisti*, LXIX (1929), 557–83, 687–714 [a somewhat abbreviated English translation: Materials for a theory of the process of tax shifting, *Review of Economic Studies*, I–II (1934–35)].

———, Di un particolare aspetto delle imposte di consumo, *Riforma sociale*, XLI (1930), 1–20 [Translation: On a particular aspect of consumption taxes, *International Economic Papers*, VI (1956), 34–49].

———, Contributo ad alcuni punti della teoria della traslazione delle imposte sui "profitti" e sui "redditi," *Studi Sassaresi*, IX (1931), 173–207; X (1931), 1–51.

———, Di un elementare problema di tempo e di alcune sue applicazioni finanziarie, *Annali di Statistica e di Economia*, IV (1936), 87–114.

———, Appunti critici sulla teoria degli effetti dell' imposta sull' offerta individuale di lavoro, *Annali di Statistica e di Economia*, IX–X (1942), 139–223.

FUBINI, R., Sulla tassazione del risparmio, *Giornale degli economisti*, LXVIII (1928), 480–93.

———, Contributo alla determinazione del concetto di imposta generale sul reddito, *Giornale degli economisti*, LXXII (1932), 297–327.

———, Contributo allo studio degli effetti dell' imposta generale sul reddito, *Giornale degli economisti*, LXXII (1932), 365–404.

PARRAVICINI, G., Imposte indirette su merci e livello generale dei prezzi, *Moneta e credito*, VII (1954), 144–64, 298–312.

RICCI, U., L'imposta unica sui consumi non necessari, *Giornale degli Economisti*, XLVII (1913), 293–326.

———, La taxation de l'épargne, *Revue d' économie politique*, XLI (1927), 860–83.

ROSSI, L., Di un caso particolare di Abwälzung, *Giornale degli economisti*, LXIX (1929), 766–78.

———, L'omogeneità dei redditi ed il fondamento teorico delle imposte, *Giornale degli economisti*, N.S. X (1951), 335–44.

SCOTTO, A., La durata del capitale fisso e gli effetti dei tributi, *Giornale degli economisti*, N.S. IX (1950), 125–65.

SENSINI, G., Le equazioni dell' equilibrio economico nell' ipotesi di sottrazioni di ricchezza operate dal Governo su determinati individui della collettività, *Giornale degli economisti*, LXX (1930), 689–709.

STEVE, S., Sul concetto di imposta generale, *Giornale degli economisti*, N.S. VI (1947), 573–626.

VILLANI, F., Il sofisma della doppia tassazione del risparmio, *Rivista di politica economica*, XLII (1952), 1–18.

25. SCANDANAVIAN SELECTION (PROFESSORS ERIK LINDAHL AND BENT HANSEN)

I. *Equity and Welfare*

A. *Equity*

CASSEL, GUSTAV, Om progressiv beskattning (on progressive taxation), *Nordisk tidskrift för vetenskap, konst och industri*, 1895, 632–52.

WICKSELL, KNUT, P.M. rörande de allmänna grunderna för en reform av inkomstloch förmögenhetsbeskattningen (memorandum on the general principles for a reform of income and property taxation), *Riksdagens protokoll*, 1919, Prop. nr 259, bil. 80–112.

LINDAHL, ERIK, Intresseprincipens tillämpning inom kommunalbeskattningen (the applications of the principle of benefit in local taxation), *Ekonomisk tidskrift*, 1921, 69–86.

WICKSELL, KNUT, Inkomstbegreppet i skattehänseende och därmed sammanhängande skattefrågor (the concept of income in taxation and other related problems of taxation), *Ekonomisk tidskrift*, 1922, 127–54.

DAVIDSON, DAVID, Om beskattningsnormen vid inkomstskatten (on the concept of the tax base in income taxation), *Ekonomisk tidskrift*, 1922, 205–52.

WICKSELL, KNUT, Några erinringar. Genmäle till D. Davidson (some comments: reply to D. Davidson), *Ekonomisk tidskrift*, 1923, 77–86.

DAVIDSON, DAVID, Replik till prof. Wicksell (reply to Prof. Wicksell), *Ekonomisk tidskrift*, 1923, 87–94.

WELINDER, CARSTEN, Inkomsten som mått på skatteförmågan (taxable income as a measure of ability to pay) *Svensk skattetidning*, 1938, 206–49.

PHILIP, KJELD, Hvori bestaar Skattebyrden (what is the burden of taxation?), *Nationaløkonomisk tidsskrift*, 1941, 173–82.

C. Public Pricing and other Aspects

ZEUTHEN, F., Socialistisk Prispolitik—offentlig Prispolitik (Socialistic price policy—public price policy), *Nationaløkonomisk tidsskrift*, 1945, 218–28.

II. Incidence and Incentive Effects

B. General Analysis

WICKSELL, KNUT, Om överflyttning av skatt (on shifting of tax), *Ekonomisk tidskrift*, 1899, 211–32; and 383–87.

CASSEL, GUSTAV, Om skatteincidens (on incidence of taxation), *Ekonomisk tidskrift*, 1899, 317–28.

ZEUTHEN, F., Indkomstfordelingens Afhaengighed af økonomiske Forhold (the dependence of income distribution on economic conditions), *Nationaløkonomisk tidsskrift*, 1925, 197–230.

RASMUSSEN, P. NØRREGAARD, Traek af Overvaeltningslaeren (aspects of the theory of incidence), *Nationaløkonomisk tidsskrift*, 1947, 174–85.

HANSEN, BENT, Ett bidrag till incidensläran (a contribution to incidence theory), *Ekonomisk tidskrift*, 1954, 195–213.

C. Taxes on Income and Profits

ZEUTHEN, F., Direkte Forbrugsskat (direct consumption tax), *Nationaløkonomisk tidsskrift*, 1924, 278–87.

PEDERSEN, JØRGEN, Direkte og Indirekte Skatter (direct and indirect taxes), *Nationaløkonomisk tidsskrift*, 1937, 23–36.

WELINDER, CARSTEN, On the future of income tax, *Nordisk tidsskrift for teknisk økonomi*, bind 12 (1948), 275–81.

D. Taxes on Products and Sales

MUTÉN, LEIF, Om bruttobeskattning (on gross taxation), *Ekonomisk tidskrift*, 1955, 25–48.

E. Taxes on Land and Property

WICKSELL, KNUT, Om arvsskatten (on the inheritance tax), *Ekonomisk Tidskrift*, 1901, 75–119.

MYRDAL, GUNNAR, Not om engångsskatt på förmögenhet (a note on capital levy), *Ekonomisk tidskrift*, 1943, 47–57.

F. *Incentive Effects*

FRISCH, RAGNAR, Den optimale arbeidsinnsatts (the optimal supply of labour), *Ekonomisk tidskrift*, 1948, 63–80.

INDEX OF AUTHORS

Index of Authors*

A

Abbott, L., 544, 556
Acworth, 291
Adams, H. C., 23, 210
Adams, T. S., 419, 542, 547, 553, 560, 562
Adarkar, B. P., 93, 101, 105
Ahman, S., 556
Albers, W., 569
Alexander-Katz, C., 560
Allen, C. L., 544
Allen, R. G. D., 146, 454
Altmann, S. D., 568
Anderson, B. M., 553
Archibald, G. C., 544
Arnold, S., 552
Auspitz, 263, 283, 368
Axelrad, S., 467

B

Bach, G. L., 494
Backman, J., 545
Bailey, M. J., 544, 550
Bajpai, F. G., 560
Balakrishna, R., 556
Balogh, T., 550, 556
Barkar, V. V., 550
Barna, T., 222, 401, 403, 414–15, 550
Barone, E., 286, 290, 436–44, 446, 569
Bastable, 173, 184, 210, 212, 262, 266, 270, 279, 341, 542, 547, 553
Bates, S., 546
Bauder, R. S., 339, 552
Beale, T., 563
Beck, M., 547, 556, 565
Behrman, J. N., 550
Beneke, R., 547
Benewitz, M. C., 556
Benham, F. C., 99, 313, 542, 546, 550
Benson, G. C. S., 93
Bergson, A., 565
Bernoulli, D., 28
Bernstein, E. M., 547
Berry, D., 123, 561
Bhargaua, R. N., 546, 559
Bickerdike, C. F., 132–38, 377–88, 545, 553
Bigham, T. C., 565
Black, D., 454, 457, 461, 511, 547, 563
Black, J. D., 373

Blackstone, 173
Bloch, H. S., 564
Blough, R., 543, 546, 556, 561, 563
Blunden, 265, 562
Boden, 215
Bodenhorn, D., 547
Böhm-Bawerk, 292
Bond, H. H., 563
Booker, H. S., 555
Borgatta, G., 569, 570
Boring, E. G., 28
Boulding, K. E., 547, 550
Bowen, H. R., 322, 525, 547, 562
Bowley, A. L., 146, 216, 560
Bowman, M. J., 494
Brabson, G. D., 550
Bradley, P. D., 547, 556
Break, G. F., 110–22, 544, 545, 555, 556
Bretherton, R. F., 565
Bronfenbrenner, M., 550, 559
Brown, E. C., 525–37
Brown, H. G., 154, 330–39, 416, 419, 546, 550, 552, 553
Brownlee, O. H., 546, 561
Buchanan, J. M., 93–109, 542, 551
Buehler, A. G., 543, 548, 562, 564
Bullock, 50
Burkhead, J. V., 548
Burns, 360
Busschau, W. J., 548
Butlin, S. J., 546
Butters, J. K., 494, 525, 548, 556, 559

C

Cabiati, A., 570
Calkins, F. G., 556
Cannan, E., 171–201, 211, 215, 224, 274, 543
Carroll, J. J., 560
Carter, C. F., 565
Cartter, A. M., 550
Carver, T. N., 20, 25, 259, 261, 263, 269, 283
Cassel, G., 543, 570, 571
Chamberlin, 343, 355
Chapman, H. H., 553
Chapman, S. J., 3–12, 22, 24, 42, 49, 543
Cheng, P. L., 565
Ciriacy-Wantrup, S. V., 553
Clark, C., 559
Clark, H., 552

* Page reference given only where source is listed.

575

*This book has been set on the Linotype in 12
and 10 point Intertype Garamond, leaded 1
point. Chapter numbers and titles are in 24 point
Garamond italics. The size of the type page
is 27 by 46½ picas.*